COLLECTED ESSAYS

VOLUME II

THE LITTMAN LIBRARY OF
JEWISH CIVILIZATION

Dedicated to the memory of
Louis Thomas Sidney Littman
who founded the Littman Library for the love of God
and as an act of charity in memory of his father
Joseph Aaron Littman
and to the memory of
Robert Joseph Littman
who continued what his father Louis had begun
יהא זכרם ברוך

'Get wisdom, get understanding:
Forsake her not and she shall preserve thee'
PROV. 4:5

COLLECTED ESSAYS

VOLUME II

HAYM SOLOVEITCHIK

London
The Littman Library of Jewish Civilization
in association with Liverpool University Press

The Littman Library of Jewish Civilization
Registered office: 4th floor, 7–10 Chandos Street, London WIG 9DQ

in association with Liverpool University Press
4 Cambridge Street, Liverpool L69 7ZU, UK
www.liverpooluniversitypress.co.uk/littman

Managing Editor: Connie Webber

Distributed in North America by
Oxford University Press Inc., 198 Madison Avenue
New York, NY 10016, USA

First published in hardback 2014
Hardback reprinted 2016
First published in paperback 2019

Catalogue records for this book are available from the
British Library and the Library of Congress
ISBN 978-1-786941-66-4

Publishing co-ordinator: Janet Moth
Copy-editing: Agnes Erdos
Proof-reading: Philippa Claiden
Indexes: Agnes Erdos
Designed and typeset by Pete Russell, Faringdon, Oxon.

Printed and bound in Great Britain by
CPI Group (UK) Ltd., Croydon, CR0 4YY

FOR

SHEON AND RENA

Preface

THE SECOND VOLUME of this collection has a long chronological stretch as it contains both my first venture into Jewish studies and my very last. The study of *Iggeret ha-Shemad* was part of my BA Honors thesis, while that on the Third Yeshivah of Bavel was written over the past two years.

The first and longest section deals with my re-evaluation of Early Ashkenaz (*c.*950–1096). Eight essays take issue with much that has been written on this subject for the past thirty-five years. My reservations are longstanding; indeed, I argued against these views with some of their proponents in the late 1970s and early 1980s. Nevertheless, I have put my critique on paper only recently for reasons that I spell out in my introductory remarks to that section. However, the notion of multiple yeshivot in geonic Bavel and their role in the founding and formation of the halakhic culture of Ashkenaz began to take shape in my mind only after I had concluded writing all that had been scheduled for this volume.

The second part of the volume deals with martyrdom, and, for me at least, the most striking thing is that the essay on *Iggeret ha-Shemad*, written in 1959, and that on martyrdom in Ashkenaz written over forty years later employ an identical technique—that of measurable deflection. This means that the author makes an argument that is patently problematic or wholly out of character, either of which would point to some force deflecting the writer's line of reasoning from its normal path. As an undergraduate I majored in Russian history, but as my university permitted writing an Honors thesis in any area in the discipline, I was free to try to make sense of an early work of Maimonides which I had read with perplexity the previous summer. I doubt very much whether I realized as a college senior the methodological problems involved in proving a bias in an author's argument when one has neither his personal correspondence nor the memoirs of his contemporaries. I simply thought that a thesis had to answer a problem and the more problems one solved, the better the thesis. Of course, one had to show that the other answers would not do, and I had learnt of Occam's razor. So it was clear to me that, other things being equal, one answer to five questions was preferable to five separate answers—one for each question. I believed then, and continue to believe now, that I had found that single answer. Not everyone agrees with me, as the numerous critiques of my essay readily evidence. (The texts of these critiques are available in PDF format on my website, <haymsoloveitchik.org>.) I have attempted to reply in this volume to my dissenters; whether successfully or not is for the reader to decide.

The concluding section has two essays on *Mishneh Torah*.

Nine of the essays are new, five others have been translated from Hebrew, and three appeared originally in English. None of the previously printed essays, whether in English or Hebrew, have been altered. Any additions or changes of position are noted either in an afterword or in the footnotes, marked by curly brackets { }. The additions to the footnotes are generally ones of fact or bibliography; those in an afterword, mostly my current reflections on the subject, responses to criticism, or reactions to other scholars' treatment of the material. All bibliographical additions have also been placed in curly brackets, with one exception. The last thirty years have seen a flood of scholarly editions of medieval halakhic works. I have updated these references without marking them. For example, a citation of the *Ḥiddushei ha-Ramban* has automatically been updated from the Meltzer edition of 1928 to the relevant volume in the series of the *Shas ha-Yisra'eli ha-Shalem*.

As closely as the previously published studies hew to the original formulations, I did not perceive them as Masoretic texts, demanding absolute fidelity of transmission. If I or the editors at Littman found a phrase infelicitous, we edited it out; if a clause seemed overcomplicated, we simplified it. On two occasions I have moved a footnote into the text and registered this in my prefatory remarks. On another occasion I have substituted two sentences for the ones in the original version as I believed that the new formulation made the same point more clearly and succinctly. (I noted the change in the footnote and also provided the reader with the initial formulation.)

The page numbers of the original essays have been supplied in the text thus |75| to enable readers to swiftly find references to passages in these articles registered in the scholarly literature of the past.

Acknowledgments

Any acknowledgment in a series of collected essays whose publication stretches back some forty-five years should begin with the 'creditors' who can never be repaid, not simply because they are no longer with us, but because their perspective and way of thinking are embedded in everything that one has written. First and foremost is my father, who bestowed upon me no less than a decade and a half of talmudic instruction—and much more; then Jacob Katz, from whom I learnt historical method. I am also under obligation to Hayyim Hillel Ben-Sasson and Joshua Prawer, under whom I studied at the Hebrew University in Jerusalem. Not all learning takes place in the classroom, and I would be sorely remiss if I did not record my obligations to Michael Bernstein, Eliezer Shimshon Rosenthal, Shraga Abramsom, and Saul Lieberman. For reasons best known to them (certainly not because of any merit of mine), they privileged me with hundreds of hours of conversation. What those sessions imparted to me, both in knowledge and method, has nourished every aspect of my scholarly life.

The idea of collecting my essays of some forty years scattered in books and journals both known and unknown (some in works possibly deserving oblivion) was first suggested to me by my cousin, Morry Gerber. When I broached the idea to Connie Webber, the managing editor of Littman, she received it enthusiastically; without her involvement, the project would not have come to fruition. I had heard from colleagues about the superb editing at Littman; what I received exceeded all expectations. I had not one, but two editors. Agi Erdos did painstaking and meticulous work, and Janet Moth then provided me with the finest English editing that I have ever received. Philippa Claiden's patient checking of the Hebrew and correcting the proofs was likewise much appreciated; Peter Russell's design has improved the readability of the text, for which I am grateful; while Ludo Craddock's handling of the bureaucratic technicalities has made them less bureaucratic and technical.

I hired Hanna Caine-Braunschvig of Jerusalem, an experienced Hebrew editor, to check all the titles, places of publication, and pages of the articles and books cited, and to keep a watchful eye on some of the other paraphernalia of scholarship. However, the intelligence of her comments on the articles and our conversations about the manner of their improvement has turned our relationship from that of author/assistant to one of collegiality. Ezra Merkin, Jerry Balsam, and Sheon Karol read and commented perceptively on every essay in the collection. I am indebted to all of them. (Jerry's eye for errant commas proved a further blessing.) Elisabeth Hollender graciously checked my German references (especially their case endings).

Without the assistance of the staffs of the Gottesman and Pollack Libraries of Yeshiva University, little of my research would have been possible. I would like to single out Zvi Ehrenyi, John Morel, and Mary Ann Linahan for special thanks. The Institute of Advanced Studies (IAS) at the Hebrew University has been my home away from home for the past twenty-five years, and much of the writing in these volumes took place within the four walls of that institution. I owe a special debt to Penina Feldman, the past administrative director of the IAS, who unfortunately did not live to see the present volume.

Given the state of the currently printed medieval rabbinic texts, no serious research is possible without sustained recourse to manuscripts. Everything that I have written in the past forty-five years is based, without exception, on the treasures of the Institute of Microfilmed Hebrew Manuscripts at the National Library of Israel in Jerusalem. Their holdings and their catalogue provide countless scholars with undreamt-of riches. The helpfulness of their staff, especially their cataloguers, is fabled. I am obliged to each and every one of them; however, I would like to note my special indebtedness to Binyamin Richler and Ezra Chwat.

I believe that the Internet has imposed a new burden of proof on authors. Whenever feasible, all, or at least the most important, sources that undergird a scholar's argument should be readily available for critical scrutiny. All the medieval sources referred to in the nine essays in Part I, and those cited in 'Kiddush ha-Shem be-Ashkenaz' and 'Maimonides' *Iggeret ha-Shemad*: Law and Rhetoric' are available in PDF form online at <haymsoloveitchik.org>, as are the different versions and editions of *Iggeret ha-Shemad* itself. Equally found there is a PDF of the several critiques levelled at my essay on *Iggeret ha-Shemad* to which I respond in this volume. Without budging from the computer, the reader can thus weigh the merits of the differing claims. I would like to thank the editors of *Dine Israel*, Arye Edrei and Suzanne Stone, and equally Barry Schwartz of the Jewish Publication Society, for allowing me to place online PDFs of these essays, which first appeared under their imprimaturs.

I wish to express my gratitude to Agi Erdos for her fine work in preparing the indexes. I would like again to acknowledge the assistance of Frank Guerra in preparing the PDFs.

I would like to thank both Cambridge University Press and Michael McCormick for allowing me to use three of the maps that appear in his book *Origins of the European Economy: Communication and Commerce, AD 300–900.*

Other than the obligation that I owe to my teachers, my greatest debt is to the president of Yeshiva University, Richard Joel, and its provost, Mort Lowengrub. The new president of Yeshiva University, Rabbi Dr. Ari Berman, and his provost, Dr. Selma Botman, have continued their policy of allowing me to devote myself full-time to study and writing. Tim Stevens, special assistant to the provost, has eased for me for the technicalities of the administrative transition. Without their gift of time and resources, this entire project —a multi-volume series of my collected essays—would simply have been inconceivable.

Contents

Note on Transliteration and Conventions Used in the Text xv

PART I

RE-EVALUATION OF ELEVENTH-CENTURY ASHKENAZ

Introduction 3

1. Agobard of Lyons, *Megillat Aḥima'ats*, and the Babylonian Orientation of Early Ashkenaz 5

2. Dialectics, Scholasticism, and the Origin of the *Tosafot* 23

3. *Minhag* Ashkenaz ha-Kadmon: An Assessment 29

4. The Authority of the Babylonian Talmud and the Use of Biblical Verses and Aggadah in Early Ashkenaz 70

5. On the Use of Aggadah by the Tosafists: A Response to I. M. Ta-Shma 101

6. Characterizing Medieval Talmudists: A Case Study 106

7. Communications and the Palestinian Origins of Ashkenaz 122

8. The Palestinian Orientation of the Ashkenazic Community and Some Suggested Ground Rules for the Writing of Halakhic History 145

9. The 'Third Yeshivah of Bavel' and the Cultural Origins of Ashkenaz—A Proposal 150

A Response to David Berger 202

PART II

MARTYRDOM UNDER CROSS AND CRESCENT

Introduction 219

10. Between Cross and Crescent 223

11. Halakhah, Hermeneutics, and Martyrdom in Ashkenaz 228

12. Maimonides' *Iggeret ha-Shemad*: Law and Rhetoric 288

13. Responses to Critiques of 'Maimonides' *Iggeret ha-Shemad*: Law and Rhetoric' 331

I. A Response to David Hartman 331

II. A Response to Yair Lorberbaum and Hayyim Shapira 338

III. A Response to Aryeh Strikovsky 347

IV. A Response to Hillel Novetsky 352

PART III

MISHNEH TORAH

14. Classification of *Mishneh Torah*: Problems Real and Imaginary 367

15. *Mishneh Torah*: Polemic and Art 378

Bibliography of Manuscripts 397

Source Acknowledgments 402

Index of Names 403

Index of Places 410

Index of Subjects 415

Note on Transliteration and Conventions Used in the Text

THE transliteration of Hebrew in this book reflects consideration of the type of book it is, in terms of its content, purpose, and readership. The system adopted therefore reflects an academic approach to transcription, such as that of the *Encyclopaedia Judaica* or other systems developed for text-based or linguistic studies. The aim has partly been to reflect the pronunciation prescribed for modern Hebrew, as well as the spelling or Hebrew word structure, and to do so using conventions that are generally familiar to the English-speaking reader.

In accordance with this approach, no attempt is made to indicate the distinctions between *tet* and *taf*, *kaf* and *kuf*, *sin* and *samekh*, since these are not relevant to pronunciation. The *dagesh* is indicated by double consonants, except when the doubling would result in a string of consonants unacceptable to the English reader's eye, as in *kitstsur*. Following the principle of using conventions familiar to the majority of readers, however, transcriptions that are well established have been retained even when they are not fully consistent with the transliteration system adopted. On similar grounds, the *tsadi* is rendered by 'tz' in such familiar words as barmitzvah. Likewise, the distinction between *ḥet* and *khaf* has been retained, using *ḥ* for the former and *kh* for the latter; the associated forms are generally familiar to readers, even if the distinction is not actually borne out in pronunciation, and for the same reason the final *heh* is indicated too. Although in Hebrew no capital letters are used, the transcription of titles and names in lower case may be strange to the English-speaking reader's eye and in this volume we therefore adopt the English system of capitalization (for example, *Shulḥan 'Arukh*).

No distinction is made between *'alef* and *'ayin* in the intervocalic position: both are represented by an apostrophe; *'ayin* is also marked at the beginnings and ends of words.

The *sheva na'* is indicated by an *e*—*perikat 'ol*, *reshut*—except, again, when established convention dictates otherwise.

The *yod* is represented by *i* when it occurs as a vowel (*bereshit*), by *y* when it occurs as a consonant (*yesodot*), and by *yi* when it occurs as both (*yisra'el*).

The definite article and those conjunctives and prepositions that in Hebrew are attached to the word have been separated by a hyphen in our transcription to help distinguish the individual elements.

Medieval Hebrew names follow the above system, whereas contemporary names are transcribed as they appear in Western literature.

The names of scholars who have published in European languages are given in Latinized form, even when referring to Hebrew articles of theirs. Thus Yaakov Katz is uniformly referred to as 'Jacob Katz' and registered in bibliographical entries as 'J. Katz'. Similarly, Yoel Miller is registered as 'J. Müller'.

YIDDISH

The transcription of Yiddish in this volume follows the conventions of the YIVO Institute.

PART I

RE-EVALUATION OF ELEVENTH-CENTURY ASHKENAZ

INTRODUCTION

ועם רבי אברהם תהיה לנו תוכחה מגולה ואהבה מסותרה

FOR SOME FIFTEEN YEARS, from about 1985 to 2000, I was occupied with putting out the halakhic writings of my father and grandfather. During this period a great deal of scholarly writing appeared about eleventh-century Ashkenaz with which I found myself in disagreement, both substantively and methodologically. I did not wish to publish criticisms until I had placed on the shelves examples of how I believed the history of halakhah should be written. (My Hebrew book on pawnbroking was, as I wrote in the first volume of this series,[1] far too compressed to have any impact, or even to have many readers.) The blocks of time available to me during that decade and a half sufficed for part-time research but not for writing. Other than an essay on Modern Orthodoxy, I published next to nothing. (*Shut ke-Makor Histori*, which appeared in 1990, had been written ten years earlier.) Having now placed in the public domain two books on the history of halakhah, both of which engage heavily with the problematic literature of the eleventh century, . I am ready to print my critique of many of the regnant theories of halakhah in Early Ashkenaz.

I find myself at variance with Reuven Bonfil's readings of both Agobard of Lyons and the *Megillat Aḥima'ats* (*Chronicle of Aḥima'ats*); I fail to see the basis of I. M. Ta-Shma's claim of a *minhag* Ashkenaz ha-Kadmon and have difficulty with a number of Avraham Grossman's determinations. The latter scholar, having written the most substantive and detailed studies of the period, bears the brunt of my critique; a few words, therefore, are in place.

Only someone who wrote, as I did, both his MA (1968, on *setam yeinam*) and Ph.D. (1973, on usury and pawnbroking) before the appearance of Grossman's books can appreciate the magnitude of his accomplishments. Any study of *setam yeinam* and usury must draw heavily on the literature of Early Ashkenaz; indeed, the halakhic positions of eleventh-century German scholars occupy more than a third of any of the half-dozen or so essays that I have

[1] *Collected Essays*, i (Oxford, 2013), 57.

written on these subjects. Ineluctably, I was obliged to work out rudimentary biographies of every figure of the period simply to know who was who and who was what to whom. I found it a time-consuming and thankless task and, after it was done, I was always worried that I may well have overlooked some significant fact. Grossman's volume on eleventh-century Germany, which appeared in 1981, changed the situation entirely, as did, some ten years later, his tome on eleventh-century France. For the first time, scholars had a *vade mecum* to that dark period. Every figure (some scarcely known before) was portrayed in detail and many were characterized; attributions of works were carefully weighed on the basis of an exhaustive use of manuscripts, and theories about eleventh-century halakhah were presented. In his book on France, Grossman further uncovered the deep involvement of Rashi and his school in the exegesis of liturgical poetry (*piyyut*) and laid bare the polemical dimension of their biblical commentaries. Scholarship is much the richer for his two volumes, and they have lightened immeasurably the labor of all scholars who now work in this period.

In matters of polemics and *piyyut* commentary, in all issues bio-bibliographical, I turn for instruction to Avraham Grossman. In matters historical or halakhic, however, I part company with my distinguished colleague, saluting him even as I turn aside.

CHAPTER ONE

Agobard of Lyons, *Megillat Aḥima'ats*, and the Babylonian Orientation of Early Ashkenaz

Agobard of Lyons: *De Insolentia Iudaeorum*

Agobard's letter to Louis the Pious, *On Jewish Insolence*, has been adduced by my eminent colleague, Reuven Bonfil, as evidence that the Jews of Lyons regulated their religious life by the Palestinian halakhah, and, by implication, so did other Jews in the Carolingian Empire at that time.[1] Sometime in the third decade of the ninth century, Agobard, archbishop of Lyons, wrote a sharp letter to Emperor Louis in Aachen, attacking the insufferable arrogance of the Jews.[2] Among the charges leveled was that meat that was deemed unclean (*immundum*) and unfit for Jewish consumption was regularly sold to Christians and called derisively 'Christian meat'. Agobard had in mind the dietary laws of *sheḥitah* (ritual slaughter) and *terefot* (the bodily defects that render the animal, even if correctly slaughtered, not kosher). His detailed description of what the Jews deemed *immundum* is the earliest report that we have of *sheḥitah* and *terefot* as practiced by the Jews of Europe. It antedates all Jewish reports by some 150 years and merits a close reading.

I would like to thank Robert Brody for reading and commenting upon this article.

[1] ''Eduto shel Agobard mi-Lyon 'al 'Olamam ha-Ruḥani shel Yehudei Eiropah ba-Me'ah ha-Teshi'it', in Y. Dan, Y. Hacker, et al., eds., *Meḥkarim be-Kabbalah, be-Filosofyah u-ve-Sifrut ha-Musar ve-he-Hagut Muggashim le-Yesha'yahu Tishby bi-Melo't Lo Shiv'im ve-Ḥamesh Shanim* (Jerusalem, 1986), 327–48, esp. 339–47. (An abridged, English version of this article is available in J. Dan, ed., *Binah: Studies in Jewish History, Culture, and Thought* 3. *Jewish Intellectual History in the Middle Ages* [Westport, Conn., 1994], 1–17. The pages relevant to our discussion are 7–14.) Note the Hebrew title of his complementary essay, cited below, n. 43 ('Be-'Italyah ha-Deromit u-ve-'Eiropah ha-Notsrit bi-Yemei ha-Beinayim ha-Mukdamim').

[2] On the date of the letter, see C. Geisel, *Die Juden im Frankenreich: Von den Merowingern bis zum Tode Ludwigs des Frommen* (Frankfurt am Main, 1998), 575–81, and van Acker's introduction to his edition of this work (see n. 3 below), 41.

Est enim Iudeorum usus, ut, quando quodlibet pecus ad esum mactant, ut subactum idem pecus tribus incisionibus non fuerit iugulatum; si apertis interaneis iecur lesum apparuerit; si pulmo lateri adheserit, vel eum insufflatio penetraverit; si fel inventum non fuerit, et alia huiusmodi, hec tamquam immunda a Iudeis repudiata christianis venduntur et insulatario vocabulo christiana pecora appelantur.[3]

Bonfil translates:

For this is the Jewish custom: when they kill any animal so as to eat it, when this animal is brought [forth] and it has not been slaughtered in three strokes [of the knife] or if a defective liver be found in its opened entrails, or [if] the lung cleaves to the wall [i.e. the ribcage of the animal] or if it [the lung] is penetrable to an influx of air or if the gall bladder is not to be found or the like—they [the animals] are [deemed] unclean and are discarded by the Jews and sold to Christians, and are called [by the Jews] by the insulting appellation 'Christian animals'.

Let us analyze the cases one by one.

1. *ut quando quodlibet pecus ad esum mactant, ut subactum idem pecus tribus incisionibus non fuerit iugulatum*—'when they kill any animal so as to eat it, when this animal is brought [forth], and it has not been slaughtered in three strokes [of the knife] . . . [the animal is deemed] unclean.'

The phrase *subactum idem pecus* ('when this animal is brought [forth]') is redundant. Can an animal be slaughtered if it hasn't been 'brought [forth]', if it isn't present? Both Gilboa and Merhavyah,[4] two scholars who had previously translated this passage, were puzzled by the phrase and simply omitted it. Bonfil took it into account; however, by the light of his translation, he must then construe the passage as referring to unsupervised delivery of meat (*basar she-nit'alem min ha-'ayin*) rather than to the slaughter of animals, which, as we shall see,[5] simply won't do. I suggest that *subactum* here is a past participle neither of *subiacio* nor *subiecio* but of *subigo*, and the entire phrase should be translated 'when [or after] this animal has been subdued, if it has not been

[3] I have reproduced the text of Agobard as cited by Bonfil, which is taken from the Monumenta Germaniae Historica, *Epistolae* 5, *Karolini Aevi (III)* (Berlin, 1899), 183. A more recent critical edition is found in Agobard Lugdunensis, 'De insolentiae Judaeorum', *Opera Omnia*, ed. L. van Acker, Corpus Christianorum, Continuatio Medievalis 52 (Turnhout, 1981), 193. The difference between the two editions in this passage is orthographic only.

[4] Agobard, Archbishop of Lyons, *Iggerot Neged ha-Yehudim*, trans. A. Gilboa (Jerusalem, 1964), 15; H. Merhavyah, *Ha-Talmud bi-Re'i ha-Natsrut: ha-Yaḥas le-Sifrut Yisra'el she-le-'aḥar ha-Mikra ba-'Olam ha-Notsri bi-Yemei ha-Beinayim, 500–1248* (Jerusalem, 1970), 81. (The translation by Gilboa was an internal publication by the press of the Student Union of the Hebrew University, Mif'al ha-Shikhpul, and was not sold outside the university. Several libraries did, however, acquire copies.)

[5] Below, pp. 13–14.

slaughtered in three strokes [of the knife]'. A brief survey of three of the five basic laws of Jewish ritual slaughter (*sheḥitah*) will explain Agobard's remark.[6]

The standard form of non-kosher slaughter before the introduction of electric stunning was to have the animal go through a narrow pass and stab it in the neck aiming for the jugular. Blood poured out from the cut artery, the animal lost strength quickly, and when sufficiently weakened, it was finished off. Whether this process took one minute or five minutes is of no import. Jewish law does not permit stabbing (*ḥaladah*);[7] it demands slitting of the throat. The 'cut' must begin from the outside, from the skin of the neck, and progress inwards (*sheḥitah mefura'at*) until most of the windpipe and esophagus are severed.[8] It equally rejects chopping (*derasah*),[9] that is, a vertical stroke severing the windpipe and esophagus, and demands instead a cutting motion, similar to that employed in slicing bread, that is to say, back and forth, horizontal strokes (*holakhah ve-hava'ah*) with a slight downward pressure.[10] The ban against vertical cutting (*derasah*) equally disqualifies instances where the knife comes down vertically on the animal's throat and those where the animal thrusts its neck upwards towards the knife. In both cases, all or part of the cut is the product of a vertical encounter between the animal's neck and the knife. Finally, *sheḥitah* must be performed on a relatively small section of the 'windpipe', from the helmet-shaped thyroid cartilage (*shippui kova'*) to the apex of the ear of the lung (*rosh kenaf ha-'unah*). Should the cut go above the former or below the latter, *hagramah* ('slanting') has occurred and the animal is deemed not kosher (*nevelah*).[11]

What this means in practical terms is that the neck of the animal must be totally immobilized during the *sheḥitah*. If the neck moves upwards, the result is *derasah*; if the animal twists its neck sideward, the *sheḥitah* takes place outside its proper zone, and the result is *hagramah*. Indeed, the two most common causes of a failed *sheḥitah* are those of *derasah* and *hagramah*. If we are talking about a steer weighing anywhere between 600 and 900 pounds, the time one can hold its neck immobile is two or three seconds at the very most. (Remember that to hold the neck down, one must also hold the thrashing feet.) Jews in Agobard's time did not have digital cameras with instant replay, so they adopted a rule of thumb of 'three strokes'. If the animal had not been slaughtered

[6] *Ḥullin* 9a. [7] Ibid. 32a. [8] Ibid. 30a. [9] Ibid. 30b. [10] Ibid.

[11] 'Yoreh De'ah', 20: 1, based on *Ḥullin* 19a. I have here followed the translation of S. I. Levin and E. A. Boyden in their copiously annotated English edition of the 'Hilkhot Terefot' of the *Shulḥan 'Arukh*, entitled *The Kosher Codes of the Orthodox Jew* (repr. New York, 1975), 26 n. 3. The reader who would like to visualize the exact location and small size of the legitimate cutting area (*mekom ha-sheḥitah*) is referred to Y. D. Lach, *Sefer Temunei Ḥol: Chullin Illuminated: A Full Color Guide to Animal Anatomy with Halachic and Scientific Discussions* (Jerusalem, 2003), 32–4.

within a time span of three strokes, one assumed that it had reared its head and that a *derasah* or *hagramah* had occurred.

Jewish ritual slaughter thus differed saliently from Gentile slaughter in two regards: it was preceded by a mini-rodeo entailing the combined efforts of several men to subdue the animal, and the slaughter itself took seconds (rather than minutes). Both of these traits are described by Agobard: 'after the animal has been subdued, if it has not been slaughtered by three cuts ... [it is deemed] unclean'.

There is, indeed, as Bonfil points out,[12] no mention in any normative text of the restriction of *sheḥitah* to 'three cuts'. However, when one reads Gentile accounts of Jewish rites, judging these accounts by reference to Jewish literary sources scarcely suffices. One must know what actually took place, for it was the performed ritual that the Gentile observed and reported. And in terms of practical execution of *sheḥitah*, the limitation to 'three cuts' is readily understandable; in fact, a limitation of that order of magnitude is ineluctable. And indeed, a similar restriction, using the same yardstick (of measuring time by the number of cuts) was employed until very recently. In my youth, after I finished studying 'Yoreh De'ah', I went to work for several months in a slaughterhouse in the Boston area to obtain first-hand knowledge of *terefot*. Some 1,130 years had passed since Agobard's letter, still there was no way of defining a maximum time limit to *sheḥitah* other than by the number of strokes allotted. The maximum allowed at the time was two strokes. If the *sheḥitah* was not consummated within that time frame, the animal was declared *nevelah*.

2. *si apertis interaneis iecur lesum apparuerit*—'if a defective liver be found in its opened entrails'

One can translate the word *lesio/laesio* as 'defective'. 'Wounded' or 'damaged' seems an even better choice. The law is that if the liver is perforated from one side to the other, even by the minutest perforation (*mashehu*), the animal is not kosher (*terefah*). A wound is a 'negative symptom' (*re'uta*), that is to say, a symptom that requires that the liver be inspected further to see if there is indeed a defect that would render the animal *terefah*. In the case of a lung, a 'negative symptom' pointing to perforation can easily be tested by inflating the lung and seeing if any air escapes or by placing it in water, as we do a tire, to see if any bubbles appear.[13] The liver, however, is a solid and there is no way to test it for minute perforations. So the Jews in Agobard's time declared that in the (rare) event of a damaged liver, the animal was not kosher.

[12] Bonfil, ''Eduto shel Agobard mi-Lyon' (above, n. 1), 344.

[13] *Ḥullin* 48a.

Bonfil asks how they knew that the liver was damaged. According to the Babylonian Talmud, one need only inspect the lung and no other organ; from this he infers that we see here a Palestinian practice whereby all of the eighteen organs whose defect would render the animal *terefah* were inspected.[14] There is a much simpler answer. The animal had to be opened, the innards taken out, salted, and prepared for consumption. In the course of taking out the innards, any defect would be discovered. Otherwise one doesn't understand how the vast literature on the various defects of the inner organs, referred to by *Pitḥei Teshuvah*, the famous supercommentary on the *Shulḥan 'Arukh*, ever arose. The Jews of Poland and Russia in the early modern and modern era certainly followed the Babylonian Talmud and not the Palestinian one. They did not have to check any inner organ other than the lung; however, if they wished to eat it, they had to open the animal and take out its innards, and any problems came swiftly to their attention.

The well-known controversy between Babylonian and Palestinian ritual about the inspection of inner organs manifested itself in two questions: first, whether there was a requirement to systematically inspect all inner organs (including the spinal cord) or just the lung; second (according to many authorities), whether or not the animal was still deemed kosher if an inner organ that required inspection disappeared before the inspection. In point of fact, however, most inner organs were inspected in the normal course of food preparation. Again, when dealing with an outsider's report, we must not confine ourselves to formal mandates of the Law, but take into account what occurred in practice; Agobard's description proves once more to be an accurate report of Jewish conduct on the slaughtering floor.

3. *si pulmo lateri adheserit*—'if the lung cleaves to the wall [literally 'the side', i.e. the ribcage of the animal]'

Agobard reports that in such an instance the Jews viewed the animal as not kosher. This ruling corresponds to the view in the Babylonian Talmud that if a lobe of the lung cleaves to the ribcage and there is no wound in the ribcage to which we might attribute the adhesion (rather than to the suction of a perforated lobe), the animal is deemed not kosher (*terefah*).[15] It is considered *terefah* even if the lobe is extracted and inflated, yet no air escapes. Only in the exceptional case that the lobe is deeply intertwined in the flesh of the ribcage (*savikh be-bisra*) is the animal viewed as kosher. The Palestinian view is that if no air escapes as a result of the inflation, the animal is kosher, for even if there was a perforation, the network of tissue of the ribcage has sealed any such hole.

14 Bonfil, 'Eduto shel Agobard mi-Lyon' (above, n. 1), 340.

15 *Ḥullin* 48a.

The Babylonian Talmud reads thus:

R. Yosef ben Manyomi said in the name of R. Nahman: if the lung adheres to the ribcage there is nothing to be feared; if, however, there is an eruption of ulcers [on the lung close to the adhesion], there is grave fear with regard to it. Mar Yehudah said in the name of Abimi: in either case there is grave fear with regard to it. What must be done about it? Rava said, Rabin ben Shaba explained to me that we must take a knife with a fine edge and separate [the lung from the ribcage]. If the ribcage has a wound, we assume that the adhesion was caused by the wound [and the animal is permitted]; if there is no such wound, then we assume that it was caused by the lung and it is *terefah*. R. Nehemiah the son of R. Yosef applied the test of putting it in lukewarm water.[16]

The Palestinian code, on the other hand, states:

If part of the windpipe [i.e. the lung] adheres to the ribcage and the slaughterer has difficulty in [cleanly] removing it [the lung] and the cluster of sinews of the ribcage are removed with it, even though there is [may be] a perforation, for the cluster of sinews seals it; and [if] it lets out no air upon inflation, [the animal] is kosher.[17]

Pirkoi ben Baboi, the self-proclaimed pupil of R. Yehudai Gaon and self-appointed admonisher of Kairouan Jewry, similarly reports that Palestinian Jews considered an animal kosher even if its lung adhered to the ribcage.[18]

While both Palestinian and Babylonian halakhah agree that an un-accounted-for adhesion reflects a prior puncture in the lung, they differ as to

[16] *Hullin* 48a.

אמר רב יוסף בר מניומי אמר רב נחמן: ריאה הסמוכה לדופן (רש"י: דבוקה בצלעות) אין חוששין לה; העלתה צמחים, חוששין לה. מר יהודה משמיה דאבימי אמר: אחד זה ואחד זה, חוששין. היכי עבדינן? אמר רבא רבין בר שבא אסברה לי—מייתינן סכין דחלש פומיה ומפרקינן לה, אי איכא ריעותא בדופן, תלינן בתר דופן, ואי לא, מחמת ריאה היא וטריפה, ואף על גב דלא קא מפקי זיקא.

The translation is that of Soncino, with minor changes by myself; e.g. I have translated *makah* as 'wound', rather than 'taint' as given in Soncino.

[17] M. Margulies and I. M. Ta-Shma, eds., *Hilkhot Erets Yisra'el min ha-Genizah* (Jerusalem, 1973), 114, #8.

[ואם היה] מקצת הקנה (כלומר הריאה) מדובק לצילעות [והטבח מת]קשה ל[העבי]רו, והרקק (כלומר רקמת גידין) הסמוך לצילעות נתלש עמו, על פי שיש בו נקב, והרקק מחופה עליו והוא עולה בנפיחה כשרה.

I have translated the passage as emended by Margulies. There is no room to quarrel with his emendations as they stem from the *Terefot de-'Erets Yisra'el* found at the end of the *Halakhot Pesukot*, ed. S. Sassoon (Jerusalem, 1951). The explanation of *rekak* as 'cluster of sinews' is that of Margulies, introduction, 103.

[18] *Ginzei Schechter*, ed. L. Ginzberg (New York, 1929), ii. 557–9, and see Ginzberg's introductory remarks, 538–40, and those of Margulies (above, n. 17), 103 n. 15. One could insist that Pirkoi refers to

the acceptable sealant. The Palestinian view is that any natural sealant will do; hence if one takes the lung out and inflates it, if no air escapes the lung, the animal is kosher. The Babylonian view is that only the exceptional sealant that results from the lung being intertwined with the flesh of the ribcage will do halakhically. Hence, there is no point inflating the lung after the slaughter, for even if no air escapes, it would only demonstrate that the presumed perforation has a temporary and legally inadequate sealant. The practice described by Agobard corresponds to the simplest reading of the talmudic passage in *Ḥullin*. Adhesion creates the legal presumption of perforation (as the Babylonian *amora*, Abimi, thought); one checks to see whether the wall has some wound (and such wounds are rare indeed), and if it does not, the animal is not kosher and inflation is superfluous. To be sure, the discussion in the Talmud on this topic is famously ambiguous, so much so that already in the mid-twelfth century R. Zeraḥyah ha-Levi, Ba'al ha-Ma'or, could preface his discussion of this *sugya* with the following words: 'The doubts and controversies [surrounding this *sugya*] have multiplied since earliest times.'[19] Nevertheless, the position described by Agobard fits one classic interpretation of the *sugya* in the Babylonian Talmud (Bavli); it cannot be squared with any construction of the Palestinian law.

4. *vel eum insufflatio penetraverit*—'or if it [the lung] is penetrated by an influx of air' (i.e. infused air penetrates the walls of the lung and exits; in other words, inflation reveals a hole in the lung)

As noted above, when a negative symptom (*re'uta*) is discovered on the lung, inflating it to see whether it is perforated is the standard test of *kashrut* in both Babylonian and Palestinian law. To be sure, there are instances when inflation is ineffective: such cases, however, are few and far between, and to this day inflation is the most frequently employed test in slaughterhouses.

5. *si fel inventum non fuerit*—'or if the gall bladder is not to be found'

The Mishnah states that if the liver is missing the animal is *terefah* and so too if the gall bladder is perforated.[20] It makes no determination about a missing gall bladder. One could argue that if perforation renders the animal *terefah*, it

some other *terefot*. From the context, however, it seems clear that he refers to those he had previously mentioned, especially the instance of the lung cleaving to the ribcage, which he had discussed at length, citing in detail the proofs advanced by R. Yehudai Gaon.

[19] 'Hilkhot Sheḥitah, Bedikah u-Terefot shel Ba'al ha-Ma'or', in *Sefer ha-Zikkaron li-Khevod Maran Ba'al ha-Paḥad Yitsḥak* (Hutner), ed. Y. Buksboim (Jerusalem, 1984), 431. For a comprehensive survey of the topic, see M. Amar, 'Dinei Sirkhot ha-Re'ah—Mekoram ve-Hitpatḥutam' (Ph.D. diss., Bar-Ilan University, 1998), 172–297.

[20] *Ḥullin* 42a.

would be all the more so if that organ was missing entirely. Conversely, one could argue that a missing spleen does not render the animal *terefah*, though a perforated one does,[21] and the same holds true for the gall bladder. Scholars have argued each way for centuries.[22]

The Palestinian *Hilkhot Terefot* found in the Cairo Genizah reads thus:[23] 'If no gall bladder was found, run your tongue along the adjacent areas; if they have a taste of the gall bladder, the animal is viewed as being kosher; if not, it is not kosher.'

This view is quoted in the *Halakhot Gedolot*,[24] possibly as a result of Palestinian influence, which we know is present in that work. It is equally possible that it is a tradition common to Babylonia and Palestine, as the same view is cited in the *'Ittur* in the name of the *She'iltot*,[25] which is free of such influences. Yet caution must be exercised, as no known manuscript of the *She'iltot* contains this passage. Such a ruling is also found in a responsum attributed to Rav Tsemaḥ Gaon in the *Halakhot Pesukot*, and again in an anonymous responsum of the Geonim that was published first by Ginzberg in his *Geonica* and then by Assaf.[26] We can't be certain then that this was an indigenous Babylonian tradition; there is no question, however, that it is a Palestinian one. Nevertheless, Agobard makes no reference to it. One may reasonably doubt whether

21 Ibid. 42a, 55a.

22 See e.g. *Sefer Ma'aseh ha-Ge'onim* (Berlin, 1910), 92–5; *Sefer Ravan*, ed. S. Z. Ehrenreich (Simleu Silvaniei, 1926), i, #134; *Sefer Ravyah—Ḥullin, 'Avodah Zarah*, ed. D. Deblitsky (Benei Berak, 1976), #1089; *Sefer Ravyah*, ed. D. Deblitsky (Benei Berak, 2005), iv, #1089 (pp. 107–8).

23 *Ginzei Schechter*, 114, #6: ואם לא היתה בה מרה, תן לשונך במקומה, אם יש בלשונך טעם מרה כש[רה] ואם לאו פסו[לה].

24 Warsaw edn. (1875), fo. 127d; ed. E. Hildesheimer (Jerusalem, 1987), iii. 141.

25 R. Me'ir Yonah edn. (repr. New York, 1956), *Hilkhot Sheḥitah, sha'ar sheni*, fo. 35d, s.v. *marah*.

26 *Halakhot Pesukot min ha-Ge'onim* (Cracow, 1896), #35; *Teshuvot ha-Ge'onim min ha-Genizah*, ed. S. Assaf (Jerusalem, 1929), 171, #137; *Geonica*, ed. L. Ginzberg (New York, 1909), ii. 29, #XII. The simplest interpretation of the difference between the formulation of the *Halakhot Gedolot*, which states the allowance with regard to a quadruped domestic animal (*behemah*) and the responsum of R. Tsemaḥ Gaon, who ruled similarly with regard to fowl (*'of*), is pure happenstance. The question put to R. Tsemaḥ Gaon concerned a fowl, hence he limited his response to fowl. Note that the respondent in *Geonica* argues from Levi's statement in *Ḥullin* 57a: 'The defects enumerated by the Sages with regard to *behemah* apply also to fowl', i.e. he derived the law of a missing gall bladder in the case of fowl from the same law in the case of *behemah*. If the principle of tasting were not operative with regard to *behemah*, how could one infer its existence with regard to fowl? Moreover, the version of the *Halakhot Gedolot* used by Avraham b. Yitsḥak, author of the *Sefer ha-'Eshkol* (d. 1158), had the allowance with regard to fowl (rather than *behemah*), exactly as in the geonic responsum cited above. If *behemah* and *'of* are identical in this matter, the two different versions of the *Halakhot Gedolot* are then of no matter; legally they say one and the same thing. If, however, the law of the gall bladder differs in these two types of animal, we must then posit two separate legal traditions in the texts of the *Halakhot Gedolot*. Occam's razor comes swiftly to mind.

such a piquant fact as the Jews running their tongues along the insides of an animal adjacent to the gall bladder would have gone unnoted by Agobard in his anti-Jewish missive to the emperor. Apparently, Jews in Agobard's time did not practice 'tongue testing'. And, indeed, a ruling that declares without qualification that a missing gall bladder renders the animal *terefah* (and omits any ameliorative tongue testing) is found in the *Hilkhot Sheḥitah* (drawn apparently from the *Hilkhot Re'u*) at the end of the *Halakhot Pesukot* and is cited in the *Sefer ve-Hizhir*.[27]

Agobard's description is again proven to be accurate—and this should not surprise us. He saw the Jews as having great influence in the court and felt that they were harassing him, indeed, were out to humiliate and even destroy him. With such a perspective, he would make every effort to see that his report was accurate, and not give the Jews an opportunity to tell the emperor, 'Have an agent of yours check out the Jewish practice in the slaughter of animals, and you will see for yourself that the Archbishop of Lyons is a liar.'

ADDENDUM

In view of Reuven Bonfil's distinguished reputation, I think it necessary to respond to his arguments concerning the Palestinian orientation reflected in the practices described by Agobard.

1. *ut quando quodlibet pecus ad esum mactant, ut subactum idem pecus tribus incisionibus non fuerit iugulatum*—'when they kill any animal so as to eat it, when this animal is brought [forth] and it has not been slaughtered in three strokes [of the knife]'

Bonfil opines that the law being referred to here is that of 'meat that has temporarily escaped observation' (*basar she-nit'alem min ha-'ayin*).[28] If one sends, via an unsupervised Gentile, meat that has no distinctive markings, it is forbidden to eat it, for fear that the Gentile has interchanged it with non-kosher meat. The Talmud states about Rabbah bar Rav Huna that before he sent meat via a Gentile he would cut it in a triangular shape, which served as a distinctive marking.[29] To sustain his argument Bonfil must then show, first, that Agobard's description fits that of *basar she-nit'alem min ha-'ayin*, and second, that

[27] *Halakhot Pesukot* (Paris, 1886), 141; *Sefer ve-Hizhir* (Warsaw, 1880), ii. 80, 'Parashat Shemini'. Robert Brody noted to me that the first source most probably drew on the *Hilkhot Re'u*.

[28] Bonfil, 'Eduto shel Agobard mi-Lyon' (above, n. 1), 344.

[29] *Ḥullin* 95b.

the triangular cut is a Palestinian tradition and not a Babylonian one. Let us examine each of these claims.

Bonfil's translation of *subactum*, 'has been brought forth', would fit the case of temporarily unsupervised meat that has just been brought again under Jewish purview; however, the context of the entire passage is the abattoir, not the Jewish kitchen. His interpretation would further mandate that *iugulare* means 'cut' rather than 'slaughter'. However, *iugulare* is derived from *iugulum* (neck) and means 'to slit the throat', not 'to cut' (analogous to the Hebrew *la'arof*, which is derived from *'oref*). Furthermore, *pecus* means 'animal' and not 'meat'. Can one imagine a variant reading of the famous verse in John (1: 14), 'et Verbum pecus factum est'?!

Second, the account of Rabbah bar Rav Huna's triangular cut appears in the Babylonian Talmud, and Rabbah bar Rav Huna himself is a Babylonian *amora*; thus, any ruling or practice of his would be a Babylonian one. Bonfil replies to these last objections in the following words:

> Rabbah bar Rav Huna is indeed a Babylonian *amora*, received his traditions [*kibbel torah*] from Rav Yosef, and it is told of him that in a quarrel with members of the household of the *resh galuta* displayed independence on the basis of the ordination [*semikhah*] that he had received from his father, who had received *semikhah* from Rav . . . which linked him directly to the traditions of Palestine.[30]

Thus, his triangular cut is a Palestinian tradition, as Bonfil puts it: 'We have here a Palestinian practice, even though no mention of this is made either in the Palestinian Talmud or in the *midrashim*, and its only remnant is to be found in the personal practice of one individual in Babylonia.'[31]

I regret to say that I have difficulty in following Bonfil's reasoning. Let us grant him the conclusion that the triangular cut is a Palestinian tradition; many *amora'im*, indeed, many of the most famous *amora'im* in the Babylonian Talmud are Palestinian, as Rabbi Yoḥanan and Resh Lakish, Rav Ami and Rav Ashi, Rabbi Yehoshua' ben Levi and Rav himself. By Bonfil's lights, everything found in their name in the Talmud Bavli is a Palestinian tradition. The Mishnah and the Tosefta are clearly Palestinian, thus all the traditions they contain are equally Palestinian. If one accepts the documentary hypothesis and doesn't believe that the Five Books of Moses were given to Moses at Mount Sinai, most of the Pentateuch is also Palestinian. Thus, almost all of the Written and Oral Law is Palestinian. If this is so, why did such towering scholars as J. N. Epstein, Saul Lieberman, and Shraga Abramson labor so

30 Bonfil, ''Eduto shel Agobard mi-Lyon' (above, n. 1), 344–5.

31 Ibid. 345.

hard, using a panoply of scholarly tools—strange variant readings and orthographies, exotic aggadic works, citations of long-lost *midrashim* by Christian polemicists, Genizah fragments, and ancient liturgy—to uncover lost Palestinian traditions, when hundreds of pages of them were readily found in the classic biblical and talmudic literature? The answer is quite simple. When we speak of 'Palestinian traditions' we refer to those rulings and practices that were unknown to Babylonian *amora'im* or were rejected by them. In other words, distinctive and exclusively Palestinian traditions found in the Palestinian Talmud, embedded in a wide and often exotic range of *midrashim*, and even in passing reports of Gentile observers. Put differently, there is no such thing as a 'pure' Babylonian tradition. Babylonia began as a Palestinian offshoot. Its traditions are thus a mixture of the teachings of Babylonian and Palestinian *amora'im*, all found in the Babylonian Talmud. 'Palestinian tradition', on the other hand, is pure Palestinian teachings (with no Babylonian admixture) and is found, as noted above, in the Palestinian Talmud, and further implied or reflected in a number of sundry sources, as early *midrashim* and Palestinian liturgy. I have serious doubts as to the Palestinian nature of the 'three cuts' of the Babylonian *amora*, Rabbah bar Rav Huna. That is, however, of no matter here. Rabbah bar Rav Huna's practice is found in the Babylonian Talmud, and hence it is part and parcel of the Babylonian tradition.

Towards the end of his discussion Bonfil raises the possibility that perhaps the passage in Agobard does, indeed, refer to the slaughtering of animals rather than to the cutting and shipping of meat, and ever so briefly suggests a relationship between the 'three cuts' of Agobard and the *Hilkhot Sheḥitah* of Eldad ha-Dani, about which he claims that 'medieval commentators (*rishonim*) had a tradition that it was of Palestinian provenance'.[32] Setting aside the dubious validity of this tradition, I would only say that I see little reason to resort to the alleged practices of the lost ten tribes of Israel to explain a description that is perfectly understandable in terms of the practice of the well-known remaining two.

2. *si apertis interaneis iecur lesum apparuerit*—'if a defective liver be found in its opened entrails'

Bonfil contends that this ruling reflects Palestinian practice,[33] for we find in the Palestinian *Hilkhot Terefot* the following ruling: 'If the liver has been wholly removed [i.e. not found upon opening the animal] or it has fully dissolved, [the animal is] not kosher. [However,] if there remains a healthy [sec-

[32] Ibid. 345–6. [33] Ibid. 348–9.

tion] of it the size of an olive, the animal is kosher, provided that [the remaining part of the liver, which is] the size of an olive is healthy.'[34]

Unfortunately Agobard's description does not match the Palestinian halakhah. The requirement of 'healthy' is made only with regard to a partial liver, the *remaining* piece the size of an olive; if an entire liver is found (as is usually the case), there is no requirement of 'healthy' in Palestinian sources. Agobard, however, does not treat the rare instance of an animal with a partially missing liver, but of a liver with a wound (*lesio*). What bearing does the above-cited passage from the Palestinian *Hilkhot Terefot* have, then, on Agobard's report?

3. *si pulmo lateri adheserit*—'if the lung cleaves to the wall [literally 'the side', i.e. the ribcage of the animal]'

Bonfil is well aware that this case corresponds to the well-known and much-discussed passage in *Ḥullin* 48a of 'the lung that adheres to the wall' (i.e. ribcage).[35] He is also aware that Agobard's description reflects the Babylonian position and not the Palestinian one, contrary to his thesis. However, he contends that this 'is impossible' (*i atah yakhol lomar kakh*), and proceeds to suggest that perhaps Agobard got it wrong or that one should emend 'unclean' (i.e. not kosher) to 'clean' (i.e. kosher).[36] I'm somewhat perplexed why Agobard should mention kosher meat, which Jews do in fact eat, when he is seeking to demonstrate the Jewish insolence of selling to Gentiles meat deemed unfit by their law for their own consumption. It is instances of non-kosher meat that he must here enumerate, not those of the kosher sort.

Alternatively, Bonfil suggests, perhaps the *vel* ('or') in the subsequent section is an error and should be elided. That is to say, there are not two instances of non-kosher meat—one if the lung adheres to the ribcage and another if air escapes an inflated lung. Only one case of non-kosher meat is described: a lung that adhered to the ribcage from which air escaped when it was subsequently inflated. There can be no appeal to variant readings, as there is only one manuscript of *De Insolentia Iudaeorum*. Of Lyons provenance and dating from the ninth century, it may well have been the personal copy of Florus, an associate of Agobard.[37] Bonfil's emendation is thus pure conjecture. A necessary emen-

34 *Ginzei Schechter*, ii. 113: ובכבד אם ניטלה כולה או נמהא[!] כולה פס[ול], אם נשתייר בה כזיית[!] בריא כש[ר], ובלבד שיהא אותו כזית בריא סמוך למרה.

35 Bonfil, ''Eduto shel Agobard mi-Lyon' (above, n. 1), 341.

36 Ibid. 342.

37 Paris, Bibliothèque Nationale, lat. 2853. The edition of Massonius (1605) and that of Baluzius (1666)—the latter incorporated by J.-P. Migne in his *Patrologia Latina* (v. 104)—were both based on the same Bibliothèque Nationale manuscript as that of van Acker. See van Acker (above, n. 3), introduction, 51–61.

dation for his thesis, to be sure, for the unemended text shows that in the 820s the Jewish community adhered to the Babylonian and not the Palestinian rite. Why should this fact be problematic? Why emend a perfectly comprehensible text? Unless, of course, the dominance of the Palestinian rite among Jews in Carolingian Europe is a premise to which facts must conform rather than a conclusion that has emerged from the facts.

4. *vel eum insufflatio penetraverit*—'or if it [i.e. the lung] is penetrated by an influx of air [i.e. infused air penetrates the walls of the lung and exits; in other words, inflation reveals a hole in the lung]'

As stated above, inflation is the standard test for *terefot* of the lung, in both the Babylonian and the Palestinian rite.

5. *si fel inventum non fuerit*—'or if the gall bladder is not to be found'

Bonfil opens by stating that the *terefah* status of the gall bladder is the position of a solitary individual (*da'at yaḥid*), and those who disagree are of the opinion that no defect whatsoever of the gall bladder would render the animal *terefah*; the gall bladder is not an organ whose defects render the animal 'non-kosher'. He writes:

> A close study of the discussion in the Babylonian Talmud reveals that they [the Palestinians] treated [instances of defective gall bladders] more severely than did the Babylonians. According to the Babylonian Talmud, not only was the gall bladder not included [among the organs whose defect renders the animal *terefah*], but one could resolve a certain problem by assuming that the claim that a pierced gall bladder [rendered the animal *terefah*] was the opinion of a solitary individual [*da'at yaḥid*]. Consequently, those who disagreed were of the view that the gall bladder was not one of the organs whose defects rendered an animal *terefah*; indeed, the animal would be kosher even if the gall bladder were entirely missing![38]

Let us first address Bonfil's notion of 'solitary opinion' (*da'at yaḥid*). He documents his thesis with a citation from *Ḥullin*: 'Who is it that includes [the piercing of the] gall bladder in the list of defects [that render an animal *terefah*]? It is R. Yossi ben R. Yehudah.'[39] He then proceeds to cite Rashi's comment on that discussion: 'Whoever considers [i.e. includes] the pierced gall bladder as one of the eighteen *terefot* mentioned in the Mishnah holds a solitary position. R. Yossi ben Yehudah is the [only] one who includes this in the Mishnah.'[40]

38 Bonfil, ''Eduto shel Agobard mi-Lyon' (above, n. 1), 341–2.

39 42b: 'מרה מאן קתני לה? ר' יוסי בר' יהודה, אפיק מרה ועייל חרותא'.

40 s.v. *marah man ka-tani lah*: 'דחשבה ניקבה במניינא די"ח טריפות במתניתין, יחידאה היא ור"י בר' יהודה קתני לה . . . ותנא דבי ר"י [ר' ישמעאל] לית ליה מרה ואפיק מרה ועייל חרותא'.

Every view in the Talmud began as one of a solitary individual. The ubiquitous phrase 'the Sages say' (*ve-ḥakhamim omrim*) does not mean that this view arose simultaneously in many different minds, but that some individual sage's view won widespread acceptance. Before an idea is accepted, it is an individual view; after its acceptance it becomes normative and universally binding. In the case at hand, the school of R. Yishma'el was of the opinion that the gall bladder was not reckoned an organ whose defects rendered the animal *terefah*. Against the view of the school of R. Yishma'el, the opinion of R. Yossi was—at that moment in the past—that of a 'solitary individual'. R. Yehudah ha-Nasi, however, accepted the view of R. Yossi and reproduced it in the Mishnah as an unchallenged ruling (*setam mishnah*), the most authoritative formulation possible in the halakhic literature. And lest someone still entertain some doubts about ruling against the school of R. Yishma'el, R. Yoḥanan, in the very next generation, emphatically restated that R. Yossi's ruling was the binding one. After the legal determinations of R. Yehudah ha-Nasi and R. Yoḥanan, no one in Palestine or Babylonia ever entertained doubts on the matter. If we may label a *setam mishnah* a *da'at yaḥid*, we will have to rewrite much of the history of halakhah.

Bonfil continues: 'In fact, in light of the discussion in the Bavli, some medieval talmudic scholars ruled that an absent gall bladder did not render the animal *terefah*, even though eventually the more stringent view prevailed on the basis of the rule that "all organs whose puncture renders the animal *terefah*, [their absence does equally]".'[41] As we have seen (above, point 5 in the original essay), the Mishnah states that if the gall bladder is pierced the animal is *terefah* and makes no mention of a missing gall bladder. The view that an animal missing a gall bladder is still kosher has nothing to do with any supposed 'doubts' as to whether a gall bladder is included in the list of organs whose defects render the animal *terefah*—that has been unquestioned since the beginning of the third century CE—but with a specific, narrow question as to whether a missing (as opposed to a pierced) gall bladder is, in fact, such a defect.

To return to Agobard. As we have seen above, the ruling that a missing gall bladder renders the animal *terefah* is found in the *Sefer Halakhot Gedolot*, the *Sefer Halakhot Pesukot*, and in the geonic responsa. It was therefore a ruling common to both the Palestinian and Babylonian traditions. The Palestinian tradition allows for tasting the surrounding area for signs of bitterness which would attest to the previous presence of a gall bladder. Babylonian law was divided on this issue. Agobard, in his accusatory letter to the emperor, makes

[41] Bonfil, 'Eduto shel Agobard mi-Lyon' (above, n. 1), 342.

no mention of Jews licking the innards of an animal before they declare an animal unclean (*immundum*) and fit only for Christian consumption. It is hard to imagine, as I have noted previously, that such a pungent and amusing detail would not have made its way into his portrayal of Jewish 'insolence and superstitions'. Agobard's account squares with one school of Babylonian halakhic thought—which disqualified missing gall bladders and knew nothing of 'tongue testing'; it cannot be squared with any Palestinian one.

Megillat Aḥima'ats

Seeing that Bonfil views his article on Agobard as being complementary—both in method and in point of fact—to his essay on *Megillat Aḥima'ats* (*Chronicle of Aḥima'ats*),[42] we need equally to examine his arguments in that article. Bonfil contends that *Megillat Aḥima'ats* reflects, among other things, the shift from a Palestinian to a Babylonian orientation that occurred in southern Italy in the mid-ninth century. The displacement of Palestinian law by the Babylonian one is reflected in two areas: 'Gentile bread' and the permissibility of fasting on the Sabbath. My distinguished colleague has addressed these issues in two articles: in an essay in Italian printed in 1983 and in a revised Hebrew version which saw the light of day in 1987.[43] The major difference lies in his wisely modifying, in light of Gilat's essay in *Tarbiz*,[44] his prior claim that fasting on the Sabbath was a Palestinian practice. It seems only proper that I should address his revised, qualified views of 1987.

Gentile Bread

Megillat Aḥima'ats reads:

> And the men began to quarrel among themselves
> Some women came out of their houses
> And with long staves for racking the oven and charred by fire,
> And with these the men and women beat one another.[45]

42 Ibid. 327.

43 'Tra due mundi: prospettive di ricerca sulla storia culturale degli Ebrei dell'Italia meridionale nell'Alto Medioevo', in *Italia Judaica*, Atti del I Convegno internazionale, Bari, 18–22 May 1981 (Rome, 1983), 135–58, esp. 143–6; id., 'Bein Erets Yisra'el le-Bavel: Kavim le-Ḥeker Toledot ha-Tarbut shel ha-Yehudim be-'Italyah ha-Deromit u-ve-'Eiropah ha-Notsrit bi-Yemei ha-Beinayim ha-Mukdamim', *Shalem*, 5 (1987), 1–30, esp. 13–19.

44 Y. D. Gilat, 'Ta'anit be-Shabbat', *Tarbiz*, 52 (1983), 1–15; repr. in id., *Perakim be-Hishtalshelut ha-Halakhah* (Jerusalem, 1992), 109–22.

45 *Megillat Aḥima'ats*, ed. B. Klar (Jerusalem, 1944), 18: **ועשו מריבה האנשים ביניהם / ותצאנה הנשים מבתיהם / ובעצים הארוכים / אשר התנור מחככים / ומן האש מחרכים / בהם היו האנשים והנשים מכים**. (Translation taken from *Chronicle of Ahimaaz*, trans., with an introduction and notes, by M. Salzman [New York, 1924], 68.)

Further we find:

> The men came (to the city) in a wagon
> The women came out from their ovens (*furnon*)
> And beat the men with their staves (*fourchons*).[46]

It is forbidden to eat bread baked by a Gentile. The Palestinian law and Babylonian law differed on whether symbolic participation by the Jew in the baking process, such as throwing a stick of wood in the fire, would neutralize the fact that most of the process had been performed by a Gentile. In the words of the famous work, *The Differences between the Men of the East and Those Who Dwell in Erets Yisra'el*: 'The Men of the East [i.e. Babylonians] forbid bread baked by a Gentile, but eat Gentile bread provided that a Jew throws [some] wood into the oven. The Men of the West [i.e. Erets Yisra'el] forbid [the case of] the wood, for a [piece of] wood neither permits nor forbids.'[47]

From the fact that the women were baking their own bread Bonfil infers that the Jews of southern Italy at the time (mid-ninth century) followed Palestinian law, for had they followed Babylonian law they could have contented themselves with throwing a piece of wood in the fire and did not need their *fourchons* and 'long sticks'. However, women throughout the Third World bake their own bread—is this because they follow Palestinian law?

Bonfil concludes his discussion by writing: 'Would it be unreasonable to assume that Italian Jews, before their practice changed [from following the Palestinian rite] to that of Babylonia observed the Palestinian stringency [*ḥumra*] in the matter of Gentile bread and baked their bread in their own homes?'[48] Frankly, I don't know the answer to the question. I do know, however, that the question assumes what most needs to be proven, namely, that Italian Jewry, indeed, once followed the Palestinian rite and subsequently switched to the Babylonian one.

[46] *Megillat Aḥima'ats*, ed. B. Klar (Jerusalem, 1944), 18 (translation taken from *Chronicle of Ahimaaz*, trans., with an introduction and notes, by M. Salzman [New York, 1924], 68). **באו אנשים בקרון / ויצאו הנשים מפורנון / והכו אנשים בפורקון**. I have translated 'ovens' rather than 'houses' as Salzman would have it and placed in parentheses the word found in the Hebrew source—*furnons*. I have similarly placed *fourchons* in parentheses, for that is the word found in the Hebrew source and which is translated by Salzman simply as 'staves'.

[47] *Ha-Ḥillukim she-bein Anshei ha-Mizraḥ u-Venei Erets Yisra'el*, ed. M. Margulies (Jerusalem, 1938), 84.

[48] Bonfil, 'Bein Erets Yisra'el u-Bavel' (above, n. 43), 14.

Fasting on the Sabbath

Megillat Aḥima'ats reads:

> There [Aaron] came upon a Jew, a Sephardi, who befriended him and offered hospitality at his home. At mealtime the Sephardi did not eat, though the day was Sabbath unto God. The master, surprised at his conduct, said, 'Today is the Sabbath unto the awe-inspiring One; why dost thou not delight thyself with that which is called a delight?' The unhappy man answered, 'O my master, do not urge me, for I am very sad, I am grieving for my son who has been taken from me for my many sins, I do not really know whether he is alive or dead.'[49]

Bonfil is aware that both in Palestine and in Babylonia some individuals fasted on the Sabbath. However, he writes: 'I think we will not err if we are of the belief that over the course of time, fasting on the Sabbath became a matter of exceptional piety [*midat ḥasidut*], mostly in the context of repentance of one's sins, in the light of the influence of Palestinian law, for Babylonians tended to disallow this practice entirely.'[50] I don't quite know the basis for this statement, but let us forget halakhah for a moment and the rival systems of Babylonia and Palestine. If one sees one's generous host not touching a morsel on the Sabbath, need one be a Babylonian to approach him and ask, 'Why aren't you eating?' And if someone's son has disappeared and he is so worried as to his son's fate that he loses all appetite and doesn't eat on the Sabbath, does this mean he is following Palestinian law?

All in all, the tales told by Aḥima'ats in his *Chronicle* tell us nothing whatsoever about the primacy of Babylonian or Palestinian law in southern Italy in

49 *Megillat Aḥima'ats* (above, n. 45), 14:

איש אחד יהודי / והוא היה ספרדי / הוליכו עמו / וכבדו כעצמו / בא עת האכל / והספרדי לא היה אוכל / ואותו היום היה / שבת הקדש ליה / הרב שאלו / להבין מלולו / שבת היום / לנורא ואי[ו]ם / ולמה לא תתענג / בקראוי ענג? / ענה העני / ואמר אי אדני / אל תענישני / כי מר נפש אני / ומתאבל על בני / שנכסה ממני / מרב עוני / ואיני יודע באמת / אם חי הוא אם מת / השיב לו בחבת / ונן כבוד לשבות / והוראני אורחות ומעגלות / שהיה רגיל לירד ולעלות / אם בחיים עודהו / אצלך אביאהו / ואם גזור הוא מארץ / אגיד לך בחרץ.

Chronicle of Ahimaaz, ed. Salzman (above, n. 45) (from which the translation is taken), 67–8.

50 Bonfil, 'Bein Erets Yisra'el u-Bavel' (above, n. 43), 18. Bonfil apparently bases himself on Pirkoi ben Baboi's words (above, n. 18), p. 564: שמתענין ביום טוב ובשבת ובשני ימים טובים של רא[ש] השנה ובשבת בין ראש השנה ליום הכפורים. However, the simplest reading of Pirkoi's statement is that Jews fast on the two days of Rosh Hashanah and on the Sabbath between Rosh Hashanah and Yom Kippur. The *vav* of *u-vi-shenei* is either the *vav* of explication, as Ginzberg would have it, or simply a scribal error, as Jacob Mann contends. (See Ginzberg [above, n. 18], 541–2, and his note on 564, to l. 16; J. Mann, 'Les "Chapitres" de ben Bâboï et les relations de R. Yehoudaï Gaon avec la Palestine', *Revue des études juives*, 70 [1920], 140, and 120 n. 4. Mann's article was subsequently reprinted in his *Collected Essays* [Gedera, 1971], 257–92. The passages under discussion are found at pp. 264 and 284.)

the mid-ninth century. Agobard's report, however, is clear evidence that the Jews in Lyons, like most probably those in or around Aachen, and possibly in wide swaths of the Carolingian Empire,[51] were guided by Babylonian law as early as the 820s.[52]

51 Note the subtitle of Bonfil's essay on *Megillat Aḥima'ats* (above, n. 43), 'Kavim le-Ḥeker Toledot ha-Tarbut shel ha-Yehudim be-'Italyah ha-Deromit u-ve-'Eiropah ha-Notsrit bi-Yemei ha-Beinayim ha-Mukdamim'.

52 A similar Babylonian orientation is found in Kairouan when it first emerges in the late 8th and early 9th centuries. See M. Ben-Sasson, *Tsemiḥat ha-Kehillah ha-Yehudit be-'Artsot ha-'Islam: Kairouan 800–1057* (Jerusalem, 1996), 36 ff.

CHAPTER TWO

Dialectics, Scholasticism, and the Origin of the *Tosafot*

MY DISTINGUISHED COLLEAGUE Avraham Grossman has repeatedly contended that the tosafist movement arose, not in the talmudic academies of France in the twelfth century as commonly thought, but in those of Germany in the eleventh century—more specifically in Worms, in the academy of R. Shelomoh b. Shimshon (also known as Rabbenu Sasson).[1] The tosafist method of study is dialectical, and Grossman's opinion is that one of the three major factors behind the rise of dialectics in the eleventh-century Jewish academies is the flourishing of Christian scholasticism at that time. I would like to analyze these two claims, both factually and methodologically.

Grossman writes:

A study of the literary oeuvre of the German scholars in the eleventh century reveals clear traces of some of the components that characterize the approach of the Tosafists. Rabbenu Gershom Me'or ha-Golah, and even more so his pupil, R. Yehudah ha-

[1] Grossman initially presented his findings at the Bar-Ilan conference on Rashi in 1988 and adumbrated them the following year in the addenda to the revised edition of his *Ḥakhmei Ashkenaz ha-Rishonim: Koroteihem, Darkam be-Hanhagat ha-Tsibbur, Yetsiratam ha-Ruḥanit mi-Reshit Yishuvam ve-'ad li-Gezerot Tatnu (1096)* (Jerusalem, 1989), 446. They were subsequently published as 'Reshitan shel "Tosafot"' in the proceedings of the conference: T. A. Steinfeld, ed., *Rashi: 'Iyyunim bi-Yetsirato* (Ramat Gan, 1993), 57–68. He republished the essay as part of his important study *Ḥakhmei Tsarfat ha-Rishonim: Koroteihem, Darkam be-Hanhagat ha-Tsibbur, Yetsiratam ha-Ruḥanit* (Jerusalem, 1995), 439–54. The only difference was that he transposed the closing section of his article on the influence of Christian dialectic to the beginning of the book (pp. 22–3) as part of his discussion of the 'Renaissance of the Twelfth Century'. However, in the closing section of his book he counted this influence as one of the three significant factors for the growth of dialectics among German Talmudists of the 11th century and made a cross-reference (p. 453 n. 81) to his discussion found at the beginning of his study. He repeated this position more recently in his article 'Temurot bi-Zekhuyot ha-Perat ba-Ḥevrah ha-Yehudit be-'Eiropah ha-Notsrit ba-Me'ah ha-Yod-Alef ve-ha-Yod-Bet', in D. Golinkin et al., eds., *Torah li-Shemah: Meḥkarim be-Madda'ei ha-Yahadut li-Khevod Professor Shamma Yehudah Friedman* (New York and Ramat Gan, 2008), 489–90.

Kohen, wrote many responsa in the form of a dialectical give-and-take [*masa u-matan*], characteristic of the Tosafists. One frequently finds 'and if you will say', 'and if you will object', 'and if someone asks', 'and should someone wish to say', and the like in their writings. As we shall see further on, this is significant evidence for their mode of talmudic study. There are other characteristics common to the Tosafists in their writings. This phenomenon is also found in the writings of R. Shelomoh b. Shimshon, who, together with R. Kalonymos, headed the academy of Worms towards the end of the eleventh century, until his death at the hands of the Crusaders in 1096. R. Shelomoh b. Shimshon also often used dialectical give-and-take in the writing of his responsa. His entire approach [*derekh 'iyyuno*] to the Talmud, in his deductions from it and in his interpretations, is very close to the approach of the Tosafists. It is hardly accidental that Rashi calls him 'a sharp and acute thinker' [*adam ḥarif u-mefulpal*].

I will content myself with one illustration that concretizes—if only externally—the frequent use of dialectical give-and-take by R. Shelomoh b. Shimshon, and, to a certain extent, his approach in talmudic studies. The example is from a responsum treating the question whether a Gentile slave can be an agent to bring a bill of divorce from the husband to the wife:

> מדפסיק ותני שאינו בתורת גיטין וקידושין אלמ' דהרי הוא כנכרי, דאיהו נמי לא הוי בתורת גיטי' וקידושין. וכי היכי דנכרי פסול בכל מילי דגט דתנן . . . נכרי נמי לאו בר היתר' נינהו דלא שייך בתורת גיטין, אלמא דפסלי תלמודא להביא את הגט דלאו בר היתר' הוא . . . וכי היכא דעבד אין נעשה שליח, הכי נמי גוי אין נעשה שליח לתרומה . . . ואינו בשום שליחות כלל. דאי איתא דעבד איתא בשליחות דהולכה ונתינה, אמאי תני דעד בר היתר' כלל . . . אלא מדפסיק ותני הכי, שמע מיניה דפסיקא ליה מילתא שאינו בתורת גיטין כלל . . . ואם בעל דין לחלוק אמאי קאמר ר' חייא בר אבא אין העבד נעשה שליח לקבל גט אשה מיד בעלה, לימ' אין עבד נעשה שליח להוליך גט וליתנו לה, ואנא ידענא דכל שכן דאין נעשה שליח לקבלה, ורבות' קמ"ל דאע"ג דנראין הדברים שהעבד מקבל גט לחברו אפי' הכי אין מקבל גט אשתו. ותו . . . השתא יש קל וחומר . . . ותו פשוט מינה דאינו כשר להולכה . . . וכיון דאשה לקבלה הכי נמי כשרה להולכה . . . ועוד נראין הדברים כן דהכשר לזה כשר לזה והפסול לזה פסול לזה . . . ועוד איש חכם יוסיף דעת ונבון תחבולות יקנה: דהא כדבעו מינה מרב אמי, מהו שיעשה שליח לקבל גט אשה מיד בעלה לא מהדר להו שום כשרות אלא מתני' דייק. (תשובות חכמי צרפת ולותיר, סי' מו) [2]

A close study of the method of analysis of the talmudic passages and their comparison with one another in this responsum and others clearly shows a similarity to the Tosafists, not only in form (the give-and-take) but even in the substantive thought.[3]

[2] I have not translated this passage for it consists of excerpts and phrases that have resonance for someone familiar with the tosafist idiom but which, strung together, have no meaning either in Hebrew or in English. They were chosen by Grossman for their style of language; they do not form a coherent passage.

[3] In Steinfeld, ed., *Rashi: 'Iyyunim* (above, n. 1), 63–4; Grossman, *Ḥakhmei Tsarfat ha-Rishonim* (above, n. 1), 447–8. (All English translations in this essay are mine.)

I would suggest that the term 'dialectics' has a number of meanings, and it is best to use it with discrimination. Clarification by dialogue, conversational or agonistic, such as Socrates employs in Plato's dialogues, is called Socratic dialectics. Comparison of parallel sources and resolution of the conflicts between them is called 'scholastic dialectics', for this was the mode of study of the medieval scholastics. The approach of the Tosafists is a classic example of scholastic dialectics, as it consists of the collation of all sources in the talmudic corpus, the discovery of contradictions between passages, and the resolution of those contradictions. At times, a distinction is made between the facts of the two cases (*hakha mairi*); at other times, a conceptual distinction is advanced, as the same legal term may contain two separate and distinct principles. However, Rabbenu Sasson, in the responsum cited above, does not deal with any talmudic contradiction, for the simple reason that no such contradiction exists. Two hundred years of tosafist scrutiny yielded no contradiction between that passage and any other one in the Talmud, and another 150 years of investigation by the great Catalonian school of dialectics (*bet midrasho shel ha-Ramban*) also turned up nothing.[4] If neither contradiction nor resolution is to be found in Rabbenu Sasson's responsum, how can he be said to be practicing scholastic dialectics?

One can clarify one's thought step by step in the form of an internal dialogue, eliminate alternative interpretations, and prove the correctness of one's conclusions; the end result is then Socratic, not scholastic, dialectics. One can repeatedly use the phrases 'one can object' (*im tomar*) and 'reply can be made' (*yesh lomar*) and all the other terms used by the Tosafists; so long as one is not raising and resolving contradictions, one is not doing what the Tosafists did. Scholastic dialectics is a method, not a vocabulary; a mode of study and analysis, not the habitual use of certain words and phrases.

Grossman says: 'R. Shelomoh b. Shimshon . . . often used the dialectical give-and-take in the writing of his responsa. His entire approach [*derekh 'iyyuno*] to the Talmud, in his deductions from it and in his interpretations, is very close to the approach of the Tosafists.' In his important study *Ḥakhmei Ashkenaz ha-Rishonim*, Grossman enumerated twenty-two or twenty-three responsa by R. Shelomoh b. Shimshon. Fourteen responsa are found in *Teshuvot Ḥakhmei Tsarfat ve-Lotir* (##43–56), and another eight or nine in *Shibbolei ha-Leket, Ma'aseh ha-Ge'onim, Or Zarua'*, and the *Sifrut de-Vei Rashi*.[5] I have studied these responsa and not a single one deals with resolving contradictions

[4] There is a dialectical problem with one of the proofs advanced in the talmudic discussion (*hiknah lo be-'eḥad mi-'evarav*), but this is a subsidiary matter in the *sugya*, and one not discussed by R. Shelomoh b. Shimshon.

[5] *Ḥakhmei Ashkenaz ha-Rishonim* (above, n. 1), 341–3.

in the Talmud. R. Shelomoh's discussions are trenchant, and in the above-cited passage he anticipates and convincingly argues a position that was later advocated by Rashi, Alfasi, and many other medieval commentators. No doubt he was a scholar of true stature, and if Rashi says so, he was also 'a sharp and acute thinker'. However, these traits by themselves do not a scholastic dialectician make.

The same holds true for Rabbenu Gershom and R. Yehudah Ba'al Sefer ha-Dinim, though I cannot go into the matter here. Admittedly, in the 200 or so responsa of the two scholars, there is one that discusses and resolves a talmudic contradiction.[6] It may equally be true that I have missed another or even several such resolutions. This, however, makes no difference. Contradictions between passages in the Talmud have been noted from the moment the Talmud was committed to writing. The Geonim resolved such contradictions, as did Alfasi and R. Yosef ibn Megas. Both Maimonides and Rashi perceived and precluded hundreds of contradictions with an added word or two in their formulations, as a perusal of the supercommentaries on their works will readily attest. However, all these scholars resolved contradictions that they 'stumbled upon', as it were—conflicting statements that they noted in the course of their learning. They did not set out to discover these contradictions in their study. They studied the Talmud vertically, as it were, page after page in the sequence found there. They did not study it 'horizontally': they did not systematically analyze, as did the Tosafists, parallel *sugyot* (talmudic discussions) so as to uncover and resolve contradictions. Dialectics is a mode of analyzing and unifying a vast, contradictory corpus, not an occasional resolution of contrarieties that one has chanced upon. I will say no more on the matter as I have expanded on this distinction elsewhere.[7]

In Grossman's view, one of the 'major causes' for the growth of the tosafist approach is the 'influence of scholasticism that flourished in the eleventh and twelfth centuries and which was characterized by intense dialectical discus-

[6] *Shitah Mekubbetset, Bava Metsi'a* (Amsterdam, 1721), 10a, s.v. *amar Rav Yohanan*. B. Z. Benedict first drew attention to this passage in his 'R. Mosheh bar Yosef mi-Narbonah', *Tarbiz*, 19 (1948), 33 (repr. in his *Merkazei Torah be-Provence* [Jerusalem, 1985], 51). Grossman conveniently reproduced the text of the first edition of *Shitah Mekubbetset* in his *R. Yehudah ha-Kohen—Sefer ha-Dinim: Teshuvotav Melukkatot mi-Mekorot Shonim* (Jerusalem, 1977), 64.

[7] *Yeinam: Sahar be-Yeinam shel Goyim—'al Gilgulah shel Halakhah be-'Olam ha-Ma'aseh* (Tel Aviv, 2003), 20–3; and in *Ha-Yayin bi-Yemei ha-Beinayim: Yein Nesekh—Perek be-Toledot ha-Halakhah be-'Ashkenaz* (Jerusalem, 2008), 116–17, 351.

sion [*masa u-matan*]'. He continues:

As to scholasticism: a noticeable revival occurred in the eleventh century, which is a transitional period in the development of scholasticism. Let us mention Gerbert of Aurillac, at the beginning of the eleventh century, and his pupil Fulbert, a contemporary of Rabbenu Gershom Me'or ha-Golah (960–1028). In fact, it suffices to point to the strong resistance of Petrus Damianus to scholasticism and to the overly fine Aristotelian distinctions [*pilpul ha-'aristoteli*] to evidence the swift growth of scholasticism in the eleventh century, a development that awakened fears in certain church circles. In his [i.e. Petrus Damianus'] view the exaggerated independence of dialectics could endanger religious faith. Against this view stood Anselm of Canterbury, who laid the foundations of scholasticism in securing religious beliefs, contending that one could use dialectics to prove the truth of Christianity.[8]

Again, we confront a blending of meanings, as one term can denote different things. If by the term 'scholasticism' one refers to the religious philosophy of the Middle Ages, that is, the attempt to use the human intellect to clarify religious dogmas as much as is humanly possible—in Anselm's famous phrase, *fides quaerens intellectum* (faith seeking understanding)—Grossman's description is correct. However, the Tosafists did not address theological issues, nor did they seek to explain and justify the religious dogmas of their faith. We are not dealing with the religious philosophy of medieval Christianity, but with a specific technique employed in the study of theology or of law or of any other discipline that rests on a corpus of canonical, binding dicta and in which a univocal, normative ruling is required. In other words, we are not dealing with 'scholasticism' but with 'scholastic method'. This method consists, as already noted, of the collation of parallel texts, the discovery of contradictions between them, and resolution by distinction (*collatio*, *contradictio*, *distinctio*). 'Scholasticism' as a school of philosophy and 'scholasticism' as a method of wresting 'harmony from discord', of resolving apparent differences in a canonical corpus, are entirely different things.

This being the case, there is no place in a discussion of tosafist method for Gerbert of Aurillac, Fulbert, or Peter Damian. Anselm is equally beside the point. Indeed, the greatness of Anselm rests precisely in his refusal to cite canonical sources (*auctores*). He sought to prove the existence of God and, to a large extent, the Incarnation on the basis of reason alone. His famous ontological argument is still being invoked and analyzed to this day.[9] The relevant

8 *Rashi: 'Iyyunim* (above, n. 1), 67–8; *Ḥakhmei Tsarfat ha-Rishonim* (above, n. 1), 450 and, in part, p. 22.

9 See e.g. A. Plantinga, ed., *The Ontological Argument: From Anselm to Contemporary Philosophers* (London, 1968) and, more recently, I. Logan, *Reading Anselm's Proslogion: The History of Anselm's*

literature is not that of the evolution of medieval thought, such as the work of David Knowles that Grossman cites, but the study of the evolution of the scholastic technique of Martin Grabmann that appeared a century ago (1909–11).[10] Undoubtedly, it needs updating in many respects; however, it remains the fundamental study of the subject. It is no accident that it was republished in 1956, again in 1961, and yet again in 1986. A perusal of the first volume, which treats developments prior to the twelfth century, yields little that could have influenced eleventh-century Jewish scholars in Germany.[11]

Argument and its Significance Today (Aldershot, 2008). The most famous discussion of the past century is that of the great Swiss theologian Karl Barth, in his *Anselm: Fides Quaerens Intellectum* (Norfolk, 1960). This study, originally written in German, first appeared in 1930.

[10] *Die Geschichte der scholastischen Methode: Nach den gedruckten und ungedruckten Quellen*, 2 vols. (repr. Darmstadt, 1956). I neither mean to imply that Anselm did not invoke *auctores* in other writings, nor that he did not occasionally use the scholastic method to the extent that it existed in his time. I am simply stating that his fame in philosophy does not stem from such writings or from such usage, but from the opposite: from his attempt to prove Christian dogma by means of human reason alone. See Grabmann's remarks, i. 258–71, 311–21.

[11] Ibid. 234–46. It is bootless to detail why neither Bernold nor Ivo could have influenced 11th-century Jewish dialectics—be it the late date of their 'dialectical' writings or the non-dialectical character of those writings—seeing that no such mode of thinking existed among the talmudists of the Rhineland in the 11th century. On the question of the dialectical nature of these writings, see e.g. C. Rolker, *Canon Law and the Letters of Ivo of Chartres* (Cambridge, 2010), 165–71, and his summary (pp. 293–302). His introductory chapter (pp. 41–7) explicates the opposing views of Paul Fournier.

CHAPTER THREE

Minhag Ashkenaz ha-Kadmon: An Assessment

IN A LENGTHY and influential article Israel M. Ta-Shma has portrayed the unique significance and force that 'custom' (*minhag*) possessed in Ashkenaz, wholly unlike the subsidiary role that it played in other west European Jewish cultures of the Middle Ages.[1] In Early Ashkenaz (*c.*950–1096) religious life was conducted according to custom and custom alone. When a conflict was detected between the prescriptions of the Talmud and popular practice, the latter prevailed—not simply by force of habit, but out of the deep conviction that the law embodied in the traditional conduct of the people should override any formal, written dictate. In the course of the twelfth century the law inscribed in the Talmud came to predominate in Ashkenaz, but only after a bitter struggle with custom. Ta-Shma attributes this distinctive view of the power of established practice to the Palestinian origins of the Ashkenazic community. The Palestinian Talmud (Yerushalmi), in sharp contrast to the Babylonian (Bavli), was of the opinion that custom overruled the dictates of prescriptive law—*minhag mevattel halakhah*.

I. Preliminary Observations

One of Ta-Shma's major sources—in one sense, *the* major source of his argument—is the *Ma'aseh ha-Ge'onim*, a collection of responsa, rulings, practices, and customs of Early Ashkenaz compiled at the turn of the eleventh and twelfth centuries by the Makirites, the four industrious sons of R. Makhir of Mainz.[2] Before evaluating his thesis, I would like to locate this singular collection—so pivotal to his argument—among the works of medieval Ashkenaz

[1] 'Halakhah, Minhag u-Masoret be-Yahadut Ashkenaz ba-Me'ot ha-Yod-Alef ve-ha-Yod-Bet', *Sidra*, 3 (1987), 85–161, repr. in id., *Minhag Ashkenaz ha-Kadmon; Ḥeker ve-'Iyyun* (Jerusalem, 1992), 13–105; references below are to the reprint.

[2] Ed. A. Epstein and J. Freimann (Berlin, 1910).

and particularly in the literature of the eleventh century. Three observations are in place.

1. Ta-Shma states repeatedly that there is nothing like the *Ma'aseh ha-Ge'onim* in the literature of Provence or in that of Spain. Indeed, there isn't. There is equally nothing like the *Sifrut de-Vei Rashi* in these cultures, and the two absences are related. Rashi's commentary on the Talmud, which gave unprecedented precision to talmudic dicta and discussions, entailed a complete audit of Jewish religious life. This was never the purpose of his commentary, only its inevitable consequence. In some instances, such as tractate *'Avodah Zarah*, his work constituted a revolution;[3] in others, the newly won clarity led to revisions of the received wisdom and practices of the Ashkenazic community. Wholly without any revisionist inclination, disliking controversy, and, perhaps above all, not wishing anything to deflect him from his great enterprise of making both the Written and Oral Law intelligible to all who sought its understanding, Rashi avoided drawing any practical conclusions in his own commentaries. His life's work was exegesis and, with the rarest of exceptions, he did not deviate from this goal. His disciples, however, had no such inhibitions, nor were they bound by Rashi's spartan literary discipline. They hastened to publicize the new conclusions that their master's commentaries entailed. We tend to forget this sweeping re-evaluation as the massive revolution of the Tosafists immediately followed that of Rashi and engendered a far more radical and enduring alteration of religious life in France and Germany. This, however, is a passport to historical misunderstanding. Disregarding the immediate implications of Rashi's oeuvre leaves the halakhic literature in the concluding years of the eleventh century and the early decades of the twelfth incomprehensible.

The disciples' work took several forms: small pamphlets of Rashi's rulings in specific areas such as the Passover *seder* or the laws of *sukkah* or *niddah*, as well as reproductions of the master's responsa and a host of his ad hoc decisions in all areas of Jewish ritual life. Rashi also brought home many rulings of the Rhineland academies where he had studied, and these, too, were included in a number of the disciples' collections. All these were collected in the numerous florilegia that issued from Rashi's academy, such as the *Maḥzor Vitry*, *Siddur shel Rashi*, the *Issur ve-Heter shel Rashi*, and the like, which have come to be known as the *Sifrut de-Vei Rashi*.

What this means is that the received way of life of Ashkenaz was under

[3] H. Soloveitchik, *Ha-Yayin bi-Yemei ha-Beinayim: Yein Nesekh—Perek be-Toledot ha-Halakhah be-'Ashkenaz* (Jerusalem, 2008), 157–66, 173–83, 208–13, 225–31, 250–61, 284–6, 347–52.

quiet but heavy pressure in the closing decades of the eleventh century and the start of the twelfth. Not that criticism was necessarily voiced, because tradition was always deeply respected; however, alternatives were being offered that tacitly but insistently laid claim to greater legitimacy. The criticism was increasing even in Germany. Consider the significance of the Mainz Commentary, printed in the Romm edition of the Talmud as *Perush Rabbenu Gershom*. As Ta-Shma has shown elsewhere,[4] in most tractates this is a multi-level work, as successive generations over the course of the eleventh century toiled on the text, each adding new layers of interpretation. In other words, the Talmud was undergoing greater and greater clarification in the eleventh century, not just in Rashi's academy but also in the very study halls of Mainz, and this newly won understanding was posing penetrating questions about the traditional norms of behavior.

No equivalent development took place in Provence. Neither R. Yehudah of Barcelona, author of the *Sefer ha-'Ittim*, nor his pupil R. Avraham b. Yitsḥak of Narbonne (d. 1159), who penned the *Sefer ha-'Eshkol*, challenged anything. To be sure, their great successors, R. Avraham b. David of Posquières (Rabad, d. 1198) and R. Zeraḥyah ha-Levi of Lunel (Ba'al ha-Ma'or, d. *c*.1186) made yeoman contributions to the understanding of the Talmud. However, R. Zeraḥyah's work took the form of a blend of critiques and essays ranged around Alfasi's text. While Rabad's commentaries on the Talmud contained profound insights, his writings reflected none of the pedagogical genius that was Rashi's alone, nor did they provide the comprehensive illumination that Rashi's terse remarks shed upon every line of the Talmud. They did have an impact on practice over the course of time, as did most serious halakhic writings, but neither in their own time nor in the years that followed did they pose any challenge to the traditional religious life of Provence. Nor do we know of any growing, collective exegesis of the Talmud in twelfth-century Midi, such as took place in Mainz a century before.

2. When reading the *Siddur Rashi* or the *Issur ve-Heter shel Rashi*, one never imagines that these were his life's work. The thought is risible, as Rashi's magnum opus is his immortal commentary on the Talmud. The responsa and the halakhic guides that he wrote are pittances when placed alongside his exegetical oeuvre. They are *Gelegenheitsschriften*, writings penned to meet the passing needs of the hour.

[4] ''Al Perush ha-Meyuḥas le-Rabbenu Gershom Me'or ha-Golah la-Talmud', *Kiryat Sefer*, 53 (1978), 356–65, repr. in id., *Keneset Meḥkarim: 'Iyyunim ba-Sifrut ha-Rabbanit bi-Yemei ha-Beinayim* (Jerusalem, 2004), i. 3–20.

We should keep the above in mind when we open the *Ma'aseh ha-Ge'onim* or read the other reports of the halakhic rulings of Rashi's predecessors and contemporaries found in the pre-Crusade literature of the Rhineland. These works, which loom so large in our eyes, are mere by-products of their scholarship, trivia when compared with their commentarial accomplishments—accomplishments that have for too long gone unappreciated. It is not simply that intellectual life in Ashkenaz is coeval with the exegesis of the Bavli, but that the earliest scholars of Ashkenaz bequeathed a new vision of talmudic exegesis, the detailed line-by-line exposition which took the form of the embedded and initial lemma (the latter commonly known as *sub verbo* or *dibbur ha-matḥil*). The Geonim had illuminated patches of the Talmud in their responsa, and small dictionaries explaining difficult talmudic terms had been written by them or in their time.[5] The North African contemporaries of Early Ashkenaz, Rabbenu Nissim and Rabbenu Ḥanan'el of Kairouan, had seen the need for more expansive works of explication. The first composed a lexicon, as it were, of obscure rabbinic concepts,[6] while the latter wrote a tractate-by-tractate commentary that explained and summarized the major sections of a talmudic *sugya*. None had attempted to explain every single line of the text of the Talmud. This was undertaken by the scholars of Early Ashkenaz. Every word of the Talmud had to be accounted for; every argument, even if entertained ever so briefly, had to be explicated. We take this comprehensive explication of the Talmud for granted, for we were introduced to it the very first day that we opened a page of the Talmud and read Rashi. However, this detailed mode of explication, this fearless promise that no phrase would be left unexplained, did not exist in the times of the Geonim, nor did the Mediterranean 'Genizah society' know of it. It was a distinctly Ashkenazic method and not of Rashi's invention. It was his predecessors, the scholars of Early Ashkenaz, who conceived this unique and daunting program of *explication de texte* and undertook to realize it in the academies of Mainz and Worms, where Rashi came to study.[7]

[5] I say 'small dictionaries', for the *Sefer he-'Arukh* was completed *c.*1100. For an example of a small dictionary, see that of R. Naḥshon Gaon in *Teshuvot Ge'onim Kadmonim*, ed. D. Cassel (Berlin, 1948), fos. 39b–42b. R. Naḥshon Gaon's authorship of that lexical handbook was determined by J. N. Epstein in 'Die Rechtsgutachten der Geonim, ed. Cassel nach Cod. Berlin und MS Michael', *Jahrbuch der Jüdisch-Literarischen Gesellschaft*, 9 (1911), 220, available in the Hebrew translation in id., *Meḥkarim be-Sifrut ha-Talmud u-vi-Leshonot Shemiyot* (Jerusalem, 1984), i. 144.

[6] *Sefer ha-Mafte'aḥ shel Man'ulei ha-Talmud* (Vienna, 1847) and reprinted in the Romm edition of the Talmud (Vilna, 1880–6) on tractates *Berakhot*, *Shabbat*, and *'Eruvin*. On this work, see S. Abramson, *Rav Nissim Ga'on* (Jerusalem, 1965), 1–90; on R. Nissim Gaon's *Sefer ha-Mafte'aḥ*, see ibid. 179–360.

[7] See Appendix I. If my proposal in Chapter 9 is correct, the use of *sub verbo* may have been part of the heritage of Early Ashkenaz.

And realize it they did. Building on their accomplishments, Rashi carried their undertaking to undreamt-of heights, and so decisively were their efforts superseded that they were mostly lost—but not entirely. We have retained their commentaries on much of the order of *Kodashim*, and on a good deal of tractates *Ḥullin*, *Bava Batra*, *Nazir*, *Nedarim*, *Mo'ed Katan*, *Ta'anit*, and *Yoma*.[8] They lack Rashi's luminous clarity, his pedagogical genius, and his capacity to cast a *sugya* in a new light with a phrase or two.[9] That said, has the commentary explicated nearly every term, have most of the arguments in those winding *sugyot* been accounted for and explained? The answer is 'Yes'—many explained for the first time and in a detail previously unimagined.

The above-mentioned tractates also reveal the novel scope of Ashkenaz's endeavors. The Talmud was not to be studied selectively, simply as a guide to proper religious conduct; such a pragmatic conception of *talmud torah* shrank the scope of talmudic learning to the areas of ritual, civil, and marital law, ignoring much of tractate *Yoma*, some 30 percent of *Pesaḥim*, and the entire order of *Kodashim* (barring, of course, *Ḥullin*). Not for these Ashkenazic Talmudists were the abridgments of Alfasi or of Rabbenu Ḥanan'el. Indeed, the scope of their endeavor exceeded even that of the academies of Sura and Pumbedita! Whether or not the list of tractates in *Kodashim* reported to be taught in the Babylonian academies reflects a serious engagement with these tractates or some pro forma instruction is an open question. However, even by this report, only four tractates of *Seder Kodashim* (other than *Ḥullin*) were included in the curriculum—*Zevaḥim*, *Menaḥot*, *Bekhorot*, and *'Arakhin*. Left unstudied in Sura and Pumbedita were *Temurah*, *Me'ilah*, *Keritut*, and *Tamid*; yet they were part of the Ashkenazic curriculum. So too was *Nedarim*, not taught in Babylonia since at least the days of R. Yehudai Gaon.[10]

[8] The commentaries on *Ḥullin*, *Bava Batra*, and *Ta'anit* were first published in the aforementioned Romm edition of the Talmud (above, n. 6). For a bibliography, see U. Fuchs, 'Le-Ma'amaro shel A. Epshtein', *Netu'im*, 6 (2000), 105 n. 3, to which should be added D. Genachowski's introduction to his edition of *Perush R. Elyakim le-Massekhet Yoma* (Jerusalem, 1964), the articles of A. Schremer, ''Al ha-Perushim le-Massekhet *Mo'ed Katan* ha-Meyuḥasim le-Rashi', in D. Boyarin et al., eds., *'Ateret le-Ḥayyim: Meḥkarim ba-Sifrut ha-Talmudit ve-ha-Rabbanit li-Khevod Professor Ḥayyim Zalman Dimitrovski* (Jerusalem, 2000), 534–54, and Y. Kohen, 'Rashi u-Veit Midrasho le-Massekhet Nedarim', *Yerushateinu*, 4 (2010), 201–50. A convenient listing of the early Ashkenazic commentaries on the Talmud may be found at the end of the latter article (pp. 235–50). The reader will also find there references to the literature on commentaries, whole or partial, on other tractates that some have attributed to the scholars of 11th-century Ashkenaz. One may question a number of the items entered and the editor's mode of argument, but this in no way diminishes the utility of the various lists he has compiled.

[9] See e.g. Soloveitchik, *Ha-Yayin bi-Yemei ha-Beinayim* (above, n. 3), 173–4, 197–8.

[10] J. N. Epstein, *Dikduk Aramit Bavlit* (Jerusalem, 1960), 14–16; A. Marmorstein, 'Mitteilungen zur Geschichte und Literatur aus der Geniza 2. Ein Fragment der Halakhot Ketu'ot', *Monatsschrift*

On what traditions the scholars of Early Ashkenaz drew in explicating these 'extracurricular' tractates we do not know (though in a subsequent essay I offer a suggestion[11]). But with a tradition or without one, they knew the task that they had to perform. Can we imagine for a moment the mobilization of energies that this Herculean task entailed? Given the meager population of

für Geschichte und Wissenschaft der Juden, 67 (1923), 134–5. As this paragraph treats both Rav Alfasi and R. Ḥanan'el together, I should qualify it by stating that, unlike Alfasi, Rabbenu Ḥanan'el does treat the topics of *kodashim* found in the tractates of *Yoma* and *Pesaḥim*. As nothing is wholly unique in history, this is not to deny that exegetes in other cultures commented on individual tractates. It is also possible, though not probable, that Rabbenu Ḥanan'el wrote a commentary on *Bekhorot*. Parts of a commentary on *Zevaḥim*, misattributed to R. Ḥanan'el, have been published from the Genizah, and R. Yosef Rosh ha-Seder reports a commentary on *Kodashim* by R. Barukh ben Yitsḥak (see S. Abramson, *Perush Rabbenu Ḥanan'el la-Talmud* [Jerusalem, 1995], 58–64, and the literature there cited. See also the index of N. Aloni's posthumous work, *Ha-Sifriyah ha-Yehudit bi-Yemei ha-Beinayim: Reshimot Sefarim mi-Genizat Kahir*, ed. M. Frenkel and H. Ben-Shammai [Jerusalem, 2005], 465, s.v. *Barukh b. Yitsḥak mi-Ḥaleb*). Significantly, though, the Mediterranean cultures did not preserve these commentaries, let alone incorporate these tractates in their curriculum. Even so great a Talmudist as R. Yosef ibn Megas had no orientation in *Kodashim*. In sharp contrast, the commentaries on *Kodashim* both of Rashi and of the Mainz school were not only transmitted intact by the Ashkenazic culture, but also formed part of its curriculum. This labor in *Kodashim* was continued unabated by their successors, the Tosafists. See p. 189 below.

Y. Sussmann, in a typically erudite essay, has pointed out that Provence, like Ashkenaz (and unlike the Jewish cultures in Muslim countries), studied *Kodashim*. I would be the last to gainsay this observation. However, two differences should be noted. First, in Ashkenaz it was not the occupation of a few figures of genius, such as Rabad of Posquières or R. Zeraḥyah of Lunel, but of the entire scholarly elite. Second, there is a world of difference between commenting on a tractate or two and undertaking to explicate the entire *Seder Kodashim*, from *Zevaḥim* to *Me'ilah*. In Provence, select parts of *Kodashim* interested a select few; in Germany the entire *seder* was part and parcel of the scholarly curriculum. (See Y. Sussmann, 'Perush ha-Ravad le-Massekhet Shekalim: Ḥidah Bibliografit u-Ve'ayah Historit', in E. Fleischer et al., eds., *Me'ah She'arim: 'Iyyunim be-'Olamo ha-Ruḥani shel Yisra'el bi-Yemei ha-Beinayim le-Zekher Yitsḥak Tverski* [Jerusalem, 2001], 131–70.) I would caution against reading too much into the letter of R. Yosef ibn Megas (written by the famed poet R. Yehudah ha-Levi) to *ḥakhmei* Narbonne requesting a commentary on *Seder Kodashim*. Rabad and Ba'al ha-Ma'or, both of whom studied in Narbonne under the famous R. Avraham Av Bet-Din, never once mention the existence of such a commentary. The letter only means that an otherwise unknown R. Ḥalfon ha-Levi told Ri ibn Megas about a commentary, and he naturally requested it. The scope and detail of that commentary are unknown, as is the far more important question of its caliber. The silence of subsequent generations of Provençal scholars in this matter, including the indefatigable collector R. Menaḥem ha-Me'iri, is deafening. (*Diwan Jehuda ha-Levi's*, ed. H. Brody [Berlin, 1901], i. 217–8, 323–4. Cf. B. Z. Benedict, 'R. Mosheh bar Yosef mi-Narbonah', *Tarbiz*, 19 [1948], 33 n. 145a, repr. in *Merkazei Torah be-Provence* [Jerusalem, 1985], 52 n. 145a; see also ibid. 18–19.) Cf. E. Kanarfogel, 'Ya'adei Limmud ve-Dimui 'Atsmi etsel Ḥakhmei ha-Talmud be-'Eiropah bi-Yemei ha-Beinayim: ha-'Issuk be-Seder Kodashim', in Y. Ben Naeh et al., eds., *Asufah le-Yosef: Kovets Meḥkarim Shai le-Yosef Hacker* (Jerusalem, 2014), 68–91.

11 See below, pp. 163–9.

the eleventh century, it could only have been a tiny band of men who attempted to do in scope and detail what had never been done before. These were men of great brilliance, but not of genius; not bearers of a Divine spark as Rashi and Maimonides were, but earners of the hard-won insight. Only a century of unremitting—indeed, unbelievable—toil could have opened up the entire Talmud in all of its complexity and brought forth the groundbreaking commentary known as *Perush Rabbenu Gershom 'al ha-Talmud*.[12] This eleventh-century commentary, at which we now scarcely glance, was radical and unprecedented. It revealed worlds that had been obscured for centuries; it revolutionized the notion of what 'understanding a *sugya*' meant and fixed that meaning to this very day.

The *Ma'aseh ha-Ge'onim* and kindred works are the small change of Early Ashkenaz, and the thoughts and writings found therein occupied no more of the time and attention of these scholars than Rashi's responsa and manuals occupied of his.

The 'small change' of Ashkenaz, *Ma'aseh ha-Ge'onim*, talks so much about 'custom', and emphasizes so strongly that it should be upheld in the face of all doubts, because their customary conduct, their habitual modes of religious practice, were under pressure at the time, which was not the case in Provence. How readily one can criticize or question long-established practice (which in any traditional society has a strong claim to truth) depends on temperament, to be sure, but also on the extent of one's conviction that one has fully grasped what the Talmud has to say on the matter. Not simply the gist of the talmudic discussion, but every word of it. That confidence could rarely arise from a commentary like that of R. Ḥanan'el, only from a successful *sub verbo* commentary, such as Ashkenaz—and Ashkenaz alone, at that time—possessed. The initial (quiet and ever respectful) critique of practice is earlier in Ashkenaz than in other cultures because the great commentarial accomplishments of Ashkenaz were earlier.

The authors/editors of *Ma'aseh ha-Ge'onim*, the Makirites (Benei ha-Makhiri), were inquisitive, even inventive at times, but by no account were they scholars of any stature, not even the finest Talmudist among them, R. Natan. No other work of the Middle Ages contains so much candid, detailed discussion by mediocrities as does the *Ma'aseh ha-Ge'onim*. It is not

12 I would not alter this formulation in light of the subsequent essay (Ch. 9). It is one thing to have an indispensable tradition of interpretation of a tractate. It is another thing to work out every step of every argument in the tractate and account for almost every phrase as the sustained use of the *sub verbo* method demands. They further had to weigh and decide between differing versions of the talmudic text that they either brought with them or found in Ashkenaz. See below, pp. 159, 196.

surprising that occasionally, when they were confronted with questions as to the justification for certain religious practices to which they had no answer, they fell back on paeans to the wisdom of their forefathers. Subtract the extravagant, defensive exclamations of the Benei ha-Makhiri from the collection of statements in praise of custom that Ta-Shma assembled, and the remainder does not differ much from what is found in other cultures.

There is nevertheless one difference, and this should not be underestimated. The Ashkenazic community did, indeed, have a higher opinion of the wisdom of their ancestors than did other settlements of the Diaspora (such as Provence and Andalusian or Christian Spain), and I would be the last to deny this. In fact, I was among the first to point out, some forty-five years ago, the deep presumption of rectitude that established practice had in Ashkenaz.[13] However, until the mid-twelfth century (or the second quarter of that century, at the earliest), the difference in the depth of that presumption between Ashkenaz and other Jewish cultures is quantitative, not qualitative. Ashkenaz, from its earliest days, did largely assume that the received practice of the community was in conformance with the law.[14] This, however, was a strong disposition rather than an ideology, and a disposition that was shared, albeit to a limited extent, by other cultures. Such justifications of popular practice are more frequent in Ashkenaz but hardly unique to it.[15] It was only when the Tosafists undertook to systematically defend—at times at the cost of all plausibility—the entire range of common practice in certain select areas, such as martyrdom, moneylending, and *yein nesekh*, that the difference between the various cultures became qualitative. This wholesale defense was characteristic of Ashkenaz alone, and with it the singularity of the Ashkenazic self-image emerged.[16]

[13] 'Minhag, Metsi'ut ve-Halakhah' (MA thesis, Hebrew University of Jerusalem, 1967). A much-expanded version appeared some forty years later in *Ha-Yayin bi-Yemei ha-Beinayim* (above, n. 3). The chapters on viticulture and communication are new, as are the geographical contextualization and the introductory history of the tosafist movement, but the crux of the study, the halakhic reconstruction and analysis of the central issues of *yein nesekh* and of the tosafist justification of communal practice in this entire area, is unchanged.

[14] It is already noticeable in the ruling of Rabbenu Gershom Me'or ha-Golah analyzed in 'Pawnbroking: A Study in *Ribbit* and of the Halakhah in Exile', 1st pub. 1972 and repr. in the first volume of this series (*Collected Essays* [Oxford, 2013], i. 57–166; see p. 112).

[15] For an instance—within the limited scope of this essay—when Provence, no less than Ashkenaz, justified popular practice, see below, n. 87.

[16] I have attempted to spell out these distinctions in greater detail in *Ha-Yayin bi-Yemei ha-Beinayim* (above, n. 3), 358–69, and in 'Religious Law and Change Revisited' (*Collected Essays*, i. 258–77).

3. Medieval Ashkenazic culture spans roughly half a millennium, *c.*950–1450, and one should never forget when dealing with the *Ma'aseh ha-Ge'onim* that far more of the halakhic writings produced in Ashkenaz in those 500 years have come down to us than of those created in the other cultures of medieval Europe. What substantive collections of responsa do we have, for example, from the Provence of the thirteenth and fourteenth centuries? Other than the *Teshuvot Ḥakhmei Provintsya* (published by Avraham Sofer) and a Paris manuscript (partially serialized by Israel Levi),[17] relatively few, especially when compared with those of Ashkenaz. Does the Provençal *Sefer Asufot* (partially published by B. Z. Benedict)[18] even begin to approach those four rich and heterogeneous collections of Ashkenazic responsa that are available under the name of *Teshuvot R. Me'ir mi-Rotenburg*? And there are three or four such collections in manuscript for every one of those four printed volumes—overlapping, to be sure, but still voluminous and varied. Is there anything in Provence vaguely resembling the florilegia of R. Mordekhai b. Hillel on so much as one tractate, not to speak of the entire Talmud? One thing is clear from the Me'iri's *Bet ha-Beḥirah*: far more significant decisions were rendered and far more original interpretations were proffered in Catalonia and Provence than have come down to us. The riches of the *Sefer ha-Terumot* vividly confirm this impression. We can see the brilliance of Provençal thought in the *Shitah lo Noda' le-Mi 'al Kiddushin*, and further glimpses can be caught in numerous passages of the work on *Bava Metsi'a* that issued from Narbonne in the mid-thirteenth century and that passed for centuries under the name of *Ḥiddushei ha-Ritva*.[19] Is it reasonable to think that Provence was creative

[17] Jerusalem, 1967; MS Paris, Bibliothèque Nationale 1391 published by I. Lévi, 'Un recueil de consultations inédites des rabbins de la France méridionale', *Revue des études juives*, 38 (1899), 103–22; 39 (1899), 76–84, 226–41; 43 (1901), 237–58; 44 (1902), 73–86.

[18] 'Mavo le-Sefer Ba'alei Asufot', *Sinai*, 14 (1950), 322–9; 'Pesakim Aḥadim mi-tokh Sefer Ba'alei Asufot', *Sinai*, 14 (1951), 191–208. Both were reprinted in his *Merkazei ha-Torah be-Provence* (Jerusalem, 1985), 105–13, 114–32. Benedict, writing at the height of the Cold War, had access only to a transcription of the Moscow manuscript (MS National Library of Israel, 4to 689). The original, MS Moscow RSL, Günzburg 73, is now readily available but holds no surprises.

[19] The first work was published in Constantinople in 1751, the second in Amsterdam in 1722. No manuscript of either of these books has been uncovered. Both, apparently, were published from *unica*. For the little that is known about the *Shitah Lo Noda' le-Mi*, see M. Benayahu, 'Ha-Shitah Lo Noda' le-Mi', *Kiryat Sefer*, 25 (1949), 126–31. The Provençal origins of the so-called *Ḥiddushei ha-Ritva 'al Bava Metsi'a* were pointed out by A. Halperin in his introduction (pp. 8–11) to the authentic version that he edited, *Ḥiddushei ha-Ritva ha-Ḥadashim 'al Bava Metsi'a* (London, 1962). The most recent editor of that work, S. Rafa'el, makes the same argument in his introduction to the *Ḥiddushei ha-Ritva le-Bava Metsi'a* (Jerusalem, 1992), 10–11. The Narbonnese provenance of the work was noted by K. Schlesinger in his introduction to his edition of *Bet ha-Beḥirah* on that tractate (Jerusalem, 1963), 9.

in the field of *Kiddushin* but not in that of *Gittin*; in *Bava Metsi'a* but not in *Bava Batra*? M. Y. H. Blau labored devotedly in publishing the Provençal manuscripts that had survived, and most of that material was banal. Fate has not been kind to Provence's halakhic heritage.

In a sense, the same holds true for Christian Spain. True, the immortal novellae of Ramban, Rashba, Ritva, and Ran have survived the ravages of time, together with a vast number of the responsa of Rashba and Rosh and a much smaller quantity of those of Ramban and Ritva. However, one is left wondering: were these all the decisions rendered in Spain in the course of three centuries? Were there no writings of lesser figures? Did not other judges pen decisions? To be sure, the unique position of *rab de la corte* (court rabbi) may have put a damper on judicial productivity, but did it stifle it entirely? What we have are the works of the great Sephardic jurists, but little of the writings of the nearly great have survived, not to speak of those of the simply talented.

One of the reasons for the different rates of survival is not far to seek: unlike the Jewish communities of France and Spain, German Jewry never experienced a kingdom-wide—more accurately, empire-wide—expulsion. When driven from one city, they moved to an adjacent one; when exiled from one territory, they took refuge in the next. When expelled, Jews had to carry their culture on their backs. Unlike in Germany, in Provence and Spain works of philosophy, science, belles-lettres, and poetry competed with halakhic writings for room on those backs.[20] Ta-Shma says, correctly, that we have nothing like the *Ma'aseh ha-Ge'onim* in other Jewish cultures. We equally have nothing akin to the inimitable *Leket Yosher* in those cultures. There were second- and third-rate scholars the world over and they, too, had pens. Compositions by such Talmudists were probably written in Provence and Spain no less than in Germany; but works of this caliber don't survive the triage of expulsion. The political vicissitudes of European Jewry, coupled with the restricted scope of German Jewish cultural interests, determined that our picture of Ashkenaz in halakhah—in the broader sense—will always be richer and more varied than the image that we possess of her sister cultures. I am not advancing any 'argument from silence'; I am simply suggesting that we

[20] The loss of the Provençal heritage was aggravated by the expulsion of 1306 just as Catalonian culture was flourishing. The cultural assonance between the two was great, the consanguinity among their members even greater, and Languedoc was swiftly absorbed by Catalonia. See my remarks in 'Rabad of Posquières: A Programmatic Essay', in E. Etkes and Y. Salmon, eds., *Studies in the History of Jewish Society in the Middle Ages and in the Modern Period Presented to Jacob Katz on his 75th Birthday* [Perakim be-Toledot ha-Ḥevrah ha-Yehudit bi-Yemei ha-Beinayim u-va-'Et ha-Ḥadashah] (Jerusalem, 1980), English section, pp. xvi–xviii. The essay will appear in the third volume of this series.

be somewhat more cautious about basing our claims for the uniqueness of Ashkenaz on pedestrian writings found in the literary remains of that culture alone. Grounding claims of singularity in the works of the Tosafists is one thing; doing it in the works of the Makirites is another.

II. Equipoise

No less important than the nature of the Ashkenazic legacy is the manner in which one goes about analyzing it. I would like to restore a sense of proportion to that analysis. A man of intellectual passion, Ta-Shma was given, at times, to heightened formulation, which occasionally did both his own case and that of others a disservice. Let me give a few examples.

1. Ta-Shma writes: 'One of their [i.e. the Tosafists'] tools, alongside analysis [*sevara*] and distinction, is free emendation of the text to the degree that they rewrite the text of the Talmud.'[21] The *Tosafot* do cite on numerous occasions the version of R. Ḥanan'el and at times advocate its adoption. They also cite, in fewer instances, the version of a *beraita* found in the Tosefta and Yerushalmi, and suggest that we should emend the Talmud in its light. Rare, however, are the occasions on which the *Tosafot* emend on their own the Talmud without supporting textual evidence. I doubt if it occurs in most tractates more than once every fifteen to twenty folios (*dappim*). In fact, if one takes all the emendations of the *Tosafot*, with or without supporting sources, the sum total of these changes per tractate is relatively small, and certainly far from constituting 'a rewriting of the Talmud'.

Ta-Shma cites an article of mine in evidence of his statement,[22] but immediately adds that in it I refer to the consequences of the tosafist dialectic. The sum total of tosafist *interpretations* did ultimately lead to a 'rewriting of the Talmud'—a wholesale revision of the understanding of the Talmud; with their infrequent emendation, however, they rewrote nothing but the words they deleted. He further cites as proof Yaacov Sussmann's article on the text of the Yerushalmi in tractate *Shekalim*.[23] But Sussmann addressed the Tosafists'

[21] *Minhag Ashkenaz ha-Kadmon* (above, n. 1), 84. In n. 118, on the phrase 'rewrites the text of the Talmud', Ta-Shma writes:

הגדרה זו לפועלם של בעלי התוספות נתן ח' סולוביציק במאמרו . . . וזאת בגלל מהפכנותם בתחום החידוש. אכן גם פועלם בתחום הגירסא יכול להיחשב כשיכתוב נכבד, ובפועל, של התלמוד, שנועד לתת ביסוס וגיבוי לחידושיהם; והכל בכלל הגדרתו.

[22] 'Three Themes in *Sefer Hassidim*', *AJS Review*, 1 (1976), 343.

[23] 'Masoret-Limmud u-Masoret-Nusaḥ shel ha-Talmud ha-Yerushalmi—le-Verur Nusḥa'oteiha shel Yerushalmi Massekhet Shekalim', in *Meḥkarim ba-Sifrut ha-Talmudit: Yom 'Iyyun le-Regel Melo't Shemonim Shanah le-Sha'ul Lieberman* (Jerusalem, 1983), 12–76.

attitude towards the text of the Yerushalmi, and perhaps other semi-canonical texts such as the *midreshei halakhah* and the like; he never made any such claim regarding the Bavli, and for obvious reasons.

2. As I have noted, Ta-Shma's entire article is based on *Ma'aseh ha-Ge'onim*, which he characterizes thus:

Ma'aseh ha-Ge'onim is a summary of Ashkenazic customs . . . In early Ashkenaz there were so many customs that a need was felt to devote an entire book to them so that they might be preserved for posterity [*le-ma'an ya'amdu yamim rabbim*]. *Ma'aseh ha-Ge'onim* is dedicated in its entirety [*kol kulo*] to [the customs] of these three cities [i.e. Mainz, Worms, and Speyer], especially the first two.[24]

One must first distinguish between a 'custom' as a communal practice that falls in the interstices of the halakhah (or even a practice that runs counter to the written law) and 'custom' in the sense of 'accustomed to ruling in a certain way'. This does not refer to any local or regional custom, but to the habitual ruling of an individual. Ta-Shma treats the two as one and the same.

Second, even if we take both of the above uses of 'custom' and treat them as one, the total of such material in the *Ma'aseh ha-Ge'onim* scarcely amounts to 20 percent of the work, if that. The word *ma'aseh* means 'ruling' or 'decision', as in the collection of Palestinian decisions entitled *Sefer ha-Ma'asim*, as Saul Lieberman pointed out long ago.[25] *Ma'aseh ha-Ge'onim* means 'the rulings of the Geonim', i.e. of the sages of Early Ashkenaz, as the term *ga'on* was frequently used in twelfth- and thirteenth-century Germany to denote the pre-Crusade scholars of the Rhineland. This, indeed, is an accurate description of the work. Some 80 percent at the least consists of halakhic discussions and rulings and has nothing to do with 'custom', in any sense of the word.

3. Finally, if I may be allowed a point of personal privilege. Ta-Shma cites my writings as evidence for the following statement:

Historically, what occurred here in the intellectual life of the Jews of central Europe [in the eleventh century] is similar to what transpired a hundred years later, when Roman law penetrated northern France in the twelfth century. As is well known, there began a legal and literary war to the death [*milḥemet ḥormah*] in northern France between the local, customary laws which struggled to survive and the newly arrived Roman law.[26]

[24] *Minhag Ashkenaz ha-Kadmon* (above, n. 1), 19–20, 23. (The entire section, pp. 22–7, from which the second quotation is taken is entitled 'Division and Unity in the Ashkenazic Custom' and addresses this topic.)

[25] 'Sefer ha-Ma'asim—Sefer ha-Pesakim', *Tarbiz*, 2 (1931), 377–9.

[26] *Minhag Ashkenaz ha-Kadmon* (above, n. 1), 89. (He then proceeds to state that a parallel struggle took place among Ashkenazic Jews between the Talmud and the prescriptive power of *minhag*. See the opening paragraph of this essay, above, p. 29.)

A few lines later Ta-Shma speaks of 'a mighty struggle' (*ma'avak 'az*) between Roman and consuetudinary law.

First, Roman law penetrated *southern* France in the twelfth century. It was not to penetrate northern France until a good century later. My article was a study of the halakhic status of the surety in usury contracts in Provence and Languedoc, and all the literature it cites deals with the Midi (and the region of Toulouse). Second, I stated in it that Roman law provided certain safeguards to the debtor that were absent from Germanic law, the law of the Germanic tribes that conquered the Roman Empire and that obtained in much of western Europe until the middle of the twelfth century (and in most parts well after that date). Many lenders insisted that borrowers renounce any protection that the Roman system afforded them. The article refers readers to the secondary literature on opposition to Roman law in southern France. It makes no mention of any 'mighty struggle', far less a 'war to the death'. *Hitnagdut* (opposition) is the word I use there, nothing more.[27]

This inclination to heightened statements can lead to a chiaroscuro picture of the past. The rich spectrum of minor differences that characterize any society tends to disappear, and binary oppositions, dramatic conflicts between irreconcilable views, take their place. Despite its great length, one wonders at times just how nuanced a portrait of Early Ashkenaz emerges from the essay on *minhag* Ashkenaz ha-Kadmon.

III. Context

Ta-Shma speaks in great detail about how religious life in Early Ashkenaz was regulated by received traditions, with no reference to the normative texts. I fully concur with his analysis. I would add only that life is lived the same way in all traditional societies. One is initiated into the group's way of life from birth and the norms of conduct are instilled from infancy. One learns, as children always do, by imitation, by doing what others do—what I have elsewhere called 'mimetically'. Millions of Jews observed the Sabbath in eastern Europe for hundreds of years without any formal knowledge of *hilkhot Shabbat.* I will expatiate on this no further, as I have portrayed the mimetic form of religious life elsewhere and simply refer the reader to that depiction.[28]

Ta-Shma would agree with this description of a traditional society but would counter that what was unique about Early Ashkenaz was that there was

[27] H. Soloveitchik, ''Arev be-Ribbit', *Zion*, 37 (1972), 15 n. 52.

[28] 'Rupture and Reconstruction: The Transformation of Contemporary Orthodoxy', *Tradition*, 28 (1994), 64–130; to be published in a separate volume by the Littman Library.

no external, critical referent. To be sure, most people in Ashkenazic society of the past 900 years have had no notion of the formal rules of the Sabbath or of many other areas of Jewish observance. Even the ordinary rabbi, busy as he was dealing with the ceaseless flow of questions that arose in the areas of civil and marital law and those regulating *kashrut*, probably had a less than adequate knowledge of many aspects of the quotidian halakhah and was only too happy to let custom rule in areas of 'Oraḥ Ḥayyim'. However, the supremacy of the written canon was acknowledged by all, and there always were some distinguished scholars who knew how that canon had ruled and to whom appeal could be made about its decisions. What was unique about eleventh-century Ashkenaz, in Ta-Shma's view, was the absence of such a notion. Practice, and practice alone, prevailed; the written law, if known at all, was entirely subordinated to practice.

It is an interesting theory, but the question is: what evidence is there for it? Precious little, so far as I can see. Indeed, a better argument can be made for the absence of a critical talmudic referent in Provence than in Ashkenaz. We know nothing about the Ashkenazic community before the latter half of the tenth century, if, indeed, such a collective existed. Michael Toch would have it that there was no Jewish community (only isolated individuals) in the Rhineland prior to that date, and that one cannot retroject the Jewish habitation from the closing decades of the tenth century onto the preceding ones. Friedrich Lotter, on the other hand, has vigorously insisted on the continuity of Jewish settlement from the early Middle Ages on.[29]

The entire controversy is about the prior physical existence of Jewish communities; intellectual life, by all accounts, begins in the last decades of the tenth century with the activities of Rabbenu Gershom Me'or ha-Golah. His responsa betoken a sovereign command of the Bavli, as do the responsa of his successor, R. Yehudah Ba'al Sefer ha-Dinim. Far more important, Rabbenu Gershom begins a massive explication of the entire talmudic corpus, including the recondite tractates on Temple service (*Kodashim*), something no other Jewish culture of the Middle Ages even attempted. As I have pointed out

[29] The issue is fully explicated in their exchange a decade ago. M. Toch, *'Dunkle Jahrhunderte'. Gab es ein jüdisches Frühmittelalter?*, Kleine Schriften des Arye-Maimon-Instituts 4 (Trier, 2001); F. Lotter, 'Totale Finsternis über "Dunklen Jahrhunderten". Zum Methodenverständnis von Michael Toch und seinen Folgen', *Aschkenas: Zeitschrift für Geschichte und Kultur der Juden*, 11/1 (2001), 215–31, and Toch's reply '"Mehr Licht": Eine Entgegnung zu Friedrich Lotter', *Aschkenas: Zeitschrift für Geschichte und Kultur der Juden*, 11/2 (2001), 465–87. Toch's position was set forth in English in an earlier article, 'The Formation of a Diaspora: The Settlement of Jews in the Medieval German Reich', *Aschkenas: Zeitschrift für Geschichte und Kultur der Juden*, 7/1 (1997), 55–78. As for the archeological findings in Cologne, see below, n. 32.

above, the Bavli was not to be studied simply for guidance in the conduct of daily religious life, as the Andalusian and Provençal Jewish culture imagined; rather, it was a sacred corpus that had to be explicated in its baffling totality. Ashkenazic communities, from the very dawn of their culture, placed the Bavli at the center of their religious and intellectual endeavors. If one adopts Toch's position that Jewish communities first appeared in the latter half of the tenth century, the intellectual elite of Ashkenaz were only too well aware of that 'brooding omnipresence in the sky', the external talmudic referent to which their actions were accountable, from the outset.

To maintain Ta-Shma's position one must adopt the view that the Jewish settlement in the Rhineland preceded its intellectual efflorescence. Indeed, Ta-Shma agrees with Grossman that the Kalonymide relocation to Mainz took place around 917.[30] That still doesn't leave much time for the formation of a mimetic tradition innocent of textual knowledge as intellectual activity begins with Rabbenu Gershom *c.*960–1028. Let us further remember that Rabbenu Gershom received his instruction from a shadowy Rabbenu Leontin, which means that one must push back talmudic knowledge in the Rhineland by a generation. Thus the intellectual origins of Ashkenaz and its settlement are reasonably coeval. Pushing back the Kalonymide translation from Lucca to Mainz to the time of Charles the Bold (around 875),[31] or even advancing Jewish settlement by a hundred years, to the 760s or 770s, as the recent archeological findings in Cologne may indicate, will not avail.[32] For a similar time gap between practice and formal knowledge is found in the

30 *Minhag Ashkenaz ha-Kadmon* (above, n. 1), 86.

31 See Grossman's discussion in *Ḥakhmei Ashkenaz ha-Rishonim: Koroteihem, Darkam be-Hanhagat ha-Tsibbur, Yetsiratam ha-Ruḥanit mi-Reshit Yishuvam 'ad li-Gezerot Tatnu (1096)* (Jerusalem, 1981), 31–44. On Rabbenu Leontin, ibid. 80–6.

32 S. Schütte and M. Gechter, 'Ursprung und Voraussetzungen des mittelalterlichen Rathauses und seiner Umgebung', in W. Geis and U. Krings, eds., *Köln: Das gotische Rathaus und seine historische Umgebung* (Cologne, 2000), 107–22, 135–7. S. Schütte, 'Die Juden in Köln von der Antike bis zum Hochmittelalter. Beitrage zur Diskussion zum frühen Judentum nördlich der Alpen', in E. Wamers and F. Backhaus, eds., *Synagogen, Mikwen, Siedlungen: jüdisches Alltagsleben im Lichte neuer archäologischer Funde*, Schriften des Archäologischen Museums Frankfurt 19 (Frankfurt, 2004), 73–116. Schütte summed up the results in a very general fashion in his 'Fouilles récents dans le quartier juif médiéval de Cologne', in P. Salmona and L. Sigal, eds., *L'Archéologie du judaïsme en France et en Europe* (Paris, 2011), 93–101. Toch, however, questions the intepretation that has been put on the archeological finds. See, most recently, M. Toch, *The Economic History of the European Jews: Late Antiquity and Early Middle Ages*, Études sur le judaïsme médiéval 56 (Leiden and Boston, 2013), 295–8. Alfred Haverkamp is equally of the belief that there is no substantive evidence to back Schütte's claims. See A. Haverkamp, 'Beziehungen zwischen Bischöfen und Juden im ottonisch-salischen Königreich bis 1090', in A. Esposito et al., eds., *Trier-Mainz-Roma: Stationen, Wirkungsfelder, Netzwerke. Festschrift für Michael Matheus zum 60. Geburtstag* (Regensburg, 2013), 63 n. 83.

Provençal community. Indeed, Narbonne is the one west European town, besides Rome, that even Toch concedes has a plausible claim to continuous Jewish settlement from the late fifth century.[33] Certainly, by the late tenth century there was a permanent Jewish community,[34] yet talmudic studies do not emerge in Narbonne (or anywhere else in Provence) until well over a century later.

Ta-Shma would reply that the crucial difference is not the time gap, but the different origins of the two communities: Ashkenaz, with its belief that custom overrules written law (*minhag mevattel halakhah*), is of Palestinian origin, whereas the roots of the Provençal Jewish community, with its credo that the written law always trumps custom, lie in Babylonia. I have already stated my serious doubts about the so-called Palestinian origin of the Ashkenazic community.[35] At the moment, one can safely say that no serious case for it has been made. I am no less doubtful about the alleged divergence between Babylonia and Palestine as to the halakhic role of custom (*minhag mevattel halakhah*). I fear that the penchant for heightened statement which I have noted above has once more come into play.

We need not, however, go into the problem, for the question that confronts us is not what the Palestinian view of custom was but rather what the Ashkenazic one was in the eleventh century. In posing this question, I come to the crux of the essay.

IV. Evidence

1. Ta-Shma devotes many pages to portraying the enormous power of *minhag* in Ashkenaz and the deep belief in its inerrancy. Towards the end of the article he points out that R. Gershom Me'or ha-Golah did not share this view of custom's infallibility and binding force, nor did these ideas obtain any purchase on the thought of R. Yitsḥak ha-Levi or of Rashi.[36] These are

[33] Toch, *Economic History of the European Jews* (above, n. 32), 68–9.

[34] Ibid. 302; F. L. Cheyette, *Ermengard of Narbonne and the World of the Troubadours* (Ithaca, 2001), 16, 56. H. Gross, *Gallia Judaica*, repr. with supplement by S. Schwartzfuchs (Amsterdam, 1969), 403–5.

[35] H. Soloveitchik, *Ha-Yayin bi-Yemei ha-Beinayim* (above, n. 3), 321–43; 'Communications and the Palestinian Origins of Ashkenaz' (below, Ch. 7), and 'The "Third Yeshivah of Bavel" and the Cultural Origins of Ashkenaz—A Proposal' (below, Ch. 9).

[36] *Minhag Ashkenaz ha-Kadmon* (above, n. 1), 87–90. (A) Rabbenu Gershom's position is even less supportive of custom than Ta-Shma realized, as he was misled by S. Eidelberg's edition of Rabbenu Gershom's responsa (New York, 1956) to attribute to Rabbenu Gershom the acquiescence to popular practice in moneylending expressed by **ומ"מ נהגו העם היתר בדבר זה**. These words, in fact, were authored a century later by R. Yitsḥak b. Asher (d. before 1133). See 'Pawnbroking—A Study in *Ribbit* and of the Halakhah in Exile' in the first volume of this series (*Collected Essays*, i. 57–166: see pp. 118 n. 140, 161 n. 118). (B) Ta-Shma writes (p. 87) that the popular practice of trade on *yom eidam* preceded

significant exceptions. Rabbenu Gershom was the greatest authority of the first generation of Early Ashkenaz (barring his teacher, Rabbenu Leontin, about whom we know next to nothing[37]); Rashi, the greatest figure of the fourth and last generation. R. Yitsḥak ha-Levi, Rashi's teacher, was unquestionably the most commanding personality of the third generation. Rashi, hardly a man given to overstatement, characterized him as 'the chief and leader of his generation by whose word they went out and they came in', an allusion to Numbers 27: 16–17: 'Moses spoke to the Lord saying . . . appoint someone over the community . . . who shall go out before them and come in before them and who shall take them out and bring them in, so that the Lord's community may not be like sheep that have no shepherd.'[38] If figures of this

Rabbenu Gershom by 'at least 200 years' and refers to his article 'Yom Eidam: Perek be-Hitpatḥut ha-Halakhah bi-Yemei ha-Beinayim', *Tarbiz*, 47 (1978), 187–215 (republished with an addendum in his *Halakhah, Minhag u-Metsi'ut be-'Ashkenaz: 1000–1350* [Jerusalem, 1996], 241–61.) I assume that he is referring to his citation in n. 15 in that article of Salo Baron's view that Agobard's report (in the 820s) of moving the market from Saturday to other days of the week (to be determined by the Jews) implies that the Jews traded with Gentiles on those other days. However, Ta-Shma rejects this inference in that very footnote, so I am at a loss to know on what this statement of 'at least 200 years' is based. Moreover, Agobard is speaking about the conduct of Louis's *missi* in and around Lyons, which had a significant Jewish presence; there is, however, no evidence that there was a Jewish community in Lotharingia at the time, or, if there was, that it had sufficient economic or political clout to move the market day. (I do believe that, when Agobard describes the arrogance of Jewish *kashrut* regulations, he would have taken care to see that these practices were those of the Jews in Louis's court. Doubly so as Agobard was very anxious about Jewish influence at the court, and would have feared—rightly—that the Jews would deny his accusations outright and ask Louis to check out their veracity locally. See 'Agobard of Lyons' [above, p. 13]. To claim that the individual Jews in the imperial court at Aachen observed *kashrut* is not the same as claiming that there was a Jewish community in Aachen or elsewhere in Lotharingia that actively participated in the fairs and markets.) Even if the excavations in Cologne point to a sizeable Jewish community in that city (and Toch and Haverkamp have both challenged this, see above, n. 32), any extrapolation of these findings to other settlements should be done with caution. Cologne may be typical or atypical, we simply do not know at present. The fact remains that there is no evidence in either Jewish or Latin sources of the existence of any Jewish community north of the Loire in the Carolingian period, let alone in Lotharingia. See the comprehensive study of J.-P. Devroey and C. Brouwer, 'La Participation des Juifs au commerce dans le monde franc (VIe Xe siècles)', in A. Dierkins and J.-M. Sansterre, eds., with J.-L. Kupper, *Voyages et voyageurs à Byzance et en Occident du VIe au XIe siècle*, Bibliothèque de la Faculté de Philosophie et Lettres de l'Université de Liège 278 (Geneva, 2000), 339–74. I would add that, while the debate between Toch and Lotter (above, n. 29) is in part methodological and in part a consequence of their larger, differing views of Jewish history in the Dark Ages, the study of Devroey and Brouwer is an 'outside' investigation of the available evidence by two fine Carolingian scholars, unlinked to any particular perspective on Jewish history.

37 See above, n. 31.

38 דָּבָּר ומנהיג לדור, על פיו יצאו ויבואו, *Or Zarua'*, ii (Zhitomir, 1862), *'Eruvin*, #140, fo. 38a; edn. Or 'Etsyon (Jerusalem, 2001), i. 495. See Grossman (above, n. 31), 282 n. 93. I have translated *dabbar* as 'chief', as *manhig* co-opted the word 'leader', and the phrase דבר לדור occurs only in the phrase

stature did not subscribe to *minhag* Ashkenaz ha-Kadmon as portrayed by Ta-Shma, just how widespread was this notion? Let us examine one by one the leaders of Ash-kenazic Jewry in the eleventh century.

Rabbenu Gershom, the first dissenter from *minhag* Ashkenaz ha-Kadmon, was one of the founding fathers of Ashkenaz, quite possibly *the* founding father (if we exclude the shadowy R. Leontin).[39] The significance of his lack of reverence for custom should, then, not be underestimated. He died in 1028; what can we say of his successors? The leading figures of the next generation, the three dominant Talmudists in the middle third of the eleventh century, were R. Ya'akov b. Yakar, R. Eli'ezer ha-Gadol, and Rabbi Yehudah ha-Kohen, Ba'al Sefer ha-Dinim. The first, R. Ya'akov b. Yakar, whom Rashi esteemed most among his teachers, died in 1064, before Rashi could fully avail himself of his riches. Impressive but with no sense of self-worth, he was characterized by Rashi as one who 'turned himself into a doormat' (*ve-hinhig* [*sic*] *'atsmo ka-'askupah ha-nidreset*).[40] Compulsively humble, shying away from any public stand, he would scarcely have been one to challenge regnant practice. Unfortunately, the responsa of R. Eli'ezer ha-Gadol are too few to admit of any assessment, and none, furthermore, deal with anything even remotely connected to custom.[41]

The third member of that trio was Rabbi Yehudah ha-Kohen, Ba'al Sefer ha-Dinim, who is characterized by Grossman as 'an individualist'.[42] While it is true that the legacy of R. Yehudah ha-Kohen is far greater—some ninety-nine responsa have come down to us, all clear and decisive rulings and written with great assurance—only three, or possibly four, deal with ritual law,[43]

דבר אחד לדור ואין שני דברין לדור, *Sanhedrin* 8a, and cited by Rashi at Deut. 31: 7. Perhaps 'commander' would be a better translation, but it seemed too strong. (The verse in Num. reads: **יפקוד ה'...** **איש על העדה אשר יצא לפניהם ואשר יבא לפניהם ואשר יוציאם ואשר יביאם ולא תהיה עדת ה' כצאון אשר אין להם רועה**.)

[39] I refrain from saying that he was the most revered name in the 11th-century Ashkenazic pantheon, as I share Agus's view that much of Rabbenu Gershom's pre-eminence is a later projection. See my remarks in the essay on pawnbroking in the first volume of this series (*Collected Essays*, i. 162 n. 126). He was, however, the major respondent (*meshiv*) of the first generation, and this is significant.

[40] *Siddur Rashi*, ed. J. Freimann (Berlin, 1912), #174, p. 80, and the parallel passages there cited.

[41] To be exact, three full responsa and a substantive report of a fourth by Grossman's count, *Ḥakhmei Ashkenaz ha-Rishonim* (above, n. 31), 226–7.

[42] Ibid. 175.

[43] See below, 'The Authority of the Babylonian Talmud', Ch. 4, n. 74. The three responsa are found in *Teshuvot R. Me'ir mi-Rotenburg*, ed. M. A. Bloch (Prague and Budapest, 1895), #913; *Ravyah 'al 'Avodah Zarah ve-Ḥullin*, ed. D. Deblitsky (Jerusalem, 1976), #1050 (= *Sefer Ravyah*, ed. D. Deblitsky [Benei Berak, 2005], iv, #1050, p. 13); *Sefer ha-Pardes*, ed. H. L. Ehrenreich (Budapest, 1924), 350. Grossman seems to be of the opinion that the responsum published in the so-called *Siddur R. Shelomoh mi-Germaiza*, ed. M. Herschler (Jerusalem, 1972), 277, was authored by R. Yehudah, as

which is the area that Ta-Shma quite properly addresses.[44] Unfortunately, none of these responsa are connected with custom of any sort, and thus have no bearing on the question of *minhag* Ashkenaz ha-Kadmon. However, we do have reports of six rulings (as opposed to actual responsa) of his in ritual law.[45] In three of them he seems to go against the reigning practice. In the matter of mourning on the second day of *yom tov*, R. Yehudah explicitly defied the custom in his community in Mainz.[46] In another, he would very much appear to be doing the same. In Chapter 4 I discuss the issue of grandchildren observing mourning for their grandparents.[47] The proponent of this practice was R. Yehudah ha-Kohen, Ba'al Sefer ha-Dinim, who wished his son to join him in mourning his father. The *Ma'aseh ha-Ge'onim* reports that his colleagues prevented him from imposing his view.[48] Grossman correctly observes that

he included it in his *Sefer ha-Dinim: Teshuvotav Melukkatot mi-Mekorot Shonim,* Kuntresim, Mekorot u-Meḥkarim (Jerusalem, 1977), 63. I doubt it. As this essay entails the tabulation of parallel passages and their identification, I have cited Ehrenreich's edition of the *Sefer ha-Pardes* and not those of Constantinople, 1802, and Warsaw, 1870. There are far fewer lines per page in Ehrenreich's work, and the pages are not double-columned as they are in the other two editions. (All passages were checked against the *editio princeps* of Constantinople.) (The single largest collection of the responsa of R. Me'ir of Rothenburg, that of Prague in 1607, was edited by Bloch and published in Budapest in 1895.)

44 *Minhag Ashkenaz ha-Kadmon* (above, n. 1), 17 n. 6. In civil law ('Ḥoshen Mishpat') custom is extremely powerful not only in Ashkenaz but in all halakhic cultures, much as 'trade usage' is in American law of contracts. Custom frequently controls the meaning of terms, the presumptions of intent of the parties, and the self-understood conditions of the deal.

45 *Ma'aseh ha-Ge'onim*, #42, p. 27, #57, p. 48, #59, pp. 49–50 (two rulings); *Shibbolei ha-Leket II*, ed. M. Z. Hasida (Jerusalem, 1969), #36, pp. 58–9; *Shibbolei ha-Leket II*, ed. S. Hasida (Jerusalem, 1988), #36, pp. 123–4; *Siddur R. Shelomoh mi-Germaiza*, 277. (The responsum found in *Sefer ha-Pardes*, 350, is the original responsum, which serves as the basis of the report in *Ma'aseh ha-Ge'onim*, #57, p. 48, which has already been counted.) I have not included the passage cited by Grossman from MS Oxford, Bodley 678, fo. 389b, that R. Yehudah ha-Kohen was upset about not having received the priestly gifts of the arm, jaw, and maw (*zeroa', leḥayayim ve-ha-kevah*). First, the obligation to give these gifts even outside the Land of Israel is clear (*Ḥullin* 130a) and is scarcely a ruling of R. Yehudah. Second, it is not at all clear that this was going against the general consensus, as R. Yehudah b. Kalonymos reports in his *Yiḥusei Tanna'im ve-'Amora'im* that prior to the First Crusade this tithe used to be given. Apparently the level of giving was simply not up to R. Yehudah's standards or, perhaps, it depended on family traditions, as Grossman suggests. See Grossman, *Ḥakhmei Ashkenaz ha-Rishonim* (above, n. 31), 194–5. (On the two editions of the *Shibbolei ha-Leket II*, see my essay on pawnbroking in the first volume of this series (*Collected Essays*, i. 160 n. 98).

46 *Ma'aseh ha-Ge'onim*, #59, p. 50; *Sefer ha-Pardes*, 263; *Shibbolei ha-Leket ha-Shalem* (Vilna, 1887), *Semaḥot*, #52, fo. 183b. (As for the attribution to the *Sefer ha-Dinim*, see my remarks in 'The Authority of the Babylonian Talmud' below, Ch. 4 n. 74.)

47 *Ma'aseh ha-Ge'onim*, #59, p. 50; *Sefer ha-Pardes*, 262–3; and see below 'The Authority of the Babylonian Talmud', 81–5.

48 *Ma'aseh ha-Ge'onim*, #59, pp. 49–50; *Sefer ha-Pardes*, 262; S. E. Stern, 'Piskei u-Minhagei

such a bar would arise only if mourning a grandparent breached customary practice.[49] Given R. Yehudah's prominent role in Mainz, he would be paid many consolation visits, and every visitor would observe his son sitting *shiv'ah*. Such a public flouting of custom could not be tolerated. Finally, it is reported that the Mainz community read the *haftarah* of the New Moon when the Sabbath of Hanukkah fell on Rosh Hodesh, 'in honor of R. Yehudah ha-Kohen'.[50] Indeed, we have his responsum on the subject—a powerful one—and it is openly dismissive of the position of *Halakhot Gedolot*.[51] (As respect must be paid, R. Yehudah finesses the issue by claiming that the ruling is a forgery for so silly a ruling could never have been given by R. Yehudai Gaon.) The clear implication of this report is that prior to R. Yehudah's writing, the Hanukkah *haftarah* was read—in accordance with the opinion of the *Halakhot Gedolot*—and it was his responsum that occasioned the change. With three out of his six rulings leaning to iconoclasm, Grossman's characterization of him as 'an individualist' may be an understatement. Be that as it may, R. Yehudah ha-Kohen can scarcely be counted as one who saw traditional practice as normative or thought custom to be inerrant.

The three dominant figures in the Ashkenazic Jewry of the next generation, those who played significant roles in the latter third of the eleventh century, were R. Yitsḥak ha-Levi (whom I have already mentioned), R. Shelomoh b. Shimshon (also known as Rabbenu Sasson, killed in the Crusade massacre of 1096), and R. Yitsḥak b. Yehudah. The first, as Ta-Shma writes, was clearly unfazed by custom. Indeed, that independent, strong-minded leader was unimpressed by established practice, and he certainly did not believe in its absolute binding authority. Nor does Ta-Shma claim that the second scholar, R. Shelomoh b. Shimshon, shared the outlook of the Makirites. Wisely so, for even if Grossman's depiction of Rabbenu Sasson is correct[52] (and, as we shall see, serious doubts can be had on the matter[53]), his stance was a question of temperament rather than ideology. R. Shelomoh b. Shimshon's halakhic

Magentsa ve-Germaiza', *Tsefunot*, 3/1 (1991), 4 (repr. in *Me'orot ha-Rishonim*, ed. S. M. Stern [Jerusalem, 2002], 185).

49 *Ḥakhmei Ashkenaz ha-Rishonim* (above, n. 31), 187.

50 *Ma'aseh ha-Ge'onim*, #57, p. 48: מפני כבודו של רבי יהודה הכהן הזקן וקימ' לן (ע"ז לא ע"א) במקום שיפול העץ שם יהו פירותיו כמו שמפורש למעלה בתשובת רבי יהודה הכהן הזקן. The responsum is not found in our copy of the *Ma'aseh ha-Ge'onim*, which is clearly truncated, but it is found in the two works cited in the next note.

51 *Sefer ha-Pardes*, 350, and *Shibbolei ha-Leket ha-Shalem*, #190, fo. 74a. The latter text ascribes it erroneously to 'R. Yehudah he-Ḥasid'. The last word should be emended to 'ha-Kohen' or 'ha-Zaken'. See my remarks below, pp. 154–6.

52 *Ḥakhmei Ashkenaz ha-Rishonim* (above, n. 31), 334–9.

53 See 'Characterizing Medieval Talmudists' (below, Ch. 6).

position was shaped by a conservative disposition, not by any theory of the near-infallibility of custom. Thus Ta-Shma's entire argument hangs upon R. Yitsḥak b. Yehudah and the Makirites. Is it wise to characterize an entire culture on the basis of one man and his acolytes? Is it wise to do so when five of the other major figures of Early Ashkenaz clearly do not share his outlook, and too little is known of the remaining two to say anything meaningful? Is one out of eight a representative sample?

Moreover, are we even certain about this one man? Ta-Shma characterizes R. Yitsḥak b. Yehudah as the central influence upon the Makirites, and claims that his spirit animated *Ma'aseh ha-Ge'onim*.[54] The question that naturally poses itself is: was R. Yitsḥak b. Yehudah a unique figure in Early Ashkenaz? Did he really possess so singular an outlook? Could there have been such a great ideological divide between him and all his predecessors and colleagues without any contemporary source noting this? R. Yitsḥak b. Yehudah's views deserve, I believe, closer scrutiny.

2. We have some eighty-three rulings of this scholar, Rashi's teacher and cousin of the Makirites.[55]

Once his son conveys a personal practice of his father, R. Yitsḥak,[56] and once R. Yitsḥak states that his father conducted himself in a certain way, though he doesn't know the reason and adds that here, in Mainz, this practice is not the accepted one.[57] On another occasion it is reported that in R. Yitsḥak's house salt was not employed in preparation of the Passover *matsot* for this was 'the custom of the forefathers' (*minhag kadmonim*).[58] All this, however, betokens no special relationship to custom. One can readily imagine scholars from any period and every halakhic culture speaking the same way.

The uniqueness of R. Yitsḥak b. Yehudah's approach is based on the way he expressed himself in no fewer than five other rulings. He, perhaps, coined the phrase 'The custom of our fathers is Torah' (*minhag avoteinu torah*) or 'Custom is Torah' (*ve-ha-minhag torah hi*). He is, undoubtedly, the first in Ashkenaz that we know of to use these phrases.[59] On two other occasions, he invoked a phrase of the Yerushalmi, 'Custom overrides halakhah' (*minhag mevattel halakhah*).

54 *Minhag Ashkenaz ha-Kadmon* (above, n. 1), 89, 331.

55 See Appendix II below.

56 *Ma'aseh ha-Ge'onim*, #56, p. 45.

57 Ibid., #3, p. 4.

58 Ibid., #24, p. 15. This was a widespread practice in many Jewish medieval cultures, though none could give a good reason for it. See Ta-Shma's suggestion in *Minhag Ashkenaz ha-Kadmon* (above, n. 1), 249–59.

59 S. Abramson, *'Inyanot be-Sifrut ha-Ge'onim* (above, n. 1), 28 n. 33. See, however, B. Lifshitz, '"Minhag" u-Mekomo be-Midrag ha-Normot be-Torah she-be-'al Peh', *Shenaton ha-Mishpat ha-'Ivri*, 24 (2006/7), 123 n. 1.

These statements can mean a great deal or very little. They can mean very little because they also terminate further discussion. Suppose a contemporary *rosh yeshivah*—wrestling, as usual, with a difficult passage in *Tosafot* or *Mishneh Torah*—was asked: 'Why should we say "Yekum Purkan"?', and he replied briefly and decisively, 'The custom of our fathers is Torah.' This may be a statement of the power of custom and its inerrancy. It could equally be a polite way of saying, 'We're going to continue saying it. And don't expect me to spend any time on your question; I have more important things to think about.'

Indeed, R. Yitsḥak b. Yehudah had more important things on his mind. Avraham Epstein, in his groundbreaking article on the *Perush Rabbenu Gershom*, in which he demonstrates that the commentary was actually the collective work of the school of Rabbenu Gershom in Mainz, portrayed R. Yitsḥak b. Yehudah as playing *the* decisive role in the work's crystallization.[60] Grossman has questioned Epstein's conclusion and, while R. Yitsḥak's role was unquestionably important, the evidence is too fragmentary to allow any certainty as to its decisiveness.[61] However, let us not forget that Rashi did turn to R. Yitsḥak b. Yehudah for help in talmudic exegesis. We have a group of thirteen queries that he sent to R. Yitsḥak, twelve of which concern talmudic passages with which Rashi had difficulty.[62] No greater compliment to exegetical prowess can have been paid in the past millennium. Indeed, if one wishes to see the casual, sovereign control of the entire Bavli assumed by the two correspondents, one need look no further than the tenth letter of this exchange.[63] Rashi asked about the disqualification of *ḥatsitsah* (the interposition of a foreign object) in the Temple service. R. Yitsḥak rattles off four places in the Talmud where this is mentioned or assumed, and discusses them without ever giving the chapter of the tractate or even the name of the tractates where these *sugyot* are found. He has no doubt that Rashi will know exactly where these passages are located in *Yoma*, *Zevaḥim*, *Menaḥot*, and *Ḥullin* and grasp the implications of his brief remarks.

[60] A. Epstein, 'Der Gerschom Meor ha-Golah zugeschriebene Talmud-Commentar', in *Festschrift zum achtzigsten Geburtstage Moritz Steinschneider's* (Leipzig, 1896), 135–41. Hebrew translation in *Netu'im*, 6 (2000), 125–31. See also J. Müller's remarks in his introduction to *Teshuvot Ḥakhmei Tsarfat ve-Lotir* (Vienna, 1881), 23–5.

[61] Grossman, *Ḥakhmei Ashkenaz* (above, n. 31), 316–18.

[62] *Ḥofes Matmonim*, ed. B. Goldberg (Berlin, 1845), 11–15; repr. by M. M. Kasher as *Teshuvot Rashi 'im Teshuvot Rabbenu Yitsḥak b. Yehudah* (Jerusalem, 1925). The responsa were taken from what is now MS Berlin, Staatsbibliothek 160. These pages are no longer to be found in the manuscript, as Paul de Lagarde accusingly noted in his catalogue (*Symmicta, I* [Göttingen, 1877], 155–9). A copy of these missing pages is found in MS Oxford, Bodley 1317. See *Catalogue of Manuscripts in the Bodleian Library*, ii: *Supplement of Addenda and Corrigenda to Vol. I (A. Neubauer's Catalogue)* (Oxford, 1994), col. 218, #1317.

[63] *Ḥofes Matmonim*, #22; *Teshuvot Rashi 'im Teshuvot Rabbenu Yitsḥak b. Yehudah*, #22.

The Mainz commentary encompassed all of the Talmud, and R. Yitsḥak was a major contributor, possibly even the one in whose school the work took final shape and was committed to writing. He was grappling with the relentless, *sub verbo* decipherment of every line of the entire Talmud, and if he did not wish to be deflected into 'customology' (*ta'amei minhagim*), it would be understandable. The scope of his learning was extraordinary, and when asked occasionally about a custom, he could draw on *midrashim* and *aggadot* and provide a reason for it.[64] To imagine, however, that he had the time (or, possibly, even the inclination) to long ponder them may well be a mistake.

Context alone will determine the meaning of *minhag avoteinu torah*. Let us therefore study the context of all of its five occurrences in the writings of R. Yitsḥak b. Yehudah.[65] (In the first instance two practices were queried and it is thus numbered I–II.)

I–II

שאילה זו שאל ר׳ מנחם בר׳ מכיר את בן דודו רבינו יצחק בר׳ יהודה:

יום מילה שחל להיות ביום תענית ציבור כגון עשרה בטבת, וי״ז בתמוז, וג׳ תשרי, מהו להתפלל פסוקי דרחמים וסליחות ולומר ווידוי כדרכו ולומר והוא רחום וליפול תחנונים ולומר א-ל ארך אפים? ואם מברכין על היין וטועמתו אם הילד, או לטעימיה לינוקא, או דילמא אין מברכין כיון שהמברך אינו יכול לטעום?

והילך תשובתו: [1] וששאל על יום המילה: כך נוהגין במקומינו שמתפללין ביום תעניות סליחות ואומר ווידוי כדרכו, ואין אומר׳ והוא רחום ולא תחנונים, ומנהג אבותינו תורה היא . . .

[2] ושליח צבור מברך על היין ואינו טועמו, ומנהג תורה היא, שאין צריך לטועמו ביום תענית ולא למיתב לינוקא דאתא למסרך אלא לשהייה עד לאורתא [ולא לשתייה לאימיה דרביא] דאמרינן בערובין היכי ניעביד (מ׳ ע״ב) ליברך עליה ולינחיי, המברך צריך שיטעום . . . וביום כפורים אם אמר זמן על הכוס כשאר ימים טובים, כיון דצריך למשתייה לשם קידוש היום ליכא למימר דלישהייה עד מוצאי יום הכיפורים, הילכך אין אומרים זמן על הכוס ביום הכפורים דלא אפשר . . . יצחק בר׳ יהודה . . .

This question was asked by R. Menahem b. Makhir of his cousin, R. Yitsḥak b. Yehudah: if the day of circumcision falls on a day of communal public fast, such as 'Asarah be-Tevet, Shiv'ah-'Asar be-Tammuz, and Tsom Gedalyah, should one recite the biblical verses of supplication and [requests for] forgiveness and make confession as is

64 See text below.

65 *Maḥzor Vitry*, ed. S. Hurwitz (Nuremberg, 1923), 624–5, with several minor emendations from *Ma'aseh ha-Ge'onim*, #64, p. 59; *Sefer ha-Pardes*, 76; *Teshuvot Rashi*, ed. I. Elfenbein (New York, 1943), #53; *Sefer Ravyah*, ed. V. Aptowitzer (repr. New York, 1983) i, *Ta'anit*, #891; *Shibbolei ha-Leket ha-Shalem*, *Milah*, #4, p. 376. The differences between the texts are entirely stylistic. It is difficult to give pride of place to any single version.

usual [on fast days] and [also] recite 'Ve-hu Raḥum' and fall [i.e. recite] Taḥanun and recite 'El Erekh Appayim'?

If one makes a blessing over [a cup of] wine, should one give it to the mother of the newborn to taste it [as is usually done] or give it to a child to taste [as one does on Yom Kippur eve] or perhaps one forgoes the blessing over [a cup of] wine, seeing that no one may taste it [and drinking from a cup of wine over which a blessing has been recited is a *sine qua non*]?

This was his [R. Yitsḥak b. Yehudah's] response:

1. As to the question of the day of circumcision, we conduct ourselves in our locale thus: on fast days we recite the [verses of] request for forgiveness; however, we do not make confession, nor recite 'Ve-hu Raḥum', and the custom of our fathers is Torah.

2. [As to the drinking of the wine:] The cantor recites the blessing over [a cup of] wine, but does not taste it, and custom is Torah, for there is no necessity to drink from it on a fast day. He may not give it to a child for that would corrupt him [i.e. the child might get the wrong impression,] [nor to the mother of the child, who is fasting]. And thus it said in [tractate] *'Eruvin*: 'What should we do? Make the blessing and leave it [undrunk]? [It is a requirement that] the wine that has been blessed must be drunk. [Give it to a child? It might corrupt him] . . . On Yom Kippur, if he recited the 'She-heḥiyanu' blessing on a cup [of wine], as done on other festivals, he must drink it in honor of the day's holiness. [Consequently] one cannot say that he should leave it for the evening [after Yom Kippur is over]. Therefore, on Yom Kippur, one does not make the 'She-heḥiyanu' blessing [at all] for it is an impossibility. [This does not hold true, however, for the cup of blessing at a circumcision on a fast day.]

Yitsḥak b. Yehudah

In this somewhat jagged passage, custom is invoked twice. The first case is one in which there is no talmudic dictum whatsoever. Supplication for forgiveness and confession of sin on fast days are near-universal practices in Jewish communities; what exactly is said and how much is said is all a matter of custom. The use of the phrase 'The custom of our fathers is Torah' does not mean here that custom trumps halakhah, as there is no halakhah here to be trumped. In this context, the sentence simply means that we have no intention of changing our ways. In matters of custom, custom prevails.

In the second case, custom is invoked to preclude the alternative explanation of a talmudic passage. The problem of reciting blessings on wine on a fast day is explored by the Talmud in *'Eruvin*. It discusses reciting 'She-heḥiyanu' on Yom Kippur on wine (*kos shel berakhah*): the one who recites the blessing cannot drink, and giving it to a child would send him the wrong message—that it is permissible to drink on Yom Kippur. Therefore one doesn't recite 'She-heḥiyanu' on wine on Yom Kippur.

This case, however, contends R. Yitsḥak, is not comparable to recitation of the circumcision (*berit*) blessings on a fast day. The wine of 'She-heḥiyanu' on Yom Kippur is a *kos shel berakhah* in honor of Yom Kippur; hence, it must be consumed on that day. The *kos shel berakhah* of a circumcision ceremony is recited in honor of the circumcision, not in honor of the fast; hence, it may be put aside and consumed after sundown, when the fast is over.

R. Yitsḥak realizes that different views are possible. Indeed, by his time other views had already been advanced, though we don't know whether he was aware of them.[66] One could contend that, inasmuch as the recitation of the blessings over wine at a circumcision is not a talmudic requirement, one forgoes the wine on a fast day. One could equally distinguish between Yom Kippur and the lesser fast days mentioned in the inquiry. One could even argue, as many were soon to do, that in the case at bar, we may in fact allow the child to drink.[67] Yom Kippur is a recurrent event; giving wine regularly to children could give youngsters the wrong impression. A *berit* falling on a fast day is not a frequent event, certainly not a cyclical one; hence we need not fear their misconstruing the drinking.

Custom is in no way being absolutized by R. Yitsḥak in this ruling. He is cutting off discussion by invoking custom. There is no point arguing about how best to draw an analogy between *berit* and Yom Kippur, as custom has already decided that question. This is an approach common to the Tosafists and, if not pushed too far, common to other halakhic cultures, both medieval and modern. When the options are roughly equal, tradition decides which way the ruling goes—if not always in theory, certainly in practice.

66 See *Otsar ha-Ge'onim*, *'Eruvin*, ed. B. M. Lewin (Jerusalem, 1931), up to 40b, pp. 30–2; *Sefer ha-'Eshkol*, ii, ed. S. Albeck (Jerusalem, 1938), 10 and notes ad loc.; *Sefer Ravyah*, ibid., and notes ad loc. Rabbenu Kalonymos of Lucca had ruled that it was permissible to forgo the blessing on wine, *Ginzei Schechter*, ii, ed. L. Ginzberg (New York, 1929), 212. However, we do not know whether R. Yitsḥak b. Yehudah knew of this responsum. Ta-Shma believes that he was aware of it (*Minhag Ashkenaz ha-Kadmon* [above, n. 1], 331). If so, R. Yitsḥak b. Yehudah had every reason to cut off what would have been, to his mind, a pointless discussion.

67 e.g. Rashbam in *Tosafot*, *'Eruvin* 40b, s.v. *dilma*; R. Eliyahu mi-Paris, *Maḥzor Vitry*, ad loc.; R. Shemu'el b. Barukh mi-Bamberg in a gloss to *Ma'aseh ha-Ge'onim*, #64, p. 60.

III

ואני שמעתי משום ר' יצחק בר' יהודה נ"ע כששאלוהו מפני מה נוהגין להפטיר ב'ויהי אחרי מות משה' והשיב כיון שנהגו נהגו, שמנהג מבטל את ההלכה.[68]

And I heard in the name of R. Yitsḥak b. Yehudah, may his resting place be in Eden, when they asked him why it is customary to read [on Simḥat Torah the *haftarah* beginning with] 'And it came to pass after the death of Moses' [Josh. 1: 1]. He replied: 'Since people are accustomed to reading it, this then is the custom [and] custom overrides halakhah.'

In the eleventh century people both in North Africa (Kairouan) and Ashkenaz discovered, to their surprise, that some of their traditional Torah readings and *haftarot* on festivals and fast days did not correspond to talmudic dictates. There was much ado about it. (See one respondent's remark: **גם בכאן [!] כבר שאלו שאלה זו כמה פעמים.**[69]) R. Yitsḥak gave the subject seven words (he did have other things on his mind); his nephews, the Makirites, thought it worth much more, as the five-page discussion in the *Sefer ha-Pardes* attests.[70] Some of the wisest words were found in a responsum of the scholars of Kairouan, cited by one of the Makirites, R. Natan:

ויש לומר שמאותו הזמן עצמו הנהיגו אלו ההפטרות, ב[י]מי אחרונים (סבור אין) [סבוראין], ראשי ישיבות [שעמדו אחרי האמוראים הנהיגו כן ויש כח בידם כי למדו תורה מפיהם (ד"א מפי האמוראים)] דקריאת הפטרות אינו לא איסור והיתר, ומה שנוהגין נוהגין. וכן אמר אביי (מגילה לא ע"ב) נהוג עלמא 'בכי תוליד', וסמכו חכמים על זה. ושלום.[71]

Reply can be made: These *haftarot* were instituted at that very time, in the days of the Latter Ones, the *savora'im*, who headed the yeshivah after the *amora'im*; [they] instituted them. And they had the authority to do so, for they had studied Torah from their [the *amora'im*'s] lips. For the recitation of the *haftarot* is not in the realm of things ritually forbidden and allowed [as are, for example, kosher and non-kosher food]. What people are accustomed to do, they do. [Furthermore,] Abbaye said, '[despite the talmudic dictum to the contrary,] people read [on Tish'ah be-'Av] 'Ki Tolid', and the Sages endorsed this position. Shalom.[72]

Seeing that this *haftarah* is widely recited, the tradition must go back to the *savora'im*, the successors of the *amora'im*, who were authorized to make such changes. Arguing alternatively, they continue: changing the *haftarot* is not the

68 *Sefer ha-Pardes*, 353.
69 Ibid. 352.
70 Ibid. 349–54.
71 Emendation on the basis of *Or Zarua'*, ii (Zhitomir, 1862), #393. R. Yitsḥak Or Zarua' attributes the concluding sentence to R. Yitsḥak b. Yehudah. However, Aptowitzer, correctly to my mind, attributes it to the responsum from Kairouan, as is clear from *Sefer ha-Pardes*. See *Sefer Ravyah*, ii, *Megillah*, #595, p. 329 n. 4.
72 *Sefer ha-Pardes*, 352–3.

equivalent of eating non-kosher food, and whatever is customarily done in *haftarah*-reading is properly done. The Talmud itself has ratified custom as the final arbiter of Torah readings and *haftarot*.

This question continued to be raised in Ashkenaz throughout the medieval period and little was said that improved on the answer from Kairouan. The *Tosafot* suggested that, perhaps, this reading was an innovation of R. Hai Gaon (d. 1038). Ri ha-Zaken (d. 1189) pointed out, in another context of dissonance between the Bavli and communal custom, that on occasion we follow the Palestinian rite. Rabbenu Tam (d. 1171) had said the same thing a generation earlier.[73] Ravyah (d. *c.*1225) cited both Ri and Rabbenu Tam and asked perplexedly: why *should* we follow the Palestinian rite in these matters? He found no good answer and ended up saying more or less what had been said some 150 years before:

> **הכי נמי סמכינן אמנהג וסמיך אגאונים ורבנן סבוראי כיון דאביי תלה לה במנהגא. ואין לנו לשנות משום [אל] תטוש תורת אמך (משלי א: ח), דזימנין דסמכו אירושלמי [ואספרים חיצונים, ודרשינן] כי לא דבר ריק וגו' ואם ריק הוא. מכם הוא ריק לפי שאין אתם יגעים בו (ירושלמי פאה פ"א ה"א, שביעית פ"א ה"ב).**

So, too, we rely on custom and upon the Geonim and the *savora'im* since Abbaye made [the reading of the *haftarah*] dependent upon custom. And one should not change, as it is written, 'and do not forsake your mother's teaching'[74] [Prov. 1: 8], for on occasion they [the Sages] relied upon the Yerushalmi and non-canonized sources [i.e. *midrashim* or *massekhet Soferim*] and they [the Sages] said [on the verse, Deut. 32: 47], 'They are not idle words for you' [literally: 'from you'] and if they are idle, it is 'from you' [i.e. on your account], for you fail to make a strenuous effort for it.[75]

Admittedly, Ri ha-Zaken's contemporary, Rabbi Efrayim of Regensburg, did seek to change a *haftarah* reading to align it with the talmudic norm. Ignored by the community, he stormed out of the synagogue in protest and declared the members worthy of excommunication.[76] But that stormy petrel —who, in his numerous disputes with his colleagues, repeatedly warned them,

73 *Tosefot R. Yehudah Sir Leon*, *Berakhot*, ed. N. Sachs (Jerusalem, 1969), i. 18a, s.v. *dalyeih*, pp. 215–16, and parallel passages cited by the editor ad loc.; *Sefer ha-Yashar*, *Teshuvot*, ed. S. F. Rosenthal (Berlin, 1898), #45: 3.

74 This verse is construed in *Pesaḥim* 50b as mandating upholding traditions: **אמר להו כבר קיבלו אבותיכם עליהם, שנאמר שמע בני מוסר אביך ואל תטוש תורת אמך**.

75 *Sefer Ravyah*, ii, *Megillah*, #595, p. 332 (the emendations are those of the editor).

76 *Teshuvot, Pesakim u-Minhagim le-R. Me'ir mi-Rotenburg*, iii: *Hilkhot Semaḥot*, ed. Y. Z. Cahana (Jerusalem, 1962), #7, pp. 34–5 (cited by Aptowitzer, *Sefer Ravyah*, ii, *Megillah*, #556, p. 273 n. 8). See id., *Mavo le-Sefer Ravyah* (Jerusalem, 1938), 322, and E. E. Urbach, *Ba'alei ha-Tosafot*, rev. edn. (Jerusalem, 1980), 200–1.

'Don't anger me!'—was hardly a typical Tosafist. He had stalked out of the synagogue in indignation on another occasion and had once sent a letter to Rabbenu Tam containing all the hairs he had torn out of his beard in anguish over some common practice.[77] Other Tosafists were quieter souls and never dreamt of changing the customary Torah and *haftarah* readings, even when they diverged from the dictates of the Bavli. This is characteristic of any traditional society and is scarcely unique to the Middle Ages. R. Yosef Kolon in the fifteenth century, for example, forcefully emphasized compliance with custom even when it conflicted with the written norm, as did R. Mosheh Isserles a century later. So did R. Avraham Gombiner a century after that, citing Ri Kolon approvingly in his *Magen Avraham*, the classic commentary on *Shulḥan 'Arukh*, 'Oraḥ Ḥayyim'.[78] Anyone who imagines that the rich and variegated corpus of religious practice is laid out upon a Procrustean bed of canonized texts, and all the numerous protuberances lopped off, has little knowledge of how a traditional society functions. Such a view also underestimates the creativity of religious communities, even the most norm-oriented ones. Were it not for that creativity—in liturgy, for example, which entailed serious halakhic problems—the religious services of Yom Kippur could be dispatched in several hours.[79] There is no such thing as perfect compliance, total congruence between deed and norm, and halakhists are only too well aware of this. If the divergences are not serious and are long-standing they acquire rectitude of their own, for legitimacy comes with age in a traditional society. There is nothing distinctive in the reply of R. Yitsḥak b. Yehudah other than its dismissive brevity.

IV

נשאול נשאל מאת רבינו יצחק על קורות ורהיטים. והתיר היתר גמור כי כן נהגו העם ואין לשנות (על) המנהג. ואם יעלה על לב לומר עדיין תעשה ולא מן העשוי, די לנו ב'תעשה' שנוטל הנסרים מעל הלטש [lattes = lates]. וגם סגן הלוי [ז"א ר' יצחק הלוי] נשאל והשיב כן, אלא שצריך לסלק את הנסרים כנגד כל הסיכוך.

והעיד אחד לפני גור אריה על הרב ר' אליעזר הגדול זצ"ל שהיה עושה סוכתו בתוך הבית ולא היה מסלק הלטש והיה בעיניו קשה מאוד על שנעשית בתוך הבית. והיה מיצר מאוד. והייתה [!] חצר בינו לבין שכינו, וקנאו כפליים בדמיה. ושאלו לגור אריה, מפני מה היה מיצר? אמר להם מפני שהיה רוצה לקיים מצוה מן המובחר.

77 *Sefer Ravyah*, #551, p. 260; *Shitah Mekubbetset*, *Zevaḥim* 18b, n. 25 (n. 26 in some recent editions).

78 *She'elot u-Teshuvot Maharik ha-Yeshanot*, ed. E. Schlesinger and S. B. H. Deutsch (Jerusalem, 1988), #148 and see #9; *Teshuvot Rama*, ed. A. Siev (Jerusalem 1971), #19; *Magen Avraham*, 'Oraḥ Ḥayyim', 690: 22.

79 See e.g. R. Langer, *To Worship God Properly: Tensions between Liturgical Custom and Halakhah in Judaism* (Cincinnati, 1998), 110–87.

R. Yitsḥak [b. Yehudah] was asked about the boards and beams [of the *sukkah*]. He absolutely allowed them [for use as roofing for the *sukkah* (*sekhakh*)], for such is the common practice, and one should not change the custom. If one is bothered by the rule of *ta'aseh ve-lo min he-'asui*, it suffices [to meet that requirement] by removing the boards above the beams. Similarly Segan ha-Levi (i.e. R. Yitsḥak ha-Levi) was asked, and he approved, provided the boards were removed from over the *sekhakh*.

And someone attested before Gur Aryeh [a moniker either for R. Yitsḥak himself or for his son, R. Yehudah] that R. Eli'ezer ha-Gadol used to make a *sukkah* in his house and did not remove the beams (only the boards or tiles), and he was sore pressed that his *sukkah* was in the house, and it did greatly distress him. There was a courtyard between him and his neighbor, and he purchased it at twice its worth [so as to make a *sukkah* outside his house, where there would be no house-beams]. They asked Gur Aryeh why he [R. Eli'ezer] was so bothered, and he replied because he [R. Eli'ezer] wished to fulfill the mitzvah in an optimal manner.[80]

To simplify somewhat for presentational purposes: for any *sukkah* to be legally valid, the amount of shade in the *sukkah* must be greater than that of sunlight. If the covering of the *sukkah* is composed of both halakhically acceptable covering (*sekhakh kasher*) and halakhically unacceptable covering (*sekhakh pasul*), the Talmud holds that one is allowed to sit also under the non-kosher *sekhakh*, provided that the requisite amount of shade comes from *sekhakh kasher*.[81] Therefore, if one removed the boards or tiles of one's house and put *sekhakh kasher* (such as cut branches) across the remaining beams (which in themselves are not *kosher sekhakh*), one has a halakhically valid *sukkah*, as the majority of the area of the *sukkah* is shaded by the branches. Both R. Yitsḥak b. Yehudah in Mainz and R. Yitsḥak ha-Levi in Worms ruled thus. R. Eli'ezer ha-Gadol was discomfited by the fact that some of the *sekhakh* under which he sat was not in and of itself *kasher*, so, at considerable expense, he bought the space that abutted his house and put up a *sukkah* that had exclusively kosher *sekhakh*. A generation or two later, when someone heard this story and asked why R. Eli'ezer had been so discomfited, he received the reply that R. Eli'ezer had sought to fulfill the imperative of sitting in a *sukkah* in an optimal manner.

The *sukkah* discussed by R. Yitsḥak ben Yehudah is halakhically valid; indeed, by the standards in Ashkenaz of the time, it was as valid as a *sukkah* could be.[82] R. Yitsḥak knew of the conduct of R. Eli'ezer, and said that in light

80 *Maḥzor Vitry*, ii, ed. S. Hurwitz, #359, p. 413; ed. A. Goldschmidt, iii (Jerusalem, 2009), #33, p. 817–18; *Siddur Rashi*, #266, p. 127; *Teshuvot Ḥakhmei Tsarfat ve-Lotir*, #20 (end).

81 *Sukkah* 9b–10b.

82 It is not clear from our story whether this was a halakhic holding of R. Eli'ezer, as Goldschmidt believes, or an intuitive religious one, as I am inclined to think. If the former, R. Yitsḥak is invoking *minhag* to decide between two views (a common function of *minhag*); if the latter, *minhag* is

of the fact that popular practice did not acknowledge a higher standard of *sukkah*, he felt that one should not introduce it, or if such a standard existed, one didn't need to concern oneself with it. R. Yitsḥak is here dealing with the question of elite conduct, not with the halakhically requisite. Animated by a strong sense of solidarity with, and faith in, popular practice, he is not prepared to admit here a higher standard of performance. There is nothing unique in his identification with the standards of the 'masses'. It is one with that of the rabbinical establishment of Ashkenaz throughout the Middle Ages. Forty years ago, Jacob Katz pointed out that in Ashkenaz, unlike in Provence, there was no gulf between popular and elite conduct, nor were the members of the religious establishment interested in cultivating one.[83]

V

מצאתי בשם ר' יצחק ב"ר יהודה: וששאלתם למה נהגו כהנים שאירע להם דבר בקרובים [ז"א אבלים] ושינו את מקומן שלא לשאת את כפיהן כל זמן שלא יושבין במקומן. על דבר זה לא מצא רבינו סמך בהדיא. ואמר לא על חינם נהגו כך, שהרי כל כהן שאינו מברך עובר בשלושה עשה, וזה יושב בטל ועובר. ואמר כמדומה לי שעל דבר זה נהגו שכל מי שעומד לברך ראוי לו שיהא שרוי בשמחה ובטוב לבב, שכן מצינו ביצחק אבינו שאמר לעשו והביאה לי ציד וגו' ולאחר שיאכל וישתה ותהא נפשו שמחה עליו אמר לברכו, לכן נראה שזה שדואג על מתו ויושב שלא במקומו אינו מברך בשמחה . . .

ואומר הרב מצוה להחזיק מנהג ראשונים בכל מה שהאדם יכול להחזיק, שכן מצינו בתלמוד ירושלמי (בבא מציעא פ"ז ה"א) שהמנהג מבטל ההלכה, וכמו כן מצינו בתלמוד בבלי שלנו דאמרינן בב"ק בהגוזל זוטא (קט"ז ע"ב) שיירא שהייתה מהלכת במדבר ועמד עליה הגייס לטורפה מחשבין לפי ממון וכו' ובלבד שלא ישנה ממנהג החמרין, אלמא מנהג מבטל ההלכה.[84]

denying the right to supererogatory behavior. I tend to discount R. Eli'ezer's view as stemming from a halakhic doctrine, for the language of the passage describes personal discomfort, not intellectual dissent. Moreover, Gur Aryeh, when questioned, should have spelled out ever so briefly R. Eli'ezer's halakhic position or at least hinted at it, rather than vaguely describing R. Eli'ezer as wishing *mitsvah min ha-muvḥar*. I do believe, however, that Goldschmidt is correct in identifying Gur Aryeh in this passage as R. Yitsḥak b. Yehudah and not his son. See his remarks, p. 818 n. 7.

[83] 'Ma'ariv bi-Zemano ve-Shelo bi-Zemano: Dugmah le-Zikah bein Minhag, Halakhah ve-Ḥevrah', *Zion*, 35 (1970), 35–60; repr. in *Halakhah ve-Kabbalah: Meḥkarim be-Toledot Dat Yisrael 'al Medoreiha ve-Zikatah ha-Ḥevratit* (Jerusalem, 1986), 175–200; English translation in id., *Divine Law in Human Hands: Case Studies in Halakhic Flexibility* (Jerusalem, 1998), 88–127. Katz's insight, based on a single example, was corroborated in the entire gamut of problems presented by the injunction against *yein nesekh*. In problem after problem, despite profound misgivings of the Tosafists as to the correctness of popular practice, they never once suggested that it was preferable for scholars (*talmid ḥakham, tsurva de-rabanan*) to live by a higher religious standard than that of the general population. They only say 'it is best to act stringently in this matter' (*ve-tov le-haḥmir, ve-nakhon le-haḥmir*), or 'the religiously scrupulous should act stringently in this matter' (*u-va'al nefesh yaḥmir*); see Soloveitchik, *Ha-Yayin bi-Yemei ha-Beinayim* (above, n. 3), 358–62.

[84] *Shibbolei ha-Leket ha-Shalem*, #23, fo. 11a–b.

And I have found in the name of R. Yitsḥak b. Yehudah: and you have asked why priests [*kohanim*] who are in mourning and who [in accordance with the laws of mourning] have changed their seats in the synagogue, do not bless the congregation [until the mourning period is over and] they return to their regular places. [The report here switches from first to third person.] Our master found nothing explicit on this matter. And he said: this is not something which would be done without [good] reason, for any *kohen* who does not bless has transgressed three [*issurei*] *'aseh*, and the aforementioned *kohen* does nothing . . .

And he said: I believe that this is done because anyone who blesses should be in a state of joy and happiness. For we find with our patriarch Isaac that he said to Esau (Gen. 27: 3–4), 'and hunt game for me',[85] and after he had eaten and drunk, his soul was happy and he blessed. Therefore, it appears to me that this [mourner] who worries about [the fate of] his dead and does not sit in his usual seat would not bless with joy . . . and the Rav [R. Yitsḥak] has said that it is incumbent to hold fast to the traditions of the Early Ones as much as possible, for we find that the Yerushalmi says [*BM* 7: 1], 'Custom overrides halakhah'. And similarly we find in the Talmud, in *Bava Kamma* in the lesser [chapter] of 'Ha-Gozel 'Etsim' [116b]: 'a caravan that was making its way in the wilderness and robbers appeared to despoil it [. . .] one calculates the costs according to the value etc. provided [that this calculation] does not violate the custom of the donkey drivers'. From this we may infer that custom overrides halakhah.

Here we are, indeed, dealing with a non-feasance, a non-performance that is transgressive. The breach here differs little from breaches in the realm of *issur ve-heter*, which, the court of Kairouan had been careful to emphasize, did not apply to changing a *haftarah*. A *kohen* who refrains from blessing the people when he should has violated an *issur 'aseh* (transgression of non-feasance), as R. Yitsḥak points out (in fact, three such *issurei 'aseh*). R. Yitsḥak then provides a rationale for popular conduct that is never mentioned in the Talmud. He seems not to be in the least upset at this flouting of a pentateuchal imperative, and appears to be quite comfortable with the current practice, simply because it is widespread. This is what religiously responsible people do, and there is no reason for them not to continue doing so. Before we draw any far-reaching conclusions, as I fear Ta-Shma has done, let us remember that we and our forefathers have conducted ourselves no differently.

It has been at least 600 years since *kohanim* ceased to bless the people not only when they are in mourning, but even when they are not. The priestly blessing should take place every day; yet other than the festivals (*yom tov*) and the High Holidays, no blessings are pronounced in Ashkenazic communities

[85] The respondent, quoting from memory, has conflated two verses.

the world over.[86] These blessings are recited only on thirteen days of the year. Are we upset about their absence on the other 343 days?[87] Not that I have noticed. Are scholars seriously bothered by this massive violation of an *issur 'aseh*? If they are, I am unaware of it. If they had to start Ashkenazic practice all over again, would they institute this massive non-blessing? Probably not. Indeed, when the pupils of the Vilna Gaon established a new Ashkenazic settlement in Palestine—which in their eyes was a barren wilderness—they followed the dictates of their master and reinstituted the daily priestly blessing. Are their descendants critical of their brethren in the Diaspora for their neglect of this pentateuchal commandment? Once again, the raised eyebrows have eluded me. Did those pupils of the Gaon who remained in Europe attempt to reinstitute the priestly blessing? One, I know from family tradition, considered it but then abandoned the idea.[88] Maybe there were others who also entertained the notion of change, but, to the best of my knowledge, none translated it into action. I fail to see how we differ in this matter from R. Yitsḥak ben Yehudah. Yet no one would argue that contemporary Orthodoxy, both centrist and *ḥaredi*, believes in the infallibility of custom. If anything, the reverse is true. Traditional practice nowadays has little presumption of rectitude, and it is under constant interrogation by the written law.[89]

Admittedly, we come after some 600 years of abstention from Birkat Kohanim, and R. Yitsḥak ben Yehudah adopted his passive stance after only seventy-five to a hundred years of similar non-feasance. However, it is not that we now react calmly to what was initially strongly condemned. If one reads Zimmer's fine study on the changing times of priestly blessings,[90] one sees that our casual attitude is no different from that of the scholars in Ashkenaz (and Provence, one should add) who first reported the desuetude of the daily priestly blessing. They recorded the fact; they didn't criticize it. No one appeared shocked, for they sensed that liturgy has a life and rhythm of its own. And they sensed correctly. Prayers arose (such as Pesukei de-Zimra and 'Ve-Yire'u 'Eineinu'), prayers disappeared (such as Birkat Kohanim); some blessings were created (such as over the Sabbath candles), others vanished (as Zvi

[86] See the study of Y. (Eric) Zimmer, *'Olam ke-Minhago Noheg: Perakim be-Toledot ha-Minhagim, Hilkhoteihem ve-Gilguleihem* (Jerusalem, 1996), 132–51.

[87] The lunar year, by which Jewish ritual is governed, has 356 days only.

[88] I heard from my father that R. Ḥayyim of Volozhin twice intended to reinstitute daily Birkat Kohanim at the yeshivah that he had founded. On both occasions, fires broke out just as he was about to implement his plan. R. Ḥayyim took this as a Divine omen to desist.

[89] H. Soloveitchik, 'Rupture and Reconstruction' (above, n. 28).

[90] *'Olam ke-Minhago Noheg* (above, n. 86), 135–9.

Groner has chronicled at length).[91] Despite all the sincere protestations of strict adherence to the written law, these rituals of recitation and silence were transmitted from generation to generation, most for well over a millennium. Some Ashkenazic scholars found rationales for these liturgical appearances and disappearances; others didn't. Few, however, were upset by them.[92] Most people pray to the God of their fathers; and when they do, they wish to pray as their fathers did.

As for R. Yitsḥak ben Yehudah's exhortation of holding fast to custom, it was entirely in place. Let us recall what I said at the outset, and what has only too often been forgotten: the Talmud was being explicated in Mainz and Worms at a level of detail that was unparalleled.[93] The new knowledge subjected established practice to unprecedented critique. To many this proved a heady brew: perhaps especially to the young, who usually welcome the dawning of a new day. A central figure, possibly *the* central figure in this recovery of the Bavli in all its grandeur and fullness, cautioned his contemporaries not to be swept away from their traditional moorings. Even here, where several *issurei 'aseh* were at stake, he advised changing nothing. An intellectual revolution was one thing; losing our links to our forefathers' way of life wholly another. Bold though he may have been in exegesis, he was still the faithful son of a traditional society. He first invoked the Yerushalmi saying 'Custom overrides halakhah'. Whether anyone in Ashkenaz at that time actually had a Yerushalmi is more than dubious. No matter; there were florilegia of it circulating, and this sufficed for his purposes.[94] Still, R. Yitsḥak b. Yehudah could

[91] 'Berakhot she-Nishtak'u' (MA thesis, Hebrew University of Jerusalem, 1964); id., *Berakhot she-Nishtak'u* (Jerusalem, 2003). (On occasion, it pays to check the printed text against the MA thesis.)

[92] The attitude to the halakhically problematic *piyyut* is analogous and has been well studied by Ruth Langer in *To Worship God Properly* (above, n. 79), 130–45.

[93] Above, p. 31–5.

[94] Such florilegia should not be confused with the *Sefer Yerushalmi*, pages of which have been found and discussed with typical erudition by Y. Sussmann in his 'Seridei Yerushalmi—Ketav Yad Ashkenazi: Likrat Pitron Ḥidat *Sefer Yerushalmi*', *Kovets 'al Yad*, NS, 12 (22) (1994), 1–8. This work contains the full text of the Yerushalmi together with numerous additions. It did not surface in Ashkenaz until the latter half of the 12th century. Ta-Shma claims that Early Ashkenaz did possess the Yerushalmi, and bases himself on Sussmann's well-known essay on the Yerushalmi's tractate *Shekalim*. If one checks the passages in Sussmann's article that Ta-Shma invokes, one will see that they refer to the late 12th-century Talmudists of Ashkenaz, not to those of the previous century. Sussmann has made the most exhaustive study of the use of the Yerushalmi in medieval Europe. To preclude any doubt as to his views, I put the question to him directly. His answer corroborated in full my own impression formed from studying for many years the literature of Early Ashkenaz, namely, that there is no evidence that Ashkenaz had the text of the Yerushalmi to any serious extent prior to the 12th century. (Ta-Shma's view is expressed in 'Sifriyatam shel Ḥakhmei Ashkenaz ve-Tsarfat', *Kiryat Sefer*, 60 [1985], 302; reprinted in *Keneset Meḥkarim: 'Iyyunim ba-Sifrut ha-Rabbanit bi-Yemei*

not rest with a dictum of the Yerushalmi—not at the very moment when the Babylonian mandate was becoming ever clearer and more peremptory. So he cited a passage that actually had little bearing on the issue at hand. The Bavli in *Bava Kamma* deals not with ritual laws or breaches of religious injunctions, but with civil matters, a field where custom reigns freely: it informs as to the meaning of terms used by contracting parties and the reasonable presumptions of intent and agreement.[95] Our debt to R. Yitsḥak b. Yehudah is, however, so great and has been so long unacknowledged that we owe him our forbearance for misapplying a passage from the Bavli to further a worthy, traditional cause.

No significant scholar of the eleventh century entertained the notion of a singular *minhag* Ashkenaz ha-Kadmon. There remain only the four busy brothers, the Makirites. Worthy gentlemen all, but who paid them heed?

APPENDIX I

ON THE USE OF *SUB VERBO* IN THE *PERUSH RABBENU GERSHOM*

In one passage of his *Ha-Sifrut ha-Parshanit la-Talmud*, Ta-Shma writes that the so-called *Perush Rabbenu Gershom* was more a summary than a *sub verbo* (*dibbur ha-matḥil*) commentary.[96] Several pages later, however, he speaks of the commentary as employing the *sub verbo* approach.[97] The Romm printers did not typeset in a *dibbur ha-matḥil* format the small-lettered, marginal commentary on the folio page of the Talmud that they published, but the *Perush Rabbenu Gershom* is clearly of the *sub verbo* type, as any sustained use of it will show. The simplest evidence is the so-called commentaries of Rashi on no fewer than four tractates, *Mo'ed Katan*, *Nedarim*, *Nazir*, and *Horayot*, printed in the standard editions of the Talmud. They, too, are products of the same German school (see the literature cited above, n. 8), and one and all explicate exclusively by means of *dibburim ha-matḥilim*.

ha-Beinayim, i: *Ashkenaz* [Jerusalem, 2005], 27–8. The references to passages in Sussmann's article on Yerushalmi *Shekalim* are given in n. 20.)

95 See above, n. 44.

96 Vol. i (Jerusalem, 1999), 39–40. A. Epstein makes the same statement in his 'Der Rabbenu Gerschom Meor ha-Golah zugeschriebene Talmud-Commentar' (above, n. 60), 123 (Hebrew trans. 'Perush ha-Talmud' [above, n. 60], 114).

97 p. 47 n. 18.

The truth of the matter is that the contrast between a paraphrastic and *sub verbo* commentary is unproductive when treating the exegesis of Early Ashkenaz, because it employs both the initial lemma (*dibbur ha-matḥil*) and an embedded one, for reasons that I will explain. The works of the German school contain, on the whole, fewer *sub verbo* entries than does Rashi's commentary, and for three reasons. First, Rashi had a far more sensitive perception of the minute ambiguities of words and phrases in the talmudic discussion which would prove a fertile breeding ground of error if each of the mistaken alternatives was not deftly dispatched. The equivocal phrase became a *dibbur ha-matḥil* which was explicated with optimum brevity. Second, Rashi's pedagogical genius lay in perceiving the tiny gaps in the talmudic presentation which made for a looseness in the argument, filling in those clefts with a word or two in a *sub verbo* and tightening the discussion. Finally, no one could match Rashi's ability to see how an obscure passage that necessitated paraphrase for all other commentators could be explicated by simply inserting in the appropriate places (i.e. under the appropriate *dibburim ha-matḥilim*) *le mot juste*. No one in the history of halakhah of the past millennium approached him in these skills.[98] Lacking this unique perception of minuscule fissures and the hermeneutical potential of their sealant, the Mainz school necessarily penned fewer *sub verbis* and blended far more often than did Rashi the running commentary with the text. Put differently, the *sub verbis* in the Mainz commentaries often do not preface the commentary but are embedded in it ('embedded lemmata') and such lemmata, if not placed in bold, are easily overlooked.[99] However, this scarcely means that these commentaries are summaries or paraphrases.

This is not a personal view of mine. All the critical editions of the *Perush Rabbenu Gershom* of the past fifty years, unhampered by the severe constraints of space and money under which the Romm printers operated in the 1880s, have published it in *sub verbo* form, whether as initial or embedded lemmata, with the *s.v.* invariably in bold.[100]

[98] See 'The Printed Page of the Talmud: The Commentaries and Their Authors', in S. Mintz, ed., *Printing the Talmud: From Bomberg to Schottenstein* (New York, 2005), 37–8; repr. in the first volume of this series (*Collected Essays*, i. 3–10: see pp. 3–4).

[99] Rashi's unique pedagogical enterprise led him to dispense almost entirely with the embedded lemma. He purposefully did not explicate the entire *sugya*, but only those numerous passages where he realized the student might legitimately go astray, leaving the rest to be mastered unaided by the student. The result was that unique mix of help and self-help that immortalized his commentary. The intentional gaps in his text dictated that almost all of his exegesis, unlike that of the *Perushei Magentsa*, should appear under initial lemma.

[100] See e.g. *Perush Rabbenu Gershom Me'or ha-Golah*, in *Kovets Rishonim le-Massekhet Mo'ed Katan*, ed. N. Zaks (Jerusalem, 1966); *Perush Rabbenu Gershom: Massekhet Ta'anit*, ed. E. Soloveichik, in

Indeed, it may well be that Ta-Shma and I do not differ substantively. Ta-Shma views a commentary that also employs embedded lemmata as a 'paraphrase'; a *dibbur ha-matḥil*, an *incipit*, after all, must be at the beginning. To my mind, a paraphrase means the restatement of a text and not an explication of it. If a commentary cites and explains the full text, by both initial and embedded lemmata, it is to all effects and purposes a *sub verbo* commentary. To give a contemporary illustration: the Schottenstein Talmud could be described equally as a paraphrase or as a *sub verbo* exegesis. The central issue for my purposes is the scope of the elucidation of the text, not whether units of that text preface the commentary or are embedded in it.

APPENDIX II

A LIST OF THE RESPONSA OF R. YITSḤAK B. YEHUDAH

Below I have tabulated the known responsa and rulings of R. Yitsḥak b. Yehudah in order to convey a sense of the scope of his judicial holdings and to sort out those which have a bearing on the inerrancy of custom. It was not compiled as a *Vorarbeit* to an intellectual biography. Two observations are therefore in place. First, the list makes no claim to being definitive. I have used the standard works of the period, and all references to manuscripts are drawn either from Grossman's writings or from my own notes and published research. Second, I have not attempted to list what is the most authentic version of the responsa or to provide parallel passages. I have simply examined sequentially the various volumes of the pre-Crusade literature together with the *Shibbolei ha-Leket* and the so-called *Siddur Rabbenu Shelomoh mi-Germaiza*, and jotted down the places where R. Yitsḥak's rulings are cited or reported. I happen to have checked, for example, the *Sefer ha-Pardes* before the *Teshuvot Ḥakhmei Tsarfat ve-Lotir*. If I registered a ruling from the former, and this ruling repeated itself subsequently in a fuller or more authentic fashion in the latter, I left the original notation of the ruling as being found in the *Sefer ha-Pardes* and

Perush ha-Raḥ: Betsah, Ta'anit, Megillah, ed. D. Metzger (Jerusalem, 1996); both editions of the commentary on *Bava Batra*, *Perushei Rabbenu Gershom b. Yehudah Me'or ha-Golah: Massekhet Bava Batra*, Or Ḥayyim edn. (Benei Berak, 1998), and *Perush Rabbenu Gershom ha-Shalem: 'al Massekhet Bava Batra 'al-pi Ketav Yad 'Attik she-be-'Oxford*, ed. T. Y. Laitner, 2 vols. (Jerusalem, 1998–9); *Perush ha-Ragmah 'al Massekhet Keritut*, ed. D. Blumenthal (Jerusalem, 2004). See also the exclusive use of *sub verbo* in two other works of pre-Crusade Ashkenaz, *Seridim mi-Perush ha-Ra 'al Ta'anit*, ed. D. Halivni (Weiss) (Jerusalem, 1959); *Perush R. Elyakim le-Massekhet Yoma*, ed. D. Genachowski (Jerusalem, 1964).

did not register its recurrence in the *Teshuvot Ḥakhmei Tsarfat ve-Lotir*. This should pose no problem for those wishing to pursue any of these topics further, as most of the parallel passages are cross-listed by the editors of the cited volumes.

In instances of two rulings or responsa in one section, the section number is cited twice; if more than two rulings are found in one section, the numbers are registered with a dash. For example, five separate rulings are found in #24, and they are registered as 8–12. As I am tabulating sources, I thought it best to register the entries from *Sefer ha-Pardes* from the Ehrenreich edition as it is more clearly printed and contains less material per page.

Ma'aseh ha-Ge'onim

1. #1, p. 3[101]
2. #2, p. 3[102]
3. #3, p. 3
4. #3, pp. 3–4
5. #14, pp. 8–9
6. #24, p. 14
7. #24, p. 14

8–12. #24, pp. 15–16

13. #27, p. 17
14. #37, p. 24[103]
15. #40, p. 25
16. #42, p. 27
17. #44, p. 29

18–21. #45, pp. 33–4

22. #49, p. 34
23. #51, p. 40
24. #54, p. 43
25. #55, pp. 43–4
26. #56, p. 45
27. #59, p. 50
28. #59. p. 50[104]

[101] Attribution to Rabbenu Sasson: A. Grossman, 'Benei Makhir ve-Sifram Ma'aseh ha-Makhiri', *Tarbiz*, 46 (1977), 129.

[102] Ibid.

[103] It is not entirely clear whether the reported assent of R. Yitsḥak is to the immediately preceding or the subsequent ruling. I incline to Aptowitzer's view (*Sefer Ravyah*, ii, *Pesaḥim*, #525, p. 156 n. 10) that it refers to the latter.

[104] I am aware that the *Roke'aḥ* (Fano, 1505), #316, reports that, when the wife of R. Yitsḥak b. Yehudah died on the first day of Sukkot, he observed mourning practices for her the next day, interrupted

mourning for the next seven days, and then observed six more days of mourning after Sukkot had passed. He is equally mentioned in the account of the 'Piskei u-Minhagei Magentsa ve-Germaiza', *Tsefunot*, 3/1 (1991), 4 (repr. in *Me'orot ha-Rishonim*, ed. S. M. Stern [Jerusalem, 2002], 185). *Roke'aḥ*'s sources for early Ashkenaz are excellent, nevertheless, I am loath to accept the attribution of this story to R. Yitsḥak b. Yehudah, unless his wife died in Worms. This account is repeated in *Ma'aseh ha-Ge'onim*, #59, p. 50, and attributed to 'R. Yitsḥak' (without 'b. Yehudah'). In the preceding line we are informed that 'Rabbenu ha-Gadol' (the moniker of the Benei ha-Makhiri for R. Yitsḥak b. Yehudah) observed mourning in such an instance. Why repeat it? Moreover, in the previous line we are told that Mainz observed mourning practices on *yom tov sheni*, while here we are told that the community refused to acknowledge the validity of such a practice, indeed, boycotted one of the leading talmudic scholars of the age on its account. (This passage in *Ma'aseh ha-Ge'onim*, #59, p. 50, is confirmed by *Sefer ha-Pardes*, 263, and in the above-cited passage in 'Piskei u-Minhagei Magentsa ve-Germaiza', the actor is explicitly named 'R. Yitsḥak b. Yehudah'. This reading is corroborated by the citation of this collection in the *Ḥiddushei Anshei Shem* in *Mordekhai*, *Mo'ed Katan*, Vilna edn., fo. 21b (cited by J. N. Epstein in *Meḥkarim be-Sifrut ha-Talmud u-vi-Leshonot Shemiyot*, ii/2 [Jerusalem, 1988], 748). MS Paris, Bibliothèque Nationale 326, fo. 60a, provides further independent confirmation of the identification, as do the excerpts from MS Bodley 1106, recently published by Y. Binder in 'Likkutim Ashkenaziyim: Pesakim u-Teshuvot, Likkutim u-Ma'asim', *Yerushatenu*, 7 (2014), 34, #1.

The writer of the passage in the *Ma'aseh ha-Ge'onim* is one of the Makirites, who opens with a citation from the *Halakhot Gedolot* (*he'etakti mi-Halakhot Gedolot*), informing us that 'Rabbenu ha-Gadol' conducted himself in conformity with the custom in Mainz and that R. Yehudah ha-Kohen disagreed. He then claims to have it on the authority of R. Shemu'el ha-Levi (*kakh horah lan R. Shemu'el*) that his father, R. Yitsḥak, also sat *shiv'ah* on the last day of *yom tov* and that *his* community (i.e. Worms) refused to recognize the legitimacy of such mourning. The writer then turns to another report about 'Rabbenu', i.e. R. Yitsḥak b. Yehudah, in matters of mourning, in which he is described as having walked barefoot to the cemetery and not just from it.

The phrase *horah lan* is, indeed, rare and the parallel passage in *Shibbolei ha-Leket ha-Shalem*, *Semaḥot*, #52, fo. 183b, and *Sefer ha-Pardes*, 263, reads *horah lo*. However, I find it inconceivable that a member of the younger generation (for he must be either the son of R. David ha-Levi or of R. Yitsḥak ha-Levi), and not a very prominent one at that, issued binding halakhic rulings to one of the leading scholars of the previous generation. For this reason, I tend to accept the more difficult reading *horah lan* or suggest the minor emendation of *horah li* or simply adopt the abbreviated language of 'Piskei u-Minhagei Magentsa ve-Germaiza', *kakh horah R. Shemu'el*. *Horah* in the sense of informing of a legal precedent (*hora'ah*) or of giving an account of it is common in the writings of the Makirites.

All this concerns the reportage of the story; in the story itself, the censorious community is Worms and the ruling that of R. Yitsḥak ha-Levi of Worms, unless, as suggested above, R. Yitsḥak b. Yehudah and his wife were visiting Worms when she died. (We find R. Yehudah elsewhere visiting Worms and issuing a ruling during his stay. See *Ma'aseh ha-Ge'onim*, #59, p. 49, and Grossman's remarks in *Ḥakhmei Ashkenaz ha-Rishonim* [above, n. 31], 177.) In that case, R. Yitsḥak b. Yehudah conducted himself according to the practice of his hometown, Mainz, contrary to that of the community in which he found himself, Worms. The Makirites received this report from a resident scholar of Worms, R. Shemu'el ha-Levi. The immediately following passage about the ruling of 'Rabbenu' to his son Yehudah after the death of the mother would then be a *sequitur*, two rulings given by one person on the same sad occasion. Cf. Grossman, ibid. 303–5. I owe the references to MS Paris, Bibliothèque Nationale 326, to his discussion; however, it fails to take cognizance of the fact that in the prior line we are already informed of Rabbenu ha-Gadol's practice and that it was in line with that of other scholars of Mainz.

29. #62, p. 56
30. #62, p. 57
31. #63, p. 57
32. #63, p. 58
33. #64, pp. 59–60
34. #64, p. 60
35. #88, p. 77[105]
36. #88, pp. 77–8 (*s.v. she-she'altem 'al shenei aḥim*)[106]
37–41. #88, pp. 81–2
42. #89, p. 84
43. #90, p. 84[107]
44–7. #92, p. 87
48. #92, pp. 88–91
49. #92, p. 92 (*s.v. u-she-she'altem 'al shetei marot*)[108]
50. MS Bodley 1103, fo. 195a (*s.v. laḥtom pi he-ḥavit*)[109]
51. MS Bodley 566, fo. 35a[110]
52. MS Montefiore 134, fo. 130a–b[111]

Sefer ha-Pardes

As the editor H. L. Ehrenreich kindly provided in his introduction both the page and line where a cited passage is found, I saw no reason to deprive my readers of this luxury.

53. p. 156, l. 9
54. p. 159, l. 31
55. p. 216, l. 25
56. p. 244, l. 20
57. p. 260, l. 9
58. p. 263, l. 15
59. p. 353, l. 3

Maḥzor Vitry

60–1. ed. S. Hurwitz, #331, p. 370; #359, p. 413; ed. A. Goldschmidt, III, #44, p. 721; #36, p. 817

[105] Attribution: H. Soloveitchik, *Yeinam: Saḥar be-Yayin shel Goyim—'al Gilgulah shel Halakhah be-'Olam ha-Ma'aseh* (Tel Aviv, 2003), 49 n. 23.

[106] Attribution: MS New York, Jewish Theological Seminary, Rabbinica 673, fo. 121c.

[107] Attribution: Grossman, 'Benei Makhir' (above, n. 101), 131.

[108] Attribution: Grossman, *Ḥakhmei Ashkenaz ha-Rishonim* (above, n. 31), 306 n. 46.

[109] Attribution: ibid. 309.

[110] Attribution: H. Soloveitchik, *Ha-Yayin bi-Yemei ha-Beinayim* (above, n. 3), 244 n. 21.

[111] Attribution: ibid.

Shibbolei ha-Leket ha-Shalem

62. #9, fo. 5a
63. #15, fo. 8a
64. #23, fo. 11a
65. #34, fo. 17a (= Rashi *Gittin* 59b, s.v. *nitpardah*)
66. #94, fo. 34a
67. #185, fo. 72a (= Rashi *Shabbat* 23a, s.v. *ha-ro'eh*)
68. #248

69–70. *Milah* #4, fo. 188b (#4 has four responsa, two of them were already registered in *Ma'aseh ha-Ge'onim*, #64; two are new)

71. *Milah* #5, fo. 188b

Shibbolei ha-Leket II, ed. M. Z. Hasida (Jerusalem, 1969)

(The new edition of H. Hasida stopped at #50.)

72. #62, p. 117

Siddur R. Shelomoh mi-Germaiza

73. p. 255
74. p. 261 (I have not taken *Ma'aseh ha-Ge'onim*, #43, p. 29, as being a responsum of R. Yitsḥak.)
75. p. 262
76. p. 281

Tosafot

77. *Berakhot* 14b, *s.v. u-manaḥ*

Sefer Ravyah, Ḥullin, ed. D. Deblitsky (Jerusalem, 1976)

78. #1103; *Sefer Ravyah*, iv, #1103, p. 148
79. #1103; *Sefer Ravyah*, iv, #1103, p. 148

Haggahot Maimuniyot

80. 'Ḥamets u-Matsah', 8: 10, n. 20

MS Jewish Theological Seminary, Rabbinica 1077

81. fo. 75a[112]

[112] Attribution: H. Soloveitchik, *Shut ke-Makor Histori* (Jerusalem, 1990), 121.

Ḥofes Matmonim

There are fifteen responsa to Rashi ##14–28: thirteen of them deal with talmudic exegesis; two contain new rulings. Thus:

82. #14
83. #25

CHAPTER FOUR

The Authority of the Babylonian Talmud and the Use of Biblical Verses and Aggadah in Early Ashkenaz

Of all the current notions about Early Ashkenaz with which I find myself in disagreement, the most incomprehensible to me is the contention that the eleventh-century Talmudists in the Rhineland were only partially guided by the Babylonian Talmud (Bavli) and frequently ruled according to their own understanding of biblical verses and *aggadot*. Equally inexplicable is its corollary: the Bavli achieved its ascendancy in the latter half of the eleventh century, as the writings of R. Yitsḥak b. Yehudah attest.

In fact, the controlling role of the Bavli is in evidence everywhere and, it should be emphasized, from the earliest days of the Ashkenazic community. The determinations of the Bavli are at all times dispositive of the question at bar, and the rare exceptions to the rule merit careful examination. For example, some ninety-nine responsa of R. Yehudah Ba'al Sefer ha-Dinim have survived. In ninety-eight of them he disposes of the issue either by invoking the Bavli specifically or by employing Babylonian dicta and notions such as *lo hadam* or *migo* (*mi-tokh she-yakhol lit'on*); in one responsum, and in one responsum alone, he employs biblical verses. Is it not plausible that this 'deviance' is due to the distinctive issue upon which he has to rule, rather than to any casualness about the authority of the Bavli or some Karaite tendency, as it were, to invoke biblical verses as he sees fit and rule on their basis? May it not be that there is either no guidance from the Bavli on the question at hand or that, under the circumstances, the invocation of the proper talmudic precedent might cause more problems than it would solve? Surely questions like these should be explored before one leaps to the radical conclusion that the Bavli was only quasi-normative in eleventh-century Ashkenaz.

Any such exploration demands substantive analysis of the responsa invoked—something that has been sorely lacking in the historiography of eleventh-century halakhah up to now. When the evidence adduced for the normative role of biblical verses and *aggadot* is subjected to such an analysis, the inference disappears.

What an in-depth examination of the responsa literature does reveal is an astonishing command of the complex corpus of the Bavli. When Ashkenaz first comes into view at the end of the tenth century and in the early decades of the eleventh, the figures of Rabbenu Gershom Me'or ha-Golah and of his pupil, R. Yehudah Ba'al Sefer ha-Dinim, appear, and one catches occasional glimpses of R. Yosef Tov 'Elem. One is struck by the sovereign mastery of the Talmud of all three, their ability to pass that corpus in its entirety before their mind's eye and invoke at times the most obscure passage to serve as precedent in resolving the question at bar. This is all the more striking seeing that—other than the misty figure of Rabbenu Gershom's teacher, R. Leon (or Leontin), with no more than some four or five gnomic rulings in his name—these men had no predecessors. Ashkenazic talmudic scholarship emerged fully grown, as it were, from Zeus's brow. That, however, is the subject of another study.[1]

Against this background, I must dissent from the now widely held view—which has arisen over the past quarter of a century as a result of the writings of Avraham Grossman—that the scholars of Early Ashkenaz did not feel bound by the Babylonian Talmud; that, on the contrary, they knowingly and openly disregarded that corpus in their rulings and resolved halakhic questions on the basis of Mishnah, aggadah, and biblical verses. This view was then expanded by I. M. Ta-Shma to include the Tosafists. I would like here to address the arguments made for Early Ashkenaz and in the next chapter those made for Ba'alei ha-Tosafot.[2]

Let me begin with several fairly obvious remarks.

First, before Rashi, the Talmud in Ashkenaz was a closed book to most people. A select few had studied in the academies of Mainz or Worms. The rest, less fortunate, had neither the knowledge nor the tools with which to

[1] See below, Ch. 9.

[2] A. Grossman, 'Zikatah shel Yahadut Ashkenaz ha-Kedumah el Erets Yisra'el', *Shalem*, 3 (1981), 67–74; id., *Ḥakhmei Ashkenaz ha-Rishonim: Koroteihem, Darkam be-Hanhagat ha-Tsibbur, Yetsiratam ha-Ruḥanit mi-Reshit Yishuvam ve-'ad li-Gezerot Tatnu (1096)* (Jerusalem, 1981), 155–8, 204–6, 429–35; id., 'Shorashav shel Kiddush ha-Shem be-'Ashkenaz ha-Kedumah', in Y. M. Gafni and A. Ravitzky, eds., *Kedushat ha-Ḥayyim ve-Ḥeruf ha-Nefesh: Kovets Ma'amarim le-Zikhro shel Amir Yekuti'el* (Jerusalem, 1993), 107–8; A. Grossman, *Ḥakhmei Tsarfat ha-Rishonim: Koroteihem, Darkam be-Hanhagat ha-Tsibbur, Yetsiratam ha-Ruḥanit* (Jerusalem, 1995), 69–70. I. M. Ta-Shma, 'Teshuvat Ri ha-Zaken be-Din Moser: Le-Tokpah shel ha-'Aggadah ba-Halakhah ha-'Ashkenazit', *Zion*, 68 (2003), 167–74, repr. in id., *Keneset Meḥkarim: 'Iyyunim ba-Sifrut ha-Rabbanit bi-Yemei ha-Beinayim* (Jerusalem, 2010), iv. 159–68.

tackle a serious talmudic topic, let alone to make sense of a tractate on their own. What this means is that most people were not familiar with talmudic Aramaic, and even less so with basic talmudic terms. To say that most understood Hebrew far better than Aramaic would be an understatement. The deep saturation of talmudic lore, idiom, and ways of thought that shaped the popular European Jewish language, Yiddish, to so large an extent that its greatest historian, Max Weinreich, called it the 'language of the way of the SHaS',[3] was centuries away. The Talmud was normative, but as a cultural force in the community at large it was only a shadow of what it was to become.

Second, the style and language of any communication are tailored to its target audience. A scholarly audience will be addressed in one way, an audience of laymen in another.

Third, unlike the Geonim in Babylonia, who headed legendary academies and whose authority reached back many centuries and had long been recognized, formally or informally, by the secular powers, the rabbinic leadership that emerged at the dawn of Ashkenaz at the turn of the eleventh century was new and without lineage, its authority untested in the freshly settled Jewish communities and unacknowledged by the surrounding Gentile society (unless individually negotiated by the local community). There was general deference to talmudic erudition and an awareness that Jewish ritual matters, as well as civil disputes among Jews, should be decided by rabbinic scholars, but between that and ancient, universally acknowledged authority that could speak *ex cathedra* lay a gulf. The less established the authority, the smaller the possibility of a simple *mandamus* and the greater the need for suasion and exhortation by the respondents to obtain conformity with their rulings by understandably recalcitrant litigants.

Let me now add two obvious principles of adjudication.

First, there is nothing wrong—or new, for that matter—in citing a *mishnah* as proof-text, if the Talmud has neither emended nor reinterpreted the text of that *mishnah*, nor modified its ruling on the basis of another tannaitic source. Indeed, if most of the community understands little, if any, Aramaic, it is wise to cite the Mishnah as much as possible. If this in itself will resolve the case at hand, do that; if the resolution entails a talmudic modification of the Mishnah, cite the Mishnah together with the modification. As much as is possible, cite resonant, authoritative words that people can understand.

Second, there is nothing wrong with quoting an aggadic source or even biblical verses as proof-text if no guidance is to be found in the halakhic

[3] M. Weinreich, *History of the Yiddish Language* (Chicago and London, 1983), 175–246. 'Shas' is an acronym for *shishah sedarim* (six orders), i.e. the Talmud.

sections of the Bavli. Such cases are far more frequent than one would imagine, as halakhah provides no more than the skeletal structure of religious life, and large tracts of religious performance are dictated by custom alone. This simple fact is never sensed by participants, as the legally requisite and the consuetudinary fuse into a single whole. Most worshippers at a Sabbath service would be astonished to discover the extent of the customary purchase of the prayer book. The same holds true for the *seder* on Passover night and for the High Holiday services. Strip the consuetudinary from the halakhically requisite, and Judaism as we know it, as Jews over the ages have known it, is unrecognizable. Customs originate from the most varied sources, but they are validated in the halakhic system (in the broad sense of the term) by being rooted in the canonical literature, in such sacred texts as the Bible and the Midrash. For this reason one is scarcely surprised to discover that the most influential customary of Ashkenaz for well over half a millennium, the *Sefer ha-Minhagim* of the Maharil (R. Ya'akov ha-Levi Moellin, d. 1427), cites verses as the source of (or validation for) various customs over 250 times, and that the Gaon of Vilna, who probably knew the sources of Jewish practices better than did R. Yosef Karo, sources *midrashim* as the basis of religious practices on hundreds of occasions in his *Be'ur ha-Gra 'al Shulḥan 'Arukh*.

Finally, an obvious methodological point: to assess how a halakhist adjudicated cases, one must investigate halakhically the cases in question. What materials lay then at hand, how did he use them, what were his options, and how have others ruled on the matter? One can scarcely write history of halakhah without going into halakhic analysis.

Let me now speak more concretely and apply these principles to the literature of the eleventh century.

If one simply reads the block of some forty responsa of Rabbi Yehudah Ba'al Sefer ha-Dinim, found in their almost pristine state in the Prague edition of the *Teshuvot R. Me'ir mi-Rotenburg*,[4] one notices two things. First, both the queries and the replies are in Hebrew—indeed, excellent Hebrew; other than talmudic citations there are few Aramaic phrases. Second, the

[4] Ed. M. A. Bloch (Prague and Budapest, 1895), ##873–913. (On the Prague and Budapest edition of *Teshuvot R. Me'ir mi-Rotenburg*, see above, Ch. 3, n. 43.) At first glance it would seem that the argument of this paragraph loses its force if one accepts the thesis proposed in 'The "Third Yeshivah of Bavel"', below, pp. 159–69. However, it should be noted that I am here addressing the recipients of responsa, not the scholars of the Third Yeshivah or their disciples. Admittedly, by the end of the 11th century, the average literate Jew (*yodea' sefer*) seems to have understood Aramaic (below, p. 160), however, the audience described here is the community some fifty to a hundred years earlier, in the days of Rabbenu Gershom (d. 1028) and his pupil, R. Yehudah Ba'al Sefer ha-Dinim.

questions are often as long as, and occasionally longer than, the responsa, and they are full of irrelevant detail. Take, for example, #880.[5]

The query is more than three times the length of the reply, and we are told, among other things, that the plaintiff's wife had little confidence in her husband's business abilities and had a higher opinion of her brother's talents; that the plaintiff wanted his wife to buy him a horse so that he could 'take to the road as other men do' but she refused his repeated requests for she saw his luck 'as never rising, only sinking'—all of which is irrelevant to the issue at hand. If the objection is raised that #880 is atypical, as the question states that they specifically appointed someone to write down the plaintiff's remarks, take #875 or #881 instead.[6] The queries are somewhat briefer but not by much, and they are equally rich in irrelevant facts. Precisely because these queries have not been edited, have not been pared down (or only minimally so[7]) to the legal essentials, to the bare-boned 'facts of the case' as they say in law school, they have proven invaluable for historians.

There is a greater concentration of such questions in the writings of R. Yehudah Ba'al Sefer ha-Dinim, but they are not unique to him. Take what is the most faithfully preserved group of responsa of his teacher and predecessor, Rabbenu Gershom Me'or ha-Golah (henceforth Rabbenu Gershom), those found in MS Montefiore 98 and published in *Teshuvot Ḥakhmei Tsarfat ve-Lotir*, for example #97 and #98, or the responsum published by Grossman from the same manuscript,[8] and we confront the same phenomenon.[9]

[5] Translations in I. A. Agus, *Urban Civilization in Pre-Crusade Europe* (New York, 1965), i. 111–14. Agus's translations are often very partial; in the fuller ones, several sentences of the original Hebrew have frequently been compressed into a single English one, and the reader thus loses the tang of the original queries.

[6] Translations ibid. ii. 714–18, 699–701.

[7] See S. Emanuel, 'Teshuvot Maharam mi-Rotenburg she-'Einan shel Maharam', *Shenaton ha-Mishpat ha-'Ivri*, 21 (1998–2000), 156–7.

[8] *Teshuvot Ḥakhmei Tsarfat ve-Lotir*, ed. J. Müller (Vienna, 1881); Grossman, 'Yaḥasam shel Ḥakhmei Ashkenaz ha-Rishonim le-Shilton ha-Kahal', *Shenaton ha-Mishpat ha-'Ivri*, 2 (1975), 195–7.

[9] Most of the responsa of R. Yehudah Ba'al Sefer ha-Dinim were preserved intact in that distinctive unit in the Prague collection, which in every way is a *unicum*. Rabbenu Gershom's responsa, on the other hand, with the clear exception of the unit in MS Montefiore 98, have come down to us via citations in later sources and have often undergone editing, both major and minor. Eidelberg's edition of Rabbenu Gershom's responsa, *Teshuvot Rabbenu Gershom Me'or ha-Golah* (New York, 1956), only complicates the matter, as he includes all and any rulings of Rabbenu Gershom reported in medieval sources, be they responsa, *obiter dicta*, commentaries, or codes. This affords a more comprehensive view of Rabbenu Gershom's halakhic oeuvre but obscures an assessment of the style and structure of his responsa-writing, especially as Eidelberg makes no effort, when confronted with differing versions—as is frequently the case—to ascertain the most original, or, more accurately, the most authentic text; e.g. Ch. 3, n. 36 above.

What this means is that, rather than being sent to a local rabbinical authority who passed them on to Rabbi Yehudah, the entire complaint of the plaintiff, or much of it, was translated by a scribe as it tumbled off the tongue of the party; he then copy-edited it—improving on the grammar and syntax—and sent it on to R. Yehudah.[10] Reason would have it that the reply followed the same course. It would be sent to the original scribe who would inform the parties of the decision and, if he was up to it, explain to them some of the reasoning.

What did most Ashkenazic Jews know in the first half of the eleventh century if they were somewhat literate? They would probably know, or certainly recognize, passages from the Bible, especially those sections that are part of the synagogue service. They could follow the crystalline Hebrew of a *mishnah* or *beraita*, even if its precise legal meaning might require explanation. From the numerous invocations of *midrashim* (a number of them ones which we might consider recondite) in the exhortations of the eleventh-century decisors, it would seem that Midrash was equally an important component of the popular imagination; its words reverberated, stirred people's emotions, and evoked in them an answering echo of assent.

We have a responsum by R. Yosef Tov 'Elem in the first quarter of the eleventh century that sheds light upon popular knowledge.[11] Two men refused to participate in the general taxation imposed by their community and were excommunicated. They traveled to an adjacent city, whose inhabitants felt that the men had been unjustly treated and revoked the ban. The two men returned triumphantly to the city with the bill of revocation and 'they cited proof from Scripture: "When the ram's horn sounds a long blast, they may go up on the mountains"' (Exod. 19: 13). This enigmatic phrase has a simple explanation. The power of one court to rescind a decree of another is derived in the Talmud from that biblical verse.[12] This authority is formulated as the rule of *kol davar she-be-minyan tsarikh minyan aḥer le-hatiro*. This long formula—or even its first three words as we now refer to this concept—was deemed by the court of the second town as being too strange and complicated to be remembered by most, so they referred to it by the biblical proof-verse, confident that this

[10] The one clear exception is #891, and most probably #887, though the plethora of irrelevant detail is the same as in the cases cited in the text.

[11] *Teshuvot R. Me'ir mi-Rotenburg*, ed. R. N. N. Rabinowitz (Lemberg, 1860), #423. I have discussed this responsum at length in *Shut ke-Makor Histori* (Jerusalem, 1990), 66–76. See also my remarks below, pp. 98–100.

[12] *Betsah* 5a, with the proviso that the second court is 'the equal of the first in wisdom and number [i.e. rank]'.

would be familiar to all, and the few cognoscenti in the community that had issued the ban would recognize the talmudic reference.

If we turn to the responsa of the next generation, those of R. Yitsḥak ha-Levi, R. Shelomoh ben Shimshon (Rabbenu Sasson) of Worms, and R. Yitsḥak ben Yehudah of Mainz, the picture changes radically.[13] The interrogators of R. Yitsḥak ben Yehudah of Mainz are primarily his nephews, 'the sons of Makhir', and Rashi. While the former were far from top-flight scholars, nevertheless they belonged to one of the most prestigious families of Ashkenaz, had acquired a fine talmudic education, and had long been the pupils and acolytes of their famous uncle. The situation repeats itself with R. Yitsḥak ha-Levi of Worms. Of the three of his responsa that have survived intact (as opposed to one- or two-line reports of his rulings), two are to Rashi and the third to R. Natan ben Makhir.[14] Some eighteen responsa by Rabbenu Sasson have survived,[15] fourteen in the singular MS Montefiore 98 and printed in *Teshuvot Ḥakhmei Tsarfat ve-Lotir*. Ten or eleven of these are replies to an otherwise unknown R. Yitsḥak ben Yitsḥak, who appears from his questions to have been a scholar of some attainment. Indeed, one of his queries is among the more perceptive in the literature of the eleventh century.[16]

[13] Only three full responsa of R. Eli'ezer ha-Gadol have come down to us (Grossman, *Ḥakhmei Ashkenaz ha-Rishonim* [above, n. 2], 226–7). One, on communal organization, was co-authored with R. Yehudah Ba'al Sefer ha-Dinim. I shall treat it at length in my discussion of the latter scholar. The second is a responsum about an apostate *kohen* who returned to Judaism, a topic about which Rabbenu Gershom wrote, and mention will be made of R. Yitsḥak's decision in my analysis of the problem. Finally, there is a scholarly exchange with R. Yitsḥak ben Menaḥem on *'edut ishah*, testimony about the death of a husband that would allow the wife to remarry. The contrast between the discussion of communal organization and that of *'edut ishah* illustrates vividly the point that I am making.

[14] We know of some ten responsa by R. Yitsḥak ha-Levi (Grossman, *Ḥakhmei Ashkenaz ha-Rishonim* [above, n. 2], 290), but only three have survived intact. For detailed attributions, see A. Grossman, 'Toledot ha-Sifrut ha-Rabbanit be-'Ashkenaz u-ve-Tsarfat ha-Tsefonit ba-Me'ah ha-'Aḥat-'Esreh' (Ph.D. diss., Hebrew University of Jerusalem, 1973), 227–8. Grossman further states there that four more responsa are to be found in manuscript, but unfortunately he provides neither manuscript references nor any citations of the texts.

[15] Grossman, *Ḥakhmei Ashkenaz ha-Rishonim* (above, n. 2), 341, speaks of some twenty; however, his own analysis reveals doubts about several of the attributions. Only *Teshuvot Rashi*, ed. I. S. Elfenbein (New York, 1943), #355 (see the editor's remarks and those of Grossman in *Ḥakhmei Ashkenaz ha-Rishonim*, 328 n. 5); *Siddur Rashi*, ed. J. Freimann (Berlin, 1912), #440; *Sefer ha-Pardes* (Constantinople, 1802), fos. 44d–45a, ibid. (Warsaw, 1870), #191; and *Shibbolei ha-Leket II*, #83, p. 168, seem clearly authored by Rabbenu Sasson.

[16] *Teshuvot Ḥakhmei Tsarfat ve-Lotir*, ##47–56. Responsum #46 may equally be addressed to the same recipient, as #47 begins *tu sha'al*. See the editor's note ad loc. The perceptive query I have in mind is that which elicited responsum #48.

Grossman states that no respondent of the eleventh century based himself so strongly on the Bavli as did R. Yitsḥak b. Yehudah and that the latter half of the eleventh century witnessed the growing influence of the Bavli.[17] It is difficult to sustain such a claim when R. Yehudah Ba'al Sefer ha-Dinim relied on the Bavli in ninety-eight of the ninety-nine rulings of his that have survived.[18] The same ratio obtains in the responsa of Rabbenu Gershom, as we shall soon see. The writings of R. Yitsḥak b. Yehudah and his contemporaries do stand in sharp contrast to those of their predecessors in their more complicated use of the Bavli. Small wonder, for these were halakhic discussions with other 'professional' Talmudists, devoid of biblical verses, invocations of Midrash, and the rhetorical exhortations that characterize some of the responsa of Rabbenu Gershom and the writings on communal organization of R. Yosef Tov 'Elem, R. Yehudah Ba'al Sefer ha-Dinim, and R. Eli'ezer ha-Gadol.

It is now time to examine the evidence advanced for the indifference to the authority of the Bavli in Early Ashkenaz.

I. Rulings Contrary to the Bavli

Let us open with the rulings that have been showcased to demonstrate that the scholars of Early Ashkenaz ruled contrary to the Bavli. The rabbinical authorities claimed to have done so are Rabbenu Gershom Me'or ha-Golah and his disciple, R. Yehudah Ba'al Sefer ha-Dinim.

Rabbenu Gershom Me'or ha-Golah

The ruling of Rabbenu Gershom that in the *kiddush-havdalah* service that is said when a festival (*yom tov*) begins on a Saturday night one should recite the blessing over aromatic spices (*besamim*) is not an innovation of Rabbenu Gershom, nor is it contrary to the Bavli.[19] There is a three-sided controversy among the Geonim as to whether one may recite *havdalah* over bread. Some say never, some say yes, if no wine is available, and some say only if it is the joint *kiddush-havdalah* ceremony, which takes place when the first night of a holiday falls on a Saturday night. The authorities validating such a recitation generally or only in a *kiddush-havdalah* setting include some of the earliest Geonim (*kama'i* in the words of the author of the *'Ittur*, though their identities are unclear[20]), better-known Geonim such as R. 'Amram, R. Tsadok, and

[17] *Ḥakhmei Ashkenaz ha-Rishonim* (above, n. 2), 319, 417–18 and *passim*. [18] See below, n. 75.

[19] Grossman, 'Zikatah' (above, n. 2), 68; id., *Ḥakhmei Ashkenaz ha-Rishonim* (above, n. 2), 157–8.

[20] *'Ittur*, in edn. R. Me'ir Yonah (repr. New York, 1955), ii, fo. 132b, and see Aptowitzer's remarks in his edition of *Sefer Ravyah* (repr. New York, 1983), ii. 146 n. 29.

R. Yehudai, one opinion in the *Halakhot Gedolot* (in both extant versions), R. Hai (at one stage of his thinking), and one might add Rabbenu Ḥanan'el of Kairouan.[21] One of the arguments cited in the name of those who validate such a recitation is the discussion of Bet Shammai and Bet Hillel in *Berakhot* 51b about the proper order of *havdalah*—whether the blessing over *besamim* precedes or follows that on light (*ner*). For reasons into which we need not enter, the proponents of reciting *havdalah* over bread contend that this controversy can be construed only as dealing with the joint *kiddush-havdalah* that is recited when a festival (*yom tov*) commences on a Saturday night. Clearly, they are of the belief that the blessing over *besamim* is said in such a ceremony. Alfasi vigorously disputes this position, but not on the basis of the simple argument that the mention of *besamim* in the passage in *Berakhot* precludes this being an instance of the *kiddush-havdalah* ceremony.[22]

In our manuscripts of the *Siddur Rav 'Amram Ga'on*, a work of controlling authority in Ashkenaz in shaping the liturgy, the recitation of the blessing over *besamim* is explicitly endorsed. In the text of that *siddur* employed by Ravan (R. Eli'ezer ben Natan of Mainz, mid-twelfth century), views both for and against are registered.[23] The recitation of a blessing over *besamim* in the joint

[21] The issue of *havdalah* on bread has frequently been discussed, and the sources for these attributions are readily found in *Ginzei Schechter*, ed. L. Ginzberg (New York, 1929), ii. 8; *Sefer Ravyah* (repr. New York, 1983), ii. 146–8; *Siddur Rav Sa'adyah Gaon*, ed. Y. Davidson et al. (Jerusalem, 1941), 126; *Otsar ha-Ge'onim*, ed. B. M. Lewin (Haifa, 1928), *Berakhot*, 77–8, 116–18; Y. Sussmann, 'Shenei Kuntresim be-Halakhah me'et R. Mosheh Boutril', *Kovets 'al Yad*, NS 6/2 (1966), 325–8; *Halakhot Gedolot*, Or ha-Mizraḥ edn. (Jerusalem, 1992), 98; *Halakhot Gedolot*, ed. A. Hildesheimer (Jerusalem, 1972), i. 68–70; I. M. Ta-Shma, *Minhag Ashkenaz ha-Kadmon* (Jerusalem, 1992), 221–33.

[22] Alfasi ad loc. (Vilna edn., fos. 38b–39a) *ika me-ravevata*. Although he does not agree with the need for its recitation, he does not see that recitation as posing any problem. S. Lieberman contends, in *Tosefta ki-Feshutah, Zera'im* (New York, 1955), i. 96, that, despite Alfasi's formulation, neither R. Yehudai Gaon nor Rabbenu Ḥanan'el actually interpreted the Mishnah as referring to a *kiddush-havdalah* service of a *yom tov* that begins on Saturday night. Their doctrine was restricted to the recitation of *havdalah* over bread (*pat*). Alfasi clearly disagrees with this interpretation, and there is every reason to assume that he had their original formulations in mind when he penned his rebuttal.

[23] *Seder Rav 'Amram Ga'on* (Warsaw, 1865), fo. 42b; ed. A. L. Frumkin (Jerusalem, 1912), ii, fo. 117b; ed. D. Goldschmidt (Jerusalem, 1971), 130, ll. 30–1. Goldschmidt suggests that these lines are a later addition, as no geonic source mentions a blessing over *besamim*, and he refers to Aptowitzer's notes in his edition of *Sefer Ravyah* (above, n. 21), 156, and Lieberman's remarks, p. 96; however, neither scholar questions the authenticity of the text. Indeed, *Ravan* (ed. S. Z. Ehrenreich [Simleu Silvaniei, 1926], ii, *Betsah* 33b, fo. 174a, whence to *Ma'aseh Roke'aḥ* [Sanok, 1912], #113) explicitly states that R. Tsadok Gaon is cited in the *Siddur* as favoring the recitation over *besamim*. In our manuscripts, the view of Rav 'Amram has been excised, and the view of R. Tsadok is cited as that of Rav 'Amram. (The other half of Ravan's citation, i.e. Rav 'Amram's explicit ruling against *besamim*—not found in our manuscripts of the *Siddur*—is reflected in some manuscripts of the *Mordekhai*; see *Mordekhai ha-Shalem*, *Betsah* [Jerusalem, 1983], #693, 109–10.) The absence of the passage endorsing the blessing over

kiddush-havdalah would also appear to be the doctrine of the Palestinian Talmud (Yerushalmi),[24] and Ravan reports that 'R. Meshullam of Mainz sent a query to the Holy City and they replied that one recites a blessing over it [i.e. *besamim*]'.[25] This view was endorsed by R. Yitsḥak ben Yehudah of Mainz in the latter half of the eleventh century, was the custom of Mainz and Cologne, and was deemed legitimate, if not necessarily correct, by Rabbenu Tam.[26]

Nowhere does the Bavli object to the saying of this blessing; its required absence is a commentarial inference. In the acronym given for the cluster of blessings recited in the *kiddush-havdalah* ceremony (*yknhz*), there is no letter *bet* for the blessing on *besamim*. This led later commentators, such as Rashbam (following Rashi's views on the subject[27]) and most of the French Tosafists, to assume that the Bavli's view was that no such blessing was to be recited.[28] However, one could equally contend, as did Rabbenu Gershom and as would Alfasi, that since the requirements for the blessing over light (*ner*) are identical with those for the blessing over aromatic spices, any stipulation that *ner* should form part of the ritual is *ipso facto* a stipulation that *besamim* should too.[29]

Grossman cites a passage in the *Shibbolei ha-Leket*, an Italian work of the mid-thirteenth century authored by R. Tsidkiyahu ha-Rofe, in which Rabbenu Gershom states that he ruled here contrary to the Bavli and in favor of the Yerushalmi.[30] Inspection of the passage immediately shows that this is not a determination of the author of the *Shibbolei ha-Leket*; it is part of a longer

besamim in the transcriptions of the *Siddur* found in the *Maḥzor Vitry* and *Siddur Rashi* (siglia *resh* and *vav* in Goldschmidt's apparatus) is not surprising as these transcriptions, as Goldschmidt himself notes (p. 15), are selective and edited to accord with the dominant French tradition, and Rashi was of the opinion that the blessing should not be recited. *Siddur Rashi*, #382, p. 185; *Sefer ha-Pardes*, Constantinople edn., fo. 13b, Warsaw edn., #133 (fo. 27b).

24 *Shibbolei ha-Leket ha-Shalem*, ed. S. Buber (Vilna, 1887), #218, fo. 92a, and validated by Lieberman (above, n. 22), who, in n. 78, questions only the authenticity of the subsequent six words of the Yerushalmi quotation. See text below.

25 Ravan (above, n. 23). The original text of the brief reply was found in the Genizah and published by A. Marmorstein, 'Notes et mélanges', *Revue des études juives*, 73 (1921), 89.

26 *Ma'aseh ha-Ge'onim*, ed. A. Epstein and J. Freimann (Berlin, 1910), #37, p. 24; *Mordekhai ha-Shalem, Betsah* (above, n. 23), #693, p. 110; *Teshuvot Ba'alei ha-Tosafot*, ed. I. A. Agus (New York, 1955), #10. (I do not know what Rabbenu Tam refers to when he writes *ve-khen nohagin be-mesivata*. It sounds like a quotation from a geonic responsum, but none has been cited.) *Or Zarua'*, ii (Zhitomir, 1862), *Motsa'ei Shabbat*, #92; Or 'Etsyon edn. (Jerusalem, 2001), i. 321.

27 See above, n. 23 end.

28 Rashbam, *Pesaḥim* 102b, s.v. *u-Shemu'el*; *Tosafot*, s.v. *rav amar*; *Tosafot, Betsah* 33b, s.v. *ki havinan*; *Tosefot R. Yehudah Sir Leon 'al Berakhot*, ed. N. Sachs (Jerusalem, 1972), ii. 52b, s.v. *ner*.

29 *Shibbolei ha-Leket ha-Shalem*, #218, fo. 92a; see my remarks above, n. 24, and Ravan, *Pesaḥim* 103a (ed. H. L. Ehrenreich, ii, fo. 164a).

30 'Zikatah' (above, n. 2), 68; *Ḥakhmei Ashkenaz ha-Rishonim* (above, n. 2), 157–8, 435.

quotation from an otherwise unknown Rabbi Ya'ir ben Me'ir (who is never cited again by R. Tsidkiyahu, or by any other medieval writer, to the best of my knowledge), who writes:

I *heard* [this is apparently an oral tradition] in the name of Rabbenu Gershom that he [*sic*] requires the recitation of the blessing over *besamim* on a *yom tov* that falls on a Saturday night, though our *gemara* doesn't require *besamim*. However, the Yerushalmi says that on a *yom tov* that falls on a Saturday night one recites [in the *kiddush-havdalah* ceremony the cluster of blessings whose acronym is] *yknbhz* [the *b* standing for *besamim*], and every place where there is a blessing over *ner* there is a blessing over *besamim*.[31]

One can't tell whether everything that this unknown author mentions in the passage above was passed on to him in the name of Rabbenu Gershom or just part of it, and the rest is his exposition. The first thing that strikes us is the reference to the Yerushalmi. Other than one late and very dubious citation by the fourteenth-century R. Ya'akov Ba'al ha-Turim,[32] Rabbenu Gershom is never quoted as relying on a Yerushalmi passage. The best test in the case under discussion here is to move back from Italy to Germany and to centuries closer to the time of Rabbenu Gershom and see how he is quoted there. The earliest discussion of the issue of *besamim* in Germany that we possess is by scholars in Rabbenu Gershom's yeshivah in Mainz some two generations after his death, which is found in the *Ma'aseh ha-Ge'onim*. They know nothing of a Yerushalmi source on the topic.[33] Neither does the twelfth-century R. Eli'ezer ben Natan of Mainz (Ravan), nor his grandson, the great R. Eli'ezer ben Yo'el ha-Levi (Ravyah). R. El'azar Roke'aḥ, the first to cite Rabbenu Gershom, makes no mention of a Yerushalmi passage; it is equally absent from the citations of Rabbenu Gershom in the *Mordekhai* and from the summation in the *Or Zarua'*.[34] This is scarcely surprising as this version of the Yerushalmi (containing the acronym *yknbhz*) is unknown to any medieval scholar other than the mysterious R. Ya'ir ben Me'ir. Furthermore, there is no need, as

[31] This passage was edited and reproduced in the *Tanya Rabbati* (Warsaw, 1873), #47, fo. 47d.

[32] *Tur*, 'Oraḥ Ḥayyim', #128; see *Teshuvot Rabbenu Gershom*, #4, p. 58 n. 2. No responsum of Rabbenu Gershom was more copied than this one, and no version in print or manuscript known to me has this Yerushalmi citation. See sources cited below in n. 61.

[33] Above, n. 26.

[34] Cited above, nn. 23, 26. Even had Rabbenu Gershom cited the Yerushalmi, it would have proven little, as David Berger has already pointed out in his review of *Ḥakhmei Ashkenaz ha-Rishonim*, *Tarbiz*, 53 (1984), 483 n. 5. If Ashkenaz had a practice of reciting the blessing over *besamim*, a passage in the Yerushalmi would have been more than adequate proof of the practice's validity, even in the tosafist period. See e.g. *Tosafot*, *Berakhot* 18a, s.v. *le-maḥar*, and the parallel passages there noted in the *Masoret ha-Shas*.

I have already noted, to assume any controversy between the Bavli and the Yerushalmi on this matter, as does the mysterious R. Ya'ir. If blessings over *ner* and *besamim* have the same criteria for recitation, any requirement regarding *ner* is by definition a requirement for *besamim*.

R. Yehudah Ba'al Sefer ha-Dinim

R. Yehudah ruled that a grandson should sit *shiv'ah* for a grandparent on the basis of a passage in *Bava Batra* that states that if a parent predeceases a grandparent and the grandparent subsequently dies, the grandchild is viewed as a direct inheritor and the property is never reckoned as having passed through the estate of the parent, and is thus not subject to any liens upon the parental estate. The Talmud invokes a verse for direct inheritance: 'Instead of thy fathers shall be thy sons' (Ps. 45: 17). R. Yehudah then cites a second proof from a passage in *Mo'ed Katan*.[35] Let us begin with the passage in *Bava Batra*.[36]

[The following statement] was sent from Palestine: [if] a son sold the estate of his father during the lifetime of the father, and [then] he [the father] died, his son [i.e. the grandson] may take [that estate] away from the buyers; and this presents a [great] difficulty in civil law; for they could say to him, 'Your father has sold and you are taking away!'

What objection is this! Could he [the grandson] not reply: 'I succeed to the rights of the father of [my] father [i.e. I inherited it directly from my grandfather and not via the estate of my father, who never owned the property and thus had no right to sell it]'? Know [that such a plea of direct inheritance is justified] for it is written: 'Instead of thy fathers shall be thy sons, whom thou shalt make princes in all the land' [Ps. 45: 17].

The Talmud, in the course of its lengthy discussion of the gnomic Palestinian directive, says: 'and as to your objection [based on the verse] "Instead of thy fathers shall be thy sons", [it may be pointed out that] this was written in connection with a blessing [i.e. has no legal connotation and cannot be cited as evidence of direct transmission from grandfather to grandson].'[37] Clearly the verse is not a proof-text—at least at this stage of the argument.[38]

[35] *Ma'aseh ha-Ge'onim*, #59, p. 49; *Sefer ha-Pardes*, Constantinople edn., fo. 49a; Warsaw edn., #290 (fo. 53d); S. E. Stern, 'Piskei u-Minhagei Magentsa ve-Germaiza', *Tsefunot*, 3: 1 (1991), 4 (repr. in *Me'orot ha-Rishonim*, ed. S. M. Stern [Jerusalem, 2002], 185). **וזה טעמו 'תחת אבותיך יהיו בניך', וחביריו משיבין לו: ההוא בברכה כתיב**.

[36] 158b–159a:

שלחו מתם . . . בן שמכר בנכסי אביו בחיי אביו ומת, בנו מוציא מיד הלקוחות וזו היא שקשה בדיני ממונות. ולימרו ליה—אבוך מזבין ואת מפיק?! ומאי קושיא? דלמא מצי אמר מכח אבוה דאבא קאתינא. תדע דכתיב 'תחת אבותיך יהיו בניך תשיתמו לשרים בכל הארץ'.

[37] Ibid.: **ודקא קשיא לך 'תחת אבותיך יהיו בניך'? ההוא בברכה כתיב**.

[38] See below, p. 83.

Grossman takes this rebuttal as proof that R. Yehudah Ba'al Sefer ha-Dinim ruled contrary to the Bavli, for did not the Talmud reply that the verse could not be cited as proof? He even claims that this is evidence of a fundamental methodological disagreement in the second quarter of the eleventh century on the right of scholars to invoke biblical verses to resolve halakhic issues, even verses which the Bavli had specifically rejected as containing any such halakhic import![39] However, all commentators noticed that the Bavli at no point disputed the Palestinian ruling. Not surprisingly, for a ruling in the form of *shalḥu mi-tam*—an official ruling issued by the Palestinian academies and sent to Babylonia—carried great weight in Babylonia. Indeed, the retention of the second day of festivals in the Diaspora (*yom tov sheni shel galuyot*) is based on just such a Palestinian directive. The Bavli was simply perplexed by the Palestinian perplexity. Why did the Palestinians see this ruling as problematic? Was this not simply a consequence of the direct inheritance of grandchildren? Admittedly, the biblical proof-text seems to have been rejected by the Bavli,[40] but did this mean that it equally rejected the principle of direct inheritance? Put differently, the Palestinian ruling is unquestionably binding, but does it have a rationale? Is it undergirded by some legal principle, or is it an incomprehensible Palestinian *mandamus*? Laws without rationales are anathema to juridical thinking and, not surprisingly, halakhists almost without exception took the Palestinian ruling as expressing the principle of direct inheritance of grandchildren, even though this principle was not rooted in any biblical verse.[41] For example, Rashbam did so in his concluding remarks on that very *sugya*, as well as Rabbenu Tam, R. Shimshon of Sens, R. Eli'ezer ben Natan of Mainz, and R. Simḥah of Speyer—to cite but some of the Ashkenazic authorities.[42] Rabad of Posquières[43] and R. Me'ir Abul'afia (Ramah)

[39] 'Zikatah' (above, n. 2), 72, and n. 52 ad loc.

[40] See below, p. 83.

[41] The question may be asked: if laws without rationales are an anathema, then why didn't the rejection of the rationale here entail a rejection of the law? The answer is that the Palestinians themselves admitted that the rule was binding despite their incomprehension (*ve-zo hi shekasheh be-dinei mamonot*, above, n. 36), as Rashbam immediately noted at the end of the *sugya* (*Bava Batra* 159b, s.v. *u-meshani*), and so did all commentators in his wake; see the next three notes.

[42] Rashbam, ibid.; Rabbenu Tam in *Tosefot ha-Rashba mi-Shants 'al Ketubbot*, ed. A. Liss (Jerusalem 1973), 91b, s.v. *de-zabna*; *Tosafot*, *Ketubbot* 91b, s.v. *de-zabna*; R. Shimshon of Sens in *Or Zarua'*, iii (Jerusalem, 1887), *Bava Kamma*, #431 (cited anonymously in *Tosafot*, *Bava Kamma* 108b, s.v. *le-vanav*); Ravan in *Bava Batra*, fo. 159a; R. Simḥah of Speyer in *Or Zarua'*, i (Zhitomir, 1862), *Hilkhot Yibbum*, #642; *Teshuvot R. Me'ir mi-Rotenburg* (Prague and Budapest, 1895), #928; *Or Zarua'*, iii; *Bava Batra*, #104.

[43] *Sefer ha-Terumot* (Venice, 1643), 48: 3: 4; ed. A. Goldschmidt (Jerusalem, 1988), 1074; *Ḥiddushei ha-Rashba 'al Bava Batra* (Jerusalem, 1960), 159b, s.v. *katav*.

of Toledo ruled similarly, as did R. Yom Tov al-Sevilli (Ritva).[44] Lest one contend that all of these authorities are later than Rabbenu Gershom, it should be added that Rav Hai Gaon also took direct inheritance of grandchildren as a halakhic given.[45] Nor did the legal intuition of the overwhelming majority of scholars err as to the nature of the Palestinian *mandamus*. The Yerushalmi in *Kiddushin* states explicitly that grandchildren inherit directly and not via the estate of the parent.[46]

As to R. Yehudah's citation of the verse 'Instead of thy fathers shall be thy sons': R. Yehudah was of the opinion, reflected in the Mainz Commentary (more commonly known as the *Perush Rabbenu Gershom*), that the rejection of the proof-verse is a function of the rejection of the principle of direct inheritance (*mi-'avuhu de-'abba ka-yaritna*), as was entertained by the *sugya* at one stage of the discussion. If the final conclusion of the *sugya* is that the binding Palestinian directive did indeed refer, as it initially assumed, to the grandchildren's direct inheritance, then one reverts to the acceptance of the proof-verse that was initially introduced.[47] One need not even resort to this interpretation, for the halakhic validity of the proof-verse is beside the point. R. Yehudah is here invoking the principle of direct inheritance of the grandchild, not the verse in isolation. The verse itself yields no inference whatsoever as to mourning (*avelut*); that inference is provided by the principle of direct

[44] *Yad Ramah 'al Bava Batra*, ed. A. O. Peled (Jerusalem, 1994), ii. 159b, s.v. *u-ve-din* (end); *Ḥiddushei ha-Ritva 'al Bava Batra*, ed. Y. D. Ilan (Jerusalem, 2005), 159b, s.v. *lo*.

[45] *'Ittur*, edn. R. Me'ir Yonah, i, fo. 10b, and see the report of R. Ya'akov Ba'al ha-Turim on the extension of this doctrine by Rav Hai Gaon from sale to debt; *Tur*, 'Ḥoshen Mishpat', 211: 3.

[46] *Kiddushin* 1: 2, Venice edn., fo. 59b–c; Academy of Hebrew Language edn. (Jerusalem, 2001), col. 1144; this was pointed out by R. Simḥah of Speyer in his responsum cited in *Teshuvot R. Me'ir mi-Rotenburg* (Prague and Budapest, 1895), #928.

[47] *Perush Rabbenu Gershom, Bava Batra* 159b, top; ed. T. Y. Leitner, 2 vols. in 1 (Jerusalem, 1999), ii. 349 ad loc. See e.g. *Tosafot, Bava Kamma* 108b, s.v. *le-vanav*. At the end of the Romm edition of the Talmud the notes of some thirty to forty leading talmudic scholars of the 18th and 19th centuries are registered. These marginalia note the slightest whisper of contradiction or apparent inconsistency in the words of Rashi and *Tosafot*. These notes have now been grouped together and arranged by talmudic folio pagination in recent editions of the Talmud, e.g. the *'Oz ve-Hadar*. Inspection of these notes on the above passage in *Bava Kamma* shows that none of these supercommentators saw the slightest difficulty in the tosafist citation of the biblical proof-verse of the direct inheritance of grandchildren. R. Shimshon of Sens similarly invokes this proof-verse when citing the principle of direct inheritance (*Or Zarua'*, iii, *Bava Kamma*, #431). Cf., however, the formulation of R. Simḥah of Speyer in *Teshuvot R. Me'ir mi-Rotenburg* (Prague and Budapest, 1895), #928 (*de-kera ika le-'ukma bi-verakhah*). The commentators do not part company over direct inheritance of grandchildren, but over the nature of the missing proof. Some contend that there is no explicit proof at all for this principle, others that there is none from the Mishnah, while a few are of the opinion that no biblical proof-verse can be adduced. Only the last, small, group of commentators would disallow a citation of *taḥat avoteikha*.

inheritance. In an age prior to standardized folio pages, one frequently referred to a law in scholarly conversation (and remember that this is the report of an oral discussion of R. Yehudah with his colleagues) by citing the verse associated with that law. Indeed, to this day one often shorthands references to laws in *Seder Kodashim* by citing the commonly associated proof-verse, irrespective of whether the proof-verse is ultimately sustained or rejected in the *sugya*.

The principle of direct inheritance is firmly established in halakhah. Indeed, other than possibly Maimonides,[48] I know of no one who challenges it. Rabbi Yehudah Ba'al Sefer ha-Dinim, an acknowledged master of civil law, knew whereof he spoke when he invoked the *sugya* in *Bava Batra*.

Turning to the second proof adduced by R. Yehudah for the mourning of grandchildren for grandparents, that from *Mo'ed Katan*,[49] let us note that both sides invoke the same passage in the Bavli, so it is rather strange to argue from this passage that they rule contrary to the Bavli. The reported discussion is perplexing, and R. Eli'ezer ben Yo'el ha-Levi, the great Ravyah, had already pointed this out in the early thirteenth century. His words were repeated by his pupil, R. Yitsḥak Or Zarua', by R. Yitsḥak's famous disciple, R. Me'ir of Rothenburg, and finally by R. Me'ir's pupil, R. Me'ir ha-Kohen, who incor-

[48] Maimonides ('Mekhirah', 22: 7), of course, rules in accord with the *shalḥu mi-tam*; however, he omits the point first made by Rav Hai Gaon and endorsed by subsequent halakhists that the son may foreclose on the property without reimbursing the current owner—a qualification that lies at the heart of direct inheritance of grandchildren. The father can equally foreclose on the house he sold because he had no right to sell the grandfather's property to begin with. However, he must reimburse the purchaser, for he took the latter's money illegally. Similarly, if the son inherits via the estate of the father, the son must reimburse the current owner. If, however, his inheritance is directly from the grandfather, the sins of his father's sale are without legal consequences for him.

[49] 20b. One naturally asks, if R. Yehudah has an explicit passage in *Mo'ed Katan* mandating *avelut*, why did he need an inference from the laws of inheritance? Moreover, he is not challenged by his disputants on this point. The real problem is the superfluous nature of the inference from *Bava Batra*, not its alleged anti-Babylonian character. One cannot argue that, seeing that *Sefer Ḥasidim*—ed. Y. Wistinetzki (Berlin, 1891), #1 (p. 2)—attests that *Mo'ed Katan* was not widely studied in the days of R. Shemu'el he-Ḥasid and R. Yehudah he-Ḥasid, the same may have been true for previous centuries. *Sefer Ḥasidim* attests only that this tractate was not a common choice of studies by laymen. It was fully on the agenda of scholars at that time, as the writings of Ravyah readily attest. The same involvement in *Mo'ed Katan* was true in earlier centuries. We have an 11th-century commentary of the Mainz school on that tractate (*Perush Rabbenu Gershom Me'or ha-Golah*, in *Kovets Rishonim le-Massekhet Mo'ed Katan*, ed. N. Zaks [Jerusalem, 1966]), and one of the earliest German *Tosafot*, those of R. Yitsḥak b. Asher of Speyer (Riva, d. before 1133) is on *Mo'ed Katan*. See E. E. Urbach, *Ba'alei ha-Tosafot*, rev. edn. (Jerusalem, 1980), 170–1. The teachings of Riva took the form of a *reportatio* by a pupil, as was common among the Tosafists; see the first volume of this series (*Collected Essays* [Oxford, 2013], i. 8, 15).

porated it into his *Haggahot Maimuniyot*, and thus both the report and its problematic nature became part of the common body of halakhic knowledge of the past 600 or so years.[50] Note, however, that no one had any difficulty with R. Yehudah's argument from *Bava Batra*; no one suspected him of ruling contrary to the Bavli or of invoking *derashot* rejected by the Bavli. All questions revolved around the argument from *Mo'ed Katan*. How R. Yehudah Ba'al Sefer ha-Dinim and his contemporaries understood the passage in question remains problematic to this day; however, all sides here invoked the Bavli and sought to rule in accordance with its dictates.

II. Biblical Verses and *Midrashim*

The evidence advanced by Grossman for these radical anti-Bavli claims is not clear. He writes that the invocation of biblical verses and *derashot* should be divided into three groups: (1) simple repetitions of *derashot* of the Talmud; (2) talmudic *derashot* expanded beyond their original scope; (3) entirely new *derashot* invented by Rabbenu Gershom.[51] The first is clearly no new mode of adjudication. Citing the law with or without the talmudic proof-verse is a question of style. Differences of style may have many reasons, and I have already discussed the different audiences addressed and the radically different authority exercised by the Geonim seated in the ancient Babylonian academies of Sura and Pumbedita and by Rabbenu Gershom in the new yeshivah of Mainz. Grossman gives one example of the second class, adding that there are 'other similar instances', and then three examples of the last class. In the footnote documenting 'the similar instances', he gives seven references but states that most of these are of the first class.[52] One of the seven is identical with one of the three instances given in the text as examples of the third class.[53] Another contradicts a responsum of Rabbenu Gershom cited by Grossman in the third class.[54] Both can't have been authored by the same person. Not knowing how my distinguished colleague classified the nine sources that he cites, I must

[50] *Sefer Ravyah*, iii, *Mo'ed Katan*, #841, p. 546; *Or Zarua'*, ii, *Avelut*, #428, fo. 88a; Or 'Etsyon edn. (Jerusalem, 2006), ii. 641; R. Me'ir of Rothenburg, *Teshuvot, Pesakim u-Minhagim*, iii, *Hilkhot Semaḥot*, ed. Y. Z. Cahana (Jerusalem, 1962), #44; *Haggahot Maimuniyot*, *Evel* 2: 4, n. 3.

[51] *Ḥakhmei Ashkenaz ha-Rishonim* (above, n. 2), 155–7, 430–1.

[52] Ibid. 156 n. 184. See similarly Grossman's discussion at p. 430.

[53] *Teshuvot Rabbenu Gershom*, #4 is identical with *Maḥzor Vitry*, #125 cited by Grossman, *Ḥakhmei Ashkenaz*, 156 n. 187.

[54] *Teshuvot u-Fesakim me'et Ḥakhmei Ashkenaz ve-Tsarfat*, ed. E. Kupfer (Jerusalem, 1973), #173, contradicts the responsum cited in the previous note. I have treated this responsum as a misattribution, but as it employs biblical verses and is clearly of 11th-century provenance, I felt obliged to address the use of these citations; see below, pp. 88–9.

examine each and every one of these references together with those instances cited in the text, testing whether they properly belong in the second or third class, the two groups that would constitute proof for Grossman's radical thesis. Needless to say, the evidence explicitly advanced in the text for the latter two classes of *derashot* of Rabbenu Gershom is equally addressed. I will conclude the essay by turning to the several responsa of R. Eli'ezer ha-Gadol and R. Yosef Tov 'Elem that have been cited to prove that these scholars invoked biblical verses and *midrashim* to adjudicate halakhic problems.[55]

Rabbenu Gershom

1. The question whether circumcision should precede or follow the blowing of the *shofar* is not one that can be decided on the basis of any talmudic source.[56] There is no discussion in the Talmud about which of these two takes temporal precedence. Nor does the answer have any halakhic consequences. Regardless of which is done first, both the *shofar*-blowing and the circumcision are perfectly valid. Absent a halakhic source, the invocation of biblical verses and *midrashim* by Rabbenu Gershom is only natural. R. El'azar Roke'aḥ provided a kabbalistic reason for *milah* preceding the blowing of the *shofar*. R. Yisra'el Isserlein (d. 1460) rejected a passage in *Zevaḥim* as a proof-text and, not possessing any halakhic source, could only repeat the reason of Rabbenu Gershom.[57] This is exactly the type of question that has been resolved for over a millennium by appeals to biblical verses and *midrashim* by figures as diverse and as Talmud-centric as Rabbenu Tam, R. Ya'akov Moellin, R. Yeḥezkel Landau, and R. Eliyahu of Vilna.

2. Does attending a wedding take precedence over attending a funeral? Rabbenu Gershom rules that the ceremony of *erusin* does not take precedence, but that of *nisu'im*, *hakhnasat kallah*, does.[58] The secondary status of *erusin* is argued on halakhic grounds, the primacy of *nisu'im* on the basis of a verse in Isaiah (45: 18), *lo tohu bera'ah*. The invocation of this verse evidencing the

[55] I forgo discussing R. Meshullam b. Kalonymos, as Grossman himself admits that he cites verses only in an exegetical or polemical context. See 'Zikatah' (above, n. 2), 70 n. 40; *Ḥakhmei Ashkenaz ha-Rishonim* (above, n. 2), 430.

[56] *Or Zarua'*, ii, 'Hilkhot Rosh ha-Shanah', #275, Or 'Etsyon edn., ii. 205; *Teshuvot Rabbenu Gershom Me'or ha-Golah*, #32. Grossman, *Ḥakhmei Ashkenaz ha-Rishonim* (above, n. 2), 156.

[57] *Sefer ha-Roke'aḥ ha-Gadol* (Jerusalem, 1960), #217 (p. 109, s.v. *u-mah*); *Terumat ha-Deshen*, ed. S. Avitan (Jerusalem, 1991), i, #266. R. Eliyahu of Vilna found the passage from *Zevaḥim* convincing; see *Be'ur ha-Gra 'al Oraḥ Ḥayyim*, 584: 4.

[58] *Orḥot Ḥayyim, Ḥelek Sheni*, ed. M. Schlesinger (Berlin, 1902), 574; *Teshuvot Rabbenu Gershom*, #34. See Grossman, 'Zikatah' (above, n. 2), 70; id., *Ḥakhmei Ashkenaz ha-Rishonim* (above, n. 2), 155.

precedence of *hakhnasat kallah* over *levayat ha-met* is not an innovation of Rabbenu Gershom. He is following a geonic tradition, reflected in the *She'iltot*, and subsequently reproduced without question or comment by such pure halakhists as R. Yosef Karo and R. Shabbetai ha-Kohen (Shakh).[59] The question here is why Rabbenu Gershom did not see the answer to the question in the passage in *Ketubbot* 17a (*ma'avirim et ha-met mi-penei ha-kallah*). Most probably because he took that passage—as Rashi was subsequently to explain it—as stating a rule of procession only. What is at bar is not the question of attendance at mutually exclusive ceremonies, but of precedence in public procession. A funeral cortège must cede the right of way to a bridal procession. And, indeed, the continuation of the *beraita* with its tale of King Agrippa graciously ceding his right of way to a bride sustains this interpretation.

I am not contending that Rabbenu Gershom knew the *She'iltot*; one needs stronger evidence than this to argue for that work's presence at so early a date in Ashkenaz. Indeed, since the author of the *She'iltot* did resolve the problem that he posed on the basis of the passage in *Ketubbot*, had Rabbenu Gershom been aware of the *She'iltot*, he would have to have countered this argument in his responsum. I am simply contending that the common perception of the precedence of *hakhnasat kallah* over *levayat ha-met*, which in tractate *Semaḥot* took the form of *kevod ha-ḥayyim kodem li-khevod ha-metim*,[60] was articulated in a parallel (Babylonian?) tradition using the biblical verse from Isaiah—*lo tohu bera'ah*.

3. There is no sure halakhic guidance concerning whether a priest (*kohen*) who has apostatized and then repented may participate in the communal priestly blessing (Birkat Kohanim) or be honored as a priest and called first to the Torah readings (*kore rishon ba-torah*).[61] The *mishnah* in *Menaḥot* 109a states that such a priest may partake in the priestly portion (*kodashim*) but may

[59] *She'iltot*, ed. N. T. Y. Berlin, i (repr. Jerusalem, 1948), #3, pp. 20–1; ed. S. K. Mirsky, i (Jerusalem, 1960), #3, p. 28: **ברם צריך—הוצאת המת והכנסת הכלה אי זה מהן קודם? הוצאת המת דהא . . . או דילמא הכנסת הכלה עדיפא משום כי לא תהו בראה לשבת יצרה**. *Bet Yosef, Shakh, Tur/Shulḥan 'Arukh*, 'Yoreh De'ah', 360: 1.

[60] *Massekhet Semaḥot*, ed. M. Higger (New York, 1931), 11: 6, p. 189; see also p. 231. See S. Lieberman, *Tosefta ki-Feshutah, Megillah* (New York, 1962), 1186–90.

[61] *Maḥzor Vitry*, ed. S. Hurwitz (Nuremberg, 1923), #125; ed. A. Goldschmidt (Jerusalem, 2004), i. 196–7; *Or Zarua'*, ii, *Nesi'at Kappayim*, #412, Or 'Etsyon edn., ii. 567–9; *Shibbolei ha-Leket ha-Shalem*, #33; *Teshuvot Rabbenu Gershom*, #4; MS Oxford, Bodley 566, fos. 59b–60a; MS Cambridge Add. 667.1, fos. 156b–c, #252 (by the foliation of the manuscript. In the photostat of the manuscript at the Institute of Microfilmed Hebrew Manuscripts of the National Library of Israel the page number given on the back of the photostat is 149); MS New York, Jewish Theological Seminary, Rabbinica 1077, fo. 63b.

not perform priestly service in the Temple. Should we draw an analogy between the synagogue service and that of the Temple? Some thought yes;[62] Rabbenu Gershom thought not. Many considered it shocking that a former apostate should bless the Jewish flock and cited biblical verses to demonstrate its odiousness. Rabbenu Gershom quoted passages to show that it was not reprehensible, and even to argue that by denying the *kohen* his rights one would be publicly humiliating him for past sins—conduct that both the Bible and the Talmud strictly enjoin (*ona'at devarim*). He further cited verses and talmudic passages to show that such rejection might even encourage recidivism and push the *kohen* back into the fold of the idol-worshippers—something the Talmud forcefully rejects.

When Rabbenu Gershom wrote: 'There is no proof from the Mishnah or from the Bible to disqualify him [the priest]; quite the contrary, there is proof from the Mishnah and Bible not to disqualify him', he was not advancing some radical new rule of adjudication.[63] He was simply stating that the Mishnah cited in support of the disqualification actually proved the reverse and that verses that have halakhic force (*lo yidḥeh even aḥar ha-nofel*)—indeed, are viewed as a halakhic mandate (*ona'at devarim*)—oppose any disqualification. Those arguing against such rights cited *divrei aggadah* and verses in abundance—see, for example, the contrary responsum, equally attributed to Rabbenu Gershom in *Teshuvot u-Fesakim me'et Ḥakhmei Ashkenaz ve-Tsarfat*[64]—and Rabbenu Gershom replied in kind.

The status of a repentant convert, and especially the priestly functions and privileges of such a penitent, were issues on which emotions ran high, and in the absence of any clear talmudic ruling, proponents from both sides cited biblical verses and *midrashim*—and with a passion. If the reader wishes to get a sense of the deep antagonism to blessings or even communal prayers by *kohanim* who have 'defiled' themselves by sin, and of the need to massively invoke law and Midrash, halakhah and aggadah, to mobilize every imaginable

62 *Otsar ha-Ge'onim*, ed. B. M. Lewin, *Gittin* (Jerusalem, 1941), 132–3, see editor's notes ad loc. (in MS Montefiore 98, fo. 78b, the responsum is attributed to R. Sherira Gaon); R. Yosef Tov 'Elem in *Shibbolei ha-Leket*, #33; R. Eli'ezer ha-Gadol, *Teshuvot Ba'alei ha-Tosafot*, #3. One should add the author of the responsum attributed to Rabbenu Gershom cited above, n. 54. The argument for the identity of blessing and service on the basis of Deut. 10: 8 made by R. Eli'ezer ha-Gadol is open to the reply that this may hold true for the priestly blessing in the Temple, but not outside it (*ba-mikdash aval lo bi-gevulin*).

63 Cf. Grossman, *Ḥakhmei Ashkenaz ha-Rishonim* (above, n. 2), 156; id., 'Zikatah' (above, n. 2), 71 (cited as one of two examples of Rabbenu Gershom's tendency to rely upon biblical verses as weighty sources in his halakhic decisions—*makor rav 'erekh bi-fesikato*). See below, n. 71.

64 Above, n. 54, #173. This may be the source of the abbreviated responsum in the name of Rabbenu Gershom in *Teshuvot Rabbenu Gershom Me'or ha-Golah*, #4.

source, canonical or otherwise, in an attempt to overcome the strong opposition, I suggest he or she study the lengthy (one and a half folio columns) responsum, seeking to permit a *kohen* who had inadvertently killed a child and had done full penance to participate in communal prayers, serve as a *sheliaḥ tsibbur*, and bless the congregation, penned by the great R. Yitsḥak Or Zarua' at the high noon of German tosafist dialectic.[65]

4. Concerning the issue of inverting an oath (*mepakh shevu'ah*),[66] Rabbenu Gershom contends that even oaths required by the Bible, such as *modeh be-miktsat*, can be inverted. Many people were reluctant to take pentateuchal oaths. One could, thus, make a false claim entailing a *modeh be-miktsat*. The defendant would predictably decline to swear, and the plaintiff could collect with no further ado. The only defense, Rabbenu Gershom argues, is to empower the defendant to demand of the plaintiff that he take a pentateuchal oath as to the truth of his claim. (The fear of falsely swearing such an oath—with its dread punishment of both the oath-taker and his descendants—often deterred even the dishonest.) This is a reasonable argument that Rabbenu Gershom bolsters with a verse from Proverbs (3: 17), 'Her ways are pleasant ways' (*derakheiha darkhei no'am*), which the Talmud construed as stating that the Torah seeks to minimize strife.[67] Rabbenu Gershom expands the application of this verse by saying that it precludes anything that is palpably unjust for this would clearly lead to strife. (Having failed to receive justice in the courts, the aggrieved defendant may be led to seek extra-judicial relief.) His position would be the same without this biblical verse and is not rendered any more cogent by its introduction. The citation is simply a rhetorical flourish. Indeed, it is strikingly similar to the use of the same verse by R. David ben Zimra (Radbaz) in the early sixteenth century, when he railed against a palpably unfair ruling on both logical and equitable grounds and concluded by stating that the verse forbade any ruling that was contrary to common sense and logic: ותו דכתיב דרכיה דרכי נועם וצריך שמשפטי תורתנו יהיו מסכימים אל השכל והסברא.

R. Yitsḥak Or Zarua' invoked the same verse when he argued that the right of abutment (*bar metsra*) exists only in situations of parity, where both parties are equally housed. It does not obtain when the abutter is housed and the

[65] *Or Zarua'*, i, *She'elot u-Teshuvot*, #112, fos. 20c–d.

[66] *Teshuvot R. Me'ir mi-Rotenburg* (Prague and Budapest, 1895), #264; *Teshuvot Rabbenu Gershom*, #31; MS Mantua, Comunità Israelitica 33, #178, fos. 25b–26a correct these texts according to MS Parma, De Rossi 425, #202, fos. 126a–127a. A text superior to the above Rothenburg texts is found in *Teshuvot u-Fesakim me'et Ḥakhmei Ashkenaz ve-Tsarfat*, #114. Agus, in his *Urban Civilization* (above, n. 5), ii. 541–2, provides a partial translation. Grossman, *Ḥakhmei Ashkenaz ha-Rishonim* (above, n. 2), 156 n. 184; see above, pp. 85–6.

[67] *Gittin* 59b (*Yevamot* 15a, 87b addresses marital strife only).

alternative purchaser is seeking living quarters. There would be no equity in an outcome which would leave one party with two houses and the other homeless. He then proceeded to cite a talmudic passage from which one may infer that, indeed, no such right of abutment exists.[68] Rabbenu Gershom no more based his ruling on biblical verses than did R. Yitsḥak Or Zarua' 200 years—or Radbaz some half a millennium—later.

5. Rabbenu Gershom mandates *avelut* (mourning) on Purim,[69] noting that the Mishnah, when enumerating the festivals on which mourning is not observed, pointedly omits Purim. As to the well-known verse in Esther (9: 13) that characterizes Purim as a day 'of feasting and rejoicing', this was construed by the Talmud not as mandating rejoicing (*simḥah*) and thus precluding mourning (as on *yom tov*) but only as banning eulogies on Purim.[70] Rabbenu Gershom saw the need to forfend an objection based on the book of Esther because his community knew *Megillat Ester* far better than the Talmud, and this verse would come quickly to most people's minds. Seeing that the Talmud reads the verse contrary to its plain meaning, and it is this reading that Rabbenu Gershom invokes, I am at a loss as to how this ruling indicates that Rabbenu Gershom drew new or, indeed, any, halakhic conclusions of his own from biblical verses.

6. A further reference by Grossman concerns guardianship (*apotropsut*) of minors.[71] Before his death Re'uven appointed Shim'on as the guardian of Re'uven's children and empowered him to allocate the inheritance between the heirs as he saw fit. Rabbenu Gershom disallowed this empowerment on the grounds that with the death of Re'uven the estate passed into the ownership of the heirs, and they had sole authority over the disposition of the estate. Shim'on remained the guardian; however, his powers were the simple ones of a guardian and these did not include any right to determine the division of the estate. Any special powers vested in him by the father ended with the latter's death. This is an elementary point in any legal system. All and any derivative powers of an appointee terminate with the death of a principal, as the dead have no legal personality. Indeed, this point is so elementary that it is difficult

[68] *Teshuvot Radbaz*, iii (repr. Warsaw, 1882), #1052; *Or Zarua'*, iii, *Bava Metsi'a*, #359; *Teshuvot R. Me'ir mi-Rotenburg* (Berlin, 1891), #229 (pp. 236–7).

[69] *Shibbolei ha-Leket ha-Shalem*, #203; *Teshuvot Rabbenu Gershom*, #33; MS Warsaw, Żydowski Instytut Historyczny 204, fos. 168a–b. Grossman, *Ḥakhmei Ashkenaz ha-Rishonim* (above, n. 2), 156 n. 184; see above, pp. 185–6.

[70] *Megillah* 5b: *simḥah—melammed she-'assurim be-hesped.*

[71] *Teshuvot Rabbenu Gershom*, #63. A very partial translation and summary is found in Agus, *Urban Civilization* (above, n. 5), ii. 570. Grossman, *Ḥakhmei Ashkenaz ha-Rishonim* (above, n. 2), 156 n. 184; id., 'Zikatah' (above, n. 2), 70, the second of the two examples given; see above, n. 63.

to cite book and verse for it. Rabbenu Gershom writes (and it is this passage that has generated the notion that he invents *derashot* of his own and rules on their basis):

Even though this law is not written explicitly in the Torah, nor is it explicit in the Mishnah, it can be inferred from the Torah and the Mishnah and also from [simple] logic. It is written [Num. 27: 8], 'If a man dies and leaves no son, turn his inheritance over to the daughter'. [Infer from this that] from the moment of death the inheritance passes [to the heirs], but in the case under discussion, the guardian allots the inheritance to the several children as *he* sees fit; he is [thus] undoing the biblical verse [mandate]. It is further written [Deut. 21: 16], 'when *he* bequeaths *his* property to *his* sons'; the *father* can bequeath his property, *not* the guardian. Moreover, if 'he [the father] bequeaths the property' [this must mean] when he was alive, but if he did not bequeath it and died, the heirs inherit. [emphasis added][72]

It is true that there is no talmudic *derashah* 'Only the father can bequeath his property, not the guardian', but Rabbenu Gershom is not formulating any new ruling; rather, seeking to bring home a legally axiomatic point to a biblically oriented community, he invokes a verse which says a *father* can bequeath his property to his heirs as he wishes, and points out that it is 'only the father, not an outsider'. An obvious point, but one which needed saying in early eleventh-century Ashkenaz, and one said best in that period when anchored in a biblical verse. Suppose someone had claimed that Sukkot begins on 20 Tishrei, and a respondent cited in reply the biblical verse (Lev. 23: 34), 'On the fifteenth day of this seventh month there shall be a Feast of Sukkot' and commented '"On the fifteenth day", but not on the twentieth', would he be ruling in accordance with a private *derashah*? Would we even consider this a *derashah*? Rabbenu Gershom is simply stating here that the basic meaning of the terms 'father', 'son', 'inheritance', and 'bequeathing' preclude any outsider from allocating an inheritance after the death of the father. He then proceeds with a sustained, in-depth analysis of the language of empowerment (*'asiyato ke-'asiyati*) in terms of 'gifts made in contemplation of death' (*matnat shekhiv mera'*) and the talmudic dictum 'carrying out the wishes of a dead man is a meritorious act' (*mitsvah le-kayyem divrei ha-met*).[73] The entire halakhic discourse is in

[72] וא[ף] ע[ל] ג[ב] דלאו בפירוש כתיב האי דינא ולא תנינא ליה בפירוש, איכא למימר (מדוקיא) [מדיוקא] דקראי (ומדוקיא) [ומדיוקא] דמתנ[יתין] דדינא הכי, וכן נמי מסברה. (דוקיא) [דיוקא] דקראי דכתיב איש כי ימות ובן אין לו והעברתם את נחלתו לבתו—משעת מיתת האב עוברת הנחלה. וכאן לכשימלך האפוטרופוס לכל אחד ואחד לפי דעתו כדי עקירת הכתוב. ועוד כתיב ביום הנחילו את בניו וכו', האב מנחיל את בניו ואין אפוטרופוס מנחיל. ועוד אם הנחיל מחיים הנחילם, ואם לא הנחילם ומת, זכו היורשים בנחלה.

[73] *Gittin* 14b. R. Shemu'el b. Me'ir, Rashbam, took issue with sections of the in-depth analysis.

categories of the Bavli. In this responsum Rabbenu Gershom addresses two separate audiences: a lay audience who must be taught that the dead have neither legal personality nor proprietary rights and a scholarly one fully at home in the complex laws of inheritance found in *Bava Batra* of the Bavli.

7. In a lengthy responsum Rabbenu Gershom validates—on the basis of talmudic rulings—the right of a community to vest a communal teacher with certain monopoly rights so as to better enable him to devote his time to study and teaching.[74] He concludes by encouraging this practice and cites the verse from Proverbs (3: 18): 'She [i.e. the Torah] is a tree of life to those who embrace her; those who support her will be blessed.' This is not a *derashah*, nor is anything learnt from it. It is simply a reminder and assurance to the community that their support of Torah (by the waiver of taxes) will not go unrewarded by God.

8. In the course of this discussion Rabbenu Gershom invokes several biblical verses emphasizing the obligation of all workers, and especially of teachers, to execute faithfully the task that they have been hired for.[75] No new conclusion is being derived from these passages; they are simply a rhetorical device prefacing a discussion of the terms of contract of teachers. They may say something about the work ethic in the time of Rabbenu Gershom, but they say nothing about his manner of halakhic adjudication.

9. A Talmud student was caught gambling on a festival day. Rather than fess up to his delinquency, he attempted to justify it with specious talmudic arguments. Rabbenu Gershom was understandably incensed and ruled that he should be punished corporally and his winnings given to charity.[76] To justify the latter, he invoked two rules. First, money earned illegally on *ḥol ha-mo'ed* should go to charity, as stated in *Mo'ed Katan* 12b. Second, any food cooked intentionally on the Sabbath is forbidden in benefit, and he cited a biblical

This responsum of Rabbenu Gershom was published from MS Montefiore 98, #97, fos. 97a–98a, and is followed by a dissent on the part of R. Shemu'el. (The copyist of the manuscript notes at the end, fo. 98b, that R. Meshullam was unconvinced by Rashbam's arguments—**וראה הרב ר' משלם את דברי רבי' שמואל ולא נתיישרו בעיניו, וקאי כוותיה דרבינו גרשם מאור הגולה**.)

[74] *Teshuvot R. Me'ir mi-Rotenburg* (Prague and Budapest, 1895), #815; *Teshuvot Ḥakhmei Tsarfat ve-Lotir*, #88; *Teshuvot Rabbenu Gershom*, #68. Grossman, *Ḥakhmei Ashkenaz ha-Rishonim* (above, n. 2), 156 n. 184; see above, pp. 185–6.

[75] *Teshuvot Rabbenu Gershom*, #72. Grossman, *Ḥakhmei Ashkenaz ha-Rishonim* (above, n. 2), 156 n. 184; see above, pp. 185–6.

[76] *Teshuvot u-Fesakim*, Addenda 2, pp. 314–15, cited by Grossman, *Ḥakhmei Ashkenaz ha-Rishonim* (above, n. 2), 156 n. 184; see above, pp. 185–6.

verse (Exod. 31: 14) to support this. Rabbenu Gershom was not inventing a *derashah*; the Talmud (*Ketubbot* 34a) cites this verse as forbidding food cooked on the Sabbath (according to the view of R. Yoḥanan ha-Sandlar). His invocation of this *derashah* has its problems, as the Talmud specifically states there that only *consumption* of the cooked food is forbidden, but not other forms of benefit. This, however, is a question of how Rabbenu Gershom used or interpreted a talmudic passage. It is not an instance of his creating a halakhic *derashah* of *ma'aseh Shabbat* on his own.

R. Yehudah ha-Kohen, Ba'al Sefer ha-Dinim

As I have mentioned above, some ninety-nine responsa of R. Yehudah have survived;[77] ninety-eight of them are decided exclusively on the basis of the Babylonian Talmud. In one and only one instance does he, together with R. Eli'ezer ha-Gadol, cite biblical verses and *midrashim*, and they cite them galore. Indeed, they seem to base their entire argument on these sources. Why would a man write ninety-eight responsa all on the basis of Bavli but only one

[77] S. Emanuel has tabulated that some eighty responsa are found in *Teshuvot R. Me'ir mi-Rotenburg* (Prague and Budapest, 1895) and noted that MS Parma, De Rossi 86, has a large number of responsa by R. Yehudah, seven of which have not been published (##217, 218, 219, 220, 223, which contains two new responsa, and #224). In a subsequent article in *Kovets 'al Yad*, he added four more, three from the same MS Parma, ##213, 222, 226, and one from *Sefer ha-Pardes*, Constantinople edn., fo. 10a; Warsaw edn., #108 end (*u-she-she'altem benei he-ḥatser*). Grossman has added some fifteen from various other sources. S. Emanuel, 'Teshuvot Maharam mi-Rotenburg' (above, n. 7), 153–7. (I have followed Emanuel's numbering of the responsa in the manuscript, see p. 154 n. 15.); id., 'Seridim Ḥadashim mi-Sefer ha-Dinim shel R. Yehudah ha-Kohen', *Kovets 'al Yad*, NS, 20 (30) (2011), 83–103; A. Grossman, *Sefer ha-Dinim: Teshuvotav Melukkatot mi-Mekorot Shonim*, Kuntresim, Mekorot u-Meḥkarim (Jerusalem, 1977), 52–66. This yields 106 responsa. However, Emanuel counted responsa from *Sefer ha-Dinim*, while we seek responsa authored by R. Yehudah himself, and not those of his teacher that he included in his collection. Thus, for our purposes, one must subtract from Emanuel's count of the Prague and Budapest edition five items, ##816, 847, 861, 865, 869, as all are responsa of Rabbenu Gershom. The attribution of the first responsum is attested to by MS Montefiore 98 (fo. 83a–b), which reads: 'from R. Gershom b. Yehudah to R. Yitsḥak b. Y' (לר' יצחק בר"י); the other four contain his signature or attribution to him in the printed text. Two entries from *Ravyah* registered by Aptowitzer, reproduced by Grossman at p. 65—*Ravyah* ##994–5—should equally not be counted, as they are also found in the Prague and Budapest collection (##868, 904) and were thus included in Emanuel's count. We are left with 99 responsa. I have discounted the report, found in *Shibbolei ha-Leket ha-Shalem*, *Semaḥot*, #52, fo. 183b, that R. Yehudah's position as regards mourning on the last day of the festivals (*yom tov ha-'aḥaron shel he-ḥag*), found in *Ma'aseh ha-Ge'onim*, #59, p. 50, comes from *Sefer ha-Dinim*. Neither *Ma'aseh ha-Ge'onim* nor *Sefer ha-Pardes* (Constantinople edn., fo. 49b; Warsaw edn., #290 [fo. 53d]) make any mention of this fact, and I would be loath to make an attribution on the basis of a report in a mid-13th-century Italian work, not to speak of an anonymous one (ומצאתי שכתב מאן דהוא).

on the basis of verses and *midrashim*? Obviously not because of any biblical or aggadic orientation. R. Yehudah's Babylonian allegiance is strikingly clear. Perhaps it is the influence of R. Eli'ezer ha-Gadol? Why, however, would he agree to use here types of sources to which, on the basis of all the considerable remaining evidence, he attributed no normative force? Perhaps this anomalous response on his part was dictated by the facts of the case, the nature of the problem that was posed. Certainly this is an avenue of investigation that should be pursued. Yet no such investigation has been undertaken. Indeed, no substantive study has been made of any of the cases where the respondents used extra-halakhic sources. Not one source that has been cited as demonstrating the non-Babylonian orientation of early Ashkenaz has received substantive analysis. I undertook an analysis of this responsum in the early 1970s, not to test the Babylonian or non-Babylonian orientation of these scholars—the current view was not then entertained—but as part of a larger study of Jewish communal organization. What that analysis yielded was (to cast the results in the terms of the issue under discussion here) that the specifics of the case dictated the nigh exclusive use of verses and *midrashim*.

1. The issue at bar in that responsum is that of communal organization, a subject in which there is little, if any, guidance to be found in the Bavli.[78] An Ashkenazic tradition linked communal organization to powers of the court (*hefker bet din hefker*) and was invoked by Rabbenu Meshullam and Rabbenu Gershom. Because of the special circumstances of the case, the respondents deemed it wiser not to refer *explicitly* to this principle, as it might have generated yet more litigation. Prevented from using the dispositive proof-text that their predecessors and teachers, Rabbenu Meshullam and Rabbenu Gershom, had employed, R. Yehudah and R. Eli'ezer ha-Gadol had to fall back on a plethora of verses and *midrashim* to bolster the power of the emerging communities to impose fines for breaches of the public order by individuals or by their households. One should further note that the respondents avoided invoking explicitly the halakhic proof-text of *hefker bet din hefker*; however, they took care to encode that principle in their responsum to give halakhic quiddity to their lengthy homilies. I will not trouble the reader with details, as I have set forth the entire analysis in *Shut ke-Makor Histori*.[79]

[78] *Kol Bo* (Naples, 1490?), #142. I assume that Grossman is referring to this responsum when he writes in *Ḥakhmei Ashkenaz ha-Rishonim* (above, n. 2), 430, that Rabbenu Gershom's student, R. Yehudah Ba'al Sefer ha-Dinim, also invoked new *derashot* for substantive halakhic purposes. Only this responsum, and putatively that of direct inheritance of grandchildren (above, pp. 90–2), invoke verses halakhically.

[79] *Shut ke-Makor Histori* (above, n. 11), 102–6, esp. p. 106. By the time I got around to publishing

2. As to the *derashah* referred to in the question of direct inheritance of grandchildren, see my discussion above (p. 91).

R. Yosef Tov 'Elem of Limoges

Let me finally turn to R. Yosef, several of whose responsa serve as the richest sources for the argument of eleventh-century adjudication on the basis of biblical verses and *midrashim*.[80] What is the subject matter of these 'anomalous' responsa? All deal with communal organization, as did the preceding responsum of R. Yehudah Ba'al Sefer ha-Dinim. Let us take each in turn.

The first responsum, addressed to the community of Troyes, deals with the question whether income from agriculture can be taxed at the same rate as income from capital, such as trade or moneylending.[81] This fairly elementary question would seem to reflect a very early stage of communal taxation and, indeed, as we shall see from another responsum of his to Troyes, communal organization in that city was in its infancy at that time. There are precious few talmudic guidelines for taxation, as many medieval Talmudists were to note. R. Yosef Tov 'Elem had only his intuition of the equitable and inequitable to go by, and he had then to clothe this instinct in rabbinic garb so as to vest it with authority. These vestments had to be especially impressive as the entire matter of taxation was new. The natural instinct in such a situation was to equalize a novel burden that still rested uneasily on the community's shoulders. R. Yosef, however, felt strongly that fairness demanded that agriculture, with its heavy physical burdens and dependence on the vagaries of the weather, should not be equated with trade and moneylending and their easeful and more predictable profits. He had thus to persuade the community of the justness of the unequal tax burdens that should be borne by agriculture and commerce. Not surprisingly, what followed was a string of citations from the Talmud and Midrash describing the burdens of agricultural employment, and

my study in 1990, the notion that 11th-century scholars had ruled on the basis of biblical verses and *midrashim* had begun to gain currency, so I added a concluding sentence in bold font and addressed the new view briefly in an added footnote, 103a—alas, to no avail.

80 Grossman, 'Zikatah' (above, n. 2), 71; id., *Ḥakhmei Tsarfat ha-Rishonim* (above, n. 2), 69–70. Again (as above, pp. 185–6) Grossman states that 'most invocations of verses are rhetorical (*ke-'asmakhta bilvad*) 'but there are places where he [R. Yosef Tov 'Elem] invoked a talmudic *derashah* and widened its scope or created a new *derashah* altogether' without spelling out which of the cited instances are rhetorical and which substantive. I have addressed the two cited instances, and to forfend any revival of this view I have concluded with a discussion of R. Yosef's responsum in *Teshuvot R. Me'ir mi-Rotenburg* (Lemberg), #423.

81 *Teshuvot R. Me'ir mi-Rotenburg* (Prague and Budapest, 1895), #941. I have provided the textual variants and discussed this responsum at length in my *Shut ke-Makor Histori* (above, n. 11), 54–65. I am here drawing upon that analysis.

a parallel string of quotations from the same sources on the facility and profitability of trade and banking. (He could just as easily have plundered the same literature for a reverse list, as did the religious kibbutz movement some eighty-five years ago.) This was followed by biblical analogies to the case at hand, midrashic exhortations for fairness and equity among Jews, and a *reductio ad absurdum* of the consequences of taxing all capital at an equal rate—not just land and money (waiting to be lent out), but even the agricultural tools of the day laborer. R. Yosef Tov 'Elem of Limoges was not turning his back here on the halakhic sources of the Bavli—for no such sources existed that could provide guidance in the novel question posed to him of apportionment of taxes.

Much the same holds true for the other responsum that the same scholar wrote to Troyes.[82] Returning from a local fair at Troyes around the year 1015,[83] some Jewish merchants from Rheims were kidnapped and held for ransom. Their families contributed as much of the ransom money as they could; to make up the difference, the community of Troyes levied a tax upon threat of excommunication on their own community and those of Auxerre and Sens, whose merchants had participated in the same fair. The cathedral of Sens had recently been sacked, and the Jewish community there had no alternative but to participate in financing its rebuilding; it was thus left with little to contribute towards the ransom. It first pleaded poverty but, more important, it challenged the authority of one city to impose a tax upon another, and the matter was referred to the prominent rabbinic authority in Limoges. (Limoges lay astride one of the three major land arteries that connected northern France with the Midi, called, aptly enough, *via limovicensis*—the Limoges Road. One took the old and well-traveled Roman road running south-west from Troyes to Auxerre and then swung south-east to neighboring Vézelay, there to pick up the famed pilgrim road to Compostella.) Communal autonomy, the right of self-governance of each and every Jewish settlement, something axiomatic in later medieval Jewish life, did not yet exist in France, and R. Yosef Tov 'Elem proceeded to establish it firmly in this wide-ranging responsum, drawing upon halakhic passages from no fewer than seven tractates of the Bavli: *Bava Batra*, *Betsah*, *Yevamot*, *Ḥullin*, *Megillah*, *Shevu'ot*, and *Mo'ed Katan*.

In addressing the issue of the poverty of the Sens community, R. Yosef invoked the standard ruling: 'one cannot decree an ordinance that is beyond

82 *Teshuvot Ba'alei ha-Tosafot*, #1, discussed at length in *Shut ke-Makor Histori* (above, n. 11), 77–86.

83 F. G. Hirschmann, *Stadtplanung, Bauprojekte und Grossbaustellen im 10. und 11. Jahrhundert: vergleichende Studien zu den Kathedralstädten westlich des Rheins*, Monographien zur Geschichte des Mittelalters 43 (Stuttgart, 1998), 178–9, 412.

the ability of the community to comply with'.[84] As Midrash had greater resonance among most people than the as yet uncommented, unexplained, gnomic text of the Bavli, he cited a verse from Job that the *midrash* interpreted as meaning that God himself does not demand of man the immensely difficult.[85] It is far from clear how this one verse can be cited as evidence for the adjudication of issues on the basis of biblical verses. Indeed, if one wishes to see the sovereign command of the Talmud and the rigorous legal thinking of R. Yosef Tov 'Elem, one could scarcely do better than study this responsum in depth. A few words here will have to suffice; the interested reader can find a detailed analysis in my aforementioned work.

Having formulated the principle of communal autonomy, R. Yosef was confronted with a problem. The tradition of self-government that he (a native of Provence ensconced in Limoges) shared with the scholars in Mainz (R. Yehudah Ba'al Sefer ha-Dinim and R. Eli'ezer ha-Gadol) distinguished between civil and religious matters. In civil matters (as, for example, taxation) each community was sovereign, but not in religious ones. Were one community to be lax in, say, the eating of matzah on the eve of Passover or observance of the Sabbath, another community would be justified in excommunicating that community until it mended its ways. The local Jewish community is a fiscal entity only; religiously, all communities are indistinguishable parts of the Jewish people, and none can go its separate way.[86] In a religious age, this rule poses few if any problems. Ransoming captives, however, is a religious imperative; indeed, it is viewed as one of the supreme acts of charity. This being so, Troyes may have been out of line fiscally, but not religiously. Its excommunication of those who failed to participate in contributing towards the ransom money was thus valid. Indeed, one needn't leave this conclusion to inference; there is an explicit statement in *Bava Batra* that one may coerce others to contribute to charity.[87]

The term for coercion used in the passage in *Bava Batra* is *kefiyyah* (*akhpei*).[88] This term occurs dozens of times in the Talmud, invariably in the

[84] אין גוזרין גזירה על הצבור אלא אם כן רוב הצבור יכולין לעמוד בה *Bava Kamma* 79b, *'Avodah Zarah* 36a.

[85] Job 37: 23 (*lo metsanuha sagi koaḥ*), *Midrash Tanḥuma* (Warsaw, 1875), 'Ki Tissa', 10; *Shemot Rabbah* (Jerusalem, 2001), 'Terumah', 34: 1 (*she-'ein ha-kadosh-barukh hu ba bi-teraḥot 'im beriyotav*), cited by Grossman in the addenda to the second edition of his *Ḥakhmei Tsarfat ha-Rishonim* (Jerusalem, 2001), 608.

[86] R. Yosef Tov 'Elem made passing reference to this principle (and took it as axiomatic) in *Teshuvot R. Me'ir mi-Rotenburg* (Lemberg), #423: ובלבד שלא תהא עבריינות של תורה. It is spelled out more fully by R. Yehudah Ba'al Sefer ha-Dinim and R. Eli'ezer ha-Gadol towards the end of the responsum in the *Kol Bo*, #142, discussed above, p. 94.

[87] *Bava Batra* 8b.

[88] Ibid.

sense of physical constraint and, a fortiori, excommunication. There is another term used interchangeably with *kefiyyah*, namely, *'issui* (as in *get me'usseh*[89]). Once, and only once—in tractate *Ketubbot*[90]—it is used in the sense of applying moral pressure on the individual. R. Yosef invokes this passage in *Ketubbot* and explains (or, more accurately, explains away) the passage in *Bava Batra* as meaning insistent exhortation, social pressure rather than actual constraint. This exegesis demonstrates an extraordinary memory on the part of R. Yosef, a capacity to pass the vast corpus of the Bavli before his mind's eye and find the solitary instance that meets the needs of the case at hand. R. Yosef, however, was not finished with his analysis. He realized that his job was only half done. The question naturally arises: why is charity different from other religious imperatives whose enforcement admits of physical coercion and excommunication? Tucked between lengthy discussions of the laws of meat and milk in *Ḥullin* is a short passage of some four lines about honoring one's parents.[91] The Talmud explains there why the courts cannot coerce filial respect. R. Yosef invokes this source and demonstrates that the principle operative in filial respect equally bars coercion in matters of charity. Neither the word *'issui* nor *kefiyyah* is mentioned in this passage; a photographic memory and purely verbal association could never by themselves have summoned it up. Only the associative memory of a creative jurist blessed with a sovereign command of the entire legal corpus and a capacity to decode underlying principles and draw an analogy between them could have produced this neutralization of coercion and annulled the excommunication of Troyes. Strange indeed that such a talmudic master should be presented in contemporary historiography as rendering legal decisions on the basis of sermonic interpretations of biblical verses and sundry *aggadot*.

Let us turn to R. Yosef's third responsum that has been invoked as proof of his sermonic approach to legal issues.[92] It, too, treats communal organization, and one can already guess the general nature of the aggadic invocation. Some members of a community, after agreeing to a certain mode of assessment of taxes, reneged and refused to pay as assessed. They were excommunicated. They betook themselves to another town, whose members apparently viewed the excommunication as unjust and annulled it. The two men returned triumphant to their city, bearing proudly the text of the written annulment and spouting the biblical verse 'when the ram's horn sounds a long blast, they may go up on the mountains' (Exod. 19: 13), which, as I have mentioned above, is

89 *Gittin* 88b.

90 *Ketubbot* 53a.

91 *Ḥullin* 110b.

92 *Teshuvot R. Me'ir mi-Rotenburg* (Lemberg), #423, discussed in detail in *Shut ke-Makor Histori* (above, n. 11), 66–76.

the proof-text for the talmudic ruling that, under the appropriate circumstances, one court may annul the decrees of another court.[93] Stymied in their attempts to enforce fiscal discipline in their community, the members turned to R. Yosef to formulate exactly what powers a community possessed, what its limits were, and whether one community could annul the excommunication of another.

Again we witness questions that could arise only in the earliest stages of communal government. This should be qualified. The responsa of R. Meshullam of Lucca speak of communities imposing fines for assault and battery.[94] This, however, is but a rudimentary form of governance. Any group, including a wolf pack, must enforce order, must have ways of containing and punishing violence among its members. The responsum of Rabbenu Gershom that speaks of excommunication for the non-return of lost property reflects a more advanced stage of governance,[95] but one that simply enforces existing rights. When the group empowers itself to tax, it steps over a crucial line. The collectivity now seeks the right of forced exactions—to divest its members of property and to excommunicate those who resist such expropriation. It marks the transition to 'governance', the advent of the social group as a coercive unit, as taxation and military service are the two hallmarks of governmental coercion. All three responsa of R. Yosef reflect the transformation of the Jewish communities in France (probably in northern France only) from manifestations of group solidarity (public order and reciprocal help) to fiscal units of governance. One suspects that the Gentile powers-that-be began to impose taxes not on individual families or clans as before, but on this burgeoning group of relatively well-to-do *alieni*, and that it was the new communal taxation by the secular government that forced the Jewish communities in France into the role of corporations of enforcement—apportioning and extracting moneys from their members.[96]

Needless to say, R. Yosef Tov 'Elem upheld the power of each and every community to conduct its own fiscal affairs unimpeded by other communities, and he mocked and castigated the second community for its purported annulment of the excommunication of the neighboring settlement. However, he realized that this coercive power was both new and radical, and that resistance to this communal intrusion into the individual pocketbook was only natural.

93 *Betsah* 5a–b.

94 *Teshuvot Ge'onim Kadmonim*, ed. D. Cassel (Berlin, 1848), ##122, 125, 135; *Ginzei Schechter*, ii. 274. These responsa are discussed at length in *Shut ke-Makor Histori* (above, n. 11), 28–37.

95 *Teshuvot Ḥakhmei Tsarfat ve-Lotir*, #97; *Teshuvot Rabbenu Gershom*, #97, discussed in detail in my *Shut ke-Makor Histori* (above, n. 11), 46–53.

96 See my discussion in *Shut ke-Makor Histori* (above, n. 11), 72–4.

He therefore invoked every available source—legal and homiletic—and threw them into the fray, hoping not only to rule legally, which he did, fully documenting his position from the relevant sources in the Bavli, but also to sway people as to the justness and necessity of the new compulsory arrangements. Did he invoke biblical verses and *midrashim*? Most certainly. Did he base his ruling upon them? Absolutely not. They served a suasive function, as these texts have through the ages; only in the eleventh century, when the Bavli was still a closed text to almost all and its idiom unknown to most, biblical and midrashic quotations had a resonance and power in Ashkenazic society that they were never to have again.

CHAPTER FIVE

On the Use of Aggadah by the Tosafists: A Response to I. M. Ta-Shma

IN the previous chapter I argued against Avraham Grossman's contention that the halakhists of Early Ashkenaz drew on occasion on biblical verses and *midrashim* as proof-texts for their rulings. I. M. Ta-Shma endorsed Grossman's position and boldly extended its scope with a new contention.

IT IS RARE that an argument marshaled against a position proves to be an argument in its favor, but such is the case with I. M. Ta-Shma's article seeking to demonstrate that the Tosafists, no less than the scholars of Early Ashkenaz, invoked aggadic sources in halakhic arguments.[1] I had argued that such arguments were, in 99.9 percent of cases, an anathema both to the halakhists of pre-Crusade Ashkenaz and to those of the tosafist movement.[2] Indeed, I would extend this statement to all medieval halakhists. Aggadah-based halakhic arguments appear only when no directive for the matter at hand can be found in the halakhic sources; for example, for many customary religious practices (*minhagim*) or in certain aspects of communal self-government—an area in which there is precious little guidance in the normative talmudic literature. In Ashkenaz, such arguments also emerge when the culturally axiomatic is challenged to account for itself before the court of the Written Word. In these rare instances, such as suicide in the face of apostasy or even the murder of children to prevent their being raised as Christians and suffer eternal death,[3] the Tosafists drew upon aggadic material to justify the self-understood correctness of the long-hallowed practice of their community.

[1] 'Teshuvat Ri ha-Zaken be-Din Moser: Le-Tokpah shel ha-'Aggadah ba-Halakhah ha-'Ashkenazit', *Zion*, 68 (2003), 167–74, repr. in id., *Keneset Meḥkarim*: *'Iyyunim ba-Sifrut ha-Rabbanit bi-Yemei ha-Beinayim* (Jerusalem, 2010), iv. 159–68.

[2] See above, Ch. 4, and below, pp. 234–5.

[3] See pp. 230–61 below.

Professor Ta-Shma adduces a remarkable responsum by Ri ha-Zaken, the great Ri, in which he was asked on what basis the Talmud (*BK* 117a) allows the execution of informers who have not endangered anyone's life or limb by their crimes but who have caused their victim only financial loss.[4] Ri advances a number of perplexing arguments, one of which is the suggestion that there may be some biblical verse justifying this execution (ואפשר שיש שום פסו[ק] ע[ל] ז[ה])! Anyone who gives an allowance on the basis of the possible existence of a permissive biblical verse, though he doesn't know what that verse is, is effectively saying that the matter is permissible, with or without such a verse. When the question at bar is nothing less than the permissibility of killing someone, we may be sure that the decisor has never in his life entertained any doubts on the matter. The 'possible verse' that is invoked is simply an *asmakhta*, a hook on which to hang something known independently from the outset.

The same holds true for Ri's justifying the execution of informers by quoting an aggadah about neck-wringing on Yom Kippur. The Talmud says that one is permitted to wring the neck of an *'am ha-'arets* (ignoramus) even on Yom Kippur that falls on the Sabbath (i.e. the holiest possible day of the year).[5] Ri has not derived any conclusions from this dictum; he has simply used the aggadic passage as another form of *asmakhta*, a crutch-like proof-text on which to lean the practice that he is defending. There is a very simple test to see whether one is deriving the validity of B from A or whether one is simply using A as an *asmakhta*. I have employed this test in my discussion of the permissibility—indeed, the merit—of committing suicide when confronted with apostasy.[6] If B is indeed derived from A, for B to be valid, so must A. If Ri did in fact derive the permissibility of killing informers from that of killing an ignoramus, the latter must be a valid halakhic ruling. Does anyone imagine that Ri would actually permit killing an ignorant Jew on Yom Kippur that falls on the Sabbath, or on any other day of the year, for that matter?[7] Clearly, he is not deducing anything from this aggadah, but, fully convinced *ab initio* of the rightness of the talmudic ruling in *Bava Kamma*—one put into action by the Ashkenazic community[8]—he seeks to ground it somehow in other tal-

[4] In *Tummat Yesharim* (Venice, 1662), #202; printed as a separate unit in Lemberg in 1812 and in Warsaw in 1897. The latter has been widely photocopied.

[5] *Pesaḥim* 49b.

[6] See below, p. 241.

[7] See the geonic response to an attempt to invoke this passage with regard to a lesser matter of lost property in *Zikkaron la-Rishonim ve-gam la-'Aḥaronim*, ed. A. A. Harkavy (Berlin, 1887), #380 (p. 197): 'Does anyone with a brain in his head think that one can do so to any ignoramus?!' אטו אדם שיש לו מוח בקדקדו סובר שכל עם הארץ מותר לעשות בו כן.

[8] See e.g. *Teshuvot R. Me'ir mi-Rotenburg*, ed. M. A. Bloch (Berlin, 1891), #137 (p. 208); *Teshuvot*

mudic texts or in some unknown biblical proof-verse. This scarcely proves Grossman's case as Ta-Shma claims.[9] Grossman claims that argument from aggadah was made in such bread-and-butter cases of halakhah as mourning on Purim, priestly blessings, inverting oaths (*mepakh shevu'ah*), guardianship of minors, and the like. In topics such as these we never find midrashic arguments being employed substantively and halakhic conclusions actually deduced from aggadah. Ri's argument for the execution of informers is not a deduction of any sort; it is simply another rare instance when the culturally axiomatic invokes a text of any sort—here of the wildest sort—as an *asmakhta*.

In an earlier article Ta-Shma defended Grossman's position from a different vantage point: the penance books of the German Pietists.[10] I attempted to dispose of his argument in a very brief footnote to a passage in my article on martyrdom (see Chapter 9 below), which I will cite here:

We further find the following story in *Kiddushin* (40a): 'Rav Kahana sold baskets. A married woman propositioned him. He said to her, "I will [first] go and adorn myself." He went up to the roof and threw himself to the earth.'

If aggadic passages may serve as normative directives in such cases, as Rabbenu Tam here assumes, suicide may then be permitted when a great man dies or when witnessing a national tragedy or to avoid mortal sin. And this does not conclude the list. There are some nine passages in the aggadic literature that narrate cases of suicide with various shades of approval. The talmudic position is far from clear if one works with aggadah, yet no discussion of the permissibility of suicide is found in the tosafist literature. Clearly, the Tosafists do not accord these sundry aggadic passages normative status; rather, they accord normative status only to those passages that treat suicide in cases of prospective martyrdom. It is the question of the permissibility of *these* suicides that is on their mind and to which they know the answer in advance,

R. Me'ir mi-Rotenburg, ed. M. A. Bloch (Prague and Budapest, 1895), #385; *Teshuvot R. Me'ir mi-Rotenburg*, ed. R. N. N. Rabbinowicz (Lemberg, 1860), #247. (On the Prague and Budapest edition see above, Ch. 3, n. 43 end.)

9 A. Grossman, 'Zikatah shel Yahadut Ashkenaz ha-Kedumah el Erets Yisra'el', *Shalem*, 3 (1981), 67–74; id., *Ḥakhmei Ashkenaz ha-Rishonim: Koroteihem, Darkam be-Hanhagat ha-Tsibbur, Yetsiratam ha-Ruḥanit mi-Reshit Yishuvam ve-'ad li-Gezerot Tatnu (1096)* (Jerusalem, 1981), 155–8, 204, 429–34; id., 'Shorashav shel Kiddush ha-Shem be-'Ashkenaz ha-Kedumah', in Y. M. Gafni and A. Ravitzky, eds., *Kedushat ha-Ḥayyim ve-Ḥeruf ha-Nefesh: Kovets Ma'amarim le-Zikhro shel Amir Yekuti'el* (Jerusalem, 1993), 107–8; id., *Ḥakhmei Tsarfat ha-Rishonim: Koroteihem, Darkam be-Hanhagat ha-Tsibbur, Yetsiratam ha-Ruḥanit* (Jerusalem, 1995), 69–70. See my discussion in Chapter 4 above, pp. 85–95.

10 'Hit'abdut ve-Retsaḥ ha-Zulat 'al Kiddush ha-Shem: Li-She'elat Mekomah shel ha-'Aggadah be-Masoret ha-Pesikah ha-'Ashkenazit', in Y. T. Assis et al., eds., *Yehudim mul ha-Tselav: Gezerot Tatnu ba-Historyah u-va-Historiografyah* (Jerusalem, 2000), 150–6, repr. in id., *Keneset Meḥkarim: 'Iyyunim ba-Sifrut ha-Rabbanit bi-Yemei ha-Beinayim* (Jerusalem, 2004), i. 388–94.

regardless of what may or may not be inferred from the passages themselves, for it is only 'logical' that they are permitted.

Revealingly, the German Pietists cited the above passage in *Kiddushin* (or another in the same vein) when they explored whether one may commit suicide as penance for a sin that merited the death penalty. Finding no such allowance in the halakhic literature, they also felt that a lacuna must exist and turned to the aggadic passages for guidance and, needless to say, swiftly found it there. Neither the Tosafists nor the German Pietists discussed the permissibility of suicide in all its permutations, only in the circumscribed cases that deeply interested them. Both turned to aggadah only in the specific instance and on the specific topics where their religious intuition had previously informed them that further norms and guidelines simply had to exist. Not surprisingly, they proceeded to find what they sought. For the German Pietists to do so was simply par for the course; their work is replete with new religious dictates encoded in Scripture and aggadah and divined by hasidic intuition. Indeed, their newly discovered *retson ha-bore* is the *raison d'être* of the movement. However, for Rabbenu Tam to do so—and on an issue no smaller than self-murder—is singular, to put it mildly.[11]

At the end of this passage there is a footnote containing the reference 'I. M. Ta-Shma, 'Hit'abdut ve-Retsaḥ ha-Zulat', the article currently under discussion, which claims that the Tosafists, the halakhists par excellence of Ashkenaz, resolved halakhic issues by recourse to *midrashim*. Can anyone adduce a single instance where an aggadah was invoked by any Tosafist to resolve a question about the thirty-nine forbidden acts of the Sabbath (*avot melakhot*) or about the possession of leavened food (*ḥamets*) on Passover, or in discussions about torts, estates, contracts, or marital law? Can anyone find R. El'azar ha-Roke'aḥ doing so?

As for the case of penance that Ta-Shma adduces in that article: R. El'azar ha-Roke'aḥ was both a Tosafist and a German Pietist, and, as a Pietist, he believed, together with his teacher/colleague R. Yehudah he-Ḥasid, that the canonical corpus did not give full expression to the Divine will in its plenitude.[12] R. Yehudah felt this to be so in many areas; R. El'azar felt it strongly in at least one—that of penance. Both proceeded to discover what they sought—what their deepest religious instincts told them *had* to exist—in the aggadic literature. However, outside of this central area of Pietistic concern—the wholly new field of penance, a subject never discussed in the Talmud—there is no use of aggadah whatsoever in serious halakhic discussions by R. El'azar

[11] Below, pp. 235–41. I have omitted the footnotes from my quotation.

[12] See H. Soloveitchik, 'Three Themes in *Sefer Hasidim*', *AJS Review*, 1 (1976), 311–25. This essay will appear in the third volume of this series.

Roke'aḥ in any of his halakhic writings—not in his well-known *Sefer ha-Roke'aḥ*, nor in his little treatise on the laws of Passover, nor in the extensive discussions in his newly available *Ma'aseh Roke'aḥ*.[13]

13 *Sefer ha-Roke'aḥ* (Fano, 1505); *R. Ele'azar mi-Vormaiza, Derashah le-Fesaḥ*, ed. S. Emanuel (Jerusalem, 2006); E. Kozma, 'Critical Editions of the Works Ma'aseh Roke'ach and Sha'are Shchitah u-Trefot by R. Eleazar of Worms', at <http://imhm.blogspot.co.uk/2010/02/critical-editions-of-works-maaseh.html>. On the *Ma'aseh Roke'aḥ*, see Emanuel's introduction to the *Derashah le-Fesaḥ*, 14–41. I exclude, naturally, those instances (mentioned at the outset of the essay) where halakhists at all times have drawn on *midrashim*, namely, when no directive for the matter at hand can be found in the canonical halakhic sources, as, for example, in many instances of customary religious practices (*minhagim*) or in most aspects of communal self-government.

CHAPTER SIX

Characterizing Medieval Talmudists: A Case Study

IN HIS INDISPENSABLE STUDY *Ḥakhmei Ashkenaz ha-Rishonim*, Avraham Grossman has characterized R. Shelomoh b. Shimshon (Rabbenu Sasson) as a decisor (*posek*) who tended towards stringency without serious regard to the economic cost of his rulings. Moreover, he 'opposed innovation, making any changes in the status quo', and he 'preserved custom studiously and defended the received communal practices with zeal'. Following Grossman, Rami Reiner recently extended Rabbenu Sasson's conservative outlook to include a blind acceptance of the *Halakhot Gedolot*.[1] Grossman and Reiner naturally document these assessments. I have doubts about the aptness of their portrayal and would like to scrutinize the various pieces of evidence that they have adduced. In treating the issues invoked by Grossman I have an unfair advantage, as I have spent many years of my life studying three of them. One could hardly expect Grossman to have spent as much time on every ruling cited in his 450-page book as I have spent on these three. My remarks, thus, should be taken as a correction but not in any way as a criticism of his scholarship.

This essay does, however, highlight a problem in writing the history of halakhah. Can one reliably characterize a halakhist by merely citing phrases employed by him without studying the thought expressed in those words? Some would argue that this would place an impossible burden on the prosopographer, as it would require a study of every topic on which every important member of the group under scrutiny has written. Use this rule, it will be said, and you will get no characterizations at all. Others would contend that no characterizations are preferable to questionable ones, especially as other scholars then use these intellectual portraits to draw new conclusions that are even further off the mark.

[1] A. Grossman, *Ḥakhmei Ashkenaz ha-Rishonim: Koroteihem, Darkam be-Hanhagat ha-Tsibbur, Yetsiratam ha-Ruḥanit mi-Reshit Yishuvam ve-'ad li-Gezerot Tatnu (1096)* (Jerusalem, 1980), 334–7.

I would like to suggest a middle path. One need not make a large-scale research project out of each topic. That clearly would place an intolerable burden on the biographer. Rather, one should study the relevant *sugya* with the basic medieval commentators (*rishonim*) to get a sense of the parameters of the issue in halakhah. Then one contextualizes the topic, focusing in greater detail on the texts of the culture in which the halakhists arose, so as to better assess the doctrine and its proponent. To give a rough yardstick of what I have in mind: evaluating a figure from Ashkenaz, for example, would entail studying a *sugya* with most of the medieval commentators who would be mentioned in the notes of a Mossad Harav Kook edition of, say, the *Ḥiddushei ha-Rashba*, and then checking the type of Ashkenazic sources that would appear in a note in Aptowitzer's edition of *Sefer Ravyah*. One need not seek to duplicate the remarkable range of Aptowitzer's references, but the fundamental works to which he refers (such as the *Sifrut de-Vei Rashi*, *Sefer Ravyah*, *Or Zarua'*, *Sefer Maharil: Minhagim*, and the like) are eminently available for reasonably swift study. I realize that opinions can readily differ. I offer this essay to illustrate the dangers of what happens when the middle path is not taken. Needless to say, the essay also has its intrinsic purpose: to correct the image of Rabbenu Sasson current in the historiography of Early Ashkenaz.

I

To document the characterization of stringency and disregard for the high price to be paid by the community for strict observance of the law, Grossman cites three rulings by Rabbenu Sasson: one on moneylending, which he states goes against the allowances of Rabbenu Gershom and Rashi,[2] a famous ruling on shipping Jewish wine, and a decision in *terefot* that was strongly disputed by Rashi.

Ma'arufya in Jewish–Gentile Moneylending

Rabbenu Sasson's ruling on moneylending is against that of Rabbenu Gershom but conflicts with nothing written by Rashi. I have discussed this ruling in my essay on pawnbroking.[3] Jews in the eleventh century still functioned as factotums or managers of Gentile business affairs (*ma'arufya* is the strange term by which medieval sources refer to them[4]). These managers provided

[2] Ibid. 335–6.

[3] See 'Pawnbroking—A Study in *Ribbit* and of the Halakhah in Exile', in the first volume of this series (*Collected Essays* [Oxford, 2013], i. 57–166: see pp. 110–12).

[4] On the origin of the term, see most recently A. Grossman, *Ḥakhmei Tsarfat ha-Rishonim:*

their co-religionists with vital access to capital. The talmudic ruling *ein sheliḥut le-goy*, namely, that a Jew could not serve as a Gentile's agent, nor could a Gentile serve as a Jew's agent, cut off the availability of such funds. In a loan between a Gentile and a Jew where a *ma'arufya* was the middleman, the Jewish manager would not be the Gentile's agent lending the latter's money, but the principal of an interest-bearing loan to another Jew.

Needless to say, this imposed an intolerable hardship on Jewish commercial activity. Rabbenu Gershom solved the problem by a judicial construction. The Jewish manager was not the Gentile's agent to lend to the Jew; he should rather be viewed as the agent of the Jewish borrower to obtain a loan from the Gentile. This is a radical step. It is roughly equivalent to claiming that the manager of a modern bank is not the agent of the bank to take the depositor's money for the bank, but the depositor's agent to give his money to the bank.[5] Not surprisingly, there were dissenting voices. Rabbenu Sasson was willing to go along with this construction if the Jewish agency was stipulated—that is, if the Jewish borrower (or lender as the case may be) stated specifically that the Jewish middleman was functioning as his agent and not acting on the Gentile's behalf.[6] This was still a considerable step for, in reality, the manager was the Gentile's agent, explicit statements or silent constructions to the contrary notwithstanding. That Rabbenu Sasson here is less bold in his allowance than Rabbenu Gershom is unquestioned; whether that makes him indifferent to the economic consequences of halakhic rulings is less obvious. All the established practices of moneylending with a *ma'arufya* could continue as before; only now one of the parties would have to recite a formula of agency. This does not seem an onerous burden or one obstructive of commerce. True, this new requirement never won acceptance. This, however, was not because it was so taxing, but because Rabbenu Sasson's authority never equaled Rabbenu Gershom's, and Rabbenu Gershom's construction was the older and the easier of the two.

Moreover, Rabbenu Sasson added a further proviso.[7] While he was of the view that agency had to be stipulated, nevertheless, if no such stipulation took place, restitution of the interest should not be ordered by his court, for in the

Koroteihem, Darkam be-Hanhagat ha-Tsibbur, Yetsiratam ha-Ruḥanit mi-Reshit Yishuvam ve-'ad li-Gezerot Tatnu, 2nd edn. (Jerusalem, 2001), 556 n. 61, and R. (Richard) Steiner, ''Akkevot Leshoniyim shel Soḥarim Yehudim mi-'Artsot ha-'Islam ba-Mamlakhah ha-Frankit', *Leshonenu*, 73 (2011), 352–7.

5 *Shibbolei ha-Leket II*, ed. M. Z. Hasida (Jerusalem, 1969), #45, p. 79; ed. S. Hasida (Jerusalem, 1988), #45, p. 169. For the parallel passages and the two editions of the *Shibbolei ha-Leket II*, see *Collected Essays*, i. 98 n. 98(C), 118 n. 140(A).

6 *Teshuvot Ḥakhmei Tsarfat ve-Lotir*, ed. J. Müller (Vienna, 1881), #56, and see 'Pawnbroking', 110–11.

7 Ibid.

final analysis the interest was being paid by the Gentile and not by his Jewish *ma'arufya*. He remained faithful to the Rhineland tradition that the enforcement of the usury injunction should be restricted to those cases where the interest was, in fact, being paid by the Jew. If the halakhic formalities of *ein sheliḥut le-goy* distorted the fiscal reality by detaching the actual from the formal principal, judicial construction should intervene to restore the real relations and turn the actual borrower (or lender) into the legal one. Failing that, the courts should never enforce usury judgments on the basis of a legal rule that misrepresented the underlying economic facts of the case. Rabbenu Sasson's position here appears eminently realistic.

Covering a Wine Cask Destined for Transportation by Gentiles

In talmudic times wine casks were made of clay. This ensured the hermetic sealing off of the wine from the air, thus allowing it to age without oxidation. No less important from a Jewish point of view, this also guaranteed that Gentile wagon drivers transporting the wine had access to the wine only through the bunghole. If the latter was sealed adequately, the wine could be shipped without Jewish supervision and the recipient was assured of its *kashrut* as long as the seal on the bunghole had not been tampered with. Europe, however, went over to using wood for barrels in the early centuries of the Common Era because wooden barrels weighed far less than their clay counterparts; northern Europe had always used barrels of this type, for there was rarely enough sun to bake an amphora, while wood was found in abundance as settlements were surrounded by vast forests.[8]

Making an airtight wooden barrel requires great skill, and the coopers of the Middle Ages were not up to the task. As a result, there were tiny spaces between the staves and, especially, between the staves and the heads (the circular top and bottom) of the barrel. Thus not only could wine not be aged but it also spoiled very rapidly, as fermentation is an anaerobic process; exposure to air only hastens oxidation and acidification. The most that could be done was to stop the small gaps with rags and straw. Nothing was easier than to insert a knife between the staves and help oneself to a bit of wine; and this was exactly what wagon drivers did.[9]

Seeking to prevent such unwanted intrusions, the rabbinical authorities of Mainz and Worms in the eleventh century demanded that each and every

[8] H. Soloveitchik, *Ha-Yayin bi-Yemei ha-Beinayim: Yein Nesekh—Perek be-Toledot ha-Halakhah be-'Ashkenaz* (Jerusalem, 2008), 82–6.

[9] Ibid. 242–4.

barrel that was to be transported without Jewish supervision be wrapped in cloth and the sack sealed. This imposed a considerable financial burden on the Jews, as every inch of cloth was hand-woven and, what's more, before the Industrial Revolution every thread of the cloth was handspun. This new requirement is associated with the name of R. Yitsḥak b. Yehudah, as Rashi famously corresponded with him about it; however, upon closer inspection it would appear that he simply lent the considerable weight of his authority to a pre-existing decree.[10] One is not surprised to discover that Rabbenu Sasson in Worms joined in insisting upon wrapped barrels.[11]

We are not dealing here with a mindless stringency. The danger was only too real. Rashi advocated abandoning the ruling because it imposed great, indeed unbearable, hardship upon the community of Troyes, and he believed that such harsh demands should be made only of the talmudically requisite.[12] To go beyond the letter of the law when genuine hardship was at stake was impermissible. This tells us a great deal about Rashi's posture in halakhic adjudication; it does not mean, however, that the proponents of wrapping were stringency seekers. If Rabbenu Sasson was indifferent to economic hardship, so too was his colleague, R. Yitsḥak b. Yehudah, as well as the rest of the German rabbinical establishment at the time. There is nothing singular in his position.

And the simple fact is that the German Jewish community continued to ship all wine sent to England in individual wrappings for another 150 years, long after both Rashi and Rabbenu Tam had announced that this was superfluous as the demand for wrapping was without talmudic basis.[13] What seemed impossible in France proved to be eminently, indeed, proudly, possible in Germany.

The argument might be made that the situation in Troyes differed from that in the Rhineland. Troyes was situated in an area inhospitable to viticulture; almost all wine for consumption had to be brought from afar.[14] Worms and Mainz, on the other hand, were located in a classically rich viticultural zone.[15] There was little need for long-distance transportation to meet the needs of consumption and, in the eleventh century, German trade in kosher wine (the Cologne–London axis) was still marginal as the Jewish community in England was in its infancy, if it existed at all.[16] This may well be true, but then we have no basis for contrasting Rabbenu Sasson's attitude with that of Rashi and speaking of the former's indifference to economic hardship.

10 Soloveitchik, *Ha-Yayin bi-Yemei ha-Beinayim* (above, n. 8), 242–4 n. 21.

11 Ibid., n. 22.

12 Ibid. 254–6.

13 Ibid. 246–50.

14 Ibid. 41–50.

15 Ibid. 37–40.

16 Ibid. 247–50.

Pelugat ha-re'ah

Grossman suggests that in the famous controversy between Rashi and his teachers—*pelugat ha-re'ah*, the debate over whether or not an animal was kosher if, after its slaughter, its lungs disappeared before inspection—the initiator of the opposition to Rashi's allowance was Rabbenu Sasson. He bases this on a passage in the *Shibbolei ha-Leket* where Rabbenu Sasson is singled out:

המורה רבנא ששון ונדיבי מלכות לותיר וכל החכמים עמו הסכימו לדעה אחת לאסור בהמה שלא נבדקה

And Rabbenu Sasson and the eminent men of the kingdom of Lotharingia and all the scholars with him [*sic*] agreed unanimously [or: arrived at a unified position] to forbid an animal which had not been inspected.

If, however, one reconstructs the sequence of events, this interpretation becomes untenable as the initiator of the clash—surprisingly enough—was Rashi.[17]

The story began in Cologne, where a ritual slaughterer had forgotten to inspect the lung before it was handled by others and inspection was thus rendered meaningless. There, an otherwise unknown R. Asher b. David ha-Levi (son of the famous R. David ha-Levi) declared the animal kosher. There was apparently no clear precedent for this case, and R. Asher passed it on to his brothers in Mainz, who thought he had ruled correctly. They were overruled by R. Yitsḥak b. Yehudah, the head of the Mainz academy, and his responsum has come down to us. He was then joined by R. Yitsḥak ha-Levi of Worms and Rabbenu Sasson. R. Yitsḥak's responsum has also been preserved. We don't know of any responsum actually written on the subject by Rabbenu Sasson; on the basis of the available evidence, it would seem that he simply concurred with the decision of his colleagues. Unbeknown to the German

[17] Determining the exact sequence of events (e.g. whether R. Me'ir of Ramerupt initially forbade an unchecked lung, and if so, at what stage of the evolving controversy this occurred) is a difficult and, perhaps, impossible task, as is establishing what the most authentic texts of some of the responsa penned in this controversy are. However, the general sequence of events is clear, as are the halakhic contents of the correspondence. In my presentation I have drawn on an unpublished seminar paper (Spring 2006) by Shemuel Herzfeld for clarification of some of these issues. See now A. Schremer, 'Shikul Da'at Hilkhati: "Pelugat ha-Re'ah" u-Meḥkar ha-Halakhah ha-Bikorti', *Dine Israel*, 28 (2011), 101–13; M. Amar, 'Ha-Maḥloket bein Rashi ve-Rabbotav bi-"Felugat ha-Re'ah" ve-Hashpa'at Laḥatsei ha-Sevivah', in A. Cohen, ed., *Rashi u-Vet Midrasho* (Ramat Gan, 2013), 168–70. Schremer sees Rashi as having been drawn into the controversy by one of the sides. However, Rabbenu Sasson played no larger a role in his reconstruction than in mine.

scholars, Rashi had allowed a similar case in Troyes. When Rashi heard of the rulings of his teachers (possibly via his son-in-law, R. Me'ir of Ramerupt, who was in Worms at the time), he wrote separately to both R. Yitsḥak and R. Yitsḥak b. Yehudah and deferentially asked the reasons for their rulings, for he had difficulty understanding what he had been told. Thus began the lengthy exchange of letters known in the history of halakhah as the *pelugat ha-re'ah*. No one organized any resistance to Rashi's allowance; the clash was occasioned by Rashi himself. It was he who informed his former teachers of his allowance and directly challenged, if ever so politely, their unanimous holding.[18]

II

To document his claim that Rabbenu Sasson was a traditionalist opposed to the innovations of his colleague R. Yitsḥak ha-Levi, Grossman cites three cases: their controversy as regards the Torah reading on Shemini 'Atseret, vinegar touched by a Gentile, and the inclusion of the biblical verses dealing with the Temple offerings in the *musaf* prayer of Rosh Hashanah.

Let us take each piece of evidence in turn.

The Torah Reading on Shemini 'Atseret

I must confess that I do not follow Grossman's claim that the reading of 'Kol ha-bekhor' on Shemini 'Atseret was an innovation of R. Yitsḥak ha-Levi, which Rabbenu Sasson tried to overturn in favor of the traditional practice of reading ''Asser te'asser'. The reading of 'Kol ha-bekhor' was the Babylonian rite, as attested by authorities such as R. Hai Gaon, the *Halakhot Gedolot*, the *Hilkhot Re'u*, and the *Siddur R. 'Amram Ga'on*. It was also the practice in

[18] Sources: A. Marmorstein, 'Ḥakham u-Fosek Italki', *Devir*, 2 (1924), 233–9, printed from MS New York, Jewish Theological Seminary ENA 2717 (subsequently reclassified as Rabbinica 1087), fos. 133b–134a (old pagination); *Sefer ha-Pardes*, ed. H. L. Ehrenreich (Budapest, 1924), 169–70; *Sefer ha-Neyar*, ed. G. Appel, rev. edn. (Jerusalem, 1994), 100–1, printed from MS New York, Jewish Theological Seminary 8259, fo. 68b; excerpted by A. Berliner from a *Sefer Issur ve-Heter* 'attributed to Rashi' in his supplementary introduction (*Likkutei Batar Likkutei*) to *Maḥzor Vitry*, ed. S. Hurwitz (Nuremberg, 1923), 174–6 (it is not found in *Sefer Issur ve-Heter*, MS Frankfurt am Main, Stadts- und Universitätsbibliothek, 8vo 69, the classic source of the work that issued from Rashi's school); *Shibbolei ha-Leket II*, ed. M. Z. Hasida, #27, 41–4; ed. S. Hasida, #27, pp. 90–5 (see above, n. 5); *Ma'aseh ha-Ge'onim*, ed. A. Epstein and J. Freimann (Berlin, 1910), #92, pp. 87–91; *Or Zarua'*, ii (Zhitomir, 1862), *Terefot*, #411, fo. 58a–b; MS New York, Jewish Theological Seminary, R. 673, fos. 126–7, printed by I. Elfenbein in *Teshuvot Rashi* (New York, 1943), #60. Elfenbein (ibid. and in ##61–2) reprinted and annotated a number of the above-cited texts.

Muslim Spain, as we are informed by R. Yitsḥak ibn Gi'at. The ruling in the Talmud to read 'Kol ha-bekhor' on Shemini 'Atseret is cited without qualification both by R. Yitsḥak of Fez (Alfasi) and by Maimonides. It was equally the rite of Italy and Provence, as attested by the *Shibbolei ha-Leket*, the *Sefer ha-'Ittur*, and the *Sefer ha-Manhig*, and the latter remarks that this was also the practice in Christian Spain.[19] If Jewish communities in Babylonia, North Africa, Italy, Provence, and both Muslim and Christian Spain, one and all, read 'Kol ha-bekhor', why should one assume that Ashkenazic practice was any different? Grossman cites a passage in the *Ma'aseh ha-Ge'onim* that tells of R. Sasson's reading "Asser te'asser' on Shemini 'Atseret in Worms against the general consensus, and which records the sons of R. Yitsḥak ha-Levi as saying that in their father's day this would never have happened.[20] My understanding of the passage is not that they are stating that 'Kol ha-bekhor' was an innovation of their father, but that any attempt to alter the established practice of 'Kol ha-bekhor' could never have occurred in the days of their father, a man characterized by Rashi as a strong-willed leader in clear control of his community: **שהיה דָבָר ומנהיג לדור ועל פיו יצאו ויבואו** ('the chief and leader of his generation, by whose word they went out and they came in').[21]

[19] The relevant sources can all be found in V. Aptowitzer's notes to *Sefer Ravyah*, ii (repr. New York, 1983), *Megillah*, #595, p. 328 n. 14, and those of C. Albeck to *Sefer ha-'Eshkol*, ed. S. Albeck (Jerusalem, 1935), i. 177 n. 13, 178 nn. 1–5. They are equally to be found in *Sefer ha-Manhig*, ed. Y. Rafael (Jerusalem, 1978), ii. 411–12 nn. 65–75. (The latter also contains, surprisingly enough, references to scholarly articles on the subject, e.g. those of Fleischer and Fried cited below.) The issue has recently been discussed by H. Y. Tesler in 'Minhagei Keri'ah be-Yom Shemini 'Atseret', *Yerushatenu*, 6 (2012), 224–43. (I differ from him with respect to the position of Rav Hai Gaon.)

[20] #52, p. 41:

ובאותו יום שמיני ספק שביעי התחיל החזן (וקורא) [וקרא] מן עשר תעשר, [ו]לא היה יום שבת, ועשה כרצון רבינו שלמה ושלא כרצון כל החכמים. וזהו טעמו של רבינו שלמה כדגרסי' במסכת מגילה (לא ע"א) ביום האחרון של חג קורא במצות וחוקים ובכור. והכי משמע ליה—היינו עשר תעשר (ו)פרש[ה] שכת[וב] בה הרבה מצות וכל הבכור. (והחולקים) [וחולקין] עליו רבותינו הלוים [ו]אומ[רים] שמעולם לא ראינו כן בפני אביהם רבינו יצחק הלוי ר"נ אלא עשר תעשר היו קור[א]ין בספק שביעי שחל להיות בשבת משום ז' גברי.

[21] *Or Zarua'*, ii, '*Eruvin*, #140; Or 'Etsyon edn. (Jerusalem, 2001), 495. See my remarks above, Ch. 3 n. 38. Rashi alludes to Num. 27: 16–17: 'Moses spoke to the Lord saying . . . appoint someone over the community . . . who shall go out before them and come in before them and who shall take them out and bring them in, so that the Lord's community may not be like sheep that have no shepherd.' The parallel passages (e.g. *Siddur Rashi*, ed. J. Freimann [Berlin, 1912], #174, p. 80; *Maḥzor Vitry*, ed. S. Hurwitz [Nuremberg, 1923], #321, p. 358; ed. E. Goldschmidt [Jerusalem, 2009], #34, p. 704; *Shibbolei ha-Leket ha-Shalem*, ed. S. Buber [Vilna, 1887], #290, pp. 271–2) lack this phrase. However, Grossman correctly points out (*Ḥakhmei Ashkenaz ha-Rishonim* [above, n. 1], 282 n. 93) that there would be no reason for a scribe to add them. Be the authenticity of the phrase as it may, R. Yitsḥak ha-Levi's boldness has been well documented by Grossman (pp. 282–5).

The person who suggested introducing the reading of ''Asser te'asser' was Rashi, and Rabbenu Sasson, far from being a conservative, emerges as someone who, seeing truth in the view of a brilliant younger colleague, was ready to put it into practice, even if it meant breaking with tradition.[22] Admittedly, Rashi believed that reading ''Asser te'asser' on Shemini 'Atseret had been the practice in the time of R. El'azar Kalir, and one could argue that this fact played a role in persuading R. Sasson. He would then have viewed himself as did Rashi: not as an innovator but as the restorer of a lost tradition. However, if he did know of the argument based on Kalir, it is astonishing that he did not cite it when the uproar in Worms occurred. In response to the suggestion that Rabbenu Sasson may have represented unawares an old Palestinian tradition, Ezra Fleischer has shown that no such Palestinian practice ever existed. Genizah documents reveal that the festival for which Kalir wrote the liturgical poem was the Sabbath of *ḥol ha-mo'ed* of Sukkot, not Shemini 'Atseret.[23]

How the Palestinian–Spanish version of the *sugya* in *Megillah* 31a,[24] which referred to other readings alongside 'Kol ha-bekhor' on Shemini 'Atseret, reached Rashi and one of the Makirites is a separate story,[25] but there is no plausible reason to assume that the reading of 'Kol ha-bekhor' on Shemini 'Atseret was an innovation of R. Yitsḥak ha-Levi. It was the traditional read-

[22] Another plausible reading of the passage could have it that the aforementioned 'R. Shelomoh' in the *Ma'aseh ha-Ge'onim* refers to Rashi, not to Rabbenu Sasson. To the natural objection—Who would introduce an innovation in Worms contrary to its traditions?—I would simply answer that someone was bold enough to do so. This would be contrarian but not inconceivable at the turn of the 12th century, when Rashi's commanding role in halakhah was apparent to all. I simply offer this suggestion to those who find an innovatory role for Rabbenu Sasson unimaginable.

[23] E. Fleischer, 'Parashat 'Asser Te'asser u-Keri'atah bi-Yemot Ḥag le-fi Minhagot Erets Yisra'el', *Tarbiz*, 36 (1967), 116–55.

[24] R. Avraham of Narbonne writes *ve-yesh be-sifrei Sefarad* and R. Hai Gaon is aware of the existence of such a version—*shama'nu ki siman hu*—probably from Palestinian copies of the Bavli, as they too had this version, though they understood it in a wholly different manner, as R. Hai goes on to explain. See *Sefer ha-'Eshkol*, 177–8; *Sefer ha-Manhig*, ii. 411–12; R. Yitsḥak ibn Gi'at, *Sha'arei Simḥah*, ed. Y. D. H. Bamberger (Fürth, 1861), i. 117. See also N. Brüll, 'Die Entstehungsgeschichte des babylonischen Talmuds als Schriftswerkes', *Jahrbücher für jüdische Geshichte und Literatur*, 2 (1876), 119–21.

[25] Rashi and, subsequently, one of the Makirites obtained a copy of this text, but did not know of the responsum of R. Hai Gaon. See Rashi, *Megillah* 31a, s.v. *korin kol ha-bekhor*; *Siddur Rashi*, #306, p. 147; *Maḥzor Vitry*, ed. Hurwitz, #384, pp. 445–6; ed. Goldschmidt, #107, pp. 939–42; *Ma'aseh ha-Ge'onim*, #52, p. 41, s.v. *u-matsati*. On the wide range of texts available to 11th-century scholars of the Rhineland and equally to Rashi, see H. Soloveitchik, *Ha-Yayin bi-Yemei ha-Beinayim* (above, n. 8), 327–43. (There is much to be learnt from N. Fried's article 'Haftarot Alternativiyot be-Fiyyutei Yannai u-She'ar Paytanim Kedumim', *Sinai*, 62 [1968], 50–66, 127–41. However, his suggestion [pp. 56–7] that a small town in Champagne, such as Troyes in the 11th century, had an independent tradition of liturgical readings unknown to Rhineland Jewry and going back to Palestine before the destruction of the Second Temple [70 CE], seems to me, at least, somewhat fanciful.)

ing of German Jewish communities in the eleventh century for the festival and continued to be so for well over half a millennium,[26] and Rabbenu Sasson, in advocating a different reading, is revealed as the antithesis of a traditionalist.

Vinegar Touched by a Gentile

Again, the picture is somewhat altered by context.[27] Expanding the ban on Gentile wine to include vinegar was not some odd stringency. Both the Rhineland and the Champagne communities were fairly close to the northern border of viticulture. If the winter lingered too long or the summer was too cloudy, the grapes did not fully mature. People, nevertheless, were desperate for some alcoholic drink. Old wine that had soured or wine made from unripe grapes was of considerable value; it could be drunk straight or with water, and the mix could still lift the spirits. As mentioned above, the barrels were poorly constructed, with air seeping in from all sides. Few wines lasted more than six months; rarer still were wines that lasted a full year. In England it was permissible to sell wine from the last harvest up until the day when the ships from France or Germany docked with wine from the new harvest. The moment they dropped anchor, all sale of old wine was forbidden as the presumption was that it had acidified. Whether this trade regulation was observed is another question, as acidified wine retained some value. We have the records of a tax assessor in Rheims in the years 1387–8: new wine is assessed in 1387 at 48 *sous* a *queue* (400 liters), wine two years old at 20 *sous* a *queue*, and three years old at 14 *sous* a *queue*. The next year (1388) the value of the same amount of two-year-old wine had risen to 40 *sous*. This is what Rabbenu Tam had in mind when he insisted that the ban on vinegar should not be lifted for 'it is a common sight—it occurs often—that some call the liquid "vinegar", while others recite over it both kiddush and *havdalah*'.[28] The difference between the taste of wine and that of vinegar, so stark and clear in subtropical Palestine and

[26] *Teshuvot, Pesakim u-Minhagim shel R. Me'ir mi-Rotenburg*, ed. Y. Z. Cahana (Jerusalem, 1962), iii. 35–6; *Sefer ha-Minhagim le-Rabbenu Avraham Klauzner*, ed. S. J. Spitzer (Jerusalem, 2006), #61, p. 53; *Sefer Maharil: Minhagim*, ed. S. J. Spitzer (Jerusalem, 1989), #13, p. 388; *Minhagot Vermaiza shel Yehudah Liva Kirkhom*, ed. Y. M. Peles (Jerusalem, 1987), 191; *Minhagim de-Kehillah Kedoshah Vormaiza le-R. Yuzpa ha-Shamash*, ed. B. S. Hamburger et al. (Jerusalem, 1992), ii. 221, 224.

[27] I have treated the ban on vinegar in *Ha-Yayin bi-Yemei ha-Beinayim* (above, n. 8), 375–9. I had doubts then whether the injunction was the product of a formal ban or arose by popular intuition, what J. Katz called 'ritual instinct' in *The Shabbes Goy: A Study in Halakhic Flexibility* (Philadelphia, 1989), 227–36 and *passim*. I now fully believe that it was the latter.

[28] *Ha-Yayin bi-Yemei ha-Beinayim*, 82–6. The citation of Rabbenu Tam comes from *Sefer ha-Yashar, Teshuvot*, ed. S. F. Rosenthal (Berlin, 1898), #45: 1: ועוד מעשים בכל יום פעמים רבות, יש שקוראין אותו חומץ ויש שמקדשין ומבדילין עליו.

Babylonia, was blurred in the temperate zone, certainly for those who dwelt close to the northern 'wine border'. Ashkenazic Jews intuitively felt that the ban on wine should include vinegary wine and vinegar itself, seeing that they both came from wine and served many of the same purposes.

For some still mysterious reason, tractate *'Avodah Zarah* was not studied in the Rhineland academies,[29] so few knew that the Talmud had exempted vinegar from the *yein nesekh* ban. R. Yitsḥak ha-Levi was the first to discover that passage in the tractate, and, never hesitating to change established practice, ruled that, henceforth, vinegar touched by Gentiles was permitted—and his pupils ruled likewise. Rabbenu Sasson did not share his colleague's radicalism and insisted on maintaining the old injunction—but not being an iconoclast does not make one a conservative, especially when there is good reason for the established practice. In fact, Rabbenu Tam, the boldest iconoclast of the Middle Ages, also urged upholding the ban on vinegar. If the argument be made that he was more put off by the arrogance of a Provençal interloper, R. Meshullam of Lunel, in allowing it than by the force of the injunction itself,[30] one should reply that the best evidence of the reasonableness of the edict is the willingness of the community to uphold it, despite the ample waivers that were available. R. Yitsḥak's allowance was followed by those of Rashi and Rashbam. Despite permission having been granted by three formidable halakhists, there is no record of any emerging popular allowance. The traditional ban on vinegar did not wear the visage of stringency. It made eminent sense to people in Champagne and the Rhineland, just as it did to Rabbenu Sasson, and they maintained it to the end.[31]

Inclusion of Certain Biblical Verses in the *Musaf* Prayer of Rosh Hashanah

R. Yitsḥak ha-Levi's insistence on including the biblical passages describing sacrifices for the New Moon in the *musaf* prayer of Rosh Hashanah encountered heavy opposition. Grossman says that the leading opponent was Rabbenu Sasson, even though he is not mentioned in any of the sources, for no one else had the authority to oppose R. Yitsḥak at the time.

This may well be, but just how 'conservative' this makes him depends on the nature of R. Yitsḥak's ruling—was it conventional or radical? Was he ruling in a vacuum, about an issue that had no controlling precedent, or was he ruling contrary to the traditions of Worms, indeed of Ashkenaz generally? If

[29] *Ha-Yayin bi-Yemei ha-Beinayim*, 133–6. See my suggestion for the reason for its omission from the curriculum of 11th-century Ashkenaz, below, pp. 191–2. [30] See ibid. 355–6. [31] Ibid. 378–9.

the latter is the case, opposition would have been only natural, and it would have been widespread. In a traditional society a new idea, however correct, simply does not translate itself overnight—or even over the course of time—into the alteration of a long-established practice. This is especially true in the area of liturgy, as the synagogue is a bastion of tradition.

Grossman himself, in his fine chapter on R. Yitsḥak ha-Levi, points out just how innovative that scholar's ruling was in the matter of recitation, in the *musaf* of Rosh Hashanah, of the biblical verses dealing with the Temple offerings of the New Moon.[32] Rashi, for example, attests that in his home town, Troyes, no verses of sacrifice were ever included in the *musaf*.[33] To change the text of the Amidah of the High Holidays is to send a gilt-edged invitation to controversy. I think Grossman is right in stating that Rabbenu Sasson was probably opposed to the innovation. However, if he was, he scarcely stood alone, and he was thereby no more a conservative than all the others in his community who opposed this change.

III

Grossman documents his claim of Rabbenu Sasson's studious, indeed zealous, defense of custom with two examples:

1. In the ritual of taking the four species of plants on Sukkot (*netilat lulav*), Rabbenu Sasson strongly forbade using an *'aravah* (willow branch) that was as tall as, or taller than, the *lulav* (palm leaf).[34] This was a new practice, and not only was he irked by it, but he also genuinely thought it was wrong. The halakhic holding, however, is in no way unique to him. It reflects the simplest reading of the passage in *Sukkah* 32b: **כדי שיהא לולב יוצא מן ההדס טפח**. His younger contemporary, R. Yitsḥak ibn Gi'at, was equally of this opinion, and he was later joined in this view by Maimonides, R. Yom Tov al-Sevilli (Ritva), and R. Nissim of Barcelona (Ran).[35] To dislike an innovation that you believe to be illegal is not what I would call a zealous defense of custom. He was opposed to the innovation not because it was new, but because he thought it wrong.

32 *Ḥakhmei Ashkenaz ha-Rishonim* (above, n. 1), 282–3.

33 Above, n. 21.

34 *Sefer ha-Pardes*, 236–7; *Shibbolei ha-Leket ha-Shalem*, #358, quoted as coming from 'Teshuvot ha-Ge'onim'.

35 *Sha'arei Simḥah*, i. 96–7; *Mishneh Torah*, 'Sukkah', 7: 8; *Ḥiddushei ha-Ritva: Sukkah, Ta'anit, Mo'ed Katan*, ed. E. Lichtenstein (Jerusalem, 1975), *Sukkah* 32b, s.v. *ve-ri amar*; Ran, *Alfasi*, *Sukkah* 32b (Vilna edn., fo. 15a), s.v. *amar*.

2. Rabbenu Sasson admitted to one of the Makirites that his argument for disposing of the *ḥamets* on the Sabbath when the first day of Passover was a Sunday (i.e. *'erev Pesaḥ* fell on the Sabbath) was compelling. Nonetheless, he ruled that since it was the practice of the *kadmonim* (forefathers) to dispose of it on Friday, one should hold fast to custom and continue doing so.[36] Passover can fall on Sunday only twice in a nineteen-year cycle, and any past practice here has none of the rootedness and sensed inalterability of the yearly performances of Rosh Hashanah. Again, I would not call his remarks here a 'zealous defense of custom', but he is assuming a traditionalist posture. Had I several other instances of this sort, I would characterize Rabbenu Sasson as 'conservative', and immediately add 'but an open-minded one, who, when he perceived that truth lay with an innovation (as in the reading of "'Asser te'asser") braved public outcry and adopted it'.

In a fine essay on the lack of influence of the *Halakhot Gedolot* in eleventh-century Ashkenaz, Rami Reiner makes one exception to this rule, Rabbenu Sasson.[37] He contends that Rabbenu Sasson was the only one of his generation who 'never dared to disagree even once with the *Halakhot Gedolot*, and it is quite probable that he viewed that work as the one that should serve as the guide, both in theory and in practice, for Jewish conduct the world over'.[38] Strong words. He draws on Grossman's characterization of Rabbenu Sasson and adduces six rulings of his as evidence: one in the text of his article and five in the footnotes.

1. Let us begin with the case cited by Reiner in the text. It deals with the question whether a test can be given to ascertain the *kashrut* of an animal that has taken a bad fall, when there is fear that it has become a *terefah* as a result. Rabbenu Sasson says that we are not sufficiently skilled to administer such a test. He then adds, 'Furthermore, you [i.e. the inquirer] have stated that this is [also] the ruling of the *Halakhot Gedolot*, and one can rely upon him.'[39]

[36] See references in *Ḥakhmei Ashkenaz ha-Rishonim* (above, n. 1), 337 nn. 52–5.

[37] 'Li-Khenisato shel Sefer "Halakhot Gedolot" le-'Ashkenaz', in H. Kreisel, ed., *Limmud ve-Da'at be-Maḥshavah Yehudit* (Be'er Sheva, 2006), 117–18. A somewhat briefer version of the article appeared subsequently as 'Mi-Halakhah le-Farshanut—Rashi ve-Halakhot Gedolot', in A. Grossman and S. Yafet, eds., *Rashi: Demuto vi-Yetsirato* (Jerusalem, 2008), 324–5.

[38] וקרוב הדבר שבעיניו היה ספר זה מורה הלכה בכל ישראל, למעשה ולהלכה כאחת.

[39] *Teshuvot Ḥakhmei Tsarfat ve-Lotir*, #54; ועוד שאמרת שכך כתוב בהלכות גדולות ויכולין לסמוך עליו.

He himself never invoked that work, indeed, he seems to have been unaware of its ruling. In the report of Rabbenu Sasson's decision in the *Or Zarua'* there is no mention of the *Halakhot Gedolot*.[40]

2. Rabbenu Sasson joined his colleagues, Rabbi Yitsḥak b. Yehudah and R. Yitsḥak ha-Levi, in the matter of *pelugat ha-re'ah*, discussed above.[41] Seeing that we have no statement by Rabbenu Sasson on the matter, simply a report claiming that he allied himself with the other scholars of Mainz and Worms, I am at a loss to see in his ruling any deference to this geonic composition. Indeed, the one who injected the *Halakhot Gedolot* into the discussion was R. Yitsḥak ha-Levi, whom Reiner quite correctly characterizes as having no hesitation in ruling contrary to that work and who invoked it only when it coincided with his own views.

3. As concerns the requirement of waiting a certain period of time (*bi-khedei she-ya'aseh*) after a festival to enjoy produce that had been picked by a Gentile during the festival: by all reports, it was R. Yitsḥak ha-Levi who insisted that this meant waiting until after the second day of the festival (*yom tov sheni shel galuyot*), even if the fruit had been picked on the first day. Rashi, in his commentary on *Betsah*, reports this position in the name of R. Yitsḥak ha-Levi and adds that 'all the people of his place share his view', which, I assume, means all the scholars of Worms, among them Rabbenu Sasson.[42] He makes no mention, however, of their ruling being based on the *Halakhot Gedolot*. In a responsum he did state that Rabbenu Sasson and R. Yitsḥak ha-Levi relied in this ruling upon the *Halakhot Gedolot*.[43] We have several reports about Rashi, but none from the pen of his opponents, R. Yitsḥak ha-Levi and Rabbenu Sasson, so it is difficult to assess whether the ruling of that work played a decisive role in their holding, or whether it was simply a convenient citation to bolster an anterior position.[44] The overall picture of R. Yitsḥak ha-Levi led both Grossman and Reiner to discount any blind obedience on his part to the *Halakhot Gedolot* and to view its invocation here as being simply a precedent which concurred with R. Yitsḥak's own independently held view. I do not know why Rabbenu Sasson's conduct should be seen any differently, unless, of course, his three remaining rulings that relate to the *Halakhot Gedolot* present a picture of the man different from the one that has emerged until now.

40 *Or Zarua'*, i (Zhitomir, 1862), *Terefot*, #416. In fact it would *seem* from the *Or Zarua'* that in disqualifying such a test he was following the ruling of his teacher: **ואמר לנו המורה והאידנא לא בקיאינן בבדיקותא ... רבינו ששון עכ"ל.**

41 See pp. 111–12 and n. 18 for the relevant documentation.

42 24b, s.v. *u-le-'erev*.

43 *Teshuvot Ḥakhmei Tsarfat ve-Lotir*, #11.

44 See the sources cited in *Ma'aseh ha-Ge'onim*, #42, p. 27 nn. 213–16; *Sefer Ravyah*, i, *'Eruvin*, #380, p. 403 nn. 1–22.

4–6. Let us turn now to those three holdings preserved in the *Teshuvot Ḥakhmei Tsarfat ve-Lotir* and cited by Reiner.[45] The first deals with the question of the recitation of 'She-heḥiyanu' (*zeman*) upon taking the *lulav* on the second day of Sukkot. Rabbenu Sasson advances a series of powerful arguments against such a recitation (not for nothing did Rashi characterize him as *adam ḥarif u-mefulpal*) and then concludes, 'And, *furthermore*, I have found [*ve-'od matsati*] written in the *Halakhot Gedolot* that one doesn't recite it [i.e. the blessing].' He is not submitting to the authority of the *Halakhot Gedolot*. That work happened to agree with his views, so he concludes his responsum with invoking it as precedent.

The second responsum is a replay of the first, only briefer and on a different topic. He argues that the Talmud in *Bava Kamma* (99a) holds for liability in cases of indirect causation and adds that the *Halakhot Gedolot* says so explicitly. The third is even more revelatory of his attitude to precedent in general and towards the authority of the *Halakhot Gedolot* in particular. Rabbenu Sasson personally was of one opinion in a disputed question of surety. However, his aged teacher (*mori ha-zaken*) was of another 'and, furthermore, the *Halakhot Gedolot*', he writes, shared the latter view. Therefore, the ruling must be in accordance with this view. He then adds a proviso which, to the best of my knowledge, is without parallel in the Ashkenazic responsa literature, namely, that if the inquirer believes that the other view is correct, he should rule accordingly and there are no grounds for any criticism for his doing so.[46]

Had the *Halakhot Gedolot* been authoritative in Rabbenu Sasson's eyes, its ruling should have bound fast his inquirer as much as it did him. Clearly, the controlling consideration here is not the holding of the geonic code, but that of his 'aged teacher', R. Ya'akov b. Yakar—an intellectual giant of surpassing humility revered equally by Rashi, who wrote of him, 'my entire intellect, my understanding, and my thinking processes were molded by him'.[47] (Is there a greater compliment in the halakhic literature of the past millennium?) Rabbenu Sasson felt himself bound by the ruling of his great mentor. All the more so, perhaps, because he knew that his teacher, for all his greatness,

[45] *Teshuvot Ḥakhmei Tsarfat ve-Lotir*, ##43, 48.

[46] **ואם דעתך נוטה לומר שערב בשעת מתן מעות לא בעי קנין, הלך אחר מה שעיניך רואות, ואין תופסין אותו בכך.**

[47] **לבי וסברתי והבנתי מפיו יצאו**. See Grossman, *Ḥakhmei Tsarfat ha-Rishonim* (above, n. 4), 127, and Marmorstein, 'Ḥakham u-Fosek Italki' (above, n. 18), 238. Grossman suggests that *libi* may be translated as 'my character'. This is, of course, a possibility. However, *lev* as the seat of intellect is a commonplace in rabbinic literature and Rashi regularly uses it in this sense in his commentaries, e.g. *libi omer li, ve-libi megamgem be-ferush zeh*. See W. Hirsch, *Rabbinic Psychology* (London, 1947), 150, and Y. Avineri, *Heikhal Rashi* (Tel Aviv, 1940–60), i. 269; iv. 125.

was consumed by a sense of utter worthlessness. Rashi, the most restrained of writers, said of him, 'I knew his stature . . . it was greater than that of all of them, but he conducted himself as a doormat made to be stepped on, and saw himself as refuse [fit for discarding] and never presumed to [wear] the crown [of Torah] which was his due.'[48] He, of all men, would have been the last to expect compliance from his students, and humility is disarming, especially when practiced by those who have the least reason to be humble. The inquirer, however, was under no such emotional constraint, owed R. Ya'akov no such deference, and was free to do as he thought best, irrespective of anything that the *Halakhot Gedolot* wrote.

[48] ידעתי [מידתו] בחר לו [?] בגדולה מכולם והנהיג את עצמו כאסקופה הנדרסת ושם עצמו שייר שיריים ולא מלאו לבו לעטרה הראויה לו. *Siddur Rashi*, #174, p. 80, and see Grossman, *Ḥakhmei Ashkenaz ha-Rishonim* (above, n. 1), 246–9. The emendation *midato* is that of the editor, J. Freimann.

CHAPTER SEVEN

Communications and the Palestinian Origins of Ashkenaz

THE CONTENTION of this essay is that the recent scholarship on communication in early medieval Europe has undermined the major tacit assumption of the reigning theory of the cultural origins of the Ashkenazic community.

Nineteenth-century Jewish scholars who pioneered the academic study of Judaism (Wissenschaft des Judentums) discovered that the Ashkenazic rite had strong Palestinian influences, and the past half-century has witnessed a vigorous reassertion of this viewpoint. It has been claimed that the underlying religious culture of Early Ashkenaz was Palestinian, and that only later, some say as late as the mid-eleventh century, did the Babylonian Talmud achieve the dominance in the religious life of Ashkenaz with which we commonly associate it. Whether one dates the Babylonian supersession in this culture to the mid-eleventh century or advances it to the mid-tenth century, the Palestinian origin of Ashkenazic culture is agreed upon by all; indeed, it may currently be called a scholarly commonplace.[1]

[1] A. Grossman, 'Zikatah shel Yahadut Ashkenaz ha-Kedumah el Erets Yisra'el', *Shalem*, 3 (1981), 57–92; I. M. Ta-Shma, *Minhag Ashkenaz ha-Kadmon* (Jerusalem, 1992), 98–103 and *passim*; R. Bonfil, 'Bein Erets Yisra'el le Bavel: Kavim le-Ḥeker Toledot ha-Tarbut shel ha-Yehudim be-'Italyah ha-Deromit u-ve-'Eiropah ha-Notsrit bi-Yemei ha-Beinayim ha-Mukdamim', *Shalem*, 5 (1987), 1–30, esp. pp. 13–19; id., ''Eduto shel Agobard mi-Lyons 'al 'Olamam ha-Ruḥani shel Yehudei 'Iro ba-Me'ah ha-Teshi'it', in Y. Dan et al., eds., *Meḥkarim be-Kabbalah, be-Filosofyah u-ve-Sifrut ha-Musar, Muggashim le-Yesha'yahu Tishby bi-Melo't Lo Shiv'im ve-Ḥamesh Shanim* (Jerusalem, 1986), 327–48, esp. pp. 339–47 (an abridged, English, version of this article is available in Y. Dan, ed., *Binah: Studies in Jewish History, Culture, and Thought*, iii: *Jewish Intellectual History in the Middle Ages* [Westport, Conn., 1994], 1–17); I. Marcus, 'The Dynamics of Jewish Renaissance and Renewal in the Twelfth Century', in M. Signer and J. Van Engen, eds., *Jews and Christians in Twelfth-Century Europe* (Notre Dame, Ind., 2001), 36–9. See also Y. Sussmann, 'Kitvei-Yad u-Mesorot Nusaḥ shel ha-Mishnah', *Divrei ha-Kongres ha-'Olami ha-Shevi'i le-Madda'ei ha-Yahadut (August 7–14, 1977): Meḥkarim be-Talmud, Halakhah u-Midrash* (Jerusalem, 1981), 236 n. 89.

I have long had my doubts about this truism on both methodological and empirical grounds which I will present in the next chapter. Here I would like to challenge its underlying premise, namely, that the nascent Ashkenazic community was located in some transalpine corner of Europe with only a tenuous connection to the East and dependent on a single cultural source whose pipeline ran from Byzantine Palestine to Byzantine southern Italy and from there through the Alpine passes to the Rhineland. The liturgical poetry of Ashkenaz was, indeed, nurtured by just such an umbilical cord, and so, it is claimed, it stands to reason that its culture generally, and its religious rites in particular, were similarly nourished.

It seems best to begin with the results of recent studies in the Ashkenazic manuscript traditions of the Babylonian Talmud. This may seem somewhat esoteric, but its relevance will soon be apparent. The work of the last forty years has been well summarized by Vered Noam:

[E. S.] Rosenthal has noted that there are two manuscript traditions [of the Talmud]: an eastern one, [best] reflected in the writings of R. Ḥanan'el [of Kairouan], and another widespread version, which he called the 'vulgata', which is reflected not only in the writings of Rashi and the Franco-German Tosafists but also in Spanish manuscripts and even in very old eastern manuscripts and Genizah fragments. This would indicate that the split in the traditions had already occurred in the East, and that the Ashkenazic tradition is an eastern one. Friedman has found that the Ashkenazic manuscripts of tractate *Bava Metsi'a* reflect the same text as that found in the writings of the Babylonian Geonim. Siegel's researches have revealed remarkable similarities between the Ashkenazic version of tractate *Megillah* and fragments from the Genizah. A striking likeness has been found to exist between the superb Sephardic manuscript of tractate *Megillah* (located in Göttingen) and the Franco-German textual traditions. Sabato has discovered two clear textual traditions in tractate *Sanhedrin*: an eastern one reflected in the Yemenite manuscripts and in the works of Rabbi Yitsḥak of Fez (Alfasi); the other reflected in the Ashkenazic tradition, which is mirrored, surprisingly, in the version used by Rabbenu Ḥanan'el [of Kairouan]: that of R. Me'ir Abul'afia [Ramah] of Toledo. He further surmised that the split had taken place quite early and in the East, and that this eastern version somehow got to Ashkenaz. This tradition has readings as good as [the Yemenite one] and at times even superior [to it]. The general picture that emerges from all these 'partial' studies [of individual tractates] is confirmed by a broad examination of the orthography of [the majority of] extant talmudic manuscripts. Friedman's morphological study has shown that many of the so-called 'Palestinian' spellings are, in fact, Babylonian, and that to a large extent this orthography is found in late Ashkenazic manuscripts. These manuscripts preserve many of the distinctive Babylonian spellings, as do the [highly regarded] Yemenite manuscripts.[2]

The upshot of all this is that either the Babylonian material that reached Yemen, the Maghreb (Kairouan), and Spain equally arrived in Ashkenaz, or Ashkenaz received its traditions from these locales. A third possibility is that it acquired some of its manuscripts independently from the East, others via the mediation of Yemen, Kairouan, and Spain. One might argue that Ashkenazic manuscripts are late—the earliest is from 1177 and most others are far later.[3] What relevance can these sources have for pre-Crusade Ashkenaz? Let us look at Rashi's emendations, made in the eleventh century, which may throw some light on this question. In the same article Noam has shown that in tractate *Sukkah* 71 percent of Rashi's emendations are confirmed by eastern or Spanish manuscript traditions. This is an extraordinarily high figure. Shai Secunda's research shows that in tractate *'Avodah Zarah* there is a 43 percent congruence of Rashi's emendations with manuscripts that, to use Friedman's typology, are either Mediterranean or of specifically Spanish provenance.[4] (Unfortunately we have no Yemenite manuscripts on *'Avodah Zarah.*) One might argue that a congruence of 43 percent could equally be random; chance would have it that at least close to 50 percent of all good emendations would be corroborated by some manuscript or other. Reply can be made that, first, there are only three and not a dozen manuscripts of this tractate. Second, Friedman has shown that one of the two manuscripts named Jewish Theological Seminary 15 is a composite. The first half (up to fo. 43) is of the 'Mediterranean' type (in Friedman's orthographical typology), while the second half (fos. 43–76) is Spanish.[5] In the first half of this manuscript the congruence of its

[2] V. Noam, 'Mesorot Nusaḥ Kedumot be-Haggahot Rashi ba-Talmud', *Sidra*, 17 (2001–2), 110–11. The work done in the last decade or so has only confirmed the picture she drew in 2001.

[3] *Talmud Bavli: Ketav-Yad Firentseh*, introd. D. Rosenthal (Jerusalem, 1972), introduction, p. 1.

[4] Shai Secunda's paper, written for a seminar of mine, contains both an analysis of the variants and emendation together with a transcription of all the manuscript readings (including those of the Genizah fragments) of the talmudic passages emended by Rashi, both as found in the printed version of his commentary and in MS Parma, De Rossi 1292. Deciding which version an author had in front of him often hinges on fine nuances. One may disagree with one point or another of Secunda's analysis, but the overall picture that he draws is, to my thinking at least, beyond question. As both the paper and the transcription variants have been placed online at <http://www.azyn.blogspot.com>, readers may draw their own conclusions.

[5] S. Friedman, 'Massekhet *'Avodah Zarah*, Ketav Yad New York, Ketav Yad she-Hu'atak bi-Shenei Shelavim', *Leshonenu*, 56 (1992), 371–4.

readings with Rashi's emendations is 47 percent; in the latter half—only 33 percent. The degree of congruence with Rashi's emendations changes noticeably with the change of the textual tradition to which it is being compared. Apparently, Rashi was working from a manuscript that had more in common with the Mediterranean type than with the Sephardic one, and that differed considerably from the one that came to be called 'Ashkenazic'. Nor is tractate *'Avodah Zarah* unique in this respect: 31 percent of Rashi's emendations in tractate *Sanhedrin* correspond to the Yemenite tradition; 13 percent are found only in the Yemenite textual tradition.[6]

Truth to tell, we need not restrict our enquiry to Rashi's emendations. Friedman has shown that in the eighth chapter of tractate *Bava Metsi'a*, Rashi's incipits reflect a 'Mediterranean' text, rather than what came to be known as the 'Ashkenazic' version of the tractate.[7] Rashi didn't import these manuscripts. They were apparently in circulation at the time and he took care to obtain them. No doubt he was a brilliant commentator and, quite possibly, he was equally talented in emendation; nevertheless, a 71 percent congruence in *Sukkah* is too high to be intuition alone, and the marked change in degree of correspondence with alternative textual traditions to which the emendations are being compared, as happens in *'Avodah Zarah*, is, again, too salient to be happenstance. It seems clear that, alongside intuition, Rashi, writing in the eleventh century, also employed a broad spectrum of manuscripts of different provenances and traditions, all of which came from places far removed from the city of Troyes, where he lived, and from the Rhineland academies of Mainz and Worms, where he had studied.

Can we push yet further back in time? I believe that we plausibly can. R. Gershom of Mainz, more commonly known as Rabbenu Gershom Me'or ha-Golah (d. 1028) issued a ban on anyone who emended the text of the Talmud.[8] Let us remember that he wrote at the dawn of Ashkenazic culture, in a period before any commentary on the Talmud had been composed. The

[6] M. Sabato, *Ketav-Yad Teimani le-Massekhet Sanhedrin (Bavli) u-Mekomo be-Masoret ha-Nusaḥ*, Sidrat 'Avodot Doktor Nivḥarot (Jerusalem, 1998), 231–78, esp. the table on p. 258.

[7] S. Friedman, *Talmud 'Arukh, Perek ha-Sokher et ha-'Umanim—ha-Nusaḥ 'im Mavo Kelali* (Jerusalem, 1997), 48, 57–69.

[8] Rabbenu Tam, *Sefer ha-Yashar: Ḥelek Ḥiddushim*, ed. S. Schlesinger (Jerusalem, 1959), introduction, 9. This paragraph may need modification in light of my suggestion as to the cultural origins of Ashkenaz, below, pp. 163–9. However, one would do well to note here, as in the chapter on *minhag* Ashkenaz ha-Kadmon (Ch. 3 above—see n. 4), that my remarks in 'Cultural Origins' address the new immigrants, the tiny elite who established the yeshivah in Mainz and who undertook to write the Mainz commentary on the Talmud. Here we are treating the local population of Mainz and of the Rhineland and the neighboring Lorraine (and even, perhaps, that of Champagne). There is no reason to suppose that these people had any meaningful command of Babylonian Aramaic.

ban issues from a time prior to the commentaries of the school of Mainz (that currently go under the name of R. Gershom), prior to the famed commentaries of Rashi and those of R. Ḥanan'el of Kairouan and R. Yosef ibn Megas. Who was so confident of his understanding of the abrupt and gnomic text of the Talmud that he would regularly presume to emend it? Who was so confident of his control of eastern Aramaic that he *could* emend the talmudic text? To give a contemporary example: what Talmudist of today could systematically emend *Bereshit Rabbah*—a text written in the dialect of third- and fourth-century Galilean Aramaic? The Babylonian Aramaic of the Talmud was as new and as alien to Ashkenazic Jews at the turn of the first millennium as the Galilean Aramaic of the *midrashim* is to us today. No doubt there were some bold souls who rushed in where angels fear to tread, but was the phenomenon so widespread that it demanded a communal ban? Is it not more plausible that if emendation was rampant, or in danger of becoming rampant, these corrections were being made on the basis of extant manuscripts? Let us assume for a moment (we shall soon see why such an assumption is plausible) that many different textual traditions were circulating in Ashkenaz in the late tenth and early eleventh centuries. Whenever a group of Jews gathered to study the Talmud, each held in his hand a different manuscript, quite possibly of a different tradition. When the group encountered a difficulty in the Talmud, nothing would have been more natural than to check the differing texts of the various members and to emend the other manuscripts according to the reading that they felt was best.

The pressing need for emendation unquestionably existed at the time. What is meant by such medieval Ashkenazic terms as 'the book [i.e. version of the Talmud] of Rabbenu Gershom Me'or ha-Golah' or 'the book of R. Yitsḥak ben Yehudah [of eleventh-century Mainz]'?[9] Not that they personally copied the book—this would not have invested the text with any authority—but rather that its readings had received their imprimatur. It had been edited by them and contained the version that they had judged best—either by their choice of manuscript reading or by their emendation. The need for an authoritative text was felt by all; the danger was that it would be attempted by the unqualified. It seems reasonable that the purpose of R. Gershom's ban was both to preserve for the few truly qualified scholars the wide range of versions

[9] Rabbenu Gershom: sources in V. Aptowitzer, *Mavo le-Sefer Ravyah* (Jerusalem, 1938), 332 n. 10. R. Yitsḥak b. Yehudah: sources in A. Grossman, *Ḥakhmei Ashkenaz ha-Rishonim: Koroteihem, Darkam be-Hanhagat ha-Tsibbur, Yetsiratam ha-Ruḥanit mi-Reshit Yishuvam ve-'ad li-Gezerot Tatnu (1096)*, 3rd edn. (Jerusalem, 2001), 316–17. See id., *Ḥakhmei Tsarfat ha-Rishonim: Koroteihem, Darkam be-Hanhagat ha-Tsibbur, Yetsiratam ha-Ruḥanit*, 3rd edn. (Jerusalem, 2001), 113, for 'the book of R. Yitsḥak ben Menaḥem'.

that were circulating and to preclude their corruption at the hands of the ignorant.

Seeing that the manuscript evidence goes back only to Rashi (d. 1105), why should we assume that different manuscript traditions were circulating in mid-tenth-century Ashkenaz generally, and in Mainz, the city of Rabbenu Gershom (d. 1028), in particular? It is the economic role of contemporary Mainz that leads to this assumption. A Jewish traveler from Spain, Ibrâhim b. Yaq'ub, who traveled around northern Europe during R. Gershom's youth (*c*.965), reported thus of Mainz:

This is a great city . . . she dwells in the land of the Franks on a river called 'Rin' . . . One sees there dirhams that were minted in Samarkand with the name of the master of the mint and the date of 301–302 [i.e. 913–14] . . . It is astonishing that a person can find in Mainz, that is to say, at the far ends of the West, perfumes and spices that originate at the far ends of the East, such as pepper, ginger, cloves, Indian nard, 'custus', and galingale. These plants are brought from India where they grow in abundance.[10]

Ibrâhim b. Yaq'ub need not have been surprised. Mainz was the final station of two of the three overland trade routes from the Near and Far East. One road led from the Black Sea through Kiev, Przemyśl, Cracow, Prague, Regensburg, and thence to Mainz. The other followed the Danube to Esztergom (Hungary), Raffelstettin (on the eastern border of the German Empire), and Regensburg, and ended equally at Mainz.[11] Jewish merchants were active in these trails; they were similarly involved in the lucrative trade of luxury goods that arrived in Mainz from the East via the port of Venice and the Alpine passes; so much so that the Venetian authorities sought to have them expelled from Mainz.[12] These trade routes led to Mainz because it was situated oppo-

[10] A. Miquel, 'L'Europe occidentale dans la relation arabe d'Ibrâhim b. Yaq'ub (Xe s.)', *Annales: ESC*, 21 (1966), 1059–60.

[11] A. Gieysztor, 'Les Juifs et leurs activités économiques en Europe orientale', in *Gli Ebrei Nell'alto Medioevo*, Settimane di Studio del Centro Italiano di Studi Sull'alto Medioevo 26 (Spoleto, 1980), i. 506–11; T. Lewicki, 'Les Commerçants juifs dans l'Orient islamique non-méditerranéen au IXe–XIe siècle', ibid. 375–401; W. G. Haussig, 'Praxis und Verbreitung des jüdischen Handels in Südrussland', in H. Jankuhn and E. Ebel, eds., *Untersuchungen zu Handel und Verkehr der vor- und frühgeschichtlichen Zeit in Mittel- und Nordeuropa*, vi: *Organisationsformen der Kaufmannsvereinigungen in der Spätantike und im frühen Mittelalter*, Abhandlungen der Akademie der Wissenschaft in Göttingen, Philologisch-Historische Klasse 183 (Göttingen, 1989), 27, 31–2.

[12] M. McCormick, *Origins of the European Economy: Communications and Commerce 700–900* (Cambridge, 2001), 796, 970; G. Caro, *Sozial- und Wirtschaftsgeschichte der Juden im Mittelalter und der Neuzeit*, 2nd edn. (Frankfurt am Main, 1924), i. 193. A letter from both the Doge and the Archbishop of Venice requested that the Jews be either banned from handling items with crosses, as they desecrated them, or expelled from the city. Caro pointed out that numerous Ottonian coins had embossed

site Ingelheim, the seat of the winter palace of Charlemagne and Louis the Pious. The importance of Ingelheim diminished somewhat under the later Carolingians, but its imperial palace returned to favor under the Ottonians. Whatever the lot of Ingelheim, the centrality and affluence of the Rhineland only increased with time. It was one of the economic pillars of the empire. In tenth- and eleventh-century Germany there were no wealthy, independent urban centers. All large, nodal points of settlement belonged either to a bishop, an abbey, or the emperor. Wealth was concentrated in the hands of the masters of these centers, and they alone had the buying power to attract large-scale luxury trade.[13] No area had a greater concentration of such hubs than the Rhineland and no region held forth a larger prospect of rich consumption, as Michael McCormick's map of transalpine coin movements strikingly illustrates (see Map 1).[14] Centrally located 'on the river called the Rin', the commercial highway of the empire, the 'great city' of Mainz in the tenth century retained its status as an emporium.

In the mid-ninth century Jewish merchants, the Radhanites, traveled to India and China. Upon their return from the East, some of them made for Constantinople to sell their treasures to the 'Romans' (the Byzantines); others headed towards 'the residence of the king of the Franks to dispose of their wares'.[15] Many scholars believe that the trade with the East was predominantly in Jewish hands; others deny this.[16] All, however, are agreed that the Jews were lively participants in this commerce.

crosses; such an injunction, then, would have effectively excluded Jews from commerce. The commercial implications of the request would also explain why the Doge of Venice joined the Archbishop of Venice in what was ostensibly a purely religious matter.

[13] T. Reuter, *Germany in the Early Middle Ages: 800–1056* (London and New York, 1991), 233; A. Haverkamp, 'Die "frühbürgerliche" Welt im hohen und späten Mittelalter: Landesgeschichte und Geschichte der städtischen Gesellschaft', *Historische Zeitschrift*, 221 (1975), 571–602. On Ingelheim, see P. Classen, 'Die Geschichte der Königspfalz Ingelheim bis zur Verpfändung an die Kurpfalz 1375', in *Ingelheim am Rhein. Forschungen und Studien zur Geschichte Ingelheims* (Ingelheim am Rhein, 1964), 87–116. For the significant archeological findings of the past decades, see H. Grewe, 'Die Ausgrabungen in der Königspfalz zu Ingelheim am Rhein', in *Deutsche Königspfalzen. Beiträge zu ihrer historischen und archäologischen Erforschung*, Veröffentlichungen des Max-Planck-Instituts für Geschichte 11/5 (2001), 155–74. I would like to thank Rainer Barzen for drawing my attention to the last work.

[14] McCormick, *Origins of the European Economy* (above, n. 12), 686.

[15] *Medieval Trade in the Mediterranean World: Illustrative Documents*, trans. with introd. and notes by R. S. Lopez and I. W. Raymond (New York, 1955), 32. For a German translation from the original Arabic account (rather than the English translation of a French translation as in the case of Lopez and Raymond's text), see the references in McCormick (above, n. 12), 689 n. 72. A Hebrew translation from the original can be found in M. Gil, *Be-Malkhut Yishma'el bi-Tekufat ha-Ge'onim* (Tel Aviv, 1997), i. 614, and see pp. 611–35 for a comprehensive discussion of the Radhanite narrative.

[16] See above, n. 12, and see the rich bibliography in M. Toch, 'Jews and Commerce: Modern Fan-

At this time, we hear of 'hordes' (*cohortes*) of merchants that traveled from Germany to Saragossa in Spain, and, not surprisingly, they stopped at Mainz.[17] We also know that in 876 Charles the Bald sent ten pounds of silver for the reconstruction of the church in Barcelona by means of his Jewish emissary, Judas. It would appear that cultivating the Spanish periphery of the empire was equally the policy of Louis the Pious two generations before, when he took under his protection Abraham the Jew from Saragossa. Historians have assumed that the release from the numerous tolls that he accorded Abraham was not simply an act of benevolence, but rather part of a policy to encourage trade with Muslim Spain or to ensure for the imperial palace a steady supply of goods from Islamic countries, similar to requirement made of merchants with imperial protection 'to appear in our palace in mid-May once every year or two'.[18] Rather than detailing each and every contact that the Rhineland had with Spain, Italy, Kairouan, Egypt, Palestine, Constantinople, and Baghdad, I would point to the map drawn by McCormick entitled 'Merchant Communications, 700–900' (Map 2), which graphically demonstrates the extent to which the Rhineland was linked with the wider world of the time.[19]

Spices and condiments from the East arrived in Mainz in abundance; so too did objects of religious significance. The Christian world attached great importance to relics, palpable remains of their sacred past, such as the hem of the robe of Jesus or of one of the Apostles, a chip of the rock on which Mary had sat, a staff that a saint or martyr had held, and the like. These fragments of wood, cloth, and stone radiated potent sanctity and were held in awe and reverence by believers; they added great prestige, even power, to those fortunate

cies and Medieval Realities', in *Il ruolo economico delle minoranze in Europa. Secc. XIII–XVIII*, Atti della XXXI Settimana di Studi, Istituto Francesco Datini, Prato (Florence, 2000), 43–58. See also the cautious formulation of J.-P. Devroey and C. Brouwer in 'La Participation des Juifs au commerce dans le monde franc (VIe–Xe siècles)', in A. Dierkens and J.-M. Sansterre, eds., *Voyages et voyageurs à Byzance et en Occident du VIe au XIe siècle*, Bibliothèque de la Faculté de Philosophie et Lettres de l'Université de Liège 278 (Geneva, 2000), 339–74.

17 McCormick, *Origins of the European Economy* (above, n. 12), 674–7.

18 F. Rörig, 'Magdeburgs Entstehung und die ältere Handelsgeschichte', in id., *Wirtschaftskräfte im Mittelalter. Abhandlungen zur Stadt- und Hansegeschichte*, ed. P. Kaegbein, 2nd edn. (Vienna and Cologne, 1971), 607–10; B. Blumenkranz, *Juifs et chrétiens dans le monde occidental: 430–1096*, Études juives 2 (Paris, 1960), 17–18.

19 McCormick, *Origins of the European Economy* (above, n. 12), 676. Our interest lies with the rich network of communication that McCormick has traced, not with any specific thesis of his—for example, that it was the growing trade in the Mediterranean rather than the upsurge of commerce in the north that proved instrumental in the economic revival of the West. See e.g. *Early European History*, 12 (2003), an issue devoted to a discussion of McCormick's book.

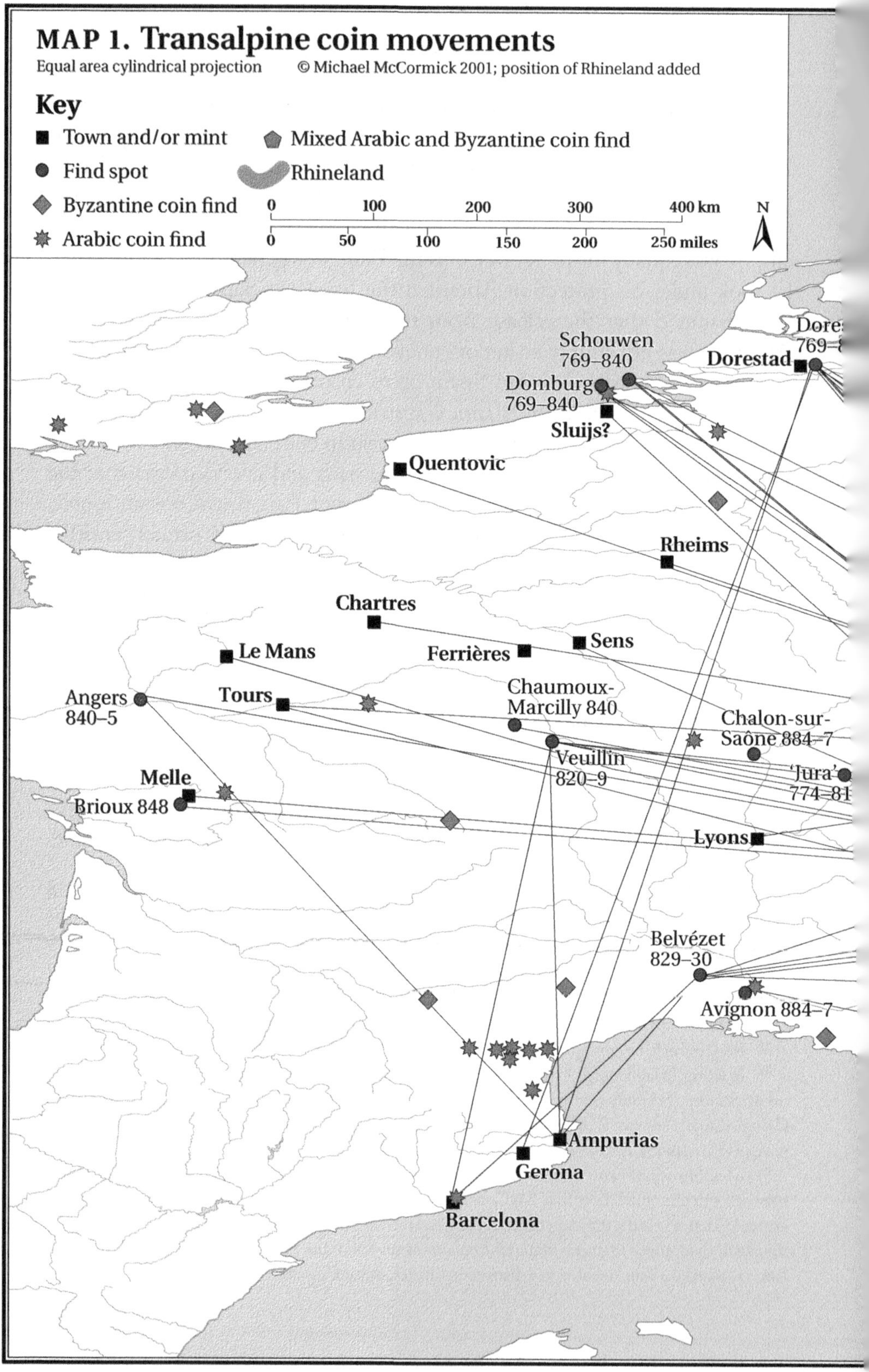
Equal area cylindrical projection
© Michael McCormick 2001; position of Rhineland added
Key
Town and/or mint
Find spot
Byzantine coin find
Arabic coin find
Mixed Arabic and Byzantine coin find
Rhineland
0 100 200 300 400 km
0 50 100 150 200 250 miles
N
Schouwen 769–840
Domburg 769–840
Sluijs?
Dorestad
Quentovic
Rheims
Chartres
Le Mans
Ferrières
Sens
Angers 840–5
Tours
Chaumoux-Marcilly 840
Chalon-sur-Saône 884–7
Veuillin 820–9
Melle
Brioux 848
Lyons
Belvézet 829–30
Avignon 884–7
Ampurias
Gerona
Barcelona

MAP 1. Transalpine coin movements

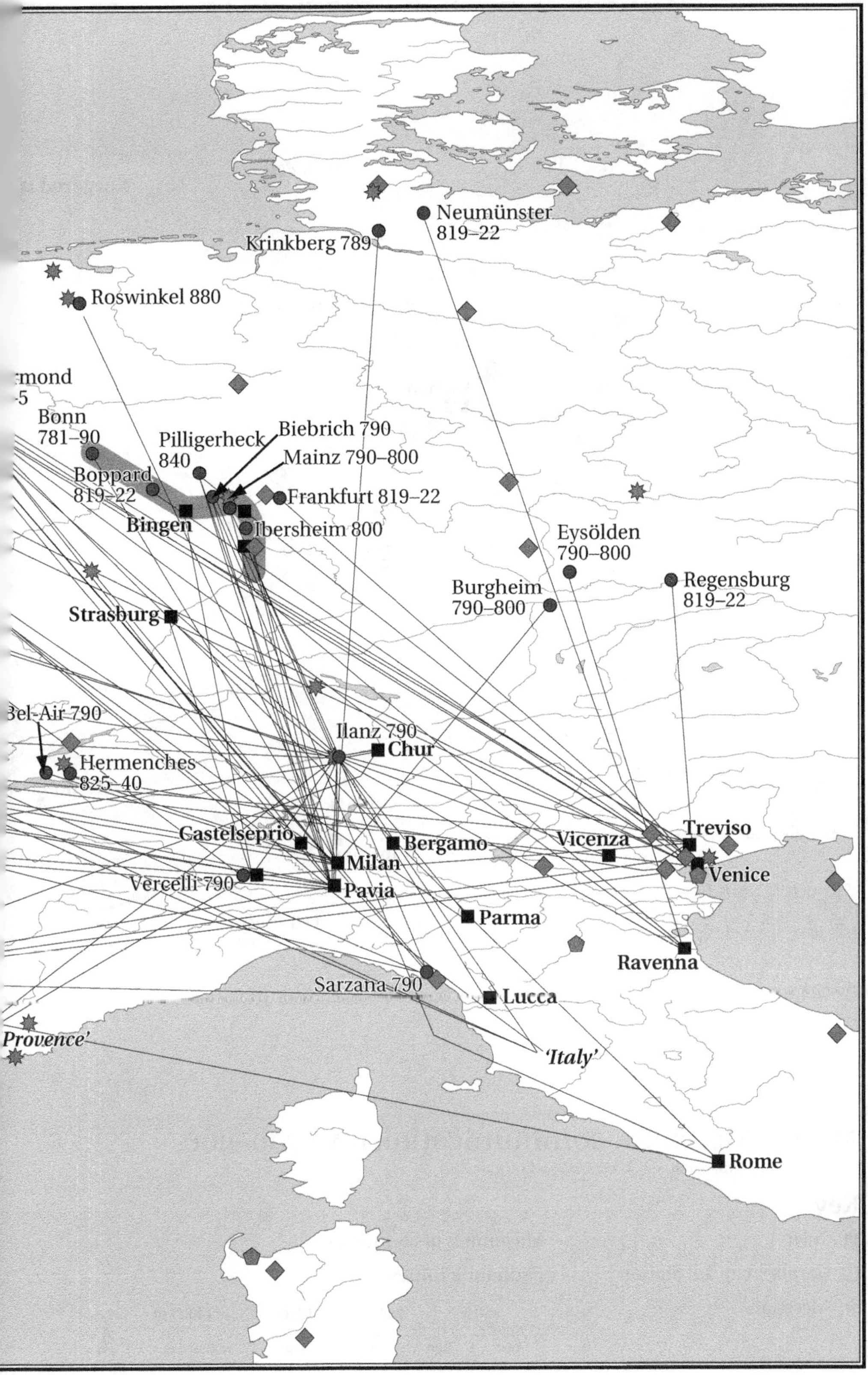

Neumünster 819–22
Krinkberg 789
Roswinkel 880
mond
-5
Bonn 781–90
Pilligerheck 840
Biebrich 790
Mainz 790–800
Boppard 819–22
Frankfurt 819–22
Bingen
Ibersheim 800
Eysölden 790–800
Regensburg 819–22
Burgheim 790–800
Strasburg
Bel-Air 790
Ilanz 790
Chur
Hermenches 825–40
Castelseprio
Bergamo
Vicenza
Treviso
Milan
Venice
Vercelli 790
Pavia
Parma
Ravenna
Sarzana 790
Lucca
'Provence'
'Italy'
Rome

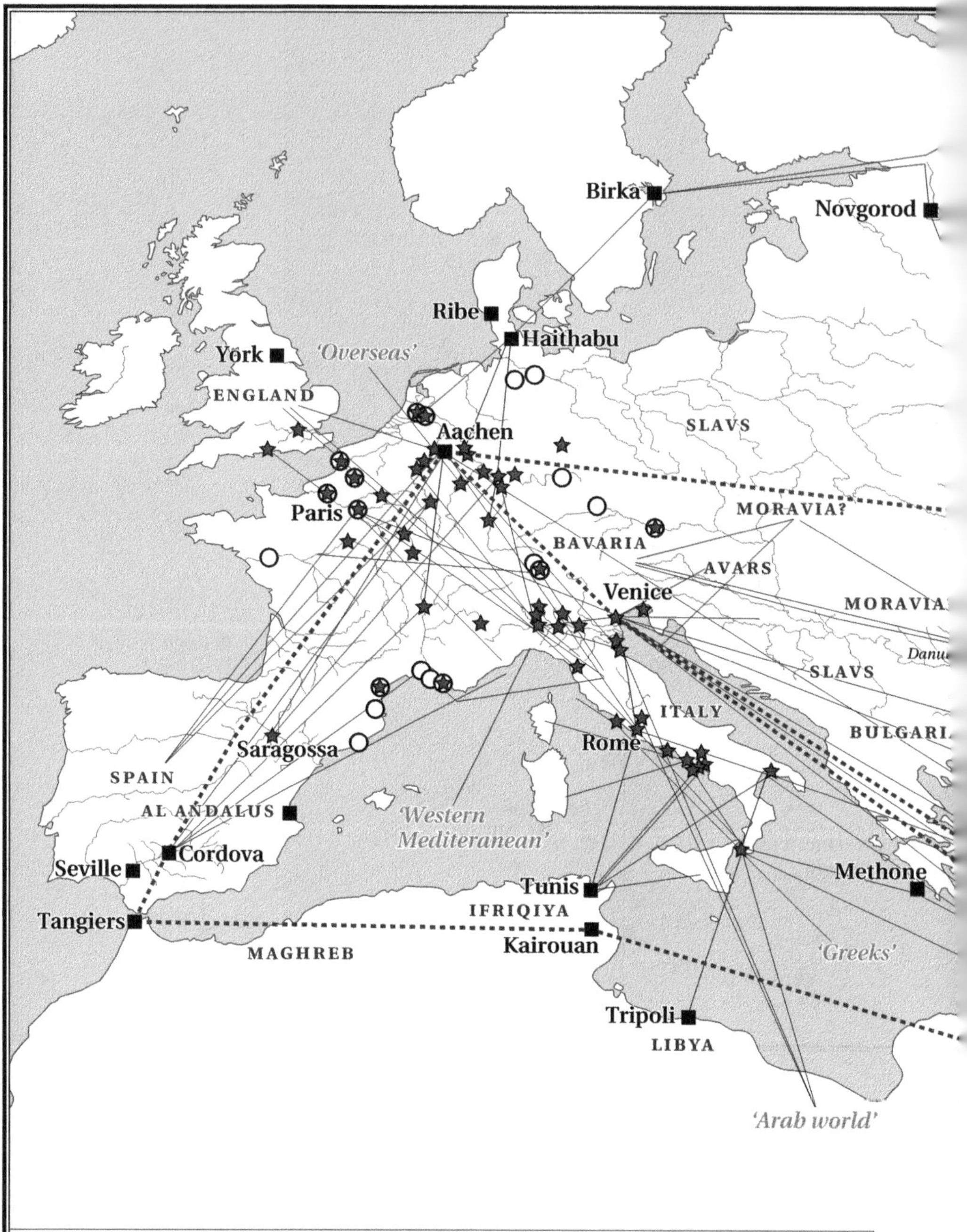

MAP 2. Merchant communications, AD 700–900

Hammer-Aitoff projection © Michael McCormick 2001

Key

■ Town

○ Carolingian Toll Station

★ Merchant

—— Movement of commerce

- - - - Radhanite routes

0 350 700 1050 1400 km

0 160 320 480 640 800 miles

N

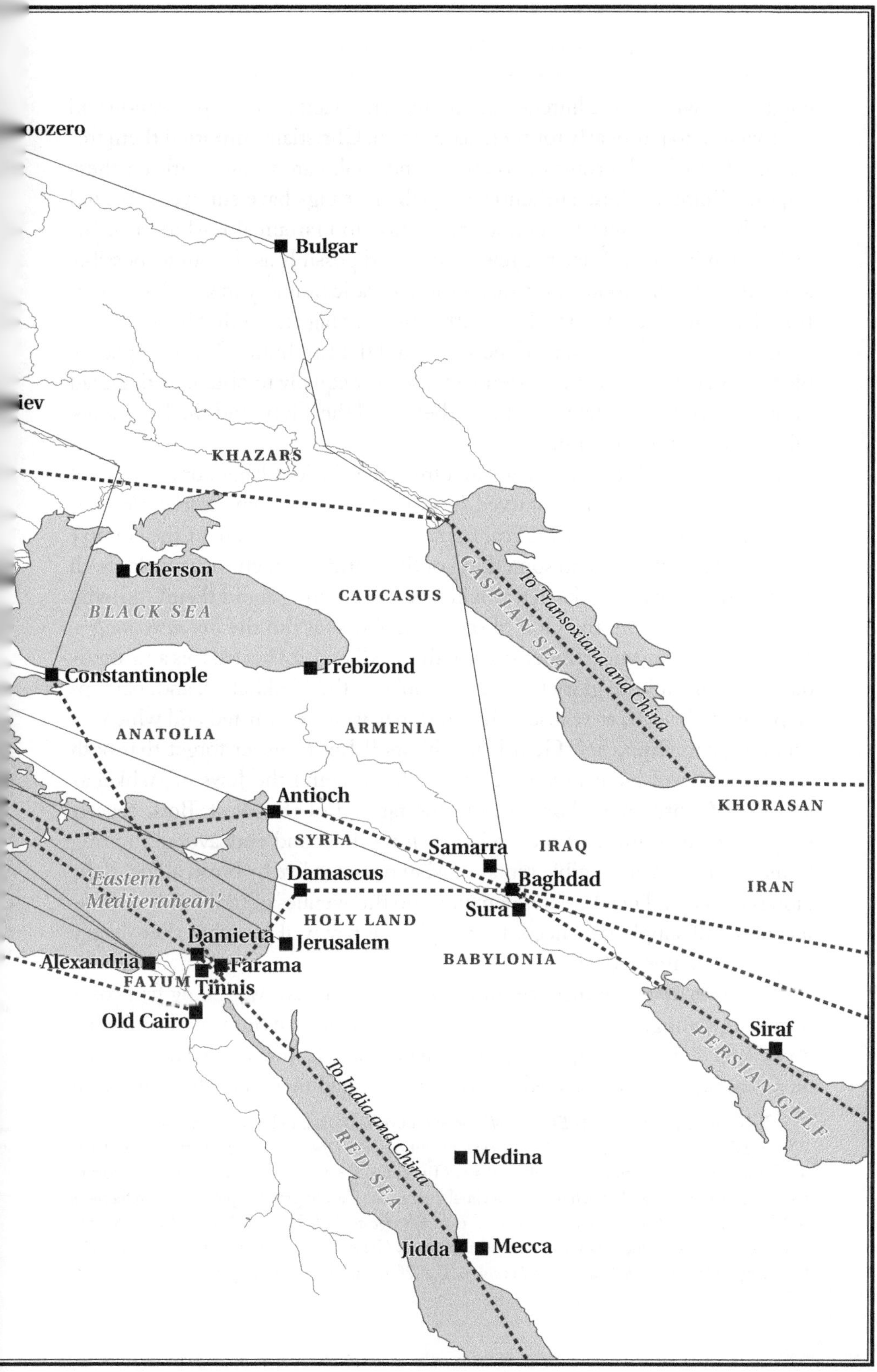

oozero
Bulgar
iev
KHAZARS
Cherson
BLACK SEA
CAUCASUS
CASPIAN SEA
To Transoxiana and China
Constantinople
Trebizond
ANATOLIA
ARMENIA
Antioch
KHORASAN
SYRIA
Samarra
IRAQ
'Eastern Mediterranean'
Damascus
Baghdad
IRAN
Sura
HOLY LAND
Damietta
Jerusalem
Alexandria
Farama
BABYLONIA
FAYUM
Tinnis
Old Cairo
Siraf
PERSIAN GULF
To India and China
RED SEA
Medina
Jidda
Mecca

enough to own them. Churches and monasteries vied for their possession and were willing to pay dearly for their acquisition. Christians imported them frequently from Mediterranean countries and took care to authenticate these imports. Some of these authenticating labels or tags have survived. Around 800, Charlemagne sent his famous delegation to Haroun al Rashid in Baghdad, which included Isaac the Jew, who served possibly as the guide, possibly as the interpreter. About this time, the aristocratic nunnery in Chelles, not far from Paris, received a relic whose authenticating tag stated that it came from an area '[between] the rivers of the Tigris and the Euphrates'.[20] Is it implausible that Isaac the Jew (or his attendants) sought equally to obtain in Baghdad or Sura or from other Jewish centers '[between] the Tigris and the Euphrates' religious objects dear to him?

Jews were not interested in a patch from the cloak of Elijah or in pieces of Moses' rod, but they were starved for knowledge: for some *midrashim* that would flesh out the sparse biblical narratives and tell them about the country from which they came and something of the world in which they would dwell after their death; for books that would reveal something about their God, who was so different from the God of their neighbors (as did the *Shi'ur Komah*—the book of the mystical dimensions of the Godhead), of his palaces and attendants and his infinite glory (as did the books of the Heikhalot), and, perhaps above all, of his law, to whose upholding they were committed and which set them so apart from their Gentile neighbors.[21] Let us never forget that both Christianity and Judaism were eastern religions, and the Jews of Ashkenaz and their Gentile neighbors lived in the far end of the West. Both eagerly sought out the sources of their religion in the East and endeavored to bring home some of their tangible remains. Man does not live by bread alone. Religion is a need and need creates demand, and the avenues of trade and communication will supply that need, for people will pay well for what they deeply desire, be it material or spiritual consignments.

Moreover, it was in these centuries that the Oral Law was being first committed to writing. In the famed Babylonian academies of Sura and Pumbedita no written texts were employed, but rather the words were recited by *tanna'im* or *garsanim*, carefully selected individuals who had meticulously memorized

[20] McCormick, *Origins of the European Economy* (above, n. 12), 313, and see pp. 283–318.

[21] See Agobard Lugdunensis, 'De judaicis superstitionibus', *Opera Omnia*, ed. L. van Acker, Corpus Christianorum Continuatio Mediaevalis 52 (Turnhout, 1981), 205–6. On the Jewish sources to which Agobard refers and which were then circulating in the Carolingian Empire, see the references in B. Blumenkranz, *Les Auteurs chrétiens latins du Moyen Age sur les Juifs et le judaïsme* (Paris, 1963), 165 n. 62. On the date of the missive, see most recently C. Geisel, *Die Juden im Frankenreich: Von den Merowingern bis zum Tode Ludwigs des Frommen* (Frankfurt am Main, 1998), 575–81.

large sections of the Talmud.[22] With the emergence of Jewish settlements in the Islamic empire, texts of the Talmud began to circulate there. One can also reasonably assume that some written guides to religious conduct existed then in Ashkenaz, but they were unofficial and non-binding, more in the nature of cribs than of codes. The tiny clusters of Jews, far removed from the major Diaspora settlements as Kairouan or Lucena, lived their life by mimetic transmission, by observing and reproducing the way of life of parents and teachers. What could have been more important, indeed epoch-making, for these meager settlements than to have received for the first time in their history some authoritative guide to the observance of the Sabbath or of Passover from the legendary academies of Sura and Pumbedita, not to speak of a tractate of the Talmud or some parts of the famed geonic codes, such as the *Halakhot Pesukot* or the *Halakhot Gedolot*? To possess such an authoritative work was truly a blessing. It also bestowed on its possessor considerable prestige and not inconsiderable religious authority.

Many routes led from west to east, not the least of which was the slave route. The Radhanites, Jews who might have originated in the environs of Baghdad, were active, possibly even played a controlling role, in this trade.[23] Around 745 a bubonic plague epidemic swept through the Islamic lands. It is estimated that Islam lost about 25–35 percent of its followers in the seven years of this scourge. There was a desperate need for labor, and the door opened wide to the slave trade. Christian Europe, in turn, saw this as an opportunity to reverse its negative trade balance with Islam. Christians were forbidden to enslave their co-religionists; however, to the east, Slavic lands were inhabited by pagans, and war parties set out to enslave and sell them to the Muslims. So ubiquitous was this trade that the word for 'slave' in English, French, German, and Italian is derived from 'Slav'.[24] Medieval Jews, in turn, called Moravia

[22] See Y. Sussmann, 'Torah she-be-'al Peh Peshutah ke-Mashma'ah: Koḥo shel Kutso shel Yod', in *Meḥkerei Talmud*, 3 (2005), 209–384; N. Danzig, 'Mi-Talmud 'al Peh le-Talmud bi-Khetav: 'Al Derekh Mesirat ha-Talmud ha-Bavli ve Limmudo bi-Yemei ha-Beinayim', in *Sefer ha-Shanah shel Universitat Bar-Ilan—Madda'ei ha-Yahadut u-Madda'ei ha-Ruaḥ*, 30–1 (2006), 49–112. In light of what I propose in Chapter 9, this paragraph describes Ashkenazic settlements prior to the arrival of the men of the Third Yeshivah. Once settled in Mainz, they naturally took advantage of the riches of that emporium. See below, p. 196, for the openness of the men of the Third Yeshivah to alternative readings in the text of the Talmud.

[23] M. Gil, 'The Radhanite Merchants and the Land of Radhan', *Journal of the Economic and Social History of the Orient*, 17 (1974), 299–328. See, however, Jacobi's critique, cited by McCormick, *Origins of the European Economy* (above, n. 12), 688 n. 71.

[24] The fullest and most recent discussion of the slave trade with Islam is that of McCormick, *Origins of the European Economy* (above, n. 12), 733–76; on the bubonic plague, ibid. 504–5, 753, and 113 n. 124.

(which was then pagan) 'the land of Canaan' after the biblical verse: 'Accursed be Canaan. He shall be his brother's meanest slave.'[25]

The current scholarly consensus is that the Jews were the major slave traders in the early Middle Ages.[26] The Christian world would not allow Muslim infidels to traverse and trade freely in its territory. The Christians living in Muslim countries were also a tolerated minority; however, they were bitterly divided into sects and it is doubtful whether one group would lend sufficient help, if any, to Christian traders of another sectarian persuasion. The Jews, however, were a tolerated minority—and a reasonably monolithic one—both in the Islamic and in the Christian worlds. The Diaspora provided Jews with an international network of contacts: communities that would welcome, house, and advise them during their stay. These local co-religionists could further serve as intermediaries between them and the different populations through which they moved. A merchant who traveled internationally also passed through many different legal systems. If he sought to do some business in these locales, he had to master their legal intricacies. The ability to have local, knowledgeable co-religionists serve as intermediaries between the merchant and the general population lightened that burden considerably. Again, a map by McCormick will serve to illustrate the multiple routes of the slave trade (Map 3).[27]

Recently historians, most notably Michael Toch, have begun to challenge vigorously the scope of Ashkenazic Jewish involvement both in international trade in general and in the slave trade in particular.[28] However, all agree that Ashkenazic Jews were predominantly traders and, more important, were purveyors to the imperial and ecclesiastical courts. They appear thus in Latin sources from the sixth-century chronicle of Gregory of Tours down to documents from the end of the tenth century from Vienne, twenty miles south of Lyons (*negotia monachorum*).[29] A similar picture emerges from the Hebrew sources of Ashkenaz, from the responsa literature that first appears at the

[25] Gen. 8: 25–6. The translation is that of the *Jerusalem Bible* (London, 1966).

[26] See the literature cited in M. Toch, 'Jews and Commerce' (above, n. 16), 43–58.

[27] McCormick, *Origins of the European Economy* (above, n. 12), 762.

[28] See M. Toch, 'Jews and Commerce' (above, n. 16), 43–58, to which add 'Wirtschaft und Verfolgung: die Bedeutung der Ökonomie für die Kreuzzugspogrome des 11. und 12. Jahrhunderts. Mit einem Anhang zum Sklavenhandel der Juden', in A. Haverkamp, ed., *Juden und Christen zur Zeit der Kreuzzüge* (Sigmaringen, 1999), 253–85. A fuller discussion of the issue of slavery is available in his Hebrew article 'Yehudei Eiropah bi-Yemei ha-Beinayim ha-Mukdamim: Soḥarei 'Avadim?', *Zion*, 64 (1999), 39–64. See also his general survey, 'The Jews in Europe: 500–1050', in the *New Cambridge Medieval History* (Cambridge, 2005), i. 555–61.

[29] J. Aronius, *Regesten zur Geschichte der Juden im Fränkischen und Deutschen Reiche bis zum Jahre 1273* (repr. Hildesheim, 1970), ##122, 129, 132–4; Blumenkranz, *Juifs et chrétiens* (above, n. 18), 15–19;

end of the tenth and the early decades of the eleventh centuries. Jews are frequently portrayed there as selling to the courts of bishops, local rulers, and even the queen of Hungary.[30] We further find there the institution of *ma'arufya*, a widely employed communal ordinance that forbade a Jew from competing with a co-religionist who until then had been the exclusive purveyor to a Gentile or his factotum. As Toch has written: 'The customers of these [Jewish] merchants [governed by the *ma'arufya* ban] came exclusively from the Christian elite, both secular and ecclesiastical.'[31]

Imagine a Gentile merchant who brings luxury items from the East to sell to local rulers in the German Empire. He knows that among the buyers there are Jewish purveyors to the court and, naturally, he would like to get on their good side. He also knows that for some reason they are eager to receive any written material, even the smallest work, from Babylonia or Palestine. Would he not take care to bring such material with him as presents or to sell it at a high price when he reached Ashkenaz? Wouldn't Jewish purveyors order on their own initiative such books or scrolls? Would they abstain from making contact with the historic, vital centers of their religion? Would they forgo such an opportunity for enlightenment, for taking instruction from the ancient and far-famed seats of learning in Babylonia?

The links with the East were not simply commercial. Numerous pilgrims and envoys also made their way to Constantinople and Jerusalem during this period. Charlemagne kept an eye on the Franks in Jerusalem, and a survey that he had instituted showed that close to one-quarter of the priests and monks in Jerusalem were of Latin (i.e. west European) origin. Between the years 700 and 900 no fewer than 239 emissaries and pilgrims made their way to sacred places in the East, primarily to Constantinople (the city richest in sacred relics) and to Jerusalem: 62 percent came from Italy and 26 percent from the Carolingian Empire.[32] Would not a Jewish pilgrim or merchant have made some effort to reach the famed, almost sacred, academies of Sura and Pumbedita, in whose halls the Talmud had been composed, and bring home some scrolls or codices? Nor did these travelers have to go so far afield as Babylonia.

J.-P. Devroey and C. Brouwer, 'La Participation des Juifs au commerce' (above, n. 16), 361–3; M. Toch, 'Jews and Commerce' (above, n. 16), 43–58, and the previous note.

30 On *ma'arufya*, see S. Eidelberg, 'Ma'arufia in Rabbenu Gershom's Responsa', *Historia Judaica*, 15 (1953), 59–67; repr. in id., *Medieval Ashkenazic History: Studies on German Jewry in the Middle Ages* (New York, 1999), 11–20.

31 M. Toch, 'Pe'ilutam ha-Kalkalit shel Yehudei Germanyah ba-Me'ot ha-'Asirit 'ad ha-Sheteim-'Esreh: Bein Historiografyah le-Historyah', in Y. T. Assis, J. Cohen, et al., eds., *Yehudim mul ha-Tselav: Gezerot Tatnu ba-Historiografyah u-va-Historyah* (Jerusalem, 2000), 43–4.

32 McCormick, *Origins of the European Economy* (above, n. 12), 129–73, esp. pp. 153–8.

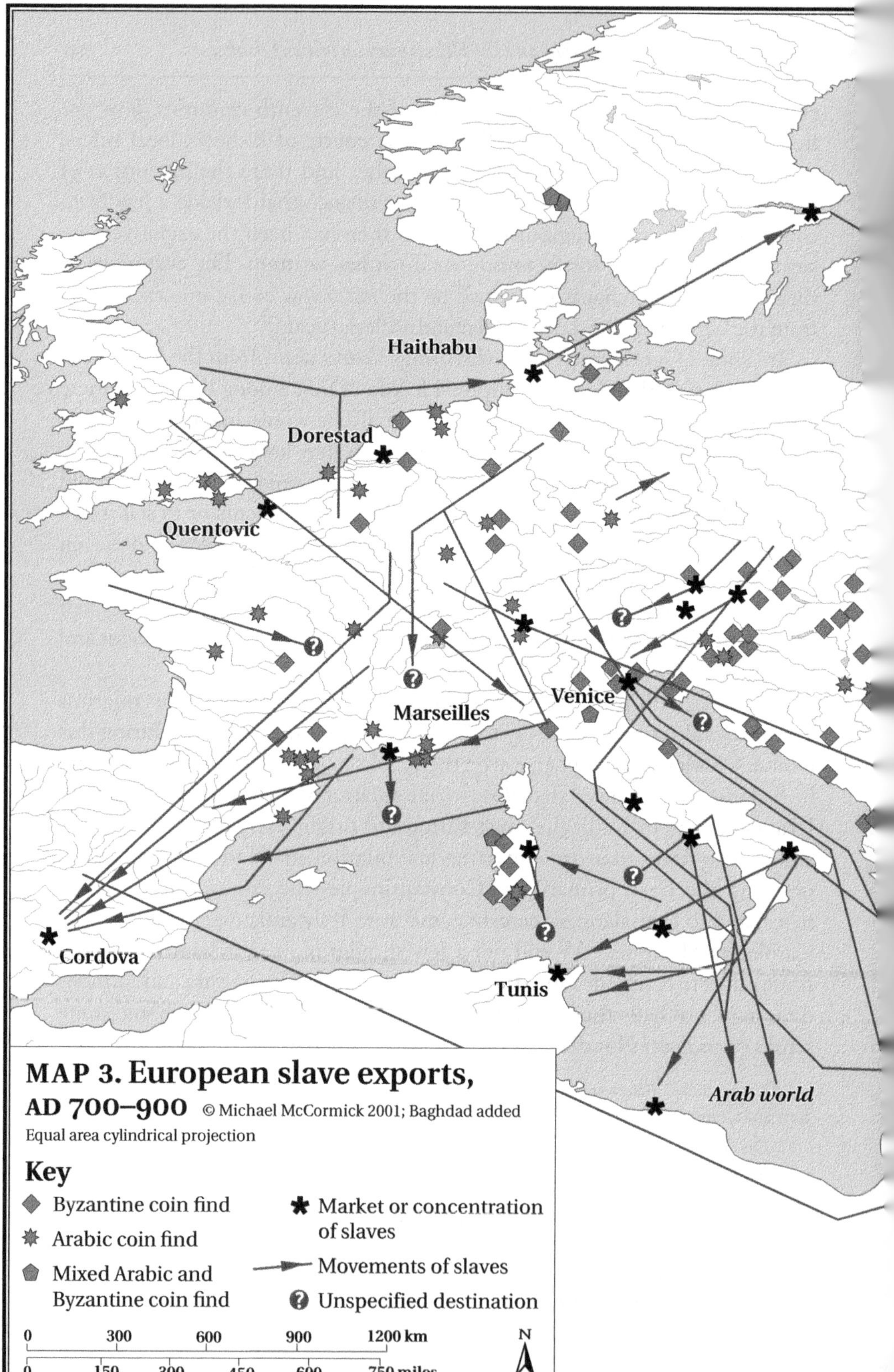

Haithabu
Dorestad
Quentovic
Marseilles
Venice
Cordova
Tunis
Arab world
MAP 3. European slave exports, AD 700–900
© Michael McCormick 2001; Baghdad added
Equal area cylindrical projection
Key
Byzantine coin find
Arabic coin find
Mixed Arabic and Byzantine coin find
Market or concentration of slaves
Movements of slaves
Unspecified destination
0 300 600 900 1200 km
0 150 300 450 600 750 miles
N

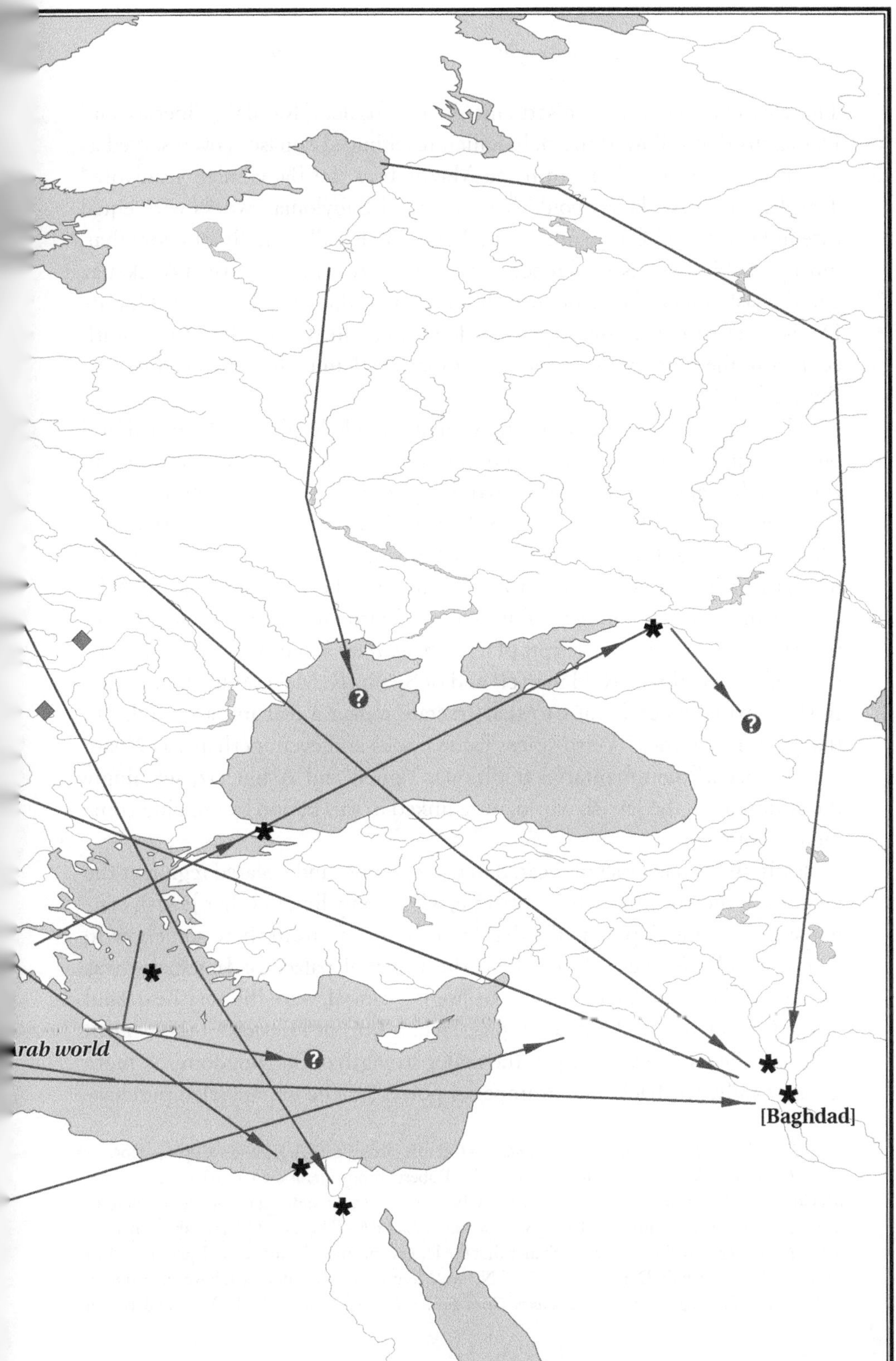
Arab world
[Baghdad]

There was no lack of Jewish settlements in Jerusalem, Ramlah, Tiberias, and Damascus that followed the Babylonian teachings. Damascus even served as an entrepôt for donations from the Maghreb to the Babylonian yeshivot.[33] Travelers from Ashkenaz could have acquired Babylonian works with equal ease in Fustat (Old Cairo) and in the Maghreb. Finally, one should note that, most probably, there is a reference to a direct, early contact between Ashkenaz and the Babylonian Geonate. Jewish merchants who visited the fair at Saint-Denis, outside Paris, sent a query in Jewish law in the middle of the ninth century to the head of one of the Babylonian academies, R. Natronai Gaon of Pumbedita.[34]

The map of the slave trade shows many roads leading to Baghdad and on the map of communication and commerce numerous lines converge on Aachen, the capital of the Carolingian Empire, as well as on the Rhineland, a major pillar of the Ottonian Empire. Is it at all surprising that a superb Spanish manuscript of tractate *Megillah* has many readings typical of Ashkenazic manuscripts or that there are striking similarities between readings in Ashkenazic manuscripts and those found in the Cairo Genizah? Is it any wonder that the Ashkenazic manuscripts of tractate *Sanhedrin* reproduce scribal traditions of the Maghreb (R. Ḥanan'el) and of Spain (R. Me'ir Abul'afia), or that Rashi's textual emendations to that tractate reflect a text in part similar to that found in Yemen? With spices came books and even, perhaps, as Noam has surmised,[35] commentarial traditions. Yemen and Ashkenaz, seemingly the antipodes of the Jewish world, were linked in this period by ongoing commercial contacts.

Early Ashkenaz was not located in some remote and isolated region at the far ends of the known earth of the time, whose only link to other Jewish centers was via some Alpine paths that led to Italy and from there somehow to Palestine. The Rhineland, in which the imperial palace of Ingelheim was located, and nearby Aachen, the Carolingian capital, were the very heartland of the Carolingian and Salian empires, what Otto of Friesing in the twelfth century called *maxima vis regni*, 'the major strength of the kingdom', or, more idiomatically, 'the backbone of imperial power'.[36] The unparalleled purchas-

[33] M. Gil, *Be-Malkhut Yishma'el bi-Tekufat ha-Ge'onim* (above, n. 15), i. 153, and see pp. 149–205.

[34] *Teshuvot R. Natronai bar Hil'ai Ga'on*, ed. Y. (Robert) Brody (Jerusalem, 1994), ii. 243, and see McCormick, *Origins of the European Economy* (above, n. 12), 650–1 and n. 44. For the meaning of 'Farangia' in this responsum, see M. Gil, *Be-Malkhut Yishma'el bi-Tekufat ha-Ge'onim* (above, n. 15), i. 625 n. 349. (There remains an outside chance that the letter concerned the market in Ephesus in Asia Minor and not that of St. Denis.)

[35] V. Noam, 'Mesorot Nusaḥ Kedumot' (above, n. 2), 117–34.

[36] O. von Freising, *Ottonis et Rahewini Gesta Friderici I. imperatoris*, ed. G. Waitz and B. von

ing power of the estates and palaces of the emperor and of local bishops and rulers attracted goods from the four ends of the earth—China, India, Babylonia, Palestine, Spain, and the Maghreb. The port of Venice further linked the Rhineland with Egypt and Yemen. Ashkenaz and 'Lotir' may well have been the richest zone of Europe and, from the point of view of demand and consumption, the economic center of Latin Christendom. Not surprisingly they served as a magnet for all the treasures of the East, including those of the spirit.

In brief, there is no more reason to assume a Palestinian base for the culture of Ashkenaz than a Babylonian one. Ashkenaz had equal access to the treasures of both of these Near Eastern Jewish cultures. From the polemical letter against the Jews that Agobard of Lyons wrote to Emperor Louis the Pious in Aachen in the third decade of the ninth century we know that in the area of *kashrut*, Carolingian Jews followed the Babylonian prescriptions when they conflicted with those of Palestine.[37] We also know that in the area of *yein nesekh*, the ban on wine that had been touched by a Gentile, the rulings of Early Ashkenaz were in keeping with those of Babylonia rather than those of Palestine.[38]

I should emphasize that this in no way precludes Palestinian influences in other spheres of religious life. We have seen that such influence exists to a small degree in prayer, and it may equally exist, to a far greater extent, in other areas. It certainly does not forestall influences in the interstices of halakhah, as in the pre-Av mourning for the destruction of the Second Temple, about which the Babylonian Talmud says nothing. Such influences, however, must

Simpson, Monumenta Germaniae Historica, Scriptores in usum scholarum 46 (Hanover and Leipzig, 1912), 28.

37 Agobard Lugdunensis, 'De insolentia judaeorum', *Opera Omnia*, ed. L. van Acker, Corpus Christianorum Continuatio Medievalis 52 (Turnhout, 1981), 193. Agobard's letter certainly is informative of the conduct of the Jews in Lyons. To my thinking, it is equally revelatory of the Jews in Lotharingia, the seat of the empire. I cannot believe that Agobard, who saw himself as being the object of persecution by influential Jews of the court, would not have taken care to see that these Jewish practices were equally observed in and around Aachen, or even more broadly, in Lotharingia generally. Otherwise, the court Jews could prove him a liar by simply asking the emperor to ascertain in local Jewish settlements if Agobard's descriptions were accurate. See 'Agobard of Lyons, *Megillat Aḥima'ats*, and the Babylonian Orientation of Early Ashkenaz', above, p. 13. (It also appeared in Hebrew: 'Berurim ba-Halakhah shel Ashkenaz ha-Kedumah: (a) Agobard, Megillat Aḥima'ats ve-ha-Halakhah ha-'Erets-Yisra'elit', in Y. Hacker and Y. Harel, eds., *Lo Yasur Shevet mi-Yehudah: Hanhagah, Rabbanut u-Kehillah be-Toledot Yisra'el* [Jerusalem, 2011], 207–18.) On the date of Agobard's missives, see most recently C. Geisel, *Die Juden im Frankenreich* (above, n. 21), 575–81.

38 H. Soloveitchik, *Ha-Yayin bi-Yemei ha-Beinayim—Yein Nesekh: Perek be-Toledot ha-Halakhah be-'Ashkenaz* (Jerusalem, 2008), 321–6.

be proven rather than assumed, for thanks to the recent discoveries mentioned above, the tacit assumption of a century and a half is no longer valid.

In retrospect, these assumptions seem only natural. Like all scholars, the nineteenth-century proponents of Wissenschaft des Judentums were only too eager to demonstrate the novel results of their discipline, to show how their findings would dispel common misconceptions. It was axiomatic in that century, as in previous centuries, that Ashkenazic Jewry had lived by the light of the Talmud, meaning of course the Babylonian Talmud, which had guided Jews for over a millennium. Nothing was then more natural when Wissenschaft uncovered the Palestinian origin of a score or so of liturgical formulas, or revealed that here and there a custom made sense only in light of Palestinian data, than to proclaim that the origins of Ashkenaz were not what they had seemed; that the religious roots of north European Jewry lay deep in Palestinian soil. Partially from unconscious Zionist motivation, partially because the Pirenne thesis had portrayed Christian Europe as being wholly cut off from the Muslim world, twentieth-century scholars viewed Ashkenaz as tenuously connected to the East. The advances in the study of liturgical poetry (*piyyut*) had further demonstrated that Ashkenazic liturgical poetry had been patterned after Italian models, and Italian models were unquestionably developments of the Palestinian ones.[39] *Piyyut* originated in Palestine, so it was assumed that Ashkenazic religious practices equally had their roots in the same soil. This then linked up with a 'founding story' that spoke of the translation of R. Kalonymos from Lucca to Mainz, and with it the establishment of Ashkenazic culture. That the story never made any claim that the halakhic traditions of Ashkenaz had originated in Italy, only its mystical ones, was overlooked. Equally overlooked or, at least, under-emphasized was its clear statement that these esoteric teachings came not from Palestine but from Babylonia, brought to 'Lombardiyah' by the mysterious 'Abu Aharon of Bagdidim' (i.e. Baghdad).[40] The roots of Ashkenaz lay in Italy; Italy had, in the Byzantine period, ongoing contacts with Palestine; ergo, Ashkenazic culture was rooted in Palestine. Thus the common notion of the cultural origins of the Ashkenazic community was born, and thus it was maintained for well over a century and a half.

Liturgy was more than simply a component of this viewpoint. The enor-

[39] E. Fleischer, *Shirat ha-Kodesh ha-'Ivrit bi-Yemei ha-Beinayim* (Jerusalem, 1975), 79–276, 425–84.

[40] Text in Y. Dan, *Torat ha-Sod shel Ḥasidei Ashkenaz* (Jerusalem, 1968), 14–20. Discussion in Grossman, *Ḥakhmei Ashkenaz* (above, n. 9), 29–44; J. Schatzmiller, 'Politics and the Myth of Origins', in G. Dahan, ed., *Les Juifs au regard de l'histoire: Mélanges en l'honneur de Bernhard Blumenkranz* (Paris, 1985), 52–4, 61.

mous progress made over the past four decades in the field of liturgical poetry, fueled primarily by the Herculean labors of the late Ezra Fleischer, has endowed that poetry with a significance greater than it deserved. Not that the importance of *piyyut* was exaggerated; it was a fundamental component of Ashkenazic culture. However, its evolution cannot serve as the bellwether of that culture generally. Developments in liturgical poetry are one thing, developments in Jewish law another, and those in religious praxis may yet be different from both. Each area demands investigation on its own terms. In liturgy itself, as distinct from liturgical poetry, we have seen that the influence of Babylonia far outstripped that of Palestine. Indeed, there is no reason even to assume that the Ashkenazic liturgy is cut from one cloth. Certainly, the different textual traditions reflected in the Ashkenazic Talmud point to variegated and multicultural origins. If any place in Europe had broad cultural exposure, free access to the cultural artifacts of both Palestine and Babylonia, and those of Fustat, Yemen, and the Maghreb too, it was the Rhineland and Lotir, the heartland and great emporium of the Carolingian and Ottonian empires.

As a coda, I would note that a recent revolutionary essay of Mendels and Edrei undermines another unarticulated assumption of the Palestinian origins of Ashkenaz.[41] It was reasonably assumed that most (though not all) settlers in northern Europe had arrived from the south, from the Mediterranean littoral with its ancient Jewish settlements. Coming from the former Roman Empire, the Jews naturally brought with them the Palestinian religious way of life, the practices reflected and formulated in the Palestinian Talmud. The customs of the Jews in the East mirrored, more or less, the Babylonian Talmud, and so it was only natural to assume that the practices of the Jews in the West reflected those of the Palestinian Talmud. However, if Mendels and Edrei are correct (and for what it is worth, I believe them to be),[42] the Jews from the empire west of Anatolia brought with them nothing other than a vague biblical

[41] A. Edrei and D. Mendels, 'A Split Jewish Diaspora: Its Dramatic Consequences', *Journal for the Study of the Pseudepigrapha*, 16/2 (2007), 91–137; 17 (2008), 163–87. An expanded German version has appeared as *Zweierlei Diaspora: Zur Spaltung der antiken jüdischen Welt*, Toldot: Essays zur jüdischen Geschichte und Kultur 8 (Göttingen, 2010).

[42] Cf. J. L. Kurtzer, '"What Shall the Alexandrians Do?": Rabbinic Judaism and the Mediterranean Diaspora' (Ph.D. diss., Harvard University, 2008), 234–318; F. Millar, 'A Rural Jewish Community in Late Roman Mesopotamia and the Question of a "Split" Jewish Diaspora', *Journal for the Study of Judaism*, 42 (2011), 364–74, and the reply of Edrei and Mendeles, 'A Split Diaspora Again—A Response to Fergus Millar', *Journal for the Study of the Pseudepigrapha*, 21 (2012), 305–11.

Judaism. Ashkenazic culture, rabbinic to the core, must then be seen not as a continuation and transformation of the Jewish religious identity of the later Roman Empire, but as a break with an indistinct and tenuous past and a fresh and sharply etched beginning. Lotir and the adjacent Rhineland saw the emergence of a new religious civilization about whose origins and nature we at present know very little.[43]

[43] See below, Ch. 9.

CHAPTER EIGHT

The Palestinian Orientation of the Ashkenazic Community and Some Suggested Ground Rules for the Writing of Halakhic History

As I explained in the preceding essay, it is currently a truism of Jewish historiography that the roots of Ashkenaz lie deep in Palestinian soil; indeed, some say, it was not until the mid-eleventh century that the Babylonian Talmud (Bavli) became normative.[1] In Chapter 7 I addressed the underlying assumption of this theory; here I would like to express the doubts that I have long entertained about this scholarly commonplace.

Let us begin with the methodological problems in the claims for the Palestinian origins of Ashkenaz.

Assume that there are roughly 200 laws regulating the observance of the numerous commandments relating to Passover; that is to say, the elimination of leavened bread, the preparation of matzah, and the observance of the *seder*. Suppose two or three are discovered to reflect Palestinian law; what this would mean is that, at most, some 2 percent of the Ashkenazic practices of Passover have Palestinian roots. However, no religious culture is a monolith, and a 2 or 3 percent admixture of the religious practices of other cultures is only natural. For example, in the lighting of Hanukkah candelabra, a field with far fewer laws than Passover, the Jews of eastern Europe follow the ruling of the Sephardic scholar Maimonides, and Sephardic Jews follow that of the famed medieval Franco-German glossators known as the Tosafists![2] Other examples of such crossovers could easily be provided. All this is common knowledge; yet no one would contend that east European religious culture has Sephardic

[1] See above, p. 122 n. 1, for the scholarly literature.

[2] *Tosafot*, *Shabbat* 21b, s.v. *u-mehadderin*; *Mishneh Torah*, 'Ḥanukkah', 4: 1; *Shulḥan 'Arukh*, 'Oraḥ Ḥayyim', 671: 2.

roots. For it is understood that to speak of influence one must have critical mass, a sufficient number of examples to rule out mere happenstance as the source of the anomalous results.

Critical mass, however, is precisely what has been lacking in the numerous articles published on the Palestinian origins of Ashkenaz. Most articles take an instance or two from a specific area, let us say, the Sabbath, another instance from a second halakhic field and a third from yet another field, show that they are of Palestinian origin, and then draw broad inferences. There is no thesis in the world which cannot be proven by such a method of sampling.

There are several areas where there does, indeed, seem to be critical mass. As I mentioned in the previous chapter, the laws of mourning for the destruction of the Second Temple during the three weeks preceding Tish'ah be-'Av are unquestionably of Palestinian origin (something medieval scholars have already noted[3]); liturgy would seem to be another such instance. Nineteenth-century scholars identified some dozen or two instances where the Ashkenazic liturgy has formulas drawn from the Palestinian rite. However, many years ago the distinguished editor of liturgical texts Daniel Goldschmidt pointed out to me that this inference was valid only in the nineteenth century, before the Genizah was discovered and its texts published. Now that we know that the differences in liturgy between the Palestinian and Babylonian rites run into the many hundreds and even thousands, the significance of a score of Palestinian formulas in the Ashkenazic rite dwindles dramatically.[4] Dwindle though it may, nevertheless there is critical mass for some claim of influence. Fifteen to twenty instances cannot be the product of chance. In most of the other examples adduced for Palestinian influence, the sparse evidence presented rarely rises above claims of the random.

The only approach that will yield substantive results is 'area study'. That is to say, to take an entire field of Jewish law, the Sabbath or Passover for example, study *all* of its laws in all their complexity, and then assess whether there are sufficient correlations with distinctive Palestinian dicta to justify a claim of influence. No such study was ever conducted by any of the proponents of the Palestinian origins of Ashkenazic culture. Several years ago I published just such a study of the laws of *yein nesekh*, the ban on all wine that a Gentile has made or even so much as touched. I did not undertake the research with

[3] *Tosefot ha-Rashba 'al Pesaḥim*, ed. E. D. Rabinovits-Te'omim (Jerusalem, 1956), 40b, s.v. *aval*; *Tosefot R. Yehudah Sir Leon 'al Massekhet Berakhot*, ed. N. Sachs (Jerusalem, 1969), i. 18a, s.v. *dalyeh*; *Or Zarua'*, ii (Zhitomir, 1862), #421, and parallel passages cited in the first two works.

[4] Goldschmidt's point was later strikingly illustrated by E. Fleischer's *Tefillah u-Minhagei Tefillah Erets Yisra'eliyim bi-Tekufat ha-Genizah* (Jerusalem, 1988).

any intent to test the Palestinian influence on Early Ashkenaz; the study had a wholly different focus. Nevertheless, two things clearly emerged: first, that prior to Rashi, Ashkenazic scholars had a very imperfect knowledge of tractate *'Avodah Zarah* in the Bavli, which governed the laws of *yein nesekh*. This should have made pre-Crusade Ashkenaz fertile soil for Palestinian influence and, even more important, for its continuance down to the closing decades of the eleventh century. Yet, and this was the second finding, the practices recorded in the pre-Rashi literature reflect entirely the prescriptions of the Bavli. In fact, several of the pre-Crusade rulings stand in stark opposition to the directives found in the Yerushalmi.[5] In other words, in an area where we would most expect a strong Palestinian presence, what we find is pure Babylonian halakhah. This does not, of course, preclude a Palestinian influence in some other areas of Jewish law, but it should preclude scholars from simply assuming such influence or advancing, as is common, wisps of evidence as proof positive of its existence.

As I pointed out in Chapter 4, the claim that Rabbenu Gershom ruled, like the Yerushalmi and against the Bavli, that the blessing over aromatic spices (*besamim*) should be included in the *kiddush-havdalah* service recited when a festival begins on a Saturday night is based upon a report in the *Shibbolei ha-Leket*, a thirteenth-century Italian work whose author studied in Germany and maintained his contacts with scholars in that country.[6] Inspection of the passage has shown, however, that the author is not citing any of his well-known German contacts, but an otherwise unknown Rabbi Ya'ir b. Me'ir—who is never cited again by the author of the *Shibbolei ha-Leket* or any other medieval writer, to the best of my knowledge. Second, this unknown scholar writes that he '*heard* [apparently he has an oral tradition] in the name of Rabbenu Gershom' that one should follow the Yerushalmi and recite the blessing over *besamim*. Not a single German report of Rabbenu Gershom's ruling states that his decision was based on the Yerushalmi—neither that of Ravan nor that of the encyclopedic Ravyah. Even more telling: the earliest report of Rabbenu Gershom's position, found in the *Ma'aseh ha-Makhiri*, edited or compiled by his great-nephews, makes no mention of the Yerushalmi. As of yet, no passage has been found in the Yerushalmi which would support the claim of the mysterious R. Ya'ir b. Me'ir.

This illustrates another methodological problem in the current halakhic historiography. There have been few, if any, discussions based on a critical editing of the sources cited. Most rulings and responsa have come down to us

[5] H. Soloveitchik, *Ha-Yayin bi-Yemei ha-Beinayim—Yein Nesekh: Perek be-Toledot ha-Halakhah be-'Ashkenaz* (Jerusalem, 2008), 133–66, 321–7.

[6] See above, pp. 79–81.

in various medieval florilegia, each with its own textual version. It is only natural to choose a text that suits one's argument. Without independently determining or reconstructing, *prior to any historical analysis*, the text closest to what the author wrote or to what was first reported in his name, the historian will simply document his preconceptions. Other than the first four volumes of the *Sefer Ravyah*, no major halakhic work and precious few minor ones of the high Middle Ages have received a genuine critical edition. Without textual editing one simply cannot write halakhic history. I don't mean editing an entire manuscript or florilegium; I simply mean editing critically the specific responsum or report of a ruling that is being introduced in the discussion. The astonishing thing is that this has rarely been done. Article after article appears on the history of halakhah in the Middle Ages without any critical evaluation of the text of the sources cited and from which conclusions are being drawn.

If I may be allowed to point to another lacuna in the current historiography of halakhah. In the essays on Agobard, *minhag* Ashkenaz ha-Kadmon, the role of biblical verses and *midrashim* in the rulings of the eleventh-century scholars of the Rhineland, and the characterization of Rabbenu Sasson,[7] I made a mini-study of each topic discussed. I had to survey the medieval halakhic literature on the topic, investigate the Ashkenazic sources in greater detail, and then attempt to locate the view of the individual in the larger halakhic landscape to understand it more fully and to better assess its distinctiveness or conventionality. I had to do this because it had not been done in any of the essays that I was discussing. While drawing conclusions about the intellectual history of Early Ashkenaz, almost no study of the past thirty-five years has examined the actual thought of this period. A doctrine is referred to, a conclusion drawn from it, but few, if any, studies have attempted to seriously engage the topic under discussion, to study it in depth and contextualize it within the legal culture of the time. Legal history cannot dispense with legal thought. It is not surprising that when the views of the various halakhists were actually studied and their background fully recovered, most of the novel conclusions drawn from them disappeared.

This lack of engagement with halakhic thought has led to a strange mode of reasoning. Not grappling with substance, historians could argue only by analogy, inferring law from poetry. Since Ashkenazic *piyyut* was Palestinian in origin, law and religious rites must equally have been Palestinian. To the best of my knowledge, no one has argued that, since Baudelaire was influenced by Edgar Allen Poe, Saint-Simon had to be influenced by Thoreau.[8]

[7] Above, pp. 5–19, 29–69, 85–100, 106–21.

[8] See above, pp. 106–7, for suggested ground rules for biographical studies of medieval halakhists.

To return to Palestine. So far I have argued that, given the questionable methodology underlying most of the claims for the Palestinian origins of the Ashkenazic community, the thesis remains unproven. I would add two obvious empirical objections. First, there is no evidence that Early Ashkenaz even possessed a text of the Yerushalmi.[9] It is true that we have no manuscripts of the Talmud from Ashkenaz that pre-date 1179; however, the scholars of pre-Crusade Ashkenaz discuss at length passages in the Bavli and debate their meaning, and it is crystal clear that they hold in front of them a text of that corpus. There are no equivalent discussions of passages in the Yerushalmi. Here and there they invoke an isolated line or two, but never do we find an actual discussion, an analysis of the give and take of a *sugya* in that work. All the cultural artifacts of the Orient were available to the men of Ashkenaz, as I outlined in a previous essay,[10] and they partook liberally of the rich midrashic, mystical, and poetic writings of Palestine. Yet they never bothered to obtain a copy of the Yerushalmi. It doesn't seem to have interested them—strange conduct for a culture that was allegedly rooted in that of Palestine and walked by the light of its teachings.

At the same time medieval scholars in Ashkenaz were actively engaged in exegeting in unprecedented detail the entire corpus of the Bavli—witness the so-called *Perush Rabbenu Gershom 'al ha-Talmud*, large sections of which are found in the standard (Romm) edition of the Talmud. This entailed, as I have outlined in '*Minhag* Ashkenaz ha-Kadmon', an enormous, almost unbelievable, expenditure of effort.[11] Why should Early Ashkenaz have labored mightily on the Bavli and ignored the Yerushalmi if they were guided all the while by Palestinian halakhah and its rite?

9 *Pace* Ta-Shma, 'Sifriyatam shel Ḥakhmei Ashkenaz ve-Tsarfat', *Kiryat Sefer*, 60 (1985), 302; repr. in his *Keneset Meḥkarim*, i (Jerusalem, 2004), 27–8. Yaacov Sussmann, who has made the most exhaustive study of Yerushalmi citations in medieval Europe, is equally of the opinion that there is no evidence of a text of the Yerushalmi in Ashkenaz before the 12th century. The so-called *Sefer Yerushalmi* first surfaces in Ashkenaz in the latter half of the 12th century, not before. See Y. Sussmann, '"Yerushalmi Ketav-Yad Ashkenazi" ve-"Sefer ha-Yerushalmi"', *Tarbiz*, 65 (1998), 37–63. See above, Ch. 3, n. 94, and below, Ch. 9, n. 16.

10 See above, pp. 122–44.

11 See above, pp. 31–3, and below, p. 159.

CHAPTER NINE

The 'Third Yeshivah of Bavel' and the Cultural Origins of Ashkenaz—A Proposal

WHILE the previous chapters were formulated in the 1980s and only now, as I explained in the Preface, have I gotten around to putting down on paper my reservations about the reigning views of Early Ashkenaz, the present essay occurred to me only as I was finishing this volume. Indeed, there are sentences, even an occasional argument, in the preceding essays that indicate that I did not yet have any notion of a 'Third Yeshivah of Bavel'. I left those passages unaltered and noted only in the footnotes the possible implications of the present essay. The previous essays are in every way self-standing, and their rejection of the current theories of the origins of Ashkenazic halakhic culture in no way hinges upon the far-ranging thesis that I propose below. I emphasize that, at the moment, this is only a proposal.

THE THEORIES that Ashkenaz was originally governed by an ancient, immutable custom or that its roots lay deep in the halakhic soil of Palestine have been weighed and found wanting.[1] The reader, however, is entitled to ask, 'While dispelling error is always beneficial, what have you to offer in its place? Ashkenaz did not emerge *ex nihilo*; it came from somewhere. Where was that "somewhere" and what was its nature? Can you suggest a new narrative of the genesis of Ashkenazic culture?'

I would like to thank Jerry Balsam, Menahem Ben-Sasson, David Berger, Robert Brody, Shulamit Elitsur, Avraham Fraenkel, Mordechai Friedman, Shamma Friedman, Elisabeth Hollender, Chaim Ilson, Sheon Karol, Paul M. Mandel, Ezra Merkin, Sara Strumsa, Yaacov Sussmann, David Rosenthal, Yoav Rosenthal, and Sara Zfatman for discussing with me various drafts of this essay. Their comments saved me from many an error. For the remaining ones, I alone bear responsibility.

[1] See above, pp. 29–100.

I believe that I can point to a key source, one of the major components of that civilization; indeed, I would argue that this source of Ashkenazic halakhah has been open to public view ever since 1881, when 'The Brothers and Widow of Romm' published in Vilna what immediately became the standard edition of the Talmud. I am further of the opinion that this starting point goes far in explaining some of the lasting characteristics of Ashkenaz, such as (*a*) the notion of *kehillah kedoshah*, a community of the righteous and the observant that I have noted in my studies of pawnbroking and *yein nesekh* (wine touched by Gentiles);[2] (*b*) its halakhic insularity—its indifference to the halakhic achievements of other Jewish communities;[3] and (*c*) its sustained apathy to the higher culture of its surroundings—its refusal to engage in the philosophical and scientific pursuits of Latin Europe.

I am not contending that the Babylonian Talmud is the sole source of Ashkenazic halakhic culture—cultural origins tend to be far more complex—I argue only for its centrality. As my thesis touches upon Geonica, and the inscription and finalizing of the texts of the Talmud and the *midreshei aggadah*, a full presentation demands a monograph, which, hopefully, will appear in the future and address issues which have not been dealt with in this essay. I would like, however, to sketch here the contours of my proposal so as to conclude my re-evaluation of Early Ashkenaz on a constructive note.

Most people engaged in Jewish studies have heard in their childhood—the story goes back to fourteenth-century Spain[4]—that Rashi's commentary was written *be-ruaḥ ha-kodesh* (inspired by the Holy Spirit). Plausibly enough, for how else could he have known all of the minute details of the countless talmudic narratives, not to speak of his command of the underlying concepts of all the talmudic discussions, many of which are assumed by the discussants in the Talmud, but are not clearly explicated anywhere? I here suggest that these astonishing feats can be explained without recourse to miracles—a proposal, if you wish, by a *litvak* to counter claims of the Holy Spirit.

Let me preface my discussion with some strange questions posed by a responsum of Rabbenu Gershom (d. 1028). It reads:

[2] *Collected Essays* (Oxford, 2013), i. 112, 239–77. [3] Ibid. 31–8.

[4] Menaḥem b. Zeraḥ, *Tsedah la-Derekh* (Warsaw, 1881), introduction, p. 6, and see J. Penkower, 'Tahalikh Kanonizatsyah shel Perush Rashi la-Torah', in H. Kreisel, ed., *Limmud ve-Da'at ba-Maḥshavah ha-Yehudit* (Be'er Sheva, 2006), 124–5.

אמנם ידעתי שכן כת[וב] בהלכו[ת] פסוקו[ת] וגם כתו[ב] בתשובת שאילתות[5]... ומה שפסקתי [בניגוד לזה] להפך שבועה אפי[לו] דאורית[א], מפני שר׳ ליאון רבי [ש]לימדני רוב תלמודי זצ״ל, חכם מופלא היה, ולא סבר ליה דלית הלכתא כמר בר רב אשי. ונראה דברי ר׳ ליאון רבי מדבריהם כי יש לומ[ר] איזה כח מרובה ... ועל כל הטעמים האילו סמכתי ולא חלקתי להפך שבועה בין דאוריית[א] לדרבנן. ועוד סמכתי על דברי רבי, ועוד שלא מצאתי בכל התלמוד שלמדתי שאין הילכתא כמר בר רב אשי במיפך שבועה. ואם בתלמוד אינו, ומסבר[א] הם אומר[ים], רואה אני את דברי ר׳ ליאון רבי שמסר לי, כי מופלא בדורו ואחרי דבר[יו] לא ישנו.

[5] Our text of the *Halakhot Pesukot*, ed. S. Sassoon, 2nd edn. with supplement by N. Danzig (Jerusalem, 1999), does not contain this passage. It is, however, found in some versions of the *Halakhot Gedolot* (Venice, 1548), fo. 233a; (Berlin, 1888–92), 490; (Jerusalem, 1972–87), iii. 61–2, and see nn. 16, 17 ad loc. It is also to be found in the *Seder Tanna'im ve-'Amora'im*, ed. K. Kahana (Frankfurt, 1935), 23, #38: 3–4. See A. (Rami) Reiner, 'Le-Hitkabluto shel Sefer "Halakhot Gedolot" be-'Ashkenaz', in H. Kreisel, ed., *Limmud ve-Da'at be-Maḥshavah Yehudit* (Be'er Sheva, 2006), 117–18. There are five possible constructions of Rabbenu Gershom's first reference. The simplest is to take it at face value and view the absence of this passage in our version as one of a number of passages that were present in the text that circulated in the Middle Ages but have since been lost. See N. Danzig, *Mavo le-Sefer Halakhot Pesukot*, rev. edn. (Jerusalem, 1999), 391–410. S. Abramson, in a posthumously published work, takes it as referring to a collection of brief responsa of R. Yehudai Gaon. (See R. Hai b. Sherira Gaon, *Sefer Mishpetei ha-Shevu'ot*, ed. S. Abramsom [Jerusalem, 2012], 291–9.) Reiner takes it as a reference to the *Halakhot Gedolot* and Danzig (*Mavo le-Sefer*, 403–4) takes it as referring to the *Seder Tanna'im ve-'Amora'im*. Kupfer suggests that it may be another collection of geonic rulings that circulated at the time and was equally entitled *Halakhot Pesukot*, i.e. *piskei halakhot* of the Geonim. For our purposes all the interpretations are one and the same. I have adopted the first interpretation only because it makes for a simpler exposition. The second reference in the responsum may refer to any one of the numerous geonic responsa endorsing this view listed in the Jerusalem edition of the *Halakhot Gedolot* at n. 16. (On the Prague and Budapest edition of the *Teshuvot R. Me'ir mi-Rotenburg*, see above, Ch. 3, n. 43 end.)

One might be tempted to contend that, since MSS Bibliothèque Nationale, 1402, Vatican 136, and Vatican 304 of the *Halakhot Gedolot*—which A. Shweka has shown to be the best manuscripts of that work—all have the opposite version, namely, that the ruling is *in accordance* with Mar bar Rav Asi, the version I have cited from the Venice 1548 edition is without significance. The issue, however, is not what the author of the *Halakhot Gedolot* thought of the question—his work is mentioned neither by the inquirer nor by Rabbenu Gershom—but whether there was a Babylonian (or 'eastern') text that contained the ruling against Mar bar Rav Asi in the text of the Talmud itself. MSS Vatican 142 and Milano-Ambrosiana C116 Sup of the *Halakhot Gedolot* corroborate the Venice reading. Shweka has shown that, for all their differences, both these families of manuscripts find corroboration in texts discovered in the Genizah and consequently are equally of eastern origin. Thus, a talmudic passage containing a ruling contrary to Mar bar Rav Asi is attested to in the East. (See A. Shweka, ''Iyyunim be-Sefer Halakhot Gedolot: Nusaḥ va-'Arikhah' [Ph.D. diss., Bar Ilan University, 2008], 357–61. I would like to thank Dr Shweka for making his thesis available to me.)

One reader has contended that Rabbenu Gershom believed that the dictum cited in the *Halakhot Pesukot*, and again by the anonymous geonic respondent—*halakhah ke-Mar bar Rav Asi be-kula talmuda bar mi-mepakh shevu'ah ve-'odita*—is simply a *sevara* (product of ratiocinative argument) of the Geonim. Rabbenu Gershom thought neither that it was found in their text of the Talmud nor that it was a geonic tradition. I find this implausible. The dictum takes the form of a classic *kelal hora'ah* (rule of adjudication). It is found, together with dozens of other such *kelalim*, in the mid-9th-century

To be sure I am aware [that such a dictum] is found in the *Halakhot Pesukot* and also in a [geonic] responsum . . . The reason [I have ruled contrary to this dictum] . . . is that my teacher, R. Leon, who taught me most of what I know of the Talmud, was a truly exceptional scholar and he did not agree with this dictum. And his position seems the more reasonable one for [the following reasons] . . . Relying upon all these reasons, I have ruled contrary to the dictum and did not distinguish in 'inverting the oath' between a pentateuchal oath and a rabbinic one. . . . And I have further relied upon the position of my teacher. Moreover, I have not found such a dictum in any place in the Talmud that I have studied. If this dictum is not found in the Talmud but is being advanced by them [i.e. the aforesaid Geonim] solely on the basis of logic, I find myself in agreement with the position of which my teacher informed me [*sic*], for he was the outstanding scholar of his generation, and one should not deviate from his articulated position.[6]

The specific topic (inverting pentateuchal oaths, *mepakh shevu'ah de-'oraita*) need not here occupy us; significant to us are the claims advanced. Rabbenu Gershom made a threefold argument of text, teacher, and logic. Let us take them in reverse order. Few people in the late tenth and early eleventh centuries would assign greater halakhic weight to their own reasoning than to that of the Geonim. Rabbenu Gershom's position here reflects notable independence but poses no intrinsic difficulty. Not so his other two contentions. His teacher, R. Leon (or Leontin, as he is sometimes called) is the authority on which he relied. This shadowy figure, familiar to subsequent generations only as the teacher of Rabbenu Gershom and without any other known accomplishment to his name, was being invoked as a counter to the authority of the *Halakhot Pesukot* and that of another (anonymous) Gaon. Does this not reflect an extravagant self-image? A new community emerged in north-western Europe and immediately claimed—no more and no less—that the holding of its founder or master teacher was superior in halakhic authority to that of the Geonim! As for text: Rabbenu Gershom was confronted with a ruling of the Geonim based on their version of the Talmud, which states explicitly that the law is contrary to the view of Mar bar Rav Asi.[7] To this he replied that

geonic work *Seder Tanna'im ve-'Amora'im*. If someone wishes to contend that all the other *kelalim* in that book are products of *sevara* rather than *kabbalah* (tradition), he has his work cut out for him. If all or most of the other *kelalim* are *kabbalah*, why assume this one is a *sevara*? On the significance of Rabbenu Gershom's invocation of *sevara*, see below, n. 7, and p. 124.

[6] *Teshuvot u-Fesakim me'et Ḥakhmei Tsarfat ve-'Ashkenaz*, ed. E. Kupfer (Jerusalem, 1973), #114; *Teshuvot R. Me'ir mi-Rotenburg* (Prague and Budapest, 1895), #264; a report of this responsum is found in R. Yitsḥak of Marseilles, *Sefer ha-'Ittur*, ed. R. Me'ir Yonah, vol. ii, 'Milveh 'al Peh', fo. 17c.

[7] One could argue that the Geonim did not claim that this was the text in the Talmud, but that they had a tradition, as exemplified by the *Seder Tanna'im ve-'Amora'im*, that the ruling was against

his version of the Talmud had no such passage. In other words, he was challenging the Geonim as to the proper text of the Talmud! How can someone thousands of miles away from Mesopotamia challenge the talmudic text of Sura and Pumbedita, the very institutions from which the text emerged? How could one possibly have a more authentic text of the Talmud than the Geonim of Sura and Pumbedita? Either Rabbenu Gershom's stance was megalomaniacal or it drew on a reality imperceptible to us, but of which he and his auditors were very much aware.

As were equally his disciples; for this independence of the Geonim, even curt dismissals of their rulings, while not quite as blatant as that which we have just encountered, are characteristic of Early Ashkenaz generally. Rabbenu Gershom's successor, R. Yehudah Ba'al Sefer ha-Dinim, rejected a holding of the *Halakhot Gedolot* by declaring that the ruling was so illogical that it was clearly inauthentic; someone else must have inserted the passage in the work.[8]

דהא מילתא מעולם לא נפיק מפומיה, דהכי כתוב התם . . . ואי סלקא דעתא דרב יהודאי אמרה, פה קדוש כרב יהודה משתעי כי האי לישנא, אלא ודאי איניש אחרינא אמרה ואסקא בשמיה.

For such a statement never issued forth from his [i.e. R. Yehudai's] mouth, for it states there . . . And should you think that R. Yehudai said it, could such a holy [i.e. wise]

the view of Rav Asi. This was certainly the position of Rav Sherira Gaon: **ונקיטי רבנן בשמועה מן הראשונים דהלכה כרב אשי בכולי תנויי לבר מן תלת, וחדא מיניהו מיפך שבועה** (*Teshuvot u-Ferushei R. Sherira Gaon*, ed. N. D. Rabinowich [Jerusalem, 2012], ii, #21 and sources cited there). The question, then, is: 'How can Rabbenu Gershom disagree with a tradition of adjudication of Sura or Pumbedita?' How can he say that, if a ruling is not found in the Talmud, the tradition of the Geonim is never better than the best argument that can be made for it? To demand of a geonic tradition that it should justify itself logically is to state that such a tradition has no intrinsic legal value. See below, p. 214.

[8] *Sefer ha-Pardes*, ed. H. L. Ehrenreich (Budapest, 1924), 350; *Shibbolei ha-Leket ha-Shalem*, ed. S. Buber (Vilna, 1887), fo. 74, #190. *Haggahot Maimuniyot*, 'Evel', 10: 10, n. 10. Much as it would suit my purpose, I do not see the basis for attributing to R. Yehudah Ba'al Sefer ha-Dinim the very sharp remarks about the *Halakhot Gedolot* found in *Or Zarua'*, ii (Zhitomir, 1862), #432. Rabbi Yehudah did disagree with the ruling (*Ma'aseh ha-Ge'onim*, ed. A. Epstein and J. Freimann [Berlin, 1910], #59, p. 50). This, however, does not make him the author of that missive. Cf. Reiner, 'Le-Hitkabluto' (above, n. 5), 98–9. See N. Danzig's discussion in his *Mavo le-Sefer Halakhot Pesukot* (above, n. 5), 261–5. A colleague has contended that the passage in the *Sefer ha-Pardes* is 'an indication of reluctance to dismiss geonic authority'. R. Yehudah's dismissal of geonic authority is more respectful than that of his predecessor or successor, but it is scarcely a reluctant one. It's a standard step in the judicial choreography of dissent, and one employed by such an unreluctant dissenter as Rabbenu Tam. See e.g. *Sefer ha-Yashar: Ḥelek ha-Ḥiddushim*, ed. S. S. Schlesinger (Jerusalem, 1959), #315. On the subsequent Ashkenazic strategy of invoking the blindness of R. Yehudai Gaon—which resulted in his inability to control the text of his book—to explain away rulings which they found incomprehensible, see Danzig, *Mavo* (above, n. 5), 10–11 nn. 73, 263 n. 114.

mouth as R. Yehudai have uttered a statement like that?! Clearly someone else said it and attributed it to him.

A generation later, when someone cited in a dispute the authority of the *Halakhot Gedolot*, R. Yitsḥak ha-Levi of Worms—who held a different position—brushed aside the ruling, saying:[9]

ואותו אדם גדול שסידר ההלכות גדולות חכם מופלא [היה], אבל לא יכולנו לעמוד על דעתו בכמה מקומות שכתב בטרפשא דכבד . . . אפשר כן הוא?! אבל אין משיבין את הארי אחר מיתה (גיטין פ"ג ע"א). ועוד כתב כנתא לא נפיק מדמא עד עולם, אפשר נשמע לו?!

That great man who compiled the *Halakhot Gedolot* was a truly exceptional scholar; however, we could not understand his opinions in a number of places. He wrote [e.g. on a certain topic] . . . Could this possibly be correct?! However, 'one does not reply to the lion [i.e. criticize an eminent scholar] after his death' [*Gittin* 83a]. He further wrote [ruled on another topic] . . . Could we possibly listen to him [i.e. pay heed to his ruling]?!

There is, to be sure, an opening courteous bow, but what follows—and one can hear the oral cadence of the transcribed remarks—is brutally dismissive, and unlike anything found in the literature of the Maghreb, Muslim Spain, or Provence in their early days, or even, one might add, in their more mature years. Admittedly R. Yitsḥak ha-Levi was an exceptionally independent *posek* (decisor);[10] however, Rabad of Posquières was no less self-reliant a thinker and had a far sharper tongue, yet he never spoke this way.

This attitude is then reflected in the collections made of the rulings of Early Ashkenaz in the first half of the twelfth century. Unlike the literature of those three other cultures, which initially gave great weight to geonic decisions and tried as much as it could to preserve the names of the geonic responders,[11] the writings of Early Ashkenaz attached little importance to the identity of geonic authors and much, if not most, of the geonic material it recorded is anonymous. Compare the carefully preserved authorship of the responsa cited in the *Sefer ha-'Ittim* or the *Sefer ha-'Eshkol* with the overwhelmingly anonymous geonic material in the *Ma'aseh ha-Ge'onim*, the *Sefer ha-'Oreh*, and the *Sefer ha-Pardes*. Here and there they will cite a responsum of a specific Gaon, but such cases are few and far between. They have material of geonic origin, but it is faceless and utilized in a haphazard fashion. The names of individual Geonim had no resonance in tenth- and eleventh-century

[9] *Ma'aseh ha-Ge'onim* (above, n. 8), #94, p. 94.

[10] See above, pp. 45–6.

[11] Indeed, as Menahem Ben-Sasson noted to me, the attitude to the words of the Geonim was so reverential in the Maghreb that they even preserved the *kuntresei teshuvot* of the Geonim, the replies in the original sequence in which they had issued forth from the academies of Sura and Pumbedita.

Ashkenaz; they evoked not reverence (as in other cultures of the Diaspora) but indifference. This is scarcely surprising, seeing that Rabbenu Gershom thought that R. Leon's opinion was weightier than that of *Halakhot Pesukot*, and that his text of the Talmud was more authentic than that of the Geonim.

What was the basis of this disregard, even disrespect, for the acknowledged leaders of world Jewry?[12] How could the scholars of Early Ashkenaz presume that their teachers understood the Talmud better than the Geonim? What privileged this tiny new community in Mainz to view its texts of the Talmud as superior to those emanating from the study halls of Sura and Pumbedita where the Talmud was created and composed? Just who did they think they were? Or more justly: Who, indeed, were they? Who were the founders of the new Ashkenazic culture that emerged in the latter half of the tenth century, and where did they come from?

I

Seeking the cultural origins of Ashkenaz one should begin by examining the cultural artifacts of Early Ashkenaz. This means that one does not start with a deeply problematic, alleged foundation myth and seek to extract what 'facts' one can from such a narrative;[13] rather, one employs the retrospective method. When faced with a relatively blank period in history whose known facts are few and far between, one begins with the picture that presents itself when the society or the culture first comes into clear view and then one works backwards, seeking things in the sparsely documented past that would explain what was found in full flourish when the curtain first rose.

[12] I should note here that with the advent of Rashi this dismissive attitude disappears. Not that Rashi deferred to the Geonim, far from it; however, his disregard expresses itself (with occasional exceptions) in general indifference to their holdings; it never eventuates in expressions of disrespect or even depreciation. This is equally true for German scholars in the 12th or 13th centuries. In fact, Ravyah is more interested in the authorship of geonic responsa than were his forefathers some century and a half before. We can often identify the author of geonic responsa cited anonymously in the pre-Crusade literature on the basis of information found in the writings of R. Yo'el and his son, Ravyah.

[13] For 150 years scholars have argued over the date and accuracy, indeed the very credibility, of the differing accounts given by R. El'azar of Worms and R. Shelomoh Luria of the transplantation by a 'Charles the Great' of R. Mosheh b. Kalonymos from Lucca to Mainz. Many discount the reports entirely, and no construction yet offered can be maintained without either changing the text or labeling certain passages as legend. See the discussions of A. Grossman, 'Hagiratah shel Mishpaḥat Kalonymos mi-'Italyah le-Germanyah', *Zion*, 40 (1975), 154–85, and the literature cited in n. 1 there; id., *Ḥakhmei Ashkenaz ha-Rishonim: Koroteihem, Darkam be-Hanhagat ha-Tsibbur, Yetsiratam ha-Ruḥanit mi-Reshit Yishuvam ve-'ad li-Gezerot Tatnu (1096)*, 3rd edn. (Jerusalem, 2001), 29–48, and M. Idel, 'From Italy to Ashkenaz and Back', *Kabbalah*, 14 (2006), 52 n. 14. On the adjective 'alleged', see below, Appendix III.

Two areas of creativity in Ashkenaz manifest themselves from the very outset, halakhah and liturgical poetry (*piyyut*). As the history of halakhah is my field, I will concentrate on the former. My thesis may or may not mesh with the parallel developments in *piyyut*; I will address this question and its implications at the conclusion of the essay.

I should state at the outset that I am neither discussing the genetic origins of the Ashkenazic community nor the origins of Ashkenazic pronunciation, but the origins of its halakhic culture. I am thus discussing a small, elite segment of that community. Indeed, as I am addressing halakhah and not *piyyut* or *sod* (esoteric lore), I am treating only a portion of that creative elite. I am also not adopting any position as to the physical continuity of Jewish settlement in the early Middle Ages, other than to remark, first, that by the 820s, the Jews in Lyons and most probably in and around Aachen were observing the laws of *kashrut* as promulgated in the Babylonian Talmud.[14] Second, by the 930s there is clearly a collective Jewish presence in the Rhineland, most probably in Mainz.[15]

The cultural history of Ashkenaz begins with Rabbenu Gershom, or, more accurately, with R. Gershom's teacher, mentioned above, the shadowy R. Leon (Yehudah[16]). Several hundred years ago there existed reports of merely three or four rulings of his, and we have no more today, despite all the extensive searches in the treasures of the Institute of Microfilmed Hebrew Manuscripts in the National Library of Israel.

The years 930–70 are, then, the proximate time of the appearance of Ashkenazic culture; for brevity's sake, I will use simply '950'. What do we see then? A rich culture emerges from nowhere—Early Ashkenaz has the entire Babylonian Talmud and is actively engaged in its exegesis. They are at home in works of Midrash such as *Bereshit Rabbah*, *Va-Yikra Rabbah*, and *Tanḥuma*, and are composing *piyyutim*. They are familiar with the mystical literature of the Heikhalot, and the Kalonymide family has imbibed the esoteric lore of Abu Aharon of Baghdad. In adjusting to the new commercial realities of

[14] On the physical continuity, see above, Ch. 3, nn. 29, 32. On *kashrut* observance, see above, pp. 5–19.

[15] J. Aronius, *Regesten zur Geschichte der Juden im Fränkischen und Deutschen Reiche bis zum Jahre 1273* (Berlin, 1902), 53–4, ##124–5. I. Elbogen et al., eds., *Germania Judaica* (repr. Tübingen, 1963), i. 175–6.

[16] On the basis of the verse in Gen. 49: 9, *leo* meaning 'lion' in Latin. On R. Leon, see Grossman, *Ḥakhmei Ashkenaz ha-Rishonim* (above, n. 13), 80–5.

Germany, the scholars of Early Ashkenaz rule boldly and move with the confident steps of the experienced, as I have noted in my essay on pawnbroking.[17]

We are confronted, then, with what might be called a 'Puritan migration'. Not in the popular sense of the word 'Puritan', certainly not in the theological sense; rather, in the exceptional education and intellectual attainments of the founding fathers and their dedication to transmitting their intellectual patrimony to subsequent generations. The men who settled in the wilderness of Boston on a new continent were embodiments of a fully developed culture and brought with them a rich library which they had thoroughly mastered. Standing on the forefront of Calvinist theology, they began writing their treatises soon after disembarkation. The settlers of 950 also stood, as we shall see, at the frontier of talmudic exegesis; they too controlled a vast and variegated library. Just as the Puritans, six to seven years after their arrival in 1630, established Harvard College for the training of ministers, so too did the settlers of 950, shortly after their arrival in their 'New World' of Ottonian Germany, set up the *bet midrash* (talmudic academy) of Mainz and began to compose the comprehensive commentary on the Talmud commonly known as *Perush Rabbenu Gershom*.

In their large library, however, there was no copy of the Yerushalmi (Palestinian Talmud), as already noted in a previous article[18]—an astonishing absence for an allegedly Palestinian-oriented community. By the middle of the eleventh century a collection of scattered statements found in the Yerushalmi had penetrated Ashkenazic circles,[19] but from the days of Rabbenu Gershom to those of the Tosafists, a period of some 125 years, there is no evidence of any copy of so much as a single chapter in a tractate of the Yerushalmi. They had the *midrashim* of Palestine galore—*Bereshit Rabbah*, *Va-Yikra Rabbah*, *Tanḥuma*—but not the Yerushalmi. A sentence or dictum from

[17] *Collected Essays*, i. 59, 82–95.

[18] Above, Ch. 3, n. 94, and Ch. 8, n. 9. See Grossman, *Ḥakhmei Ashkenaz ha-Rishonim* (above, n. 13), p. 428, and his list at n. 74. I do not know the basis for his remark on p. 157 that Rabbenu Gershom had a text of the Yerushalmi. A solitary citation of the Yerushalmi may well have come from a florilegium, and that alleged citation has been shown to be spurious (see above, pp. 79–81). R. Yehudah Ba'al Sefer ha-Dinim never cites the Yerushalmi, as Grossman notes at p. 204. As noted in the preceding chapter (n. 9), the leading authority on the diffusion of the Yerushalmi in the Middle Ages, Yaacov Sussmann, shares my view that there is no indication of an actual text of the Yerushalmi circulating in Ashkenaz before the 12th century.

[19] This should not be confused with the *Sefer Yerushalmi* described by Y. Sussmann in '"Yerushalmi Ketav-Yad Ashkenazi" ve-"Sefer Yerushalmi"', *Tarbiz*, 65 (1998), 37–63. This work contains the full text of the Yerushalmi's tractate *Berakhot* and *Seder Mo'ed* together with much extraneous material. It does not surface in Ashkenaz until the latter half of the 12th century in the circle of Rabbenu Yo'el and Ravyah.

that corpus is occasionally evoked, but never the analysis of a *sugya*, of an actual talmudic discussion, in the Yerushalmi. No one in Early Ashkenaz was interested in having a copy of the Yerushalmi, to say nothing of explicating it.

The Bavli (Babylonian Talmud), on the other hand, was the center of their intense attention, and they were actively engaged in its interpretation. Indeed, their curriculum of the Babylonian Talmud exceeded that of all the other communities of the Diaspora. It included the entire *Seder Kodashim* (the order of Temple service), none of which was part of the traditional talmudic curriculum of the Jews of Muslim North Africa, Muslim Spain, or Christian Provence. Ashkenaz, the alleged offshoot of Palestinian culture, had, from the outset, a greater Babylonian orientation in talmudic studies than any of these renowned bastions of the Bavli.

Ashkenaz also had a radically new vision of what comprehension of the Talmud meant. As noted in my essay '*Minhag* Ashkenaz ha-Kadmon',[20] the Bavli was neither to be summarized nor abridged as Rabbenu Ḥanan'el and Rav Alfasi thought. It had to be grasped in its entirety; every nook and cranny of it had to be illuminated; every thought and interpretation, however briefly entertained by the *amora'im*, had to be understood in all its detail. They introduced line-by-line exegesis in the form of the initial lemma (*dibbur ha-matḥil*) and the embedded lemma. The tool in itself is insignificant; what was revolutionary was its scope. No summary but a phrase-by-phrase explication of all the winding *sugyot* of the Talmud with almost no expression left unexplained.

They equally did not distinguish in their exegetical enterprise between halakhah and aggadah. Every line of aggadah had to be explicated in as precise a fashion as the halakhic passages. We take this for granted as we do the detailed exegesis, for from our very first encounter with the Talmud we find this in Rashi. This should not blunt our sensitivity to its radical originality. To the best of our knowledge the *aggadeta* of the Bavli had lain outside the systematic exegetical enterprise of the Talmudists of both North Africa and Spain. It also was beyond the ongoing purview of Provence's greatest exegete, Rabad of Posquières.[21]

[20] Above, p. 32, and see Ch. 3, Appendix I (pp. 62–4) on the use of the *sub verbo* in the Mainz commentaries.

[21] I must emphasize the word 'systematic' because there is, of course, some treatment of aggadah in Rabbenu Ḥanan'el's commentary. One cannot argue that the reason that the scholars of Spain and the Maghreb did not explicate the *aggadeta* of the Talmud was that they focused exclusively on halakhic topics of practical import. Seeing that they didn't explicate *Seder Kodashim*, one can scarcely be surprised that they didn't explicate aggadic passages. Rabbenu Ḥanan'el, for example, commented on *Ḥagigah* and on all the passages on *Kodashim* in both *Yoma* (70 percent of which treats matters of

Let us, for a moment, turn the clock ahead by some 140 years and cast a glance at Rashi in the closing decades of the eleventh century. As every child who has studied *Ḥumash* knows, Rashi frequently says *ke-targumo*, that is, '[its meaning is] as the Targum Onkelos has translated it'. I was in the third grade when I first encountered this expression in Rashi's commentary and remember looking at the incomprehensible Aramaic phrase in Onkelos and asking, 'How does this help?' Sixty-five years have passed and only now do I have an answer. It is a simple one: Rashi assumes that the average literate reader (what we would now call a *yodea' sefer*) of his day understood most words or phrases in Aramaic. And, one might note, in no other culture of the Diaspora did Targum Onkelos play so large a role in biblical exegesis as it did in Ashkenaz.[22]

Let us now turn south to Rome and to Rashi's contemporary, R. Natan of Rome. It is a truism, at least since Alexander Kohut's great edition of the *Sefer he-'Arukh*, that the three major sources on which R. Natan drew were the Geonim—especially Rav Hai Gaon—Rabbenu Ḥanan'el of Kairouan, and Rabbenu Gershom, together with the work of his school, *Perushei Magentsa*.[23] That Rav Hai and his father would know recondite Aramaic terms is understandable—they were, after all, native Babylonians and the *rashei yeshivah* of Pumbedita. Rabbenu Ḥanan'el's knowledge is equally understandable; he was the heir to over 200 years of Babylonian tutelage and sustained correspondence between Kairouan and the academies of Sura and Pumbedita. But what could German Jews in Mainz possibly know about problematic Aramaic expressions? R. Natan carefully registers the interpretations of no fewer than nine subgroups of Rabbenu Gershom's yeshivah—*ḥakhmei Magentsa*, *rav shel hakhmei Magentsa*, *rabbanei Magentsa*, *moreh shel Magentsa*, *talmidei Magentsa mi-pi ha-moreh*, *benei Magentsa*, *ḥasidei Magentsa*, and *talmid ḥakham mi-*

Kodashim) and *Pesaḥim* (30 percent of which addresses topics in *Kodashim*). Clearly, whatever was included in the North African curriculum—irrespective of its practicality—fell within his interpretative purview.

22 Elisabeth Hollender made this observation to me. By way of illustration, I would point out that P. Toledano wrote a doctorate at University College London, in 1980 entitled 'Rashi's Commentary to the Pentateuch and its Relation to the Targumim, with Special Reference to Targum Onkelos'. It is difficult to conceive of someone doing a similar study on the commentary of Ibn 'Ezra or that of Kimḥi, not to speak of the works of the earlier exegetes of Muslim Spain. For an up-to-date bibliography on the topic of Toledano's thesis, see E. Weisel, 'Ma'amado shel Targum Onkelos be-Toda'ato ha-Parshanit shel Rashi', *Tarbiz*, 75 (2006), 345, n. 1. (To forfend any misunderstanding, I am arguing from the significance of Targum Onkelos in Torah exegesis and not from its liturgical use—or partial disuse—in Torah readings on the Sabbath and festivals; see e.g. J. Penkower, 'Tahalikh Kanonizatsyah' [above, n. 4], 134 ff.)

23 *Arukh Completum*, ed. A. Kohut (Vienna, 1926), i. 11–14 (introduction); viii. 5–27 (appendix, 'Nerot ha-Ma'arakhah').

Magentsa. Why this fuss over the interpretations of Magentsa? What traditions could anyone from Mainz posses that would explain gnomic terms and obscure references in the Talmud? How could R. Natan possibly view them as a source of talmudic lexicography on a par with Rav Hai Gaon?

Shift back now to the mid-tenth century and the original characteristics of Ashkenaz. I have noted that the new settlers saw no difference between the aggadic sections of the Talmud and the halakhic ones and exegeted both in equal detail. We take this, too, for granted because we find a commentary on both sections on every printed page of the Talmud that we have seen since early youth. Think, however, what this entails lexically. The halakhic portions of the Talmud are strongly formulaic, as is any unpunctuated text. If one knows some thirty to forty idiomatic phrases in Jewish Babylonian Aramaic, most halakhic passages will pose few linguistic problems. (Understanding their legal content is a different matter.) However, the aggadic narratives entail a wide-ranging and detailed knowledge of the Aramaic language—all the terms of different household utensils, farm equipment, agricultural practices, domestic animals, flora and fauna, to mention just a few areas of life that are reflected in the narratives of the *aggadeta*. We are talking about a vocabulary of some 10,000–12,000 words, if not more. (Actually, much more, as one should count meanings rather than words or roots [*shorashim*]. Most words have multiple meanings, and commanding a language means precisely controlling the numerous meanings of its words, as well as of its idioms.) Unless these settlers had a vast dictionary, alongside which the *Sefer he-'Arukh* would seem a Berlitz phrase book, and unless this enormous dictionary and even the memory of it got lost in the Mainz academy within one generation, we must conclude that these immigrant founders of Ashkenazic culture were Aramaic speakers.[24] Precisely because Aramaic was their native tongue, they could readily undertake what the scholars of Kairouan, Fez, and Lucena (all native Arabic speakers) could only attempt with trepidation, namely, to exegete the entire Talmud, leaving no phrase, halakhic or aggadic, unexplained.[25]

[24] One could scarcely identify this huge, lost dictionary with the *alpha-beta de-R. Makhir*. A simple glossary would have been supplanted by the Mainz Commentary or that of Rashi, but hardly a massive dictionary, just as the *Sefer he-'Arukh* was not supplanted by them. See e.g. MSS Vienna, Österreichische Nationalbibliothek 39 and 40, Leiden 4722, Modena Estense 39 and Oxford, Bodley 1515, all Ashkenazic manuscripts of that work by R. Natan of Rome. If R. Makhir studied under Aramaic-speaking teachers or ones with a full command of Aramaic and who were bearers of an exegetical tradition, as did his more famous brother, Rabbenu Gershom, one understands how he made a glossary of some of the more difficult terms and why it was viewed as generally reliable. See n. 25 below. On R. Makhir b. Yehudah, see Grossman, *Ḥakhmei Ashkenaz ha-Rishonim* (above, n. 13), 102–5.

[25] This is not to claim that all their descriptions of talmudic realia are correct or that their

Did the second or third generation have an active or passive command of Aramaic? Did they actually speak Aramaic or simply understand that language fully? If it was not spoken in the home, had it been the language of instruction and discussion in the *bet midrash* for several generations? These are good questions and have implications; however, they make no difference to my argument here. A century after the arrival in Ashkenaz any fluency in Aramaic that might have existed was gone; nevertheless, they were still reciting liturgical poetry (*piyyut*) in that language. We are familiar with 'Akdamut' and 'Yetsiv Pitgam'. These are but the 'saving remnants' of the hundred or so pages of Aramaic religious poetry found in Yonah Fraenkel's comprehensive edition of the Ashkenazi *maḥzor* of Shavuot and in the additional fifty pages in that of Passover, poems that were recited before the Torah reading on the seventh day of the holiday.[26] To be sure, almost all of the Aramaic poetry is of Palestinian and Italian origin.[27] This is only natural, seeing that the tradition of liturgical poetry in Ashkenaz is, as we shall see, of Palestinian origin as mediated by Italy. The Aramaic of the few liturgical poems composed in Ashkenaz leaves more than something to be desired, but the aspiration to write religious verse in that language is significant[28] and clearly the sounds of

traditions in these matters were uniform and univocal. The settlers of Ashkenaz were thoroughly conversant with Babylonian Aramaic of the 10th century; the words that they commented upon had been spoken more than half a millennium earlier. The meaning of many words, and certainly their nuance, changes over so long a period of time. Utensils cease to be used, different ones take their place. Opinions could and did readily differ in Early Ashkenaz in the reconstruction of meanings (see Grossman, *Ḥakhmei Ashkenaz ha-Rishonim* [above, n. 13], 102–5). Even accurate linguistic knowledge is no guarantee of the accuracy of a commentary. To recognize, for example, words as names of flora and fauna is one thing; to correctly identify these plants is another, not to speak of knowing their exact structure and peculiarities, all of which may be necessary for a specific exegesis (as, for example, the signs of *bosar* and *ḥanatah*). Nevertheless, the advantage in talmudic exegesis that these settlers had over native Arabic speakers is incalculable.

26 *Maḥzor Shavu'ot: le-fi Minhag Benei Ashkenaz le-Khol 'Anfeihem*, ed. Y. Fraenkel (Jerusalem, 2000), 385–591; *Maḥzor Pesaḥ: le-fi Minhag Benei Ashkenaz le-Khol 'Anfeihem*, ed. Y. Fraenkel (Jerusalem, 1993), 608–61. (I halved the number of pages in my description in the text, as the liturgical poems are printed, in an interlinear fashion, both in the original Aramaic and in Hebrew translation.)

27 See the rich Palestinian literature of Aramaic liturgy that Y. Yahalom and M. Sokoloff have recently brought to light in their joint publication *Shirat Benei Ma'arava: Shirim Aramiyim shel Benei Yisra'el ba-Tekufah ha-Bizantit* (Jerusalem, 1999). See also Y. Schirmann, 'Piyyut Arami le-Faytan Italki Kadum', *Leshonenu*, 21 (1957), 212–19; S. Abramson, 'He'arot le-"Fiyyut Arami le-Faytan Arami Kadum"', *Leshonenu*, 25 (1967), 31–4. I wish to thank Avraham Fraenkel for pointing out to me that barring the poems of R. Me'ir, *sheliaḥ tsibbur* of Worms, the Aramaic poetry recited in Ashkenaz was not locally produced.

28 This impulse is not to be confused with the *jeu d'esprit* that led R. Shemu'el ha-Nagid to compose a few Aramaic poems, e.g. the letter of consolation to Rabbenu Ḥanan'el in *Divan Shemu'el ha-Nagid: Ben Tehillim*, ed. D. Yarden (Tel Aviv, 1966), 256–60.

Aramaic were not alien to Ashkenazic ears. The average listener probably understood as much of these Passover and Shavuot *piyyutim* as he understood of the intricate and highly allusive Hebrew ones of Kalir recited on the High Holidays.

Given their command of Babylonian Aramaic, their ignorance of and indifference to the Yerushalmi, and their exclusive preoccupation with the Bavli, the founding fathers of Ashkenazic halakhah clearly hailed from Babylonia rather than from Palestine. And indeed, Aramaic was still spoken in the smaller towns of Bavel in the eleventh century—how much more so the century before, when the Ashkenazic migration took place (decades before the move of the yeshivah of Pumbedita to Baghdad towards the end of the tenth century and of the yeshivah of Sura sometime after).[29]

I have noted above that the curriculum of Ashkenaz included from the outset the order of *Kodashim*,[30] which was never part of the program of study of the other Jewish cultures of the Diaspora. More significantly, the Ashkenazic curriculum also included tractates *Nazir*, *Temurah*, *Karetot* (more commonly called *Keritut*), *Me'ilah*, and *Tamid*—all edited in a dialect other than that of the rest of the Talmud (which medieval commentators already noted and called *lashon meshunah*), and, what is far, far more important, they were not part of the curriculum of Sura and Pumbedita.[31] The Ashkenazic curriculum also included *Nedarim*, a tractate edited in the same dialect as the above-mentioned five tractates and also not taught in the two famed Babylonian yeshivot since 750.[32] What is significant is not that the pilgrim settlers of Ashkenaz

[29] J. N. Epstein, *Dikduk Aramit Bavlit* (Jerusalem, 1960), 16–17; J. Blau, ''Al Ma'amadan shel ha-'Ivrit ve-ha-'Aravit bein Yehudim Dovrei 'Aravit ba-Me'ot ha-Rishonot shel ha-Islam', *Leshonenu*, 21 (1962), 281–2. On the move to Baghdad, see R. Brody, *The Geonim of Babylonia and the Shaping of Medieval Culture* (New Haven, 1998), 31, 36. (These dates are given for presentational reasons only, as I shall soon argue that new settlers came from places other than Sura and Pumbedita.)

[30] Above, pp. 33, 159.

[31] I wish to emphasize here as in the text that I am not addressing the *editing* of these tractates in amoraic or savoraic times—this may well have taken place in Sura and Pumbedita—but their *subsequent absence* from the curriculum of those famed yeshivot in the geonic period. See A. Marmorstein, 'Mitteilungen zur Geschichte und Literatur aus der Geniza 2. Ein Fragment der Halakhot Ketu'ot', *Monatsschrift für Geschichte und Wissenschft der Juden*, 67 (1923), 134–5. For the objection that perhaps only one of the two famed yeshivot omitted these tractates from their study programs, see below, p. 187. Marmorstein is of the opinion that *Nedarim* and *Nazir*, which are both missing from the printed list, were equally not taught. N. Danzig and A. Shweka also believe that *Nazir* was not taught. See N. Danzig, *Mavo le-Sefer Halakhot Pesukot* (above, n. 5), 427; A. Shweka, ''Iyyunim be-Sefer Halakhot Gedolot: Nusaḥ va-'Arikhah' (Ph.D. diss., Bar Ilan University, 2008), 86 n. 11. The best study of this dialect is that of Y. Breuer, 'The Babylonian Aramaic in Tractate *Karetot* according to MS Oxford', *Aramaic Studies*, 5 (2007), 1–45.

[32] Danzig, *Mavo le-Sefer Halakhot Pesukot* (above, n. 5), 425–7; R. Brody, *Teshuvot R. Natronai bar*

possessed copies of these volumes, but that they were actively involved in exegeting them, including those that are of great difficulty. The commentaries of Early Ashkenaz upon these tractates have survived and were published in 1881 by the Romm Press in what has been the standard edition of the Talmud ever since. The writers were working off a commentarial tradition—hardly all-encompassing, but still a sturdy, substantive tradition—without which one cannot make sense of the abrupt, almost telegrammatic text of any talmudic tractate, not to speak of the highly recondite ones of *Temurah* and *Me'ilah*. This is doubly true if one attempts, as they did, a detailed line-by-line commentary. To be sure, there is no lack of groping in their treatment. It could not be otherwise. They attempted the unheard of, and it is not surprising that its execution was incomplete and replete with problems. No one before or, indeed, after them (barring their 'disciple', Rashi) had ever attempted to work out in light of a more general body of knowledge the entire give and take of each and every *sugya* in the Talmud. As great as their commentarial skills were (and they have hitherto been wholly unappreciated), without a core knowledge of the crux of each *sugya* their exegesis would have been impossible. Whence came this commentarial tradition? Not from Sura and Pumbedita; the *lashon meshunah* tractates were not taught there.

It may be argued that there were some outstanding scholars in these famed yeshivot who did command these tractates—witness the citations from these texts in the *Halakhot Gedolot*. Perhaps one of these scholars, or even several of them, were members of the founding group of Ashkenaz. It is a possibility. However, we confront the novel curriculum of Ashkenaz, which is unlike that of any other diaspora community (all of whom received their guidance from Sura and Pumbedita), and, more importantly, unlike that of Sura and Pumbedita. We would then have to say that this scholar or scholars from Sura and Pumbedita not only instructed the founding fathers in the *lashon meshunah* tractates, but equally persuaded to incorporate them into their curriculum, induced this new settlement in distant Germany to have a larger talmudic curriculum than the two great yeshivot from which they had sprung. Perhaps. The simpler interpretation, to my mind, is that Ashkenaz was not settled by disciples of Sura and Pumbedita, but by disciples of what I would call the

Hilai Ga'on (Jerusalem, 1994), ##185, 253. The Ashkenazic commentaries on *Nedarim* and *Nazir* have been printed under the name of Rashi since 1520. That the attribution to Rashi was an error has been common knowledge for centuries; its Early Ashkenazic provenance was demonstrated by J. N. Epstein in 'Perushei ha-Rivan u-Ferushei Worms', *Tarbiz*, 4 (1933), 153–78; it was reproduced in his collected essays *Meḥkarim be-Sifrut ha-Talmud u-vi-Leshonot Shemiyot* (Jerusalem, 1991), iii. 35–60.

'Third Yeshivah of Bavel',[33] in which these tractates were regularly studied. The new settlement in Ashkenaz simply reproduced the intellectual traditions and study patterns of its original habitat, replicating the old in the new setting, as immigrants usually do.

One might contend that we have evidence only that the *lashon meshunah* tractates were absent from the curriculum of either Sura or Pumbedita, but not of both. Perhaps the founders of Ashkenaz came from the one that did study these tractates. I have never before heard it claimed that Sura and Punbedita had different curricula, but that is of no matter. The essential point is that if they did hail from one of these two institutions, why were they so dismissive of the authority of the heads of both? Their attitude is quite understandable, as we shall soon see, if they heralded from elsewhere, from another time-honored Babylonian yeshivah.

J. N. Epstein contends that *Nedarim* was edited in Maḥoza, but does not commit himself with regard to the other five tractates that are characterized by *lashon meshunah*.[34] The name of the town or towns is not important in itself; even less so as I am addressing, and this must be emphasized, not the editing of these tractates in the amoraic or savoraic period but their exposition and instruction in the time of the Geonim.[35] What is important is the awareness where the settlers did *not* come from. They did not come from Sura and Punbedita. Equally important is the realization that these two famed academies had no monopoly on either talmudic knowledge or talmudic education.

Why have we not heard of this 'Third Yeshivah',[36] why have we no record of it? For the same reason that we have no record of at least two other crucial *battei midrash* in Bavel that were operating, as we shall soon see, at the same time and

[33] The phrase 'Third Yeshivah of Bavel' is not of my own minting; it was suggested to me by Sara Zfatman. 'Third Yeshivah' is a shorthand device, employed simply for brevity; see below, p. 172, and Appendix I, pp. 194–7.

[34] See his *Mavo le-Sifrut ha-'Amora'im* (Jerusalem, 1962), 69–70, 72–83, 131–44. The various theories of the editorship of *Nedarim* have been conveniently summarized in S. Rybak, 'The Aramaic Dialect of *Nedarim*' (Ph.D. diss., Bernard Revel Graduate School, Yeshiva University, 1980), 1–20.

[35] See above, n. 29. Put differently, six tractates were not part of the geonic curriculum. They all share a common linguistic denominator, which reflects a different editorial origin. Whether or not there is a link between this editorial otherness and the absence of these tractates from the curriculum is irrelevant to my argument.

[36] Truth to tell, as we know nothing of the structure of this institution, the Hebrew phrases *bet midrash* or *ohel torah* would be more apt. Since neither of these terms has made its way into English, I employ 'yeshivah'.

were engaged in no less a task than inscribing the final version of the Bavli that has come down to us.[37] And that reason is simple. Most of our knowledge of the Geonim and their world comes from the Cairo Genizah. We are endlessly indebted to its riches; however, they have also distorted somewhat our perspective. The Genizah tells us how the Geonim and Babylonia appeared to people in the West, that is to say, Palestine (*ma'arava*), Egypt, the Maghreb, and Spain; it tells us nothing of how the Geonim appeared to people in the East, to the deeply settled communities in Babylonia and its surrounding territories. It informs us of the doings of the official centers of Torah of the time, but reveals nothing of the activities of the unofficial ones, especially if they took care to issue their works anonymously. In the West, all authority—both formal and informal—resided in the two famed Babylonian yeshivot. They had a monopoly on rabbinic decision-making and were viewed as the font of rabbinic knowledge. However, do we have any reason to assume that they had an equivalent monopoly of knowledge and of intellectual activity in Bavel itself? Is there any basis for thinking that they were seen as having an exclusive hold on religious authority by the residents of the ancient center of Jewish civilization, Babylonia? Many of its communities had been in existence for well over half a millennium before the emergence of any Geonate. Their religious leaders had been resolving their halakhic problems and adjudicating their civil conflicts for centuries, in some instances for close to 600 years; why should we assume that they now looked upon the freshly minted Geonate as the new arbiter of all things Jewish? Sura and Pumbedita may have been seen as the exclusive source of authority, the sole living embodiment of the Talmud, in Fustat, Kairouan, and Lucena, but not, I suggest, in much of Bavel itself, at least not in certain significant circles.

Suppose the tsar of Russia had had a generally benevolent, or at least a neutral, attitude to the Jews, and in 1880 had conferred the status—de jure or de facto—of ultimate arbiters of things Jewish upon the *rashei yeshivah* of Volozhin and Mir. Does one imagine that Vilna, Cracow, Lublin, or Brisk (Brest-Litovsk) would have deferred to these two institutions? Or would they have indicated, in deed if not in word, that they had been handling their affairs quite well for hundreds of years and were quite capable of continuing to do so? Would the yeshivot and *battei midrash* in these cities have closed their doors? Mir and Volozhin would have been the fonts of rabbinic knowledge and the supreme decisors for the emerging Russian Jewish diaspora in England, America, and South Africa, but scarcely for the Jews in the Russian Empire itself.

[37] See below, pp. 170–2; Appendix I, pp. 194–6.

Suppose again that, a century later, the Russian Empire had undergone a second Mongolian conquest and all the literature of Russian Jewry had been destroyed, leaving us to construct Jewish life in this period on the basis of a *genizah* in Paris or London through which the intellectual traffic between the Russian diaspora and Volozhin and Mir had been channeled. Would we have had any inkling of the importance of a Vilna or of the stature and achievements of the scholars of Cracow and Lublin? What would we even know of the communities themselves—their institutions, their rabbinate, their local history and politics? How does this differ from the state of our knowledge of Bavel in the geonic period? Look at the historiography of the past century. We have had major studies on the Jews in Kairouan, Alexandria, Fustat, and Palestine in this period, but none of Jews outside Baghdad and the two great yeshivot. We have books and monographs on the history of the Geonim and the Geonate, but not a history of Jewish Babylonia. The rest of Bavel, however, did not cease to exist with the anointing of Sura and Pumbedita. Let us never forget that the vast hinterland of Baghdad/Sura/Pumbedita contained the largest Jewish community in the world, and its history surely merits reconstruction to the full extent of our powers. As there are few documents, this can be done only by inference—by the retrospective method which I have employed and by drawing inferences from other disciplines, which I shall attempt. However, we are running ahead of ourselves; let us return to the Third Yeshivah.

The Third Yeshivah is hidden from our view, but can we be sure that it was hidden from the view of some of its contemporaries for centuries? Is it plausible that there should be scholars who commanded the entirety of Shas (the Talmud) and, as retiring as they may have been, were unknown to scholars and laymen alike, generation after generation? Might they not have had pupils who settled in various parts of Bavel, even in parts of the far-flung Diaspora, and later turned to them for guidance? Zvi Groner once remarked to me many years ago, 'How do we know that all the nameless responsa in the Genizah and elsewhere were authored by the Geonim of Sura and Pumbedita?' How indeed? These responsa may never have been signed to begin with, for anonymity had been the hallmark of amoraic culture. The most famous responsum of talmudic times is 'They sent from there [i.e. Palestine], "Take care to observe the custom of your forefathers"', that is, continue to observe the second day of the holiday (*yom tov sheni shel galuyot*), even after the institution of the lunar calendar.[38] The authors of that historic missive are not recorded.

[38] *Betsah* 4b: שלחו מתם הזהרו במנהג אבותיכם בידיכם. See also *Bava Batra* 158b.

Signing responsa is a geonic innovation,[39] and, as we shall see, there is reason to believe that scholars of the Third Yeshivah, the masters of *Nedarim*, *Nazir*, and *all* of *Seder Kodashim*, were not enamored of some of the new ways of the Geonim.

The numerous rulings examined in the course of my study of pawnbroking show the scholars of Early Ashkenaz dealing creatively and with quiet assurance with the numerous forms of Jewish entrepreneurial activity in the German Empire, fields of endeavor for which little halakhic guidance can be found in the Talmud.[40] Novel forms of debt transference are validated and de facto property rights bestowed on the ubiquitous Gentile pawn. These are the rulings of experienced decisors, not of men who have just stepped out of an ivory tower. To be sure, the scholars of the Third Yeshivah were not creating new fields of halakhah as did the Geonim, for example, in warranty and partnership. Nor were they ordaining new rules in debt collection and dowry. They did not carry the burden of adjusting an agricultural legal system to that of a worldwide commercial one as did the heads of Sura and Pumbedita. However, the men of the Third Yeshivah seem to have received over the centuries sufficient queries from pupils or followers to regularly bring them into contact with new economic realities and apprise them of both the need for, and the varied means of, legal adjustment to changed circumstances. This knowledge and experience was put to good use when they were called upon to regulate the activities of their co-religionists in the 'New World' of Ottonian Germany. The responsa of Early Ashkenaz are, from the very outset, neither the writings of novices nor the rulings of the unworldly.

Whether the tractates of *Zevaḥim*, *Menaḥot*, *Bekhorot*, and *'Arakhin*—which *were* part of the curriculum of Sura and Pumbedita—were studied there in the same depth as were *Shevu'ot* and *Bava Metsi'a* is open to question. These famed academies had to forge a code of commerce with little precedent to guide them. The Talmud treats an agricultural society, as was the Jewish community both in Roman Palestine and in Persian Babylonia. The Geonim of Sura and Pumbedita had to deal with the consequences of the Muslim conquest, which, in a relatively brief span of time, transformed an agricultural economy into an expanding mercantile one which rapidly attained international scope. The questions that now poured in from the new, distant Jewish communities in the Muslim empire dealt with religious practices and civil and marital law and inquired little about the niceties of the Temple service in the days of yore. It would not be surprising, then, if the four trac-

[39] See below, pp. 175–6. [40] See *Collected Essays*, i. 59, 82–95.

tates of *Seder Kodashim* in their curriculum were treated in a perfunctory manner.[41] The Third Yeshivah of Bavel had no formal standing, bore no official responsibilities. Free of the burden of leadership and adjudication—of waging war with the Karaites, of providing religious guidance to a new, far-flung Diaspora and adjudicating its innumerable disputes—this school could divide its time equally between all tractates.

Unsurprisingly, the Ashkenazic culture, from its outset, did the same. It treated *Zevaḥim*, *Menaḥot*, *Bekhorot*, and *'Arakhin*, plus the five other tractates dealing with Temple law that were not part of the Sura-Pumbedita curriculum, in identical detail and with the same attention as the other, more relevant, *sedarim* of the Talmud. They also addressed tractate *Nedarim*, which Sura and Pumbedita had neglected.[42] There was no selectivity in their talmudic enterprise. Every line of every tractate had to be mastered to an equal degree. The talmudic canon of the founders of Ashkenaz was thus larger and more comprehensive than that of the two famed Babylonian academies, and all of it was studied with equal care.

The founders of the halakhic culture of Ashkenaz came from the Third Yeshivah of Bavel and were very much aware of this fact, as the responsum of Rabbenu Gershom clearly demonstrates. In it he shows no deference whatsoever to the Geonim. Quite the contrary, he believed that his text of the Talmud was more trustworthy than that of Sura and Pumbedita and the authority of his teacher, R. Leon, superior to that of the heads of those institutions. There was no megalomania whatsoever in the responsum of Rabbenu Gershom. His was the voice of a group that had textual and commentarial traditions stretching back as far as did those of the two renowned yeshivot, and that had preserved more faithfully than had those institutions the fullness of the amoraic curriculum. It is, then, not at all surprising that their traditions of interpretation were placed on a par with those of Rav Hai Gaon by no less an exegetical and linguistic connoisseur than the author of the *Sefer he-'Arukh*.[43] R. Leon, Rabbenu Gershom, *u-vet midrasham be-Magentsa* represented a group that was as Babylonian as Rav Hai and whose traditions were as ancient as those of Pumbedita.

[41] For the commentary attributed to Rabbenu Ḥanan'el on *Bekhorot* and the reports of R. Yosef Rosh ha-Seder, see above, Ch. 3, n. 10. What is registered in the index of N. Aloni, *Ha-Sifriyah ha-Yehudit bi-Yemei ha-Beinayim: Reshimot Sefarim mi-Genizat Kahir*, ed. M. Frenkel and H. Ben-Shammai (Jerusalem, 2006), 491: *Perush Kodashim la-Rashbaḥ*, 30: 31–2, is actually a biblical commentary on *parashat* 'Kedoshim'.

[42] See above, n. 31.

[43] See above, pp. 160–1, and below, p. 188.

II

Strictly speaking my essay ends here. Why the men of the Third Yeshivah arrived in Ashkenaz—by chance or by choice—is irrelevant to my argument. The significant fact is that in the mid-tenth century they and their traditions of learning did arrive there, and this heritage explains—without recourse to the Holy Spirit—Rashi's command of the entire vocabulary of Jewish Babylonian Aramaic including words of Persian origin, his detailed knowledge of talmudic realia, and his grasp of legal concepts that are employed but never fully explicated in the Talmud.[44] What is problematic is the emigration to Mainz: why would some men of the Third Yeshivah, such dedicated students of the Bavli, ever wish to leave Bavel?

We will be better able to answer this question if we consider just how much of Bavel has been obscured by the twin towers of Sura and Pumbedita. I would suggest (and I do no more than that, as I am an expert neither in geonic history nor in the history of the talmudic text) that the imposing height of these two institutions has blocked the view of not only the Third Yeshivah of Bavel, whose talmudic range exceeded their own, but also other yeshivot or *battei midrash* that were actively involved—indeed, played a decisive role—in the copy-editing of the talmudic text. The editing—gathering the various amoraic discussions on a topic, determining under which *mishnah* they should be registered, and deciding upon their sequence—was clearly over by 700, or by 750 at the very latest. The copy-editing, the final fixing of the talmudic text that we currently possess, continued in the geonic period, perhaps even as late as its closing years, in the 1030s, as no clear *terminus ad quem* can be given. The study of this involved process is in its infancy. Only two tractates have been analyzed in their entirety in light of all the available manuscripts and *testimonia*.[45] We have, in addition, a half-dozen or so analyses of individual chapters of various tractates.[46] Just from this limited material a complex picture emerges. Some chapters show minimal variation between the families of manuscripts, some show differences between a 'dynamic' edition and a

44 See above, pp. 151, 160.

45 M. Sabato, *Ketav-Yad Temani le-Massekhet Sanhedrin (Bavli) u-Mekomo be-Masoret ha-Nusaḥ*, Sidrat 'Avodot Doktor Nivḥarot (Jerusalem, 1998); R. Shustri, 'Mesorot ha-Nusaḥ shel Massekhet Sukkah, Bavli' (Ph.D. diss., Bar-Ilan University, 2009).

46 e.g. E. S. Rosenthal, *Talmud Bavli, Massekhet Pesaḥim: Ketav-Yad Sasson-Lunzer u-Mekomo be-Masoret ha-Nusaḥ* (London, 1985); id. 'Toledot ha-Nusaḥ u-Ve'ayot ha-'Arikhah be-Ḥeker ha-Talmud ha-Bavli', *Tarbiz*, 57 (1988), 1–36, and his subsequent article cited above, n. 33; S. Friedman, *Perek ha-Sokher et ha-'Umanin: Bavli Bava Metsi'a Perek Shishi*, 2 vols. (New York and Jerusalem, 1990–6); S. Y. Wald, *Perek Elu 'Overin: Bavli Pesaḥim Perek Shelishi* (New York and Jerusalem, 2000).

'static' one, and in some the same material is occasionally found in different sequence and sometimes, though much more rarely, the different manuscripts reflect different traditions.

Allow me to explain at the risk of gross oversimplification. There are, for example, several ways of introducing a question from tannaitic sources into a discussion (*sugya*), two of them being *ve-raminhu* and *metivei* (commonly pronounced *metvei*). One can find a family of manuscripts that will present all the queries from tannaitic sources with *metvei*; another group of manuscripts will systematically present the identical material with *ve-raminhu*. One expression is as good as the other; it is simply two different ways by which the identical *sugya* has been transmitted. Other than differences of this type, the two manuscript families present fairly identical texts. In other chapters of the same tractate or of another tractate, one will get a family with a more expansive version, another with a more conservative, terser one. For example, the Talmud points out a contradiction between the dicta of Rabbi A and Rabbi B. The Talmud replies in one family of manuscripts, 'No problem; this refers to case X, that refers to case Y.' In a second family the text reads: 'No question, the dictum of Rabbi A refers to case X, that of Rabbi B refers to case Y.' Again, there is no difference in meaning; one text is simply more reader-friendly (if the original formulation was written) or more listener-friendly (if the original text was oral) than the other. In other words, the Talmud underwent different final 'copy-edits' and this is reflected in the extant manuscripts. In all the above cases the sequence of the discussion, the various queries and replies, follow the same order in all manuscripts. (Indeed, there are mnemonic devices, or *simanim*, still embedded in the printed text of today which hark back to times of orality, when the Talmud was recited rather than written, and refer to the sequence of material to be cited in the *sugya*.) However, there are tractates in which one finds instances of difference in the sequence of a *sugya*, and occasionally even passages where the manuscripts reflect not simply differences of style, but also of content.

It is highly unlikely that Sura and Pumbedita played any role in committing the Talmud to writing, let alone in copy-editing such a text. They were so deeply invested in oral transmission, as Yaacov Sussmann and others have shown, in their continued possession of 'reciters' (*garsanim*) of fabled memory, in their nigh millennium-old monopoly of the living voice of the Talmud, that they would justly have feared that any involvement in inscription would be perceived as lending an imprimatur to such written texts and undermine their pre-emptive claims to authenticity. It was equally clear, however, that they neither opposed nor criticized the inscription of the Talmud. They maintained only that the Vox Talmudica, the time-hallowed oral text as recited in the two famed yeshivot, was the ultimate arbiter.[47]

For centuries everyone assumed that the written versions of the Talmud that we possess originated in Sura and Pumbedita. There was no reason, therefore, to think that any other institutions were involved in the creation of the written talmudic corpus, or even to contemplate their existence. Once this assumption has been discredited—and discredited thoroughly in 2005 by Sussmann's great article—the conclusion appears inevitable. The initial inscription of this vast corpus in the pre-geonic period (before 700–750) and its two final copy-editings—the manuscripts divide into two versions—in the geonic era took place *outside* Sura and Pumbedita. As we shall probably never penetrate the mists of the sixth and seventh centuries, and some scholars contend that the talmudic text was both inscribed and copy-edited in the same era, let us focus on the geonic period (750–1038). The massive undertaking of copy-editing almost every line of the talmudic corpus was carried out in Bavel in this era in two different locations, in two different institutions—yet there was no reference to any of this in the Genizah.[48] What I have 'discovered', as a result of the *lashon meshunah* tractates taught in Ashkenaz, is not the Third Yeshivah of Bavel but the Fifth Yeshivah of Bavel. As Yoav Rosenthal's doctorate has recently shown the strong likelihood of the existence of yet a third editorial tradition, there is probably now a sixth one.[49] The Third

[47] Y. Sussmann, '"Torah she-be-'al Peh", Peshutah ke-Mashma'ah: Koḥo shel Kutso shel Yod', *Meḥkerei Talmud*, 3 (Jerusalem, 2005), 209–384; N. Danzig, 'Mi-Talmud 'al Peh le-Talmud bi-Khetav', *Sefer ha-Shanah Bar Ilan*, 30–1 (2006), 49–112.

[48] When the notion of a polycentric Bavel crystallized in my mind, I contacted Shamma Friedman and said that I wished to run some ideas of mine past him. He said that my timing was excellent as he wished to drop by and give me his volume of collected essays that had recently come out. After I outlined the ideas in this essay, he smiled and said, **ברוך שכיוונתי, אבל הסתי**, which translates roughly as, 'I'm glad to discover that we both thought along the same lines; however, I hesitated.' He took out the book he had just inscribed, *Sugyot be-Ḥeker ha-Talmud ha-Bavli: Asufat Ma'amarim be-'Inyanei Mivneh, Herkev ve-Nusaḥ* (Jerusalem, 2010), turned to his introduction, where (p. 13), in the midst of a description of the way the manuscripts break clearly into two families, there appears a sentence which reads: **יש לראות תהליך זה כאילו מתרחש, לשבר את האוזן, בשני מרכזים שונים בבבל** ('One should see this process as if, to speak metaphorically, it took place in two different centers in Bavel'), which, however, is not followed up—understandably, as the author is an eminent scholar of texts, not a historian whose task is to think institutionally. For the objection that these other institutions were housed in Sura and Pumbedita, see below, Appendix I, pp. 194–6.

[49] 'Massekhet Karetot (Bavli): le-Ḥeker Mesoroteiha' (Ph.D. diss., Hebrew University of Jerusalem, 2004), 155–207. I would like to thank Dr Rosenthal for providing me with a copy of his thesis and further discussing it with me. I have written 'strong likelihood' because he has informed me that, while it is true that the reading in Genizah fragment JTS ENA 2093/5–6 is so different from those of the other manuscripts that it seems to represent, alongside the *Halakhot Gedolot*, a different editorial

Yeshivah of Bavel was itself no monolith but was composed of several differing *battei midrash*, as the *lashon meshunah* of *Temurah* is found only in the *lishna aḥarina* of that tractate.[50]

The quantity of talmudic texts whose manuscripts have been closely studied is less than 10 percent of that corpus, and it has yielded already four to five *battei midrash* engaged in finalizing the text of the Talmud. Would it be unreasonable to assume that a study of the remaining 90 percent would reveal another four or five such institutions?[51] An entire cluster of academies was engaged in finalizing the text of the Talmud outside of Sura and Pumbedita. If one of the versions did emanate from one of those two famed institutions, or from the two jointly, clearly the editors of the other versions, who were located in other *battei midrash*, were in no way deferential and felt their edition to be equal to that of Sura and Pumbedita.

Some have entitled 'transmission' what I have here called 'copy-editing'. The difference in terminology may be important to some views of the history

tradition, nevertheless the entire fragment is only two pages long and, while close to the text found in the *Halakhot Gedolot*, it is not identical with it. Thus, a caveat should be entered that there remains an *outside possibility* that there are only two textual traditions of *Karetot*. He further warned about a natural misinterpretation of the argument made in the essay. While suspending judgment as to my claim that a separate editorial tradition implies the existence of a separate institution, the reverse, he noted, is certainly not true: the existence of a separate institution does not in any way imply a separate editorial tradition. There can be five institutions with only three traditions. For example, we have no idea what tradition of 'copy-editing', if any, obtained in Sura or Pumbedita. In *Karetot*, for example, a geonic responsum cites a passage of the Talmud as is found in the above-cited Genizah fragment (Rosenthal, 'Massekhet Karetot', 100 n. 22, 146 n. 100).

Similarly, there is no reason to assume that the institutions which *taught* the *lashon meshunah* tractates (some of whose scholars moved to Ashkenaz) had any distinctive textual traditions. Indeed, the Ashkenazic text as reflected in the Mainz commentary on *Karetot* corresponds to one of the two families of manuscripts that characterize most tractates, only that both here employ *lashon meshunah* (ibid. 55–74). One might add that they equally could have been copy-edited in the same *battei midrash* that produced the final form of the other tractates. It is difficult to conceive that the same persons would edit different parts of one corpus in dissimilar dialects. However, finding texts in *lashon meshunah* that needed copy-editing, there is every reason to do so in that dialect, and this can be accomplished with little difficulty.

50 The phrase *lishna aḥarina* ('another version [reads]') is found a few times in many tractates. In *Temurah*, a tractate of only thirty-four folios, they simply abound. There are no fewer than twenty-three of them in the standard printed text; another nineteen are found in MS Florence, BNC Magl. II 1.8, and yet more in R. Betsal'el Ashkenazi's notes to *Seder Kodashim*, printed in the Romm Talmud under the title *Shitah Mekubbetset*. It is these alternative versions which contain the *lashon meshunah*. See E. S. Rosenthal, 'Li-Leshonoteiha shel Massekhet Temurah', *Tarbiz*, 58 (1989), 326–7.

51 Indeed, Y. Elman's analysis would point to yet a seventh *bet midrash*. See his 'Resh Pesaḥim ba-Bavli u-va-Yerushalmi: She'elot be-'Arikhah u-ve-Hithavut', in A. Amit and A. Shemesh, eds., *Melekhet Maḥshevet: Kovets Ma'amarim be-Nos'ei 'Arikhah ve-Hitpatḥut shel ha-Sifrut ha-Talmudit* (Ramat Gan, 2011), 9–25.

of the talmudic text. From the point of view of this essay it is irrelevant. Call it what you will, various centers were empowered to give the final shape to a 'fixed but fluid text, fixed in content and basic formulation but open to rephrasing'.[52] The authority to give final form to the central normative text of a religion is no minor matter. As any lawyer will tell you, draftsmanship can be determinative, and no junior scholar would be permitted to undertake such a task. Such copy-editing could only be done by someone who had a sovereign command of this normative corpus, and whose editing, one could be sure, would never alter in the slightest way the content of the canonical text. We are talking, then, about master scholars who had the full confidence of the talmudic elite; and to all appearances, they were neither members nor representatives of the two renowned academies, committed as those institutions were to their sole possession of the living Vox Talmudica.

This is no less true of other works in the Jewish canon. Research on the *midrash* of *Eikhah Rabbati*, for example, has pointed to extensive editorial revision in Babylonia which does not seem linked to the yeshivot of Sura and Pumbedita, as the Geonim appear to be unaware of *Midrash Rabbah*.[53] The inscription of the Talmud was certainly over by the mid-eighth century; however, it is difficult to assign any dates to the completion of its massive copy-editing, as it is equally difficult to give a *terminus ad quem* to the editorial work on the *midreshei aggadah*.

If one seeks a text stating the existence of multiple centers of rabbinic activity, none is to be found. However, the different dialects employed in editing, the different modes of copy-editing, and the variety of the genres of the classical literature that were undergoing revision lead the historian to infer the activities of such institutions. Textual edition and the study of history have been operating in separate spheres; they need to be joined. The significant progress that has been made in the past two generations in reconstructing the editorial processes that rabbinical literature underwent has historical implications which reflect a far more complex reality than what seems at first to emerge from the Genizah.[54] When these textual studies are coupled with

[52] The formulation is that of Shamma Friedman in a personal communication.

[53] Paul D. Mandel, '*Midrash Lamentations Rabbati*: Prolegomenon, and a Critical Edition to the Third Parasha', Ph.D. diss., 2 vols. (Hebrew University of Jerusalem, 1997), i. 127 ff. (A much briefer presentation of points relevant to this discussion may be found is his 'Between Byzantium and Islam: The Transmission of a Jewish Book in the Byzantine and Early Islamic Periods', in Y. Elman and I. Gershoni, eds., *Transmitting Jewish Traditions: Orality, Textuality and Cultural Diffusion* [New Haven, 2000], 78–100.) Version A, the tradition that shows strong Babylonian influence, substitutes Esav/Yishma'el for Esav/Se'ir, which would indicate that the reworking was done after the Arab conquest. I wish to thank Dr Mandel for making his thesis available to me.

[54] See above, n. 49.

Sussmann's monograph, which strongly precluded the involvement of Sura and Pumbedita in any textual editing, indeed, with any talmudic inscription at all, the multi-institutional rabbinic landscape, the decentralized, even diffuse, intellectual activity in Bavel become ever more apparent.

Babylonia and 'Sura and Pumbedita' are not one and the same thing, even though it initially may appear that way from the vast repository in Cairo. The Genizah is full of the products of these large-scale editorial undertakings, but of the institutions that were engaged in these activities, that produced these texts, there is not a word. They go entirely unnoted—for some significant *battei midrash* prized, as we shall very soon see, anonymity. If one goes by names—personal and topographical—the Genizah reflects simply the coming and going of the couriers in the two famed yeshivot; toponyms and signatories, however, are not an accurate gauge, by any means, of the massive, ongoing rabbinic enterprises that were under way all over Bavel (and Palestine, for that matter). Put differently, Sura and Pumbedita had a duopoly on authority in the Diaspora; they never had one on the intellectual activities of Babylonia. Bavel, in the three long centuries of the Geonim (750–1038), must be seen as it actually was—in all its richness and variety, not reduced to what it seemed to be to the distant eyes of the West. In matters rabbinic, Bavel was polycentric, and dynamically so. Indeed, those unsung bastions of learning were engaged in nothing less than constructing the 'portable homeland' of the Jews and shaping their civilization to this day.

Such were the institutional consequences of looking historically at the results of textual studies. The anonymity of the men engaged for generations in this huge editorial undertaking yielded a cultural inference, which, in turn, may lead us to the solution of our original question: why the migration? Why would the men of the Third Yeshivah—tenth-century devotees of the amoraic heritage—leave the land of their fathers, the country where Jews had dwelt for close to a millennium, and venture to the land of Edom, settling in what was to them the end of the world, the Ottonian Rhineland?

The scholars involved in the geonic period in this extended enterprise of copy-editing were nameless, and intentionally so. They were continuators of the *savora'im* and *setama'im*, the faceless men who so decisively shaped Jewish history. Few, if any, have had the impact on Jewish culture as those who had 'put together' the Talmud—gathered the records of the scattered discussions, determined which *sugyot* would be included in the canon and which not, where they would be entered and in what sequence, and, perhaps, even composed some or all of the innumerable anonymous passages of the Talmud. Yet the *savora'im* and *setama'im* are nameless, or as close to nameless as is humanly possible. To seek to perpetuate one's memory by linking it to the timeless texts of *torah she-be-'al-peh* was to them an act of sacrilege, for it meant turning an ultimate into an instrument, and an instrument of self-aggrandizement at that. They were the guardians of the Divine word, and to commemorate themselves by means of that word was to betray their trust. It was far worse than taking money or being publicly honored for one's editorial toil. Any material benefit derived from the Torah disappeared with the death of the beneficiary; attaching one's name to that Torah constituted an endless—in a sense, an eternal—breach. The names of a few people about whom we know nothing is all we have for a period of some 200–225 years of unremitting toil and of an importance without parallel in Jewish history.[55]

Like their savoraic predecessors, the copy-editors saw themselves as servants of the text, toilers in the vineyard of the Lord deserving of no recognition. This ongoing insistence on anonymity by the editors and copy-editors of the rabbinic heritage—and remember that we have no *terminus ad quem* for this copy-editing, which may well have gone on throughout the geonic period—meant that the savoraic culture had not disappeared with the rise of the Geonate; it had continued for many centuries in numerous *battei midrash*, and, most probably, also in sectors of the general population of Babylonia. Signing one's name and the recognition that accompanies authorship are hallmarks of the Geonate. The Geonim were leaders and, of necessity, politicians; two professions in which neither modesty nor anonymity is a virtue. This indicates that two different cultures had existed side by side throughout the geonic period and tension between them would have been inevitable. What the dedicated, unnamed men of the 'other' yeshivot thought of the assertive and attention-calling institution of the Geonate with its pomp and circumstance, its authored books and signed responsa, is unrecorded but, perhaps, may be imagined. 'Paris is not France' is a time-worn admonition of historians; perhaps 'Baghdad and Sura-Pumbedita are not Bavel' should be another. Bavel in the geonic period may well have had no single civilization with an agreed-upon set of values and unified mores; on the contrary, it was probably a divided, and possibly even a much-contested, ground.

[55] The importance of the *savora'im* is unquestioned; the exact nature of their work and the length of the savoraic perod, which I have taken as beginning *c*.425, is a much-contested issue which fortunately has no bearing on our argument. For a recent bibliography on the savoraic question see A. Hakohen, 'Le-'Ofyah shel ha-Halakhah ha-Savora'it: Sugyat ha-Bavli Resh Kiddushin u-Masoret ha-Ge'onim', *Dine Israel*, 24 (2007), 161–4 nn. 1–5.

I would like to explore this possibility and proffer a hypothesis or two that students of Geonica might deem worth considering. If subsequent research confirms these conjectures, it would round out our picture of the early years of Ashkenaz and shed further light on some long-term characteristics of that culture.

Once again, it seems best to employ the retrospective method. Let us turn back to Early Ashkenaz, observe some of its original traits, and then return to Babylonia and search for answers to our questions.

The Geonate was not an authoritative institution in Ashkenaz, which is entirely understandable in light of what we now know of the founding fathers. There is, however, a difference between not reflexively submitting to the religious governance of the Geonim and adopting a casual, at times even dismissive, attitude to their rulings. This posture is already apparent in the writings of Rabbenu Gershom, the most prominent of the first generation of Ashkenazic scholars. He did not learn to take the Geonim lightly in the Rhineland. A Rhenish scholar had no more basis for disregarding the Geonim than did a Spanish, Provençal, or North African one, and the scholars, early or late, of all of these last three cultures revered the Geonim. It would seem, therefore, not to be an attitude that was developed but rather received, one that the original settlers had brought with them from Bavel and had imparted to their disciples. What was there in the conduct of the Geonim in Sura and Pumbedita that generated the disrespect or, at the very least, the absence of respect, among the men of the Third Yeshivah?

A second striking feature of Ashkenaz from the outset down to the eighteenth century is its indifference to the culture of its surroundings. A research group at the Advanced Institute in Jerusalem spent an entire year looking for evidence of some interest and could find almost none. Nor did they uncover any reason for this incuriosity and lack of involvement.[56] Unlike Jews of other cultures, Ashkenazic Jews, for close to a millennium, displayed no serious interest in, and had no sustained engagement with, the rich intellectual life of the Gentiles around them—not in medicine, not in astronomy, not in philosophy; far less did they adopt the poetic or belletristic models of their environment. Works on medicine did circulate, but they were read for pragmatic purposes; Ashkenazic Jews did not view medicine as an area worthy of exploration and advancement for its own sake and were equally uninterested

[56] The results of their year-end conference were published in 2009 as the eighth volume of the *Simon Dubnow Institute Yearbook*. See esp. the introduction of the editor, G. Freudenthal (pp. 17–26). See also R. Leicht, 'The Reception of Astrology in Medieval Ashkenazi Culture', *Aleph*, 13 (2013), 201–34, esp. the summary, pp. 232–4.

in other sciences of medieval Europe, let alone its philosophical thought. This is so unique and long-standing a trait of Ashkenaz that it seems to be part of its cultural DNA.

Casual or 'de facto' indifference alone—there was no vibrant culture in the Rhineland at the time to attract them[57]—will not explain this aversion. Provence too was initially indifferent to the surrounding culture. The refugees from Spain fleeing the Almohad persecution arrived in Provence in the mid-twelfth century and brought with them the Judeo-Arabic culture of Andalusia. Hebrew translations were swiftly made of the classic works of Spain, and within some seventy-five years large sectors of the Provençal intelligentsia were deeply engaged in the surrounding culture of the society in which they were embedded: in medieval science and philosophy, even penning works in such new and alien genres as secular poetry and belles-lettres. Ashkenaz was immune to such involvements. Indifference rather than opposition reigned at the outset of Ashkenazic history; there wasn't much to oppose. For a century or more, the lack of interest was low-key and relaxed. That casualness, however, is deceptive: it was the ease of an ideology in repose. Principled indifference is a deep-rooted characteristic of Ashkenazic culture, almost a genetic trait. This profound opposition to any involvement with the surrounding civilization would be readily understandable if the founding fathers of Ashkenaz left Babylonia precisely to escape the encroachments of the Judeo-Arabic culture in Bavel.

With these Ashkenazic characteristics in mind, let us return to Bavel and attempt to see it as it was seen not in the West but in the East, at least by some. Were I writing in French, I would switch here into the subjunctive mood, for all the retrospective method yields at the outset is a working hypothesis. What happened in a later stage is possible, or probable, only if X existed in a previous one. One then proceeds to ask whether the existence of X in that earlier stage is likely and whether traces of it can be detected *once attention is focused on their discovery*. Geonica is not my field. I can only address the question of X's plausibility and leave to students of Geonica the task of verifying or denying its factual existence. For this reason the title of this essay characterizes it as 'a proposal'. The question I address is: is it plausible, even probable, that some people in Babylonia in the tenth century looked askance at the Geonate and were also adamantly opposed to involvement in the culture of its surroundings?

[57] The flourishing culture of the cathedral schools of the 10th century was confined to a tiny elite. It was not remotely comparable in scope to that of 10th-century Baghdad. See C. S. Jaeger, *The Envy of the Angels: Cathedral Schools and Social Ideals in Medieval Europe, 950–1200* (Philadelphia, 1994), 36–179, and the literature there cited.

We take the existence of the Geonate for granted. It is worth remembering that the Geonate is prescribed neither by the Torah nor by the Talmud. It is a creation of the Abbasid Caliphate, de facto or de jure. Around 750 an anointed officialdom of talmudic studies emerges with claims to a monopoly of religious knowledge and authority. Such claims may have won full acceptance in the West; however, is it a stretch to imagine that a Babylonian *bet midrash* with an independent talmudic tradition broader than that of the new hegemons and stretching back well into the amoraic period may have viewed such contentions of suzerainty as absurd, even found it offensive? Could not the men of the Third Yeshivah have legitimately asked, 'Why should the relocation of capital of Gentile rulers determine talmudic authority?'

In 750 the Abbasids shifted their capital from Damascus to Baghdad, and around that time the Geonate, after a shadowy existence of perhaps a century and a half, emerged suddenly in full view. Historians have reasonably linked the two developments: the relocation of the Caliphate to Baghdad brought the Geonate, as history knows it, into existence. Such an institution was in the interests of the Caliph. To the extent that the Jewish communities in the far-flung Islamic Empire were subordinate to establishments in the Caliph's backyard, they were all the more subject to his direct control. Granting such hegemony would be a natural component of the centralization of Abbasid power. Nor need there have been any formal conferral of authority.[58] In an absolute autocracy, being looked upon with favor by the ruler is empowerment enough, especially for members of a wholly dependent, tolerated minority.

Certainly the move of the Abbasids transformed the Geonate, as the scope of its potential authority increased immensely. The vast expanse of the Islamic empire gave a new urgency to the old struggle between Palestine and Babylon for religious hegemony. The Geonate could be transformed into an institution of international significance. Of necessity, it had to become politically oriented, to acquaint itself with the center of power newly located in its vicinity. True, the Exilarch was charged with political leadership, but the relations of the Geonim with the Exilarch were not always the best, and if they were to entrust their material fate to another institution, they would swiftly have lost their independence. The Geonim or, more accurately, their representatives and well-wishers, had to now walk the corridors of power and familiarize themselves with its major players, their ambitions, whims, and desires. With power came the public displays of difference, the pomp and

[58] Some previous historians linked the rise of the Geonate to the enforcement of their authority by the Caliphate. R. Brody, in *The Geonim of Babylonia* (above, n. 29), 334–40, argues that there is no evidence in the sources of any such grant of authority.

circumstance with which all authority surrounds itself so as to place distance between the leaders and the led and inculcate the notion that rulers and ruled occupy different planes of existence. The greater the power, the more meaningful are the fine gradations of proximity to it. Hierarchies become more intricate, rankings more defined and formalized. Some of this may already have existed in the earlier days of Sura and Pumbedita, but it was greatly intensified by the new closeness to the political and administrative center which controlled an empire stretching from India to the Pyrenees.[59]

As inevitable as these new developments may have been and as positive as some of their results were to prove, some might look with unease, even distaste, at the transformation. Abbaye and Rava had never called themselves 'Geonim', and Rav and Shemu'el had lived, taught, and led the Jewish community without the trappings of authority or rituals of power. Where there is power, there are power struggles, and some of them were quite loud and nasty. Geonic politics had more than its share of unbecoming moments, which shed no luster on either the Geonate or the religion that it represented.

Responsa is a genre created by the Geonim and, together with the halakhic monograph, it is their most permanent legacy to the halakhic literature. It allowed them to link the scattered communities of the far-flung Diaspora and provide guidance to those at great distance from any center of Torah. The subject of a responsum, however, is determined by the inquirer. As noted above, the new forms of enterprise of the emerging commercial world raised endless questions in commercial law, and the recently established communities in North Africa and Spain needed practical guidance in marital law and in religious matters.

The Geonim rose to the challenge; the attention of Sura and Pumbedita, certainly that of their most creative minds, turned in new directions. This, however, entailed concentration on the laws which were currently relevant and inattention to that which was currently irrelevant. Not that the latter disappeared from the curriculum, but one might question how much serious thought was being devoted to the study of *Zevaḥim* and *Menaḥot*, *Bekhorot*, *'Arakhin*, and *Nazir*.[60] Put differently, the amoraic intellectual heritage was trimmed to contemporary needs; the energies of the ancient academies were now focused on an abridged Talmud. Some may well have seen in this reduction a cultural loss and wanted no part in this diminution.

The emergence of the Geonate, the rise of an entirely new genre of

[59] N. Danzig, *Mavo le-Sefer Halakhot Pesukot* (above, n. 5), 1; Brody, *The Geonim of Babylonia* (above, n. 29), 10–11, 185–6.

[60] *Nazir*, as noted above (n. 32), may not have been in the curriculum altogether.

halakhic writings, the responsa, and the notion and legitimacy of personal authorship were simply part of a far wider transformation. My previous contrast between the savoraic culture and that of the Geonim regarding anonymity should be seen as one of the differences between the Judeo-Iranian civilization of some half of a millennium and the new, emergent Judeo-Arabic one.[61] We tend to think of such transformations primarily in terms of high culture, language, and intellectual life, for literary remains are all that we have. These are, indeed, extremely important, as we shall see. However, 'culture' in the broader sense means the entire way one perceives the world and how one feels and acts in it. It shapes the relationship between husband and wife, standards of private and public comportment, notions of honor and shame, rest and relaxation, child-rearing and education. Any major cultural shift involves a radical transformation of the proprieties of behavior and of accustomed ways of thinking. Some find living on the cusp of such a *bouleversement* exhilarating; others find it deeply unsettling, indeed, deserving of unrelenting resistance.

The Judeo-Iranian culture had contained its inevitable share of acculturation, as the writings of Yaakov Elman and his colleagues have brought home to us.[62] But for those brought up in this culture (and for those who later sought to preserve it) it appeared autochthonous and wholly Jewish, much as the *shtrayml* appears to contemporary Hasidim to be as Jewish a garment as the *tallit*, and not the headgear of Polish noblemen of the eighteenth century. The new way of life that was emerging would have appeared to some deeply conservative people as a rejection of the customary Jewish modes of conduct and a repudiation of the time-hallowed ways of thinking and feeling. It was untraditional and thoroughly alien, and it was best to place as great a distance as possible between themselves and these powerful forces of negative change. In this group, I suggest, were some of the scholars from the Third Yeshivah of Bavel.

As bad as these changes may have seemed, the worst was yet to come. Indeed, I would suggest that it was the final phase of this metamorphosis that triggered the migration to Ashkenaz, though one may reasonably assume

[61] Sussmann, in "'Torah she-be-'al Peh'" (above, n. 47), 328 n. 31, has remarked on the simultaneous developments occurring around the mid-8th century, coeval with the time of the transfer of the Abbasid capital from Damascus to Baghdad: the emergence of the Geonate, the inscription of the Talmud (at least for communities in the Diaspora), and the first appearance of halakhic works other than the Talmud, such as the *She'iltot* and *Halakhot Pesukot*. All of which join in pointing to the decline of one culture (that of the *savora'im*) and the emergence of another (that of the Geonim).

[62] See e.g. Y. Elman, 'Acculturation to Elite Persian Norms and Modes of Thought in the Babylonian Jewish Community of Late Antiquity', in Y. Elman et al., *Neti'ot le-David: Jubilee Volume for David Weiss Halivni* (Jerusalem, 2004), 31–56.

that the disruptive cultural changes of the preceding century had alienated some from their surroundings and eased the decision to relocate. I emphasize again that we are probing an inference of the retrospective method, namely, that opposition to involvement in the higher culture of the host society was part of the ethos of the founding fathers, and asking whether it is probable for such an ideology to have developed on Babylonian soil by the mid-tenth century.

The new Judeo-Arabic culture progressed from a transformation of mores to a menacing transformation of *Weltanschauung*. In the tenth century the conservative forces in Bavel were confronted not simply with a world of new values and a novel way of life, but with a culture that was diverging radically from that of the *amora'im*. A new paideia was forming—and with it a new elite—that had a different intellectual agenda: philosophy, science, biblical exegesis, and grammar. Talmudic studies occupied only a portion of it. These new cultural horizons had been legitimated, in the 'conservative' view, by the appointment in 928 to the Geonate of Sura of Rav Sa'adyah.

Jews in tenth-century Babylonia faced a situation similar to that confronted by German Jewry in the eighteenth century and by east European Jewry in the nineteenth. An inward-turning, relatively self-contained culture of close to a millennium was confronted with a new, 'modern' one of a vastly higher cultural level than that of the Sassanian society that had previously enveloped it. It proffered a more rational mode of belief, a more 'sophisticated' notion of God, a far clearer account of the workings of the natural world, and fresh, novel forms of literary expression—all of Gentile origin. One of the bearers of this new intellectual agenda was the Egyptian Sa'adyah ben Yosef al-Fayummi, and his appointment as the Gaon of Sura was the equivalent of appointing R. David Tsevi Hoffmann as the *rosh yeshivah* of Volozhin.

Is it unreasonable to assume that there were many in the tenth century (among them some scholars of the Third Yeshivah) who resisted, just as did large numbers of Jews some 800 or 900 years later? It would be astonishing if this were not the case. Such a conflict may not have occurred in the relatively new Jewish communities in the West, and hence no record of it is to be found in the Genizah. In the East, however, in Babylonia itself, such cultural and ideological contentions seem inevitable. What long-entrenched civilization surrenders without a protracted struggle? A centuries-old way of life and millennium-old *Weltanschauung* never lack ardent defenders. To some, perhaps even to many, in Babylonia it appeared that nothing less than the Judaism of time immemorial, the Judaism of Rav and Shemu'el, of Abbaye and Rava, and that of all the *amora'im* and *savora'im* was being destroyed. Small wonder, as the source and inspiration of the new paideia was wholly Gentile. This new-begotten culture and all its enticements had to be shunned entirely. Nothing was more dangerous, in their view, than any involvement in it. One's entire energies should be dedicated now as before to *talmud torah* and to it alone. Jews must continue to be engaged, as they had always been, in grasping and interpreting that vast repository of Divine law and authentic Jewish culture—the Talmud, both its halakhah and aggadah.

III

Why, as the tenth century neared its mid-point, a small segment of this group moved to the Rhineland, of all places, we may never know for certain. No more than we would know why a group, gathered around John Winthrop, embarked for the strange and distant New World, if we did not have the journals of Winthrop and the records of the Massachusetts Bay Company. One thing seems clear. Without an offer of support for these scholars and their institution, the move would scarcely have been undertaken. Nor is such an offer difficult to imagine. The Rhineland was the richest area in the Ottonian Empire,[63] the greatest power in western and central Europe at the time. There was a Jewish collectivity in Mainz by the 930s, and many Jews were actively engaged in the vigorous trade, both local and international, that converged on that city.[64] It would require only a forceful advocate or two—remember how very small the Jewish population was in this period—for such a group of affluent and widely traveled merchants to decide to seek, as it were, their own place in the sun, to create a cultural center befitting their economic position, something to match that of their co-religionists in Islamic countries among whom they traveled and who, in all probability, looked upon these uneducated 'Franks' with contempt.

We may even have a record of what finally triggered a decision that had been a while in the making. A query was sent by men of the Rhineland to 'the communities in Erets Yisra'el' in 960 about the time of the advent of the messiah. They received the following reply: 'As to the coming of the messiah you were [*sic*] not worth replying to . . . It were better that you had asked us about the deep [topics] of [the tractates] *Yevamot* and *'Eruvin*.'[65] They had asked a deeply serious question in all sincerity, had sent an emissary with their query on a long and dangerous voyage, and had been treated like yokels. This may have been the last straw: never again would they be humiliated as country

[63] See above, pp. 122–41. [64] See above, pp. 127–8.

[65] וטוב היה לכם לשאול לנו בעמקי יבמות ועירובין.

bumpkins.[66] A twelfth-century scholar, R. Yitsḥak b. Dorbelo, first reported this query, and some scholars have questioned its authenticity. I have always been inclined to view it as genuine, seeing that it is the most insulting comment that we possess on the patriarchs of any Jewish community in the Diaspora. It is not something that their descendants would invent; quite the reverse—it is a document of which most would prefer not to know, and that is why it surfaced by accident only some two centuries later in Worms. If this dismissive reply was, indeed, the turning point, the straw that broke the camel's back—and this is no more than a conjecture—we would have 960 as the *terminus post quem* for the emigration.[67]

Why such an offer was made in the mid-tenth century is not difficult to imagine. Why the most fearless and adventurous of the Babylonian expatriates (all others, I assume, declined to journey thousands of miles to an unknown location in a vastly differing climate) might have been inclined to accept is equally understandable. Though, I repeat, without further information we shall never know what turned inclination into decision.

As the fourth or fifth decade of the tenth century drew near, the future in Bavel looked bleak. The Abbasid Empire was unraveling: Baghdad had been ravaged by a flood of unparalleled dimensions and was then racked by bloody turmoil as warring groups took and retook the city. Its economic hinterland was in decline, its people emigrating, seeking their livelihood elsewhere.[68] As for matters of the spirit, the situation was even worse. Pumbedita was now in chaos; its incessant politics had effectively dug the grave of the institution, and Sura had attempted to stave off dissolution in 928 by appointing an 'infidel', the Egyptian Sa'adyah, as its head. The new Arabic civilization was becoming ever more sophisticated, and, despite all the material problems of those years, its influence was ever more pervasive. Cultural contamination now threatened the devotees of the old order; they had to find some way to escape from the osmosis with the environment.

The hardiest and most committed of this segment of the Jewish population began to entertain the unthinkable—emigration, if only the opportunity presented itself. But where were they to go, what opportunities should they seize? Emigration to the backwater of the Holy Land and especially Jerusalem and its environs, to which some had, perhaps, retreated, was out,[69] as Jeru-

[66] For the account of Yitsḥak Dorbelo, see A. Z. Eshkoli, *Ha-Tenu'ot ha-Meshiḥiyot be-Yisra'el* (Jerusalem, 1956), 155–8.

[67] See below, n. 76.

[68] E. Ashtor, *A Social and Economic History of the Near East in the Middle Ages* (London, 1976), 169–76; id., 'Un mouvement migratoire au haut Moyen Age: migrations de l'Irak vers les pays méditerranéens', *Annales d'histoire économique et sociale*, 27 (1972), 185–214.

[69] *Ginzei Schechter*, ed. L. Ginzberg, ii (New York, 1929), 556.

salem had become, in the tenth century, the center of the Karaites, much of whose vibrant intellectual life drew on the alien, insidious Arabic culture from which these culturally conservative scholars had so sought to insulate themselves.[70] Most new settlements in the Islamic world were founded after the Arab conquest, and even if the settlements had antedated the coming of Islam, they had nothing, not even a residual element, of the ancient civilization from which they, the saving remnant, had issued. There was less of a chance of their retaining the old world—the world of the *amora'im* and *savora'im* (as they thought it to have been)—in these locales than in Babylonia. The only alternative was the land of Edom.

Such a decision—to continue the modern analogy in a subjunctive mood—would have been much like that of Akiva Yosef Schlesinger in the latter half of the nineteenth century. The struggle with the forces of Enlightenment and modernity in Hungary, indeed, in Europe generally, was a lost cause. The only solution was to retreat to a cultural backwoods, Palestine of the Ottoman Empire.[71]

Not that the Babylonian resisters would have moved precipitously to distant and wholly unknown lands. That would have been folly. As we now know that there was no lack of communication at this time between the Rhineland and Babylonia,[72] it seems reasonable to assume that inquiries were made of merchants and travelers as to the nature of the new land and its inhabitants, and, of no less importance, just how serious these 'Franks' were, how intent these sincere but unschooled Jews were on establishing a Jewish culture in the land of Edom. The emigration to Germany may well have taken place over a period of time. The route they followed awaits further research. Some may well have taken the Black Sea route, moved through Byzantium, and acquired some literature there; others may have opted for the Mediterranean route and traveled either via Italy and, in the ancient Jewish settlements of the peninsula, picked up some books and camp followers, or via Provence to Arles and up the Rhone. Whether it was a one-time move or emigration in waves, whether the Babylonians took one route or many, things came together, crystallized, in the middle of the tenth century with the founding of the yeshivah in Mainz.

If the Ottonian merchants of the land of Edom entertained high ambitions, if they wished to avoid creating simply a pale imitation of Kairouan or

[70] H. Ben-Shammai, 'The Karaites', in J. Prawer and H. Ben-Shammai, eds., *The History of Jerusalem: The Early Muslim Period—638–1099* (Jerusalem and New York, 1996), 211 n. 41.

[71] See M. Silber, 'Pe'amei Lev ha-'Ivri be-'Erets Hagar', *Kathedra*, 73 (1994), 84–105 and the bibliography cited there.

[72] For the numerous contacts between the Rhineland and Babylonia, see above, pp. 122–41.

Fustat which would always be viewed as inferior to its parent community, no better choice could have been made by the founders of the new northern Jewish civilization than inviting the expatriates of the Third Yeshivah of Bavel. Intended or not, what occurred in tenth-century Ottonian Germany was a true *translatio studii* (the epoch-making relocation of a cultural center) from Babylonia to the Rhineland, only what was being translated was not the Babylonia of the tenth century but the Bavel of the *amora'im* and *savora'im*—as envisaged by the immigrant founders.

These men felt no deference to the Geonim. For Ashkenaz was founded by an 'anti-geonic' group, as it were; perhaps better, a 'non-geonic' group. Its founding fathers were a body of scholars who had never accepted the monopolistic claims of the Geonim to rabbinic authority. They had discountenanced the hierarchical ways of discussion in the academies of Sura and Pumbedita at the time and took care that in the new yeshivah which they founded in the Rhineland a far more informal, even intimate, atmosphere prevailed.[73] They may not have been critical of the geonic preoccupation with applied halakhah; it was, after all, a historical necessity. However, they had no use for it as an ideal. Realistic jurisprudence was an overriding need; it should not become a pre-emptive occupation. Ad hoc rulings were one thing; devoting one's energies to writing halakhic monographs on new actualities another. Grasping the totality of halakhah was the true goal of talmudic studies, not simply application of sections of it. Their Talmud was larger, their curriculum broader by six tractates than that of the academies of Sura and Pumbedita, and all of the Talmud was studied and mastered equally. Power had never tempted them, and they had remained untainted by the corruptions of politics. Above all, they had never defiled their intellectual inheritance by steeping themselves in the so-called 'wisdom of the Gentiles' and presenting their heritage in its light. In view of the vast transformation that attended the full arrival of the Judeo-Arabic culture in Babylonia, they may well have felt that they were not leaving Bavel; Babylonia had left Bavel. They were taking Bavel—the true Bavel, the Bavel of old—with them.

IV

In what ways did this 'Puritan migration', the transplanted men of the Third Yeshivah of Bavel, leave their imprint on Ashkenaz?

[73] See A. Grossman, 'Ha-Yeshivot be-Bavel, be-Germanyah u-ve-Tsarfat ba-Me'ot ha-Yod ve-ha-Yod-Alef', in R. Feldhay and I. Etkes, eds., *Ḥinnukh ve-Historyah: Heksherim Tarbutiyim u-Politiyim* (Jerusalem, 1999), 79–99.

That Ashkenaz sprang from a Babylonian transplantation seems a firm conclusion. Otherwise, how does one account for their sovereign command of Babylonian Aramaic, their capacity to explicate with ease and in detail the aggadic portions of the Talmud with their vast, variegated vocabulary, something no other diaspora seemed capable of doing? Why else would the author of the *'Arukh* view the explications of Rabbenu Gershom and the *Commentaries of Mainz* as on a par with those of Rav Hai? That these Babylonian settlers stemmed from the Third Yeshivah seems a reasonable inference. Otherwise, whence the source of the Ashkenazic commentarial traditions of the *lashon meshunah* tractates? Why else is the talmudic curriculum of the new settlement in the distant lands of Germany greater than that of Sura and Pumbedita, the fountainheads of all rabbinic knowledge in the Diaspora? (Both inferences are independent of the cause of the transplantation, whether it was ideological or simply a historical 'accident'.) The argument might be advanced, as I noted before, that, perhaps, only one of the two famed yeshivot omitted these tractates from its curriculum, and that the settlers of Ashkenaz came from the one that included them. This, however, would leave unexplained the dismissive attitude to the Geonim that emerged so clearly from the writings of Rabbenu Gershom and those of his pupils.[74] Rabbenu Gershom saw his teacher as being clearly superior to the Geonim, which would accord with the latter's representing the Third Yeshivah of Bavel, but scarcely had his master been himself a product of either Sura or Pumbedita.

With the emigration of the Third Yeshivah in the mid-tenth century, the self-effacing values of the *savora'im* and *setama'im* were implanted in the Rhineland and lasted as long as did the culture of Early Ashkenaz, that is to say, until the massacre of its scholars and the destruction of their yeshivot in the First Crusade (1096). We well know who were the leading Talmudists of the eleventh century—Rabbenu Gershom, Rabbenu Yehudah Ba'al Sefer ha-Dinim, R. Ya'akov ben Yakar, R. Yitsḥak ha-Levi, Rabbenu Sasson, and R. Yitsḥak b. Yehudah.[75] Their names bulk large in the literature of *Siddur of Rashi*, the *Maḥzor Vitry*, and *Ma'aseh ha-Ge'onim*. Rashi, however, didn't travel to the Rhineland and sit at their feet for the 'small change', as it were, of the *Sifrut de-Vei Rashi*, to acquaint himself with their ad hoc rulings on issues of ritual. He spent his youth and early manhood there to apprise himself of their traditions and accomplishments in talmudic exegesis so as to provision himself for his great commentarial enterprise. Yet, as frequently as the names of various scholars appear in the halakhic literature of the eleventh century, the

[74] Above, pp. 151–5.

[75] See Grossman, *Ḥakhmei Ashkenaz ha-Rishonim* (above, n. 13).

astonishing fact is that they are totally absent from the Mainz commentary on the Talmud, the so-called *Perush Rabbenu Gershom*, written in the very same academies by the very same men. The most that one receives is an occasional 'and the master said' (*ve-'omer ha-rav*), 'and the teacher explained' (*ve-ha-moreh piresh*), and the like; never a specific name.[76] The rabbinic figures mentioned above were second-, third-, and fourth-generation Europeans and made no pretense to anonymity, had no hesitation whatsoever in signing and co-signing hundreds of responsa. However, the moment they stepped over the threshold of the *bet ha-midrash* and engaged in talmudic exegesis, they became faceless. In the study hall, in the bastion of the Third Yeshivah, the ethos of the old country, the mores of the *savora'im* and *setama'im*, still obtained.

Indeed, it would seem that it was forbidden by some to quote any explanation on any part of the rabbinic corpus—Talmud, Midrash, or Targum—in the name of a specific person. R. Natan, author of the *Sefer he-'Arukh*, cupped his ears whenever he heard the name Magentsa. It was as close as he, a denizen of Rome, could ever get to 'the horse's mouth', as it were, to the living speech of native Aramaic speakers. It made no difference to him whether the explanation of a word or term stemmed from 'the commentaries of Magentsa', 'the scholars of Magentsa', 'the rabbi of the scholars of Magentsa', 'the rabbis of Magentsa', 'the teacher of Magentsa', 'the pupils of Magentsa in the name of the teacher', 'the sons of [*benei*] Magentsa', 'the righteous of [*ḥasidei*] Magentsa', or just 'a scholar from [*talmid ḥakham mi-*] Magentsa'—all their explications, if accurately transmitted, were of equal value.[77] However, rarely is there any mention of a name. He openly names his Provençal sources—R. Mosheh ha-Darshan of Narbonne and R. Mosheh b. Ya'akov b. Mosheh b. Abun of Narbonne—and his Italian sources—R. Mosheh of Bari, R. Moshe Kalfo of Bari, R. Mosheh of Pavia—but not those of Magentsa. It is as if most of his numerous German sources had been enjoined from using in their accounts any proper names, forbidden to attribute any interpretation of the sacred sources to a particular individual. Rashi, entirely European and wholly his own man, did not feel bound by this, but most of the 'reporters' of R. Natan seem to have been.[78]

[76] A. Epstein, 'Der Gerschom Meor ha-Golah zugeschriebene Talmud-Commentar', in *Festschrift zum achtzigsten Geburtstage Moritz Steinschneider's* (Leipzig, 1896), 125–6; Hebrew translation in *Netu'im*, 6 (2000), 114–16.

[77] See above, pp. 160–1.

[78] R. Natan of Rome does name R. Meshullam b. Kalonymos once, R. Meshullam b. Mosheh b. Iti'el once, and Rabbenu Gershom any number of times. (See *Arukh Completum* [above, n. 23], introduction, i. 14–15.) Mentioning the name of R. Meshullam is not surprising as he was from Lucca and not part of the Third Yeshivah. The name Iti'el is very distinctive and known in only one family.

Let us turn now to the long-term imprint of the Babylonian migration.

The Third Yeshivah bequeathed to Ashkenaz a program of study that for centuries had not distinguished between ritual law (*Seder Mo'ed*), marital and civil law (*Nashim u-Nezikin*), and that of Temple service (*Kodashim*). This is attested to by the writings of Rashi and the Tosafists, who commented on and analyzed the tractates of all four orders (*sedarim*) in equal detail. The Catalonian school of Naḥmanides and his disciples was, as already noted, the true intellectual successor of Ri and Rabbenu Tam,[79] and openly acknowledged their debt.[80] Nevertheless they could not escape their heritage, that of Provence and Spain, and their great sets of novellae (*nimmukim* or *ḥiddushim*) are confined to the three orders of *Mo'ed*, *Nashim*, and *Nezikin*.[81]

A R. Iti'el is mentioned as part of the Luccan transplantation and was related to the same R. Meshullam b. Kalonymos. (See Grossman, *Ḥakhmei Ashkenaz ha-Rishonim* [above, n. 13], 31, 45–6, 388.) His comments are upon a *mishnah* in *Pe'ah* and lie far from the beaten path of the Mainz commentary. Rabbenu Gershom is the notable exception to this rule of German anonymity. Why, I don't know; it may reflect a remarkable sense of independence on his part or the prominence of his contribution to the talmudic exegesis of Mainz, which precluded his being submerged in any crowd. Either of these would point to his occupying a position of special prominence in Mainz, something that Grossman claims and which I have challenged. See my *Collected Essays*, i. 162 n. 126.

A similar dichotomy is noticeable in the Mainz commentary. The German figures are anonymous, with the exception of Rabbenu Gershom, who is mentioned by name in the commentary on *Ḥullin*. See Epstein, 'Der Gerschom Meor ha-Golah zugeschriebene Talmud-Commentar' (above, n. 76), 122; Hebrew translation, 124–5. There may be one solitary breach to this rule: an enlarged version of the so-called *Perush Rabbenu Gershom 'al Bava Batra* published from MS Oxford 416. A gloss in that manuscript informs us that an anonymous scholar (*rebbi*) told the author of a joint interpretation given by one of the Makirites, R. Natan b. Makhir, and an otherwise unknown R. Binyamin (*Bava Batra* 101b, ed. T. Y. Leitner, 2 vols. in 1 [Jerusalem, 1999], ii. 25; Or Ḥayyim edn. [Jerusalem, n.d.], 120). One doesn't know whether this gloss contains material that the scribe erroneously left out of the body of the text or whether it is a later addition of the 12th century. Furthermore, the Benei Makhir were acolytes of the heads of the Mainz yeshivah, not *rashei yeshivah* themselves. It may be significant that it is a nameless mentor (*ve-'amar li rebbi*) who transmits this interpretation to the writer, not the authors of the interpretation themselves.

Foreigners fared differently. The Italian immigrant R. Kalonymos Ish Romi (from Rome), who came to Mainz after the death of R. Ya'akov b. Yakar in 1064, is mentioned once by an anonymous teacher (*ha-moreh*) in the commentary on *Bava Batra* at 14b, s.v. *shivrei* (ed. Leitner, i. 38; Or Ḥayyim edn., 39). R. Yitsḥak ha-'Orliani (from Orléans) is cited as is Rav Hai Gaon. R. Yitsḥak did study with R. Eli'ezer ha-Gadol of Mainz; however, his traditions and standing were independent of Mainz. He came from one of the oldest and most prestigious families in France, and this is reflected in the respectful way in which R. Eli'ezer addressed him. See A. Grossman *Ḥakhmei Tsarfat ha-Rishonim: Koroteihem, Darkam be-Hanhagat ha-Tsibbur, Yetsiratam ha-Ruḥanit* (Jerusalem, 1995), 82–3, 107–20.

79 See *Collected Essays*, i. 32.

80 See e.g. Ramban's introduction to his 'Kuntres Dina de-Garmi' in *Ḥiddushei ha-Ramban le-Makkot, Kuntres Dina de-Garmi, 'Avodah Zarah, Sanhedrin*, ed. M. Herschler (Jerusalem, 1970), 105.

81 I should add, of course, together with their *ḥiddushim* on three tractates of great, indeed

If the knowledge of Ashkenaz was more comprehensive than that of Sura and Pumbedita and all the Diaspora communities that took their instruction from them, what could any of those settlements teach them about Torah? Ashkenaz's talmudic curriculum was far wider, its detailed knowledge of both halakhah and aggadah far greater (by virtue of its line-by-line exposition). This is the starting point of the halakhic insularity of Ashkenaz.[82] The teachings of the founders and their disciples were then transmuted by Rashi's genius into what was universally acknowledged to be *the* definitive commentary on the Talmud. This was followed by the revolutionary labors of Rabbenu Tam and Ri, which revived talmudic dialectic and ushered halakhah into a new golden age. These later developments only confirmed the Ashkenazic notion of halakhic superiority. What could a R. Mosheh b. Maimon of Córdoba or a R. Shelomoh ibn Aderet of Barcelona possibly teach them?

If my hypothetical reconstruction of the events in Bavel is equally correct—and this is for scholars of Geonica to decide—the men of the Third Yeshivah of Bavel had emigrated to escape the alien civilization of the Judeo-Arabic world, and in the distant climes of the north they would be free to erect what to their thinking was an authentically Jewish one. They came with a notion of setting up a New Jerusalem or, perhaps more accurately, a New Bavel. They would establish, in the wildernesses of Germany, free from all corrupting influences, a perfectly observant community. Whence the distinctive notion of ***kehillah kedoshah*** that permeates the thought of Ashkenaz and which is, as I noted some forty years ago, already perceptible in the writings of Rabbenu Gershom.[83] In other words, this self-image is coeval with the existence of the Ashkenazic community.[84]

Religious simplicity and scrupulous observance of the law were achievable in tenth- and eleventh-century Germany, with one exception, namely, in the sphere of Jewish–Gentile relations. The Talmud had laid down strict laws intended to minimize trade relations with Gentiles; they restricted the use of Gentile servants, banned Gentile midwives and nursemaids, and forbade all trade in Gentile wine (*yein nesekh, setam yeinam*), indeed, banned all benefit from such wine. This was doable in amoraic Babylonia, where Jews were an agricultural class and constituted a large segment of the population. In Ger-

controlling, practical significance, *Berakhot* (from *Seder Zera'im*), *Ḥullin* (from *Seder Kodashim*), and *Niddah* (from *Seder Toharot*). On the study of *Seder Kodashim* in other cultures, see above, p. 33, n. 10, and cf. E. Kanarfogel, 'Ya'adei Limmud ve-Dimui 'Atsmi etsel Ḥakhmei ha-Talmud be-'Eiropah bi-Yemei ha-Beinayim: ha-'Issuk be-Seder Kodashim', in Y. Ben-Naeh et al., eds., *Asufah le-Yosef: Kovets Meḥkarim Shai le-Yosef Hacker* (Jerusalem, 2014), 68–91.

[82] See *Collected Essays*, i. 31–8.

[83] Ibid. 112.

[84] Ibid. 246–7 and see 258–77.

many, however, the Jewish community was predominantly, if not entirely, commercial, and their trading partners were inevitably Gentiles. The Jewish community was minute; it could in no way provide the numerous hands required to run a household in the days before plumbing and electricity. Finally, the major source of wealth in the Rhineland was the wine trade, payments in kind were ubiquitous, and the most common unit of payment was the wine barrel. The ban on drinking Gentile wine was observed with a passion; that on trade was widely disregarded.

Admittedly these talmudic bans were rabbinic ordinances and not pentateuchal ones; however, few of them could be overcome or sidestepped. For example, the Mishnah had banned all trade for the three days preceding and following a Gentile religious holiday. This meant that no trade was ever possible in a Christian society as Sunday, the day of rest, occurred every seven days. The men of the Third Yeshivah could not advocate that the well-to-do traders of Ashkenaz become warriors or tillers of the soil like the 'two-footed beasts' of the Middle Ages, the peasants. Nor could they preach that housewives do without help. They confronted the choice between cultural contamination of the whole of Judaism in the lands of Islam or breach in one area of rabbinic law in lands of Christendom. Had not the entire purpose of the migration been to escape osmosis with a tainted environment and preserve unsullied the *Weltanschauung* of their fathers? They were first and foremost ideological purists, and, not surprisingly, they preferred a community of unblemished beliefs over one of perfect performance (as, I believe, would our contemporaries in Benei Berak and Stamford Hill).

Halakhic non-compliance, however, posed problems. Many in Ashkenaz might say, 'If a breach in one area is inevitable, a breach or two in other areas will make no difference.' All the hopes for a *kehillah kedoshah*, for a New Bavel, would then be lost, and much of the very purpose of emigration would be for naught. The founders adopted the policy expressed in the talmudic dictum: 'Better that they sin ignorantly [i.e. out of ignorance of the law] than knowingly [i.e. despite knowledge of the law].'[85] They removed the tractate which treats Jewish–Gentile relations, *'Avodah Zarah*, from the curriculum of Early Ashkenaz. This is the reason for the strange fact that had so baffled me in my work on *yein nesekh*: the tractates of *Zevaḥim*, *Temurah*, *Me'ilah*, and *Nazir* were taught in the yeshivah of Mainz, but not that of *'Avodah Zarah*![86] (You

[85] מוטב שיהו שוגגין ולא מזידין. *Betsah* 30a and parallel passages cited there. This is not to say that this principle was explicitly invoked; we have, after all, no record of their thought. Rather, they adopted the principle expressed in that saying.

[86] *Collected Essays*, i. 177–8; *Ha-Yayin bi-Yemei ha-Beinayim: Yein Nesekh—Perek be-Toledot ha-Halakhah be-'Ashkenaz* (Jerusalem, 2008), 133–5.

cannot teach the *entire* Talmud from *Berakhot* to *Niddah* and accidentally omit *'Avodah Zarah*. Its absence had to have been intentional.) A hundred and thirty years or so later Rashi could return *'Avodah Zarah* to the Ashkenazic curriculum. The communal image had been safely established. Didn't Rashi announce to his students that 'the entire congregation are holy, every one of them' (Num. 16: 4)? If one received a gift of food on the holidays from one's co-religionist, there was no need to inquire as to its *kashrut* (whether it was picked on the holiday itself or the day before: in the former case it would be forbidden to eat it during the holiday; in the latter one, its consumption would be permitted), for not only did all Jews scrupulously observe the laws of *kashrut*, but they were equally familiar with its intricate details.[87]

Finally, there is Ashkenaz's avoidance of any involvement with the higher culture of its environment. Let me not be misunderstood. Acculturation took place inevitably; it was assimilation that was opposed. The terms are not significant; differentiating between the two notions is. Acculturation (as I am using it here) is an unconscious process; over the course of time significant ways of thinking and feeling receive their impress from the environment. Assimilation is the conscious involvement in the higher culture of the society and the acceptance of all or some of its values. (Total assimilation would be conversion; partial assimilation, in contemporary America, would be Modern Orthodoxy's acceptance of secular education and humanistic values.)

Every minority becomes acculturated. Its manner of speech and vocal register, its taste in dress and furnishings, its palate, its concepts of honor and shame, many of its notions of personal comportment are adopted from the environment. The humor of Sholem Aleichem is also Russian humor, as *chulent* is a Russian dish. Ashkenazic Jews were medieval French or German Jews, not nineteenth-century Polish or Hungarian ones. Things could not be otherwise. However, any engagement with the intellectual life of their Gentile neighbors, any participation in what we call medieval Western culture, was taboo. Principled indifference was part of the cultural DNA of Ashkenaz for it had been founded by men who sought, above all, intellectual and ideological isolation. They had fled the encroaching culture of Islam, and had not journeyed thousands of miles to a strange new world to be caught up in that of Christianity. So deep was that desire, so profound the aversion to alien 'wisdom', that it became their most enduring legacy. It stamped Ashkenazic culture for some 800 years.

Ashkenaz was thus what Louis Hartz once termed a 'fragment society'.[88]

87 *Ma'aseh ha-Ge'onim* (above, n. 8), 83.

88 L. Hartz, *The Founding of New Societies* (New York, 1964).

A small, at times even tiny, segment of a larger society detaches itself and creates a new civilization in a wilderness, as did the Puritans in America or several waves of Dutch and English settlers in South Africa. Freed from the complex, inhibiting whole—entrenched institutions and hierarchies, deep structures of social and cultural restraint—the fragment develops unimpeded, exfoliates without hindrance, and stamps the society that it established for centuries.

V

Is this the entire story? Clearly not, because the second major area of cultural creativity of Early Ashkenaz, composition of liturgical poetry (*piyyut*), cannot be explained by a Babylonian migration of the mid-tenth century. The Palestinian origins of the Ashkenazic *piyyut* are undeniable. That genre's proven route is from Palestine, to southern (Byzantine) Italy (Bari, Otranto), to northern Italy (Lucca), and thence to the Rhineland. One has to assume the migration of an Italian elite. This brings us back to the 'foundation story' which links the esoteric traditions (*torat ha-sod*) of Ashkenaz with the transplantation of the Kalonymides from Lucca to Mainz. Of the three possible dates that one can assign to that migration, 917 is the most plausible, as Avraham Grossman has argued.[89] One could contend that there were three separate transplantations—halakhic, liturgical, and esoteric—that coalesced in the mid-tenth century. The Kalonymide family, the bearer of the esoteric traditions, however, was equally involved in liturgical composition, and the *piyyutim* of R. Meshullam b. Kalonymos noticeably influenced those of R. Shim'on b. Yitsḥak of Mainz, a contemporary of Rabbenu Gershom.[90] One can then plausibly argue (though any final determination is up to experts in *piyyut* and *sod*) for a two-stage founding of Ashkenazic culture. The liturgical-esoteric stratum was laid in 917, and was then reinforced by the migration from Le Mans to Mainz of the Abun family, which produced the famed *paytan*, R. Shim'on b. Yitsḥak.[91] The dominant halakhic stratum was laid around 950–60 by the scholars of the Third Yeshivah.

[89] See above, n. 13.

[90] E. Fleischer, 'Azharot le-Rabbi Binyamin (Ben Shemu'el) Paytan', *Kovets 'al Yad*, NS 11/21 (1985), 40–1, and more generally id., *Shirat ha-Kodesh ha-'Ivrit bi-Yemei ha-Beinayim*, reprint with supplementary bibliography (Jerusalem, 2007), 425–73.

[91] This information is provided by the anonymous medieval chronicle transmitted by R. Shelomoh Luria in his *Teshuvot Rashal* (Lublin, 1574/5), #29. See Grossman (above, n. 9), 86–94. Hanna Caine-Braunschvig has pointed out to me that if 917 is taken as the date of the Kalonymide transplantation, the authenticity of the 960 letter to the 'communities in Erets-Yisra'el' (above, p. 183) would be somewhat dubious. It is difficult to imagine (though, of course, not impossible) that a community headed by R. Meshullam b. Kalonymos, or one that contained him, would pen such an inquiry.

The two or three settlements blended easily. Both composition and recitation of *piyyut* had already made serious headway in Babylonia by the mid-tenth century, as the writings of Be'eri and Elitsur have shown us—Rav Sa'adyah's *siddur*, for example, composed after his accession to the Geonate, contains *piyyut*.[92] The calm acceptance, even embrace, of *piyyut* by the halakhic leaders of Early Ashkenaz is explicable in light of the growing success of liturgical poetry in their homeland. Nor is there any problem in the acceptance by the men of the Third Yeshivah of certain Palestinian practices, primarily in the area of liturgy. I have already noted that Talmudists throughout the ages viewed liturgy as having a life of its own, and despite their sincere devotion to halakhic correctness they have been singularly reluctant to alter established liturgical practices.[93] As for the few other ritual practices that deviated from the Babylonian norm, it would have been folly to have split the tiny Jewish settlement of Mainz, to have wasted, at the very least, precious political capital over some practices whose only sin—if it could be called a sin—was that they followed the Palestinian rite. A new group of settlers with a vaulting ambition of setting up a new amoraic society, as it were, who had traveled vast distances at great personal risk in the hope of founding a *kehillah kedoshah*, a model religious community, would have been doubly hesitant to risk its entire enterprise over some ritual minutiae which could even show themselves to be rooted in the ancient literature. Wisdom lay in silence.

APPENDIX I

YESHIVOT IN BAVEL

One can, of course, insist that these were not different centers but different groups, all of whom were housed under the roof, or were otherwise under the wing of Sura and Pumbedita, if it is reasonable to assume that these two institutions were the only yeshivot in Babylonia. I think that such an assumption is worth questioning.

Josephus' statement that there were 'innumerable *miriades*' (units of tens of thousands) of Jews in Babylonia well over a century before Rav established his academy in Sura is clearly hyperbolic.[94] While hard numbers are notoriously

[92] T. Be'eri, 'Shirah 'Ivrit be-Bavel ba-Me'ah ha-'Asirit ve-ha-'Aḥat-'Esreh le-'Or Mimtsa'ei ha-Genizah', *Te'udah*, 15 (1999), 23–36; id., *He-Ḥazan ha-Gadol asher be-Bagdad: Piyyutei Yosef ben Ḥayyim Albardani* (Jerusalem, 2002); S. Elitsur, 'Le-'Ofyo ve-li-Netivot Hashpa'ato shel ha-Merkaz ha-Paytani be-Bavel: Hirhurim be-'Ikkevot Sefareiha shel Tovah Be'eri', *Tarbiz*, 79 (2010/11), 229–48. On Sa'adyah, see ibid. 232 n. 12.

[93] See above, p. 56.

[94] *Antiquities of the Jews*, Loeb Classical Library 6 (repr. Cambridge, Mass., 1978), xi. 133.

difficult to come by, the clear impression in the Talmud is of a large Jewish population. There is no reason to assume that the numbers dropped in the geonic period. Is it reasonable that only two yeshivot serviced such a large community? Scholars attended the gathering of *kallah* in Sura and Pumbedita, where tractates, or chapters thereof, were studied intensively and outstanding issues in these areas resolved. These scholars came intellectually equipped; where did they receive their education? Clearly, other yeshivot or *battei midrash* of all sorts provided this instruction. Why should we assume that they were all of a 'secondary school' level? Editing clearly was done in places other than Sura and Pumbedita, and these famed academies employed the written texts of the others on occasion.[95] Doesn't such sustained editorial labor, even textual intervention, reflect a sovereign command of the material? Why should we not assume the existence of other important seats of learning, not officially sanctioned as were Sura and Pumbedita, but still of high intellectual caliber? Everything we know of the final textualization of the Talmud points to their vibrant activity.

To the argument that the editing of the Talmud was concluded long before the tenth century, there are two replies. First, some inscriptions of the Talmud were concluded by the mid-eighth century, at the latest, and that copies of these inscriptions were circulating throughout the Diaspora is unquestioned, but that does not mean that all the various versions of the Talmud that we currently know of were then in circulation. To the best of my knowledge no one can provide a *terminus ad quem* for all the differently copy-edited versions of the Talmud that have come down to us. Second, even granting that all the current versions—and then some—were inscribed and copy-edited by the mid-eighth century, why should we assume that the yeshivot or *battei midrash* that fixed their final form then closed their doors? These texts are far too elliptical to be self-explanatory; they demand an interpretative tradition to be understood. In other words, they must be taught. (To give a modern example: note the different fates of the Soncino translation of the Talmud and that of Steinsaltz, or the ones published in the Schottenstein series. The first had very restricted sales and its purchasers were primarily libraries; the other two sell in the many thousands and the overwhelming majority of those who buy them are individuals. Soncino is a translation and a very fine one, but nothing more. Without some commentary, however, the telegraphic text of the Talmud, even if fully understood lexically, has little meaning. The Steinsaltz and Schottenstein editions explicate the translated text.) Who, in the geonic period, could

95 Sussmann, '"Torah she-be-'al Peh"' (above, n. 47), 209–384.

better provide this instruction than the institutions that had preserved these texts for centuries and had finally given them their written form? The most natural answer to the question 'Where did the students of the *kallah* receive their education?' is, 'In the various *battei midrash* that had been involved from time immemorial in the oral transmission of the Talmud and had centuries-old traditions of the meaning of that often cryptic text.'

In conclusion I would only add that Robert Brody has observed to me that, while the Jews of Spain or North Africa did not easily entertain the notion of multiple texts of the Talmud, variant readings are part and parcel of the Ashkenazic commentarial tradition. He is unquestionably correct. Textual variants in Ashkenaz were taken almost as a given and deciding between them was perceived as an inevitable component of the exegetical enterprise. Authority seeks to speak in a single voice, and the impression given in the responsa that issued forth from the two great yeshivot is that there is one authoritative text of the Talmud, and while written texts do circulate, the living Vox Talmudica is to be found within the four walls of Sura and Pumbedita.[96] The Third and other yeshivot of Bavel had no need to speak in authoritative tones and were actively involved in 'editing' (and expounding) the written texts of the Talmud. They knew only too well the measure of fluidity of the text and even the occasional differences between the versions, and they imparted this awareness to the Ashkenazic community.

Indeed, one may wonder whether the men of the Third Yeshivah and other *battei midrash* in Bavel shared this aversion to writing, which Sussmann has so magisterially chronicled.[97] Sussmann himself wondered why this persistent orality long after both Christian and Muslim cultures had turned to inscribing their canon, and he hesitantly proffered some suggestions.[98] One may also propose that the orality of a vast text furthers a monopoly of authority. Texts can be transported to distant lands and commentaries then written which open them to the understanding of the broader public. A recited text is inhospitable to commentarial exposition, and how many people exist who have phonographic memories and can accurately recite verbatim huge amounts of 'text', especially if it lacks the rhythms and alliterations of poetry? Diffusion of the 'text' of the Talmud is thus sharply limited and its explication greatly complicated. Furthermore, who is to certify these 'reciters' in a distant country, and

[96] I emphasize that I am speaking of the overall impression. The Geonim mention occasionally differing versions of the talmudic texts. See, for example, R. Brody, "Sifrut ha-Ge'onim ve-ha-Tekst ha-Talmudi", in Y. Sussmann and D. Rosenthal, eds., *Meḥkerei Talmud: Kovets Meḥkarim be-Talmud u-vi-Teḥumim Govlim* (Jerusalem, 1990), i. 237–304.

[97] Sussmann, 'Torah she-be-'al Peh' (above, n. 47).

[98] Ibid.

what guarantee is there that errors have not slipped into their repertoire over the course of the years? *Tanna'im* (reciters, Hebrew) and *garsanim* (reciters, Aramaic) function best in temples of authority, ancient centers of learning, which had in the past, when orality was obligatory,[99] developed the necessary controls to ensure the integrity of the transmission, true and tried techniques that are still in place. If Sura and Pumbedita were to establish the authority of the Bavli over the far-flung Diaspora, they had to project their uniqueness and authority by all possible means. Working quietly in the hinterland and making no claims to power, what need had the other yeshivot and *battei midrash* of Bavel of the mystique of orality?

APPENDIX II

UNCOVERING WRITINGS FROM THE DARK SIDE

Granted, some may say, that Bavel, like the moon, has her dark side, how can we ever get a glimpse of it? I have already noted (see p. 167 above) that it is reasonable to assume that some of the anonymous material in the Genizah comes from these unnamed *battei midrash*. The first task, then, is to identify such writings. To my untutored eye, three criteria loom large, and I offer them hesitantly as suggestions to experts in several fields—Geonica, the history of the talmudic text, and Aramaic—who may accept, refine, or even reject them and suggest others. I would propose arranging all the citations of the Talmud found in geonic writings into two groups—those that are known to be authored by the heads of Sura and Pumbedita and those that remain anonymous, taking care to distinguish between actual quotations and partial geonic rewrites of the passage.[100] Where there are parallel citations of a talmudic passage, do the citations differ? If one is lucky enough to have identical quotations from both Sura and Pumbedita, but the quotation in some of the anonymous material differs, that would be a first step towards isolating material emanating from the hinterland of Bavel. Second, the same two groups should be analyzed in terms of their halakhic rulings. There may well have been more controversies in the era of the Geonim than there were between the actual Geonim. Finally, using early Eastern geonic manuscripts as described by

[99] *Gittin* 61b: *devarim she-be-'al-peh iy ata rasha'i le-'omram bi-khetav.*

[100] See M. Morgenstern, 'Ha-'Aramit ha-Bavlit ha-Yehudit bi-Teshuvot ha-Ge'onim: 'Iyyunim be-Torat ha-Hegeh, bi-Tetsurat ha-Po'al, be-Khinnuyim u-ve-Signon' (Ph.D. diss., Hebrew University of Jerusalem, 2002), 11–13. Needless to say, pride of place should be given to the reports found in early Eastern geonic manuscripts (see next note).

Matthew Morgenstern,[101] the faceless and the identified groups should be studied with regard to the four 'registers' (some might call them 'dialects'[102]) that he has discerned in geonic writings: 'the talmudic idiom (in citations), an informal style employed in legal discourse, a formal style employed in legal pronouncements and a highly formal style used only in the introductions of collections of responsa'.[103] Morgenstern has treated the material as an undifferentiated mass, as representative of one set of writers. If one disaggregates that mass and distinguishes between the clearly authored and the anonymous material, do both groups still have all four styles? If they do not, that would be a third step towards identification of the non-Sura/Pumbedita material. If they do, is there any sharp difference between these two groups in the frequency of use of these different styles?

No single characteristic will suffice to identify the writings from the dark side, only a convergence of such characteristics. When a responsum or a work differs linguistically from those that emanated from the two yeshivot and has equally a different ruling or an alternative textual tradition, the chances are that it was produced by one of the nameless yeshivot of Bavel. Hopefully, experts in various fields can devise other yardsticks of differentiation between the sources of the period and thus enlarge the possibility of intersections of distinguishing traits—finally giving the unsung *battei midrash* of Bavel their rightful place in the sun.

APPENDIX III

THE FOUNDATION MYTH OF ASHKENAZ

There is still a missing piece in our reconstruction. Why did Ashkenaz not retain some proud memory of its origins in the Third Yeshivah of Bavel? Why is there not a whisper of this in Ashkenazic sources? I have no answer to this question at the moment, and for this reason, I have characterized this essay as a 'proposal'. However, I would like to distinguish between this issue and the so-called 'foundation myth' of Ashkenaz.

My thesis accords well with the widely held view that the transplantation of the Kalonymides as recounted by R. El'azar of Worms in the 1220s is rooted

[101] *Studies in Jewish Babylonian Aramaic Based on Early Eastern Manuscripts*, Harvard Semitic Studies 62 (Winona Lake, Ind., 2011), 40–54.

[102] Morgenstern, 'Ha-'Aramit ha-Bavlit' (above, n. 100), 13–15.

[103] *Studies in Jewish Babylonian Aramaic* (above, n. 101), 35.

in fact,[104] for I, too, assume an independent settlement in Mainz by the Kalonymides, probably in 917, which antedated that of the Third Yeshivah by a generation and which brought to Ashkenaz the traditions of esoteric knowledge (*sod*) and, possibly, that of liturgical poetry (*piyyut*).[105] I take this translation from Lucca as a probability, and if someone in the Middle Ages wished to link it to Charlemagne and give it thereby greater grandeur, this would in no way controvert anything advanced in this essay. However, I don't believe that the tale told by R. El'azar meets the basic requirements of a foundational myth.

First, the story of the transplantation was told by R. El'azar in the introduction to his *Perush ha-Tefillot* for the purpose of authenticating the traditions of *sod* that he was about to disseminate. By contrast, the tale of the four captives in *Sefer ha-Kabbalah* accounts for the emergence of the acknowledged mastery of the Talmud in Spain and Kairouan which legitimated the religious autonomy of those two communities.[106] The halakhah was both the written and unwritten constitution of the Jewish community. It was the basis of Jewish existence and its importance was realized by all. Any story that validated the community's claim to independence and authority in this realm merits the adjective 'foundational'.

Mastery of arcane *sod* is a different and much lesser matter, at least before the widespread diffusion of Lurianic kabbalah in the seventeenth century. Moreover, the mystical traditions of El'azar Roke'aḥ had been for centuries intensely esoteric. Until he decided to go public, only one or two families and a very limited number of outsiders were privy to its teachings. How many people in Ashkenaz knew at all about this esoteric lore and how many cared about its truth? More important, how much broad authority did these traditions convey? Would the Ashkenazic community have felt itself delegitimized had R. El'azar's claims been proven false? The French and English communities were unimpressed by his teaching and, in their prayer, ignored its demands

104 H. Breßlau, 'Diplomatische Erläuterungen zu den Judenprivilegien Heinrichs IV.' *Zeitschrift für Geschichte der Juden in Deutschland* (1887), i. 154–9; Grossman, *Ḥakhmei Ashkenaz ha-Rishonim* (above, n. 13), 29–44 and the literature there cited; id., 'Mythos Dor ha-Meyassedim bi-Tefutsot Yisra'el bi-Yemei ha-Beinayim u-Mashma'uto ha-Historit', in *Ha-Mythos ve-ha-Yahadut: Historyah, Hagut, Sifrut*, ed. M. Idel and I. Grunwald (Jerusalem, 2004), 123–42; J. Schatzmiller, 'Politics and the Myth of Origins: The Case of Medieval Jews', *Les Juifs au regard de l'histoire: mélanges en l'honneur de Bernhard Blumenkranz*, ed. G. Dahan (Paris, 1985), 52–4. Cf. I. G. Marcus, 'History, Story and Collective Memory: Narrativity in Early Ashkenazic Culture', *Prooftexts*, 10 (1990), 165–88.

105 Above, p. 156.

106 *A Critical Edition with Translation and Notes of the Book of Tradition (Sefer ha-Qabbalah) by Abraham Ibn Daud*, ed. G. G. Cohen (Philadelphia, 1967), 46–51.

with equanimity.[107] Did R. Mosheh Tachau's challenges to the Kalonymide traditions threaten for even a moment the basis of Ashkenazic religious authority?[108]

Finally, a foundation narrative, mythical or otherwise, is a 'laying on of hands', an authentication of legitimacy. Who authenticated, however, the authenticity of R. El'azar's traditions? 'Abu Aharon ben R. Shemu'el ha-Nassi.'[109] And just who is this 'Abu Aharon' (or 'Adon Aharon' in some versions) and why should one pay him any heed? Who is he to guarantee that R. El'azar has the keys to the Heavenly Gates of Prayer (*sha'arei tefillah, sha'arei raḥamim*)? R. El'azar says nothing about him, apparently knew nothing about him. Indeed, until the discovery of the *Megillat Aḥima'ats* some seven centuries later,[110] there was no reason to believe that such a strangely named individual had ever existed. The impression received is that R. El'azar put down as accurately as possible what he knew, with no attempt to gild in any way his family tradition. His knowledge stopped with Abu Aharon and with it his narrative. If this abrupt ending weakened his claim to authenticity in the eyes of his readers, so be it. He could only honestly set down what he had been told. Clearly, this was not a tale told to impress outsiders; it was an account rendered to his circle of readers, people who believed the author to begin with.

Be that as it may, one may still ask: why is there no foundational narrative of the Third Yeshivah, no tale explaining the *halakhic* independence of the Ashkenazic community? The answer is simple: there was no need for one. The Spanish and Kairouan communities had been under the tutelage of Sura and Pumbedita for centuries, hence they needed a story, mythic or otherwise, to legitimate their independence, to demonstrate that it was the Divine will itself that they attain halakhic autonomy.[111] Ashkenaz had never experienced Babylonian subordination and the men of the Third Yeshivah, and their disciple (or disciple's disciple) Rabbenu Gershom never acknowledged the

[107] S. Emanuel, 'Ha-Pulmus shel Ḥasidei Ashkenaz 'al Nusaḥ ha-Tefillah', *Meḥkerei Talmud*, 3 (2005), 591–625.

[108] *Ketav Tamim: Ketav Yad Paris H711*, Merkaz Dinur–Kuntresim, Mekorot u-Meḥkarim 16 (Jerusalem, 1984).

[109] Y. Dan, *Torat ha-Sod shel Ḥasidut Ashkenaz* (Jerusalem, 1968), 15–16; Grossman, *Ḥakhmei Ashkenaz ha-Rishonim* (above, n. 13), 72. The texts from sources of different periods were gathered by Neubauer in 1891 and little to nothing has been added since. See A. Neubauer, 'Abou Ahron: le babylonien', *Revue des études juives*, 23 (1891), 230–7.

[110] *Megillat Aḥima'ats*, ed. B. Klar (Jerusalem, 1945).

[111] *A Critical Edition* (above, n. 106), 189–262; G. Cohen, 'The Story of the Four Captives', *Proceedings of the American Academy of Jewish Research*, 29 (1960–1), 55–131; M. Ben-Sasson, *Tsemiḥat ha-Kehillah ha-Yehudit be-'Artsot ha-'Islam: Kairouan, 800–1057* (Jerusalem, 1997), 410–24.

geonic supremacy; indeed, he viewed them as scholars inferior to his own masters.[112] Their independence was to them axiomatic and their sense of superiority had been so long ingrained as to be almost casual.

They would, however, never speak of their own merits. If any group ever believed in low profile, indeed, anonymity, it was the founding fathers of Ashkenaz, heirs of the *savora'im*, *setama'im*, or call the editors of the Bavli what you will. Few groups in Jewish history can match their impact on Jewish civilization. Yet fewer were more intentionally unknown than they. Signing one's name and the recognition that accompanies authorship are hallmarks of the Geonate, a Caliphate creation (*de facto* or *de jure*) and not for the men of the Third Yeshivah the new ways of the Caliphate, either its culture or its attention-drawing innovations.

That Ashkenaz neither had nor needed any 'foundation myth' seems to me clear; that we do not know the names of the settlers does not surprise me;[113] that the traditions of Ashkenaz did not preserve with pride their origin in the Third Yeshivah of Bavel surprises me very much. This means, as I said at the outset, that my reconstruction is incomplete, and the essay remains—even as regards Ashkenaz—a proposal only.

[112] See above, pp. 153–4. The story of Rabbenu Gershom's marriage to Rav Hai Gaon's sister is late. It is first registered in a late 13th- or early 14th-century source. See Y. N. Epstein, '"Ha-He'etek" she-bi-Teshuvat Rashal #29', *Meḥkarim be-Sifrut ha-Talmud u-vi-Leshonot Shemiyot II* (Jerusalem, 1988), ii. 372–3. The Ashkenazic sense of superiority to Babylonian geonic culture is reflected in a later tale, where R. Meshullam b. Kalonymos declines the hand of Rav Hai's sister and returns to Ashkenaz and makes a local marriage. It is found in an early 16th-century manuscript (National Library of Israel 28[vo] 3182) and is reproduced and discussed by S. Zfatman in *Rosh ve-Rishon: Yissud Manhigut be-Sifrut Yisra'el* (Jerusalem, 2010), 441–2, 453–4. Zfatman points out that, as no one who lived after R. El'azar Roke'aḥ (d. *c.*1230) figures in that collection of tales, the stories *may* then date from the latter half of the 13th century.

[113] It may be that a few of the names were retained in the family traditions of the Makirites; this is expressed in an internal correspondence between the brothers, found in *Ma'aseh ha-Ge'onim*, #61, p. 55, and in the parallel passages cited in the notes ad loc., and equally in a source not available in 1910 to the editor of the *Ma'aseh ha-Ge'onim*, the *Shibbolei ha-Leket II*, published in the 1930s by M. Z. Hasida, p. 114. (On this typescript edition of the *Shibbolei ha-Leket II*, see *Collected Essays*, i. 160 n. 98.) The text is not without problems. See A. Grossman, *Ḥakhmei Ashkenaz ha-Rishonim* (above, n. 13), 370 n. 44. (If this identification is correct, it would point to a Provençal figure among the earliest settlers and a possible link between the two settlements.)

A RESPONSE TO DAVID BERGER

AT THE Sixteenth Congress of the World Union of Jewish Studies in Jerusalem in July 2013, I presented a précis of the first part of this essay arguing both for the existence of a Third Yeshivah in Bavel and its role in the founding of the halakhic culture of Ashkenaz. The lecture awakened considerable discussion, and a number of scholars who were unable to attend requested by e-mail from Professor David Berger, the respondent, the written text of his remarks. He graciously complied with a return attachment. Given the nature of e-mail, these attachments had a wide circulation, though Professor Berger never intended this—people of our age discover daily that they live in a new era. Effectively, his response was on the internet, in the sense that anyone in the field could obtain a copy of the text, and many did. Professor Berger's widely disseminated queries and questions were penetrating and merit, indeed demand, a serious reply. This rejoinder also serves another purpose: placing the lecture and a central thesis of the essay in their proper context.

I should add that Professor Berger has read and approved of my formulations of his queries and objections.

In one sense, Professor Berger was at a disadvantage as he had only the text of the lecture, which was a précis of the first third of the essay, and that text was without footnotes, wherein further evidence was cited and qualifications made. Moreover, he—understandably enough—was not familiar with the chapters that precede this essay and upon which it rests, and of which it serves as the culmination.

Let me recap the conclusions that form, in part, the basis of the thesis of the Third Yeshivah. No serious case has ever been made for the Palestinian roots of the Ashkenazic culture, as I have detailed in Chapter 8 and in the closing pages of Chapter 7. There is equally no evidence of any *minhag* Ashkenaz ha-Kadmon as I have argued in Chapter 3. The Bavli is the controlling authority from the very outset, and Early Ashkenaz never ruled on the basis of biblical verses or *aggadot* where a halakhic source in the Bavli was available, as I have contended in Chapters 4 and 5. That the cultural roots of Ashkenaz are Babylonian is the conclusion of the first eight essays, and one that I had entertained for over a quarter of a century, in fact, closer to a half-century, seeing that never in my life had I encountered any area of *Oraḥ Ḥayyim* or *Yoreh De'ah* where I could discern in the literature of Early Ashkenaz a substantive influence of the Yerushalmi or, even more broadly, of what is called 'Palestinian halakhah'. (I exclude *Ḥoshen Mishpat* and *Even ha-'Ezer* only because there is very little, if any, eleventh-century German literature on these fields.) I am not contending that there is no such area of Palestinian influence, only that no one has ever demonstrated its existence, and I personally have yet to come across it. I spelled out the requirements for such a proof both in Chapter 8 in this volume and in the ninth chapter of my book *Ha-Yayin bi-Yemei ha-Beinayim*.[1] To be sure, here and there is a Palestinian ruling—halakhic purity, like racial purity, is an impossibility—and there certainly was Palestinian influence in the interstices of Babylonian law, as in the three weeks between Shiv'ah 'Asar be-Tammuz and Tish'ah be-'Av. However, as far as the woof and warp of Jewish life in Early Ashkenaz is concerned, Palestinian law, for all practical purposes, didn't exist. The lack of any copy of the Yerushalmi or discussion of a *sugya* of the Yerushalmi in this period is simply emblematic of its overall absence, and it was in this heraldic sense that these two facts were invoked in this essay.

If my arguments against both the Palestinian origins of the Ashkenazic culture and the existence of any ancient Ashkenazic custom are weighed and found wanting, the contentions of this concluding essay are considerably weakened. However, if these two notions have been laid to rest, and the Rhineland cleared of Palestinian devotees and blind adherents to the traditional, the Babylonian origins of Ashkenazic halakhic culture are then almost a given—and it is culture and not genetics or pronunciation that we are investigating—and one can start probing whether or not we can identify this source more precisely, as I began doing as I was nearing the end of the first eight essays above.

I had never subscribed to the Palestinian thesis or that of ancient custom, though I have only recently gotten around to registering my disagreement. It was clear to me ever since my graduate school days that Ashkenaz was a Babylonian-oriented community from the start, but I had always been baffled as to the nature of its 'Babylonianism'. Rabbenu Ḥanan'el (Raḥ), R. Yehudah of Barcelona, author of the *Sefer ha-'Ittim*, not to speak of R. Avraham of Narbonne, author of *Sefer ha-'Eshkol*, were continuations of the geonic culture, as was Alfasi. He had his quarrels with geonic rulings, to be sure; however, his point of departure was those rulings, and he wrote and thought much as they did. The works that issued forth from Kairouan, Fez, Lucena, and Narbonne came from the same climate of opinion as did the writings of the Geonim; the

[1] Above, p. 191 n. 86.

writings of the Rhineland reflected a wholly different intellectual atmosphere. The *Perushei Magentsa* did not resemble any geonic commentary, though I could not then put my finger on what made them distinctive and set them so apart from the rest. The discussions found in the *Ma'aseh ha-Ge'onim*, the responsa of Rabbenu Gershom, and those of R. Yehudah Ba'al Sefer ha-Dinim were qualitatively different from those of their contemporaries in the other centers of the Diaspora; and this was not simply because these Ashkenazic writers were far more independent of geonic authority than the others. The writings of Early Ashkenaz were the work of people who did not look over their shoulders; they made little reference to Babylonian predecessors and none to contemporaries in other centers of the Diaspora. In short, they were the product of a culture that had long dwelled alone. This I felt early on; however, I never pursued why it was so. 'Who were the founding fathers, and from where exactly in Bavel did they come?' was a question that I had long entertained but never investigated.

As I concluded writing the eight critiques of the reigning theories of Early Ashkenaz and the methods that have hitherto been employed in analyzing its literature, the significance of the distinctive curriculum of Ashkenaz, the *lashon meshunah* tractates, hit me. The founders were teaching tractates not taught in Sura and Pumbedita; clearly they came from elsewhere, and that elsewhere had to be some third yeshivah. Why, however, did this yeshivah never show up in the Cairo Genizah?

I had, over the years, followed the writings of Eliezer Shimshon Rosenthal and Shamma Friedman and their respective schools on the editorial work being done on the Talmud, which systematically broke down to two distinct families.[2] I had naturally read the writings of Robert Brody and Neil Danzig on the text of the Talmud in geonic times, and, of course, the rich essays of Yaacov Sussmann.[3] I realized suddenly that the work of the textual editors was of historical interest, for it had institutional implications—and major ones at that. More generally, the significant progress that has been made in the past two generations in reconstructing the editorial processes that the rabbinical literature underwent had not been integrated into the historical picture. The

[2] Above, p. 170 n. 46.

[3] R. Brody, 'Sifrut ha-Ge'onim ve-ha-Tekst ha-Talmudi', *Meḥkerei Talmud*, 1 (Jerusalem, 1990), 237–304; N. Danzig, 'Mi-Talmud be-'al Peh le-Talmud bi-Khetav: 'al Derekh Mesirat ha-Talmud ha-Bavli ve-Limmudo bi-Yemei ha-Beinayim', *Bar Ilan, Sefer ha-Shanah*, 30–1 (2006), 49–112; Y. Sussmann, 'Torah she-be-'al Peh' (above, p. 172 n. 47) and id., 'Kitvei-Yad u-Masoret-ha-Nusaḥ shel ha-Mishnah', *Divrei ha-Kongres ha-'Olami ha-Shevi'i le-Madda'ei ha-Yahadut: Meḥkarim ba-Talmud, Halakhah u-Midrash* (Jerusalem, 1981), 215–50.

two disciplines—textual edition and history—had been operating in isolation, each unaware of the findings of the other, to the detriment of both.

From Sussmann's memorable article 'Torah she-be-'al Peh' that appeared a decade ago,[4] it was clear that Sura and Pumbedita would scarcely have had a hand in the actual final copy-editing of the Talmud. They were committed to their monopoly of the living Vox Talmudica, and bestowing any imprimatur on the written word would have weakened their insistent claims to a monopoly on authenticity. It was no less evident, however, that they neither resisted nor censured the inscription of the Talmud. They insisted only that the final authority was the living oral tradition, the ancient text recited by the *garsanim* of Sura and Pumbedita.

The implications of Sussmann's findings were clear and revolutionary. People had assumed from time immemorial that the written texts of the Talmud in all their variety had emerged from the two famed yeshivot of Bavel. There was no reason to imagine that any other significant yeshivot or *battei midrash* had existed in the post-talmudic era. It was now obvious that this age-old assumption was mistaken. If so, the initial inscription of the Talmud in the shadowy pre-geonic period (before 700–750, at the very latest) and the final copy-editing—more accurately copy-editings, for there were two distinct versions—of this vast corpus in the geonic period took place *outside* Sura and Pumbedita. We have no information from, and almost none about, the sixth and seventh centuries, and one school is of the opinion that there were no two stages; inscription and copy-editing took place in roughly the same epoch. Let us, then, concentrate on the geonic period (750–1038). Copy-editing of the Talmud is a massive undertaking. Anyone who has ever had his manuscript copy-edited by the most intelligent editor knows how carefully he or she has to go over the changes to make sure that there has been no alteration in the intended meaning or even in the finer nuances of the original. All the more so in law, where the slightest change of language can have far-reaching implications. Only scholars of the highest caliber could undertake such an operation. If one studies the variants in the critical editions one sees that this tightening of the text affected almost every line, and every touch-up had to be checked and rechecked for possible modification of meaning. The editors succeeded notably. It is astonishing how little, if any, difference there is between the differently edited versions. The length of time and the magnitude of effort that went into this enterprise are impossible to estimate.

Clearly, a massive undertaking was taking place in Bavel in the geonic period in two different locations, in two different institutions—yet there was

[4] Above, p. 172 n. 47.

no reference to this in the Genizah.[5] What I had 'discovered' as a consequence of the unique talmudic curriculum of Ashkenaz was, as I wrote, not the Third Yeshivah of Bavel but the Fifth Yeshivah of Bavel. As Yoav Rosenthal's doctorate has recently shown the strong probability of the existence of yet a third editorial tradition, there was now in all likelihood a sixth one. What was more, the editorial enterprise encompassed another field—*midreshei aggadah*. Much of the rabbinic corpus was being edited, copy-edited, and given final form in this period. The Jewish canon was being definitively shaped in any number of *battei midrash* in Bavel, and all of this went unnoted in the Genizah. It was clear just how partial a picture of Bavel the Genizah yielded. Or, more accurately, the picture was partial if one judged its contents on the basis of personal names and toponyms; if, however, one judged it by the hundreds, indeed, thousands of pages and fragments of the Jewish canon found in the Genizah which cannot plausibly be linked to Sura and Pumbedita, a far more complex academic landscape emerged.

Such were the institutional consequences of bringing textual studies to bear on history; the anonymity of the men engaged in this huge editorial undertaking stood in stark contrast to the assertive authorship of the Geonim and pointed to cultural differences. Two disparate civilizations had existed side by side throughout the geonic period and tension between them was inevitable. The old adage 'Paris is not France' warns of projecting the center onto the periphery. Bavel was anything but a cultural monolith. All that is needed, then, is to translate the adjective 'geonic' into 'Judeo-Arabic', and savoraic (and stamaitic) into 'Judeo-Iranian', and the differences of comportment (anonymity or self-projection) became ones of *Weltanschauung*, and the reason for the Third Yeshivah's emigration appears quickly on the horizon.

Once the Third Yeshivah of Bavel was firmly established in my mind, I began looking for further signs of Babylonian origins, in language, in the absence of geonic mystique and even the discounting of any geonic pre-eminence, and this chapter opened with what I had found. This section—in an abridged form—constituted my lecture at the Congress, and from this shortened version it appeared that I had based my inference of Babylonian origins strongly on linguistic grounds and the indifference to the Geonate. My respondent at that session was, as I mentioned at the outset, Professor David Berger, who registered characteristically trenchant reservations about my thesis and

[5] Above, pp. 170–3.

offered, if ever so tentatively—possibly even as devil's advocate—a counter-thesis of his own.

Though the linguistic argument and disregard of the Geonim scarcely served as the basis of my central contention, I stand behind these characterizations nonetheless. I divide my reply to Professor Berger's objections into three sections: interpretation, language and curriculum, and finally the founders' attitude towards the Geonim.

Interpretation

What struck me most in the so-called *Perush Rabbenu Gershom* was both its unique curriculum and the radical, new, and sweeping conception of what talmudic interpretation entails, to which I have drawn attention in Chapter 3 above. Professor Berger and I are in agreement that the Talmud is far too abrupt and telegraphic a text to be comprehended by simply grasping the words alone. The major positions taken in the Talmud are easily enough understood and need little explanation, but detailed line-by-line explication of every passing idea in the *sugya*—and this is the unique accomplishment of the Mainz commentary—chapter after chapter, tractate after tractate until the commentary encompasses the entire Babylonian Talmud can be achieved only with the aid of some interpretative tradition. Indeed, what we lack in the Yerushalmi is precisely an interpretative tradition. The text of the Yerushalmi is not especially difficult; most of the vocabulary was understood by commentators medieval and modern. *Bereshit* and *Va-Yikra Rabbah* are written in the same Galilean Aramaic and posed few problems to scholars with wide-ranging knowledge. The discussions in the Yerushalmi are far briefer and less involved, and, in one sense, less 'sophisticated' than those of the Bavli, yet no genius has ever succeeded in making the Yerushalmi an accessible text. The accurate, literal translations that have appeared no more open up the Yerushalmi to serious, legal comprehension than the Soncino translation has the Bavli.

This being the case, where did R. Leon—who, Professor Berger suggests, was the founder of the Mainz school and not the Babylonian émigrés from some Third Yeshivah—receive his instruction? Not in Ashkenaz—there was no scholarly community there—but elsewhere. Where was that elsewhere and where did he get his instruction in the *lashon meshunah* tractates? Professor Berger suggests that, as his name seems to be of Italian or French origin (we will come to this point later), he had traveled from one of those lands to Babylonia and acquired his education in Sura and Pumbedita, and since, as I noted in the lecture, there were individuals besides the scholars of the Third

Yeshivah who did know the *lashon meshunah* tractates (passages from them are cited in the *Halakhot Gedolot*), he studied at their feet and, instead of returning home, he settled in Mainz and founded the yeshivah there. Given the tiny number of Jews in Mainz in the mid-tenth century, Professor Berger claims, an exceptional person could have a disproportionate influence.

I think that is an unnecessarily complicated scenario; however, it makes no difference to my central argument as to the origin of Ashkenazic culture whether the men of the East came West (as I presented it) or a man of the West went East and returned home (as Professor Berger would have it), as long as what he brought back with him to the West was the amoraic heritage in its entirety.[6]

Professor Berger admits that to do all this R. Leon would have had to be a man of exceptional talent and, furthermore, of striking independence to have broken the consensus of the scope of the talmudic curriculum of institutions no less authoritative than Sura and Pumbedita and added to it the *lashon meshunah* tractates. Professor Berger suggests—admittedly very hesitantly and stating that it is an imperfect analogy—that R. Leon resembled the Gaon of Vilna. I think the example is a good one, for it provides us with a yardstick by which to measure the stature of R. Leon, as proposed by Professor Berger. The Vilna Gaon was a scholar of awesome proportions and did, indeed, break away from the traditional curriculum of his culture and turn his attention to the 'underprivileged' texts of classical halakhah. Professor Berger contends that R. Leon need not have been as brilliant as the Gaon to have accomplished what he did. I beg to differ. R. Leon, by Professor Berger's proposal, founded a school of exegesis that lasted for well over a century and served as the basis of Rashi's masterpiece. If anyone in the halakhic pantheon of the past millennium was unable to set down his thoughts on paper, it was R. Elijah of Vilna. For all his talent, he lacked the ability to share his insights with others in a comprehensible fashion. Have any of his 'writings' (if one can use that term for his inscriptions), including those on the Yerushalmi, opened up that corpus and enabled others to go beyond him? His written legacy was a series of gnomic notes or contradictory, occasionally muddled reports of pupils, real and self-proclaimed. R. Leon, who had mastered all of Shas, and, though coming from France or Italy, nevertheless acquired a sovereign (if passive) command of Jewish Babylonian Aramaic, who further established *Kodashim* in its entirety as an integral part of the Ashkenazic talmudic corpus and, on top of all this, laid the foundations of the groundbreaking, comprehensive,

[6] It would make a difference, of course, to the claim of the existence of the Third Yeshivah. I attempt to counter this argument further on.

line-by-line commentary of the Mainz school on the entire Talmud, had to have been of a stature greater than the Vilna Gaon.

An individual of such Olympian stature is, of course, a possibility. History, however, is not a question of logical possibilities but of historical probabilities. Granting that such an extraordinary figure could have existed, is his existence more probable than the existence among the founding fathers of an exegetical tradition which they began to commit to writing soon after their arrival? The halakhah of Early Ashkenaz is Babylonian, the founders understand the Babylonian Talmud in its entirety—isn't the simplest conclusion that they came from Babylonia? They know the *lashon meshunah* tractates—isn't the natural inference that they are the product of *a bet midrash* in Babylonia where the entire Talmud, including the *lashon meshunah* tractates, was taught?[7]

Advancing claims for the extraordinary talents of R. Leon, Professor Berger cites my remarks to him about Maimonides' comments on R. Yosef ibn Megas. ('When a genius stands in awe of someone, that someone should be taken very seriously.') First, as Professor Berger himself noted, R. Gershom is not Maimonides. Second, and far more important, Maimonides' remarks about Ibn Megas do not bear comparison with those of Rabbenu Gershom about R. Leon. Maimonides, a man scarcely given to compliments, says of Ibn Megas, 'As God is my witness, that man's understanding of the Talmud astonishes all those who contemplate intently his words and the depth of his insight, so much so that I can say of him and his way of thinking [2 Kgs. 23: 5]: "there was no king ever like him before".'[8] I take such an evaluation—without parallel in the history of halakhah—very seriously. Rabbenu Gershom, however, says nothing of this sort about his teacher.[9] Implicitly he says that Rabbenu Leon has a full command of the Talmud; explicitly he simply states that he is the finest scholar or decisor of his generation and he relies on his judgment over that of all others, including those long deceased. A similar statement could have been uttered by a Hungarian rabbi in the latter half of the nineteenth century about Maharam Shick, a Galician rabbi about R. Shaul Natan Natanson, or an American rabbi in the past generation about R. Moshe Feinstein. What is striking is not the characterization of

7 Professor Berger's demographic argument is unquestionably correct. In view of the minute size of the Jewish community of Mainz at the time, the influence of one exceptional figure could be decisive. Demography, however, cuts both ways. The smaller the demographic pool, the less the chance of abnormality, negative or positive. One figure of near-genius in a population of 50,000 is quite possible; one figure of near-genius in a population of a hundred is highly improbable.

8 וחי ה' כי הבנת אותו איש בתלמוד מפליאה כל מי שמתבונן בדבריו ועומק עיונו, עד שאפשר לומר עליו 'לפניו לא היה מלך כמוהו' בשיטתו.; *Perush 'al ha-Mishnah le-Rabbenu Mosheh ben Maimon*, ed. Y. Kafih, *Seder Zera'im* (Jerusalem, 1963), introduction, p. 47.

9 Above, p. 153.

Rabbenu Leon, but to whom he is being compared and found superior—the author of the *Halakhot Pesukot* and some anonymous Gaon (probably R. Sherira) in the high tide (*c.*1000) of the geonic period. If you believe the Geonim to be the ultimate arbiters of halakhah, the unique possessors of traditions going back close to a millennium, Rabbenu Gershom's reply is astonishing; if you believe the Geonim to be simply very learned scholars of a different culture, the reply is quite natural. It is what a nineteenth-century Hungarian scholar would say to a Galician one who invoked the authority of R. Natanson or other—by then long deceased—Galician luminaries.

What has to be emphasized, and perhaps I did not do so sufficiently either in the lecture or in this concluding essay, is the radically new notion of what understanding the Talmud entails. First, it does not mean simply grasping the important statements in a *sugya*; it means understanding every momentarily entertained hypothesis in the *sugya*; it means comprehending every line of the winding discussions of the *setama* of the *sugya*. Second, it includes the systematic exegesis of aggadah in its curriculum. Third, it entails a refusal to distinguish between *Kodashim* and the three other *sedarim* of the Talmud. No other diaspora entertained such notions. Just as the Genizah has obscured our vision of Babylonia in the round, so too has Rashi obscured our realization of the unprecedented vision of *talmud torah* bequeathed to Ashkenaz by its founding fathers. Since we find early on this concept of Talmud study embodied in Rashi, we take it for granted. We should not. It did not constitute the premises of *talmud torah* in the other cultures of the Diaspora. By Professor Berger's suggestion, this radical conception of *talmud torah* would also have to have been the invention of R. Leon, for such an approach is not reflected in any work of the Geonim. We would also have to assume that R. Leon both envisioned and succeeded in establishing in the cultural wasteland of Ottonian Germany a *bet midrash* with a curriculum greater than that of the famed academies of Bavel in which he had studied. All of which seems a bit much. Indeed, R. Leon's stature and accomplishments, as suggested by Professor Berger, appear to me to be a *deus ex machina*, or if you wish, a secularized version of the explanation of Divine inspiration (*ruaḥ ha-kodesh*) that has been given for some 750 years to the question how Rashi could possibly have known all that he did.[10]

Language

Professor Berger suggests that the founding fathers need not have been native Babylonians; they could well have come from elsewhere and attained the

[10] Above, p. 151.

necessary knowledge of Aramaic both from studying the Targum of the Tanakh and from studying Talmud with some oral tradition, which, we are in agreement, such study required. Let us take each point separately. The Bible's vocabulary is that of narrative (both national and dynastic) and of poetry. It does not address the quotidian as the aggadah does constantly. Moreover, the Bible, as Erich Auerbach pointed out some sixty years ago, does not see.[11] No detail is mentioned unless it is essential to the narrative. I think the only description of the inside of a room in an ordinary house that we have in the Bible is that of the Shunamite (2 Kgs. 4: 10): bed, table, chair, and lamp. The aggadah sees and sees in detail. On the basis of the Midrash and aggadah, Samuel Krauss was able to publish a multi-volume study of talmudic realia.[12] I doubt very much if one could produce a volume on biblical realia on the exclusive basis of the text of the Bible. As for knowledge of Aramaic gained from studying Talmud with an oral tradition: I would simply note that this was equally true of all the other Jewish centers in the West, such as Fustat, Kairouan, Lucena, and Barcelona. Nevertheless, they did not undertake to explicate the entire aggadah of the Talmud. The simplest answer is that the other centers had no interest in doing so systematically; Ashkenaz by chance did. Above I suggested a reason why such a massive and lexically challenging task could be more readily undertaken by the founding fathers of Ashkenaz than by the scholars of the other Jewish communities.

Professor Berger then suggests that perhaps they spoke Western Aramaic, which would have enabled them to grasp the meaning of the Eastern Aramaic in which the Talmud is written. I have no problem with this suggestion. The central question is not what language these people spoke but what culture they brought with them and implanted in Ashkenaz. It is clear that they introduced the Bavli and a curriculum of the Bavli larger than that of Sura and Pumbedita. If one wishes to have these scholars, bearers of the Babylonian heritage in its entirety, stop off a generation or two in Palestine, I have no objection.

I spoke of the founding fathers as being 'Aramaic speakers'. Professor Berger contends that there is no evidence of their active command of the language. Strictly speaking, he is right. A sovereign passive mastery of Aramaic will account for their exegetical scope and accomplishments. However, if the simplest interpretation of the data is that some erudite Babylonians came from Bavel to Ashkenaz, their fluency in spoken Aramaic is then a given. Why not take advantage of its explicatory power? Indeed, I do believe that their command was active, and further think—though I have not advanced this

[11] *Mimesis: The Representation of Reality in Western Literature* (Princeton, 1953), 3–24.

[12] *Talmudische Archäologie*, 3 vols. (Leipzig, 1910–12).

claim in the essay—that Aramaic was for a long while the language of instruction in the *bet midrash*. To give a modern example: when European *rashei yeshivot* went to Israel, the United States, and Central and South America, the instruction was for several generations in Yiddish. (In Israel it still is.) Understandably, as the purpose of studying under these masters was to absorb the rich Jewish culture from which they came and which they embodied. Serious interaction with them—intellectual or personal—demanded mastery of their spoken language. No less important is the simple fact that the most effective way to absorb a culture is to speak its language. Could Aramaic—the language of some books in the Holy Scriptures and that of the Talmud—possibly be less Jewish than Yiddish?! The Talmud is in Aramaic, and the greater one's command of that language, the more accessible that fountainhead of Jewish culture becomes. What also led me to this conclusion are Rashi's remarks in his commentary on the *Ḥumash* (Pentateuch).[13]

Rashi's frequent use of *ke-targumo*, I contended, assumed that the average educated layman of his day, what we would call today a *yodea' sefer*, understood most words or phrases in Aramaic, and that this reflected a tradition of spoken Aramaic somewhere in the past, even though active command of the language was clearly gone by the mid-eleventh century. Professor Berger believes that even without a spoken tradition, a literate person could understand Targum on the basis of his Jewish studies. Indeed, he claims that most people in the audience at the time of the lecture could understand Targum. I beg to differ with Professor Berger about the knowledge of *yod'ei sefer* of today and also of yesteryear. How many people today, including those with an advanced talmudic education, would know the meaning of עללא, צבע, or אחסנתא? (The Aramaic for the common biblical, indeed pentateuchal, words תבואה, כבס, and ירושה.) Why assume that the *yod'ei sefer* in Rashi's time knew more?

As I have said, an active command of the language is not essential to the linguistic argument; a passive command—an understanding of some 10,000–12,000 words of Jewish Babylonian Aramaic—is. Professor Berger argues that, before we can say that the founding fathers displayed such mastery, we must determine the accuracy of the identification of the innumerable realia provided by the Mainz commentary. I addressed this in a note above and will briefly restate it here.[14] First, some 500 years separate the Aramaic known to the founders and the Aramaic of the text they were interpreting. The 'pilgrim fathers' of Ashkenaz spoke or knew the Aramaic of the tenth century; the text they were interpreting stems from the third to fifth centuries. Words fall into disuse in the course of half a millennium, and meanings change. Second, they

13 Above, p. 160. 14 Above, p. 161 n. 25.

may well have known, for example, the identification of many fruit trees, but had no clear idea of the stages of their ripening that are so essential to the halakhah, such as *semadar*, *boser*, and *ḥanatah*. There are, no doubt, numerous specific errors in their explication. However, one who studies a tractate with the Mainz commentary understands it correctly, not only its essentials but also most of its details, not to speak of the innumerable involved discussions in that volume.

Attitude to the Geonim

Professor Berger feels that R. Yitsḥak ha-Levi's remarks about the *Halakhot Gedolot* contain two respectful statements,[15] and in light of them he does not perceive the rhetorical questions אפשר כן הוא?! אפשר נשמע לו?! 'Could this possibly be true?', 'Could one possibly follow this ruling?!'[16] as being necessarily disrespectful. I feel obliged to disagree with him. There are various ways to register disagreement while preserving the forms of traditional deference. One, for example, is to claim that the author himself never penned these words; they were added by an errant pupil or scribe. The leading Ashkenazic scholar in the preceding generation, R. Yehudah Ba'al Sefer ha-Dinim, leveled a withering critique of a doctrine found in the *Halakhot Gedolot*, but took care, at least, to conclude on such a grace note.[17] R. Yitsḥak ha-Levi declined to do even that. He simply says that the author of the *Halakhot Gedolot* was a great scholar who occasionally wrote nonsense. I have here given, perhaps, a slightly sharper edge to R. Yitsḥak's remarks than they actually possess; however, I do not see how they can be viewed as anything other than dismissive, and brutally so. I am unaware of any similar remarks about geonic rulings in the literature of other cultures or even in that of Ashkenaz in later centuries. Rashi ignored the Geonim, but never spoke disrespectfully of them, and in the post-First Crusade culture of Ashkenaz the tone was entirely different, even while the independence of geonic authority continued.

Finally, Professor Berger questions my reading of the responsum of Rabbenu Gershom with which I opened the lecture.[18] He says that Rabbenu Gershom never stated that his text was better than that of the Geonim. What he said was that no such rule as 'the law is not like Mar bar Rav Asi in the matter of *mepakh*' was to be found in his text of the Talmud. If it's not in the text of the Talmud, the issue depends, then, on *sevara* (logical argument) and the stature of the *posek*.

Professor Berger is correct. Because of the time constraints of the lecture, I could only present one interpretation of Rabbenu Gershom's ambiguous

[15] Cited above, p. 155. [16] Ibid. [17] Above, p. 154. [18] Above, pp. 151–2.

remarks. In the essay, I addressed the alternative interpretation in a footnote,[19] which I will briefly recap. Rabbenu Gershom is clearly arguing against a dictum that stated that the ruling is contrary to Mar bar Rav Asi in the matter of *mepakh shevu'ah*. As we do not possess the original query, only Rabbenu Gershom's reply, it is not clear whether the Geonim claimed that this dictum is found in the Talmud (as, indeed, it appears in some versions of the *Halakhot Gedolot*), or that they stated, as did Rav Sherira Gaon,[20] that they had an ancient tradition according to which the law was contrary to Mar bar Rav Asi—a tradition that is equally found in the earlier geonic work on the rules of adjudication of talmudic controversies, the *Toledot Tanna'im ve-'Amora'im* (in the entry preceding that of *ya'al kegam*).[21] If they claimed that this rule was found in their talmudic text, Rabbenu Gershom is stating that his text of the Talmud is superior. If they invoked an ancient tradition, Rabbenu Gershom's silence is striking. He is in effect saying, 'So what of it? What difference does it make to us? There are three and only three factors to be considered here: text, *sevara*, and the stature of the decisor. Your ancient tradition binds you; it means nothing to us.' Rabbenu Gershom views the Geonate and its venerated practices in much the same way as a Hungarian *posek* would look upon the avatars and customs of Polish Jewry.

Professor Berger also raised the issue of R. Leon's name: it is clearly not Babylonian, but rather, as linguists have told him, of Italian or French origin. This is an excellent point, and I must admit that the lecture and, indeed, the first section of the essay may give a wrong impression, which should be corrected. I do not believe that R. Leon was a founding father. I believe the founding fathers chose to remain anonymous, for they came from a culture which prized anonymity; indeed, they viewed it as a *sine qua non* for all those engaged in the sacred labor (*melekhet shamayim*) of editing and expounding the Divine word. Furthermore, no magic carpet brought them to the Rhineland. As I wrote elsewhere in the chapter:

> The emigration to Germany may well have taken place over a period of time. The route they followed awaits further research. Some may well have taken the Black Sea route, moved through Byzantium, and acquired some literature there; others may have opted for the Mediterranean route and traveled either via Italy and, in the ancient Jewish settlements of the peninsula, picked up some books and camp followers, or via Provence to Arles and up the Rhone. Whether it was a one-time move or emigration in waves, whether the Babylonians took one route or many, things came together, crystallized in the middle of the tenth century with the founding of the yeshivah in Mainz.[22]

[19] Above, p. 153 n. 7.

[20] Ibid.

[21] Ibid.

[22] Above, p. 185.

Nothing would have been more natural than to have acquired, in the course of their long journey, an immensely talented acolyte. They may have enrolled him in their ranks in Italy or France or possibly even in the Rhineland, for French was the spoken language or the language of choice of the Jews in the Rhineland from the outset until at least the second quarter of the thirteenth century. The Rhinelander with the bluest blood, the Kalonymide, R. El'azar ben Yehudah (d. *c.*1230), still glossed his *Sefer ha-Roke'aḥ* with French words, as did the authors of the so-called *Perush Rabbenu Gershom*. Louis Brandin, who analyzed these glosses, insisted that many reflect pronunciation older than that found in Rashi and thus must be dated to the early eleventh century, if not the closing decades of the tenth—the years associated with the activity of Rabbenu Gershom. The use of French may already have been the rule a generation earlier.[23]

I would like once again to thank Professor Berger for the careful reading he gave to the text of my lecture and for his perceptive critique that forced me to clarify obscurities in my presentation and restate my position more comprehensively, and, I hope, more convincingly.

[23] 'Les Glosses françaises (Loazim) de Gerschom de Metz', *Revue des études juives*, 42 (1901), 238. He believes these findings contradict A. Epstein's view that *Perush Rabbenu Gershom* is a collective work stretching well over a century and argues against it. (A. Epstein, 'Der Gerschom Meor ha-Golah zugeschriebene Talmud-Commentar' [above, n. 76], 115–43; Hebrew trans. pp. 107–33.) The two assessments, however, do not necessarily clash. The first layer of any such commentary would be the lexical one; the explication of the legal arguments of the tractate constitutes the later sediments, each improving upon its predecessor.

PART II

MARTYRDOM UNDER CROSS AND CRESCENT

INTRODUCTION

As noted in the preface, both my article on *Iggeret ha-Shemad*, which I wrote as an undergraduate, and that on martyrdom in Ashkenaz, composed a decade or so ago, employ the same criterion of 'measurable deflection' to discern whether something extraneous to the halakhic system is impinging upon the thought of a halakhist. That is to say, in order to avoid a simplistic sociology of law that attributes, with little ado, legal conclusions to personal inclinations or some social or economic need, one must be able to point to some uncharacteristic flaw, or, at the very least, some measurable swerve in the line of argument that would indicate the operation of a force deflecting the author's analysis from its normal course and leading him to unexpected conclusions. Unsurprisingly, this yardstick plays a significant role in other studies of mine published in the intervening years, such as 'Can Halakhic Texts Talk History?' and 'Pawnbroking: A Study in *Ribbit* and of the Halakhah in Exile'.[1]

There has been some misunderstanding concerning the nature of this tool, and a word or two may be in place. 'Measurable deflection' is not a jurisprudential criterion, as some have thought, but an evidentiary one. That is to say, whether law develops immanently, and the judge's role is that of an outsider simply ascertaining what the normative texts say on the problem—as the judicial formalists believe—or whether the judge is consciously or unconsciously a social or religious engineer interpreting the pliable normative texts in such a manner that the results conform to his *Weltanschauung*—as the judicial realists contend—has been a long-standing question in jurisprudence. However, the issue between the formalists and the realists is the nature of the predominant mode of adjudication; each readily admits that 'predominant' does not mean universal and that there are any number of exceptions to the system's usual manner of operation. Measurable deflection addresses the question, When does a historian have the right to say that a specific decision of a specific judge was shaped by external considerations? How judges generally act is a jurisprudential question; why Judge X ruled as he did in Case Y is a

[1] *Collected Essays*, i. 57–166, 169–223.

historical one. Even in law, 'general propositions do not decide specific cases', as Justice Holmes pointed out long ago.[2]

This is not to argue that such extraneous forces are not, consciously or unconsciously, in operation even when one cannot detect an angle of deflection; only that the historian has no basis for claiming that they are. Nor is it to assert that there is no other criterion for detecting the workings of some larger purpose which shapes the conclusions of a major jurist. A sustained pattern of rulings all tending towards the same end could equally be used, provided that criteria for what constitutes 'a sustained pattern' are established and observed. Obviously, one cannot cite some ten holdings or doctrines that point, shall we say, to a policy of leveling the playing field between debtors and creditors without taking into account those rulings that point in the other direction. Less obvious but no less important is taking into consideration those rulings which could equally have been bent, had the jurist been so inclined, to the purpose of such a leveling, yet were not shaped to that end. Meeting the last criterion is no easy task, to put it mildly; however, to attribute a larger goal to a jurist without taking into account the opportunities of its attainment that went unrealized is the equivalent of judging a batter by the number of his hits without taking into consideration the number of times that he went to bat.

It has been furthermore contended that in advancing the criterion of measurable deflection I 'assume a constant jurisprudential system at all times and that historical information can be drawn from halakhic texts only when they "deviate" from how the rules of jurisprudence are supposed to operate. [This] method assumes that Jewish law as a historical fact operates only [in] the way it is supposed to. If there [is] no uniform set of rules and practices in historical fact, there can be no meaning to the term "deviation".' The principle of measurable deflection restricts 'inferring historical realia' to instances where there are '"deviations" from a universal halakhic norm'.[3]

First, 'historical information' and 'historical realia' can be inferred from halakhic sources without any need whatsoever for deviance from a halakhic norm. Historians have been doing this for well over a century and a half. I thought that, occasionally, inferences had been drawn improperly, and wrote an entire book setting forth ground rules on extracting historical data from responsa, never mentioning any criterion of measurable deflection.[4] This yardstick is to be applied only with regard to attributing judicial holdings to extra-judicial considerations.

[2] *Lochner v. New York* (1905) 198 US 45 at 76.

[3] I. G. Marcus, 'Israeli Medieval Jewish Historiography: From Nationalist Positivism to New Cultural and Social Histories', *Jewish Studies Quarterly*, 17 (2010), 280.

[4] H. Soloveitchik, *Shut ke-Makor Histori* (Jerusalem, 1990).

As to the charge that the use of such a gauge is based on some unchanging Platonic idea of halakhah, I would simply note that there are as many different ways of doing halakhah as there are to doing history. Nevertheless, there is a difference between an academic work of history of any school and a campaign biography. In any discipline there exists some outer boundary beyond which one cannot go and still claim that it is a work of history, philosophy, halakhah, or whatever. One simple criterion is that it must obey the laws of logic. One cannot commit the fallacy of the 'undivided middle', namely, argue that since (a) all tailors have two feet and (b) John has two feet, therefore (c) John is a tailor. One cannot infer the existence of D from the existence of A and then proceed to rule as if D existed but not A. Neither can one state in the same ruling, indeed in the same breath, that Q both does and does not exist.[5] Furthermore, most legal systems operate with a hierarchy of sources. No court in the United States can rule contrary to an explicit article in the US Constitution. Similarly in halakhah, one cannot rule contrary to an unambiguous ruling of a *mishnah*. Breaches of this sort answer to the criterion of measurable deflection, and it is such sins in argumentation to which I have drawn attention in these essays. 'Jewish law as a historical fact' has, indeed, abided 'at all times' by the rules of logical consistency and hierarchy of sources, and deviation from them indicates that some extraneous force is at work deflecting the argument from its normal course. When one finds a cluster of such breaches on a given issue, the conclusion appears ineluctable.

[5] H. Soloveitchik, *Yeinam: Saḥar be-Yeinam shel Goyim—'al Gilgulah shel ha-Halakhah be-'Olam ha-Ma'aseh* (Tel Aviv, 2003), 56–7.

CHAPTER TEN

Between Cross and Crescent

In this brief essay I pointed to one reason for the differing self-images of the Jews of Christian Spain and those of Islamic countries when confronted with mass conversion on the part of their communities. Avraham Grossman then incorporated this insight into a more comprehensive explanation. The issue has recently been revisited and cast in a new light in an essay by Menahem Ben-Sasson.*

Both the Jews in Christian Spain and those of Islamic countries experienced religious persecution. Though the tenets of both Islam and Christianity forbade conversion by force, religious zealotry and political advantage occasionally converged and resulted in sustained attempts to compel mass conversion by the threat of death or exile. Many Jews willingly paid the price of their beliefs and, at times, entire communities were wiped out because they refused to renounce their God. A large number of Jews did, however, convert; indeed, sometimes the majority of the Jewish population went over to the other faith. So it fell in Spain in the 'great persecution' of 1391 and again in the expulsion of 1492; it happened equally in mid-twelfth-century Maghreb under the Almohads, and again in Yemen in the latter half of the twelfth century.[1]

* A. Grossman, 'Kiddush ha-Shem ba-Me'ot ha-Yod-Alef ve-ha-Yod-Bet: Bein Ashkenaz ve-'Artsot ha-'Islam', *Pe'amim*, 75 (1998), 27–46; M. Ben-Sasson, 'Zikkaron ve-Shikhehah: 'al Kiddush ha-Shem be-'Artsot ha-Natsrut u-ve-'Artsot ha-'Islam bi-Yemei ha-Beinayim ha-Mukdamim. 'Iyyun ba-Beḥinot ha-Mashvot—bi-Tefisat ha-Musag, ba-Teguvah la-'Erua' u-vi-Shemirat ha-Zikkaron', in Y. Hacker et al., eds., *Rishonim ve-'Aḥaronim: Meḥkarim be-Toledot Yisra'el Muggashim le-'Avraham Grossman* (Jerusalem, 2010), 47–72. The rich bibliography of the latter essay renders the updating of my footnotes superfluous.

[1] On the Almohad period, see D. Corcos, 'Le-'Ofi Yaḥasam shel Shalitei ha-'Almoḥadon la-Yehudim', *Zion*, 32 (1967), 137–60, and the bibliography contained therein. On Yemen, see S. D. Gotein, *Ha-Temanim—Historyah, Sidrei Ḥevrah, Ḥayyei ha-Ruaḥ—Mivḥar Meḥkarim*, ed. M. Ben-Sasson (Jerusalem, 1983), 44–9. The subject of conversion to Islam was discussed in considerable detail in the winter issue of *Pe'amim*, 42 (1990). See esp. the articles of N. Levzion, M. Ben-Sasson, and J. Tobi.

The common phenomenon of mass conversion elicited, however, radically different responses. In Spain, the large-scale defection of both the common folk and the religious and cultural elite shattered the community's self-image, broke its pride, and generated a constant, corrosive brooding over why it had been unequal to the challenge and betrayed its covenant with God.[2] In one sense one might say that Iberian Jewry and its diaspora, together with its historiography, have never fully recovered from the trauma of mass conversion. In Islamic countries, however, nothing of the sort occurred. No doubt, many were racked with guilt and wrestled with a heavy conscience. However, these feelings produced no outpouring of self-criticism or self-examination, no pained inner reckoning with their deepest beliefs. Quite the contrary: rather than self-laceration, we find encouragement and solace—to the extent that their emotions assumed written form, the literature they produced is that of consolation.[3]

Ineluctably we are led to ask: why the difference? To my thinking, the answer lies in the different status of martyrdom in these two religious cultures. The question is not, and this must be emphasized, the legal status of *kiddush ha-shem*, but rather its place in the hierarchy of the two cultures' religious values. Halakhic status and religious significance are two entirely different things. Take the eating of pork, for example. Legally, the ban on pork is no different from the ban on the consumption of any other non-kosher animal. In fact, it is far less serious than eating unsalted meat—meat that has not been purged of blood.[4] Religiously and emotionally, however, eating pork is viewed, and not simply by religious people, as a turning of one's back on Judaism, as some ultimate act of disavowal of Jewish tradition and sentiment. I doubt if we shall ever know in full the reasons for this profound Jewish revulsion for the pig. However, I do believe that one can suggest a reason for the differing emotional hold of *kiddush ha-shem* among the Jews of Christian Europe and those in the Muslim world.

[2] Still fundamental is the article of H. H. Ben-Sasson, 'Dor Golei Sefarad 'al 'Atsmo', *Zion*, 26 (1961), 23–64; repr. in id., *Retsef u-Temurah* (Jerusalem, 1984), 198–238; {Y. Hacker, 'Ga'on ve-Dika'on: Ketavim be-Ḥavayatam ha-Ruḥanit ve-ha-Ḥevratit shel Yotse'ei Sefarad u-Portugal ba-'Imperyah ha-'Otomanit', in R. Bonfil et al., eds., *Tarbut ve-Ḥevrah be-Toledot Yisra'el bi-Yemei ha-Beinayim: Kovets Ma'amarim le-Zikhro shel Ḥayyim Hillel Ben-Sasson* (Jerusalem, 1986), 541–86.} The self-laceration and justification continued until the early 17th century; see e.g. I. Tishby, *Meshiḥiyut be-Dor Golei Sefarad u-Portugal* (Jerusalem, 1985), esp. p. 44 n. 108.

[3] See e.g. *Iggeret ha-Neḥamah shel R. Maimon Avi ha-Rambam*, ed. B. Klar (Jerusalem, 1945); 'Iggeret ha-Shemad shel ha-Rambam', in *Iggerot ha-Rambam*, ed. Y. Shilat (Jerusalem 1987), 25–58.

[4] In the view of most medieval halakhic authorities (*rishonim*). See Maimonides, *Sefer ha-Mitsvot*, ed. S. Frankel (Jerusalem, 1995); 'Hassagot Ramban', *shoresh* 9, and the classic medieval commentators on *Makkot* 16b.

Judaism had long proclaimed the principle of martyrdom, that the highest act of belief is the sacrificing of one's life and that such self-immolation is the ultimate act of love for God.[5] In this area, Christianity, too, saw martyrdom as the peak of religious life and the ultimate test of one's faith in God.[6] Islam, however, had a different view. There is, of course, an imperative to die for Allah. This imperative, however, obtains in the field of battle, where one's death advances the spread of Islam. Death off the battlefield, death that contributes nothing to the war with infidels or to the expansion of the faith, was seen as a highly meritorious act, a mark of the religious elite, but it was never viewed as an iron-clad demand made of every believer, and certainly not a cornerstone of the faith. In times of religious persecution the principle of *taqiyya* (caution) obtained—that is to say, to dissimulate until such time as one was free again to conduct oneself openly as a Muslim. There is no religious laxity in the principle of *taqiyya*, simply a different religious perspective, namely, that in times of persecution the survival of the true believer is more important than his serving as a 'witness'. *Taqiyya*—a major theme in Shiite religiosity, one might add—went (and, to this day, still goes) hand in hand with profound piety and total religious dedication.[7]

In the religious climate of Islam, in which Jews had dwelt for many centuries, it was only natural for a failure to live up to the imperative of martyrdom (*kiddush ha-shem*) to appear to most people as an offense so serious that it constituted a 'desecration of the Divine name' (*ḥillul ha-shem*) for which, God

[5] See e.g. S. Spiegel, 'Mi-'Aggadot ha-'Akedah: Piyyut 'al Sheḥitato shel Yitsḥak u-Teḥiyato le-Rabbi Efrayim mi-Bona', in *Sefer ha-Yovel li-Khevod Aleksander Marks li-Melo't lo Shiv'im Shanah* (New York, 1950), ii. 471–549. English translation: *The Last Trial: Legends and Lore of the Command to Abraham to Offer Isaac as Sacrifice: The Akedah*, trans. J. Goldin (New York, 1967).

[6] See the old but still valuable entry *martyre* in A. Vacont et al., eds., *Dictionnaire de théologie catholique* 10 (Paris, 1928), cols. 220–54. For a more recent bibliography, see J. Höfer and K. Rahmer, eds., *Lexikon für Theologie und Kirche* 7 (2nd edn., Freiburg, 1962), s.v. *martyr, martyrium* (cols. 127–32, 134–8).

[7] *Encyclopedia of Islam*, s.v. *takiyā*, s.v. *shahīd*. For a more recent discussion, see E. Kohlberg, 'Some Imāmī-Shī'ī Views of Taqiyya', *Journal of American Oriental Society*, 95 (1975), 395–402; see also E. Mayer, 'Anlaß und Anwendungsbereich der *taqiyya*', *Der Islam*, 57 (1980), 246–80; W. M. Watt, 'Suffering in Sunnite Islam', *Studia Islamica*, 50 (1975), 5–19. Hava Lazarus-Yafeh has drawn my attention to Bernard Lewis's remarks in his *The Jews of Islam* (Princeton, 1975), 82–4. Lewis deals with the phenomenon of conversion; I deal with the communal self-image after conversion. In addressing the latter subject, one should always take into account that in Islam the insistence on conversion was more a question of religious solidarity and unity than one of belief. It demanded, above all, public conformity to Islam; the personal beliefs of the individual were secondary, as was, to a large extent, his personal conduct in the privacy of the home. See A. J. Wensinck, *The Muslim Creed* (Cambridge, 1932), 29–31. Maimonides emphasized this point in his 'Iggeret ha-Shemad' (above, n. 3), 41, 53. See also M. Ben-Sasson, 'Zikaron ve-Shikheḥah' (above, p. 223, n.*), 28–9.

had warned, there would be no cleansing. However, this 'desecration' seemed no worse than swearing falsely, where God had also served notice—in the Ten Commandments no less—'that He will not cleanse those who take his name falsely'. In times of persecution one was absolutely forbidden to dissimulate and deny one's faith; however, if one was unequal to the call of martyrdom, this yielding would simply be one more cardinal sin among others.[8] Certainly, there was no treason in such dissimulation. One had sinned greatly by choosing life over a martyr's death, but in doing so one had betrayed neither one's God nor one's people.[9]

In Christian Spain the situation was radically different. There the religious climate had raised the status of martyrdom to new heights. Sacrifice of one's life was seen as the ultimate religious act, the supreme test of man's faith in God. If Gentiles demanded of themselves so high a measure of devotion to 'the hanging corpse', could Jews demand any less for 'the one true and living God'? The religious atmosphere in Spain had not dulled the importance of martyrdom, nor diminished its centrality. Quite the contrary, it had made its call ever more insistent. Martyrdom thus played a pivotal role for Jews and Christians alike; yet when the moment of truth arrived, the ideal went unrealized. For reasons both known and still unknown, the Spanish Jews could not live up to the demands of martyrdom, and their conversion appeared to them as an unpardonable sin—a betrayal of God and His people. Their failure cast doubt upon the depth and integrity of their past religiosity and called into question their spiritual health in the 'good years'. They lost faith in their faith; they lost confidence not in their beliefs but in their own believing, and probed incessantly for the cause of their spiritual rot.

If we broaden our scope and extend it from Christian Spain to Latin Europe, we might propose that Ashkenaz knew well the demands of martyrdom, and when their time came, proved equal (or thought that they had proved equal) to its challenge.[10] The Islamic Jewish community, when simi-

[8] See *Mishneh Torah*, 'Yesodei ha-Torah', 5: 1–10, and the first chapter of 'Teshuvah'.

[9] Significantly we do not find in the letters from the Genizah maledictions following the mentioning of a convert's name, such as *shem resha'im yirkav* or *shehik 'atsamot*, that are so liberally bestowed in Ashkenazic literature. The relation to converts in Genizah literature is neutral and matter-of-fact. Menahem Ben-Sasson remarked to me that one finds evidence of the different attitude towards conversion of the Jews under Islam in that there is no parallel in their history to the mass martyrdom of much of the Jewish tribe in Arabia in 627, the Banu Qurayza. Not only was this event not imitated; the collective memory of Islamic Jewry retained no recollection of it. We know of this event from Muslim sources only. See *Encyclopedia of Islam*, v. 436, s.v. Ḳurayẓa Banū. {See now M. Ben-Sasson's article, 'Zikkaron ve-Shikhehah', mentioned at the outset, for a full development of this theme.}

[10] See I. G. Marcus, 'From Politics to Martyrdom: Shifting Paradigms in the Hebrew Narratives

larly summoned, often could not meet that call; however, in the religious atmosphere of their culture this failure seemed a grievous sin but hardly a treasonable one. The tragedy of Spanish Jewry was that it believed, no less than did Ashkenaz, in the central importance of martyrdom, but could not live up to its demands. Its conversion was perceived as perfidy, a betrayal of God and of His people. And that sense of guilt has haunted the Spanish diaspora and its historiography for centuries.

of the 1096 Crusade Riots', *Prooftexts*, 2 (1982), 40–52; the third chapter of A. Mintz, *Ḥurban* (New York, 1984), esp. pp. 91–2; H. Soloveitchik, 'Religious Law and Change: The Medieval Ashkenazic Example', *AJS Review*, 12 (1987), 214–16; repr. in the first volume of this series (*Collected Essays* [Oxford, 2013], i. 239–57).

CHAPTER ELEVEN

Halakhah, Hermeneutics, and Martyrdom in Ashkenaz

UNLIKE CHRISTIANITY, which underwent centuries of persecution before the conversion of the Emperor Constantine (313)—and the second-century Church Father Tertullian could rightly say, 'The blood of martyrs is the seed of the Church'—Judaism emerged from national slavery, not religious persecution. There were instances of religious persecution, to be sure, but these occurred relatively late in the history of Judaism and did not have a formative influence. Not surprisingly, the tannaitic and amoraic dicta on martyrdom are few and elicited next to no discussion in the yeshivot of Sura and Pumbedita. Nor did suffering death at the hand of infidels constitute an axial religious event in Judaism as it did in Christianity (crucifixion). Martyrdom lies just beneath the surface of Christianity, as its '*imitatio dei*' can readily take the form of picking up the cross, re-enacting the Via Dolorosa, and achieving martyrdom. Things changed dramatically in the second millennium of the Common Era. In a western Europe without heathens, there was no opportunity for Christian martyrdom. However, in the now thoroughly Christianized western Europe, martyrdom became a defining feature of Jewish existence. Beginning with the First Crusade (1096), religious persecution became the constant companion of the Jew, and martyrdom a significant component of Jewish self-perception, even of self-definition. The article below seeks to show how the sustained, lethal pressure for religious conversion and the tragic modes of Jewish defiance led some medieval Talmudists and more than one modern scholar to read the rabbinic texts of the first millennium through the spectacles of the second.

What further emerges from this study is the extent to which on occasion major—indeed, overwhelming—considerations do not register on the legal radar. The fate of the children in this world and, above all, their eternal death in the world to come, the absurdity of suffering a martyr's death and having one's offspring brought up as Christians or Muslims and lost forever to the Jewish people, are not meaningful categories in talmudic law. Not surprisingly, as in the large, deeply settled Jewish communities of talmudic times, both in the Holy Land and in Babylonia, the child of the martyr would be brought up by relatives or neighbors and the continuance of Judaism assured. Not so in medieval Europe or the Maghreb. Powerful forces were thus at work in medieval martyrdom which could not find expression in the traditional, normative idiom. Ineluctably, they created new idioms or refashioned (if you wish, distorted) old ones. Thus, discussions of martyrdom are often halakhically problematic, if by halakhah one means the classic, talmudic norms that govern quotidian Jewish conduct.

In my essay 'Religious Law and Change: The Medieval Ashkenazic Example' (*AJS Review*, 12 (1987), 208–10; repr. in *Collected Essays*, i. 242–4), I remark that there was no halakhic basis for the conduct of the Ashkenazic communities in the First Crusade, and that the justifications for the mass suicides and murder of children by their parents proffered by the Tosafists were *ex post facto* rationales. This aroused considerable criticism. The brief documentation in one footnote (n. 8) that I then provided answered neither the numerous critiques nor the counter-theories that were advanced. Some contended that the conduct of the Rhineland communities in 1096 was a product of the Palestinian orientation of Ashkenaz, and it was unhistorical to judge their actions by the standards of the Babylonian Talmud (Bavli). Others argued that aggadah had regularly been invoked in halakhic discussions by the Tosafists, and its presence in texts dealing with martyrdom was thus hardly an aberration. I sought in this essay to set forth in detail why I found the tosafist arguments wanting and why I thought that the other explanations that were being offered would not bear scrutiny.

Much of the analysis contained in this essay was presented at a series of seminars on martyrdom sponsored by the Collège de France and the École des Hautes Études en Sciences Sociales in May and June 1999. I would like to thank Barber Johanssen and Maurice Kriegel for inviting me to give the series. A subsequent presentation at a seminar on Jewish hermeneutics held by the program of Jewish studies at the University of California, Los Angeles, in March 2000 helped clarify some issues. My thanks to David Myers for his kind invitation and to Arnold and Ora Band for hosting my stay in Los Angeles. I am further indebted to David Berger, Benjamin Z. Kedar, Amnon Linder, and Kenneth Stow, who were kind enough to read and comment upon the manuscript.

All the sources cited here have been scanned and are available on my website <haymsoloveitchik.org> under the title 'Kiddush ha-Shem be-Ashkenaz'.

This essay was originally published in two installments in *JQR*—this accounts for the break in the original page numbering at the beginning of Part II. In the original publication the Hebrew text of a passage cited in translation in the body of the essay was omitted in the footnotes. It is registered here in note 18, rather than in an

ungainly 17a. Thus all references in the prior scholarly literature to footnotes in the article after 17 are found under the cited number plus one.

A HISTORIAN has no right to claim extraneous influences unless he or she can show that the conclusion arrived at by the thinker is so atypical that unless something had impinged, consciously or unconsciously, upon his thought he could never have arrived at the conclusion that he did. I have called this elsewhere detecting an angle of 'measurable deflection'.[1] If, however, the halakhist's line of reasoning is a valid one, and one could envision another jurist without such a *parti pris* arriving at the same conclusion, the historian has no right to attribute it to outside forces. This is not to say that in such instances the individual was not influenced by an extraneous force, |77| only that the historian has no basis for claiming that he was.

The question that next poses itself is: How does one know what a typical mode of reasoning is for a specific jurist or thinker? Often this is a major stumbling block, but not when studying the great set of medieval French glosses known as the *Tosafot*.[2] These dialectical glosses have dominated the study of the Talmud since their promulgation in the early thirteenth century and have been printed alongside the Talmud since the 1530s. All serious talmudic study begins with the study of these glosses, and the contradictions that they have pointed out and the solutions they have propounded are the staples of halakhic thought to this day. Any student of the Talmud lives in daily, intimate contact with the *Tosafot*. There are few if any thinkers whose thought processes are so familiar to us. Indeed, generally the epistemological problem is not whether we can reconstruct their normal train of thinking but whether we can think in a mode other than tosafist, so deeply have they imprinted themselves on our minds, so thoroughly have they shaped our approach to halakhic issues. This is not to say that we understand every gloss, nor that all their arguments are convincing, even to sworn dialecticians. However, the difficulties that we encounter are usually subtle, not gross errors of inference, and certainly not strings of gross errors. When we do encounter an agglomeration of logical

[1] 'Can Halakhic Texts Talk History?', *AJS Review*, 3 (1978), 174–5; repr. in the first volume of this series (*Collected Essays* [Oxford, 2013], i. 197–9).

[2] A brief overview of the tosafist movement with characterizations of the two major figures who will dominate our discussion, Rabbenu Tam and Ri, may be found in my article 'Catastrophe and Halakhic Creativity: Ashkenaz—1096, 1242, 1306 and 1298', *Jewish History*, 12 (1998), 72–8, repr. in *Collected Essays*, i. 12–17. The comprehensive study is the two-volume work of E. E. Urbach, *Ba'alei ha-Tosafot*, rev. edn. (Jerusalem, 1980).

leaps and far-fetched interpretations on a specific topic, then (and only then) are we justified in saying that a sensitive subject is deflecting the course of tosafist thought from its usual exegetical channels.

Some fifteen years ago I argued that there are occasions when cultural norms shape the perception of halakhah, even on the part of its greatest thinkers. There is no pure empiricism in halakhah any more than in other disciplines. The simplest text, if it leads to unbelievable conclusions, will be either discounted or reinterpreted. The more outlandish the conclusions of the straightforward interpretation, the less plausible need be the reinterpretation. Despite its improbability, it will carry the air of verisimilitude to those who share the shock at the alternative. This does not happen often, but it does happen—even in such important areas of Jewish law as martyrdom. |78|

The strange reasoning of the Tosafists on the subject of martyrdom does not, I contended, bear legal scrutiny. Both their justification of suicide when fearing that one might yield to torture and apostatize and their even more surprising defense of parents slaughtering infants to prevent them from being reared as Christians were *ex post facto* justifications of the conduct of Jewish communities during the First Crusade.[3] To have ruled otherwise the Tosafists would have had to conclude that the venerated martyrs of 1096, whose actions had been held up as an ideal of Jewish conduct in times of persecution, were, in reality, suicides and murderers who should either be denied burial in a Jewish cemetery or be buried with criminals at its far end. This was a ridiculous, indeed impossible, conclusion for the Tosafists. It denied their deepest feelings, and, more significantly, their deepest religious intuition. Any interpretation that would retain the lofty status of the *kedoshim*, or 'holy ones' as the martyrs were called, would prove far more persuasive to them than the straightforward reading of the law.[4]

The matter seemed fairly obvious to me, and I contented myself with one long footnote of documentation.[5] This was evidently a mistake. Much to my surprise, my claim stirred considerable controversy. Charges were leveled that

[3] References to recent literature can be found in Y. T. Assis et al., eds., *Yehudim mul ha-Tselav: Gezerot Tatnu ba-Historyah u-va-Historiografyah* (Jerusalem, 2000); A. Haverkamp, ed., *Juden und Christen zur Zeit der Kreuzzüge* (Sigmaringen, 1999), and in *Der Erste Kreuzzug 1096 und seine Folgen. Die Verfolgung von Juden im Rheinland*, Schriften des Archivs der Evangelischen Kirche im Rheinland 9 (Düsseldorf, 1996). {See now E. Haverkamp, 'Martyrs in Rivalry: The 1096 Martyrs and the Theban Legion', *Jewish History*, 23 (2009), 336 n. 5.}

[4] 'Religious Law and Change: The Medieval Ashkenazic Example', *AJS Review*, 12 (1987), 208–13, repr. in *Collected Essays*, i. 239–57: see pp. 242–6. As the main purpose of this essay is methodological, I will keep the length of notes to a minimum, omitting strings of citations and of parallel passages, as well as variant readings in the sources that are irrelevant to the issue at hand.

[5] Ibid., n. 8.

I had no right to argue that the Tosafists consciously sought to reinterpret the halakhah or that they simply manipulated sources to their advantage—for, as my critics claimed, the arguments justifying suicide, and possibly even murder, were halakhically valid by their notions of argumentation (rather than mine), or, as others pointed out, the Tosafists had a viable Palestinian tradition that guided their conduct.[6]

Clearly, the subject needs to be treated in far greater detail. Let us, then, carefully examine the tosafist writings on martyrdom |79| and see whether their hermeneutical sins on this topic are indeed so scarlet. But first a cautionary word. We are about to engage in legal analysis, testing analogies and making distinctions. Legal distinctions often appear to the uninitiated as hair-splitting, and perhaps justly so. To medieval men, however, lives—and often eternities—hinged upon these distinctions. Whether one faced an eternity of bliss or death depended, in their mind, on whether one's actions were viewed as suicide or martyrdom. The consequences of these small distinctions were incalculably large and we would do well, therefore, to pay them heed.

I

Like canon law and most legal systems,[7] Jewish law recognizes two types of coercion: absolute and relative. 'Absolute coercion' means someone throwing me down in front of an idol; 'relative coercion' means that I choose to bow down to the idol because I fear that I will otherwise be murdered. In the former, the individual's body is the object of another's action; in the latter, the person's will is the object of coercion, for in relative coercion the individ-

[6] A. Grossman, 'Shorashav shel Kiddush ha-Shem be-'Ashkenaz ha-Kedumah', in Y. M. Gafni and A. Ravitzky, eds., *Kedushat ha-Ḥayyim ve-Ḥeruf ha-Nefesh: Kovets Ma'amarim le-Zikhro shel Amir Yekutiel* (Jerusalem, 1991), 99–130; I. M. Ta-Shma, 'Hit'abdut ve-Retsaḥ ha-Zulat 'al Kiddush ha-Shem: Li-She'elat Mekomah shel ha-'Aggadah be-Masoret ha-Pesikah ha 'Ashkenazit', in *Yehudim mul ha-Tselav* (above, n. 3), 150–6 {repr. in id., *Keneset Meḥkarim* [Jerusalem, 2005], i. 388–94}; E. Kanarfogel, 'Halakha and Metziut (realia) in Medieval Ashkenaz: Surveying the Parameters and Defining the Limits', *Jewish Law Annual*, 14 (2003), 193–224. (I would like to thank Professor Kanarfogel for making his manuscript available to me before publication.)

[7] For canon law (where 'relative coercion' is termed 'conditional coercion'), see S. Kuttner, 'Kanonistische Schuldlehre von Gratian bis auf die Dekretalen Gregors IX', *Studi e Testi*, 64 (Vatican, 1935), 301–7, cited in B. Z. Kedar, *Crusade and Mission: European Approaches Toward the Muslims* (Princeton, 1984), 73 n. 89; {E. F. Vodola, '"Fides et culpa": The Use of Roman Law in Ecclesiastical Ideology', in B. Tierney and P. Linehan, eds., *Authority and Power: Studies on Medieval Law and Government Presented to Walter Ullman on his Seventieth Birthday* (Cambridge, 1980), 83–97; A. M. Kleinberg, 'Depriving Parents of the Consolation of Children: Two Legal *Consilia* on the Baptism of Jewish Children', in Y. Hen, ed., *De Sion Exhibit Lex et Verbum Domini de Hierusalem: Essays on Medieval Law, Liturgy, and Literature in Honour of Amnon Linder* (Turnhout, 2001), 129–35.}

ual must choose to actively abjure his religion to avoid death. This distinction is maintained in the martyr imperative, where the victim is given a choice between compliance and death. Compliance involving absolute coercion does not require martyrdom; compliance involving relative coercion, where action is demanded of the individual, does. For example, should someone say 'Stand still so I can throw you down in front of the idol; otherwise, I will kill you', there is no imperative of martyrdom. A threat of 'Bow down or I will kill you', on the other hand, demands a martyr's response.[8] |**80**| In other words, Jewish law demands martyrdom *only* in the case of coercion of the will, where the victim must act upon a choice he has made, not in cases of coercion of the passive body.

Maimonides' classic statement of martyrdom runs thus: martyrdom is always demanded when one is confronted with a choice between death, on the one hand or, on the other, apostasy, commission of murder, or a grievous sexual crime (adultery or incest). In a time of religious persecution or if one is coerced publicly, one must suffer death rather than commit any religious infraction, even one less severe than apostasy and the like. Maimonides adds the ruling that voluntary martyrdom is forbidden. In those cases where transgression is permitted under the threat of death, one *must* transgress; otherwise one is viewed as having committed suicide.[9]

[8] *Tosefot ha-Rashba 'al Pesaḥim*, ed. E. D. Rabinovits-Te'omim (Jerusalem, 1955), 25b, s.v. *mah*; *Tosefot ha-Rashba mi-Shants 'al Ketubbot*, ed. A. Liss (Jerusalem, 1973), 3b s.v. *ve-lidrosh*; *Tosafot Yeshanim*, *Yoma* 82a, s.v. *ḥuts*; *Tosafot, Sanhedrin* 74b s.v. *ve-ha*. {The reader might well object that the two cases given in the text are not comparable. In an instance where an individual is seized and thrown down before an idol the individual is wholly passive, whereas in the case of 'Stand still so I can throw you down in front of the idol; otherwise, I will kill you', the individual has chosen to stand still. The distinction is factually correct, but legally irrelevant. What the individual has willed in the latter case is to stand still—which is no crime. This enables someone else to subsequently throw him down before an idol. However, the individual thrown down has neither performed the criminal act of prostration nor even 'willed' it, in the sense of instructing the body to perform it. (Enabling a crime is neither doing nor even 'willing' it.) One who bows down under the threat of death has both willed and committed that act of prostration.} This is certainly so in the case of idolatry, which is the subject of our essay. Whether it is equally true for rape or murder is another question. See *Entsiklopedyah Talmudit*, xxii (Jerusalem, 1997), s.v. *yehareg*, cols. 87–94. There is a view that a married woman, if given the choice, is obliged to suffer death to avoid rape despite the fact that the woman is wholly passive. Nevertheless, adulterous intercourse has taken place, albeit contrary to the woman's will. Idol worship, on the other hand, means bowing down to an idol, so being thrown down doesn't constitute worship. A similar distinction is made by some between being thrown upon a baby and killing him and being thrown down in front of an idol. A tortious act has occurred in the former case, irrespective of wish or will, but no such thing has occurred in the latter. I should emphasize that this view exists only in instances where someone is given a choice between the passive use of his body and death {as in 'Stand still or lie still or I will kill you'}. Where no such choice is proffered and one's body is seized and used against one's will, the individual is held blameless by all accounts.

[9] 'Yesodei ha-Torah', 5: 1–4.

The tosafist statement of martyrdom would comport with most of Maimonides' rulings, which in turn merely restate the laws found in the Talmud. However, the Tosafists would demur from Maimonides' personal ruling against voluntary martyrdom and make three further allowances.[10] Their statement would run thus: in all cases where one is permitted to transgress and not die, one may, nevertheless, choose to die rather than transgress. Furthermore, when confronted with a martyr's choice and fearing that one may yield, one may commit suicide to avoid apostatizing. The imperative is operative even if one is threatened with torture, not simply death. Finally, parents may kill their children to prevent them from falling into Gentile hands and being raised as idolaters.

What are the bases of these rulings? If one studies Maimonides' sources, to which the standard commentaries are a sure guide, one sees that they are all in the famous halakhic discussion in *Sanhedrin* (74a–b), the locus classicus of the laws of *kiddush ha-shem* (literally, sanctification of the Name, i.e. martyrdom). However, if one studies the sources of the tosafist position, one will note immediately that those sources are aggadic. Indeed, there is no discussion of contemporary martyrdom in the *Tosafot* on the classic passage in *Sanhedrin*, nor is there a reference to this *sugya* in all their discussions of contemporary martyrdom. |81| As all remarks of the Tosafists on voluntary martyrdom, torture, and suicide are comments on aggadic portions of the Talmud, a word on the place of aggadah in halakhic argumentation is appropriate.

Some have argued, for reasons that are beyond me, that the Tosafists viewed aggadic sources as having normative force and that their use of these in legal discussions was only natural and legitimate.[11] Let us for the moment accept this premise [which I have addressed in Chapters 4 and 5 above]. I trust, however, that its proponents will agree that the conclusions drawn from aggadah must follow logically from the material being cited. One may broaden the corpus from which one derives conclusions, but the mode of logical inference remains unchanged. Thus the methodological considerations outlined above are still applicable. If the inferences drawn by the Tosafists from aggadic material are systematically and grossly flawed, we are justified in suspecting that some extraneous factor strongly impinged upon their thought processes. The traditional view, and one to which I subscribe, would characterize the relationship between halakhic and aggadic passages in tosafist thought

[10] *Sefer Mitsvot Katan* (Constantinople, 1509), #3; R. Avraham ben 'Azri'el, *'Arugat ha-Bosem*, ed. E. E. Urbach (Jerusalem, 1963), iii. 194–5. See below, pp. 261–74.

[11] Grossman, 'Shorashav shel Kiddush ha-Shem' (above, n. 6), 99–131; Ta-Shma, 'Hit'abdut ve-Retsaḥ ha-Zulat' (above, n. 6), 150–6.

thus: aggadic statements have no validity when opposed by halakhic ones. However, when the normative passages in the Talmud provide no guidance, one may then fall back on the aggadic portions for guidance, seeking some precedent in the sacred texts, some guide in the canonized literature for conduct in new and uncharted waters.[12] However, whatever the status of aggadah, the conclusions derived from it must flow logically from the passage cited.

To return to our case: clearly, Maimonides saw the passage in *Sanhedrin* as comprising the totality of the 'martyr imperative'. He did not feel that anything was missing. By contrast, the Tosafists felt that the passages in *Sanhedrin* did not represent—indeed, could not represent—the whole of *kiddush hashem*. Therefore they fell back on the aggadic passages. For even those who claim that aggadah is an integral part of the tosafist legal system will admit that the Tosafists did not regularly invoke aggadic passages in their discussion. They resorted to aggadah only when they felt that these sources contained information that added to or modified the conclusions of the halakhic passages of the Talmud.

What led the Tosafists to believe that the normative passages in the Talmud do not represent the whole of the laws of martyrdom? **|82|** Was it textual problems (they were, after all, exegetes and dialecticians) or was it contemporary events and conduct? Let us explore the first alternative. Perhaps they found that the narrative or aggadic passages in the Talmud presented a pattern of conduct that was at variance with the normative one. If some of these passages were indeed tales of the martyrdom of great *tanna'im*, this would clearly indicate that the sparse normative passages of the Talmud were but imperfect reflections of the halakhic reality. Their presentation is dominated by three talmudic stories: that of the 400 boys and girls in *Gittin*, the famous story of R. 'Akiva's death found in *Berakhot*, and the passage in *'Avodah Zarah* describing R. Ḥanina ben Tradyon's conduct during his agonizing death at the hands of the Romans. Let us take each one in turn.[13]

[12] See the sources cited by R. Ḥezekiah Medini, *Sedei Ḥemed, kelalim* (Benei Berak, 1963), *ma'arekhet ha-'alef*, ##95, 37, and those referred to in the *Entsiklopedyah Talmudit*, i (Jerusalem, 1947), s.v. *aggadah*, cols. 132–3.

[13] The entire tosafist discussion on suicide in the face of torture and apostasy assumes that, when not confronted with these options, suicide is strictly forbidden. Whether this injunctive stand was rooted in passages in *Semaḥot*, 2: 1–5 (see below, n. 24) or was simply a cultural norm of the Ashkenazic community is beside the point. See E. Kupfer, 'Le-Toledot R. Mosheh ben R. Yom Tov Abir London', *Tarbiz*, 40 (1971), 385–7; repr. in *Sefer Hilkhot Semaḥot ha-Shalem*, ed. A. Dov and Y. Landau (Jerusalem, 1976), 104–5, sect. 89. On the medieval background, which may well have contributed, if not to the proscription of suicide then to the deep aversion to it, see A. Murray, *Suicide in the Middle Ages*, ii: *The Curse of Self-Murder* (Oxford, 2000).

We read in *Gittin* (57b):

On one occasion 400 boys and girls were carried off for immoral purposes. They divined what they were wanted for and said to themselves: 'If we drown in the sea shall we attain the life of the future world?' The eldest among them expounded the verse, 'The Lord said: I will bring again from the Bashan, I will bring again from the depths of the sea . . . I will bring again from the depths of the sea, those who drowned in the sea' [Ps. 68: 23]. When the girls heard this they all leapt into the sea. The boys then drew the moral for themselves, saying [by a fortiori reasoning], 'If these, for whom this is natural, act so, shall not we, for whom it is unnatural?' They also leapt into the sea. Of them the text says, 'Yea for thy sake we are killed all day long, we are counted as sheep for the slaughter' [Ps. 44: 23].[14] |83|

Taken at its simplest, the story reports that 400 children facing a life of forced prostitution chose to commit suicide. There is no intimation that they were given any choice, nor that they feared that, ultimately, their will might be broken and they might become willing sexual participants. No doubt such a fear is a very real one—indeed, white slavery (forced prostitution) is based on breaking the will by degradation—but that fear is not operative in our narrative. They committed suicide not in order to avoid idolatry but in order to escape a life of sexual exploitation. Moreover, while homosexual relations fall within the martyr imperative, heterosexual relations between Jew and Gentile do not. True, in the course of generations, some scholars did advance such a claim; however, no such position is to be found in the writings of the Tosafists. In fact, we have a famous ruling by Rabbenu Tam, the very reinterpreter, as we shall see, of the *Gittin* passage, that such sexual relations do not require martyrdom.[15] If the girls drowned themselves not to avoid a life of shame but to fulfill the martyr imperative, from fear that their will would be broken and at some point they would engage in sexual relations willingly, their suicide was pointless, for being forced into heterosexual relations with Gentiles does not demand martyrdom.[16]

14 מעשה בד׳ מאות ילדים וילדות שנשבו לקלון, הרגישו בעצמן למה הן מתבקשים. אמרו אם אנו טובעין בים, אנו באין לחיי העולם הבא? דרש להן הגדול שבהן: ׳אמר ה׳ מבשן אשיב אשיב ממצולות ים׳, ׳מבשן אשיב׳ מבין שיני אריה אשיב, ׳ממצולות ים׳ אלו שטובעין בים. כיון ששמעו ילדות כך, קפצו כולן ונפלו לתוך הים. נשאו ילדים ק״ו בעצמן ואמרו, מה הללו שדרכן לכך, אנו שאין דרכנו לכך על אחת כמה וכמה. אף הם קפצו לתוך הים. ועליהם הכתוב אומר ׳כי עליך הורגנו כל היום נחשבנו כצאן טבחה׳. All talmudic translations are those of the Soncino Talmud, with minor changes by the author.

15 *Tosafot Sanhedrin* 74b s.v. *ve-ha*. The original formulation was found in Rabbenu Tam's *Sefer ha-Yashar*, absent from the printed version. Fortunately a citation is found in a responsum of R. Shemu'el b. David ha-Levi published by E. Kupfer in *Teshuvot u-Fesakim me'et Ḥakhmei Tsarfat ve-'Ashkenaz* (Jerusalem, 1973), 288–9.

16 Cf. Grossman, 'Shorashav shel Kiddush ha-Shem' (above, n. 6), 114.

The passage in *Berakhot* (61b) reads:

When R. 'Akiva was taken out [for execution], it was the time of the recital of the Shema'. While they flayed his flesh with iron combs, he was accepting the heavenly yoke [i.e. reciting the Shema']. His students said to him, 'Master, to this extent?!' He replied, 'All my life I was troubled by the verse "with all thy soul—even if He takes thy soul", and I thought, when will I have an opportunity to fulfill it? Now that I have the opportunity, should I not fulfill it?' . . . A *bat kol* went forth and proclaimed, 'Happy art thou R. 'Akiva for thou art destined for life in the world to come.'[17]

The famous story of R. 'Akiva poses the same problems: he was given no choice. The Romans were not interested in converting him to emperor worship, but in executing him. |84| The torture meted out to him was punishment for deeds past, not an attempt to coerce him to abjure his God. It was not an instrument of religious duress but a ritual of violence, to give horrific expression to their outrage at his disobedience. R. 'Akiva's famous reply may express total and loving acceptance of God's will regardless of its harshness, or it may be joy at one's death not being a meaningless event but rather the very climax of one's religious life. It is not, however, a statement that the worst of deaths must be chosen to avoid forswearing one's faith.

The death of R. Ḥanina ben Tradyon is no less a case of Roman reprisal than that of R. 'Akiva. Indeed, by talmudic accounts, they died at the same time and for the same breach of the Roman decree against teaching Torah. We find in *'Avodah Zarah* (18a):

Upon their return they found Rabbi Ḥanina ben Tradyon sitting and occupying himself with the Torah, gathering large multitudes, and a Torah scroll was resting on his lap. They took him, wrapped the Torah around him, encircled him with bundles of branches and set them afire. They brought tufts of wool, soaked them in water, and placed them on his heart so that he should not expire quickly . . . His students asked him, 'What do you see?' He replied, 'The parchment burns but the letters fly [up to

17 **בשעה שהוציאו את ר' עקיבא לחריגה זמן ק"ש [קריאת שמע] היה, והיו סורקים את בשרו במסרקות של ברזל, והיה מקבל עליו עול מלכות שמים. אמרו לו תלמידיו, רבינו, עד כאן? אמר להם, כל ימי הייתי מצטער על פסוק זה 'בכל נפשך' אפילו נוטל את נשמתך, אמרתי מתי יבא לידי ואקיימנו, ועכשיו שבא לידי לא אקיימנו? היה מאריך באחד עד שיצתה נשמתו . . . יצתה בת קול ואמרה, אשריך ר"ע שאתה מזומן לחיי העוה"ב [העולם הבא].** {As to the authenticity of the phrases **מצטער על** and **מתי יבא לידי ואקיימנו** see S. Safrai, 'Kiddush ha-Shem be-Toratam shel ha-Tanna'im', *Zion*, 44 (1980–1): *Sefer Zikkaron le-Yitsḥak Ba'er*, 36–7; repr. in id., *Bi-Yemei Bayit Sheni u-vi-Yemei ha-Mishnah: Meḥkarim be-Toledot Yisra'el* (Jerusalem, 1994), 415–16. (Yonah Brander brought this to my attention.) For subsequent discussions of this problem, see the works cited by A. Tropper in his *Ka-Ḥomer be-Yad ha-Yotser: Ma'asei Ḥakhamim be-Sifrut Ḥazal* (Jerusalem, 2011), 112 n. 2. The two phrases in question appear already in the citations of this passage both in the *Tosefot ha-Rashba mi-Shants 'al Ketubbot* 33b, s.v. *ilmalei*, and in the *Yalkut Shim'oni* (Jerusalem, 1980), #837.}

heaven]. [They said to him,] 'Open your mouth and let the fire enter you.' He replied, 'It is better that He who gave [life] should take it rather than a person should inflict injury upon himself.'[18] |85|

Despite the considerations I have outlined, all of the above cases are taken by the Tosafists as instances of martyrdom—of refusal to apostatize when faced with the threat of death. In so doing, the Tosafists read things into the text that simply are not there.

My remarks thus far have been general. A closer study of the actual arguments of the Tosafists only increases our perplexity. We are fortunate in having numerous and reliable reports of the thoughts of the greatest of the Tosafists, the man who single-handedly revived talmudic dialectic, R. Ya'akov of Ramerupt, commonly known as Rabbenu Tam (d. 1171). The earliest *Tosafot* (gloss) that has come down to us is that of R. Elḥanan, martyred in 1184. We are doubly fortunate. This *Tosafot* is possibly the very first one written in the school of Dampierre, home of the tosafist movement. Moreover, it was written at the feet of the master, R. Yitsḥak of Dampierre, commonly known as Ri (d. 1189), and under his direction, constituting what in medieval times was called a *reportatio*.[19] In this gloss to the story of R. Ḥanina ben Tradyon's death we have a report of the position of Rabbenu Tam, who, in the matter of martyrdom as in so many other matters, had a decisive influence on the course of tosafist thought.[20]

18 **בעת חזרתן מצאוהו לרבי חנינא בן תרדיון שהיה יושב ועוסק בתורה ומקהיל קהלות ברבים וספר תורה מונח לו בחיקו. הביאוהו וכרכוהו בספר תורה, והקיפוהו בחבילי זמורות והציתו בהן את האור, והביאו ספוגין של צמר ושראום במים והניחום על לבו כדי שלא תצא נשמתו מהרה . . . אמרו לו תלמידיו: רבי, מה אתה רואה? אמר להן: גליון נשרפין ואותיות פורחות. אף אתה פתח פיך ותכנס בך האש. אמר להן: מוטב שיטלנה מי שנתנה ואל יחבל הוא בעצמו**. See the Afterword, p. 283, #1.

19 B. Smalley, *The Study of the Bible in the Middle Ages*, 2nd edn. (repr. Notre Dame, Ind., 1964), 200 ff.; P. Glorieux, 'L'Enseignement au Moyen Âge: Techniques et méthodes en usage à la Faculté de Paris au XIIIe siècle', *Archives d'histoire doctrinal et littéraire du Moyen Âge*, 43 (1968), 65–186.

20 *Tosefot R. Elḥanan 'al 'Avodah Zarah*, ed. D. Fränkel (Husiatyn, 1901), 18a, s.v. *mutav*: **ואר"ר יעקב דהיכי דחובל והורג את עצמו מחמת שמתיירא שלא יכפוהו הגוים ע"י (א)יסורי' ומכות ומיתה רעה יותר לעבור ע"ד [על דת] (תורה) וירא שלא יוכל לעמוד בחם, מותר כגון קפצו כולם ונפלו לתוך הים דגיטין. דאע"ג דמשם אין ראיה כ"כ שע"כ הי' יכולים השבאים לנהוג בהם קלון כדאמר שנשבו לקלון, מ"מ סברא היא דשרי, ומצוה היא**. (I have taken **ע"ד** as denoting **על דת** and as being the original version, for that is the term used by R. Elḥanan's colleague, R. Shimshon of Sens, in the parallel passage cited below in n. 45. This was the technical term for forced apostasy; see below, nn. 56, 58. I take the word **תורה** as a scribal emendation explaining what **על דת** meant.) {(A) **על דת** is equally found in Rabbenu Tam's formulation given by the *Gilyonei ha-Tosafot* as cited by R. Yom Tov al-Sevilli, *Ḥiddushei ha-Ritva 'al 'Avodah Zarah*, ed. M. Goldstein (Jerusalem, 1978), 18a, s.v. *ha*. MS London, Montefiore 65, from which both the Husiatyn edition and the newer and more accurate one of Y. Kreuzer (Jerusalem, 2003) was published, reads **על דברי תורה**, as Kreuzer accurately registers it. In view of all the medieval parallels and the existence of a technical term that fell into disuse, I still believe that the original text of the *Tosefot R. Elḥanan* had *'al dat* and that it was corrupted in the process of scribal transcription.

[*Incipit:*] 'It is better that He who gave [life]': Rabbi Ya'akov [i.e. Rabbenu Tam] says that in the case where someone kills himself because he fears that he may be driven to apostasy as a result of either torture or [threat of] painful death, fearing that he would not withstand them, it is permissible to do so. As in the case of those who 'jumped into the sea' [*Gittin* 57b].

Although the simplest reading of the Tradyon passage would seem to clearly imply that taking one's own life is forbidden, Rabbenu Tam glosses the text to qualify this conclusion. Suicide is permitted; indeed, it is a halakhically commendable course of action when faced with the prospect of cracking under torture and forswearing one's faith. He cites proof from the tale of the 400 children, despite all the problems that I have noted in analogizing that case to one of religious persecution. It is hard to avoid the tentative inference that this was a premise of Rabbenu Tam rather than a conclusion—a premise derived from sources other than the Talmud. The lines in the gloss immediately following say as much.

It is difficult to know whether the concluding lines in the *Tosafot of R. Elḥanan* are the words of Rabbenu Tam himself or reflect the thoughts of his famed nephew, R. Yitsḥak of Dampierre:

Even though that proof-text is not much of a proof, seeing that their captors could have used them sexually against their will as the language indicates: 'were taken captive for sexual use', nevertheless, it is logical that it [i.e. suicide] is permitted, indeed, one who has acted so has acted meritoriously [*sevara hi u-mitsvah*].

The analogy of the proof-text of suicide is challenged here. No will needed to be broken in the instance of the 400 children: the prospect confronting them was repeated rape, pure and simple. |**86**| Put differently, they chose death because their fate was sealed; there was no way that they could avoid what would be done to them. However, the case of martyrdom presented by Rabbenu Tam, namely, yielding under torture, deals with 'relative' rather than 'absolute' coercion; not with passive objects of a *force majeure* but with active subjects freely choosing their fate. One is confronted with the choice of torture or apostasy. This case is wholly different from that of the helpless victim of rape. His body is not being used; rather, his will is being tested. He may well withstand the test. Many martyrs have suffered excruciating pain without

The scribal error may have been generated by the passage in *Sanhedrin* 110b, which speaks of *Rabbi 'Akiva ve-ḥaverav she-masru 'atsman li-sheḥitah* [or *li-zeviḥah*] *'al divrei Torah*. (**B**) Binyamin Richler's outstanding article 'Kitvei Yad shel Tosafot 'al ha-Talmud', in A. (Rami) Reiner et al., eds., *Ta-Shema: Meḥkarim be-Madda'ei ha-Yahadut li-Zikhro shel Yisra'el M. Ta-Shema* (Alon Shevut, 2012), 831, #233, registers a fragment of *Tosafot* on *'Avodah Zarah*, 18a–20b, which would include a *Tosafot* parallel to the one under discussion here. Unfortunately, the fragment is only of folios 19a–20b.}

abjuring, and nowhere do we find any allowance to commit suicide for fear that one's will might be broken and one might agree to abandon the faith. 'Nevertheless', continues Ri (or possibly Rabbenu Tam himself), despite the absence of proof, 'it is logical [*sevara*] that it [suicide] is permitted'. Wherein lies the logic? 'Logic' (*sevara*) may be inductive, deductive, or axiomatic. No principle has been enunciated from which the permissibility of suicide logically follows. Nor can the permissibility flow from induction, because the analogy from the 400 children has been shown by the Tosafists themselves to be mistaken. Clearly, the legitimacy—indeed, the meritorious nature—of such a suicide is axiomatic to the writers. The Tosafists' conclusion is openly and avowedly based on a cultural norm, on a religious given of the society in which they live.[21] |87|

The formulation *sevara hi* ('it is logical'), an explicit statement of its axiomatic and unprovable nature, was a bit too blatant and was omitted in

[21] Cf. Grossman, 'Shorashav shel Kiddush ha-Shem' (above, n. 6), 114. A colleague has suggested that Rabbenu Tam may have been arguing on the basis of an a fortiori deduction (*kal va-ḥomer*). If suicide was permitted in the face of sexual degradation where no martyr imperative obtains, suicide in the face of grievous sexual crimes (*gillui 'arayot*) and apostasy, which mandate martyrdom, should certainly be permitted. I find this interpretation unpersuasive on several grounds. First and foremost, Rabbenu Tam makes no mention of any a fortiori principle. Nor is there so much as a hint of one in any of the subsequent reports of his position published in the writings of the Tosafists. Tosafist literature spans close to a century and a half, from R. Elḥanan (d. 1184) to R. Asher (d. 1327), and from editors who were not historians but jurists and scarcely hesitant to add a word or two if it gave greater valence to the position they were presenting. Yet no editor thought it necessary to add two brief words (*kal va-ḥomer*) to modify the original position. The passage in *Gittin* was seen by Rabbenu Tam, as well as by his successors, as a proof-text in itself and not as the basis of an a fortiori deduction. This is scarcely accidental. Such an argument would immediately encounter the objection that an identical a fortiori applies to the talmudic case at hand. The statement of the boys in the *Gittin* narrative should have then read: מה הללו שאינן מצווין על כך, אנו שמצווים על כך, על אחת כמה וכמה. One can scarcely contend that such a legalistic reading is inappropriate for an aggadic passage, for the very premise of the argument is that this passage has normative force. A passage that has legal content must be read according to strict rules; otherwise one could draw almost any conclusion that one wished from most aggadic texts.

Second, were the suggested a fortiori reasoning valid, suicide might equally be permitted in the face of the prospect of desecration of the Sabbath or of eating pork. If the instance of 400 youths is one of *gillui 'arayot*, this entails an allowance of suicide when one is confronted with apostasy or murder. What suspends the injunction against suicide is the common severity of the prospective crimes. If, however, the 400 youths are confronted with no serious crime, what then annuls the suicide injunction? Not the primal, carnal violation of body and self, for the suspension is being extended to apostasy, where no such violation takes place. The overwhelming horror at, and disgust with, the threatened act becomes the controlling factor. Why then should a similar horror of eating pork not allow suicide? Once one treats the narrative as being of normative force and contends that it sanctions suicide in the instance of the 400 youths, one must have a criterion that determines the scope of the sanction.

subsequent reports of the Tosafists, who rested content with simply saying that such suicide was a meritorious act (*mitsvah hi*).[22]

Let us look ahead for a moment. Rabbenu Tam's position on suicide when one is confronted with the prospect of being tortured to renounce one's faith is well known and widely cited. He was, after all, one of the greatest Talmudists of the past millennium. He adduced his evidence from an aggadic passage that allows suicide when one is confronted with the prospect of rape or sexual degradation. Yet one looks in vain for any mention of such an allowance in the literature. While they were far from being historians, subsequent scholars intuitively felt that the allowance of suicide when confronting the prospect of apostasy was very seriously intended by Rabbenu Tam, but the permission granted in the instance of prospective rape was far from certain, and suicide was much too serious a matter to be allowed on dubious grounds. They sensed that the proof-text was interpreted to yield a conclusion outside itself—on apostasy, not on rape and sexual degradation. In other words, the conclusion drawn from the aggadic precedent was to be taken seriously, but not the precedent itself. As we shall see, this is a phenomenon that repeats itself in Rabbenu Tam's arguments about martyrdom.[23]

Let us return to Rabbenu Tam and note his very selective use of aggadah. As a dialectician, he is bothered by the conflict between the tale of Rabbi Ḥanina ben Tradyon and that of *Gittin*. |88| However, if the permissibility of suicide is on his mind, and as there is a lacuna in talmudic law—no statement about the permissibility or the forbidden nature of suicide may, strictly speaking, be found in the halakhic sections of the Talmud[24]—he is of the belief that aggadic passages may serve as the basis for normative inferences. The issue is then far more complex than he has presented. For example, in *Ketubbot* (103b) we are told:

> On the day that Rabbi died a *bat kol* went forth and announced: 'Whosoever has been present at the death of Rabbi is destined to enjoy the life of the world to come.'

[22] *Tosafot 'Avodah Zarah* 18a, s.v. *ve-'al*. *Tosefot Rash mi-Shants* in *Shitat ha-Kadmonim 'al 'Avodah Zarah*, ed. M. Y. H. Blau (New York, 1969), i. 18a, s.v. *mutav* (cited below, n. 45) also omits *sevara hi*, but speaks only of the permissibility of suicide, not of its being meritorious.

[23] See below, pp. 248–9. {It should be noted that we are dealing here with heterosexual rape. The threat of homosexual rape may allow suicide; see A. Y. Kook, *Mishpat Kohen* (Jerusalem, 1937), #144.}

[24] The Talmud in *Bava Kamma* 91b forbids inflicting bodily injury on oneself—which would include, of course, suicide—indeed, it derives the ban from the same words in the same verse as suicide; however, this general injunction standing alone has nothing of the force and bite of an injunction against 'self-murder'. *Semaḥot* (ii: 1–5) strongly forbids suicide, but this tractate, while far from being aggadic, had only a quasi-binding authority. See *The Tractate 'Mourning' (Semaḥot) (Regulations Relating to Death, Burial and Mourning)*, trans. D. Zlotnick (New Haven and London, 1966), 33.

A certain fuller, who used to come to him every day, failed to call that day, and as soon as he heard this, he went up to the roof, fell down to the ground, and died. A *bat kol* came forth and announced: 'That fuller is also destined to enjoy the world of the life to come.'[25]

And in *Ta'anit* (29a) we read:

When the First Temple was about to be destroyed bands upon bands of young priests with the keys to the Temple in their hands assembled and mounted the roof of the Temple and exclaimed, 'Master of the Universe, as we did not have the merit to be faithful treasurers these keys are handed back to Thy keeping.' They then threw the keys up to heaven. There emerged the figure of a hand and received these keys from them. Whereupon they jumped and fell into the fire.[26]

We further find the following story in *Kiddushin* (40a): 'Rav Kahana sold baskets. A married woman propositioned him. He said to her, "I will [first] go and adorn myself."|89| He went up to the roof and threw himself to the earth.'[27]

If aggadic passages may serve as normative directives in such cases, as Rabbenu Tam here assumes, suicide may then be permitted when a great man dies or when witnessing a national tragedy or to avoid mortal sin. And this does not conclude the list. There are some nine passages in the aggadic literature which narrate cases of suicide with various shades of approval. The talmudic position is far from clear if one works with aggadah,[28] yet no discussion of the permissibility of suicide is found in the tosafist literature. Clearly, the Tosafists do not accord these sundry aggadic passages normative status; rather, they accord normative status only to those passages that treat suicide in cases

25 ההוא יומא דאשכבתיה דרבי נפקא בת קלא ואמרה: כל דהוה באשכבתיה דרבי מזומן הוא לחיי העוה"ב. ההוא כובס כל יומא הוה אתי קמיה, ההוא יומא לא אתא, כיון דשמע הכי, סליק לאיגרא ונפל לארעא ומית, יצתה בת קול ואמרה אף ההוא כובס מזומן הוא לחיי העולם הבא.

26 משחרב הבית בראשונה, נתקבצו כיתות כיתות של פרחי כהונה ומפתחות ההיכל בידן, ועלו לגג ההיכל ואמרו לפניו: רבונו של עולם, הואיל ולא זכינו להיות גזברין נאמנים, יהיו מפתחות מסורות לך, וזרקום כלפי מעלה, ויצתה כעין פיסת יד וקיבלתן מהם, והם קפצו ונפלו לתוך האור.

27 רב כהנא הוה קמזבין דיקולי, תבעתיה ההיא מטרוניתא, אמר לה, איזיל איקשיט נפשאי. סליק וקנפיל מאיגרא לארעא.

28 See B. A. Brody, 'A Historical Introduction to Jewish Casuistry on Suicides and Euthanasia', in id., ed., *Suicide and Euthanasia: Historical and Contemporary Themes* (Amsterdam, 1989), 40–6; A. J. Droge and J. D. Tabor, *A Noble Death: Suicide and Martyrdom among Christians and Jews in Antiquity* (San Francisco, 1992), 97–112. I must here retract a statement in the opening presentation of my article 'Religious Law and Change' (above, n. 4), 208 (*Collected Essays*, i. 242): 'Life is not optional in Judaism.' It was clearly not optional in the viewpoint of medieval Ashkenaz as noted (above, n. 24); however, that scarcely justified my sweeping formulation. {For further instances of suicide for noble reasons in the Yerushalmi and midrashic literature, see S. Lieberman, *Tosefta ki-Feshuta*, *Bava Kamma* (New York, 1988), 110–11.}

of prospective martyrdom. It is the question of the permissibility of *these* suicides that is on their mind and to which they know the answer in advance, regardless of what may or may not be inferred from the passages themselves, for it is only 'logical' that they are permitted.

Revealingly, the German Pietists cited the above passage in *Kiddushin* (or another in the same vein)[29] when they explored whether one may commit suicide as penance for a sin that merited the death penalty.[30] Finding no such allowance in the halakhic literature, they also felt that a lacuna must exist and turned to the aggadic passages for guidance; needless to say, they swiftly found it there. Neither the Tosafists nor the German Pietists discussed the permissibility of suicide in all its permutations, only in the circumscribed cases that deeply interested them. Both turned to aggadah only in the specific instance and on the specific topics where their religious intuition had previously informed them that further norms and guidelines simply had to exist. **|90|** Not surprisingly, they proceeded to find what they sought. For the German Pietists to do so was simply par for the course; their work is replete with new religious dictates encoded in Scripture and aggadah and divined by hasidic intuition. Indeed, their newly discovered *retson ha-bore* is the *raison d'être* of the movement.[31] However, for Rabbenu Tam to do so—and on an issue no less significant than self-murder—is singular, to put it mildly.[32]

[29] The story of R. Ele'azar b. Durdaya in *'Avodah Zarah* 17a, and that of the nephew of R. Yose b. Yo'ezer in *Bereshit Rabbah* 65: 27, ed. J. Theodor and C. Albeck (repr. Jerusalem, 1965), 742–3.

[30] e.g. S. Y. Spitzer, 'Teshuvat R. Yehudah he-Ḥasid be-'Inyanei Teshuvah', in Y. Buksboim, ed., *Sefer ha-Zikkaron le-ha-Rav Shemu'el Barukh Werner* (Jerusalem, 1996), 202. See *Sefer Ḥasidim*, ed. Y. Wistinetzki (Berlin, 1891), #18 (p. 23). (This is based on a Parma manuscript [De Rossi, 1133] twice the size of the standard *Sefer Ḥasidim* [below, n. 104]; the Berlin edition is referred to below as *SHP*.) See also the conduct of R. Mosheh b. Yom Tov's son recounted in the text published by Kupfer, 'Le-Toledot R. Mosheh' (above, n. 13). {Not surprisingly a new *derashah* emerged in hasidic literature; see the so-called *Perush ha-Roke'aḥ 'al ha-Torah*, ed. Y. Klugmann (Jerusalem, 1978), i. 133: **יכול כשאול ת"ל אך; יכול כחנניא מישאל ועזריה ת"ל אך; יכול אף ההורג את עצמו מחמת תשובה ת"ל אך**. The work, published from MS Oxford, Bodley 268, issued from the school of the German Pietists. However, it was not authored by R. El'azar of Worms; see Y. Dan, 'He'arot', *Kiryat Sefer*, 59 (1984), 644. Echoes of the Pietist position can be found in *Teshuvot R. Ya'akov Weil*, ed. Y. S. Domb (Jerusalem, 2001), #114, as A. Gross has pointed out in his *Struggling with Tradition: Reservations about Active Martyrdom in the Middle Ages* (Leiden and Boston, 2004), 22. The crime for which the brother of the inquirer, R. Shimshon, was executed is not clear from R. Ya'akov's response. The responsum is reproduced, with the signature of R. Ya'akov Weil, in *Teshuvot R. Mosheh Mints*, ed. Y. S. Domb (Jerusalem, 1991), #107, and the running head states that he was executed by Gentile authorities for the murder of another Jew.}

[31] H. Soloveitchik, 'Three Themes in Sefer Hasidim', *AJS Review*, 1 (1976), 311–25; the article will be reprinted in the third volume of this series.

[32] Cf. I. M. Ta-Shma, 'Hit'abdut ve-Retsaḥ ha-Zulat' (above, n. 6), 152–3, and my reply, cited above, n. 11.

The comments on the death of R. Ḥanina ben Tradyon are not the only record of the thoughts of Rabbenu Tam on the subject of *kiddush ha-shem*. In *Pesaḥim* (53b) the Talmud asks: 'Why did Ḥananyah, Misha'el, and 'Azaryah see fit to throw themselves [i.e. submit to being thrown] into the fire?' and proceeds to give an aggadic (i.e. midrashic) answer. Here, too, we have a *reportatio* by R. Elḥanan's colleague, the great R. Shimshon of Sens.

[*Incipit*:] 'Why did Ḥananyah, Misha'el, and 'Azaryah see fit': [summary of question] Rabbenu Tam asks what is the basis for this question. Submitting to martyrdom rather than bowing down to the idol erected by Nebuchadnezzar was not optional but obligatory. Ḥananyah, Misha'el, and 'Azaryah suffered martyrdom not because they chose to do so or for the midrashic reason given by the Talmud, but because they were halakhically bound to do so.

[Reply:] And Rabbenu Tam explained that the statue erected by Nebuchadnezzar was not idolatrous [i.e. not to be worshipped as a divinity] but rather a monument erected in his own honor. Therefore the Talmud asks, 'Why did they see fit?' seeing that it was not entirely idolatry [*ve-'einah 'avodah zarah gemurah*], and even here there was 'sanctification of the name' [*kiddush ha-shem*, i.e. fulfillment of the martyr imperative], that they so clove to the worship of the creator that they would bow down to him alone . . . and for this reason we find the Talmud saying (*Ket.* 33a), 'Had they lashed [Rashi: tortured] Ḥananyah, Misha'el, and 'Azaryah, they would have worshipped the idol.' And had it been idolatry, God forbid, they would have bowed down.[33] |**91**|

A word on the passage in *Ketubbot* cited by Rabbenu Tam. In a wholly different context, discussing the severity of various punishments, the Talmud entertains the possibility that there may be punishments worse than death and cites in support a statement by Rav that had Ḥananyah, Misha'el, and 'Azaryah been tortured, they, too, would have worshipped the idol. This passage shocks Rabbenu Tam: how dare one impugn the resolution of these martyrs—for it is accompanied by the rarest of remarks in the highly impersonal literature of the *Tosafot*, 'God forbid!' The shock is understandable, but the lengthy reply and reinterpretation are not. The simplest way of handling this passing remark would have been a brief gloss stating: 'Not to be taken literally' (*lav davka*), or 'A rhetorical exaggeration only' (*guzma be-'alma nakat*). That is to say, the point of the passage is that there are things worse

[33] *Tosefot ha-Rashba 'al Pesaḥim* 53b, s.v. *mah ra'u*. As it was written at the master's feet, the text dates from before Ri's death in 1189. **ור"ת פירש דצלם שהעמיד נבוכדנצר לאו ע"ז הוה אלא אנדרטא העמיד לכבוד עצמו, והלכך מתמה מה ראו הואיל ואינה ע"ז גמורה ומסיק (ו)ק"ו מצפרדעים שאף בכאן הי' קדושת השם שכל כך [היו] נדבקים [ב]יראת יוצרם שלא להשתחוות כי אם לו . . . והיינו נמי דאמר באלו נערות אלמלא נגדו לחנני' מישאל ועזרי' פלחו לצלמא, ואלו ע"ז הי' חס ושלום שישתחוו.** (The emendations are those of the editor on the basis of parallel *Tosafot*.)

than death; the example of Ḥananyah, Misha'el, and 'Azaryah should not be taken literally. But a simple *lav davka* will, apparently, not do. The text is too dangerous to be allowed to stand uninterpreted or, more accurately, 'uninterpreted away'. Something more is at stake. Fortunately, we also have a gloss on this passage, and we are doubly fortunate that it, too, is a *reportatio* by the same R. Shimshon of Sens. It provides us with the source of Rabbenu Tam's reinterpretation.

'Had they lashed Ḥananyah, Misha'el, and 'Azaryah, they would have worshipped [*palḥu*] the idol.'

[*Incipit:*] 'Had they lashed': How does the Talmud know this? For was it not said (*Ber.* 61a) that when they led R. 'Akiva out [to his execution] he said, 'All my life I was troubled as to when I would have the opportunity to fulfill [the verse "And thou shalt love God, thy God,] with all thy soul" [which has been interpreted as meaning "even if He takes your soul", i.e. even at the cost of your life].' From this one can infer that the clause 'with all thy soul' includes even the cases where they will torture someone harshly, as they did R. 'Akiva, whose flesh they flayed with iron teeth, and how much more so [is martyrdom required] in instances of simple lashes. And Rabbenu Tam says that the idol was not actually idolatrous ['*avodah zarah mamash*], but one made to honor the king. |92| And that is what is intended in the [question in] tractate *Pesaḥim*, 'Why did Ḥananyah, Misha'el, and 'Azaryah see fit'.[34]

The real issue is not the reputation of Ḥananyah, Misha'el, and 'Azaryah, but the obligation to endure torture rather than forswear one's faith. Rabbenu Tam reasons that since the Talmud would never have suspected these three martyrs of acting contrary to halakhah, the simplest reading of the passage would imply that apostasy under torture is permissible. This, however, is impossible, as the story of R. 'Akiva proves. Hence the interpretation of Rabbenu Tam.

Even granting Rabbenu Tam's assumption that the case of R. 'Akiva is one of death freely chosen, problems nevertheless remain. R. 'Akiva's conduct may be paradigmatic, but how do we know that it is mandatory? Surely one would not deny martyrdom to one who, while choosing an agonizing death over conversion, nevertheless screamed in pain rather than smiling blissfully during

[34] *Tosefot ha-Rashba mi-Shants 'al Ketubbot* 33b, s.v. *ilmalei*:

תימא מנא ליה לתלמודא הא, דהא אמרינן בהו כשהוציאו את ר' עקיבה אמר כל ימי הייתי מצטער על פסוק זה [אימתי] יבא לידי ואקיימנו בכל נפשך, אלמא דבכל נפשך מיירי [אפילו היו] מייסרין את האדם (א') ביסורין קשין דומיא דר' עקיבא שהיו מסרקין בשרו במסרקי ברזל, וכ"ש לנגדא. ואומר ר"ת שלא היה אותו [צלם ע"ז ממש] אלא עשוי לכבוד המלך היה, והיינו דאמר בפסחים מה ראו חנניא מישאל ועזריה וכו'.

(The emendations are those of the editor on the basis of the printed *Tosafot*.)

his torture. R. 'Akiva's tranquility is the expression of a religious ideal, not of a demand with which one must comply in order to merit the title of martyr. If R. 'Akiva's repose was optional—exemplary but not mandatory—his willingness to endure torture may equally have been optional. How does one know that one *must* choose an agonizing death rather than convert? Perhaps the martyr imperative only applies in cases of a swift death, but when one is threatened with long agony compliance is, strictly speaking, permitted. Choosing death is heroism enough for the halakhah. The saintly will, of course, opt for martyrdom when confronted with torture, as did R. 'Akiva, but no such fearsome demand is made of the average man or woman. True, the same proof-text is adduced by R. 'Akiva as it is in *Sanhedrin* for the classic demand for martyrdom, but this passage can also be cited, and is, indeed, cited, for the most widely divergent laws.[35] From one and the same verse the most varied prescriptions can be derived, as a glance at the *midreshei halakhah* will swiftly reveal.[36] And, surely, there is no imperative more subject to gradations—from the requisite to the preferred to the exemplary to the heroic—than that of loving God: 'And thou shalt love the Lord with all thy heart and all thy soul and all thy might.'

The simplest reading of the passage in Daniel is that the idol of Nebuchadnezzar was indeed an idol and its worship was idolatry. |93| The simplest reading of the passage in *Ketubbot*, if read literally and taken as halakhically informative, is that torture is not included in the martyr imperative. Martyrdom demands only death, not protracted agony. R. 'Akiva's memorable endurance was paradigmatic but not mandatory. Indeed, we find just such an interpretation proffered in the *Shitah Mekubbetset*, a massive sixteenth-century compendium of medieval commentaries:

And in the *Notebooks* [*Kuntresim*] it is written thus: 'Had they lashed': R. Eli'ezer explained that the Torah only obligated one to die [for one's religion], as it is written, '"*with all thy soul*"—even if He takes your soul'. However, one is not obliged to suffer more than death [i.e. torture]. And [the author of the *Notebooks* goes on to comment] he [R. Eli'ezer] interpreted the text well. And that which Rabbenu Tam cited as an objection to his [R. Eli'ezer's] interpretation, namely, the passage about R. 'Akiva [which says] that they tore R. 'Akiva's flesh with iron teeth and he did not worship, does not seem to me to be a problem. There [in R. 'Akiva's case] it was a case of 'limited beating'; since they flayed his flesh, it was clear that he would die swiftly and he

[35] e.g. the injunction of *lo tukhlu le-'ekhol bi-she'areikha*; see Maimonides, *Sefer ha-Mitsvot* (repr. Benei Berak, 1995), Injunctions ##141–7.

[36] e.g. *Torat Kohanim*, ed. I. H. Weiss (Vienna, 1862), up to Lev. 11: 34. See also Rashi's remarks on that verse.

thus falls under the rubric of 'even if He takes your soul' [i.e. the martyr imperative]. However, the passage of 'Had they lashed' refers to 'endless beatings [without death]', such as incarcerating them for a year or two and beating them daily. This is more severe than death or lashes, and the Torah did not oblige one to suffer martyrdom in such a case. End quote [i.e. here ends the citation from the *Notebooks*].[37]

In my analysis I have distinguished between swift death and slow death by torture; the *Notebooks* distinguishes between death and endless torture not eventuating in death. The point is one and the same. One cannot translate R. 'Akiva's sufferings into the demands of *kiddush ha-shem*. We do not know who the author of the *Notebooks* is, nor even with certainty who 'R. Eli'ezer' is. What we do know is that their position had no resonance in Jewish law. |**94**| Despite its textual persuasiveness, this posture towards martyrdom seemed so anomalous that it simply dropped from view and is mentioned only in the encyclopedic *Shitah Mekubbetset*.[38] This, however, may tell us more about the religious atmosphere in the Middle Ages and its consequent hermeneutics than about the dictates of *kiddush ha-shem* in the Talmud.

Let us now turn to Rabbenu Tam's reinterpretation of the passages in *Pesaḥim* and *Ketubbot*. He proposes that the idol was simply a statue of the king to which one bowed in honor and not that of a God to whom one bowed in worship. If so, why did Ḥananyah and his friends decline to bow and risk death? A case could be made that bowing down before the statue of a saint, let alone one of the Virgin Mary, would fall under the sway of *kiddush ha-shem*, and martyrdom, if not necessarily obligatory, would certainly be permissible

[37] *Shitah Mekubbetset 'al Ketubbot* (repr. Jerusalem, 1961), 33b; ed. Y. Y. Har-Shoshanim-Rosenberg (Jerusalem, 2002), 812, s.v. *u-ve-kuntresin katuv*:

ובקונטריסין כתוב וז"ל: אלמלא נגדוהו. פירש ה"ר ר' אליעזר, דלא חייבה תורה אלא למסור עצמן למיתה, כדכתיב בכל נפשך אפילו הוא נוטל את נפשך, אבל להחמיר עליהם יותר ממיתה לא היו חייבים. ויפה פירש. ומה שהקשה עליו רבינו תם ז"ל מרבי עקיבא וחבריו שסרקו את בשרו במסרקות של ברזל ולא פלח. וראה לי דלא קשה מידי, דהתם הכאה שיש בה קצבה הויא, דכיון שסרקו את בשרו ברור הוא שימות במיתה גמורה במהרה וההיא הויא כמו נוטל את נפשך, אבל הא דאמר רב אלמלי נגדוהו כו', פירושו, הכאה בלא מיתה קאמר, כגון שהניחום שנה או שנתים ויכו אותם בכל יום, והויא הכאה שאין לה קצבה שהיא חמירא יותר ממלקות ומיתה, ובהא לא חייבתו תורה דלאו נוטל את נפשך הוא. עד כאן.

{Cf. *She'elot u-Teshuvot Maharil*, ed. Y. Satz (Jerusalem, 1951), #72 (p. 95)}. A similar position (with the identical argument) is advocated by the late 16th-century Polish scholar, R. Manoaḥ Hendel b. Shemaryahu, in a responsum published by A. Berger in Y. Buksboim, ed., *Sefer ha-Zikkaron li-Khevod ha-Rav Ya'akov Betsal'el Zholti* (Jerusalem, 1987), 334–6.

[38] R. Me'ir of Rothenburg does not adopt a similar position in *Teshuvot Maharam* (Prague and Budapest, 1895), #938. There he addresses coercion in contracts, not the martyr imperative. (On the Prague and Budapest edition of *Teshuvot R. Me'ir mi-Rotenburg*, see above, Ch. 3, n. 43.)

under the doctrine of voluntary martyrdom that the Tosafists advocated.[39] There is a devotional element in bowing, for these figures are objects of religious reverence and supplication, and martyrdom may even be demanded when the object is merely linked with the Divine, even if its role is restricted to mediation.[40] If religious devotion is not at stake, why then the refusal? If I am told that I must bow down to a statue of Abraham Lincoln on pain of death, what forbids me from doing so? What would even forbid a sincere communist, when the cult of personality was in full swing, from bowing to a statue of the 'great leader and eagle of the human race', Joseph Stalin?[41] Ri (and possibly Rabbenu Tam) realizes the problem and states that the statue was 'not wholly idolatrous' (*lav 'avodah zarah gemurah*). I'm not sure what partial idolatry is, but it too should fall under the martyr imperative.[42] Ri's successors sensed the problem in the formulation and they wrote instead, 'it was not actually idolatry' (*lo hayah 'avodah zarah mamash*). |95| But if so, why suffer martyrdom? Rabbenu Tam is caught between Scylla and Charybdis. The moment religious significance is attached to the idol, martyrdom becomes obligatory; the moment it is removed, the refusal to prostrate oneself becomes incomprehensible, indeed suicidal.[43]

Rabbenu Tam was one of the most influential halakhists of the past millennium, yet one will listen in vain for any echo of his doctrine that martyrdom is

[39] See below, p. 276.

[40] It would fall under the category of *avizaraihu de-'avodah zarah* (*Sanhedrin* 74b), which might be loosely translated as 'derivatives of idolatry'.

[41] See *Sanhedrin* 61b. (Bowing to Haman was forbidden because he demanded to be worshipped as a god.)

[42] If not falling within the category of *'avodah zarah* itself, it would clearly fall under its derivative, *avizaraihu de-'avodah zarah* (*Sanhedrin* 74b). The simplest line of criticism of Rabbenu Tam's doctrine would be to point out that Nebuchadnezzar's decree created a state of religious persecution (*she'at ha-shemad*), during which anything linked in any way with idolatry falls under the martyr imperative. However, Rabbenu Tam, in a passage not found in our *Sefer ha-Yashar* but cited by German Tosafists in the Middle Ages (above, n. 15) contends that *she'at ha-shemad* demands that *all* religious practices be proscribed, not just one. It's an incomprehensible doctrine nowhere cited by the Tosafists. It may well have been a passing thought of Rabbenu Tam. For this reason, I have deemed it best not to raise the issue of *she'at ha-shemad* in any internal critique of Rabbenu Tam's position but rather that of *avizaraihu*. {I now believe that this understanding of the cited passage in the *Sefer ha-Yashar* is in error. From the concluding remarks of Rabbenu Tam, it seems clear, to me at least, that the phrase *ke-she-gozrim 'al kol ha-mitsvot* is a scribal error, and that the text should read instead *ke-she-gozrim 'al aḥat min ha-mitsvot*. No new theory of *she'at ha-shemad* is being advanced there. See the Afterword, p. 283 #1.}

[43] Cf. Kanarfogel, 'Halakha and Metziut' (above, n. 6), 206 n. 42. It is one thing to use a *midrash* on Ḥananyah, Misha'el, and 'Azaryah as a rhetorical flourish to statements conforming with talmudic law, as did Maimonides. It is a wholly other one to employ *midrashim* to determine new halakhic norms.

permitted in cases involving prostration before a statue made in honor of a ruler. Though they were anything but historians, halakhists sensed—as I have mentioned above—that the purpose of Rabbenu Tam's remarks was deflective rather than interpretative; the negation was more seriously intended than the assertion. He was out to forbid apostasy under torture. Any interpretation would do, and it need not be taken too seriously, as long as religious defection under all circumstances was precluded.[44]

So speak the great figures of the tosafist movement, Rabbi Ya'akov Tam and Ri (Rabbi Yitsḥak of Dampierre). Only one figure of the next generation, indeed, of the entire tosafist movement, Rabbi Shimshon of Sens, could perhaps equal those two giants of dialectic. We are fortunate that yet another *Tosafot* of Rabbi Shimshon of Sens has come down to us, and in it we have what seem to be his own thoughts and not those of his teacher, Rabbi Yitsḥak of Dampierre, on suicide in times of religious persecution. He writes on the story of Rabbi Ḥanina ben Tradyon:

> Rabbenu Tam says that where someone is afraid lest he be forced to forswear his faith, he is permitted [to take his own life], like those [400 children] who were captured for immoral purposes who jumped into the sea. And further [i.e. another proof-text] we find in the Midrash: 'one might have thought that the aforesaid applies also to the case of Sha'ul, [therefore] the word 'but' comes [and teaches that it does not apply].'[45] |**96**|

R. Shimshon first reports Rabbenu Tam's position and then, apparently aware of the difficulty in the analogy of the 400 children, adduces his own proof-text for Rabbenu Tam's position, namely, the *midrash* on Sha'ul which allows suicide in times of religious persecution. A brief word of explanation is here in place. The biblical verse (Gen. 9: 5) 'But for your own lifeblood I will require a reckoning' is expounded in *Bereshit Rabbah* (ad loc.) as prohibiting suicide. The *midrash* then continues in the passage cited by R. Shimshon and excludes Sha'ul's case from the enjoinment.

Let us turn to the relevant passage in 1 Samuel (31: 3–4), which reads: 'The fighting grew fierce around Sha'ul and when the archers overtook him, they wounded him critically. Sha'ul said to his armor bearer: "Draw your sword and run me through or the uncircumcised will run me through and abuse me." But his armor bearer was terrified and would not do it; so Sha'ul took his own sword and fell on it.'

44 See above, p. 241.

45 *Tosefot Rash mi-Shants* 18a, s.v. *mutav*. **אומר"ת דבמקום שמתיירא פן יכריחוהו לעבור על דת שרי כהנהו דפ' הניזקין שנשבו לקלון וקפצו לתוך הים, ועוד אמרי' במדרש יכול כשאול ת"ל אך**. See also *Tosefot Ḥakhmei Angliyah 'al 'Avodah Zarah*, ed. S. Schreiber (Jerusalem, 1971), 18a, s.v. *ve-'al*.

What has the story of Sha'ul to do with suicide in times of religious persecution? His case may demonstrate, and indeed the point has been variously argued, the right of God's anointed king to commit suicide rather than fall into captivity and be subjected to torture, which would constitute a national humiliation; or the right of any man or woman facing protracted torture to opt for self-destruction; or even, perhaps, the right of someone who is mortally wounded to opt for a swift death—but it cannot prove any right to suicide as an alternative to apostasy.[46] The Philistines had not forced Shimshon to worship Dagon; they simply reduced him to a mill slave and an object of mockery. There is no indication that they intended to do otherwise to Sha'ul, should he have survived. That R. Shimshon of Sens, the outstanding exegete of *Zera'im* and *Toharot* and Maimonides' only equal in this field, could read the *midrash* as he did shows to what extent the greatest of the Tosafists were captives of their convictions in the matter of martyrdom and read every text in their light.[47] |97|

Let us address the issue of killing one's children rather than allowing them to fall into the hands of idolaters (i.e. Christians). Though this dramatic subject appears in the Crusade chronicles, is celebrated in liturgy, and became a widely accepted Ashkenazic practice in the period, nevertheless, we do not find its advocacy in mainstream tosafist literature. One must wait for a fourteenth-century gloss to discover the rationale advanced over the course of centuries, though it is clear that arguments permitting and counter-

46 See Kimḥi's commentary on the passage in 1 Sam. in the standard *Mikra'ot Gedolot* editions of the Bible and see *Piskei Rosh, Mo'ed Katan* 3: 94. For a survey of the various interpretations given to Sha'ul's death in medieval literature, see Y. Goelman, 'Hishtakfut Moto shel Sha'ul be-Sifrut ha-Halakhah', in *'Arakhim be-Mivḥan Milḥamah: Musar u-Milḥamah bi-re'i ha-Yahadut: Kovets Ma'amarim le-Zikhro shel Ram Mizraḥi* (Jerusalem, 1985), 233–51.

47 Cf. Grossman, 'Shorashav shel Kiddush ha-Shem' (above, n. 6), 113. Reports of Rabbenu Tam's position, albeit with R. Shimshon of Sens' proof-text, reached R. Yom Tov al-Sevilli (Ritva) in 14th-century Spain. Given the sensitivity of the topic and the price that many had willingly paid, his reaction was naturally muted; nevertheless, his incomprehension is clear. He writes: **והם דברים שצריכין תלמוד ועיון גדול, אלא שכבר הורה זקן. ושמענו בשם גדולי צרפת שהתירו כן הלכה למעשה.** *Ḥiddushei ha-Ritva 'al 'Avodah Zarah*, ed. M. Goldstein (Jerusalem, 1978), 18a, s.v. *ha de-'amrinan* (p. 81). This passage is missing in the older, standard editions, but its existence was known through 16th-century *testimonia*. There may also be a muted criticism of this interpretation of the Sha'ul reference in *Bereshit Rabbah* by the author of the *Ḥizkuni* in his brief comments on Gen. 9: 5; see *Ḥizkuni: Perush ha-Torah le-Rabbenu Ḥizkiyah ben Mano'aḥ*, ed. C. B. Chavel (Jerusalem, 1954), 25. His remarks, however, are too gnomic for us to know with any degree of certainty. {Jeffrey Woolf has recently drawn attention to the damning evaluation of voluntary martyrdom by Emmanuel of Rome in his 'Kedoshim ba-Tofet: 'Immanu'el mi-Roma 'al Mit'abdei Ashkenaz', *Pe'amim*, 133–4 (2013), 11–25. On the date of Emmanuel's work, see T. Dunkelgrün, 'Dating the *Even Bohan* of Qalonymos ben Qalonymos of Arles: A Microhistory of Scholarship', *European Journal of Jewish Studies*, 7 (2013), 39–72.}

arguments forbidding it had circulated in the Ashkenazic community long before. The classic reasoning would seem to have been broached by R. Eli'ezer ben Yo'el (d. *c.*1230), the outstanding dialectician of medieval Germany.[48] Some of the arguments were known already to R. Me'ir of Rothenburg (d. 1293), the greatest respondent and decisor of the medieval Ashkenazic community, who proceeds to advance his own rationale. Perhaps nothing illustrates better the factors at work than his responsum:[49]

A Jew asked our teacher R[abbi] M[e'ir], may he live [long]: is penance required of someone who slaughtered his wife and four children during the great massacre at Koblenz [April 2, 1265],[50] the blood-soaked city, |**98**| because they asked him to kill them for they saw that God's wrath had been kindled and the enemies [Christians] began slaughtering the children of the living God [i.e. Jews]? He, too, wished to kill himself [and die] with them, but God [wished otherwise] and saved him by the Gentiles [i.e. they stopped him from killing himself].

And he [Rabbi Me'ir] wrote to him: 'I'm at a loss as to how to rule. Certainly one who kills himself for the Unity of God is permitted to do so, for it is written, "I might have thought [that even suicide in a case similar to Sha'ul's] is forbidden, [therefore] comes the word 'but' to teach otherwise [i.e. that it is not forbidden]". We further find

[48] See below, n. 59.

[49] יהודי אחד שאל את מהר"מ שיחיה, אם צריך כפרה על ששחט(א) אשתו וד' בניו ביום הרג רב בקופלינש עיר הדמים, כי כך ביקשוהו יען ראו כי יצא הקצף מלפני ה' והתחילו האויבים להרוג בני א-ל חי הנהרגים על קדוש השם. וגם הוא רצה להרוג את עצמו במית(ו)תם אלא שהצילו ה' על ידי גוים.

וכתב לו: לא ידענא שפיר מה אידון ביה, כי ודאי ההורג עצמו על ייחוד ה' רשאי לחבול בעצמו, ואמ' יכול כשאול? ת"ל אך. ואמרינן מעשה בד' מאות ילדים וילדות שנשבו לקלון וכו' עד והפילו עצמם בים (וכן) [וכו']. (אם) [אף] גם היא עלתה לגג ונפלה ומתה, יצתה בת קול ואמרה: אם הבנים שמחה, וכהנה רבות. אבל לשחוט אחרים צריך עיון למצוא ראייה להתיר, ומשאול אין ראייה לאיסור אחרי שציוה דוד להרוג אותו (וכן) בן איש גר עמלקי, שנאמר אנכ[י] מות(ו)תתי משיח ה', [דדילמא מלך משיח] שאני. ועוד דבלאו הכי היה חייב מיתה דדואג האדומי היה כדכתיב דמך על ראשך, דמים בנוב עיר הכהנים.

מיהו דבר זה פשט היתירו, כי שמענו ומצאנו שהרבה גדולים שהיו שוחטין את בניהם ואת בנותיהם. וגם רבי' קולנימוס עשה כן בקינה המוגוולג . . . וצ"ל לחביא ראייח לחתיר, דכי היכי דוזמ' יכול כשאול? ת"ל אך, ה"נ [הכי נמי] נימא דההורג את חבירו על קידוש השם מותר, דבההוא קרא כתיב ומיד האדם ומיד איש וגו'. [ו]אך [ד]רישא דקרא אכולי' קרא דבתרי . . . ומי (שמטעינן) [שמטעינו] כפרה, הוא מוציא לעז על החסידים הראשונים. ואחרי שכוונת(ו) [יצרו] היה לטובה, מרוב אהבת יוצרינו יתברך שמו פגע ונגע (במעמד) [במחמד] עיניו, גם הם חילו פניו על ככה . . .

[וצור ישראל ינקום את נקמתינו ונקמת תורתו ונקמת דם עבדיו השפוך במהרה בימינו ויראו (עינו) [עינינו] וישמח לבינו] מאבב"ש.

Teshuvot, Pesakim u-Minhagim R. Me'ir mi-Rotenburg, ii, ed. Y. Z. Cahana (Jerusalem, 1960), *Teshuvot*, #59. The emendations and additions are those of the editor, mostly on the basis of manuscripts.

[50] Z. Avneri, ed., *Germania Judaica*, ii: 1 (Tübingen, 1968), 410–11, and see S. Salfeld, *Das Martyrologium des Nürnberger Memorbuches* (Berlin, 1898), 130–1.

the story of 400 boys and girls who were captured for immoral purposes etc. and they threw themselves into the sea. And [the subsequent story in that passage from *Gittin* of the mother of seven children who died for their faith; after witnessing their deaths] 'she threw herself off the roof and a Heavenly Voice went forth and said, "Happy is the mother of children" [Ps. 113: 9].' And many other [passages] like these. However, to kill other people requires further scrutiny to find allowance. One can't cite any proof that such killing is forbidden from [the story of] Sha'ul's [death], i.e. from David's killing the Amalekite convert [who reported] 'I have killed the anointed of the Lord.'[51] For perhaps the anointed of God is different [i.e. one cannot kill an anointed king, but others under these circumstances may be killed] . . .

However, the allowance in this matter is widespread and we have found that many great people regularly killed their sons and daughters. And [they were] celebrated by Rabbi Kalonymos in his dirge [beginning] . . . And it would appear to me to cite a proof of its permissibility; just as we say that the verse [in Genesis forbidding suicide] authorizes it [under certain circumstances] on the basis of the story of Sha'ul, so we may say that it equally authorizes one to kill another for the sake of *kiddush ha-shem*, for we derive the injunction against murder from the concluding words of that very same verse (Gen. 9: 5) . . . And the exclusionary [i.e. permissive] 'but' [in the verse] refers to both the beginning and concluding [clauses of the sentence] . . .

And whoever imposes penance upon him [i.e. the father] speaks evil of the pious of preceding generations, since his intention was to do good **|99|** and he hurt those who were most dear to him only out of an abundance of love for our Creator, may He be blessed, and they begged him to do so . . . And one should not be severe with him [the father] at all.[52]

May the Rock of Israel avenge our plight and the plight of his Torah and the plight of the blood of his servants swiftly in our days, and may our eyes see it [God's vengeance] and our hearts rejoice.

MbB [= Me'ir ben Barukh], may he [i.e. Barukh] live [long]

R. Me'ir's analysis is written after the tragic fact, and he opens by admitting that he is at a loss as to what to say. Then, gathering strength, he offers his own justification for such tragic but time-honored conduct. It is hardly surprising that his arguments are shot through with inconsistencies. Indeed, the contra-

[51] Apparently some supported the commandment that killing others was forbidden by citing the subsequent account of David's killing the Amalekite convert who informed him that he himself had killed Sha'ul upon Sha'ul's request.

[52] For an echo of this responsum a century or so later, see *Nimmukei R. Menaḥem mi-Merseburg*, regularly printed at the end of *Teshuvot R. Ya'akov Weil* (Jerusalem, 1959), end: **דין: מי ששחט אשתו ובניו בשעת הגזירה אין להחמיר עליו [בתשובות המשקל] כלל, כ"ש [כל שכן] שאדם רשאי להרוג עצמו על קידוש השם. ראובן מרצונו קיבל דינו שנקרו עיניו. ויש בני אדם שקורין לו רוצח ולבניו בני רוצח, יש לגעור בהן והעובר על ככה במזיד חייב נידוי.**

dictions are as blatant here as in the glossatorial comments of Rabbenu Tam. When confronted with a proof against the practice of slaughtering others from the Sha'ul narrative, R. Me'ir points out immediately, and quite correctly, that nothing can be inferred from Sha'ul's case for he was God's anointed king. Yet a line later he advances the permissibility of suicide for anyone confronting religious persecution based on that very same narrative. R. Me'ir perceives the non-comparability of royalty and commoners when the argument is against the killing of others but not when the argument is in its favor.

R. Me'ir's justification of murder using the previously cited *midrash* about Sha'ul is similarly incomprehensible. First, however, a word of introduction. The verses from Genesis were spoken to Noaḥ and his sons and have been interpreted by the Oral Law as applying to all Gentiles (the Noahide Laws). The specific demands on Jews were spelled out at Sinai and not after the Flood. However, as something could not be forbidden to Gentiles and at the same time permitted to Jews, the lacunae in the Sinaitic revelation may be filled by those restrictions found in the Noahide Laws. Now, there is no injunction in the Sinaitic revelation against suicide, hence this is an open area. The Talmud equally makes no normative statements about suicide. The Midrash, however, informs us that it is forbidden by the Noahide Laws, which *ipso facto* means that it is forbidden also to Jews. This being so, any allowance found in the suicide injunction holds for Jews no less than for Gentiles. |**100**|

R. Me'ir argues that the injunction against murder is derived from the final clause of the very same verse in Genesis that forbids suicide. Ergo, he argues, if the injunction against suicide is waived in times of religious persecution, so, too, is the injunction against murder. It would not be difficult to contest R. Me'ir's inference. However, even if it is correct, it would apply only to Gentiles, who received their laws in the revelation to Noaḥ after the flood, but not to Jews, who received their laws at Sinai, where God said to them (Exod. 20: 13), 'Thou shalt not kill.'[53] The suicide injunction for all derives from Genesis, and the prohibition of murder found there is for Gentiles only. No allowance for murder found in Genesis can apply to Jews. R. Me'ir's argument is valid only if one forgets the Seventh Commandment. We well understand why he began by saying that he was at a loss for an answer.

As we are about to leave the classic period of the Tosafists and venture into recently published fourteenth-century glosses and anonymous medieval works of unknown time and place, we would do well to address here the question that I initially posed. I think we can safely say that the classic writings of

[53] The Ten Commandments, having been addressed to Jews ('who took thee out of Egypt'), are viewed by the Oral Law as binding for Jews only.

the Tosafists, indeed, the very doctrines and arguments of their four greatest figures, Rabbenu Tam, R. Yitsḥak of Dampierre (Ri), R. Shimshon of Sens, and R. Me'ir of Rothenburg, all show such massive and atypical gaps in reasoning that we may conclude that something is deflecting their thought process from its normal course.[54] That something is, as I have suggested elsewhere, the conduct of their community in the persecutions of the Crusades that became culturally normative, indeed axiomatic, for the entire Ashkenazic world of the Middle Ages, so much so that they could not for a moment entertain the notion that their people's tragic sacrifices were not all sanctioned, even mandated, by the halakhah, and all scholars—great and small—read the talmudic texts in that light.

I trust that it will be equally clear that the Tosafists were not simply manipulating the sources to extract an allowance or making 'an emotional accommodation to their community's elevated self-image'. Rather, they were wholly, indeed passionately, convinced of the correctness of their interpretation. The principle undergirding their thought processes here is that of *reductio ad absurdum.* |**101**| The simplest readings of the relevant passages led to the impossible conclusion that the saintliest of martyrs, whose deeds were being held up as religious ideals, were, in reality, criminals. Obviously, then, the simplest reading was wrong. The entire point of this exercise has been to illustrate how convictions, when held so widely and so deeply as to constitute cultural axioms (and their converse, cultural absurdities), shape the hermeneutical process, however unwittingly, of even the greatest halakhists. I add this only because my previous remarks have been seriously misunderstood.[55]

Let us return to the sad matter of slaughtering children to prevent their being reared as Christians. At first blush, we do hear dissenting voices. In an anonymous medieval biblical commentary of Ashkenazic origin (though its exact time and place of origin cannot be determined) we find a striking passage that achieved widespread diffusion in the late Middle Ages. It is quoted in a Provençal work of the early fourteenth century, the *Orḥot Ḥayyim*, and again in a vast commentary on Maimonides' code written in Provence in the late fourteenth century.[56] After citing the allowance for slaughtering children

[54] If the report of R. Mosheh of Zurich is accurate (see below, n. 59) then R. Eli'ezer ben Yo'el (Ravyah), arguably the greatest of German Tosafists, should be added to this distinguished list.

[55] See Grossman, 'Shorashav shel Kiddush ha-Shem' (above, n. 6), 108, and Kanarfogel, 'Halakha and Metziut' (above, n. 6), 211.

[56] *Orḥot Ḥayyim*, ed. M. Schlesinger (Berlin, 1902), ii. 26–7: *Mezukkak Shiv'atayyim* (MS) fo. 71a by R. Yosef ben Sha'ul of the Kimḥi family, currently in the collection of Victor Klagsbald, Jerusalem. I would like to thank Mr Klagsbald for graciously allowing me access to the manuscript.

in times of persecution, our author proceeds:

And there are those who forbid [such slaughtering] . . . And they explain thus [the *midrash* on Sha'ul]: 'one might have thought that the aforesaid applies also to the case of Sha'ul, who surrendered himself to death, [therefore] the word "but" comes and teaches that one is not allowed to commit suicide, and what Sha'ul did, he did contrary to the opinion of the Sages.' [Signed] R. S. son of R. Avraham, known as Uchmann. There once was a rabbi [or teacher] who slaughtered many children in a time of persecution for he feared that they would be baptized. And there was another rabbi [or teacher] with him and he was furious at him and called him 'murderer', but the latter ignored [his remarks]. And that rabbi [or teacher] said, 'If I'm right, he [the slaughterer] will die a horrid death.' And so it happened. The Gentiles seized him and first flayed his flesh and then put sand between the skin and the flesh. And the persecution was halted and if he had not killed the children, they would have been saved.[57] |**102**|

The range of controversy, however, may well be smaller than first seems. Note that the rabbi in the story is not a parent—not even a family member. He is a stranger, though one of some religious authority. Power over life and death in these tragic instances seems generally to have been accorded by popular religion to parents alone. Almost all reports are of parental slaughter.[58] This might be attributable to some notion of *patria potestas*, but more probably to the instinctive feeling that only one who had to sacrifice his or her deepest attachments could be authorized to take such a step.

Be that as it may, it is in the early fourteenth century that we find the classic rationale for the slaughter of children—though since there is very little, if anything, that is original in the eclectic glosses of Rabbi Mosheh of Zurich to the *Semak*, it had probably been offered long before: |**103**|

And holy ones who slaughtered themselves and their children when they came to be tested, for they did not rely on their inner fortitude [*'al da'atan*] . . . and they feared that

[57] ויש שאוסרין ומפרשים כן: יכול כשאול—שמסר עצמו למיתה? ת"ל אך, פירוש שאינו יכול לחבול בעצמו כלל. ושאול שלא ברשות חכמים עשה. מהר"ש בר אברהם המכונה אוכמן. ומעשה ברב אחד ששחט הרבה תינוקות בשעת השמד, כי היה ירא שיעבירום על דת. והיה רב אחד עמו והיה כועס עליו ביותר וקוראו רוצח, והוא לא היה חושש. ואמר אותו רב אם כדברי יהרג אותו רב במיתה משונה. וכן היה, שתפסוהו עכו"ם והיו פושטין עורו ונותנין חול בין העור והבשר. ואחר כך נתבטלה הגזרה, ואם לא שחט אותן התינוקות היו ניצולין.

Tosafot ha-Shalem 'al ha-Torah: *Otsar Perushei Ba'alei ha-Tosafot*, ed. Y. Gellis (Jerusalem, 1982), i. 262. Cf. Grossman, 'Shorashav shel Kiddush ha-Shem (above, n. 6), 116; Kanarfogel, 'Halakha and Metziut' (above, n. 6), 211–16.

[58] The only other report known to me where children are killed by someone other than their parents and where, as in the case above, the outsider is a figure of religious authority, is that of R. Natan Eiger of Tübingen; see Y. Y. Yuval, *Ḥakhamim be-Doram* (Jerusalem, 1989), 173.

the Gentiles would force them to apostatize and that they would thereby desecrate the Name of God—they all have a share in the world to come and they are martyrs in the full sense of the word [*kedoshim gemurim*] . . . and from here [i.e. from their current state of innocence, which is similar to that of the soon-to-be-invoked case of the 'rebellious son'] they find support in a time of persecution to slaughter children, who do not know right from wrong, for we fear lest they assimilate among the Gentiles, becoming Gentiles, and it is 'preferable that they die virtuous rather than die as sinners'. For so we find with regard to the 'rebellious son' [Deut. 22: 18–21] that he is stoned for he is destined to rob [and murder in the course of robbery] his fellow creatures and desecrate the Sabbath [*San.* 72a].[59]

[59] **ואותם הקדושים ששחטו עצמן וזרעם כשבאו לידי ניסיון מפני שלא רצו לסמוך על דעתן . . . והיו יראים שיעבירום הגוים על דת ויהיה שם שמים מתחלל על ידיהם, כולם יש להם חלק לעולם הבא וקדושים גמורים הם . . . ומכאן סמכו לשחוט הילדים בשעת גזירה שאינם יודעים בין טוב לרעה לפי שאנו יראים פן ישתקעו בין הגוים בגויתן כשיגדלו, מוטב שימותו זכאים ואל ימותו חייבים, שכן מצינו גבי בן סורר ומורה שעל שם סופו ללסטם הבריות ומחלל שבתות, לפיכך הוא בסקילה. עד כאן לשון האבי העזרי.**

Semak Zurich, ed. Y. Y. Har Shoshanim-Rosenberg, i (Jerusalem, 1973), #6, p. 57 n. 19. Rabbi Mosheh of Zurich attributes this argument to R. Eli'ezer ben Yo'el (Ravyah, d. *c.*1225). Such a passage has yet to be found in the latter's works in print or manuscript. However, a similar allowance is, perhaps, found in his name in some manuscripts of a French work of the later 13th century, the *Kitsur Sefer ha-Mitsvot* of R. Avraham ben Efrayim. (MSS Paris, Bibliothèque Nationale 392 [written 1271], 393, 1408. The signature **אבי העזרי** is missing in MS Parma, De Rossi 813 and Moscow, RSL, Günzburg 1.) This passage, however, is missing from a second version of that work, MS Vatican 176. Nevertheless there seems no reason to doubt its accuracy. As for the astonishing line of reasoning contained therein: if Rabbenu Tam could argue the permissibility of suicide from the case of the 400 captives, Ravyah could equally argue for the allowance of murdering children from the case of the 'rebellious son'. The same mindset and hermeneutical process is at work. {It may well be that Ravyah gave this ruling orally, as it was, as we shall see (text, below, pp. 259–60), the most apt description of the contemporary situation. However, he recoiled from penning a ruling that invoked as precedent something that the Talmud had labeled a practical impossibility. An oral ruling would circulate on the periphery.} See also Ravyah's liturgical poem celebrating the joy that, to his mind—and also to the mind of his Ashkenazic brethren—both Avraham and Yitsḥak experienced at the time of the *'akedah*, cited and analyzed by S. Elitsur in her enlightening article "Akedat Yitsḥak: be-Vekhi o be-Simḥah? Hashpa'at Masa'ei ha-Tselav 'al ha-Sippur ha-Mikra'i ba-Piyyut', *'Et ha-Da'at*, 1 (1997), 22–3. See also *Ḥiddushei ha-Ritva 'al 'Avodah Zarah* (cited partially above, n. 47), 18a, s.v. *ha de-'amrinan*, in the name of *Gilyonei ha-Tosafot*. The passage from R. Avraham b. Efrayim's work was published by A. Y. Havatselet in Y. Buksboim, ed., *Sefer ha-Zikkaron le-Yitsḥak Yedidyah Frankel* (Jerusalem, 1993), 260–1. The passage is missing from MS Vatican 176, from which Havatselet claims to have published his text. He inadvertently added this passage from manuscripts of the second version of the *Kitsur Semag*. {The note requires immediate correction. No manuscript of the *Kitsur* has an allowance of killing children, only that of suicide, some attributing it to Ravyah, others not, with MS Vatican 176 being the exception as it makes no mention of either suicide or murder. The breakdown of the manuscripts is as the note states, except that MS Paris, Bibliothèque Nationale 393, like the Parma and Moscow MSS, does not contain this attribution to Ravyah. The *Kitsur Sefer ha-Mitsvot* of

Note that R. Mosheh refers to 'themselves and their children'. He mentions the widespread practice of parents, and it is this that he seeks to sanction. The problem with his analogy is simply that the law of the rebellious son was declared inoperative by the Oral Law, a declaration that found expression in the famous talmudic dictum 'there has never been, nor could there ever be a case of the rebellious son' (*lo hayah ve-lo 'atid lihyot*).[60] The inconceivability of punishing someone—and especially of meting out capital punishment—not for the commission of a crime but on the basis of a prognosis of crime made those biblical verses a halakhic impossibility. If the Palestinian sages of the first and second centuries could not condemn a rebellious son to death as the Pentateuch had ordered, how could a medieval parent condemn an innocent babe to death on the basis of this law? R. Mosheh's subliminal unease is noticeable from the redundant emphatic, *kedoshim gemurim* ('martyrs in the full sense of the word'). People who died for the 'sanctification of the Name' were, in point of simple fact, martyrs and no insistence on the matter was needed; indeed, it would sound tastelessly out of place. (Who suspected them of being anything else but martyrs?) Only if the case at bar was stretching the notion of martyrdom would the stressed affirmation be apropos. As Agnon once pointed out, only a Jew can be a *goy gamur*.

Much has been written about the killing of children—perhaps needlessly, for our shock should be less than it is. Just walk the children's ward of any hospital. |**104**| Children are being subjected to the most punishing chemotherapy in the hope of prolonging their lives. What parent would not condemn his child to several years of pain to gain for him a healthy life for some sixty, seventy years? And what are seventy years in comparison with an eternity? Convinced of the palpable reality of the afterlife, feeling its almost graspable closeness (and the chronicles breathe this assurance), husbands killed wives and parents dispatched their children with a swift stroke of the knife, certain that they were bestowing upon them the gift of eternal bliss.[61] If the afterlife is a fact, martyrdom is a bargain.

R. Avraham b. Efrayim has since been published from MS Vatican 176 by Y. Horowitz under the title *Kitsur Sefer Mitsvot Gadol* (Jerusalem, 2005), see p. 32 and the editor's n. 24 ad loc.}

[60] *Sanhedrin* 71a. See M. Halbertal, *Mahapekhot Parshaniyot be-Hithavutan: 'Arakhim ke-Shikkulim Parshaniyim be-Midreshei Halakhah* (Jerusalem, 1997), 46–66. {See the Afterword to this chapter, p. 285, #3.}

[61] e.g. E. Haverkamp, ed., *Hebräische Berichte über die Judenverfolgungen während des Ersten Kreuzzugs*, Monumenta Germaniae Historica. Hebräische Texte aus dem mittelalterlichen Deutschland 1 (Hanover, 2005), 285, 331, 355–9, 363, 377–9, 395, 413, 417, 431; A. M. Habermann, ed., *Gezerot Ashkenaz ve-Tsarfat* (Jerusalem, 1945), 31, 33, 35–7, 45, 47–9, 51, 55, 96, 102, 104. {To those modern souls who seem shocked by this conduct—and they have grown somewhat more vocal recently—I would point out

Then there was the revulsion. Franco-German Jewry saw themselves as living among murderous barbarians, little different from beasts.[62] The pride of place given to the warrior in feudal society was, in their eyes, an endorsement of violence and bloodshed.[63] Trial by ordeal revealed a people bereft of rational thinking and a society devoid of justice. Christians of the Midi, proud heirs of a millennia-old Roman culture, despised the northern barbarians; Ashkenazic Jews despised them even more. Perhaps the view of the 'natives' held by white settlers in Africa in the late nineteenth century came closest to those of Jewish parents in the medieval German Empire. The thought that their child might grow up as a murderous savage filled them with horror.

And, of course, there was Christianity, the religion of the 'hanging corpse' with its veneration of the 'whoring mother'. For a tiny minority to survive it must heighten every difference with the surrounding society and infuse it with loathing. Trinity was polytheism and the statues and figurines of Jesus in churches and homes were idolatry incarnate.[64] Every aspect of the Christian religion was subjected to ridicule and disgust,[65] |105| and the most difficult emotion to overcome is neither hatred nor contempt but disgust.[66] Without

William March's *The Bad Seed* (New York, 1954) in which a mother, discovering that her little daughter is a serial poisoner, kills her (or believes that she has killed her) and then commits suicide. The book became a million-copy best-seller. Readers found the mother's dilemma tragic, her solution harrowing but understandable—as did the viewers of the very successful Broadway play and Warner movie that were made of the novel. One may equally turn to Margaret Garnet's killing of her daughter to prevent her being returned to the South and to a life of slavery, which inspired Toni Morisson's *Beloved* (New York, 2000). See M. Reinhardt, *Who Speaks for Margaret Garnet* (Minneapolis and London, 2010). In both cases the mothers' thinking was 'this-worldly', as it were; neither of them believed, as did the parents in the Middle Ages, that the child's eternal fate was at stake.}

[62] e.g. the letter of 'Ovadyah ben Makhir in S. Spiegel, 'Mi-Pitgamei ha-'Akedah: Kedoshei Blois ve-Hitḥadshut 'Alilat ha-Dam', in M. Davis, ed., *Mordecai Kaplan: Jubilee Volume on the Occasion of his Seventieth Birthday* (New York, 1953), 286; 'Piyyutei Rabbi Barukh ben Shemu'el mi-Magentsa', ed. A. M. Habermann, in *Yedi'ot ha-Makhon le Ḥeker ha Shirah ha-'Ivrit*, 6 (1945), 96; the *seliḥah* of Avraham b. Shemu'el of Speyer in D. Goldschmidt and A. Fraenkel, eds., *Leket Piyyutei Seliḥot* (Jerusalem, 1993), i. 20 and *ad libitum*.

[63] e.g. A. M. Habermann, ed., *Piyyutei Shim'on ben Yitsḥak* (Jerusalem, 1938), 160–2.

[64] J. Katz, 'Sheloshah Ma'amarim Apologetiyim', *Zion*, 23 (1958), 181–94, repr. in id., *Halakhah ve-Kabbalah* (Jerusalem, 1984), 277–90.

[65] e.g. A. Sapir-Abulafia, 'Invectives against Christianity in the Hebrew Chronicles of the First Crusade', in P. W. Edbury, ed., *Crusade and Settlement* (Cardiff, 1985), 66–72 {repr. in id., *Christians and Jews in Dispute: Disputational Literature and the Rise of Anti-Judaism in the West (c. 1000–1150)*, Variorum Series (Aldershot, 1998), article XVIII.} For a list of derogatory terms for Christianity and its figures and symbols, see the appendix to Mordekhai Breuer's edition of the *Sefer Nitsaḥon Yashan* (Jerusalem, 1978), 195. For the obscene, Jewish retelling of the Gospels that has circulated since at least the 9th century, see S. Krauss, *Das Leben Jesu nach jüdischen Quellen* (Berlin, 1902).

[66] Moshe Halbertal once made this observation to me.

this primal, visceral reaction, the pressure to convert might become too strong. Much of the intuitive rejection of conversion in Ashkenazic communities came from the revulsion towards Christianity instilled from childhood.

Jews were, moreover, aliens and infidels in the society in which they found themselves, and their suffering filled them with bitterness. Rome had first destroyed their Temple and dispersed them in exile and now Rome (Christianity) was oppressing them daily. Esau, the symbol of Rome in talmudic literature, became identified with Christianity, and this fused identity, this charged symbol, only heightened Jewish hatred of the millennia-old arch-enemy.[67] Conversion was treason. It meant more than changing one's religion; it meant joining the persecutor, enlisting in the forces of the enemy. Having one's children brought up as Christians meant not only having them raised as savages, worshipping idols and venerating corpses, but also becoming the bloodstained persecutors of the Chosen People. And after a barbaric and sin-filled life, they would be condemned to an eternity of death. A swift stroke of the sword was perhaps seen as the greatest kindness that a parent could bestow upon a child.[68] **|106|**

Of all the arguments, that of the rebellious son is the most absurd and at the same time the truest. What had been inconceivable to the Palestinian sages of the first and second centuries—how could one foretell with absolute

[67] See G. Cohen, 'Esau as Symbol in Early Medieval Thought', in A. Altman, ed., *Medieval and Renaissance Studies* (Cambridge, Mass., 1967), 19–48, and repr. in the author's *Studies in the Variety of Rabbinic Cultures* (Philadelphia, 1991), 243–70.

[68] Modern research has not much emphasized the Jewish fear that their children would be raised as Gentiles, although the Crusade chronicles speak of it openly; e.g. **ארבעה ילדים יש לי, גם עליהם אל תחסו, פן יבאו הערילים הללו ויתפשום חיים ויהיו מקויימים בתעותעם.** in *Hebräische Berichte* (above, n. 61), 355; *Gezerot Ashkenaz* (above, n. 61), 34; **אלא כדי (להנצל) [להציל] בניי מיד בני עוולה, ושלא יהיו מקויימים בתעותם** (*Hebräische Berichte*, 377; *Gezerot Ashkenaz*, 37); **ונציל את בנינו מידם . . . אולי יהיו אילו מקויימים בטעותם** (*Hebräische Berichte*, 285; *Gezerot Ashkenaz*, 95). S. Goldin and B. Z. Kedar have justly redrawn attention to this salient consideration: S. Goldin, 'Yeladim Yehudim u-Misyonarizatsyah Notsrit', in Y. Bartal and Y. M. Gafni, eds., *Eros, Erusin vo-'Issurim; Miniyut u Mishpaḥuh ba-Historyah* (Jerusalem, 1998), 97–118. B. Z. Kedar, 'The Forcible Baptisms of 1096: History and Historiography', in K. Borchardt and E. Bünz, eds., *Forschungen zur Reichs-, Papst- und Landesgeschichte: Peter Herde zum 65. Geburtstag von Freunden, Schülern und Kollegen dargebracht* (Stuttgart, 1998), i. 187–200. Whatever problems there may have been in converting Jewish children against the wishes of the parents, if the parents were dead and no *patria potestas* existed, there was no conceivable bar to the validity of their conversion nor any practical bar to their being reared as Christians. See Kedar, ibid. 196–8; F. Lotter, 'Tod oder Taufe', in Haverkamp, ed., *Juden und Christen* (above, n. 3), 115–22, and W. Pakter, *Medieval Canon Law and the Jews* (Ebelsbach, 1988), 314–31. {See now David Berger's remarks in 'Jacob Katz on Jews and Christians in the Middle Ages', in Jay M. Harris, ed., *The Pride of Jacob: Essays on Jacob Katz and his Work* (Cambridge, Mass., 2002), 50; repr. in his *Persecution, Polemic and Dialogue: Essays in Jewish–Christian Relations* (Boston, 2010), 60.}

certainty that a child would become a murderer?—had become only too real for the tiny Jewish minority in medieval Europe. They could predict with frightening accuracy that a child would live a life of crime and infamy. Death in this world was a small price to pay to forestall a life of sin and death for an eternity; any caring parent would pay that price willingly.

This traumatic resolution may not have been taken suddenly and without warning but possibly had been in the process of formation for a decade or so prior to the First Crusade. B. Z. Kedar has noted that while most of the other *privilegia* granted by Henry IV to the communities of Worms and Speyer had long precedent behind them, the protection against forced baptism of their children was entirely new[69]—so new that six years earlier the recently formed community of Speyer had not sought such protection in its founding charter from the city's bishop, Rüdiger.[70] In Kedar's words:

> One may propose . . . that the forcible baptisms of 1096 did not arise *ex nihilo*, but that in the preceding decade, or even earlier, there came into being a streak of popular spirituality that led some Christians of the Rhineland to believe that it was their duty to baptize the offspring of the Jews even against their will. Such attempts at Christianization may well have been prompted by eschatological considerations; they may have been connected in some way with a wave of popular piety that . . . appears to have been especially prevalent in Germany's rural areas; Bernold of Constance mentions this movement under the year 1091.

A sword of Damocles may well have been hanging over the Jewish community for close to a decade and a decision may have been slowly, if indistinctly, forming in the minds of some, possibly of many. When the First Crusade struck, the Jewish community was suddenly confronted not with the nightmare of an individual tragedy but with the horror of the mass baptism of its offspring. In the heightened religious atmosphere, |**107**| a grim decision swiftly crystallized, born of desperation, defiance, and hope for a better life for the blameless children. Once that decision was taken, the suicides and the spouse-killing followed as a matter of course. What mother would wish to survive the sacrifice of her children by her own hand, what father would not wish to join them in the world to come?

The problem of the conversion of children highlighted the radically changed circumstances within which the halakhah now had to operate. In

69 Kedar, 'The Forcible Baptisms of 1096', 198–200.

70 J. Aronius, *Regesten zur Geschichte der Juden im Fränkischen und Deutschen Reiche bis zum Jahre 1273* (Berlin, 1902), #170, p. 73; A. Linder, *The Jews in the Legal Sources of the Early Middle Ages* (Detroit and Jerusalem, 1997), 400.

tannaitic times the Jews were in their own land, or, more precisely, the society in which the *tanna'im* lived and which they addressed resided in their own land. When oppressed by an occupying force far smaller than the indigenous population, the children of the martyrs would be raised by their own countrymen. In Exile, however, they would be raised by the murderers. The consequences of mass martyrdom were frightening. One would die for one's God, only to have one's child raised in the persecutor's faith. There were two paths open to the Jews. They could convert with their children and hope to raise them quietly as Jews until such time as they could flee or return openly to Judaism, or they could die as martyrs and take the children with them. During the Crusade both roads were taken.[71] There was even someone who chose the first route, saw his compatriots and their families massacred, and, out of guilt and shame, chose the second route for both his children and himself.[72]

The choice that now confronted the Jews probed the limits of the halakhah. The laws of martyrdom treat the issue of when one is obliged to lay down one's life. What happens after one is dead is irrelevant from a legal point of view but only too relevant in real life. The fate of the child of the now-dead martyr was outside the purview of halakhah but remained at the very center of Jewish concerns for religious continuance. Halakhah could not adequately address that burning question, so Jews addressed it on their own. Their solution was then endorsed by the halakhists; some even rationalized it after a fashion. The inadequacy of their answers was not simply because they were given after the bloody fact, but also because the received halakhah itself was inadequate to resolve the tragic question raised by their present condition: what was the point of Jewish martyrdom if the children would be reared as Christians? |**108**|

[End of Part I of the original article in *Jewish Quarterly Review*]

II

Having addressed the rationales for suicide and slaughter of kin offered by the Tosafists in the centuries following the first Crusades, let me now turn to

[71] Example of the first path: **מהם שאמרו: נעשה רצונם לפי שעה ונלך ונקבר את אחינו ונציל את בנינו מידם, כי תפשו הילדים אשר נשארו מתי מעט, לאמור אולי יהיו מקויימים בטעותם**, *Hebräische Berichte* (above, n. 61), 284–5; *Gezerot Ashkenaz* (above, n. 61), 95–6. Note also the full understanding and acceptance of their conduct by those Jews who refused to convert described in the immediately following passage: **אך הם לא סרו אחרי בוראם ולא נטו לבם אחרי הצלוב ודבקו בא-להי מרום**.

[72] *Hebräische Berichte*, 375–81; *Gezerot Ashkenaz*, 36–8.

the thoughts of the actors themselves; the rationales, if any, of the tragic protagonists. |278| Avraham Grossman opens his article on *kiddush ha-shem* by forcefully stating that no Jewish community in the Middle Ages 'dealt so extensively with this subject' (of martyrdom) as did the pre-Crusade Ashkenazic one.[73] To the best of my knowledge, not a single line—in print or in manuscript—discussing martyrdom is found in the literature of that community. Apparently, it is also to the best of Grossman's knowledge, seeing that he adduces no eleventh-century text that treats the subject. Thirty-five years of study of the pre-Crusade literature have yet to yield either of us a single deliberation on *kiddush ha-shem*.[74] Did the martyrs weigh their actions halakhically or did they act intuitively in a heightened state of religious dread and exaltation? We simply don't know, for not a word of justification is to be found in any of the numerous speeches in the Crusade chronicles. The argument has been made that they knew the passage in *Gittin* about the 400 boys and girls. No doubt they did; but there is no evidence that this passage played any role in the grim events that followed, no indication in the sources that desperate Jews of Mainz and Worms drew from it the strange conclusion that Rabbenu Tam drew a half-century later.

Much has been made of the existence of a Palestinian tradition justifying suicide and the murder of one's wife and children.[75] The key argument advanced is the midrashic passage about Sha'ul. Admittedly, *Bereshit Rabbah*, where the passage is found, is Palestinian; however, that *midrash* has nothing to do with suicide in times of religious persecution. The argument is also made that the mass suicide at Masada—described by Josephus and transmitted to the medieval Jewish community by *Sefer Yosippon*—served as precedent and justification, |279| for *Sefer Yosippon* was viewed as a halakhic source and possessed normative force. This claim raises both methodological and factual problems. It rests upon a note found in a very fine fifteenth-century Italian

[73] Grossman, 'Shorashav shel Kiddush ha-Shem' (above, n. 6), 99.

[74] Both Grossman, implicitly, and I. Marcus, explicitly, criticize my article 'Religious Law and Change: The Medieval Ashkenazi Example', *AJS Review*, 12 (1987), 208–13 {repr. in *Collected Essays*, i. 239–57}, for anachronistically judging 11th-century conduct by the halakhic standards of the 12th. I am somewhat perplexed by the criticism seeing that the article dealt exclusively with the Tosafists, assessing the rationales that they advanced in light of their own standards of evidence. No 11th-century rationales were ever evaluated for the simple reason that none exist. (Marcus's critique is registered in 'The Dynamics of Jewish Renaissance and Renewal', in M. A. Signer and J. Van Engen, eds., *Jews and Christians in Twelfth-Century Europe* [Notre Dame, Ind., 2001], 36.)

[75] Grossman, 'Shorashav shel Kiddush ha-Shem' (above, n. 6); id., 'Bein 1012 le-1096: ha-Reka' ha-Tarbuti ve-ha-Ḥevrati le-Kiddush ha-Shem be-Tatnu', in *Yehudim mul ha-Tselav* (above, n. 5), 55–73. A briefer English version is found in *Juden und Christen zur Zeit der Kreuzzüge* (above, n. 3), 74–91.

manuscript of the *Yosippon* that reads: 'And thus I have found written in a copy [of *Sefer Yosippon*] written by the great R. Gershom.'[76] David Flusser, the editor of the critical edition of *Yosippon*, announced that the scribe had in mind R. Gershom Me'or ha-Golah (d. 1028). Possibly; it doesn't make much of a difference. The manuscript would still be far and away the best one regardless who its scribe was, and no one would begrudge a scholar who devoted decades of his life to *Sefer Yosippon* the pleasure of thinking that he had arrived at the direct copy of a late tenth-century text written by Rabbenu Gershom Me'or ha-Golah himself. If, however, the argument is to be made that *Sefer Yosippon* had halakhic force in Ashkenaz *because* it was copied by Rabbenu Gershom Me'or ha-Golah, that is a very large claim indeed, and one must ask: on what basis do you state that it was copied by Rabbenu Gershom? The strength of evidence required for a claim depends on the weight of the argument that it is to support.

When great halakhic figures in the Ashkenazic culture refer to 'Rabbenu Gershom', we know that they have Rabbenu Gershom Me'or ha-Golah in mind. If they give the appellation 'great' to someone, we can assume that he was indeed a major thinker. Do we, however, have any idea whom an anonymous scribe in fifteenth-century Italy had in mind when he wrote 'the great Rabbenu Gershom'? Do we know that his assessment of 'greatness' is of any worth? All we know is that he copied it from a manuscript written by a Rabbi Gershom whom the scribe esteemed as a great man. It may well have been R. Gershom Me'or ha-Golah, who lived in Mainz close to half a millennium(!) earlier, and whose autographed manuscript made its way somehow to Italy and into our scribe's possession.[77] It may equally have been Rabbi Gershom, author of the *Sefer ha-Shalman*, of whose talmudic scholarship R. Menaḥem ha-Me'iri, no mean Talmudist himself, writes admiringly.[78] By the same measure, it may have been some local Italian luminary revered by his contemporaries.

Even assuming that the manuscript was, in fact, transcribed by R. Gershom Me'or ha-Golah, what gives the transcribed work halakhic force? **|280|** Admittedly, Rabbenu Gershom copied the Mishnah; it is no less true that he also copied some tractates of the Talmud, but these works had canonical

76 *Sefer Yosippon*, ed. D. Flusser, 2 vols. (Jerusalem, 1978–80) i. 4: כדברים האלה מצאתי כתוב בספר רבינו גרשום הרב הגדול מכתיבת ידו.

77 Though unlikely, it is not impossible. See e.g. A. Grossman, *Ḥakhmei Ashkenaz ha-Rishonim: Koroteihem, Darkam be-Hanhagat ha-Tsibbur, Yetsiratam ha-Ruḥanit mi-Reshit Yishuvam ve-'ad li-Gezerot Tatnu (1096)* (3rd edn., Jerusalem, 2001), 451, addendum to pp. 158–61.

78 *Seder ha-Kabbalah le-R. Menaḥem ha-Me'iri*, ed. S. Z. Havlin (Jerusalem, 1992), 140.

authority in Ashkenaz on their intrinsic merit, not because of the prestige of their scribe. It would be astonishing if a historical work had normative force in a legal system. In fact, it doesn't. A hundred and seventy years ago Leopold Zunz registered all the citations from the *Sefer Yosippon* in the halakhic literature that had been published. The work has been twice revised and updated, in 1892 and again in the Hebrew edition in 1947.[79] An examination of the citations shows that in every instance it is used either for geographical or for historical information. It was an invaluable database, indeed, almost the only source available to Ashkenazic scholars to fill in some of the factual lacunae in the Talmud or flesh out an elliptical narrative. The published literature has more than quadrupled since the last update; nevertheless, the picture of the work as having empirical rather than normative authority remains unaltered. I know of no place in the halakhic literature of Ashkenaz where *Sefer Yosippon* is ever invoked halakhically. Every rule has its exception and there is no reason why our case should be different. Should such an instance be found, the questions that need to be asked are: is the person citing it a well-known or a peripheral, even anonymous, figure? Is it being invoked as support for a halakhic truism or is it cited as a challenge to the verities of the canonized literature? Finally, is the issue that occasioned its invocation trivial or significant? Let us never forget that *Sefer Yosippon* is being relied on here by historians to sanction nothing less than murder.

At times one hears of *Sefer Yosippon* being described a bit more cautiously as having 'authoritative' and 'canonical' force in early Ashkenaz.[80] I am not quite

[79] *Die gottesdienstlichen Vorträge der Juden, historisch entwickelt* (Berlin, 1832), 151 note f. In the revised Hebrew translation of the 1892 edition, *Toledot ha-Derashot be-Yisra'el ve-Hishtalshelutan ha-Historit*, ed. C. Albeck (Jerusalem, 1947), 320–1. {The recent exhaustive study of Saskia Dönitz of the diffusion of *Sefer Yosippon* confirms my assessment; see S. Dönitz, *Überlieferung und Rezeption des Sefer Yosippon* (Tübingen, 2013), 239–46. This work, however, considerably undermines the value of the Rothschild manuscript, which, following Flusser, I have characterized above (p. 263) as 'far and away the best' manuscript.}

[80] This is my rendering of Grossman's **בעל סמכות וקדושה** in 'Shorashav shel Kiddush ha-Shem' (above, n. 6), 119, and again at p. 117 **'מקודשת'**. {Dönitz analyzed in detail (*Überlieferung und Rezeption* [above, n. 79], 246–61) the value attached by *Sefer Yosippon* to dying in battle for one's God as opposed to passive martyrdom (not to speak of suicide and murder of children) and has shown that it is a heroic, warrior death rather than quiescence and self-destruction that is valued and encouraged by that work. For this reason she rejects any significant influence of *Sefer Yosippon* on the conduct of Rhineland Jewry in 1096, or, more accurately, on the high value that the Crusade chronicles assigned to the Ashkenazic community's singular mode of martyrdom—suicide and murder of children. If any further proof were needed to discount the *Sefer Yosippon* as a source of this Ashkenazic practice, it can be found in the recent work of a research group at Scholion at the Hebrew University. Basing themselves in part on the work of the late S. Sela and in part on their own searches for passages from *Sefer*

sure just where to locate that fine line between 'authoritative' and 'normative'. However, the same strictures apply. In no place in the Ashkenazic literature is *Sefer Yosippon* invoked prescriptively. There is no hint in the numerous matter-of-fact citations that its authority ever went beyond factual accuracy.

Others contend that while it is true that *Sefer Yosippon* had no normative force in Ashkenaz, nevertheless, the heroism at Masada made a deep impression upon Palestinian culture and came, in time, to be seen as paradigmatic. This ideal was then transmitted to Ashkenaz by way of Italy and *Sefer Yosippon*. |**281**| This may well be true, but there is no evidence for it. Masada is never mentioned, to the best of my knowledge, in the entire Palestinian literature—halakhic, midrashic, or liturgical. Nor does this massive, multi-volume corpus ever endorse or even mention suicide and murder of children in times of religious persecution.

Surprisingly, none of the advocates of the so-called Palestinian posture regarding martyrdom mention the Yerushalmi. It would seem only reasonable that the Palestinian Talmud should be the first place to look for Palestinian attitudes and positions. A discussion of martyrdom is in fact found in the Yerushalmi, in two parallel and almost identical passages (so any fears of scribal error or omission are diminished, if not eliminated altogether).[81] The discussions are almost identical with those of the Bavli, as are their conclusions. Almost—but not quite. It would appear that the Yerushalmi forbids voluntary martyrdom, a topic about which the Bavli is silent.[82] |**282**| In other words, to the extent that the Yerushalmi differs from the Bavli, it differs in being more, rather than less, restrictive in the range of instances where martyrdom is permitted! The close congruence between the Bavli and the Yerushalmi should hardly surprise us here. The rules of martyrdom given in the Bavli come from Palestinian sources. The requirement of martyrdom in times of religious persecution (*she'at ha-shemad*) and in instances of public coercion (*be-farhesya*) is stated by R. Yoḥanan, a Palestinian *amora*, and the

Yosippon in the Genizah, they have concluded that there is good reason to think that *Sefer Yosippon* was as widely diffused and 'canonical' in Islamic lands as in Latin Europe, yet no suicide or murder of children arose there. See M. Ben-Sasson, 'Zikkaron ve-Shikheḥah shel Shemadot: 'al Kiddush ha-Shem be-'Artsot ha-Natsrut u-ve-'Artsot ha-'Islam bi-Yemei ha-Beinayim ha-Mukdamim', in Y. Hacker, B. Z. Kedar, and Y. Kaplan, eds., *Rishonim ve-'Aḥaronim: Meḥkarim be-Toledot Yisra'el Muggashim le-'Avraham Grossman* (Jerusalem, 2010), 51–2. {See also the Afterword, p. 284, #2.}

[81] *Sanhedrin* 3: 5, *Shevi'it* 5: 2; fos. 21b, 35a–b in the Venice edn.; cols. 1281–2 and col. 190 in the edn. of the Academy of Hebrew Language (Jerusalem, 2001). {It is indicative of the vagaries of contemporary scholarship in halakhic matters that the Palestinian tradition of martyrdom has been widely advocated for some three decades without anyone bothering to check the Yerushalmi.}

[82] See below, pp. 276–80.

famous *beraita* stating that 'it was resolved by a majority vote in the upper chambers of the house of Nitza in Lydda' that martyrdom is incumbent in all cases of forced idolatry, murder, and adultery or incest is, of course, Palestinian.[83] Even subsidiary discussions in the Bavli are either by a Palestinian *amora* or echo a Palestinian position.[84] In other words, the Palestinian position on martyrdom is found in the Bavli! Methodologically speaking, it is one thing to talk about a distinct and radically differing Palestinian tradition when there is a lacuna in the Yerushalmi. It is far more problematic when the topic is as fully discussed in the Yerushalmi as it is in the Bavli, and yet not a hint is to be found of any dissenting Palestinian tradition. There are no two traditions of martyrdom—an expansive Palestinan tradition and a restrictive Babylonian one. There is one, and only one, tradition: a Palestinian one, found equally in the Bavli and the Yerushalmi, and it is restrictive.

Having disposed of Palestinian influences, what evidence can we find for Italian ones? The answer: a bit, though scarcely enough to make a case. To be sure, the origins of the German community in liturgical poetry and theosophy are Italian and the famous and influential family of the Kalonymides—poets, scholars, and guardians of the esoteric lore of Ashkenaz—were proudly of Italian origin. This, however, is not true in halakhah, and, as for other areas, we simply do not know. *Sefer Yosippon* does describe the suicides at Masada, and we have one report, from Otranto in southern Italy possibly from the tenth century, in which a communal leader slit his own throat to avoid baptism. But no one has yet found any Italian precedent for the slaughtering of others, not to mention murdering one's children. *Sefer Yosippon* was known in Ashkenaz and there is an echo of it in two speeches of First Crusade martyrs who refer to entering Paradise as '[going] towards the Great Light'.[85] Was this simply an

83 *Sanhedrin* 74a–b. {The two sentences at the end of this paragraph replace the following in the original text: 'Not only does the evidence for the allowance of suicide and murder fail to meet the heightened standards demanded by the latter case, it fails to meet even the basic requirements of the former.' The new formulation makes the central point more clearly.}

84 The question whether the martyr imperative applies also to a Noahide is asked of Rav Ami, a Palestinian *amora*, and, understandably enough, is found in the Yerushalmi (above, n. 81). Even Rava's position of *hana'at 'atsmo* is equally advocated by the Yerushalmi (ibid.). The only position in the entire *sugya* of martyrdom that is not reproduced in the Yerushalmi is that of *kark'a 'olam*, which, as it is advanced by Abbaye contrary to Rava, would ordinarily be disregarded. For the Palestinian context of the Noahide question, see S. Lieberman, 'The Martyrs of Caesarea', *Annuaire de l'Institut de Philologie et d'Histoire Orientales et Slaves*, 7 (1939–44), 395–446. The Yerushalmi may well be less demanding of the Noahide than is the Bavli, at least according to Rashi's interpretation; see the so-called *Ḥiddushei ha-Ran 'al Sanhedrin* (Sulzbach, 1762), 75a, s.v. *ve-'im ita*.

85 *Hebräische Berichte* (above, n. 61), 289, 377; *Gezerot Ashkenaz* (above, n. 61), 37, 97: (אל המאור הגדול), and *Hebräische Berichte*, 287; *Gezerot Ashkenaz*, 97: (נבא ונראה באור הגדול). Cf. *Sefer Yosippon*

idiom of *Sefer Yosippon* that had entered the religious language of Ashkenaz, a turn of phrase used by individual speakers or by the authors of two of the Crusader chronicles some fifty years later? Or does it rather betoken, as the advocates of Italian influence would have it, a profound cultural saturation with the text and its values, an identification sufficiently powerful to impel mothers and fathers to slaughter their own children? The last suggestion is possible, but some might prefer sturdier evidence.

Truth to tell, we hardly know whether the above phrase was even uttered by any protagonist in the tragedy of 1096. I proudly count myself among the positivist historians, those thoroughly un-modern souls who take the accounts in the Crusade chronicle as being selective and hortatory but fairly accurate as far as they go. This, however, is not to say that I take the lengthy speeches by the participants in those chronicles as precise reportage. They appear to me as being more like the speeches found in Thucydides, correct in their overall thrust but reflecting what the writer imagines the participants would or ought to have said. |283| Even were I to believe in their overall accuracy, I would scarcely vouch for every phrase. Yet the entire link to *Sefer Yosippon* hinges on a two-word phrase in an exhortation.

Ironically the only source that links the conduct of the Jews to the account in Josephus is William of Newburgh, a Christian chronicler of the Third Crusade.[86] This is not surprising, as the Latin version of Josephus was viewed as a 'fifth Gospel' or 'little Bible' by early Christian writers, and copies were abundant in medieval Christian circles.[87] No medieval Jewish writer however, made that connection.

If I read the Crusade chronicles correctly, the Jewish community itself was amazed at its own deeds. So great was the surprise and so urgent the need for commemoration that it momentarily awakened the Ashkenazic community from its historiographical slumber. The literary outburst that mass voluntary martyrdom generated was unprecedented; never again were so many, such

(above, n. 76), 301, l. 26, and note ad loc. For a discussion of this term in *Yosippon*, see E. R. Wolfson, 'The Theosophy of Shabbetai Donnolo, with Special Emphasis on the Doctrine of *Sephirot* in *Sefer Ḥakhmoni*', *Jewish History*, 6 (1992), 295–6.

[86] William of Newburgh, 'Historia Rerum Anglicarum', in R. Howlett, ed., *Chronicles of the Reign of Stephen, Henry II and Richard II*, Rolls Series, no. 82 (London, 1884), i. 320: 'Verum qui Josephi de Judaico bello legit historiam satis intelligit ab antiqua Judaeorum superstitione, cum forte tristior casus incumberet, illam nostri temporis manasse vesaniam.'

[87] H. Schreckenberg, *Die Flavius-Josephus-Tradition in Antike und Mittelalter* (Leiden, 1972), 122–54 (William of Newburgh is not registered there). The documentation for 'little Bible' and 'Fifth Gospel' is found in id., 'The Works of Josephus and the Early Christian Church', in L. Feldman and G. Hatai, eds., *Josephus, Judaism and Christianity* (Detroit, 1987), 317.

lengthy, and such vivid chronicles to be written in that culture. The community's surprise was only natural. Everyone was astonished by the First Crusade: the French nobles, the German bishops, the Emperor, and the Pope himself.[88] No one anticipated the religious enthusiasm, the bellicosity, the mass mobilization, let alone the sustained intensity. Historians have struggled for close to two centuries to explain this eruption, and it remains somewhat of a mystery to this day.

Some of the religious atmosphere of the times can be reconstructed, but much still eludes us. It was thick with spiritual exaltation, possibly even with popular messianic overtones.[89] Certainly, the air was suffused with self-sacrifice for God, with the promise of remission of all sins and, perhaps, even with an assurance in the minds of most (if not necessarily in the thought of theologians) of eternal bliss that would come with the martyr's crown.[90] |284| The Jews may well have shared some of this exaltation, heightened as it was by very real messianic expectations in the next few years—by calculations foretelling the advent of the millennium by 1102.[91] When it became clear that they would be the first to pay the price for the newly found form of Christian devotion, many were determined not to be outdone by the 'corpse worshippers' in dedication and self-sacrifice. They, too, could die for their God and offer up not only their life and property, but also their priceless children on the altar of God's devotion. Their baptism would further be taken by the uncircumcised as confirmation of the promise of the Gospels and their conversion hasten, in their persecutors' mind, the long-awaited *eschaton*. Never would they allow their tormentors this satisfaction; never would they be befouled by the impure waters or allow their children to be raised in barbarism and eternal

[88] H. E. Mayer, *The Crusades* (Oxford, 1988), 9–36.

[89] See S. Schein, 'Die Kreuzzüge als volkstümlich-messianische Bewegung', *Deutsches Archiv für Erforschung des Mittelalters*, 47 (1991), 119–38.

[90] Whether the notion that death conferred martyrdom on the Crusader antedated the Crusader expedition or was formed in its course is a much-disputed issue. See, most recently, J. Flori, *Pierre l'Ermite et la première croisade* (Paris, 1999), 216–21, and the literature there cited. However, all agree that the Crusader's death—as a faithful soldier of his Divine lord—was seen as a noble one and that it achieved for him remission of all his sins. How thick or thin a line differentiated this in public preaching and popular perception from 'martyrdom' is moot.

[91] *Hebräische Berichte* (above, n. 61), 247; *Gezerot Ashkenaz* (above, n. 61), 24, 72; S. Emanuel, 'Ḥeshbon ha-Luaḥ ve-Ḥeshbon ha-Kets: Pulmus Yehudi–Notsri bi-Shenat 1100', *Zion*, 63 (1998), 151–7.

[92] D. Malkiel's argument in 'Destruction or Conversion: Intention and Reaction, Jews and Christians, in 1096', *Jewish History*, 15 (2001), 257–80 {reiterated in his *Reconstructing Ashkenaz: The Human Face of Franco-German Jewry, 1000–1250* (Stanford, 2009), 73–94}, leaves unexplained why Jews committed suicide in community after community and went so far as to murder their spouses and children. By his reading, we must posit some overwhelming aversion to death by Gentile hands,

error.[92] And if the preceding decades had witnessed the kidnapping and forced conversion of their children, as the imperial *privilegia* of 1090 would lead one to suspect,[93] many in these communities had long contemplated, and some had even resolved, what their response would be *in extremis*, |285| when confronted with the certainty of the forced conversion of their children.

We may well understand some of their vehement emotions, but what impelled them, what allowed them to act upon these feelings? When and how did the iron enter their souls to execute these dread resolutions? We simply don't know. The Jewish response to the First Crusade is much like that Crusade itself: the magnitude of the events dwarfs their known causes. In the elevated thoughts and grim deeds of all the protagonists there are 'depths of light and darkness which posterity can observe with reverence or with horror, but which its short fathom-line cannot plumb'. Rather than create centuries-long traditions of martyrdom where none existed or turn wisps of Italian evidence into proofs strong as Scripture, let us simply admit to our own ignorance.

III

I have discussed so far the literature of the Tosafists; I would like to turn now to their codes. The *Sefer Yere'im*, authored by R. Eli'ezer of Metz, a pupil of Rabbenu Tam, makes no mention of any of his teacher's rulings on *kiddush ha-shem*.[94] The great tosafist code of the mid-thirteenth century, the *Sefer Mitsvot Gadol*, equally makes no mention of the teachings of Rabbenu Tam and Ri on the subject, even though the work is saturated with their thought, and their doctrines are generally writ large on every page.[95] The popular abridgment of that work, the *Semak*, does speak of the permissibility of voluntary martyrdom, but makes no mention of suicide or of the necessity of enduring

strong enough to overcome both the instinct of self-preservation and the inhibitions of murder of one's own children! Seeing that there is no prior or subsequent record of such an aversion, the conduct of the Jewish communities in the First Crusade becomes a series of Jonestown massacres. Later generations then rewrote history and turned the demented into heroes by attributing their deeds to a horror of Christianity and baptism. To my thinking the supposed conflict between the sources is illusory. Once the massacres began, conversion may not have helped in many cases and there was undoubtedly no lack of bloodlust among the Crusaders. They lusted, however, for the blood of 'Jews', not that of 'New Christians', to use an anachronism. Given the passions aroused, not every 'New Christian', nor even every newly Christianized community, would have been spared. Generally speaking, however, both Jewish and Latin chroniclers believed that timely conversion would have averted much of the bloodbath.

93 See B. Z. Kedar's article, 'The Forcible Baptisms of 1096: History and Historiography' (above, n. 68).

94 *Sefer Yere'im ha-Shalem*, ed. A. A. Schiff (Vilna, 1891), ##340, pp. 403–5.

95 *Semag ha-Shalem*, ed. E. Schlesinger (Jerusalem, 1995), Imperatives ##3, 5; Injunction #2.

torture.[96] In fact, other than in the gloss of R. Perets of Corbeil, who justifies, though he does not advocate, suicide, and in one version of the wholly uninfluential, indeed generally unknown, *Kitsur Semag* of R. Avraham ben Efrayim, who similarly justifies the murder of children in almost identical language to that of R. Mosheh of Zurich,[97] |286| we will search in vain the codificatory literature, down to and including the *Shulḥan 'Arukh*, for any mention of suicide or of enduring torture, not to speak of committing murder.[98] To say that voluntary martyrdom is permissible is to state an option; to advocate suicide or suffering torture is another matter. Any good *posek* knows how far his writ runs, and who is to dictate the choice if the law is not crystal clear? As deep as his conviction may be, the wise judge holds his peace. The laws of martyrdom found in the Talmud are indeed binding, and any codifier must mention them. To do less would be to misrepresent the law. Eliciting conduct above and beyond that norm is the task of the educator, not the jurist. Preferring suicide and torture to apostasy became a cultural norm in Ashkenaz—it was never made a legal one. Needless to say, neither did the slaughter of children.

Yet in one area and among one very influential group of Tosafists, conduct beyond the talmudic norm *was* made prescriptive. One cannot leave the topic of *kiddush ha-shem* in Ashkenaz without noting the emergence, in the latter half of the thirteenth century, of a new demand—suffering death to avoid dressing as a Gentile or denying one's Jewishness, an obligation wholly unknown to prior generations, tested as they had well been in *kiddush ha-shem*.

The Yerushalmi offers two explanations as to why the Mishnah in *'Avodah Zarah* assumes that Jewish men in captivity are in mortal danger but Jewish women are not. The first is that, while men are generally killed, women's lives are spared—they are kept in captivity for sexual use. Second, a woman can claim to be Gentile, while a circumcised man cannot.[99] This passage is discussed by R. Elḥanan and his successors—R. Shimshon of Sens and the editors of our printed *Tosafot*—all with no sense that it had any bearing on

96 *Sefer Mitsvot Katan*, #3. The numerous manuscripts register no significant variants. Admittedly, MS London, British Library 1056 (arguably the oldest extant manuscript) lacks the passage on voluntary martyrdom. However, unless this is an earlier version of the *Semak*—the popular acronym of *Sefer Mitsvot Katan*—which would be very surprising, the presence of this passage in all other manuscripts of the work attests to its authenticity.

97 Ibid. One should emphasize (in contradistinction to the text of the *Semak* referred to in the previous note) that the gloss found in the standard editions of the *Semak* permitting suicide is *not* that of R. Perets of Corbeil but is a later addition by an unknown editor. The gloss is not found in the earliest dated manuscripts of the *Semak*, such as MSS Parma, De Rossi 189 (dated 1297), Oxford, Bodley 877 (dated 1297), and Oxford, Bodley 875 (dated 1299).

98 'Yoreh De'ah', 157.

99 *'Avodah Zarah* 2: 1, fo. 40c in the Venice edn.; col. 1383 in the edn. of the Academy of Hebrew Language (above, n. 81).

the issue of martyrdom.[100] |287| R. Yitsḥak Or Zarua' of Vienna (fl. first half of the thirteenth century), however, cites this Yerushalmi passage and writes that the two interpretations stem from an underlying controversy concerning whether one is permitted to present oneself as a Gentile in times of danger.[101] This is an atypical way for medieval scholars to understand a talmudic passage. The Talmud sometimes says that a disagreement on A reflects a disagreement on B, but the usual approach taken by talmudic commentators is to attribute a difference of opinion to some disagreement about a principle in the area under discussion, not to make it the function of a problem in a wholly different legal domain. The impression received is that the problem of posing as a Gentile was being raised in the time of R. Yitsḥak, and he was searching for some text in which to anchor the problem. Be that as it may, a generation later a pupil of R. Me'ir of Rothenburg reports his teacher to have ruled that dressing as a Gentile to avoid danger was strictly forbidden.[102] Something is clearly at work here. *Sefer Ḥasidim* gives the unmistakable impression that the use of Gentile dress to escape harm was common practice in Germany—aggadic passages could be adduced to validate this practice.[103] Moreover, *Sefer Ḥasidim* does not see anything wrong with it. The only proviso that the author of that work attaches to the practice is to insist that Jews prepare for this contingency by ensuring that such 'Gentile clothes' contain no *sha'atnez*.[104]

R. Me'ir's pupil, R. Asher (d. 1327), echoes his teacher's remarks in his *Pesakim* on *Bava Kamma*, and in *'Avodah Zarah* he writes forcefully about the very Yerushalmi passage that the *Or Zarua'* had discussed: 'one cannot infer

[100] *Tosefot R. Elḥanan 'al 'Avodah Zarah* 25b, s.v. *ika*, end. Note the phrase 'and I saw in the Yerushalmi'; it is R. Elḥanan speaking here rather than his father, Ri. *Tosefot Rash mi-Shants 'al 'Avodah Zarah* 25b, s.v. *ishah*; *Tosafot*, *'Avodah Zarah* 25b, s.v. *ika*.

[101] *Or Zarua'*, iv (Jerusalem, 1887), *'Avodah Zarah*, #143.

[102] *Haggahot Maimuniyot*, 'Yesodei ha-Torah', 5: 3, n. 5.

[103] *Ta'anit* 22a, *Me'ilah* 17a, *Bereshit Rabbah*, #82, cited by R. Margaliot (below, n. 104), though one should note that the pungent closing reply: **אלא שאין דרכו של אדם לאבד את עצמו לדעת** is absent in most manuscripts and equally in the *Yalkut Shim'oni*; see C. Albeck's remarks in his and J. Theodor's edition of *Bereshit Rabbah*, ii. 984–5. Indeed, R. Y. Ḥaviva, in *Nimmukei Yosef*, *Alfasi*, *Bava Kamma* 113b (Vilna edn., fo. 40b), arguing for the permissibility of such dressing, cites this passage from *Bereshit Rabbah*. See also *Sefer ha-'Eshkol*, ed. S. Albeck (Jerusalem, 1935), ii. 132.

[104] {*SHP*, ##203–5}, *Sefer Ḥasidim*, ed. R. Margaliot (Jerusalem, 1964), #199. (This is an annotated edition of the *Sefer Ḥasidim* published in Bologna in 1538; it is referred to below as *SHB*.) R. Yisra'el Isserlein in the late 15th century already noted that the position of *Sefer Ḥasidim* is contrary to the ruling of R. Asher. See *Terumat ha-Deshen*, ed. S. Avitan (Jerusalem, 1991), #197. {Note should be made of *SHP*, #258, where the Pietist states that it is *middat ḥasidut* (an act of piety, over and above the legally requisite) to identify oneself as a Jew whenever one is taken for a Gentile. This supererogatory demand, however, is a general one and is not restricted to instances when knowledge of one's Jewish identity might result in persecution or death.}

from this Yerushalmi that it is permissible to pass oneself off as Gentile, for this is certainly apostasy'.[105] This opinion does not go unqualified in the late Middle Ages, but such was the influence of R. Asher that this view is cited in the *Shulḥan 'Arukh*.[106] |288|

The lights were going out for the Jews in western Europe in the latter half of the thirteenth century. The conversionary offensive of the Church, backed by royal power and coupled with a ruthlessly enforced policy of exorbitant tallage, had broken the back of the Jewish community in England by the 1260s.[107] At the same time, Louis IX's campaign against Jewish moneylending, together with his deep-seated animosity towards Jews and Judaism, had seriously weakened the French Jewish community as well.[108] The following decades witnessed the brutal mass seizures of Alphonse of Poitiers in the 1280s; the blood libel and execution of the Jews of Troyes in 1288 and the expulsion from Gascony; the further expulsion from Anjou and Poitiers in 1289; the accusation of host desecration in Paris in 1290; the expulsion from Nevers in 1294, and, finally, the expulsion from the Kingdom of France in 1306.[109] In Germany the breakdown of imperial power, which had largely stood as a bulwark against the rising tide of popular antisemitism, boded ill for the Jewish community. In 1287 the Good Werner pogroms occurred—the first large-scale regional massacre of Jews in Germany since the First Crusade, some two centuries before.[110] This proved to be only a prelude to the even

[105] *Piskei ha-Rosh*, *Bava Kamma* 10: 11; *'Avodah Zarah* 2: 4. {Rabbenu Asher sees a statement of one's faith, or implying the same with one's dress, as identical with a profession of faith. Most halakhists would view this as a legal stretch. Saying that one is a Christian may be a statement that one has in the past converted to Christianity or that one has been born to Christian parents. Even the avowal of a past conversion is scarcely identical with the recitation of the Credo, which constitutes the formal acceptance of Christianity. It is the latter, the criminal act of apostasy (*ha-mekabbel 'alav le-'eloah* [*San.* 60b]) or that of *'avodah zarah* that falls within the martyr imperative, not an account of such earlier offenses. Narrative statements about past sins would not even fall within the orbit of *avizraya*. *Avizraya* must be linked in some way with an act of worship, a *ma'aseh 'avodah zarah*. It must entail some devotional element such as invoking the intercession of a saint or acceptance of some lesser figure in the religion's hierarchy, such as acknowledging Mary as the Queen of Heaven.}

[106] See *Haggahot Mordekhai*, *Sanhedrin*, #719 (Vilna edn., fo. 23b); *Terumat ha-Deshen*, #197; 'Yoreh De'ah', #157: 2. {See also the discussion in the inner gloss of the *Semak*, MS JTS, Rabb. 653, fos. 10v–11r, in the name of an 'old book' (*sefer yashan*).}

[107] R. Stacey, '1240–1260: A Watershed in Anglo-Jewish Relations', *Bulletin of the Institute of Historical Research*, 61 (1988), 135–50.

[108] W. C. Jordan, *The French Monarchy and the Jews from Philip Augustus to the Last Capetians* (Philadelphia, 1989), 142–76, esp. p. 161.

[109] Ibid. 179–235.

[110] G. Mentgen, 'Die Ritualmordaffäre um den "Guten Werner" von Oberwesel und ihre Folgen', *Jahrbuch für Westdeutsche Landesgeschichte*, 21 (1995), 159–98.

bloodier Rintfleisch massacres (1298) that destroyed scores of communities in Franconia, Bavaria, and Austria.[111]

The Jewish badge, which had not hitherto made its way into any German legislation, was made mandatory by the Schwabenspiegel issued around the year 1275. This had been preceded a few years earlier, in 1267, by the decrees of the church councils of both Vienna and Breslau. Two years later Louis IX began strict enforcement of the badge in France, and Philip IV made it a source of royal revenue, demanding in 1281 that the Jews pay a yearly fee for the badge.[112] |289| Being marked by one's dress as a Jew was becoming more of a trial every day—not only of humiliation but also of danger. Did some Jews in Germany seek to elude the stigma and peril and achieve some anonymity and safety by dispensing not simply with the Jewish badge but more generally with their distinctive dress? Nothing would be more natural. The first to raise the issue of non-identification and seek some legal resolution to the question was R. Yitsḥak Or Zarua', who was in Paris at the time of the proclamation of the edicts of the Lateran Council. He reports the discussions on the halakhic issues that would arise by the wearing of the badge on the Sabbath.[113] His anchoring of the question of non-identification in the Yerushalmi may be an attempt to find guidance in the canonical literature for the emerging problems of self-denial by word or by garb. Initially, the badge requirement was rarely implemented and was, hence, little discussed. However, some fifty years later, both in France and in Germany, it began to be enforced, and in a perilously hostile atmosphere wherein being marked as a Jew invited insult and even injury. Is the reaction of R. Yitsḥak's pupil, R. Me'ir of Rothenburg, a response to this new imposition and to the growing temptation to disengage from one's religious identity in the public arena? It is an attractive conjecture but no more than that. In this singular, late thirteenth-century development in the laws of martyrdom there is a perceptible angle of measurable deflection. Something is clearly impinging on the thought processes of two great Talmudists, R. Me'ir of Rothenburg and R. Asher, as was earlier the case in the thinking of even

[111] F. Lotter, 'Die Judenverfolgung des "König Rintfleisch" in Franken um 1298. Die endgültige Wende in den christlich-jüdischen Beziehungen im Deutschen Reich des Mittelalters', *Zeitschrift für historische Forschung*, 15 (1988), 385–422.

[112] S. W. Baron, *A Social and Religious History of the Jews* (New York and Philadelphia, 1952–83), ix. 27–32, xi. 96–106; G. Kisch, *The Jews in Medieval Germany* (repr. New York, 1970), 295–9; R. Strauss, 'The "Jewish Hat" as an Aspect of Social History', *Journal of Jewish Social Studies*, 4 (1942), 59–72. The overall situation in England was, if anything, even worse; see R. C. Stacey's summary article with bibliography, 'Yahadut Angliyah ba-Me'ah ha-Shelosh-'Esreh u-Ve'ayat ha-Gerush', in D. S. Katz and Y. Kaplan, eds., *Gerush ve-Shivah* (Jerusalem, 1993), 9–25.

[113] *Or Zarua'*, ii (Zhitomir, 1862), 'Hilkhot Shabbat', #3.

greater figures, Rabbenu Tam and Ri, on suicide—but what that force was we cannot say with certainty.

IV

Having already mentioned that *Sefer Ḥasidim* permitted dressing as a Gentile, I would like to address briefly the posture of Ḥasidei Ashkenaz regarding martyrdom and then conclude my study with a discussion of the tosafist stance on voluntary martyrdom, not simply for the sake of comprehensiveness, but also because it further illustrates the caution one must use in arguing for an 'angle of measurable deflection'. **|290|**

Martyrdom has sometimes been presented as central to the thought of the German Pietists, and emphasis has been given to the depth of their aspirations to attain it.[114] Surprisingly, one would not know this from their writings on *kiddush ha-shem*. They make no mention of either suicide or the slaughter of kith and kin. They know, as did the Tosafists, of the permissibility of voluntary martyrdom, but nowhere do they advocate it. On the contrary, they decry those who purposely place themselves in situations where martyrdom will be required of them.[115] The willingness to suffer martyrdom is taken as a given, and the Ḥasid writes, in advising how to resist temptation: 'Think if you were living in a time of persecution, you would be suffering death or torture for . . . [love] of God . . . and if they wished to kill you or torture you, in which we [Jews] choose death over life, you would suffer, how much more so [should you be ready to suffer in this case of temptation] where [the cost] is not so great.'[116] But other than forbidding men to dress as monks or priests to avoid the danger of being killed as a Jew—though a woman was permitted to dress

[114] Y. Baer, 'Ha-Megamah ha-Datit-Ḥevratit shel *Sefer Ḥasidim*', *Zion*, 3 (1938), 14–15; repr. in id., *Meḥkarim u-Masot be-Toledot 'Am Yisra'el* (Jerusalem, 1986), 188–9; Y. Dan, 'Be'ayat Kiddush ha-Shem be-Toratah ha-'Iyyunit shel Tenu'at Ḥasidut Ashkenaz', in *Milḥemet Kodesh u-Martirologyah be-Toledot Yisra'el u-ve-Toledot ha-'Amim* (Jerusalem, 1968), 121–9; id., *'Al ha-Kedushah: Dat, Musar u-Mistikah ba-Yahadut u-ve-Datot Aḥerot* (Jerusalem, 1997), 272; Grossman, 'Shorashav shel Kiddush ha-Shem' (above, n. 6), 111.

[115] *Sefer Ḥasidim* (above, n. 30), #251. *SHP*, #251, cites two views as to the permissibility of knowingly entering situations that will demand martyrdom; however, #776 speaks out against doing so, as does *SHB* (above, n. 104), #955. Both express only opposition to such danger-fraught conduct. This is not an unusual occurrence. *SHP* will present two views in one passage and in another rule in accord with one of the positions. In such cases *SHB* usually adopts the decision found in *SHP*. See e.g. *SHP*, ##1714, 857, 181–5, and *SHB*, ##317, 684–6, 188–9.

[116] *SHP*, #2 (pp. 4–5), *SHB*, #155 (p. 157). See, for a later period, the remarks of R. Ya'akov Molin: **ומעשים בכל יום המתפרצים בבני עמנו בג"ע [בגלוי עריות] ואקידוש הי"ז [ה' יתעלה זכרו] זהירים טפי מאחריני**. *Teshuvot Maharil*, ed. Y. Satz (Jerusalem, 1980), #72 (pp. 94–5).

as a nun in order to avoid rape[117]—they have no special teaching about martyrdom. When one chooses martyrdom, and in what circumstances it must be endured, are not subjects to which the German Pietists gave any special thought or about which they made any special demands. The Pietist suffered martyrdom on the same occasions as did the non-Pietist.

Ḥasidei Ashkenaz discuss the rewards that await a person who wages war on his basic instincts, suffers humiliation for his hasidic principles, and avoids looking at women, but they speak little, if at all, of the rewards of the martyr. |291| The hasid is never defined by any special aspiration for martyrdom or even willingness to suffer for his faith.[118] There are various passages defining *ḥasidut* and the traits that make for a hasid.[119] In most of them, no mention is made of martyrdom; in one or two, the desire to sanctify the Name is mentioned, but alongside a series of other characteristics, such as abandoning all worldly concerns or acting for the common weal (*le-zakkot et ha-rabbim*).[120] In no passage, however, is martyrdom given pride of place. To be sure, the hasid preferred to end his life as a martyr, and in the absence of such bliss he consoled himself with the thought that the willingness to suffer martyrdom was equivalent in God's eyes to martyrdom itself.[121] This, however, is a common enough aspiration among the deeply religious, Jewish or Christian, Catholic or Protestant.[122] There is little that is unique in the hope that death will be the climax of one's life rather than a meaningless ending, or in the desire to freely surrender one's life for the love of God rather than to be stripped of it helplessly for no purpose. The German Pietists knew, as pietists around the world have always known, that dying for God was easier than living for Him. 'Spiritual martyrdom'—the continuous sacrifice of one's most basic instincts

[117] *SHB*, ##199–201; *SHP*, ##259–61 {#202 equally forbids wearing a cross}.

[118] Martyrdom is never mentioned in 'Shoresh ha-Ḥasidut' of R. El'azar of Worms. In fact, it is mentioned only once in passing in the entire 'Hilkhot Ḥasidut' found in R. El'azar's *Sefer ha-Roke'aḥ* (Jerusalem, 1960). It is noticeably absent from the many descriptions and ruminations on the soul's fate in the afterlife found in the *Ḥokhmat ha-Nefesh* (Safed, 1913).

[119] e.g. *SHP*, #2 (p. 5), 975–8, 982, *SHB*, ##7, 9, 10; *Sefer ha-Roke'aḥ*, 'Hilkhot Ḥasidut', 'Shoresh ha-Ḥasidut'; {*Perush ha-Tefillot* cited by Urbach in his introduction to *'Arugat ha-Bosem*, iv. 103. See *Perushei Siddur ha-Tefillot la-Roke'aḥ*, ed. M. Herschler and Y. A. Herschler (Jerusalem, 1992), ii. 513.}

[120] *SHP*, #815 (p. 206), *SHB*, #14, taken from *Sefer ha-Roke'aḥ*, 'Shoresh Ahavah'.

[121] *SHP*, ##263–4, *SHB*, #222.

[122] See L. Gougaud, *Dévotions et pratiques ascétiques du Moyen Age* (Paris, 1925), 200–19. Gregory the Great's determination, 'unum in mente, aliud in mente simul in actione', is cited on p. 203; E. Randolph Daniel, 'The Desire for Martyrdom: A *Leitmotif* in St. Bonaventure', *Franciscan Studies*, 32 (1972), 74–87. For a rich discussion, see B. S. Gregory, *Salvation at Stake: Christian Martyrdom in Early Modern Europe* (Cambridge, Mass., 1999).

for the love of God—occupied a far larger role in hasidic thought than physical martyrdom ever did.[123]

At the outset of the essay I made mention of Maimonides' position forbidding voluntary martyrdom. It is an open question what the Talmud intended when it ruled: 'With all other commandments [that is, other than idolatry, murder, and incest and adultery] should one be threatened "transgress or be killed," [one should] transgress [*ya'avor*] and not be killed.' |292| One can translate *ya'avor* equally as 'he may transgress' or 'he must transgress', as Hebrew knows no difference in the imperfect tense between the jussive and the imperative. Unlike suicide, where the position itself is problematic, involuntary martyrdom questions arise from the mode of argument and not from the doctrine itself.

Maimonides' restrictive ruling awakened opposition in the German Empire almost as soon as his work became known there.[124] Whether it generated opposition in France is not clear. In the early decades of the thirteenth century Ri's successor in Dampierre, R. Yitsḥak ben Avraham, assumed as a matter of course that voluntary martyrdom was forbidden.[125] In the next generation R. Mosheh of Coucy, author of the *Semag*, pointedly avoided taking a stand on the issue or even mentioning it. Even though he based his work in part on the *Mishneh Torah* and wrote with that book open in front of him, editing and transcribing large sections of it into his own oeuvre, he made no mention of the issue. Things began to change in the mid- to late thirteenth century. Our printed *Tosafot* dating from that period adds that voluntary martyrdom is permitted.[126] The tosafist position seems to have emerged without the negative stimulus of the *Mishneh Torah*, and its position was bolstered by a misquotation from the Yerushalmi.[127] This misquotation merits our attention.

In tractate *Sanhedrin*, and again in *Shevi'it*, the Yerushalmi in effect repro-

[123] Cf. A. Rush, 'Spiritual Martyrdom in St. Gregory the Great', *Theological Studies*, 23 (1962), 572–5, 579–80.

[124] Avraham ben 'Azri'el, *'Arugat ha-Bosem*, iii. 194–5.

[125] See below, n. 134. This may equally have been the position of R. Shemu'el ben Me'ir, Rashbam, a century earlier; see S. Japhet and R. B. Salters, *The Commentary of R. Samuel ben Meir, Rashbam, on Qoheleth* (Jerusalem, 1984), 101 (on 7: 15). Controversy exists as to whether the commentary was actually authored by Rashbam. I tend to believe that it was. I was referred to this passage by S. Goldin, *'Alamot Ahevukha, 'Al-Mavet Ahevukha* (Lod, 2002), 238; English translation: *The Ways of Jewish Martyrdom* (Turnhout, 2008), 232.

[126] Between the years 1244 and 1251; see *Tosafot, 'Avodah Zarah* 9b, s.v. *hai*. (There is no certainty as to the dates, as these *Tosafot* underwent final editing in the seventh or eighth decade of the 13th century in the school of R. Perets of Corbeil.)

[127] *'Avodah Zarah* 27b, s.v. *yakhol*. It is not to be found in the two earlier *Tosafot* on this tractate, *Tosefot R. Elḥanan* 18a, s.v. *mutav*; and *Tosefot Rash mi-Shants* 18a, s.v. *mutav*.

duces the discussion and rulings of the Babylonian Talmud. Only one additional story is narrated there, which runs thus:

R. Ba bar Zamina was sewing at [the home of] someone in Rome. He [the Roman] brought him some non-kosher meat [*nevelah*] and said, 'Eat it.' |293| He [R. Ba] replied, 'I won't eat it.' He [the Roman] said, 'Eat it or I will kill you.' He [R. Ba] replied, 'If you wish to kill me, do so, I will not eat non-kosher meat.' He [the Roman] then said, 'Who informed you that had you eaten, I would have killed you? A Jew [must conduct himself as] a Jew, a Gentile [as] a Gentile.' R. Mena commented [on this story]: 'Had R. Ba known of the Sages' ruling [that only the injunctions of murder, incest, and idolatry demand martyrdom, but no other], he would have departed [this earth, i.e. been killed].'[128]

Note that the text states that 'he would have departed', not that 'he might have departed'. The Yerushalmi assumes that given the rabbinic dictum allowing such transgression, R. Ba would have had no choice but to eat. Even if one were to argue that the Yerushalmi intended to say 'he might have departed', if one credits R. Ba with sufficient religious zeal to have refused to eat non-kosher food even at the risk of his life had he only been permitted to run that risk, the implication would again be that one may not suffer martyrdom voluntarily. Otherwise R. Ba would have declined to eat even if he had known the permissive ruling of the Sages. This is the way most commentators have understood the narrative. Be that as it may, the story certainly does not state that one may volunteer for martyrdom, for clearly R. Ba did not know of the permissive ruling of the Sages when he refused the forbidden food. Yet in the middle of the thirteenth century this Yerushalmi is cited by the Tosafists as proof positive that voluntary martyrdom is permitted.

The Tosafists cite the passage of the Yerushalmi without the concluding sentence: 'Had R. Ba known of the Sages' ruling' and so forth. Presumably they had a different text in front of them. The reading of our version is, however, corroborated by *testimonia* coming from a wide variety of rabbinic cultures: Provence, Spain, and North Africa.[129] The possibility that France had a different version is laid to rest by a citation of the Yerushalmi identical

[128] ר' בא בר זמינא הוה מחיט גבי בר נש ברומי, אייתי ליה בשר נבילה, אמ' ליה אכול. אמ' ליה לי נא אכיל, אמ' ליה אכיל דלא כן אנא קטיל לך, אמ' ליה אין בעית מיקטול קטול, דלי נא אכיל בשר נבילה, אמ' ליה מאן מודע לך דאילו אכלתה הוינא קטלין לך, או יהודי יהודי או ארמאי ארמאי. אמ' ר' מנא אילו הוה ר' בא בר זמינא שמע מיליהון דרבנן מיזל הוה בהדא.

Sanhedrin 3: 7, *Shevi'it* 4: 2; 21b and 35a–b in the Venice edn.; col. 1282 and col. 190 in the edn. of the Academy of Hebrew Language.

[129] See B. Ratner, *Ahavat Tsiyyon vi-Yerushalayim*, *Shevi'it* (Vilna, 1907), 29–31.

with our text in an early thirteenth-century French work.[130] |294| It would seem that this citation stemmed from a florilegium of the Yerushalmi that was then in circulation and that mixed authentic and inauthentic, full and truncated citations of the Yerushalmi.[131]

Was this abbreviated version an attempt to alter the negative view of voluntary martyrdom found in the Yerushalmi and to bring it in line with the religious intuition of Ashkenaz? Perhaps, though voluntary martyrdom was hardly the flashpoint of the Christian–Jewish encounter. There may well have been instances of Gentile ruffians forcing Jews to eat non-kosher food and desecrate the Sabbath, just as they occasionally threw Jewish children and old men into the water as mock-baptism,[132] but that was hooliganism. The purpose of Christian persecution, to the extent that it was purposive and not simply an expression of hatred, was not to achieve Jewish transgression but Jewish conversion. Moreover, abbreviated quotations of the Yerushalmi are common enough in the halakhic literature of the Middle Ages, whether of Ashkenazic, Provençal, or Sephardic provenance, and our instance would scarcely be the first passage from the Yerushalmi whose meaning was altered by abridgment.[133]

Furthermore, this shortened text initially appears in the late twelfth and early thirteenth centuries in contexts unrelated to martyrdom. R. Yitsḥak, the brother of R. Shimshon of Sens, assumed that voluntary martyrdom is forbidden. Possessing, however, the same abbreviated text of the Yerushalmi as did his successors, he attempted to explain the passage by suggesting that if one is required to eat forbidden foods, coerced to ingest a tabooed substance, the revulsion may be such that one is permitted in such an instance, though in no other, to refuse. After a moment's thought, though, this seemed too radical a notion; he averred the passage to be difficult and left it at that.[134] Similarly,

[130] The *Kuntres Aḥaron* of the *Yalkut Shim'oni* cited by Ratner, ibid. The variant reading in *Shevi'it*, הוה מיכל, is of no worth, seeing that this is simply an emendation by the scribe of the Leiden manuscript. The original text had מיזל just as the *testimonia* have מיזל or variants thereof. See the text in the edition of the Academy of Hebrew Language (above, n. 81), col. 190, ii. 24–5, and Ratner, *Ahavat Tsiyyon* (above, n. 129), 29–31.

[131] See now the two comprehensive studies of Y. Sussmann, '"Yerushalmi Ketav-Yad Ashkenazi" ve-"Sefer Yerushalmi"', *Tarbiz*, 65 (1995), 37–64, and 'Seridei Yerushalmi—Ketav-Yad Ashkenazi; Likrat Pitron Ḥidat "Sefer Yerushalmi"', *Kovets 'al Yad* NS 12/22 (1994), 3–120. The few extant fragments of this collection do not contain our passage.

[132] J. Aronius, *Regesten zur Geschichte der Juden im Fränkischen und Deutschen Reiche bis zum Jahre 1273* (repr. Hildesheim, 1970), 319–20, #757.

[133] Any perusal of the tomes of Ratner, *Ahavat Tsiyyon* (above, n. 129), will yield innumerable examples.

[134] *Or Zarua'*, ii, 'Hilkhot Shabbat', #108.

R. El'azar of Worms cites the same truncated version as one of many talmudic passages affirming that the definition of the hasid is one who willingly forswears the permissible.[135] |295| Significantly, neither R. El'azar of Worms nor R. Shimshon of Sens cites this text in his discussion of martyrdom; it makes its first appearance in France in the *Tosafot* published in the standard Talmud, which date from the mid- to late thirteenth century.[136] In Germany it first appears in *Sefer Ḥasidim*, of approximately the same period.[137] However, the permissibility of voluntary martyrdom had been advanced there since at least the beginning of the thirteenth century,[138] and, given the force of the German statement, it is clear that this position needed no bolstering from any Yerushalmi source.[139] It seems wisest to simply note the appearance of a truncated text without rushing to any conclusions as to how it came to be shortened. The Franco-German position permitting voluntary martyrdom was an indigenous development and not the result of an altered text. Nor was the altering of the text necessarily a product of the newly evolving position on elective martyrdom.

At approximately the same time, R. Yitsḥak of Corbeil composed his much-copied *Sefer Mitsvot Katan*, commonly known by its acronym, *Semak*. In it, he advocates the permissibility of voluntary martyrdom, writing:

And other transgressions [other than murder, idolatry, and forbidden sexual relations] he may transgress and not be killed; however, it would be an act of piety not to transgress [and be martyred]. One cannot argue that since the Talmud said 'transgress and be not killed' [this is an imperative] and one who disobeys the rule is viewed as having committed suicide. Seeing that his intention is for God's sake, [this deed] is viewed as

135 *Sefer ha-Roke'aḥ*, 'Hilkhot Ḥasidut', 'Shoresh Yiḥud ha-Shem', 23.

136 Above, n. 126.

137 *SHB* (above, n. 104), #219, *SHP* (above, n. 30), #249. Any dating of *Sefer Ḥasidim* in either of its published versions is, of course, conjectural. {Whether the Pietists understood the allowance to be restricted to ingesting forbidden foods, as entertained momentarily by R. Shimshon of Sens, or the case of forbidden foods serves simply as an example of a general allowance (as the Tosafists thought) is not clear. Personally, I would incline to the former, seeing that *Sefer Ḥasidim* is scarcely hesitant about making large generalizations from the texts it cites. Indeed, much of the movement's rooting its doctrines in classic texts is based on this tendency.}

138 R. Avraham ben 'Azri'el, in *'Arugat ha-Bosem*, iii. 194–5, cites the permissibility as the unanimous position of his teachers.

139 Needless to say, the Yerushalmi passage didn't hurt and Rabbenu Asher (Rosh), who was intellectually of the French school for all his German lineage, cited it approvingly in his *Piskei Rosh, 'Avodah Zarah*, 2: 9. R. Ḥizkiyah of Magdeburg is of two opinions about the topic: see *Haggahot Asheri, Ketubbot* 1: 3.

a righteous one. The proof of this is from [the deed of] Sha'ul and further proof from that of R. Yehudah he-Ḥasid.'[140]

Clearly, R. Yitsḥak was either unaware of the text of the Yerushalmi then circulating or knew that the citation was inaccurate. |296| That, however, did not stop him from advocating voluntary martyrdom, though proofs he had none. As I have already shown, the case of Sha'ul proves nothing;[141] that of R. Yehudah he-Ḥasid even less. The permissibility of voluntary martyrdom was, then, a deeply held conviction of R. Yitsḥak of Corbeil, not an inference from any authoritative source.

The change in, or crystallization of, the French position on voluntary martyrdom emerged at the same time as the new German doctrine concerning the denial of one's Jewishness. The two developments may have been parts of one and the same phenomenon—a hardening of normative positions on martyrdom generated by the conversionary offensive of the Church and royal power in France and England in the mid-thirteenth century,[142] coupled with the rapidly devolving position of the Jews in all of north-western Europe during the closing decades of that century. A plausible suggestion, but given the current state of the evidence it must remain only that.

140 *Sefer Mitsvot Katan*, #3:

ושאר מצות בצנעה יעבור ואל יהרג, אבל מדת חסידות שלא יעבור. ואין לומר מאחר שאמרו חכמים יעבור ואל יהרג, אם יעבור פיהם דמו הנה נדרש, כי מאחר שכוונתו לשמים, צדקה תחשב לו. וראיה משאול, ועוד ראיה מר' יהודה החסיד.

{Seeing that the manuscripts vary as to the documentation for Sha'ul and R. Yehudah he-Ḥasid (see next note), I have followed the text of the *Semak* as found in the *Semak Zurich*, which, I have come to realize, often provides the most authentic readings because the massively annotated *Semak Zurich* was copied so little.} (On MS London, British Library 1056, see above, n. 96.)

141 Above, pp. 249–50. The story of R. Yehudah he-Ḥasid referred to in the printed *Semak* (or in the glosss to the *Semak*, e.g. in many manuscripts and also in the text of the *Semak Zurich*) is not to be found in either of the two printed versions of *Sefer Ḥasidim* (above, nn. 30, 104), but the absolute aversion to the use of God's name for any personal purpose is well attested in hasidic literature. See under the entry *hashba'ot* in J. Freimann's introduction to the 1924 Frankfurt am Main edition of *SHP*, and also E. Kanarfogel, 'German Pietism in Northern France', in Y. Elman and J. S. Gurock, eds., *Ḥazon Naḥum: Studies in Jewish Law, Thought and History Presented to Dr Norman Lamm on the Occasion of his Seventieth Birthday* (New York, 1997), 217–18. However, nothing done by R. Yehudah he-Ḥasid could be of normative import, to put it mildly.

142 The material is now conveniently and sensitively summarized in the first chapter of S. L. Einbinder's *Beautiful Death: Jewish Poetry and Martyrdom in Medieval France* (Princeton, 2002). {A further hardening of position is found in the 'Likkutim' of the *Semak Zurich*, #3, n. 10. This was brought to my attention by Yehudah Galinsky. However, I have neither found the passage in the *Mordekhai* to which the author refers nor do I know the date of the composition of the 'Likkutim'.}

Nevertheless, the tragic middle decades of the thirteenth century, during which some 5 to 10 percent of the population of English Jewry converted,[143] as did significant numbers of French Jews,[144] did leave some trace in the writings of the Tosafists. While not necessarily playing a role in the emergence of new halakhic positions (the issue at bar in this essay), a hypersensitivity to any profession of Christianity is noticeable in a remark of the printed *Tosafot* on *'Avodah Zarah*, which date approximately from the years 1244–51.[145] |297| There is a controversy among the *tanna'im* whether idolatry demands martyrdom in all circumstances or only when one is being constrained to worship publicly (*be-farhesya*). From a passage in *'Avodah Zarah* (54a), it would appear that the ruling is in favor of R. Yishma'el, who held that martyrdom was incumbent only in public situations. The *Tosafot of R. Yehudah of Paris*, written before 1189, notes this possible inference without ado and simply remarks that the final ruling is according to R. 'Akiva, who holds that when idolatry is at stake, martyrdom is incumbent under all circumstances, public or private.[146] Our printed *Tosafot* makes the same point but exclaims: 'God forbid that one should be permitted to worship idols [when constrained privately (*be-tsin'ah*).'[147] Anyone with the slightest familiarity with the writing of the Tosafists knows how extremely rare such exclamations are in the impersonal language of their glosses. To be sure, Christian missionary efforts had scarcely aimed at single, one-time confessions of the faith, after which the Jew would return home and resume his old way of life. Nevertheless, the notion of even a fleeting profession of Christianity, however coerced, evoked a shudder in mid-thirteenth-century northern France that it had not elicited some fifty years earlier.

[143] R. Stacey, 'The Conversion of Jews to Christianity in Thirteenth-Century England', *Speculum*, 67 (1992), 269–73; J. Shatzmiller, 'Jewish Converts to Christianity in Medieval Europe 1200–1500', in M. Goodich, S. Menache, and S. Schein, eds., *Cross-Cultural Convergences in the Crusader Period: Essays Presented to Aryeh Grabois on his Sixty-Fifth Birthday* (New York, 1995), 316–19.

[144] W. C. Jordan, *Louis IX and the Challenge of the Crusade* (Princeton, 1979), 155–7.

[145] See above, n. 126. As noted there, these lines may equally date from the closing decades of the 13th century.

[146] In *Shitat ha-Kadmonim 'al Massekhet 'Avodah Zarah*, i. 54a, s.v. *ha*.

[147] *'Avodah Zarah* 54a, s.v. *ha*. The revelatory nature of the phrase *has ve-shalom* in tosafist literature was already noted by Jacob Katz in *Exclusiveness and Tolerance: Studies in Jewish–Christian Relations in Medieval and Modern Times* (Oxford, 1961), 83–4. {I incline to a mid-13th-century date for this sensitivity, as R. Mosheh of Coucy is cited as attempting, in his *Sefer Mitsvot Gadol*, to forfend any notion that there was an amoraic opinion which held that the martyrdom imperative obtained only in instances of public idolatry—a possibility that did not bother his teacher, R. Yehudah of Paris. The passage cited is not found in any text of the *Sefer Mitsvot Gadol*, in either print or manuscript. S. Abramsom conjectures that it was found in the *Tosafot* of R. Mosheh on *'Avodah Zarah*. See S. Abramson, ''Inyanot be-Sefer Mitsvot Gadol', *Sinai*, 80 (1977), 208.}

The actions of the First Crusade martyrs can be viewed only in retrospect; they have little or no explanatory antecedents. There was no Palestinian tradition and precious little evidence of any Italian influence that would have presaged the course of the bloodstained events, or that could account, even in part, for the conduct of the Rhineland communities. We have only writings after the fact, and they are silent as to the actors' reasons. Not that the Crusade chronicles suffer from lack of speeches, but they are hortatory rather than explanatory. The protagonists (or those who later put words into their mouths) saw no need to justify their actions—only to encourage others to follow suit. The correctness of their deeds was axiomatic to their successors, the Tosafists.

'Hard cases', observed Justice Holmes, 'make bad law.' Tragic ones, one might add, make for even worse law. Law is designed for ordinary situations, not extraordinary ones. The starker the choice, the more dire the alternative, the worse law functions. Aware of its own limitations, law tries to avoid judging cases of extreme circumstances, for example, when group survival is set against individual survival—when one person in a lifeboat must be cast overboard so the others may remain alive.[148] When supreme values are at stake —man's ultimate allegiance (to God, king, or country) opposes the primal instinct for survival or the equally primal impulse of parental love—and the choice is left wholly up to the individual, the rational dictates of the law and its effective reach usually break down. The response is not reasoned but intuitive and unpremeditated. Not only does law generally not control these choices, often it does not even seek to judge them. When called upon to do so, its deliverances are more often than not as instinctive and culturally determined as the actions upon which it has been asked to deliver a verdict.

AFTERWORD

A RETRACTION, A NOTE ON A RECENT DOCTORATE, AND A REPLY TO RABBI Y. GROSSMAN

The essay was completed and submitted to the *Jewish Quarterly Review* (*JQR*) before the appearance of Simha Goldin's comprehensive study of martyrdom in Ashkenaz in the high Middle Ages, *'Alamot Ahevukha: 'Al-Mavet Ahevukha* (Lod, 2002), now translated and published as *The Ways of Jewish Martyrdom* (Turnhout, 2008). Had this fine study been available to me when I was composing this essay, I would have added a footnote here and modified a phrasing there, but scarcely altered the argument, as we are in general agreement. In one sense, my narrow-gauged,

[148] A. W. B. Simpson, *Cannibalism and the Common Law: The Story of the Tragic Last Voyage of the Mignonette and the Strange Legal Proceedings to which it Gave Rise* (Chicago, 1984).

methodological essay on the uses of legal texts for the study of cultural axioms simply buttresses a number of points in Goldin's broad empirical study.

Shortly after the appearance of this essay, Abraham Gross published two studies: *Struggling with Tradition: Reservations about Active Martyrdom in the Middle Ages* (Leiden and Boston, 2004) and *Spirituality and Law: Courting Martyrdom in Christianity and Judaism* (Lanham, Md., and Oxford, 2005). Written independently of my own study, they share with it a common perspective. My understanding of the forces moving the Jewish community to suicide and murder of their own children when confronted with the possibility of apostasy is similar to that of David Berger in his article 'Judaism and General Culture in Medieval and Early Modern Times', in J. J. Schachter, ed., *Judaism's Encounter with Other Cultures: Rejection or Integration* (Northvale, NJ, and Jerusalem, 1997), 114; reprinted in Berger's *Cultures in Collision and Confrontation: Essays in the Intellectual History of the Jews* (Boston, 2011), 85.

1. I must retract the statement that R. 'Akiva and R. Ḥanina ben Tradyon were executed for resisting the Romans and were not victims of religious persecution. Both narratives of their martyrdom state that they had defied a Roman ban on teaching Torah. Following the editor Efraim Kupfer, I discounted this as being the basis of Rabbenu Tam's position because it took his statement in *Sefer ha-Yashar* (above, n. 15) as defining *she'at ha-shemad* as a general religious persecution, not simply the interdiction of a single *mitsvah* or several *mitsvot*. I now think this understanding to be mistaken (see n. 42 above), and Rabbenu Tam's position differs in no way from that of the Tosafists. If this is so, the cases of R. 'Akiva and R. Ḥanina ben Tradyon are cases of *she'at ha-shemad*. My other objections remain in place. (The position, advocated by some Spanish Talmudists, that there is no *she'at ha-shemad* on positive commandments cannot be retrojected onto Rabbenu Tam as there is no evidence of his having ever entertained this view, especially as it runs against the simplest reading of the above-cited passages and that of R. Yehudah b. Bava in *Sanhedrin* 14a. Rabbenu Tam equally never contended that martyrdom is permissible whenever it serves a larger communal purpose (*she-ha-sha'ah tserikhhah le-khakh*).

2. Eitan Reich, in his recent Ph.D. thesis, 'Mesirat ha-Nefesh 'al Kiyyum ha-Mitsvot: Ide'ologiyot u-Temurot mi-Sifrut Ḥazal 'ad Ashkenaz ha-Kedumah' (Bar Ilan University, 2011), has contended that while it is true that the Palestinian and Babylonian teachings about the obligation of martyrdom are one and the same, the aggadic material shows a sharp divergence between the outlook of Erets Yisra'el and that of Bavel. The former endorses voluntary martyrdom and even suicide (though not infanticide), while the latter does

not. The Palestinian literature repeatedly holds up and encourages martyrdom as a religious ideal; the Babylonian is far more circumspect in this matter. Ashkenaz was deeply influenced by the Palestinian outlook.

I have no quarrel with this argument. The Ashkenazic response to the First Crusade came from somewhere. Simply sharing in the religious exaltation of the time and proudly manifesting a willingness to suffer death for their God equal to that of any Crusader—real as these motivating factors may have been—will not suffice to explain the deeds of the Rhineland community in 1096. That 'somewhere' from which the response arose may well have been the midrashic world, which formed, as noted before (above, p. 75), a large component of their imaginative world. I registered my objections to the exaggerated notions of the influence of Palestinian halakhah on Early Ashkenaz (above, p. 264); I never dealt with aggadah or ideology. While there are, in my view, areas where the religious outlook of Ashkenaz was deeply influenced by certain circles in Babylonia (see above, Chapter 9), Ashkenazic culture was scarcely a monolith. There is no reason why the outlook on martyrdom should not be an area where Palestinian influence bulked large.

Dr Reich, however, does not argue simply for influence of the midrashic literature on the unique Ashkenazic notion of *kiddush ha-shem*, but also insists on the crucial role played by *Sefer Yosippon*. Presently, I find Dönitz's skeptical evaluation of the role of martyrdom in *Sefer Yosippon* (above, n. 80) the more persuasive one. Reich has interesting, indeed important, observations about the differences between the text of *Sefer Yosippon* that circulated in Latin Europe and that which was current in Muslim lands. However, as the earliest Ashkenazic manuscript dates from 1282, there is no way of knowing whether the passages encouraging suicide and the murder of one's children were introduced before or after the First Crusade or even after the mass martyrdom in York in 1190, by which time the virtue of such conduct had become culturally axiomatic in the Franco-German community. Moreover, not only was *Sefer Yosippon* not 'quasi-canonical' in Early Ashkenaz, there is no evidence that it had any cultural impact whatsoever on the Rhineland communities. One or two historians have claimed such an influence, but they have offered no proof of it. As already noted in the text (p. 264), there is not a single passage in print or manuscript that would indicate that this work was viewed as anything more than a sourcebook for historical and geographical details of Jerusalem in the closing decades of the Second Temple. Nor is there any indication in the sources that *Sefer Yosippon* played a role in the mass martyrdom of the First Crusade or in any subsequent one. Let us never forget that the asserted influence must be great enough to permit mass murder, not to speak of impelling parents to kill their own children. However, a doctorate is but the first draft of a book, and one awaits with great interest Reich's published presentation.

3. R. Yitzhak Grossman, in his blog *Bein Din le-Din*, has correctly taken issue with my formulation (p. 252). 'It is hardly surprising that his arguments are shot through with inconsistencies . . . R. Me'ir perceives the non-comparability of royalty and commoners when the argument is against the killing of others but not when the argument is in its favor.'[149] It is invalid, he says, for an injunction concerning God's anointed does not necessarily carry over to ordinary people, since what it is forbidden to do to a king may yet be permissible to do to a commoner. However, a liberty that one is allowed to take with a king (i.e. killing him under certain circumstances) applies, a fortiori, to a commoner under the same circumstances. He is correct. The subsequent objection raised in the text against R. Me'ir's argument, namely, the Sinaitic rather than the Noahide injunction against murder, however, retains its force.

Rabbi Grossman further takes me to task in the same blog for my concluding claim about the argument from the case of the 'rebellious son' (*ben sorer u-moreh*, above, p. 257), especially the clause that I have here italicized: 'Of all the arguments, that of the rebellious son is the most absurd and at the same time the truest. *What had been inconceivable to the Palestinian sages of the first and second centuries*—how could one foretell with absolute certainty that a child would become a murderer?—had become only too real for the tiny Jewish minority in medieval Europe.' There is no evidence that the *tanna'im* of second-century Palestine found *ben sorer u-moreh* inconceivable—very rare yes, perhaps even impossible, but not inconceivable. How does one know that the Tosafists were of the opinion that the ruling is in favor of Rabbi Yehudah that the rebellious son 'never was and never will be' (*lo hayah ve-lo 'atid lihyot*)? Rabbi Grossman further challenges my citation of Halbertal's book as documentation,[150] saying that what Halbertal thinks or what I think is irrelevant, the question being what the *tanna'im* thought, or, more accurately, what the Tosafists thought the *tanna'im* thought. He is definitely correct about the last point. I happen to agree with Halbertal's understanding, but his book does not make any argument for the Tosafists' view of the matter, and that is what it is necessary to document.

What happened was that once, while studying, I made a mental note that

[149] Dated Aug. 22, 2008. The text of the blog of some six years ago was moved for storage purposes to <seforim.traditiononline.org> and may be viewed there. It is also found on my website (<haymsoloveitchik.org>) in the file 'Bein Din le-Din'.

[150] M. Halbertal, *Mahapekhot Parshaniyot* (above, n. 60).

'*Tosafot*' had taken for granted that *ben sorer u-moreh lo hayah ve-lo 'atid lihyot*, and I had this in mind when writing the passage under discussion. However, I could not remember at the time where the passage was found. I left the footnote blank and then forgot about it. The editors at *Jewish Quarterly Review* e-mailed me that footnote 60 was blank. I pulled out Halbertal's book, found the relevant pages and registered them as a reference—improperly. This is what happens when one cuts corners.

The reference that had slipped my mind was the responsum of R. Yitsḥak of Dampierre, Ri ha-Zaken, found in the Provençal collection *Temim De'im*.[151] R. Asher ben Meshullam from Provence sent Ri a number of questions dealing with the treatment of informers (*mosrim*). One shocked query was: how could the Talmud ever allow a snitch who had passed on information *only* about financial matters to be put to death?[152] In reply, Ri invoked an aggadic passage that one may wring the neck of an ignoramus (*'am ha-'arets*) even on the Day of Atonement that falls on a Sabbath and further argues that any such *moser* is automatically suspect of robbery and murder (*ḥashud lelastes ve-laharog*).[153] Rather than accuse a mild-mannered individual who informs only on financial matters of also plotting murder, and permit his execution for this intention, Ri could have simply argued that this first step of snitching leads finally to thievery and murder, as we find in *ben sorer u-moreh*. Yet, astonishingly, Ri never invokes either the ruling of the Mishnah that the rebellious son is executed for capital crimes that he is destined to commit (*ben sorer u-moreh nidon 'al shem sofo*) or its famous explication in the *beraita* of R. Yosei ha-Gelili (*San.* 72a), 'The Torah foresaw the final intentions of the rebellious son . . . he goes out to the highway and robs people' (*higi'ah torah le-sof da'ato shel ben sorer u-moreh . . . yotse le-farashat derakhim u-melastes et ha-beriyot*), even though both beg to be invoked, as this slippery slope is exactly what was feared in the instance of the informer. Such a passage would certainly have been more apt than the wild, aggadic exaggeration of neck-wringing on Yom Kippur (*Pes.* 49b). Indeed, realizing the weakness of his argument, Ri adds, 'and there may be some verse [permitting] this'. (An astonishing statement that I treat in 'On the Tosafists' Use of Aggadah: A Reply to I. M. Ta-Shma'; see Chapter 5 above.) Instead of some conjectured, unknown biblical verse, why not simply invoke an authoritative *mishnah* or *beraita* that states *nidon 'al shem sofo*? Apparently, those passages and that law could not, to Ri's thinking, be invoked. The only reason that I can think of is because he was of the opinion that *ben sorer u-moreh lo hayah ve-lo 'atid lihyot*.

[151] In *Tummat Yesharim* (Venice, 1622), #202. (It was published separately as *Temim De'im* in Lemberg in 1812, and again in Warsaw in 1897. The numbering of the sections is identical with the first edition.)

[152] *Bava Kamma* 117a.

[153] *Pesaḥim* 49b.

R. Grossman cites Mei'ri and Maimonides as not ruling like R. Yehudah. In evaluating an Ashkenazic argument, Ri is more relevant than Me'iri or Maimonides, let alone R. 'Ovadyah Bartenura, whom Rabbi Grossman mentions, especially as this is not a conscious legal position taken by Ri, but rather a self-evident assumption on his part that needed no explicit formulation. I would prefer to have proof in the popular lore of medieval Ashkenaz (though I don't know where I should look to find it) or in the writings of Ravyah (if he, indeed, advanced this argument from *ben sorer u-moreh*) but, absent that, I think a self-understood, halakhic 'given' of so central a figure as Ri Ba'al ha-Tosafot is valid documentation.

As for the clause 'What had been inconceivable to the Palestinian sages of the first and second centuries' (above, p. 259), I think it is defensible. *Ben sorer u-moreh*, according to the *setam mishnah*, *nidon 'al shem sofo*. This runs contrary to every principle in Jewish law and, indeed, in most Gentile law. People are executed for crimes that they have committed, not for crimes that they might commit—preventive detention for the criminally inclined perhaps, but preventive execution?! If I find *tanna'im* attempting to make the implementation of this law impossible,[154] does it strain the imagination to think that they did so because it contradicts their elementary sense of right and wrong? I, for one, think not.

Rabbi Grossman argues that we find a similar ruling about *nig'ei battim* and there is no ethical problem in this realm. Indeed, there isn't; however, no one claimed that all instances of 'never was and never will be' (*lo hayah ve-lo nivra*) are a result of ethical issues. Only those in which we find this type of problem, such as *ben sorer u-moreh* and, to add to the roster, the 'apostate city' (*'ir ha-niddaḥat*) as R. Eliezer Berkovits has contended (as noted by R. Grossman). As for the similar requirement of identity for the *shenei se'irim* of Yom Kippur (*Yoma* 62a–b), the *Tosafot Yeshanim*, s.v. *shenei* (ad loc.), to which R. Grossman draws attention, have already pointed out that finding what to our eyes are identical animals is difficult but possible, whereas finding a mother who looks just like the father is an impossibility, and that makes all the difference.[155] An exegesis that makes execution of a law more difficult may be simply a matter of interpretation; an exegesis that makes execution impossible has that in mind to begin with. One plausible reason that one might have sought to render a Divine directive inoperable is that such a dictate appeared inconceivable for a just God.

[154] *Sanhedrin* 71b. See the *Tosafot Yeshanim*, *Yoma* 62a, s.v. *shenei* (cited by R. Grossman) and *Tosefot ha-Rosh* cited in the next note.

[155] This view is equally stated in the *Tosefot ha-Rosh*, *Yoma* 62a, ed. S. H. Villman (Jerusalem, 1996), and the *Ḥiddushei ha-Ritva*, *Yoma* 62a, ed. E. Lichtenstein (Jerusalem, 1996).

CHAPTER TWELVE

Maimonides' *Iggeret ha-Shemad*: Law and Rhetoric

I PUBLISHED part of my BA Honors thesis some twenty years after it was written, in a rabbinical jubilee volume that took so long to be printed that it turned into a memorial volume. Though respectfully buried, the article had a surprising afterlife, generating more comment—mostly negative—than anything else that I have written. The numerous criticisms are available on my website; my replies to them follow on the heels of the essay.

|281|

THIS WAS MY FIRST VENTURE in Jewish studies many years ago and was cast, understandably enough, in a somewhat tosafist mold. Were I to write it now, I would perhaps drop the two-section format of question and answer and opt for an integrated contextual approach. Not only would the questions be posed less stridently, but an attempt would also be made to show the peculiar interplay between the halakhist and rhetorician at work in *Iggeret ha-Shemad.* Nevertheless, I stand now as then by the contention of the essay as to the nature of Maimonides' letter, and I offer it, with its youthful exuberance, in tribute to one who, while ripe in years, remains young in spirit.

LAW

THE MOROCCAN JEWS had been under persecution for well over a decade when Maimonides arrived in Fez in or around the year 1159. The |282| same religious fanatics who had driven him from his native Córdoba and set him on his decade of wandering held sway over North Africa. The Almohads, as these disciples of Ibn Tumrat were called, sought a society of true believers only which left no room for infidels. The inhabitants of the lands

The BA Honors thesis was submitted in spring 1959 and is on file in Pusey Library, Harvard University. Barring one contention, which proved unpersuasive upon rereading, the text has been left as originally written. The notes, however, have been altered. I have compressed some and expanded

that they seized were given, in effect, the choice between Islam, exile, or death. Some Jews suffered martyrdom, others fled, but most simply repeated the *shahada* after the soldiers—'There is no God but Allah, and Muhammad is the prophet of Allah'—and attempted to maintain their religion in the secrecy of their homes.[1]

Some time after Maimonides' arrival a letter was widely circulated in the Moroccan community and caused great consternation among the Marranos.[2] It seemed that someone had inquired of a scholar outside the Almohad rule

others in view of the different audiences addressed and the secondary literature currently available. The halakhic references have been heavily reduced in light of the appearance of the six-volume *Sanhedrei Gedolah* (Jerusalem, 1968–76), the *'Einayim la-Mishpat 'al Sanhedrin* (Jerusalem, 1971), the recent edition of the *Sefer ha-Madda'*, ed. Y. Cohen and M. H. Katzenelenbogen (Jerusalem, 1964), and the latest volumes of the *Entsiklopedyah Talmudit*, all of which are copiously annotated and obviate the extensive references that were necessary in 1959. {The essay appeared in a memorial volume to Rabbi Joseph Lookstein that had originally been planned as a Festschrift, and I submitted it when the honoree was still alive. Hence the present tense—'remains young in spirit'.}

The various editions of *Iggeret ha-Shemad* as well as all the halakhic sources cited in this essay have been digitized and are available on my website <haymsoloveitchik.org>.

[1] The subject of my essay is Maimonides' defense of the forced converts of the Almohad persecution, rather than the nature of the persecution itself. The details of the Almohad demands—their scope, intensity, and duration—remain obscure. Contemporary statements are vague, and specifics are found only in much later and often geographically removed sources. See A. Halkin, 'Le-Toledot ha-Shemad bi-Yemei ha-'Almoḥadin', in *Joshua Starr Memorial Volume: Studies in History and Philology* (New York, 1953), 101–10; S. W. Baron, *A Social and Religious History of the Jews* (New York, 1951–75), iii. 124–6, 289–92; D. Corcos, 'Le-'Ofi Yaḥasam shel Shalitei ha-'Almoḥadon la-Yehudim', *Zion*, 32 (1967), 137–61, and the literature there cited. A convenient Hebrew translation of many of these sources may be found in B. Z. Dinur, *Yisra'el ba-Golah*, 2: i (Tel Aviv and Jerusalem, 1965), 313–23. The best evidence for the nature of the persecution at the time of the writing of *Iggeret ha-Shemad* would seem to be that work itself. It would have been absurd for Maimonides, seeking to counsel the Jews of Morocco and to raise their spirits, to have addressed them on a set of facts other than those they experienced daily. It would seem unwise, then, to project backward a harsher and more extreme persecution on the basis of R. Yosef ibn 'Aknin's remarks a generation later (cf. Halkin, 'Le-Toledot ha-Shemad'), and equally unwarranted to deny that sometime prior to 1165 the Almohads demanded of the Jews the recitation of the *shahada* (cf. Corcos, 'Shalitei ha-'Almoḥadon', 155–60). {See now M. Ben-Sasson, 'Li-Zehutam ha-Yehudit shel Anusim—'Iyyun be-Hishtamdut bi-Tekufat ha-'Almoḥadon', *Pe'amim*, 42 (1990), 16–37; M. A. Friedman, *Ha-Rambam, ha-Mashiaḥ be-Teman ve-ha-Shemad* (Jerusalem, 2002), 23–31; J. L. Kraemer, *Maimonides: The Life and Work of One of Civilizations' Greatest Minds* (New York and London, 2008), 83–98; S. Stroumsa, *Maimonides in his World: A Portrait of a Mediterranean Thinker* (Princeton, 2009), 53–62.}

[2] My use of this term is anachronistic, as it was first employed centuries later to designate the New Christians in Spain. The word has lost all of its original derogatory connotations in English and has achieved a full measure of respectability, even of honor, in the vocabulary of religious persecution. I find it preferable stylistically to 'pseudo-Muslim', 'crypto-Jews', and other such terms often used by historians to describe the unwilling converts to the Muslim faith. The Hebrew term *anusim* will be used synonymously with Marranos.

how one should conduct oneself in this time of persecution. The reply was harsh and unequivocal: Islam was a form of idolatry and thus came under the imperative of martyrdom. Those who had failed the test had desecrated the name of God and had worshipped false gods. They merited the penalty the Jewish law prescribes for the latter transgression—death by stoning. While they lived they were to be |283| considered apostates and subject to all the onerous disqualifications that this status entailed. Their silent prayers to the God they had denied were loathsome in His eyes, and all their clandestine religious observances were not worth a farthing. Nothing could ever alter this, short of an outright repudiation of Islam and a public manifestation of Jewishness.

The reply to this was Maimonides' *Iggeret ha-Shemad* (Letter on Persecution).[3]

[3] The Arabic original of this work has been lost, and what we possess are Hebrew translations only. *Iggeret ha-Shemad* (or *Ma'amar Kiddush ha-Shem*, as it was sometimes called) was first published by Abraham Geiger from MS Munich 315 in his *Moses ben Maimon: Studien* (Breslau, 1850) and soon after by Z. H. Edelmann from MS Oxford, Bodley 2218 in *Ḥemdah Genuzah* (Königsberg, 1856). It was subsequently reprinted by A. L. Lichtenberg in his *Kovets Teshuvot ha-Rambam ve-'Iggerotav* (Leipzig, 1859) and in a popular, heavily annotated edition by M. D. Rabinowitz entitled *Iggerot ha-Rambam* (Tel Aviv, 1951), which was subsequently incorporated into the set of *Rambam la-'Am* (Jerusalem, 1960). Y. Kafih has edited the work on the basis of the above editions together with several (unspecified) Yemenite MSS in his *Iggerot Rabbenu Mosheh b. Maimon*: *Makor ve-Targum* (Jerusalem, 1972). The differences between the several editions are slight, and no text has any distinct edge over the others. For convenience's sake, I have made reference to the readily available edition of *Rambam la-'Am*, primarily because there is less text per page in that edition than in any other, and hence the passage intended is more easily found. On the few occasions when the text of another edition made for a more felicitous translation, I have adopted it. For further MS references, see A. Freimann, *Union Catalog of Hebrew Manuscripts and Their Location*, ii (New York, 1964–73), #438, which should be supplemented by the card index of the Institute of Microfilmed Hebrew Manuscripts of the National Library of Israel in Jerusalem. {Y. Shilat lists and discusses the various MSS in the introduction (pp. 28–9) to his edition of the *Iggeret*, see below.}

{Since this essay was published two new editions and a new translation of *Iggeret ha-Shemad* have appeared. Yitsḥak Satz published an annotated edition with halakhic comments in *Sefer ha-Zikkaron le-Maran ha-Ga'on R. Ḥayyim Shemulevits*, ed. Y. Buksboim (Jerusalem, 1980), 229–60. Yitsḥak Shilat published a large part of *Iggeret ha-Shemad* in *Sinai*, 95 (1984), 157–64, in a medieval translation that differed from that of Geiger and Edelmann. He subsequently put out a useful, quasi-critical edition of the work in his *Iggerot ha-Rambam* (Jerusalem, 1987), i. 25–59, using as a base text MS Jewish Theological Seminary 2380. (No criticism is implied by my characterization, as it is impossible to produce a truly 'critical' edition seeing that we lack the Arabic original.) In 1985, Abraham Halkin published an English translation of the work in *Crisis and Leadership: Epistles of Maimonides* (Philadelphia, 1985), 15–45, with an introduction by David Hartman (pp. 46–90), highly critical of my essay. (I have attempted to reply to his remarks: see Ch. 13, Part I, below). A previous English translation of much of the *Iggeret* by Leon Stitskin appeared in *Tradition*, 14 (1973), 107–12; 16 (1977), 95–120, followed by a full translation in hardcover in *Letters of Maimonides*, translated and edited with

'And we saw fit', writes Maimonides,

> to cite his relevant arguments . . . and to omit what merits no reply. And one of these is his claim that one who admits to the mission [of Mohammed] has by this denied the God of Israel. And he cited support from what our sages said, 'Whoever admits to idolatry, it is as if he denied the entire Law [Torah].' [But] in making this analogy he makes no distinction between one who willingly admits to idolatry without compulsion . . . and one who says of an ordinary mortal that he is a prophet, under compulsion, from fear of death.[4]

Maimonides, in his rebuttal of the charge that the Marrano is an apostate in the full sense of the word, forwards two distinctions: first |**284**| that the profession of the prophetic character of Mohammed is not a form of idolatry, and, second, that in any event it is done under compulsion. As the second point is a recurrent theme in the responsum, I leave it for later consideration after we have seen more instances of its invocation and are better able to weigh its merits. Let me address, for the moment, only the first point.

Maimonides claims that his antagonist has failed to notice the obvious: that all the Marranos have done is admit the prophetic nature of Mohammed's mission; they have in no way assented to any idolatry. Admittedly this is correct, but is this difference of fact legally significant? Mohammed's prophetic character is the first and fundamental article of faith in the Muslim religion, and subscription to it is *ipso facto* subscription to Islam. If Islam itself is idolatry, then anything that officially conveys belief in it is also idolatry. The true issue is not, then, the specific content of the formula (acceptance of Mohammed's prophetic character), but what the recitation of the formula constitutes (acceptance of Islam).

introductions and notes by L. D. Stitskin (New York, 1977), 40–69. A French translation in Les Dix Paroles series of Verdier, edited by C. Mopsic, appeared some six years later: Moïse Maimonide, *Épitres*, trans. J. de Hulster (Lagrasse, 1983), 7–43. (It was subsequently reprinted by Éditions Gallimard, Paris. It is this imprint which is currently available.)

In my notes I have retained the references to the pagination of the *Rambam la-'Am* edition (referred to below as *IH*) and added references to Shilat's edition, designated by S, and to Halkin's translation, designated by H. Thus, a notation of '*IH* 46; S 55; H 68' means the passage is found in the *Rambam la-'Am* edition at p. 46; in that of Shilat at p. 55, and in Halkin's translation at p. 68. While systematically including references to Halkin's translation for the reader's convenience so that he can judge the context in which the citations appear—and context, as we shall see, is important in evaluating the thrust of Maimonides' words—I have nevertheless retained, both in the text and in the footnotes, my own translations of the *Iggeret* as found in the original article. I have detected no substantive difference in any citation between my translation and that of Halkin. Readers, however, can decide for themselves.}

[4] *IH* 31; S 31; H 15–16.

One would expect that Maimonides would now proceed to discuss the nature of Islam and its status in Jewish law, but nothing of the sort is forthcoming. In the very next sentence he turns to a different problem; the lines I have cited constitute almost the entire rebuttal. Almost, but not quite. Several pages later, after Maimonides has more or less finished his formal reply to his opponent's charges, he digresses a moment to show the incoherencies and irrelevancies that fill the letter of accusation.

To a single question he made many replies, [and ones] that have nothing to do with the matter. He cited support from [the laws of] perjured witnesses [*'edim zomemim*], cursing of mother and father, the commandment of fringes [*tsitsit*], plowing with ox and donkey, and the breeding of animals; as if it had been asked of him that he should compile and count therein all the commandments. And he also said that the Ishmaelites [Muslims] have an idol in Mecca and in other places, as if he had been asked whether one should make a pilgrimage to Mecca. And he similarly said that the madman [Mohammed] killed 24,000 Jews, as if he had been asked whether he [Mohammed] would have a share in the world to come. And many [irrelevancies] like these.[5]

The paragraph is highly effective, but insofar as our problem is concerned it is rhetoric and not argument. If Maimonides wishes to say |285| in his sarcastic remark about pilgrimages that a religion is to be judged by its principles and not by cultic aberrations, he should say so more explicitly, and then proceed to show that the fundamentals of Islam are monotheistic.

One could demur and argue that I am working with illegitimate preconceptions. Because we know that later in his life, in a famous responsum, Maimonides declared Islam to be monotheistic,[6] I have assumed that he is pressing the same point here. But the total absence of any such discussion should show us that he is not advancing this point at all. What he is claiming is that, regardless of the nature of Islam, the Jews in Morocco simply haven't subscribed to it. All they have done is to repeat a well-known formula, and this does not imply any adherence to the Islamic faith.

Perhaps this objection is well taken (though I doubt it), but it only substitutes one silence for another. The assumption that the acceptance of the

[5] *IH* 43–4; S 42; H 21.

[6] *Teshuvot ha-Rambam*, ii, ed. J. Blau (Jerusalem, 1960), #448. {See now D. Novack, 'The Treatment of Islam and Muslims in the Legal Writings of Maimonides', in W. M. Brinner and S. D. Ricks, eds., *Studies in Islamic and Judaic Traditions* (Atlanta, Ga., 1986), 233–50; id., 'Maimonides on Judaism and Other Religions', the Samuel H. Goldenson Lecture delivered February 23, 1997 at the Hebrew Union College-Jewish Institute of Religion, Cincinnati, Ohio; E. Schlossberg, 'Yaḥaso shel ha-Rambam el ha-'Islam', *Pe'amim*, 42 (1990), 38–60.}

fundamental article of a creed is not equivalent to the acceptance of the faith itself is a highly debatable one,[7] and would require at least as much discussion and proof as that of the status of Islam.

Moreover, the defense fails to fill another large gap in the Maimonidean position. Even assuming that Islam is not idolatry, or if it is, that Jews are not subscribing to it, it is undeniable that they are assenting to the prophetic character of Mohammed. They subscribe perhaps to no more, but certainly to no less. The acknowledgment of the mission of Mohammed, however, is a denial of the supremacy of the Mosaic revelation.[8] The distinctiveness of Judaism has lain precisely in its insistence on the eternal validity of the Pentateuch as interpreted by the Oral Tradition. When this is superseded, Judaism is superseded. For this reason, denial of the supremacy of the Old Testament is, in the eyes of Jewish law, and naturally, then, of Maimonides,[9] the rankest of heresies.

Maimonides asserts elsewhere in his letter that the heterodoxy that denies prophecy comes under the term 'idolatry' as used in the |**286**| laws of *kiddush ha-shem*.[10] Why should the *shahada*, with its assertion of the primacy of Mohammed's prophecy, be any different? The contemporary nature of Judaism changes little whether one asserts that there never was a revelation or, alternatively, that it had occurred but has now been superseded. Both statements would seem to be equally treasonable. A distinction, perhaps, can be made between the two cases, but the burden of proof certainly rests with its proponent. No defense of Marranoism in Muslim countries can go very far without a precise analysis of the nature of heresy and its place within the domain of martyrdom.

Maimonides' assumptions as to the character of heterodoxy and of Islam may very well be correct, but the *Iggeret ha-Shemad* sets forth little justifica-

[7] The word 'acceptance' may raise some eyebrows, but at this stage of the discussion use of this term will cause the least confusion. For the ultimate justification of its use, see below, n. 17.

[8] This point was made by A. Geiger in his *Moses ben Maimon* (above, n. 3), 18, and reprinted in his *Nachgelassene Schriften* (Berlin, 1876), iii. 51. {Ritva in *Ḥiddushim 'al Pesaḥim*, ed. Y. Levovits (Jerusalem, 1983), 25b, s.v. *mah*, states explicitly that acceptance of Islam is heresy and fully subject to the martyr imperative. Y. Satz, in his edition of *Iggeret ha-Shemad* (above, n. 3), 231 n. 7, points out that this position was endorsed by R. David ben Shelomoh ibn Zimra in *Teshuvot Radbaz*, iv (Warsaw, 1882), #1123, and asserted once again, as Satz perceptively notes, in *Magen Avraham*, 'Oraḥ Ḥayyim', 128: 54.

[9] 'Teshuvah', 3: 8. {*Mishnah 'im Perush le-Rabbenu Mosheh b. Maimon, Nezikin*, ed. Y. Kafih (Jerusalem, 1965), *Sanhedrin* 11: 1, introduction, 215–16, *ve-ha-yesod ha-teshi'i*; *Hakdamot ha-Rambam la-Mishnah*, ed. Y. Shilat (Jerusalem, 1996), 144–5; see also *Teshuvot ha-Rambam*, i, ed. J. Blau (Jerusalem, 1960), #149, pp. 284–5, and C. Adang, *Muslim Writers on Judaism and the Hebrew Bible: From Ibn Rabban to Ibn Ḥazm* (Leiden, 1996), 192–222.}

[10] *IH* 39–41; S 37–40; H 20–1.

tion for them. The crux of his opponent's position that Islam is idolatry is casually dismissed, and the profound difficulties in his own position are simply ignored.

A few pages later Maimonides drops, in passing, another line of argument:

> But the persecution which we are in, we do not simulate that we worship idols but [only] that we believe in what they [our coercers] say. And they are already fully aware that we do not believe this under any circumstances, only we deceive the king, [as it is written], 'and they did flatter him with their mouth: and they lied unto him with their tongue' [Ps. 78: 37].[11]

In the second part of the responsum this becomes a major point in the defense, and Maimonides dedicates an entire section to it:

> But this persecution does not oblige [us to perform] any act, only speech . . . Because this coercion does not require of any man action, only speech. And they are already fully aware that we do not believe in this speech, and it is only uttered by people to save themselves from the king, to satisfy him with some empty words . . . [Consequently,] if one should come and ask us whether he should profess or die, we say to him: 'Profess and be not killed.'[12]

If Maimonides were still claiming that Islam is not idolatry, then this line of reasoning would be wholly gratuitous. Moreover, the first quotation is the closing part of a section discussing a talmudic narrative involving |287| idolatry, and the transitional sentence, which I have already quoted—'But the persecution which we are in, we do not simulate that we worship idols, but [only] that we believe in what they [our coercers] say'—almost explicitly concedes the present persecution to involve idolatrous beliefs, though not actions.

It would seem, then, that Maimonides is shifting his line of defense. He is now contending that, even admitting that Allah and Mohammed are, for some reason, 'strange gods', the Marrano profession of the *shahada* still does not constitute apostasy. Any claim to the contrary fails to take into consideration three salient features of the contemporary religious oppression: the Jews are not required to actually serve false gods, but only to assert verbally their belief in them; the religious formula is repeated not out of conviction but out of expediency; and the Almohads themselves realize the empty nature of the profession.

The first thing that catches our attention is the total absence of talmudic citations. Maimonides has pointed out some unique facets of the Moroccan persecution, yet he has not shown that these are of legal significance. One

[11] *IH* 41; S 41; H 20. [12] *IH* 61–2; S 53–4; H 30.

wonders whether the silence is because the principles to which he is appealing are self-evident or because they are non-existent.

In his first point, Maimonides is attempting to claim that apostasy must be committed by deed and not just by word. The Talmud itself takes up the definition of idolatry and in a well-known *mishnah* explicitly rejects such a distinction: 'These are the ones to be stoned . . . The idolater [is culpable] no matter whether he worships or sacrifices or burns incense or pours out a libation or bows himself down to it or accepts it as his god, or says to it, "Thou art my god".'[13] The *mishnah* asserts that idols can be as effectively worshipped by mouth as by hand or foot and that Jewish law recognizes no difference between them.[14] **|288|**

Maimonides makes a second point, a second distinction, writing: 'and it is only uttered by people to save themselves from the king, to satisfy him with some empty words'.[15] There is a fundamental difference, he contends, between idolatry and other injunctions. In homicide, for example, it is obvious that intent plays a decisive role, separating first-degree murder from manslaughter. Nevertheless, it does not affect the nature of the act itself. Killing constitutes the objective act of taking another's life: the subjective intent affects only the extent of the individual's culpability for the act. The case is different with idolatry. Worship, by definition, is fundamentally, if not exclusively, a psychological state, and any mechanical performance must be accompanied by the thought of adoration for it to be considered an act of worship. This being so, the *anusim*, Maimonides now claims, have never committed apostasy, for their profession of faith was not done out of belief, but out of compulsion, and is, hence, absolutely meaningless!

This is a tour de force. Unfortunately, Maimonides has won far too much. If one can never be compelled to worship 'strange gods', why should one ever be required to lay down one's life rather than submit? If idolatry committed under coercion is of no account, then the entire concept of martyrdom for one's religion becomes meaningless and should never have existed to begin with. But we know only too well that it does. Maimonides' neat theory is contradicted by the massive, bloody fact of Jewish law—the imperative of 'Be killed and do not transgress' (*yehareg ve-'al ya'avor*).

13 *Sanhedrin* 60b.

14 ''Avodat Kokhavim', 3: 4. See *Leḥem Mishneh* ad loc., whose author rejects any modification of the efficacy of verbal assent, and his position is borne out by Maimonides' formulation in 'Shegagot', 1: 2. See, though, M. Krakowski, *'Avodat ha-Melekh* (Vilna, 1931), ad loc. Islam, however, is a known religion, and both the *Leḥem Mishneh* and *'Avodat ha-Melekh* are in agreement that in instances of a known religion (as opposed to a private one) the spoken word alone constitutes an act of idolatry.

15 *IH* 61; S 53; H 30.

Moreover, in a subsequent passage in *Sanhedrin* (64a), the Talmud states—and Maimonides, both in his *Perush ha-Mishnayot* and in his Code, repeats—that if one should participate in a foreign religious service with the specific and exclusive intent to mock, one has nevertheless transgressed the injunction against idolatry.[16] In other words, there is no |289| difference in the eyes of Jewish law whether someone partakes (to use a Christian example) of the Eucharist to satisfy his religious convictions or to laugh at transubstantiation; in both cases he is held culpable. Willy-nilly we are compelled to conclude that idolatry does not require a subjective state of belief, but rather that the quiddity, the very essence of the transgression, lies in the mechanical act itself.[17]

Maimonides' third point, that the Almohads themselves are aware of the

[16] ''Avodat Kokhavim', 3: 5. See *'Avodat ha-Melekh* ad loc. The author of *Kesef Mishneh* wishes to restrict the obligation to a sin offering only (*ḥattat*). Even if this interpretation is correct, the restriction arises out of the difficulty of Maimonides' envisioning a state of *mezid* coexisting simultaneously with that of **מיכוין לביזויה**. Regardless of how one classifies the intent, the criminal act remains that of idolatry, otherwise one would be **מביא חולין לעזרה**. Interestingly, even this consideration of the problematic coexistence of 'intent' and 'contempt' occurred to Maimonides only later in his career. In the first edition of his *Perush ha-Mishnayot* he wrote simply *ḥayyav*. It was in his later editions that he added (as he did in *Mishneh Torah*) the word *ḥattat*. In other words, at the time of his writing *Iggeret ha-Shemad* he viewed the 'intent to mock' case as fully and unqualifiedly culpable. (See *Mishnah 'im Perush le-Rabbenu Mosheh b. Maimon, Nezikin*, ed. Y. Kafih [Jerusalem, 1965], *Sanhedrin* 7: 6, n. 9.)

[17] The issue whether the crime of idolatry demands an inner state of belief is a moot one and revolves heavily about the problematic *sugya* of **העובד מאהבה ומיראה פטור** (*Sanhedrin* 61b, *Shabbat* 72b, *Keritut* 3a). Basically, there are two views—yes and no—and these doctrines, in their varying shades, can be found in the classic commentaries on the aforementioned passages, taken together with the works cited in the first note and the cross-references contained therein. Maimonides' opinion in *Mishneh Torah* (''Avodat Kokhavim', 3: 5–6) is anything but clear, and the contradiction between his formulation of the 'intent to mock' law (**מיכוין לביזויה**) in sect. 5, with that of *mi-'ahavah u-mi-yir'ah* in sect. 6, is one of the oldest cruxes of Maimonidean scholarship and has not been fully resolved to this day (e.g. A. I. Karelitz, *Ḥazon Ish* ad loc., and the works cited above, nn. 14, 16). For our purposes much of this is irrelevant, for the problem only arises if one rules that *ha-'oved mi-'ahavah u-mi-yir'ah patur*. Maimonides initially held, however, that the perpetrator is *ḥayyav* (thus in the *mahadura kamma*, see *Mishnah 'im Perush le-Rabbenu Mosheh b. Maimon* [above, n. 9], *Sanhedrin* 7: 6, n. 3), and this view, taken together with the law of mockery, leads ineluctably to the conclusion that the external act alone suffices for culpable idolatry. I happen to be of the opinion that this was Maimonides' view even at the time of his composition of *Mishneh Torah*, for otherwise his famous a fortiori from the *Sifra* ('Yesodei ha-Torah', 5: 4), exculpating acts committed under duress, even in instances of **יהרג ואל יעבור**, would no longer hold. Be that as it may, my argument revolves about Maimonides' early views, and these are crystal clear.

The example of the Eucharist may not be the most apropos one according to some interpretations of *mekhaven le-vizuyeh*. But this in no way affects my argument, and so I have used it for convenience's sake.

hollow nature of the profession, is equally inadmissible. Every act of religious persecution involves a situation where the coercer is aware of his victim's psychological resistance. If someone, for example, should stick a revolver in my back and order me to kneel to his god, if he possesses even a glimmer of intelligence he must realize that I do not believe in his idol, nor do I wish to bow to it. If I did, he would hardly need to threaten to get me to worship it. Nevertheless, I am solemnly enjoined to surrender my life rather than bend to his deity—a fact that is inexplicable by the Maimonidean standards of apostasy. Maimonides' position throws out the baby of martyrdom together with the bathwater of 'unwarranted' charges of apostasy.

Since it would be foolish to assume that Maimonides, immersed in the problem of apostasy and martyrdom, forgot its most elementary definitions and circumstances, we are led to the conclusion that **|290|** these three points were not meant to be taken separately, but only in conjunction with one another. Placed side by side, our problems mutually resolve themselves. Maimonides is not contending that there can be no apostasy via speech, nor is he contending that there can be no idolatry without inner conviction. What he is claiming is that there can be no apostasy via speech without inner conviction. It is in this respect that speech differs from deed, not in general. A glance again at his statement should convince us that this is what he is driving at.

> But this persecution does not oblige [us to perform] any act, only speech . . . Because this coercion does not require of any man action, only speech . . . [Consequently,] if one should come and ask whether he should profess or die, say to him: 'Profess and be not killed.'[18]

Maimonides almost explicitly states that were the persecution to focus on heathen acts rather than on speech, there would be no escape from the duty of martyrdom, regardless of one's inner disbelief.

In the section in the latter half of the responsum directed to this point, Maimonides introduces no support for his novel contention. His casual discussion in the first part, however, follows, in a somewhat abrupt fashion, the narration of a story mentioned in the Midrash and the Talmud. It chanced that R. Eli'ezer was seized by the Romans for heresy. As he ascended the gallows the general said to him, 'Is it possible that such a wise man should believe in such nonsense [i.e. Jewish law]?' R. Eli'ezer replied, 'I take the Judge's word for it [*ne'eman 'alai ha-dayyan*]', meaning that he remained firm in his belief in the words of the Supreme Judge. The general, however, took 'Judge' with a

[18] *IH* 61–2; S 53–4; H 30.

small *j*, taking it to mean that R. Eli'ezer had agreed with him, and he thereupon released him.[19]

The fact that Maimonides introduces this as a defense of Marranoism indicates that he does not conceive of the events as being just a lucky coincidence, but thinks that R. Eli'ezer actually intended to deceive his would-be executioner.[20]

I take it that Maimonides now |**291**| reasons that if verbal apostasy does not require inner belief, then the great sage was guilty of dastardly cowardice by yielding to his persecutor and renouncing God. R. Eli'ezer's conduct becomes explicable only if we assume that there is no commandment of martyrdom where lip service alone is involved. It is with this intent that Maimonides prefaces his word–deed distinction with the talmudic narrative.

The story, however, proves more than Maimonides wants. He has set down two conditions that strip an oral profession of faith of the elements of heresy—inner disbelief and realization of this on the part of the coercer. It should be clarified, however, whether either of these can by itself remove the charges of apostasy or whether both are required in any given situation.

Let us construct a hypothetical situation. Someone thrusts a revolver in my back and commands me to worship his god. I myself had been contemplating this step and, viewing, perhaps, this action as a Divine sign or intercession, I decide then and there to embrace his faith. And so I proceed to repeat the formula as he has commanded me with deep inner conviction. For personal reasons, however, I do not wish to give him this satisfaction and I allow neither my face nor voice to betray my new belief. My coercer leaves with the disgruntled impression that my recital had no meaning for me.

Common sense, I think, would say that I have not been faithful to my religion but have renounced it, and I am an apostate despite my coercer's mistaken impression. It is apparent, then, that Maimonides' second condition—the constrainer's opinion of the meaninglessness of the Jew's assertion—certainly cannot by itself annul the heretical moment. What of the first condition?

[19] *IH* 40–1; S 37–41; H 29. See *Midrash Kohelet* 1: 8 and *'Avodah Zarah* 16b–17a for precise details of the story. See also S. Lieberman, 'Roman Legal Institutions in Early Rabbinics and in the *Acta Martyrum*', *Jewish Quarterly Review*, 35 (1944), 19–24. {To the above-mentioned primary sources one should add Tosefta, *Ḥullin*, 2: 24, ed. M. S. Zuckermandel (Halberstadt, 1880), 503. The secondary sources should be supplemented by P. Schäfer, *Jesus in the Talmud* (Princeton, 2007), 41–50, and the literature there cited, to which one should add D. Jaffé, *Le Judaïsme et l'avènement du christianisme: Orthodoxie et hétérodoxie dans la littérature talmudique Ier–IIe siècle* (Paris, 2005), 117–28.}

[20] It should be emphasized that Maimonides is not arguing for the permissibility of a *double entendre* in cases of duress. In fact, he pointedly omits this aspect and for good reason. R. Eli'ezer's case could not be advanced as a defense of the recitation of the *shahada*.

The answer is again apparent. If the speaker's inner disbelief suffices by itself to annul the treasonable nature of his confession, even if his coercer is under the false impression that he has renounced his old religion, then what need is there for Maimonides' second condition? If the person's profession is said with conviction, despite his oppressor's view to the contrary, he is an apostate; if it is said without conviction, again despite his oppressor's opinion to the contrary, he is not an apostate. The coercer's opinion becomes irrelevant, capable of neither mitigating religious treason when it is present nor of bestowing it when it is absent. By setting forth a second condition, Maimonides makes plain that both the disbelief of the speaker and the skepticism of the coercer are required in any given situation to relieve one of the onus of heresy.

But both were not present in the instance of R. Eli'ezer. The general |**292**| was under the impression that the sage agreed with him. We have, then, inner disbelief coupled with outer dissimulation, which, as we have seen, still constitutes, in Maimonides' opinion, apostasy. Maimonides draws upon the story for support by claiming that if one denied his set of principles, R. Eli'ezer would stand convicted of idolatry, but we see that if one admits them, the sage has in no way been vindicated.

Maimonides could, of course, discard his second qualification, but he doesn't; on the contrary, he seems to attach more importance to it than to the first. As it stands, his sole support is itself a rebuttal. Maimonides cannot both prove his position and maintain it, or at least he hasn't done so.

It may be a plausible assumption that words, unlike deeds, possess no intrinsic weight and attain significance only through the intention of the utterer—and then again, it may not. At any rate, such a supposition is a very novel one, and it detaches a sizable area of conduct from the domain of martyrdom which has hitherto been supposed to belong to it. An assumption with such wide-ranging implications needs support: either persuasive logical exposition or hard documentation. One cannot just assert it and assume that by so doing one has refuted the opposite view.

But this is precisely what Maimonides has done. He has adduced either no evidence or insufficient evidence, and as for ratiocination, the few lines that I quoted at the outset, if they may be called explication, are all that we are given. Significantly, in all his subsequent voluminous writings—the *Perush ha-Mishnayot*, the *Sefer ha-Mitsvot*, and the *Mishneh Torah*—no mention whatsoever is made of such a theory. Indeed, in the subsequent 700 years of Jewish legal history, no one, so far as I have been able to ascertain, has ever advanced a similar view.[21] If there is anything to Mill's famous contention that an |**293**| idea

[21] We are not dealing here with the problem of mental reservations with regard to ambiguous

containing a grain of truth tends, even if forgotten or suppressed, to be rediscovered over the course of the ages, then the judgment of history is completely against Maimonides' contention.

On the whole, the word–deed distinction would appear to be an artificial one, contrived for the exigencies of the moment—at its best suggestive, but certainly unable to bear the heavy burden of argument that Maimonides assigns to it.

Maimonides next moves to refute the charge that had caused the greatest consternation amongst the Marranos. It was alleged that their clandestine attempts to fulfill the law were utterly worthless and that they could expect no recompense or reward whatsoever for their religious observances, 'and so too other commandments, if one should do them he will not receive the reward for the doing of any one of them'.[22] The most worthless of all were their prayers, and, indeed, their supplication was almost criminal! 'If one of the Marranos should pray, he has no reward for that prayer, indeed, he has committed a sin.'[23] By telling the *anusim* that their double life was meaningless, the unknown accuser was cutting their last link with Judaism, and Maimonides devotes more space to the rebuttal of this point than to any other, for, as he writes:

statements, such as occupied the thought of late medieval thinkers, nor with the issue of whether stating that one is a Gentile constitutes apostasy (see 'Yoreh De'ah' 157: 2 and references there given, esp. the *Yam shel Shelomoh*), but with the contention that inner disbelief neutralizes an explicit confession of faith. Here the silence of generations is deafening. Explicit statements to the contrary are to be found in *Teshuvot R. Me'ir mi-Rotenburg*, ed. M. A. Bloch (Berlin, 1891), #80; *Teshuvot Maharil*, ed. Y. Satz (Jerusalem, 1980), #72. Indeed, to the extent that distinctions have been made between word and deed in matters of idolatry, the thrust has been in the latter direction, namely, that confessions under duress are held more culpable than deeds. The most explicit advocate of this position is the *Tosafot Yeshanim, Shabbat* 72b. A number of other thinkers tend in this general direction (e.g. R. Me'ir Abul'afia [Ramah] in *Yad Ramah, Sanhedrin*, ed. Y. Zilber [Jerusalem, 2000], 61b; R. David Bonfid in the so-called *Ḥiddushei ha-Ran 'al Sanhedrin*, ed. Y. Sklar [Jerusalem 2003], 61b; *Tosefot R. Yehudah mi-Paris* in *Shitat Kadmonim 'al 'Avodah Zarah*, ed. M. Y. H. Blau [New York, 1969], ii. 260), though it is not clear with regard to our particular case to what extent, according to Ramah, *she'at ha-shemad* by itself would constitute a גלי דעתיה (I would tend to think that it would), or to what extent the statement of אלי אתה must, according to R. David Bonfid and R. Yehudah of Paris, be accompanied by one of the four archetypal forms of worship (I would incline to the negative). For these reasons, the three above scholars cannot be cited as denying the Maimonidean contention, but to the extent that they speculate on this subject they distance themselves from, rather than move towards, Maimonides' novel contention. {I now have serious doubts whether the doctrine I attributed to Ramah was actually entertained by him.}

As to Maimonides' views about misleading statements, see *Sefer ha-Mitsvot*, Imperative 9. {See the Afterword to this essay, #4.} R. Shabbetai Kohen's remarks in his *Nekuddot ha-Kesef*, 'Yoreh De'ah' 148: 1, have clearly no bearing on our problem.

22 *IH* 46; S 43–4; H 22. 23 *IH* 45; S 43; H 22.

We feared that this [i.e. the opponent's] responsum (which drives man away from God) would reach the masses, and they shall discover therein that there is no reward for their prayer, so they shall cease praying. And similarly other commandments, if they shall do them, they will not be rewarded for any one of them [so they will cease from performing them].[24]

His defense consists of citing several stories mentioned in the Talmud. **|294|**

The Bible has already noted that Ahab, the son of Omri, who denied God and worshipped idols, of whom the Lord has testified, 'but there was none unto Ahab [in wickedness]' [1 Kgs. 21: 25], when he fasted two and a half hours, as our sages of blessed memory remarked [*Ta'an.* 25b], the Heavenly decree against him was cancelled, as it is written, 'And the word of the Lord came to Elijah the Tishbite, saying, "Seest thou how Ahab humbleth himself before me? Because he humbleth himself before me, I will not bring the evil in his days"' [1 Kgs. 21: 28–9]. And the Holy One, blessed be He, did not withhold the reward of his fast.

And Eglon, the king of Moab, who oppressed Israel, because he gave honor to the God of Israel; when Ehud said to him, 'I have a message from God unto thee', he [Eglon] rose from his stool.[25] The Lord rewarded him [with] a good reward and He gave . . . the Messiah [to arise] from his seed, for Ruth the Moabite was his daughter as they [the Rabbis] have said [*Naz.* 23a]. The Holy One, blessed be He, did not withhold his reward.

And the wicked Nebuchadnezzar, who killed as many Jews as the sands along the sea, and who destroyed the house [which was] the footstool of the Lord [i.e. the Temple], because he ran four steps [in order to see] that the name of God should precede that of Hezekiah, as they [the Rabbis] said, 'he ran after him four steps' [*San.* 96a], his reward was that he ruled for forty years . . . The Holy One, blessed be He, did not withhold his reward.

And if the Lord has rewarded these well-known heretics for the smallest of good deeds, Jews who are caught in religious persecution and fulfill the commandments in secret, how shall the Lord not reward them for this? Does he [the opponent] see no difference between one who fulfills a commandment and one who does not, between one who worships God and one who does not? Yet so it would appear from his words [when he writes], 'but when the Marrano prays he sins'.[26]

Our attention is immediately caught by the nature of the material Maimonides employs. His entire defense rests on aggadic sources. Homiletic disquisitions are not the stuff of which legal arguments are made. Their amorphousness and subjectivity make them unamenable to a serious juridical system. They may be used occasionally with some effectiveness in a peroration, as

24 *IH* 46; S 43–4; H 22.

25 See Judg. 3: 20.

26 *IH* 46–9; S 45–6; H 22–3.

the *coup de grâce* of a sharp legal duel, but |295| they lack the firmness and substantiveness to bear the brunt of juridical combat. Maimonides is too fine a halakhist not to realize that if there is any moot point in his position, none of his citations can be called upon for effective support. If he uses them it must be because the points are beyond doubt and need no justification, and he invokes these stories as illustrations of an uncontestable principle.

The message of these homiletical passages is that when man appears before the Heavenly court (and he does so every day), he is judged not on the basis of his predominant actions but for all of them—every petty crime or act of merit is taken into consideration. This is nothing but the idea of Divine retribution, and the *midrashim* quoted by Maimonides vividly portray its exactness. In essence Maimonides is arguing, and very persuasively so, that to claim that the Marranos' observances are meaningless and that they may expect no recompense is to deny the incontrovertible principle of *sakhar va-'onesh*—Divine retribution. The charge of the opponent is, then, a patent falsehood and verges dangerously on heresy.

To this rebuttal there can be no reply. It is final and overwhelming. So total is Maimonides' victory that our suspicions are at last aroused. The upshot is that underneath the opponent's religious garb there lurks a base anarchist, one who believes that apostasy is an invitation to all types of licentious action, for once one has become a heretic God is blind to one's merits or misdeeds. One begins to wonder whether his opponent, for all his faults, was so blind or so unprincipled as to deny Divine retribution.

A momentary digression will enable us, perhaps, to resolve our doubts. Every Jew is commanded to eat unleavened bread (matzot) on the night of Passover. Suppose an atheist should be invited to a house in which the festival is celebrated. Upon arrival he says to himself: 'Of course, I do not believe in the Mosaic revelation, much less in the Divine nature of the Bible. The entire holiday is the holdover of a tribal superstition. But I am a guest, so I'll participate in the ritual tonight and eat whatever I'm supposed to.' The question that poses itself is whether he will, by his social supping, have fulfilled the commandment of eating matzot.

If charity is given not out of a sense of religious obligation but from a desire to help a fellow man, little doubt can be entertained as to its merits. However, when we come to purely ritual performances, the meaningfulness of one's deeds becomes much more suspect. One |296| wonders whether one can fulfill one's religious duty via some technical act though one denies one's religion, or whether the act takes on substance only within the context of conviction. In short, can one be 'observant' without believing?

The instinctive answer, I think, would be in the negative. Fulfillment of a commandment becomes meaningful within, and only within, the matrix of admission of its Divine and obligatory character. A commandment whose essential nature has been denied is meaningless when performed, for ritual without belief is a game and not a religious act.

At any rate, this is the opinion, I venture to suggest, of Maimonides' opponent and the point he was actually making. His position was not just a vague forecast of the millennial fate of the Marranos, but a consequence of his previous stand. The Jews in Morocco had admitted the prophetic character of Mohammed's mission. They had by this disavowed the eternal validity of their religion and their law, and for this they were to be deemed apostates. This led to one inescapable conclusion: that their religious observances were of no value. Having denied their religion, their attempts to fulfill its dictates were not only worthless but ridiculous: indeed, they bordered on mockery. There is no room in the faith, he claimed, for Orthodox Jewish heretics.

In this charge he was assessing not simply the moral standing of the Marrano generally, but also the meaningfulness of his religious conduct, the precise legal standing of his actions. He was focusing on the deed as much as on the man. The conclusions at which he arrived were highly negative, and he spared nothing to make this brutally clear to his readers. With his gift for effective statement he summed up his position in a phrase calculated to drive deepest into the hearts of simple people: 'even if he performs a commandment he will receive no reward for it'.[27]

Maimonides, in accordance with his practice of not repeating an entire argument, justly quotes this sentence as the gist of his opponent's position. But by quoting it in isolation he transforms the entire charge.[28] |297| What had been a rhetorical flourish, a flashy expression to accent the denouement of a closely knit argument, now becomes the entire argument and a different one at that. The point at issue ceases to be the juridical quality of religious observance

[27] The phrase 'no reward for his deeds' has a dual meaning. It may be used technically to express the idea that an action is juridically worthless, as in *Berakhot* 26a: שכר תפילה יהבי ליה, שכר תפילה בזמנה לא יהבי ליה, that is to say, קיום תפילה יש לו, קיום תפילה בזמנה אין לו. Or it may be used colloquially, to state that a seemingly meritorious deed is actually worthless. In the latter sense it would correspond roughly to our modern secular expression 'he deserves no credit for it'. {On religious meaninglessness of orthopraxis by actual atheists (not by Marranos, who have been coerced to utter heretical statements but who in reality fully believe in the Divine dictates of the Torah): Y. Satz (above, n. 3) has drawn attention (p. 232 n. 13) to Naḥmanides' remarks in his *Perush la-Torah*, Deut. 28: 14, and Dov Frimer (in a personal communication) to R. Elhanan B. Wasserman's endorsement of this view in *Kovets Shi'urim: Shi'urim she-Ne'emru ba-Yeshivah* (Tel Aviv, 1963), #47: 12.}

[28] For a further indication that Maimonides transformed the nature of his opponent's charge, see below, pp. 318–19.

and becomes that of Divine retribution. A substantive, legal, terrestrial claim becomes a metaphysical assertion touching upon the ways of celestial book-keeping. The opponent's entire charge is transcendentalized until it is a ghost of its former self: and Maimonides then finds very little difficulty in exorcising it.

Maimonides' rebuttal of his antagonist's claims, to which he devotes the first half of his responsum, is to a great extent composed of these three points of prophecy and idolatry, word and deed, and reward and punishment. Abusive epithets and homiletic diversions occur sometimes in the treatise, but while the former are amusing and the latter occasionally moving, neither has much relevance to the problem at hand. But there remains a major theme, still unanalyzed, that runs through the letter like the thread of Ariadne—that of free will and coercion. It will be remembered that when refuting the fundamental charge of idolatry leveled against the Marranos, Maimonides also notes that anything that has been perpetrated has been done under constraint and allowances have to be made for this circumstance.[29] He touches upon it again in reference to a charge involving Sabbath desecration,[30] and it comes strongly to the fore against the claim that the *anusim* had, by their religious transgressions, forfeited their right to serve as witnesses, when Maimonides writes:

> And they had disobeyed God not because they sought convenience or benefit, nor have they abandoned the Law and distanced themselves from it to attain rank or temporal enjoyment [but only because] 'they fled from the sword, from the drawn sword and from the bent bow and from the grievousness of war' [Isa. 21: 15].[31] |**298**|

And finally it occurs again, in a more subdued fashion, in his defense of the religious observances of the Moroccan Jews, when he remarks that if willful sinners have been recompensed for their slight merits, certainly the oppressed community may expect that its attempts to remain true to its faith will not be disregarded.[32]

[29] Above, p. 291.

[30] *IH* 31–2; S 32; H 16. The charge of *ḥillul Shabbat* had been leveled by his antagonist and apparently with devastating force, for Maimonides refers to it no fewer than three times in the *Iggeret* (*IH* 31–2, 63, 67; S 32, 53, 59; H 16, 30, 33). He even closes the *Iggeret* with words of consolation for the *meḥallel Shabbat*. The cutting edge of the charge was the famous talmudic dictum (*Ḥullin* 5a) that the status of a Sabbath violator was the same as that of an idolater. Sabbath violation, moreover, is the only tort where no distinction is made between *le-te'avon* and *le-hakh'is*, and hence an argument in defense of the Marranos that any specific sin incurred as a result of dissimulation was still committed solely out of a desire to live, and therefore its performer had at worst the status of *mumar le-te'avon*, was inapplicable to *ḥillul Shabbat*. Maimonides' only defense remained, then, that of duress.

[31] *IH* 38; S 34; H 19.

[32] *IH* 48–9; S 45; H 23–4.

The refutation, however, is strangely lacking. It points out that the *anusim* acted only out of fear of death, but his opponent was fully aware of this and nevertheless leveled the charge of apostasy. The bone of contention is not the existence of the Almohad terror, but whether it suffices to relieve one of legal culpability. The Talmud clearly outlines under what circumstances one is obliged to suffer death rather than transgress and under what circumstances one is not. However, it does not discuss the scenario where someone declines to be a martyr and chooses rather to perform what is demanded of him. Is such a person to be held legally responsible for his deeds?

Ordinarily the problem can never arise, for the threat of death (*pikuaḥ nefesh*) renders the criminal act permissible. But in the case of idolatry or murder one is mandated not to yield. In yielding the individual has, no doubt, acted illegally, but has he done so willingly? Left alone he would never have killed the man or worshipped the idol; he acted only to save his life. On the one hand, we have the undeniable threat of death (*pikuaḥ nefesh*); on the other, we have the indisputable imperative of 'Be killed and do not transgress'. Put briefly: does an action taken under the threat of death relieve man of responsibility, even in those instances where he is supposed to suffer martyrdom? The resolution of this problem is far from self-evident. A defense of Marranoism in the early 1160s cannot rest with the simple statement of the fact of persecution, but must proceed to invest it with halakhic significance; yet Maimonides concludes his vindication of North African Jewry without having even attempted to do so.

The second half of the letter is devoted to a formulation of some of the most common terms employed in the discussion of martyrdom and a systematic presentation of the fundamental laws governing one's conduct in the time of persecution. Surprisingly, it is in this constructive portion of the missive that we encounter, in a sudden pocket of polemic, Maimonides' justification for his stand on coercion.

Breaking off his calm presentation, he suddenly recalls his |299| opponent's earlier charge of disqualified witness and a new one that the Marranos have merited death by their idolatrous worship, and he writes:

> But if he did not let himself be killed, but transgressed because of coercion, he has not acted properly . . . but he is not subject to any punishment, for we do not find anywhere in the Law . . . that one who is coerced is punished, only one who acts willingly . . . nor is he disqualified from testimony . . .
>
> But should anyone contend or think [that] because our sages have said 'Be killed and do not transgress', if one transgresses he incurs the death penalty; [know that] this is a total error. For it is in no way so, but rather as I will [proceed to] tell you: the person

is commanded to [let himself] be killed, but if he does not let himself be killed he has not incurred the death penalty; for even one who worships strange gods under coercion has not incurred [even] *karet*, and certainly the courts cannot kill him. This fundamental principle has been set forth in the *Torat Kohanim*, '"And I will set my face against *that* man" [Lev. 20: 3]; *that* man [who performs willingly] and not one who acts out of coercion . . . and under constraint.' Desecration of the Name is an injunction, for it is written in the Pentateuch: 'And you shall not swear by My name falsely [for] you shall not profane the name of your God; and I am the Lord' [Lev. 19: 12]. Nevertheless the Mishnah [*Ned.* 3: 4] states that one may take a [false] vow to 'murderers, robbers, and [illegal] publicans'.[33]

Maimonides' opponent had advocated the view that the imperative of *kiddush ha-shem* conflicts with and destroys the law of *pikuaḥ nefesh*. Once we enter the awesome domain of martyrdom, the principle of self-preservation is annulled *in toto*, hence all acts that require martyrdom, for any reason, retain their full criminality. Maimonides' erudition disposes of this contention easily. He adduces a passage from the *Sifra* stating that idolatry committed under coercion is non-culpable. As the worship of false gods certainly falls within the realm of prescribed martyrdom, it is obvious that regardless of the martyr imperative, the |**300**| deed is still viewed in that source as involuntary, and for this reason the performer is not held legally responsible.[34]

[33] *IH* 59–60; S 51–52; H 29–30. I have omitted, for simplicity's sake, the reference to *terumah* in the Mishnah, as it in no way affects the line of argument.

[34] There should be no doubt as to the force of Maimonides' argument, which he reproduces in 'Yesodei ha-Torah', 5: 4. With the exception of the isolated remarks of R. Mosheh ha-Kohen (*Hassagot ha-Ramakh 'al ha-Rambam*, ed. S. Atlas [Jerusalem, 1969], ad loc.) and the counter-interpretation of the *Sifra* by R. David Bonfid (*Ḥiddushei ha-Ran 'al Sanhedrin* 61b, s.v. *itmar*), which attracted no followers, Maimonides' views won widespread acceptance. Centuries later a problem was detected in this proof in view of some obscurity in the *Mishneh Torah* as to the status of Moloch worship; see Y. Y. L. Perlman, *Or Gadol* (Vilna, 1924), 34 ff. and the literature there cited. But this in no way affected the acceptance of Maimonides' doctrine of non-culpability in instances of duress. How deeply Maimonides felt on this matter can be seen in the *Sefer ha-Mitsvot*, Injunction 294, and in 'Sanhedrin', 20: 2, where he contends that the courts are specifically enjoined from punishing the coerced. (Cf. Naḥmanides' critique in *Sefer ha-Mitsvot*, *shoresh* 8 and Injunction 294.) In his *Mishnah 'im Perush le-Rabbenu Mosheh b. Maimon*, *Mo'ed*, ed. Y. Kafih (Jerusalem, 1963), *Yoma* 8: 6, Maimonides adds that not only is someone coerced held not culpable, but he is also in no need of atonement (*kapparah*). {One should add R. Yitsḥak b. Asher of Speyer—Riva—to the small list of those who disagreed with Maimonides' position on coercion in instances when martyrdom is demanded; see Avraham b. 'Azri'el, *'Arugat ha-Bosem*, ed. E. E. Urbach (Jerusalem, 1963), iii. 195. The second reply, *ve-yesh mefarshim*, in *Tosafot*, *Sanhedrin* 61b, s.v. *rava*, and *Tosefot ha-Rosh*, *Sanhedrin*, ed. S. H. Vilman (Jerusalem, 1978), 61b, would seem equally to disagree. However, that position was not developed out of disagreement with the first reply, but was advanced independently by R. Eli'ezer of Metz in his *Sefer Yere'im ha-Shalem*, i, ed. A. A. Schiff (Vilna, 1892–1902), #100. It happens to be juxtaposed in *Tosafot* to the first resolution but was not in any way generated by it. Dov Frimer has drawn

But Maimonides does not rest content with this proof; he seeks to advance another, and with it writes some of the most astounding lines in his entire career. He claims (and justly so) that false oaths constitute a *ḥillul ha-shem* (desecration of the Name);[35] nevertheless, the Mishnah states that one is permitted to swear falsely under coercion. This, he asserts, is decisive evidence that one is not held culpable even where desecration of the Name is involved.

It is true that swearing falsely constitutes a desecration of the Name, and it is certainly correct that yielding to one's persecutor when one must not also involves a violation of the same injunction. However, Maimonides' antagonist did not claim that there is culpability whenever *ḥillul ha-shem* is involved—only when the obligation of martyrdom is present, which, by destroying the principle of *pikuaḥ nefesh*, retains for the act its full criminal nature. The very point of the passage cited by Maimonides is that this form of desecration does not require martyrdom; hence his opponent would be the first one to grant that the swearer is absolved of all obligation, despite the fact that he has transgressed on *ḥillul ha-shem*. Maimonides has committed the elementary logical fallacy of the 'undistributed middle', that is to say, he has employed the flawed 'syllogism' of (*a*) John and Jim are both tailors, (*b*) John has a big nose, (*c*) therefore, Jim has a big nose. Similarly, Maimonides has incredibly argued that (*a*) both swearing falsely and breaching the martyrdom imperative constitute desecration of the Name; (*b*) the injunction against swearing falsely is lifted in cases of coercion; (*c*) therefore, the injunction against breaching the martyrdom imperative is lifted in cases of coercion!

Coupled with this logical error is a factual one, no less astonishing. It is universally admitted that the coercion that relieves the individual of legal responsibility for his deeds must be the actual threat of death. Something chosen as an alternative to |**301**| a lesser threat,[36] such as loss of money, is deemed by all hands as voluntarily performed. The Mishnah deals with a case in which the threat of death is not necessarily present. For this reason it sets

my attention to the dissenting view of Don Crescas, brother of Rivash, published in the latter's collection, *Teshuvot ha-Rivash*, ii, ed. D. Metzger (Jerusalem, 1993), #387 (p. 546), s.v. *u-va'al din* and notes ad loc. Contrast this with Rivash's own position endorsing that of Maimonides expressed in *Teshuvot Rivash*, i, ##4, 11, 171. With all respect, I find the interpretation of *Tosafot, 'Avodah Zarah* 54a, s.v. *ha* proffered by R. Shemu'el Strashon in his *Haggahot Rashash* ad loc. forced. *Le-mitah* in *Tosafot* means the obligation to suffer death, i.e. the imperative of martyrdom; it does not mean incurring the death penalty if that imperative was disobeyed.}

35 'Yesodei ha-Torah', 5: 10 and commentaries ad loc.

36 I have omitted the much later controversy over whether the threat of loss of limb reaches the level of 'coercion' sufficient to relieve one of culpability (see *Shakh*, 'Yoreh Deah' 157: 3, and references there cited).

forth the three types of coercers—murderers, robbers, and illegal publicans—all portraying different gradations of constraint: the murderer threatens with death, the robber with other penalties, and so on.[37] It is obvious, then, that the principle at work in the passage on taking a false oath has absolutely nothing to do with the problem of coercion at all; indeed, as Maimonides himself recognized and explicitly stated in his *Perush ha-Mishnayot* and his *Yad ha-Ḥazakah*—together with all his contemporaries and successors, whether of the Franco-German, Provençal, Spanish, or Moroccan schools—the law here embodied concerns the effectiveness of mental reservations vis-à-vis certain vows.[38] The *mishnah* is totally unrelated to the issue at hand, and Maimonides' reasons for its introduction are nigh incomprehensible.

In my discussions of word–deed distinctions, Divine retribution, and culpability for actions performed under duress, I have covered large areas in the second half of *Iggeret ha-Shemad*. A look at the remaining aspects of this section will round out my survey of Maimonides' letter.

To make his readers aware of the central shift that is taking place in the responsum, from polemic to constructive formulation, Maimonides prefaces his discussion with a brief table of contents.[39]

I have seen fit to divide my remarks on this topic into five sections. The first section: the differences between commandments in a time of coercion [i.e. which commandments require martyrdom and under what circumstances]. The second section: the definition of *ḥillul ha-shem* and its punishment. The third section: the status of those killed for the sanctification of the Name and that of the *anusim*. The fourth section: [the nature of] this persecution [as compared with that of] other persecutions; and how it befits a man to act in it. The fifth section: how a man should watch himself [i.e. view himself] in this persecution. |**302**|

The ability which Maimonides displays in encompassing a problem in both its theoretical and its practical aspects is admirable, but his presentation is

37 Cf. commentaries ad loc. and see S. Lieberman and E. Y. Kutscher, 'Taggarin, Ḥaramin, Ḥaragin', *Leshonenu*, 27 (1963), 34–9.

38 i.e. דברים שבלב, see *Shevu'ot* 3: 2, *Nedarim* 4: 2, and the standard commentaries on the passage in *Nedarim*. {I have overstated my case. Maimonides, in *Perush ha-Mishnayot*, simply explains the cases of the Mishnah but gives no explanation whatsoever for the allowance. He states the rationale of mental reservations only in *Mishneh Torah*. As this explanation is also given by all other commentators, I see no reason why not to retroject the interpretation expressed in *Mishneh Torah* upon his earlier *Perush ha-Mishnah* and view it as reflecting Maimonides' opinion from the very outset of his career. Satz (above, n. 3), 254 n. 78, has attempted to explain Maimonides' strange proof from the *mishnah* in *Nedarim*. I find his suggestion unpersuasive.}

39 *IH* 50; S 46; H 24, something which he fails to do in his rebuttal, where it would have been somewhat more useful.

nevertheless odd. Systematic organization was always Maimonides' forte, indeed, his most distinctive intellectual trait, yet by all standards the discussion should not have begun as it did. The first section is hardly an independent topic but one subsumed under 'desecration of the Name'. The proper order would have been to begin with the definition of *ḥillul ha-shem* and then proceed to discuss the obligation of martyrdom as one of the subdivisions of this large and comprehensive rubric.

Though the position may be mystifying, the content of the first section is not. It constitutes a masterly presentation of the times and places when one must lay down one's life rather than yield to the coercer. The three immutable injunctions of idolatry, murder, and incestuous or adulterous relations (*gillui 'arayot*), the principle of persecution (*she'at ha-shemad*), and that of public coercion (*be-farhesya*) are all explained and skillfully interwoven with the relevant talmudic texts. In some ways the clarity of Maimonides' discussion here exceeds that of his later *Mishneh Torah*.[40]

Writing next on *ḥillul ha-shem*, he says:

Desecration of the Name . . . shall be divided into two classes: [one] of universal [application] and one of special [application]. The universal one [applying to all men] shall be divided into two portions: one of them [is] when a man sins for the sake of defiance [*le-hakh'is*], i.e. [should he sin] not out of any desire for pleasure or benefit but because this injunction is insignificant and contemptible in his eyes, he has desecrated the Name . . . The second: if a man conducts himself in mundane matters in such a manner so as to start bad rumors flying, even though he has committed no sin, he has desecrated the Name . . . and so they said in *Yoma* [86a] . . .

The special [class, i.e. that applying only to a limited body of people] shall be divided into two sections. The first: when a scholar does that which is permitted to all men, but ill behooves a man like him to do for . . . more is expected of him—he has desecrated the Name . . . The second: when a scholar conducts himself in a vulgar and repulsive fashion in his business dealings, and he receives men angrily and insultingly . . . he has desecrated the Name . . . And *ḥillul ha shem* is a grave sin . . . [for unlike] |303| all other transgressions neither the Day of Atonement, nor suffering nor repentance can atone for it . . . [only] with death is it fully atoned, as they have said: 'But if he has been guilty of desecration of the Name' [*Yoma* 86a].[41]

Though the rumor-preventing conduct on the part of the ordinary man was never repeated by Maimonides in his subsequent writings, nor mentioned by any of his predecessors or successors, the definition of *ḥillul ha-shem* is nevertheless a highly comprehensive one, and we find in it much of the material that

[40] The syntax in 'Yesodei ha-Torah', 5: 2 is not flawless, as the *Leḥem Mishneh* (ad loc.) already sensed.

[41] *IH* 52–6; S 47–50; H 25–7.

went into the shaping of the *Sefer ha-Mitsvot* and the *Mishneh Torah*.[42] Only one little thing is lacking: the commandment of martyrdom. Throughout the entire definition not one reference is made to it, and the impression left is that it does not constitute a violation of the injunction of 'thou shalt not desecrate my holy Name'. Nor does Maimonides' discussion of *kiddush ha-shem* contribute to a different notion. 'Sanctification of the Name is the opposite of desecration. This [takes place] when a man performs any commandment without mixing with it [i.e. the performance] any motive other than the sheer love of God and His worship.'[43] It is true that martyrdom is a form of altruism, but no one reading this definition would conclude that simply because one must act disinterestedly, one is obliged to suffer death.

The preface, then, was no accident. Maimonides quite intentionally preceded his analysis of *ḥillul ha-shem* with a discussion of martyrdom because he did not wish to treat the latter as a subdivision of desecration. This runs counter to all previous opinions and Maimonides' own subsequent views, and, indeed, is in direct contradiction to the talmudic texts in *Sanhedrin*, which he himself cites in the letter. Then, immediately after, he writes:

> The third section: on the status of those killed for the sanctification of the Name . . . Know that [in] all cases where our sages have said 'be killed and do not transgress', if he [let himself] be killed, he has sanctified the Name . . . as Ḥananyah, Misha'el, and 'Azaryah . . . and about them was said: 'Gather |304| my saints unto me, those who have made a covenant with me by sacrifice' [Ps. 50: 5] . . . and about them was said, 'Yea for thy sake are we killed all the day long' [Ps. 45: 23]. And the Lord [shall place] this man, that is to say, one who has been killed for sanctification of the Name, in the ranks of the highest.[44]

He is now of the opinion that suffering death for one's faith constitutes sanctification of the Name, yet in his lengthy formulation of that commandment he has made no reference to it whatsoever!

For some bewildering reason, the aspect of *kiddush ha-shem* and *ḥillul ha-shem* which had loomed the largest in the eyes of all Talmudists (Maimonides included) from time immemorial is blithely and completely banished from Maimonides' presentation, and then quietly admitted through the back way, accompanied even with a bit of mournful fanfare.

The letter continues: 'But if he did not let himself be killed, but transgressed because of coercion, he has not acted properly, but has desecrated the Name under coercion, but he is not subject to any punishment.'[45] It then goes

[42] Injunction 63; 'Yesodei ha-Torah', 5: 5, 10, 11; 'Teshuvah', 1: 4.

[43] *IH* 55; S 49; H 26–7.

[44] *IH* 57–8; S 50–1; H 28.

[45] *IH* 59; S 52; H 28.

on to reject the theory that in instances where martyrdom is obligatory, the individual will be held responsible for his deed. Maimonides concludes this pocket of polemic, and with it the third section, with a forceful rejection of any culpability for acts committed under coercion.

Maimonides initially devotes the next part of the responsum to establishing the fact that this oppression differs from most others, in that only word, and not deed, is required of the Jews. He reiterates that even the greatest of sinners will be judged based on not only their misdeeds but also the meritorious acts that they have committed, and that the Marranos should in no way relinquish their religious observance. He then very movingly tells the Moroccan community that while technically, perhaps, they are not under religious persecution, nevertheless they should make every possible effort to leave the country and settle in a place where they can fulfill the word of God without fear and hesitation. With a strange mixture of rebuke, encouragement, and consolation, Maimonides closes his responsum, writing:

|**305**| Section five: I will explain how it is fitting for a man to view himself in these days of persecution. Everyone who cannot escape ... [for various reasons] and stays in this place, he must view himself as one who has desecrated the Name of God, though not willingly, but [by his continued presence and not fleeing] he comes close to [desecrating it] willfully, and he is an outcast in the eyes of God and will be punished for his wicked deeds. But he should always have in mind that if he performs a commandment, the Holy One, blessed be He, will reward him doubly, for he certainly performs it for the sake of Heaven only and does not seek to show off his religiosity. And one cannot compare the reward [i.e. merit] of one who performs it knowing that if he is discovered he will lose his life ... But nevertheless his mind should not rest until he leaves that place ... But still [one who stays] ... should not be despised or kept at a distance, but brought nearer and encouraged in the performance of commandments ...

From the day when we were exiled from our land ... our persecutions have never ceased ... But the Talmud says, 'persecutions tend to pass away'. May God annul this one and realize in our time what he said [to Jeremiah]: 'In those days and in that time, saith the Lord, the iniquity of Israel shall be sought for, and there shall be none: and the sins of Judah, and they shall not be found: for I will pardon them whom I shall preserve' [Jer. 50: 20]. So may it be His will, amen.[46]

RHETORIC

Had this letter come down to us unattributed, we would have written it off as the work of a talented amateur, who combined, as dilettantes often do, wide erudition with astonishing lapses of ignorance, facile presentation with funda-

[46] *IH* 67–8; S 58–9; H 33–4.

mental organizational confusion. However, we know it to have come from the pen of a 'Moses ben Maimon of Córdoba', whom posterity has numbered among the mighty of the earth and whose writings to this day bear witness to the wisdom of the judgment.

To claim that at this point he had not yet acquired his vast talmudic knowledge is to disregard his monumental *Perush ha-Mishnayot*, written during this very period, while to assert that he simply forgot the most elementary definitions of apostasy and *kiddush ha-shem* is to shut one's eyes to his having written large sections of his commentary on the Mishnah during his wanderings without |**306**| the aid of books, and yet without flaw in their references. Of all the charges that were leveled against the author of the *Mishneh Torah* and the *Moreh Nevukhim* (and they were legion), weakness of memory has never been numbered among them.

Ineluctably, we are led to the conclusion that Maimonides was aware of the incorrectness of his position. Perhaps, as some historians have claimed,[47] he was himself a Marrano, and, stung by the accusation, he willfully twisted or omitted the facts to vindicate his own conduct. Yet for a man who had the most recondite of legal passages at his fingertips, it would have been child's play to cover his tracks more effectively. When a great scholar takes it into his mind, for one reason or another, to defend a false position, the resultant product is far beyond the criticism of a schoolboy. The errors in Maimonides' letter bulk too large, the missing links or arguments are too apparent, for this to be an *apologia pro vita sua*.

As a legal defense *Iggeret ha-Shemad* is inexplicable, but not as a work of rhetoric, in the classic (and medieval) sense of the term—as a pamphlet aimed not at truth but at suasion, at moving people by all means at hand towards a given course of action.[48] *Iggeret ha-Shemad* is not a halakhic work, not a responsum, but, to use a modern term, a propagandist tract, written with a single purpose in mind—to counteract the effects of a letter of indictment that had gained great currency and threatened to wreak havoc on the Moroccan community.[49]

[47] For references to the literature, see Corcos, 'Shalitei ha-'Almoḥadon' (above, n. 1) and Y. L. Maimon, *Rabbenu Mosheh ben Maimon* (Jerusalem, 1960), 18 nn. 2–4, and references in the article by S. Z. H. Halberstam reprinted in the latter work, p. 242 ff. {See now M. A. Friedman, *Ha-Rambam, ha-Mashiaḥ be-Teman* (above, n. 1), 31–7, to which add A. Mazor, 'Hit'aslemuto mi-'Ones shel ha-Rambam: Yedi'ah Ḥadashah', *Pe'amim*, 110 (2007), 5–8.}

[48] 'Rhetoric is the faculty of discerning in every case the available means of persuasion' (Aristotle, *Rhetoric*, i: 2 [1355b]). It is this meaning which obtained in the Middle Ages under the Aristotelian influence. Our current use of the word as connoting 'artificial elegance of speech' or 'declamation without earnest feeling' is a later development.

[49] The writer took measures to see that his work was widely disseminated: *IH* 34; S 34; H 17.

Though that letter has not come down to us, we can, from Maimonides' passing remarks, reconstruct what he was up against. The desultory form which he so criticized contributed, one suspects, to the letter's wide circulation.[50] The reader's indignation was aroused by the account of the massacres that Mohammed had visited upon the Jews, and his interest was awakened by the description of the idolatrous rites that |307| took place in Mecca.[51] The letter was fairly bursting with scholarly talmudic citations, ranging from the law of perjured witnesses (*'edim zomemim*) to those regulating the breeding of animals. Most of this was irrelevant, as Maimonides sarcastically noted,[52] but it caught the eye of the untrained masses and impressed them.

The letter's effectiveness stemmed, however, from more than just its colorful flaws. In an era when religion was the ultimate human concern, guilt will have weighed heavily on the mind of the Marrano. When first confronted with the choice between death and an alien creed, he perhaps told himself that whatever he might say or do, nothing would alter his adherence to Judaism. But his life became one of constant pretense, and every dissimulation brought home to him that he had, in effect, surrendered his faith.

The burden of religious treason is too great for most consciences to bear, and the Marrano divested himself of it by thrusting the responsibility on to the shoulders of circumstance. He consoled himself with the thought that there was no alternative. But the relief that this afforded was illusory, for if he was acquitted of apostasy at the bar of his conscience, he stood convicted of moral cowardice. All that the attendant circumstances can plead is that it was to save his own life that he betrayed his religion.

The only escape from this agonizing indictment was simply not to confront it, but to go about one's everyday life without questioning its implications too deeply. The people ceased to think and to judge, that they might not be judged. Thus the intellectual life of the Marrano community was soon overtaken by a pained, forced stillness, and its members went about their daily tasks with their eyes hooded in a cloak of uneasy silence and self-deception.

The letter tore off those protective blinders. Its unequivocal and peremptory tone forced the *anusim* to look squarely at their surroundings, and its harsh, brutal language pointed out to them the full criminality of their religious dissimulation. It boldly articulated what the community had long feared but had attempted to suppress, and its effect was correspondingly devastating.

The purpose of the letter had been to startle the Jews into realizing the heinousness of their deeds, and by this to summon them to live up to the |308|

50 *IH* 30, 34–5, 43–4; S 30, 34, 42; H 15, 17, 21.

51 *IH* 44; S 42; H 21.

52 *IH* 35, 43–4; S 34, 42; H 17, 21.

challenge of martyrdom. But living outside North Africa,[53] the author overestimated the courage of the Marranos. For some reason or another, unlike their north European brethren, the Jews of the Moroccan community were not equal to their awesome duty.[54] They were aware now of the gravity of their sin, but it drove them not to heroism but to despair. Overwhelmed by their guilt, they began to wonder if they should not concede to Islam altogether, for 'however strictly they observed the ordinances of their religion, they were still to be considered idolaters and sinners and could expect no pardon'. The entire Moroccan Jewish community was in danger of outright apostasy.

To avoid this catastrophe, Maimonides entered the fray. It mattered little now whether they were or were not technically 'apostates', for if something was not done they would soon be so in fact. As long as they persisted in their Judaism, even if technically speaking their efforts were worthless, they could very easily be brought back into the fold when the persecution had passed. At any rate, their children and future generations would not be lost forever to the people of Israel.[55] And while this last point was indeed irrelevant to the legal question of *yehareg ve-'al ya'avor* ('he should be killed and not transgress'—the imperative of martyrdom), it had no small bearing on the simpler issue of Jewish survival. Some means had to be found to alleviate the community's profound sense of guilt and to tell its members that they had not abandoned its faith.

Maimonides undertook to assuage the bruised feelings of the persecuted people, and the long torrent of abuse that marks the letter was directed towards that end. He hoped to lighten the suffering of the Marranos by pointing out that their accuser was far from the scholarly saint they thought him

[53] *IH* 29; S 30; H 15, and again a sarcastic reference to this fact on p. 60 (S 52; H 30).

[54] See G. D. Cohen, 'Messianic Postures of Ashkenazim and Sephardim', in M. Kreutzberger, ed., *Studies of the Leo Baeck Institute* (New York, 1967), 117–58, repr. in his *Studies in the Variety of Rabbinic Cultures* (Philadelphia, 1991), 271–97. {M. Cohen, *Under Cross and Crescent: The Jews in the Middle Ages* (Princeton, 1994), 162–94. This dichotomy, both as regards messianic postures and choice of martyrdom, has been challenged in recent years, with the pendulum swinging too far in the other direction. See D. Berger, 'Ha-Meshiḥiyut ha-Sefardit ve-ha-Meshiḥiyut ha-'Ashkenazit bi-Yemei ha-Beinayim: Beḥinat ha-Maḥloket ha-Historiografit', in Y. Hacker et al., eds., *Rishonim ve-'Aḥaronim: Meḥkarim be-Toledot Yisra'el Muggashim le-'Avraham Grossman* (Jerusalem, 2010), 11–28. English translation: 'Sephardic and Ashkenazic Messianism in the Middle Ages: An Examination of the Historiographical Controversy', repr. in id., *Cultures in Collision and Conversation: Essays in the Intellectual History of the Jews* (Boston, 2011), 289–311. For bibliography on the martyrdom dichotomy, see P. Tartakof, 'Jewish Women and Apostasy in the Medieval Crown of Aragon, c.1300–1391', *Jewish History*, 24 (2010), 31 n. 86. For a fresh perspective on this dichotomy (together with a full bibliography, esp. of the Islamic dimension), see M. Ben-Sasson's fine article in the same volume, 'Zikkaron ve-Shikheḥah shel Shemadot: 'al Kiddush ha-Shem be-'Artsot ha-Natsrut u-ve-'Artsot ha-'Islam bi-Yemei ha-Beinayim ha-Mukdamim', 47–72.}

[55] *IH* 29; S 30; H 15.

to be. His letter, they were told, was 'weak and tasteless, without form or content, and with an array of arguments so lacking that even empty-headed women could perceive it', written by a 'muddle-headed' man who had 'veritably abused the Divine gift of speech' by his 'blasphemy and reviling and long-winded foolishness and madness'.[56] To us this may seem in poor taste, for Maimonides did not possess that dagger-like wit which rescues sharp |**309**| polemic from degenerating into sheer abuse,[57] but he obviously deemed the invective necessary, and it most probably had its effect.[58]

[56] *IH* 30–1, 33; S 30–2; H 15–16.

[57] He was no match in this respect for his contemporary, Rabad of Posquières, nor even for his later successor R. Shelomoh ibn Aderet (Rashba) in his *Mishmeret ha-Bayit*.

[58] It would be the rankest pedantry to point out that Aristotle had noted the utility of denigrating one's opponent in debate whenever possible. How to make a good argument for a bad case requires no knowledge of Aristotle, as anyone who has ever caught a child with his fingers in a cookie jar well knows. Nevertheless, here and there—as in the use of 'example', the misuse of homonyms (e.g. *sekhar mitsvah*), the employment of sham enthymemes (e.g. the 'syllogism' with the 'undivided middle')—references will still be made to the *Rhetoric*. The point of these references (which could be easily multiplied) is not to imply that without some knowledge of this work Maimonides would not have written as he did, or that he wrote according to a preconceived model. This would be nonsense. They serve, rather, the purpose of underlining that, given the goal of the *Iggeret*, given its very nature, the tools employed would be viewed as fitting and legitimate by one raised in the Aristotelian tradition. Rhetoric was a recognized literary and intellectual genre and Maimonides could well feel that his mode of argumentation, no less than his ultimate goal, was in one sense valid, and that in writing as he did, he stood not only religiously, but intellectually as well, in a reputable tradition—a tradition in which, given every instinct and inclination of his, he would ideally have preferred not to involve himself, but a respectable one nonetheless.

Aristotle's *Rhetoric* had been translated and commented upon by Maimonides' time, and knowledge of it was part and parcel of any philosophical education of the period. Unwilling to rely upon my layman's knowledge (or, more accurately, non-knowledge) of this matter, I turned to my colleague Professor Arthur Hyman, who was kind enough to allow me to quote his reply:

> That Maimonides was familiar with the philosophical rhetorical tradition of his day is evident from his *Treatise on Logic*, in chapter 8 of which he discusses the rhetorical syllogism and the art of rhetoric. He points out that the art of rhetoric uses the analogical syllogism and that the enthymeme is one of the forms of the rhetorical syllogism. In the tenth chapter of the *Treatise* he mentions the 'Book of Rhetoric' as the sixth part of the medieval Aristotelian logical canon. He also cites the *Rhetoric* in *Guide* III. 49, but this citation deals with an ethical rather than a methodological point.
>
> The logical tradition upon which Maimonides drew contained a number of full or partial works devoted to rhetoric, and most of the Islamic philosophers whom Maimonides mentions in his well-known letter to Shemu'el ibn Tibbon (edited by Alexander Marx in the *Jewish Quarterly Review*, 25 [1934–5], 374 ff.) wrote on this discipline. Al-Farabi, whom Maimonides praises for his excellence in logic, wrote works on rhetoric, and two of these were published recently (Al-Farabi, *Deux ouvrages inédits sur la Rhétorique*, ed. J. Langhade and M. Grignaschi [Beyrouth, 1971]). Similarly, Avicenna wrote on rhetoric as did al-Ghazali. And Averroes, Maimonides' contemporary, composed an Epitome and Middle Commentary on the *Rhetoric*. There also existed among the Muslims a literary rhetorical tradition, though this subject has been less investigated by scholars.

But the greater impression by far was achieved by Maimonides in his masterly use of midrashic material. With vast erudition he selected tales and narratives from *Yoma*, *Pesaḥim*, *Berakhot*, *Bava Batra*, *Keritut*, *'Avodah Zarah*, *Megillah*, *Shabbat*, *Bereshit Rabbah*, *Shemot Rabbah*, and *Va-Yikra Rabbah*, *Midrash Ḥazit*, *Midrash Ma'aseh Ḥanukkah*, and yet other sources, some of which are still unknown to this day.[59] With them he |310| conjured up before the eyes of his readers the figures of Moses, Elijah, and Isaiah, the images of Israel in bondage in Egypt and the captured tribes in Babylon, and soon the condemned R. Eli'ezer and the persecuted R. Me'ir came to the Marrano, like Job's friends, 'to mourn with him and to comfort him'. The *anusim* were quietly led out of the protective shell in which they had encased themselves and were made to feel part of a historic community which received them willingly.

Maimonides did not overestimate, however, the effectiveness of either abuse or homiletics. He knew that they did not impinge in any way upon the core of his opponent's position. The impact of the letter had lain in the bold fashion in which it had asserted that Moroccan Jews formed a community of apostates for they had, by their profession of Islam, denied both their religion and their God. So long as these charges remained unanswered, the missive would continue to wreak havoc among the people.

The task of rebuttal was, at the same time, a dangerous one. The conviction of the Jews in Islamic countries (again unlike that of their north European co-religionists) tended to weaken under persecution. The simple folk could not understand why, if they were God's chosen people, they should be subject to such oppression. They began to wonder whether the mightier hand of the Muslims was not of some Divine significance, and 'whether God had not indeed superseded his revelation at Sinai with a newer one at Mecca'. Only a few years before, Maimonides' father had written, immediately upon his arrival at Fez, his *Letter of Consolation*, in which he exhorted the Moroccan community not to interpret its suffering as a sign of rejection by God, but to be firmly aware of the truth of its religion, of the primacy of Moses among the prophets, and of the immutable nature of his revelation.[60] A decade later

[59] *IH* 48, 64; S 45, 55–6; H 23, 31.

[60] *Iggeret ha-Neḥamah*, trans. from the Arabic by B. Klar, introd. and notes Y. L. Fishman (Jerusalem, 1945). An English translation by L. M. Simmons (together with the original Arabic text) may be found in the *Jewish Quarterly Review*, OS 2 (1890), 66–101 (Arabic text, pp. 335 ff.). {On this letter, see bibliographical note at the outset of M. Ben-Sasson's article 'Tefillatam shel Anusim', in Y. M. Gafni and A. Ravitzky, eds., *Kedushat ha-Ḥayyim ve-Ḥeruf ha-Nefesh: Kovets Ma'amarim le-Zikhro shel Amir Yekuti'el* (Jerusalem, 1993), 153–66, esp. pp. 155–64, and E. Schlossberg, 'Yaḥaso shel R. Maimon, Avi ha-Rambam, la-'Islam ve-li-Shemadotav', *Sefunot*, NS, 5 (1991), 95–107.}

Maimonides was to repeat these same points to the persecuted Jewish community of Yemen, where masses had been on the verge |311| of conversion because of the doubts raised by their downtrodden position.

Any attempt to alleviate the sense of guilt by playing down the idolatrous element in Islam might have proved, under the circumstances, a cure worse than the disease. If, indeed, Islam was monotheistic, and by assenting to it they were not worshipping false gods, many would have wondered whether the whole attempt to preserve their religion was worth the risk. The Almohad persecution, moreover, posed special dangers, for their relentless monotheism, 'their uncompromising insistence on the absolute unity of God', rendered their conception of Islam all the more attractive.[61] The distinctive nature of Judaism had to be preserved, yet at the same time those who had professed Islam had to be told that they were not apostates. Wherever Maimonides turned, he was confronted with the specter of assimilation, whether from despair or from indifference.

A legitimate way out might perhaps have been found if he had been allowed to make full use of his vast erudition and penetrating intellect; but that, too, was out of the question. Any recondite scholarship or subtle line of reasoning would be totally lost upon the untutored masses. All the points had to be elementary,[62] and of immediate meaning to the crowd, or nothing would be gained for the cause of Judaism. Maimonides faced the task of reconciling opposites and of doing it in a few easy steps.

He thereupon sidestepped the entire issue and avoided any discussion as to the nature of Islam, but focused his attention upon the manner in which the Jews had allegedly subscribed to it. He could here advance several simple, albeit specious, distinctions that would capture the imagination of the crowd. First he asserted that the people had not assented to the Islamic faith but only to the prophetic character of Mohammed. On close scrutiny the two are synonymous, but he knew that the ones he was trying hardest to reach would not be of the type who would have too many second thoughts. The insufficiencies of his first contention were, however, a trifle too apparent, and he decided not to bank too heavily upon it. He chose, rather, to base his position on a far more suggestive thesis: the distinction between word and deed coupled |312| with the idea of inner disbelief. The concept is a persuasive one, at first blush, and its rejection required a knowledge of the formal definition of idolatry, and the 'intent to mock' law, all of which Maimonides could be sure that his readers would lack. He hammered home these points as he knew they

[61] Cf. S. W. Baron's remarks, *History of the Jews* (above, n. 1), iii. 292 n. 7 end; viii. 315 n. 28 end.

[62] *Rhetoric*, i: 2 (1357a).

were just of the type that would impress his public, and then he bolstered them with (specious) support from a talmudic narrative, so that every Marrano could say to himself, 'I have not acted worse than the great R. Eli'ezer.'[63]

The charge that had caused the greatest consternation was more difficult to reply to. The anonymous writer had driven home, with great effectiveness, the accusation that the religious practices of the Marranos were absolutely worthless, and their prayer simply blasphemy. Prayer, with its confession and supplication, was the great purgative of the *anusim*. Maimonides recognized this no less than had his father, who had emphasized in his letter to the same oppressed communities how vital it was to maintain this intimate link with a living and cleansing God, for without it the burden of guilt and despair would be overwhelming.[64] But Maimonides could discover no ad hoc distinctions with which to deflect his opponent's charges. The polemical gifts of the accuser came unexpectedly to his aid. His antagonist had summed up his views in a sentence wisely calculated to go straight to the hearts of the masses: 'even if he performs a commandment he will receive no reward for it'.[65] Maimonides picked up the phrase and turned his opponent's flank. As I have mentioned above, he cited the statement quite justly as the core of the accusation, but in doing so he estranged it from its context and altered its very nature.[66] No longer did the claim now center upon the legal worth of the Marranos' ritual but upon the nature of Divine bookkeeping.

Having transformed the charge, Maimonides could dispose of it with ease, yet he took care never to press his advantage too hard. He refused to mention even once the central issue of reward and punishment, and rested content with simply citing the aggadic passages and letting them tell their own tale. On the surface, the simplest line of defense would have been to charge that the accusations ran counter not just to several *midrashim* but to the |313| incontrovertible principle of Divine retribution, and then to swing into a crushing offensive by pointing out that the very person who had condemned whole communities for heresy was himself a heretic, since by his accusations he had denied one of the fundamental tenets of the faith. Maimonides eschewed doing so, for to bring out too clearly the fatal absurdity of his antagonist's claim would serve only to make his own victory suspect. He declined to delin-

63 *Rhetoric*, ii: 24 (1401b, and cf. Geiger, *Moses ben Maimon* [above, n. 3], 18).

64 *Iggeret ha-Neḥamah* (above, n. 60), 18 ff., 38 ff., 59 ff. (*Jewish Quarterly Review* [above, n. 60], 73–7, 85 ff. and M. Ben-Sasson's article there cited). Maimonides refers to prayer no fewer than three times in the *Iggeret*: *IH* 32, 45–6; S 33, 43–4; H 16, 22.

65 See above, pp. 300–5.

66 On the use of homonym in polemics (in our case Maimonides' citation of the ambiguous term *sekhar mitsvah*—above, n. 27), see *Rhetoric*, ii: 24 (1401a).

eate too sharply just what it was he was refuting for fear that his readers might become aware that this was not at all what had been charged. He left his opponent's argument untouched in form but vitiated in substance, so that when the time came, despite its outer impressiveness, it would topple dramatically under the blow of a few tales.

Aware that his whole position was of a flimsy and makeshift nature, with little more than an aggadic loincloth to cover its nakedness, Maimonides took care to quietly lay the foundation for a more substantial, if less showy, defense. When mentioning that the Jews had only professed belief in the mission of Mohammed, he remarked, almost as an afterthought, that at any rate it was done under coercion; he dropped this remark again when he insisted that if willful sinners had been rewarded for their good deeds, certainly the *anusim* would be. In both these instances Maimonides' main effort was directed along different and more popular avenues of thought, but nevertheless, by his reservations, he had erected a second, unobtrusive line of defense to which the Marranos could retreat in the instance that all the *verbo–acto*, transcendental contentions failed and they were compelled to admit the criminality of their actions.

As this constituted the true core of his entire position, Maimonides could hardly omit it, yet its introduction into the argument had its pitfalls. Precisely because it was of such a high legal caliber if placed alongside the other claims, their shabbiness would manifest itself by contrast. The substantive nature of this issue, with its nigh-irrefutable support from the *Sifra*, would bring out the rickety character of the rest of his defense. He thereupon mentioned it continually in his rebuttal, but only as another plausible suggestion, and left its development and juridical justification to the second half of the responsum, where, thanks to the solid nature of that section, the proof would not cast any inconvenient reflections upon its immediate surroundings, with, of course, the added benefit that he could, by its repetition, rake his opponent once more over the coals.

The latter portion of the letter, however, was not composed just as a **|314|** setting for the principle of non-culpability for acts committed under coercion, though it did prove extremely useful for this point; its writing had far deeper purposes. Maimonides had been fortunate that the accusations had lent themselves, via a few deft twists, to rebuttal; however, he also knew that this might not always be the case. He might find himself hard pressed to defend the Marranos with equal persuasiveness were another letter to start circulating stating similar charges in a different fashion. For the effectiveness of this letter of accusation was not a coincidence, but resulted from its strident tone shattering the fragile self-imposed silence that had settled over the Moroccan community. So long as the Marranos continued their willful ostrich policy, they would always be exposed to sudden waves of despair, some of which might sweep them, as this one seemed to be doing, to the shores of Islam. The people had to be made to confront the facts of their persecution and to acknowledge their double life. It was to this end that Maimonides devoted the second part of *Iggeret ha-Shemad*: to set forth what the Law demanded of them, to analyze the contemporary persecution, and to discuss 'how it is fitting for a man to view himself in these days of persecution'.

Once more, that task was not an easy one. By yielding to its oppressors the community had undoubtedly desecrated the Name, and this constituted, not only legally but even colloquially, the gravest of all sins. The simple mention of *ḥillul ha-shem* was enough to make most people blanch. The masses would have to get themselves accustomed to hearing of its dire consequences, and so Maimonides was forced to dwell on it at inordinate length.

> Desecration of the Name is a great sin. He who commits it in error is punished in the same measure as one who commits it intentionally, as the Rabbis have said [*Avot* 3: 4] . . . All sins the Lord waits for man [to repent], except that of desecration, where retribution is swift, and so [the Rabbis] have said: 'no loan of time is granted when the Name of the Lord has been desecrated.' . . . And this [sin] is more [severe] than all others, for neither the Day of Atonement, nor suffering nor repentance atone for it . . . but only death, for so the Rabbis have said: 'Anyone who has been guilty of desecration, then penitence has no power etc.' . . . as it is said: 'Surely this iniquity shall not be expiated by you till you die [Isa. 22: 14]' [*Yoma* 86a].[67] **|315|**

But this necessary admission invited despondency, for if every day they were guilty of crimes so heinous that only death would suffice for their expiation, of what use were their painful, secret, danger-laden efforts to lead a religious life?[68]

Maimonides' solution was to concede the dreadful nature of *ḥillul ha-shem* but to dissociate martyrdom from it. He opened his discussion with a masterly analysis of the instances requiring surrender of one's life, but by its position he removed from it the onus of desecration, and in his definition of *ḥillul ha-shem* he similarly omitted all mention of the laws of 'Be killed and do not transgress'.[69] To cover the large gap in his discussion, he stretched the material at hand to the limit. He split the conduct of scholars into two sections, though actually it is apparent from the Talmud and from Maimonides' subsequent works that both instances evince the same principle of unbecoming behavior;

[67] *IH* 55–6; S 49–50; H 27.

[68] *IH* 67; S 58; H 33.

[69] See above, pp. 308–9.

then he fabricated a new concept of 'gossipy conduct' and included that within the category of *ḥillul ha-shem*.[70] The result was that he could clutter up his definition with four categories of desecration in the hope that the absence of martyrdom would thereby go unnoticed. The tactic was so risky that he dared not repeat it, and circumvented the difficulties in *kiddush ha-shem* by a different method. He defined it simply (and in a sense quite |316| accurately) as altruism—a formulation broad enough to admit martyrdom, but so general that no one could ever infer without prior knowledge that it was necessarily included within it.[71]

Having surmounted the major barrier, Maimonides then took care to cover his tracks. Reference to the relationship between martyrdom and *ḥillul ha-shem* could not be omitted altogether; its truancy would be noticed, and once suspicions were aroused the entire effect of the letter would be jeopardized. So he took care to write in the third section:

But if he did not let himself be killed, but transgressed because of coercion he has not acted properly, but has desecrated the Name under coercion, but he is not subject to any punishment, for we do not find anywhere in the Law . . . that one who is coerced is punished, only one who acts willingly. But should anyone contend that because the sages said 'Be killed and do not transgress', then if someone transgresses he incurs the death penalty, [know that] this is a total error. For it is in no way so . . . And this fundamental principle has been set forth in the *Torat Kohanim*.[72]

[70] *IH* 52–5; S 47–9; H 26 (and above, pp. 302–3). 'Fabricated' is indeed a sharp word. But its use seems justified in view of Maimonides' other writings, all prior and subsequent halakhic literature (to the best of my knowledge), and the very nature of *ḥillul ha-shem*. The talmudic text cited (*Yoma* 86a) clearly refers to scholars, and no one before or after, Maimonides included, ever construed it as referring to ordinary folk. In the voluminous literature cited in the entry on *ḥillul ha-shem* in the *Entsiklopedyah Talmudit* (vol. xv, cols. 340–60), no such doctrine makes its appearance. Nor is its absence accidental. *Ḥillul ha-shem* occurs when the bearer of God's name, as it were, degrades it or betrays it in the eyes of others. It applies, for example, when a Jew, a representative of the true religion, discredits his nation or his God in the eyes of Gentiles, or if a scholar, the living embodiment of Torah, dishonors that which he represents in the eyes of the masses. *Ḥillul ha-shem* is, as it were, a class injunction. It regulates the conduct of one group in the presence of another. If, however, Jacob the tailor should act in a fashion that makes Joseph the tailor suspect him of eating pork, he has lapsed into the offense of **הרחק מן הכיעור ומן הדומה לכיעור** or that of **והייתם נקיים**; however, those two imperatives are light years away from the injunction of *ḥillul ha-shem*. Conduct that invites gossip is indeed forbidden by the halakhah; however, Divine punishment of the direst sort does not await those who transgress it, nor is death its only expiation as it is for *ḥillul ha-shem* (above, p. 320). Cf. *Bi'urei ha-Maharshal 'al ha-Semag*, Injunction 2 (repr. in the 2-vol. photostat of the 1547 Venice edn. of the *Semag*). {A more recent edition of that work is found in the *Sefer Mitsvot Gadol ha-Shalem*, Makhon Yerushalayim/Makhon Shelomoh Aumann edn. (Jerusalem, 1993). The cited passage is found on p. 402.}

[71] *IH* 55; S 49; H 26–7.

[72] *IH* 58–9; S 51–2; H 29.

What struck the reader was not that the Marrano had transgressed upon *ḥillul ha-shem*, but that he had only done so under coercion. Before the reader could realize that Maimonides had just conceded what he had been tacitly denying throughout his earlier formulations, Maimonides swung into a discussion of free will and constraint, and the recollection of the remarks that had been quietly dropped along the way crowded into the reader's mind. A sudden turn to slashing polemic, and then a brilliant stroke of erudition disproving the culpability of actions committed under duress, and the *éclat* was so great that the still, small voice of desecration went unheard. Yet so frightful must its tone have been to the *anusim* that Maimonides deemed it necessary to silence it altogether; and so immediately after his *coup* he openly raised the issue of *ḥillul ha-shem* that he had tried so hard to avoid. And while the pyrotechnics were taking place, he quietly drained the charge of its substance. What was then introduced was not the desecration arising from yielding to one's persecutors, but that arising from swearing falsely.[73] This was, of course, a sheep in wolf's clothing but he knew that to the ignorant masses, the |317| outer skin of *ḥillul ha-shem* would make the two indistinguishable, and with the defeat of one they would feel themselves rid forever of the dread charge of having desecrated the Name.

Feeling he had dealt sufficiently with the theoretical aspects of martyrdom, *ḥillul ha-shem*, mixed actions, and the like, Maimonides deemed it wise to close his responsum with a treatment of the more immediate problems at hand. He turned to the points uppermost in his readers' minds: the nature of the contemporary persecution, how one should act in response to it, and how the Marrano should regard himself.

He first reasserted that the Almohad oppression, as it demanded only verbal assent and not active participation in Islam, did not constitute 'persecution' or 'idolatry' as used in the laws of martyrdom. But this was no longer a debated point as in the first half of the letter; it was now set forth as an accepted legal fact on a par with the laws regulating the conduct of scholars and the like in the preceding three sections. Then again, in the context of stating self-evident principles, he reassured the *anusim* that their attempts to remain faithful to their religion would not go unheeded and that they should never be overwhelmed with guilt. He then proceeded to practical advice and told them that the proper conduct and solution was not assimilation out of despair but flight to a land where they would be free to practice their religion, and averred that

[73] *IH* 60; S 52; H 29–30. Shalom Rosenberg of the Hebrew University has drawn my attention to the sham enthymeme of the 'undivided middle' in *Rhetoric*, ii: 24 (1401b).

he was giving this advice to himself no less than to his readers. Indeed, several years later Maimonides did manage to escape.

He concluded the letter with the following passage:

> Section five: I will explain how it is fitting for a man to view himself in these days of persecution. Everyone who cannot escape . . . [for various reasons] and stays in this place, he must view himself as one who has desecrated the Name of God, though not willingly, but [by his continued presence and not fleeing] he comes close to [desecrating it] willfully, and he is an outcast in the eyes of God and will be punished for his wicked deeds. But he should always have in mind that if he performs a commandment, the Holy One, blessed be He, will reward him doubly, for he certainly performs it for the sake of Heaven only and does not seek to show off his religiosity.[74]

Maimonides is telling the members of the community that while they should not look complacently upon their situation they should nevertheless remain firm in their |**318**| religious observance and serene in the knowledge that the Lord would take note of it.

Or so the closing section appeared to the masses. But no halakhist could have failed to decode the message Maimonides tapped out in his final paragraph—that he was disowning the entire responsum. The *anusim* had indeed desecrated the Name of God, and all his prior formulations of *ḥillul ha-shem*, his prophecy–idolatry and word–deed distinctions, were to be discounted. As every one of his readers had been under the Almohad persecution for years, the presence of the saving grace of coercion was highly dubious, for he implied that coercion most probably could only be claimed in instances when it had been unavoidable, but not when one had the opportunity of flight and had declined it. And he went so far in some versions of his great code, the *Mishneh Torah*, as to say so explicitly and in the most unrelenting fashion: 'However, if an individual is able to save himself from the power of the wicked king and does not do so, he is like a dog that returns to his vomit. He is called a willful idolater, is excluded from the world to come, and descends to the lowest depths of Gehinnom.'[75]

---

[74] *IH* 67–8; S 58–9; H 33–4.

[75] 'Yesodei ha-Torah', 5: 4: **אבל אם יכול למלט נפשו ולברוח מתחת יד המלך הרשע ואינו עושה, הוא ככלב שב על קיאו. והוא נקרא עובד עבודת כוכבים במזיד. והוא נטרד מן העולם הבא ויורד למדרגה התחתונה של גיהנם** and from there to 'Yoreh De'ah' 157: 1 end. Note that Maimonides defines the case as one of outright **מזיד** rather than **קרוב למזיד** as in the *Iggeret*. (In his closing passage, he took care not to employ even the recognizable **קרוב למזיד**, e.g. *Bava Kamma* 32b, *Makkot* 7b, 9a, but chose rather some circumlocution that eventuated in a Hebrew translation of **אלא קרוב הוא להיות ברצונו**.) In some MSS of *Mishneh Torah* this passage is missing. See the variant readings and notes in the edition

Almost every charge of his opponent was correct, yet the purest and greatest Sephardic scholar of the ages sat down at his table and |319| wrote a letter in which he distorted the facts to whose ascertainment he had dedicated his life, in the hope of saving a host of sinners from despair and conversion. 'God is my witness, and He is a sufficient witness ... that I would not have replied ... [but] that I feared that this letter, which casts one away from God, would reach the masses.'[76]

AFTERWORD

What emerges here, as in the essay on martyrdom in Ashkenaz (Chapter 11 above), is the powerful but silent role played by the destiny of the children of the Moroccan community. Maimonides opens his *Epistle on Martyrdom* by stating that the question before him was whether or not a man should 'admit to the mission of Mohammed so that he should not die and his sons and daughters not sink without trace among the Gentiles [*ve-yittam'u banav u-venotav ba-goyim*]', yet their fate—upon which hinges nothing less than Jewish continuance—never figures so much as once in his arguments. As overriding a concern as national survival may be, it is not a halakhic category. It goes unregistered on the halakhic seismograph because religious continuance was not at stake in the formative years of the halakhah—in Palestine of the tannaitic period and in the old diaspora of Babylonia of the *amora'im*. Jews constituted a large percentage of the population of those countries, and the children of martyrs would be raised as Jews by their neighbors. In Christian and Muslim lands, however, Jews were demographically insignificant, and the offspring of those who died for their faith would be brought up by the very infidels who had killed the parents. What was the point of martyrdom in the new diaspora of the Cross and Crescent if the children were to be reared as Gentiles? Potent, insistent forces were thus at work beneath the surface of the

of *Sefer ha-Madda'* by Kohen and Katzenelenbogen referred to at the outset of the essay {and those in the Shabse Frankel edition of *Sefer ha-Madda'* (Jerusalem, 2001), 'Yesodei ha-Torah', 5: 4. Y. Shilat suggests in the notes in his *Rambam Meduyyak*, i (Ma'aleh Adumim, 2004), ad loc., that this passage is an early scribal addition to the Maimonidean text. If so, the sentence in the text to which this note is appended, together with its accompanying citation, should be deleted.} (The remarks of R. Shim'on Duran, *Sefer ha-Tashbets*, i, ed. Y. Katan [Jerusalem, 1998], #63 end, are overtly tendentious, see *Or Gadol* [above, n. 34], 51.)

76 *IH* 44–6; S 43–4; H 22. (On the phrase ודי בו עד, see Kafih's note in his edition [above, n. 3], 112, and M. Goshen-Gottstein, *Taḥbirah u-Milonah shel ha-Lashon ha-'Ivrit she-bi-Teḥum Hashpa'atah shel ha-'Aravit* [Jerusalem, 1951], 44. Professor Goshen-Gottstein was kind enough to draw my attention to his remarks there.)

literature of *kiddush ha-shem* of the past millennium, forces that could silently recast—if you wish, skew—the content of the standard halakhic vocabulary until its categories accurately reflected the tragic reality which they addressed.

Rereading this essay after many years, I find that I have one major reservation. I do not think that I erred in claiming that *Iggeret ha-Shemad* is a work of rhetoric, and that Maimonides employed techniques of argument that would be unacceptable in a strictly legal work. I still am of the opinion that the positions taken by Maimonides in this epistle contradict those that he espoused in his early writings, notably, that *ha-'oved mi-'ahavah u-mi-yir'ah* is culpable.[77] Finally, I continue to think that the equation of heresy (*minut*) and idolatry (*'avodah zarah*) found in the *Perush ha-Mishnayot* and *Mishneh Torah* was justifiably invoked in my essay.[78] Some people are never young. Read, for example, the letters of Gershom Scholem or those of Max Weber written when they were some 14 years of age, and you have the feeling that you are dealing with an adult whose basic *Weltanschauung* is already formed.[79] Though we have no such correspondence of Maimonides, the feeling that I have is that he was never young and that his basic religious and halakhic outlook was formed very early in his life, probably in his teens but certainly by his early twenties. If this is correct, one is justified in retrojecting the extension of the injunction against idolatry from cult to ideology onto Maimonides at the time that he penned the *Iggeret ha-Shemad*, and invoking it against him. Indeed, his remark in the *Iggeret* that '*minut* is a more serious crime than idolatry' clearly adumbrates the famous position that he adopted in subsequent writings.[80]

However, does all this constitute the proper yardstick by which to judge the *Iggeret ha-Shemad*? Should the criterion be the personal, if weighty, views of Maimonides or the rules of conventional halakhah at the time that Maimonides wrote? Put differently: Would there—should there—be any compunction on the part of a halakhic decisor (*posek*) facing a situation where a despairing community was in danger of converting to forestall this catastrophe by

[77] *Mishnah 'im Perush le-Rabbenu Mosheh b. Maimon, Nezikin*, ed. Y. Kafih (above, n. 9), *Sanhedrin* 7: 6, n. 9.

[78] Ibid. 11: 1 introduction, pp. 209–17; Y. Shilat, *Hakdamot ha-Rambam la-Mishnah* (Jerusalem, 1994), 140–6; 'Teshuvah', 3: 6–8.

[79] G. Scholem, *Lamentations of Youth: the Diaries of Gershom Scholem, 1913–1919*, ed. and trans. A. D. Skinner (Cambridge, Mass., 2007); M. Weber, *Jugendbriefe* (Tübingen, n.d.).

[80] *IH* 43, 45; S 37, 41; H 20–1.

assuaging its guilt with formulations that comported well with contemporary halakhic canons, though not with his own?

I must admit that most decisors would probably mount such a defense with no pangs of conscience, indeed, view such advocacy as obligatory, as 'sacred labor' (*melekhet shamayim*). If so, the relevant question is: did the recitation of the *shahada* constitute apostasy in pre-Maimonidean halakhah? And the answer is: most probably not.

First, the talmudic passage of 'intent to mock' (*mekhaven le-vizuyeh*) must mean that there is culpability in acts of idolatry even without any inner belief, if one rules that *ha-'oved mi-'ahavah u-mi-yir'ah* (as understood by Rav Hai Gaon and Maimonides[81]) is liable (*ḥayyav*), as Maimonides did in his early versions of his *Perush ha-Mishnayot*. That, however, is the view of Abbaye; Rava believes that he is not culpable (*patur*). Normally the ruling would be clearly in favor of Rava, unless there were compelling reasons to the contrary. Maimonides, in his youth, felt that there were such reasons, but subsequently recanted this view, and the consensus of other scholars has been equally in favor of Rava. If so, then idolatry is credal rather than cultic, and he who says what he says or does what he does without inner belief is no idolater. As for the *sugya* of *mekhaven le-vizuyeh*: in light of Rava's unequivocal ruling, it has to be interpreted away (and that is what many *rishonim* did) or in a culture that does not subscribe to dialectic, one disregards it and follows the *sugya de-shemateta'*, the controlling *sugya*. Discussants such as Abbaye and Rava are certainly far weightier than a relatively unknown R. Menasheh and his *bet midrash*. Moreover, the controversy between Abbaye and Rava is a classic one and cited repeatedly in the Talmud (*San.* 61b, *Shab.* 72b, *Ker.* 3a); the *sugya* of *mekhaven le-vizuyeh* is found only once (*San.* 61b).

Second, that Islam was not idolatry would probably have been agreed upon by most hands at that time; one did not need Maimonides' *Epistle to 'Ovadyah the Convert* to make that point. This was certainly true of the radical monotheism of the Almohads, who identified themselves as *muwahhidun*, 'those who proclaim the true unity of God', as opposed to the *mujassima*, 'those who profess a corporeal understanding of God'. True monotheism, according to the Almohads, did not allow even for an anthropomorphic God, even if this God were to have all the other traits of a monotheistic God—solitary, all-powerful, all-good, and all-knowing.[82]

As for the denial of the supremacy of the Mosaic revelation entailed by the

81 *Sanhedrin* 64a; 61b; *'Arukh* s.v. *A–H–V*; *Mishneh Torah*, 'Avodah Zarah', 3: 6.

82 See Stroumsa, *Maimonides in his World* (above, n. 1), 51–9. The translation in quotes is taken from that work, p. 52.

recitation of the *shahada*: the revolutionary redefinition of 'idolatry' to include a large range of heterodoxies, the radical leap from idolatry as cultic acts (including speech acts), as found in the Mishnah and Gemara, to mistaken views of the Deity and Revelation is the distinctive perspective of Maimonides. Anyone ruling on the basis of the Talmud would not classify heresy as idolatry per se. Heresy is, indeed, very serious, and the heretic may well forfeit his place in the world to come,[83] but this does not make it identical with, nor subsumed under, the rubric of idolatry. Certainly, most halakhists would adopt a strict construction of the term 'idolatry' when faced with the ominous imperative of martyrdom (*yehareg ve-'al ya'avor*). Human lives are at stake in this far-reaching redefinition of that word. One cannot transfer the profound conviction in the absolute necessity of theological correctness from Maimonides to most, if any, of his contemporaries. Thus, for most halakhists, the recitation of the *shahada* would not fall into the category of the martyrdom imperative for two reasons. First, it is recited without inner belief; second, heresy is not included in this imperative.

There are, then, three separate questions, and the third is one I did not ask in the essay. First, is the *Iggeret ha-Shemad* a work of rhetoric? Did Maimonides use modes of argument, such as the enthymeme of the undistributed middle, cite irrelevant sources, such as the *mishnah* in *Nedarim*, and make distinctions—for example, between word and speech—without solid basis, all to persuade his community that it had not abandoned its God? The answer to this is 'Yes'.

Second, are some of the views expressed in the *Iggeret* incompatible with those held by Maimonides in his early years, and most probably with several of his later beliefs? The answer is again 'Yes'.

Third, did Maimonides defend an untenable halakhic position? The answer is 'No', if 'tenable' is defined not by what he, the halakhic revolutionary, thought, but by what were, most probably, the dominant halakhic categories at the time that he penned the *Iggeret*.

I would add a fourth question: is this surprising? Scarcely, as most halakhists, confronted with the danger of mass conversion, would most probably have done the same thing.

What does this mean? It means that the argument in the essay is correct, but the conclusions are far less startling. Maimonides allowed himself, as would have probably most halakhists, to write a work of polemic that conflicted with his own halakhic views, because he knew that his despairing community had not—by both the traditional and the reigning standards of the

[83] Mishnah, *Sanhedrin* 11: 1.

time—fallen from the faith, and was not guilty of the terrible sins for which it had been publicly and brutally damned.

RESPONSES TO CRITICISMS

1. After reading the several critiques of the essay, I realize that I had failed to emphasize that the yardstick by which to judge the *Iggeret ha-Shemad* was Maimonides' early writings, such as the first edition (*mahadura kamma*) of his *Perush ha-Mishnayot*. In fact, I had relegated Maimonides' early positions to the footnotes (nn. 16, 17)! Whether the commission of idolatry requires inner conviction is still open to question in the *Mishneh Torah*, where Maimonides ruled that *ha-'oved mi-'ahavah u-mi-yir'ah patur* ('one who worships an idol out of fear of another person or to seek his favor is not guilty of idolatry').[84] However, if one rules, as did Maimonides in the first edition (*mahadura kamma*) of his Mishnah commentary, that *ha-'oved mi-'ahavah u-mi-yir'ah ḥayyav* (that in the above instance of fear or favor, the worshipper is guilty of idolatry),[85] the strictly formal definition of idolatry becomes inevitable. The act of idolatry per se, irrespective of intent, constitutes a crime, as, indeed, the simplest reading of the story of R. Menasheh (*Sanhedrin* 64a) would indicate. Maimonides' cultic perception of idolatry becomes yet more obvious when one sees that in the *Perush ha-Mishnayot* he initially ruled that *mekhaven le-vizuyeh* (one who participates in an idolatrous ceremony in the spirit of mockery) is fully culpable, unlike his holding in the *Mishneh Torah*, where he qualifies the culpability by ruling חייב ומביא קרבן על שגגתו.[86]

2. My formulation at p. 295 is a poor one and has lent itself to misinterpretation.

Maimonides makes a second point, a second distinction, writing: 'and it is only uttered by people to save themselves from the king, to satisfy him with some empty words'. There is a fundamental difference, he contends, between idolatry and other injunctions. In homicide, for example, it is obvious that intent plays a decisive role, separating first-degree murder from manslaughter. Nevertheless, it does not affect the nature of the act itself. Killing constitutes the objective act of taking another's life: the subjective

[84] ''Avodat Kokhavim', 3: 6.

[85] See *Mishnah 'im Perush le-Rabbenu Mosheh b. Maimon, Nezikin*, ed. Y. Kafih (above, n. 9), *Sanhedrin* 7: 6, nn. 3, 9.

[86] ''Avodat Kokhavim', 3: 5.

intent affects only the extent of the individual's culpability for the act. The case is different with idolatry. Worship, by definition, is fundamentally, if not exclusively, a psychological state, and any mechanical performance must be accompanied by the thought of adoration for it to be considered an act of worship. This being so, the *anusim*, Maimonides now claims, have never committed apostasy, for their profession of faith was not done out of belief, but out of compulsion, and is, hence, absolutely meaningless!

This is a tour de force. Unfortunately, Maimonides has won far too much. If one can never be compelled to worship 'strange gods', why should one ever be required to lay down one's life rather than submit? If idolatry committed under coercion is of no account, then the entire concept of martyrdom for one's religion becomes meaningless and should never have existed to begin with. But we know only too well that it does. Maimonides' neat theory is contradicted by the massive, bloody fact of Jewish law —the imperative of 'Be killed and do not transgress' (*yehareg ve-'al ya'avor*).

Unless one reads the passage very closely, it sounds as if I were claiming that if inner conviction is necessary for idolatry, there can be no martyr imperative. This is clearly wrong. Many—possibly most—commentators think that belief is a *sine qua non* for the crime of idolatry; nevertheless, they hold that martyrdom is still incumbent. What I was contending was that if one claims that inner disbelief *annuls* the imperative of martyrdom—as Maimonides seems to do in this passage when he argues that the inner disbelief in the *shahada* relieves the Moroccan community of the duty of martyrdom[87]—no martyrdom imperative will ever exist, for all religious persecution entails coercing disbelievers.

3. It is equally clear from the same critiques that I had also failed to emphasize sufficiently the centrality of the fallacy of the excluded middle and the baffling invocation of the Mishnah in *Nedarim*. If these two critiques are correct, the *Iggeret ha-Shemad* is still primarily a work of rhetoric, whether or not my other objections are sustained.

4. Isaac Chavel (in a private communication) drew my attention to Maimonides' position on *kiddush ha-shem* in his *Sefer ha-Mitsvot*. Maimonides' formulation there is, indeed, strange. He defines *she'at ha-shemad* not simply as persecution of the Jewish religion—as everyone, including Maimonides himself in the *Mishneh Torah*, has understood the term—but as a sweeping ordinance requiring all faiths to worship the God of the oppressor. This

[87] I write 'seems to do' for I immediately go on to say (above, p. 297) that Maimonides is actually arguing that it is the conjunction of three facts, one of which is inner disbelief, which annuls the imperative of martyrdom.

matches the case of the Almohad persecution as Christians, no less than Jews, were coerced to recite the *shahada* under the threat of death. Moreover, in the *Sefer ha-Mitsvot* Maimonides specifically forbids deceiving the oppressor into believing that one has accepted his faith—the exact opposite of what he argued in the *Iggeret ha-Shemad*.

Chavel sees the dicta of *Sefer ha-Mitsvot* as a reaction to and rejection of what Maimonides had argued in the *Iggeret*. Or, put differently—and closer to Dr Chavel's formulation—it comprises an idealized picture of what should have been the response of the Jews to the Almohad persecution. This is a fairly radical assessment, yet Maimonides' formulation of the martyrdom imperative in *Sefer ha-Mitsvot* is so out of line with everything we know about *kiddush ha-shem* (including all else that Maimonides wrote) that Dr Chavel's conclusion on this point seems reasonable.[88]

5. Herbert Davidson solves all problems by arguing that the *Iggeret ha-Shemad* was not written by Maimonides.[89] His contention that the author lived outside the lands of Islam runs up against the problem that the person who composed the *Iggeret* knew of Mohammed's massacre of the Jewish tribe Banu Qurayza at Yathrib (now known as Medina), an event recorded in Muslim sources alone.[90]

[88] Dr Chavel is more bothered than I am by Maimonides' contradictory stand in the *Iggeret* on voluntary martyrdom. Maimonides felt strongly about the issue; so much so that he did the rarest of things in *Mishneh Torah*: he repeated the injunction against such a deed twice in one chapter (5: 1, 4). However, this position was his own, rooted perhaps in the Yerushalmi (*Sanhedrin* 3: 7, *Shevi'it* 4: 2; 21b and 35a–b in the Venice edn.; col. 1282 and col. 190 in edn. of the Academy of Hebrew Language), but still a personal one. To retract or waffle in a work of polemic about a purely personal position is one thing; to write something contrary to the common canons of halakhah is another. It is the latter issue that I address.

[89] *Moses Maimonides: The Man and his Work* (Oxford, 2005), 501–9. He first articulated this position in Ezra Fleischer et al., eds., *Me'ah She'arim: Studies in Medieval Jewish Spiritual Life in Memory of Isadore Twersky* (Jerusalem, 2001), English section, 125–33.

[90] *IH* 44; S 42; H 21. See M. Ben-Sasson, 'Tefillatam shel ha-'Anusim' (above, n. 60), 155 n. 5.

CHAPTER THIRTEEN

Responses to Critiques of 'Maimonides' *Iggeret ha-Shemad*: Law and Rhetoric'

I

A RESPONSE TO DAVID HARTMAN

DAVID HARTMAN'S essay first appeared in the journal *Maḥshevet Yisra'el* in a poor Hebrew translation that did not do justice to his ardent style.[1] He later published the original English version as an introduction to a new translation of the *Iggeret ha-Shemad* in a work entitled *Crisis and Leadership: Epistles of Maimonides*.[2] I have thought it best here to cite the original English version, rather than to translate back into English the deficient Hebrew translation of the English original. (I nevertheless provide page references equally to the original Hebrew version, designated *MY* in the footnotes, to which my reply was originally addressed.) It is customary in academic circles to invite the object of an article's criticism to respond, so the editors of *Maḥshevet Yisra'el* solicited a reply from me. I have translated my original rejoinder,[3] moved a long quotation from a footnote into the body of the text where it seemed more apropos, and, in one instance, added two paragraphs where I thought the original version had been too elliptical. I have identified the additional two paragraphs in the footnotes.

[1] D. Hartman, 'Iggeret ha-Shemad le-Rabbenu Mosheh ben Maimon—Aspaklaryah le-Murkavut ha-Pesikah ha-Hilkhatit', *Meḥkarei Yerushalayim be-Maḥshevet Yisra'el*, 2 (1983), 362–403, referred to as *MY* below.

[2] *Crisis and Leadership: Epistles of Maimonides*, trans. and notes by A. Halkin, discussions by D. Hartman (Philadelphia, New York, and London, 1985). A much-improved Hebrew translation subsequently appeared under the title *Manhigut be-'Itot Metsukah: 'al Iggerot ha-Rambam* (Tel Aviv, 1989).

[3] 'Beḥanim li-Fesikah Hilkhatit: Teshuvah le-Dr D. Hartman', *Meḥkarei Yerushalayim be-Maḥshevet Yisra'el*, 3 (1984), 683–7.

I WOULD LIKE TO THANK David Hartman for bringing to the attention of scholars an article of mine that had lain unread in a *Gedenkschrift*. I am doubly grateful that he saw fit to devote some forty pages of discussion to an essay that I had written in my schooldays.

Despite the obvious differences between us in style and temperament, I believe we are of the same opinion as to the terrible problem that the Jews of the Maghreb confronted under the rule of the Almohads. It also seems to me that we are in agreement on the motives of Maimonides and that he was right in doing what he did. Our disagreement lies in how one should characterize Maimonides' deeds: as an act of religious leadership or as the rendering of a halakhic judgment. This matter needs to be addressed both methodologically and substantively.

Methodological Considerations

The crucial issue that lies at the very heart of our disagreement is whether there are outer limits to an intellectual discipline which cannot be breached and whether we can lay down some ground rules for arguments within a discipline.

Everyone agrees that political theory takes into account the entire spectrum of considerations—logical, social, and psychological—that Dr Hartman dwells upon at length. Its broad playing field allows a wide range of intellectual maneuver and the most contradictory views can be advanced with comparable claims to legitimacy. However, should a political theorist argue that (1) all revolutionaries are mortal; (2) Goldberg is mortal; (3) therefore Goldberg is a revolutionary, this contention would not be political theory but rhetoric. The problem is that Maimonides employs precisely this kind of argument (i.e. the fallacy of the undivided middle) in the *Iggeret ha-Shemad*. Without plunging into the thorny problem of the ground rules of halakhah, we can safely state two of them: (1) the argument must abide by the elementary rules of logic; (2) a halakhic conclusion cannot contradict an explicit *mishnah*, when the *mishnah* has been understood in one and the same fashion by all commentators of the past millennium. Maimonides breached both ground rules in his *Iggeret ha-Shemad*.

Hartman contends that Maimonides 'gathered a wide assortment of sources from Jewish tradition', both halakhic and aggadic, and 'integrated them in light of a comprehensive view of Judaism', weighing both the political and psychological implications 'in the clear and penetrating light' of the relationship of the individual to his community and of the community's relationship to God, as well as of 'the historic destiny of the Jewish people'.[4] Truer words have never been written. The Satmar Rebbe, however, did the same in his *Va-Yo'el Mosheh*. His work is the most brilliant contemporary example of a similar fusion of diverse material from Jewish sources. The problem with his book, and what precludes it from being seen as a halakhic work, is the absence of critical ground rules. No rules are set forth as to what can be introduced as evidence, nor are there any canons of inference and deduction that would allow critical scrutiny of the author's argument. In the absence of such ground rules, numerous questions inevitably arise. For example: what *midrash* may one adduce as proof for one's position and what *midrash* is inadmissible? What is the weight of one aggadic passage as opposed to another? What are the acceptable and unacceptable methods of fusing halakhah and aggadah? Just how far may one depart from the simple meaning of an aggadic passage 'in light of a comprehensive view of Judaism'?

My distinguished colleague identifies religious leadership with halakhah. However, not every act of religious leadership, as desirable and even as necessary as it may be, is *ipso facto* halakhic. Truth to tell, Dr Hartman's underlying assumption is identical with what is now called *da'at Torah*: that for the decision of a religious leader to be considered a halakhic one it suffices for him to render it in the language of the traditional sources. It is scarcely fortuitous that in Dr Hartman's essay, as in the numerous proclamations that issue forth from Benei Berak, the words 'halakhah' and 'Judaism' are used interchangeably.

Substantive Considerations

In Hartman's essay there is not a single substantive halakhic discussion, either in the text, or in the footnotes. This is somewhat surprising, seeing that half of my own essay was devoted to examining the numerous halakhic problems in Maimonides' stance. I expressed my doubts as to its halakhic validity; however, opinions can differ on this matter, and it is a pity that Hartman refrained entirely from addressing this central problem.

In the second section of my essay, discussing the manner in which Maimonides dealt with the religious and literary problem that he confronted in his attempts to save his community from despair, I pointed out two techniques that he employed. My eminent colleague ignores five of the seven halakhic

[4] Some of the phrases in the original Hebrew version which I cited were not reproduced in the English or in the second Hebrew translation. However, these themes run like an Ariadne's thread throughout Hartman's essay; see e.g. *Crisis and Leadership* (above, n. 2), 47, 64–5, 78, 82–3; *Manhigut* (above, n. 2), 35–6, 48, 58, 61, 65; *MY* 367–8, 381–2, 397, 402. Indeed, these are the central themes in Hartman's essay.

difficulties to which I drew attention in the first half of my essay (including the logical fallacy and the astonishing reading of the *mishnah* that I have mentioned above). Instead, he concentrates his criticism on the two rhetorical techniques I pointed to and on my conjectural reconstruction of one of the actual charges of Maimonides' opponent. Even if we grant the validity both of my colleague's presentation of my views and of his criticism, little is changed, for I scarcely based my arguments on the points 'refuted'.

Let me take, first,[5] Hartman's attack on my hypothetical reconstruction of one of the charges of Maimonides' adversary.[6] Maimonides rebuts the claim that after someone has apostatized God is indifferent to that person's good or evil acts. I questioned whether anyone had advanced such an extreme claim, and doubted whether Maimonides' opponent was the religious anarchist that Maimonides makes him out to be. I *suggested* that the argument of the opponent had focused on the invalidity of the religious performances of the Marranos. Maimonides, by focusing on the formulation *sekhar mitsvah*, turned a terrestrial, halakhic argument into a celestial one of Divine retribution.[7] It matters not in the least whether the terrestrial, halakhic argument is right or wrong. If his opponent in fact advanced one argument—good or bad—and Maimonides answered another, Maimonides' reply is rhetoric. The central point is that he did not address his opponent's argument; its correctness is irrelevant. I have no objection to Hartman's holding forth eloquently against the opponent's viewpoint (I, too, entertain reservations about it), but how does this rebut the charge of rhetoric?

Let us further remember that the entire argument is but a conjecture of mine. A plausible one, I believe, but still only a conjecture. Moreover, nothing hinges on it. Assume the surmise to be in total error, and we are still left with Maimonides' avoidance of the issue of the supremacy of the Mohammedan prophecy, the blatant logical error—not to speak of his unacceptable reading of the *mishnah* in *Nedarim* which I have previously mentioned.

The only charge that Hartman confronts directly is Maimonides' strange definitions of *kiddush ha-shem* and *ḥillul ha-shem*,[8] definitions that can be characterized only as '*Hamlet* without the prince of Denmark'. Even were we to accept my colleague's view of *kiddush ha-shem* in *Mishneh Torah*,[9] the questions posed remain unanswered. Hartman writes: 'The ultimate sacrifice of

[5] This paragraph and the one that follows were not in the original Hebrew text.

[6] *Crisis and Leadership* (above, n. 2), 57–67; *Manhigut* (above, n. 2), 41–50; *MY* 374–80. See above, pp. 302–3.

[7] *MY* 361–7; pp. 302–3 above.

[8] *Crisis and Leadership* (above, n. 2), 67–82; *Manhigut* (above, n. 2), 50–64; *MY* 384–401.

[9] *Crisis and Leadership*, 67–75; *Manhigut*, 52–8; *MY* 384–93.

one's life under extreme circumstances does not exhaust the significance of *kiddush ha-shem*.'[10] True enough, but one can scarcely omit such sacrifice from the definition of *kiddush ha-shem*, as did Maimonides in his *Iggeret ha-Shemad*.

As to the interpretation of *kiddush ha-shem* that my distinguished critic attributes to Maimonides:[11] if Hartman wishes to express his own idea of *kiddush ha-shem* and claim it for Maimonides, attaching it to one of the great figures of the Jewish past and relying on the timeless axiom that the new is only a swerving back to recapture something that had been previously lost, I have no quarrel with him. This is common practice in traditional societies, and he is only doing to Maimonides' words what that great thinker did to the words of the talmudic sages (*ḥazal*). If he wishes, however, to engage in textual exegesis, to uncover what Maimonides actually said, he is doing intellectual history, and the ground rules of history-writing apply—the first of which is that the interpretation proffered must conform in some way to the words of the author being interpreted.

The interesting notion of *kiddush ha-shem* that Dr Hartman attributes to Maimonides revolves around my eminent colleague's interpretation of the last section of the fifth chapter of *Yesodei ha-Torah*, #11, where Maimonides discusses what he describes as 'the other things that are included in the class of *ḥillul ha-shem*', the axial passage of my colleague's argument. I have some reservations about his reading of the passage, as it requires making a number of prior assumptions: first, one must assume that it is speaking of the *ḥasid* and not the *talmid ḥakham* or *ḥakham*. Second, we must disregard all of the parallels to this passage in the fifth chapter of *De'ot*, which, from beginning to end, speaks only of the *talmid ḥakham* and *ḥakham* and never once mentions the *ḥasid*. Third, we must ignore the numerous forms of meritorious conduct described in section 11 and fix only on 'habitually acting beyond the strict requirements of the law' (*li-fenim mi-shurat ha-din*). Fourth, one must assume that when Maimonides writes in the concluding section of the chapter, 'there are other things that are included in *ḥillul ha-shem*', this does not mean that he is turning to a secondary (albeit significant) meaning of the term, but to its main, indeed fundamental, one, and that it is this basic meaning that undergirds the previous ten sections of that chapter. In other words, what is written at the end is really written in the beginning, and 'other things' means the 'main thing'.

The question of the definitions of heresy and idolatry and their place in *kiddush ha-shem*, the question of word versus speech, and the need for inner

10 *Crisis and Leadership*, 74; *Manhigut*, 57; *MY* 392.

11 *Crisis and Leadership*, 67–75; *Manhigut*, 52–5; *MY* 384–93.

conviction in idolatry and heresy and its consequences for the martyr imperative were discussed at length in my article. Indeed, some eight pages were devoted to them. Dr Hartman disposes of all of this in one sentence:

Assessing the impact of the community's submission to the Almohads upon the character of its members was in many respects a more important *legal* consideration than whether Islam was technically a form of idolatry or whether public pronunciation without conviction constitutes religious worship.[12]

If one excises the word 'legal' from the passage, I could not be more in agreement. Indeed, I myself wrote something quite similar.[13] If, however, one does insert the word 'legal', not to speak of emphasizing it,[14] then one is obliged to offer halakhic support for one's claim—unless one assumes that any consideration that one believes is good for Judaism is *ipso facto* halakhic, which brings us back to the question of ground rules that I raised at the outset.

Last but not least: Dr Hartman writes with captivating enthusiasm, and it is difficult not to be impressed by his emotional involvement with his argument and his existential identification with his own ideas. However, this enthusiasm leads him, at times, to present the opinions of those with whom he polemicizes without quite the precision that one might ideally hope for. For example, he writes:

The entire epistle has no basis in Halakha; its intellectual roots [Soloveitchik claims] lay rather in the Aristotelian tradition and specifically in Aristotle's *Rhetoric*, with which Maimonides was familiar.

Rhetoric was a recognized literary and intellectual genre, and Maimonides could well feel that his mode of argumentation, no less than his ultimate goal was, in one sense valid, and that in writing as he did, he stood not only religiously, but intellectually as well, in a reputable tradition—a tradition that, given every instinct and

[12] *Crisis and Leadership*, 64; *Manhigut*, 48; *MY* 382.

[13] See p. 314 above: 'To avoid this catastrophe, Maimonides entered the fray. It mattered little now whether they were or were not technically "apostates", for if something was not done they would soon be so in fact. As long as they persisted in their Judaism, even if technically speaking their efforts were worthless, they could very easily be brought back to the fold when the persecution had passed. At any rate, their children and future generations would not be lost forever to the people of Israel. And while this last point was indeed irrelevant to the legal question of *yehareg ve-'al ya'avor* ('he should be killed and not transgress'—the imperative of martyrdom), it had no small bearing on the simpler issue of Jewish survival. Some means had to be found to alleviate the community's profound sense of guilt and to tell its members that they had not abandoned their faith.'

[14] In the original Hebrew version to which I responded, the word 'legal' was italicized. In the English version published a few years later, the adjective 'legal' was present as before, but it was no longer italicized. The italics are equally absent from the Hebrew translation of 1989 (above, n. 2).

inclination of his, he would ideally have preferred not to involve himself in, but a respectable one nonetheless.[15]

This citation is not drawn from the body of my essay (which makes no mention of Aristotle whatsoever) but is excerpted from a footnote. The following is the full text of that note:

It would be the rankest pedantry to point out that Aristotle had noted the utility of denigrating one's opponent in debate whenever possible. How to make a good argument for a bad case requires no knowledge of Aristotle, as anyone who has ever caught a child with his fingers in a cookie jar well knows. Nevertheless, here and there—as in the use of 'example', the misuse of homonyms, the employment of sham enthymemes —references will still be made to the *Rhetoric*. The point of these references (which could be easily multiplied) is not to imply that without some knowledge of this work Maimonides would not have written as he did, or that he wrote according to a preconceived model. This would be nonsense. They serve, rather, the purpose of underlining that given the goal of the *Iggeret*, given its very nature, the tools employed would be viewed as fitting and legitimate by one raised in the Aristotelian tradition. Rhetoric was a recognized literary and intellectual genre, and Maimonides could well feel that his mode of argumentation, no less than his ultimate goal, was in one sense valid, and that in writing as he did, he stood not only religiously, but intellectually as well, in a reputable tradition—a tradition in which, given every instinct and inclination of his, he would ideally have preferred not to involve himself, but a respectable one nonetheless.[16]

15 *Crisis and Leadership* (above, n. 2), 73; *Manhigut* (above, n. 2), 56; *MY* 390.

16 p. 315 n. 58 above.

11

A RESPONSE TO YAIR LORBERBAUM AND HAYYIM SHAPIRA

|163|

THE ESSAY by Yair Lorberbaum and Hayyim Shapira that appeared recently in *Dine Israel* is less a criticism of my arguments in 'Maimonides' *Iggeret ha-Shemad*: Law or Rhetoric' [reproduced in Chapter 12 above[1]] than a jurisprudential analysis of sorts.[2] Such articles usually do not generate a reply. Indeed, when their essay first appeared in a Hebrew Festschrift over a decade ago I ignored it, especially as Festschrifts are sites of dignified interment.[3] The publication of an English version in a law journal, however, provided a far wider dissemination to their analysis and to what, in my view, was a somewhat distorted presentation of my article. After some thought, I concluded that a short corrective was in place. I will first address the jurisprudential aspects of the essay and then, very briefly, two criticisms of my own essay.

It is very flattering to have an essay that one has written as an undergraduate analyzed years later and shown to rest on deep jurisprudential foundations.[4] I picked up Lorberbaum and Shapira's article with curiosity and anticipation: what could I and David Hartman, I wondered, or, for that matter, Maimonides |164| and his opponent, have to do with the philosophy of Ronald Dworkin and Herbert Hart? Could I have actually intuited in my youth the thoughts of either of these famed jurists?

My learned colleagues contend that underlying my position are the jurisprudential assumptions of Herbert Hart, and that underlying Hartman's

[1] {My essay was originally published in L. Landman, ed., *Rabbi Joseph Lookstein Memorial Volume* (New York, 1980), 281–318.}

[2] Y. Lorberbaum and H. Shapira, 'Maimonides' *Epistle on Martyrdom* in Light of Legal Philosophy', *Dine Israel: Studies in Halacha and Jewish Law*, 25 (2008), 123–69. {The authors of the critique, when referring to what I had written, naturally registered the page numbers of my original article. These page references have been placed in round brackets in the text and the passage's location in the present volume placed in square brackets.}

[3] 'Iggeret ha-Shemad la-Rambam: Vikuaḥ Soloveitchik–Hartman bi-Re'i ha-Filosofyah shel ha-Mishpat', *Meḥuyyavut Yehudit Mitḥadeshet: 'al 'Olamo ve-Haguto shel David Hartman* (Tel Aviv, 2001), i. 345–73.

[4] It was part of my BA Honors thesis, on file in Pusey Library, Harvard University.

argument are those of Ronald Dworkin. They do this by having me agree with Maimonides' opponent and Hartman with Maimonides. (Why they need to identify me with Maimonides' opponent instead of simply addressing the latter's position will become clear later on.) Passing for the moment my putative identity with Maimonides' opponent, let me address the position of Hartman/Maimonides, for Hartman does, indeed, identify himself with Maimonides' position in *Iggeret ha-Shemad*.

The analysis of Lorberbaum and Shapira is based upon a lengthy article that I wrote on *Iggeret ha-Shemad*; however, it appears, to me at least, that the entire point of it has eluded them. This is perhaps my own fault; the essay 'Maimonides' *Iggeret ha-Shemad*: Law and Rhetoric' may be too long and not clearly written. However, I have also written, in reply to David Hartman's critique, a brief essay of five pages (inclusive of quotations), in which I highlighted the crux of my article and my basic differences with Dr Hartman. Perhaps it, too, was unclear. I will open by citing the start of that short essay and the reader can judge:

> The crucial issue that lies at the very heart of our disagreement [i.e. that between Hartman and myself—HS] is whether there are outer limits to an intellectual discipline which cannot be breached and whether we can lay down ground rules for arguments within a discipline.
>
> Everyone agrees that political theory takes into account the entire spectrum of considerations—logical, social, and psychological—that Dr Hartman dwells upon at length. Its broad playing field allows a wide gamut of intellectual maneuver, and the most contradictory views can be advanced with comparable claims to legitimacy. However, should a political theorist argue that (1) all revolutionaries are mortal; (2) Goldberg is mortal; (3) therefore Goldberg is a revolutionary, this contention would not be political theory but rhetoric. The problem is |**165**| that Maimonides employs precisely this kind of argument (i.e. the fallacy of the undivided middle) in the *Iggeret ha-Shemad*. Without plunging into the thorny problem of the ground rules of halakhah, we can safely state two of them: (1) the argument must abide by the elementary rules of logic; (2) a halakhic conclusion cannot contradict an explicit *mishnah*, when the *mishnah* has been understood in one and the same fashion by all commentators of the past millennium. Maimonides breached both ground rules in *Iggeret ha-Shemad*.[5]

Having failed to get my point across to my two colleagues with a hypothetical from political theory, perhaps I will succeed with one from law. Suppose a

[5] 'Beḥanim li-Fesikah Hilkhatit: Teshuvah le-Dr D. Hartman', *Meḥkerei Yerushalayim be-Maḥshevet Yisra'el*, 3 (1984), 683–4; translated and printed above as 'Reply to David Hartman' (the original was prefaced by a two-paragraph introduction).

judge sentenced a man to twenty-five years of imprisonment on the basis of the following argument: (1) all terrorists have two feet; (2) this man has two feet; (3) therefore this man is a terrorist, and this ruling was then upheld by the superior courts. Would Lorberbaum and Shapira see the man as having been convicted by a valid legal system, with which they have only a difference of opinion? Do they think that Dworkin would ponder the jurisprudential foundations of such a system? Furthermore, Maimonides' statements contradict an explicit ruling in the Mishnah. Does Dworkin treat a legal system where a local judge in Washington, DC can rule that the president of the United States is elected for a two-year term, and everything done after that period is not binding, for when the Constitution of the United States says 'four years', it means 'two years'? If *Iggeret ha-Shemad*, by reason of the aforementioned breaches, is not law but rhetoric, what does Dworkin have to do with it? Jurisprudence does not deal with the unarticulated assumptions of rhetoric, polemic, or the literature of consolation. If one wishes to apply jurisprudential analysis to *Iggeret ha-Shemad*, one must first address the question whether or not the *Iggeret* is a legal work.

The authors announce that they are treating the meta-halakhic aspects of the issue and that they will take no stand as to the halakhic correctness of the arguments.[6] However, halakhic error—indeed, occasional absurdity—is the crux of my argument. I checked Maimonides' arguments against the rulings of the Talmud as understood in his writings, especially those of his earlier years, and found them to be in contradiction to his position in the *Iggeret*. I checked his line of reasoning by the rules of simple logic and found it, in one instance, to be absurd. It is on the basis of these determinations that I advanced the claim that the |**166**| *Iggeret* is a work of polemic and not of law. If I am correct, there is nothing about which to be jurisprudential. The accuracy or error of my halakhic analysis is thus prejudicial, in the classic sense of the word, to any such analysis. Yet Loberbaum and Shapira fail to address this issue. They simply assume that Maimonides' position in *Iggeret ha-Shemad* is legally valid and proceed to philosophize about it. I don't begrudge them their philosophizing, but they are assuming what needs most to be proven.

Not only is there no substantive engagement, but these two crucial points —the use of an argument entailing the fallacy of the undivided middle and the presence of mishnaic interpretations that run counter to the very words of the Mishnah (and, naturally, counter to every interpretation of the Mishnah of the past millennium, *including* that of Maimonides)—are never mentioned in my colleagues' presentation of my argument and analysis of its assumptions.

[6] p. 134.

To be sure, Lorberbaum and Shapira do pen the following note:

Soloveitchik rejects Maimonides' argument from *Nedarim* 3:4, see ibid. (299–300) [above, pp. 307–8].[7]

That is an understatement. I said that the argument from *Nedarim* 3: 4 made no sense, either logically or hermeneutically. To quote from the pages referred to by my colleagues:

But Maimonides does not rest content with this proof; he seeks to advance another, and with it writes some of the most astounding lines in his entire career . . . Maimonides has committed the elementary logical fallacy of the 'undistributed middle'. . . Coupled with this logical error is a factual one, no less astonishing. It is universally admitted that the coercion that relieves the individual of legal responsibility for his deeds must be the actual threat of death. Something chosen as an alternative to a lesser threat, such as loss of money, is deemed by all hands as voluntarily performed. The Mishnah deals with a case in which the threat of death is not necessarily present . . . It is obvious, then, that the principle at work in the passage on taking a false oath has absolutely nothing to do with the problem of coercion at all; indeed, as Maimonides himself recognized and explicitly stated in his *Perush ha-Mishnayot* and his *Yad ha-Ḥazakah*—together with all his contemporaries and successors, whether of the Franco-German, Provençal, Spanish, or Moroccan schools |**167**|—the law here embodied concerns the effectiveness of mental reservations vis-à-vis certain vows.

Since Maimonides the halakhist did not write nonsense, I inferred that he was not arguing halakhically; he was not seeking to make a cogent argument but to dispel a mood of despair and a dangerous loss of hope.

My colleagues' formulation 'Soloveitchik rejects the argument from *Nedarim* 3:4' is not accidental; it reflects the necessary assumption of their entire essay. There are no fundamental problems with Maimonides' arguments that preclude the *Iggeret* from being a halakhic work. The proof that he adduces from *Nedarim* is logically and legally sustainable; it is merely Soloveitchik's personal view, they claim, that this argument is incorrect.

Such are my reservations about the Hartman–Maimonides–Dworkin thesis.

As for the Soloveitchik–Maimonides' opponent–Hart thesis, let us turn to the question raised earlier: why identify me with the position of Maimonides' opponent? Why not write simply about the jurisprudential underpinnings of Maimonides' disputant? The answer is quite simple. Unless I am identified with his opponent, the crucial correlation of that individual's position with

[7] n. 17.

Ish ha-Halakhah and my family tradition of talmudic analysis collapses. Maimonides' opponent could scarcely be influenced by a work published in 1944 or by a school of thought that arose in the late nineteenth century. It would also appear somewhat rash to set forth the jurisprudential philosophy of an anonymous twelfth-century figure of whom we have but one holding, and next to nothing of that holding in his own words. Yet, other than identification on my part with *one* supposition underlying my *conjectured reconstruction* of *one* of the numerous accusations that Maimonides was seeking to neutralize (see below), there is not a word of personal identification with the rest of the charges. I was vindicating neither the opponent's charges of heresy, nor his contention that the prohibition of idolatry may be violated without inner belief. I was judging those two central contentions not by what I thought but by Maimonides' own statements. The question that I posed was the extent to which Maimonides' positions in *Iggeret ha-Shemad* are compatible with his other writings, especially his earlier ones. To the extent that they are incompatible (not to speak of their being logically flawed), *Iggeret ha-Shemad* is rhetoric. What I thought about these questions was and is irrelevant. For this reason, these views were never expressed in my study. |**168**|

My silence proved no bar for my colleagues. The problem of the necessary identity of my position with that of Maimonides' opponent was handled with ease, as the following examples illustrate.

1. Take the statement of culpability for acts committed under duress that the above-cited note 17 (see p. 341, line 2, above) was meant to document. This is a crucial holding, for without it I could scarcely agree with Maimonides' opponent as to the status of the Marranos as apostates, their disqualification as witnesses, and, arguably, the worthlessness of their religious practices. They write: 'Soloveitchik thinks that the Maimonidean argument as to the sinner's exemption from all punishment in those situations where he ought to have sacrificed his life has no real basis'.[8] Readers can turn to the cited pages in my essay above, where I write the exact opposite:

Maimonides' opponent had advocated the view that the imperative of *kiddush ha-shem* conflicts with and destroys the law of *pikuaḥ nefesh*. Once we enter the awesome domain of martyrdom, the principle of self-preservation is annulled *in toto*, hence all acts that require martyrdom, for any reason, retain their full criminality. Maimonides' erudition disposes of this contention easily. He adduces a passage from the *Sifra* stating that idolatry committed under coercion is non-culpable. As the worship of false gods certainly falls within the realm of prescribed martyrdom, it is obvious that,

[8] p. 134.

regardless of the martyr imperative, the deed is still viewed in that source as involuntary, and for this reason the performer is not held legally responsible. [above, p. 306]

And in note 34 I expanded on the matter:

There should be no doubt as to the force of Maimonides' argument, which he reproduces in 'Yesodei ha-Torah', 5: 4. With the exception of the isolated remarks of R. Moses ha-Cohen (*Hassagot ha-Ramakh 'al ha-Rambam*, ed. S. Atlas [Jerusalem, 1969], ad loc.) and the counter-interpretation of the *Sifra* by R. David Bonfid (*Ḥiddushei ha-Ran 'al Sanhedrin* 61b, s.v. *itmar*), which attracted no followers, Maimonides' views won widespread acceptance. Centuries later, a problem was detected in this proof . . . But **|169|** this in no way affected the acceptance of Maimonides' doctrine of non-culpability in instances of duress.

2. Lorberbaum and Shapira further write: 'Soloveitchik argues that performing a commandment without faith and without inner conviction is lacking in value. Ritual without faith, he states, is like a game and not a religious act.'[9] To this statement they append a note: 'To be precise, Soloveitchik attributes this argument to the sage against whom Maimonides argues; however, from the general tone of his words, it is clear that he himself accepts this argument. See Soloveitchik, "Law and Rhetoric" (294–296) [above, pp. 302–4]'.[10] So far, so good. However, they then proceed to state—and, again, it is an important building block of their argument:

As mentioned above, Maimonides attributed value to the Marranos' fulfillment of the commandments by drawing a distinction between willful idolatry and compelled idolatry. Soloveitchik argued that this is not a real defense, as the Marranos had failed in their obligation to sanctify God's name and had engaged in idolatry and hence were considered as apostates, such that there was no value to the commandments which they fulfilled. The performance of commandments is of value only if it is accompanied by acknowledgement of the God who gave the commandments and the obligation to obey him. Such recognition is lacking among the Marranos.[11]

Not so. There are two separate issues. (1) Does the performance of religious rituals require belief? (2) Were the religious rituals of the Marranos performed in a state of disbelief? If the reader will review my remarks on the pages cited by my colleagues [above, pp. 302–3], he will see that I answered 'Yes' to the first question, but said nothing about the second. I do believe that the performance of religious ritual by a genuine atheist is of no religious value; that, however, is not the bone of contention in *Iggeret ha-Shemad*. What is at bar in that work is

[9] p. 133. [10] n. 16. [11] p. 135.

whether there is religious value to the performance of *mitsvot* by someone who has been |170| coerced by the threat of death to assert disbelief, yet still believes with all his heart and soul. Maimonides' opponent believed that it was of no value; not I.

As I say above, I would very much like to have intuited in my youth the jurisprudential assumptions of the famed Herbert Hart. I simply do not see how I have.

Let me now turn to two criticisms, one factual and one methodological, that my colleagues make of my argument.

1. They write:

> On this point Soloveitchik seems to contradict himself; he initially argues against Maimonides that the definition of idolatry does not depend on inner faith, but rather upon the technical nature of the act, so that even one who is forced to do so is considered an idolater; further on he argues that in order for commandments to be of any religious value, they must be accompanied by inner conviction. Why does idolatry not require inner conviction, whereas it is a necessary precondition for the value of one's fulfillment of commandments?[12]

I fail to follow the logic of their argument. If I believe that paganism or idolatry is cultic rather than credal, why must I believe that Judaism, or Christianity for that matter, is the same? I point this out with regret, for my colleagues' line of reasoning would greatly alleviate the current problems of conversion in Israel.

Far more important, I never claimed that idolatry is cultic. I said that Maimonides, in his early years, was of the belief that idolatry was cultic. Previously, Lorberbaum and Shapira identified my position with that of Maimonides' opponent; now they identify it with that of Maimonides. The only justification of such an identification would be if what I wrote had little basis in Maimonides' actual writings but was a clear projection of my view onto that great Talmudist. Let us therefore examine the basis of my claim that Maimonides, early in his career, took paganism as being cultic.

Most of us began studying the Talmud with the second chapter in *Bava Metsi'a*, 'Elu Metsi'ot'. Very soon we came to the famous controversy of Abbaye and Rava of *ye'ush shelo mi-da'at* and were told by our *rebbe*—|171| often with great fanfare—that this controversy is one of only six places in the

12 pp. 135–6.

entire Talmud where the ruling is according to Abbaye. In all the hundreds and hundreds of other controversies between the two, the ruling always follows Rava. And we all felt privileged to study such a unique controversy. It is no exaggeration to say that every schoolboy knows that *Abbaye ve-Rava, halakhah ke-Rava*.

The question whether idolatry is cultic or credal is, in fact, a controversy between Abbaye and Rava (and not one of the famous six):

It has been taught: If one engages in idolatry through love or fear [of man, but does not actually accept the divinity of the idol], Abbaye said that he is culpable; but Rava said that he is not culpable. Abbaye ruled that he is culpable since he has worshipped it; but Rava said he is not culpable: if he has accepted it as a god, he is culpable; but not otherwise.[13]

Maimonides, in the early version of the *Perush ha-Mishnayot*, ruled like Abbaye![14] Did I have an alternative to stating that Maimonides initially viewed idolatry as cultic?

2. Loberbaum and Shapira further write,

The validity of his [i.e. Soloveitchik's] argument depends on his succeeding in demonstrating that all (or at least most) of Maimonides' arguments in the *Epistle* [i.e. *Iggeret ha-Shemad*] are flawed and that these flaws are obvious. Hence in order to confute Soloveitchik's argument it is sufficient to show that at least part of Maimonides' arguments has a firm basis, and where he does in fact 'err', his error is a reasonable one.[15]

Three brief points: first, is breaking an elementary rule of logic and then ruling contrary to a *setam mishnah* 'reasonable'? Perhaps that is why Loberbaum and Shapira have omitted these central points from their summary of my argument. Second, how can one demonstrate that a legal argument has a 'firm basis', or that a legal error is a 'reasonable one', if one avowedly eschews legal argument as my colleagues do?[16] Third, to show that the *Iggeret ha-Shemad* |172| was a rhetorical work, written to persuade a community on the verge of religious despair that they had not betrayed their God, I need only demonstrate that some arguments of Maimonides are so out of line that one cannot

[13] *Sanhedrin* 61b: איתמר העובד עבודת כוכבים מאהבה ומיראה, אביי אומר חייב, רבא אומר פטור. אביי אמר חייב—הא פלחיה. רבא אמר פטור—אי קיבלה עליה באלוה חייב, ואי לא, לא. {There are, of course, different interpretations of this controversy. I adopt here, naturally, the interpretation of Maimonides, who (following Rav Hai Gaon) understood it as being the question of cultic performances without inner belief. See *Mishneh Torah*, ''Avodah Zarah', 3: 6; *'Arukh*, ed. A. Kohut (Vienna, 1937), s.v. *A–H–V*.}

[14] *Mishnah 'im Perush le-Rabbenu Mosheh b. Maimon, Nezikin*, ed. Y. Kafih (Jerusalem, 1965), *Sanhedrin* 7: 6, p. 184 n. 3.

[15] p. 134.

[16] Ibid.

imagine that they were advanced seriously. As I have stated above, Maimonides did not pen halakhic absurdities, and if absurdity there is in *Iggeret ha-Shemad*, then that work was not penned as a halakhic defense. Some of Maimonides' arguments are impossible, some problematic or (as in the distinction between heresy and idolatry) possible but unproven. One argument alone is both cogent and proven—that of coercion. Why did Maimonides present all the others? I addressed the nature of the piece as a whole, not whether buried in the plethora of rabbinic citations there is one from the *Sifra* (proving the non-culpability of coerced idolatry) which is deeply relevant.[17]

Even the *Sifra* passage is insufficiently developed to afford the Marranos relief, for all that Maimonides' remarkable erudition has proven is that coerced acts are not punishable, not that they are non-tortuous. Punishment is one thing; sin is another, and the sting of the opponent's charges lay as much in the sinfulness of the Marranos' deeds as in their culpability. Maimonides, indeed, seems to be of the opinion in his *Perush ha-Mishnayot* that religious breaches committed under duress have no need for atonement.[18] This would form the natural complement to the argument from the *Sifra*. However, he does not advance it in his defense of Moroccan Jewry—and for an obvious reason. If their conduct has not been sinful, why should Jews flee Morocco, as he insists that they must? Maimonides was caught between the Scylla of overwhelming guilt and the Charybdis of guiltless inertia[19]—whence the deeply moving but problematic *Iggeret ha-Shemad*.

[17] See my remarks above, pp. 305–6.

[18] *Mishnah 'im Perush le-Rabbenu Mosheh b. Maimon, Mo'ed*, ed. Y. Kafih (Jerusalem, 1964), *Yoma* 8: 6, p. 266. (I say 'seems' because Maimonides uses the term *patur* [exempt, relieved of] in the Arabic original, which seems awkward here. *Patur* from what? From the context the only thing he could be relieved of is the need for repentance or the need for Yom Kippur and suffering to lessen the sin and death to finally atone for it. All of this would imply that the coerced sinner does not need atonement. From the context it is clear that Maimonides is referring only to religious infractions, *bein adam la-makom*, not to breaches in one's duty to one's fellow man, *bein adam le-ḥavero*.)

[19] This was pointed out in the essay {above, pp. 316–17}.

III

A RESPONSE TO ARYEH STRIKOVSKY

IF DRS HARTMAN, LOBERBAUM, AND SHAPIRA avoided halakhic engagement with my essay, not so Rabbi Aryeh Strikovsky.[1] He tackles my argument head on. He agrees that there is a strong suasive element in the *Iggeret* and that Maimonides was confronted by the unenviable task of minimizing the gravity of the Marranos' actions—which hinged ultimately on the portrayal of Islam as monotheistic—while not downplaying the seriousness of converting to that religion. He is also in agreement that the *Iggeret* is structured to facilitate this dual purpose. While admitting that it has a rhetorical function—an attempt to lighten the Marranos' guilt for their recital of the *shahada* and living outwardly as Muslims—he insists that it is equally a valid halakhic defense of the conduct of the Jews under the Almohads and takes issue with my halakhic analysis, registering a number of legal arguments in defense of Maimonides' position.

In Rabbi Strikovsky's alternative reading Maimonides made the following argument:

> In my opinion, says Maimonides, Islam is not an idolatrous religion and the *shahada* is nothing but an empty declaration about Mohammed's prophecy. If you will contend that one who proclaims the *shahada* transgresses by [dissimulating his Jewishness and] appearing to be a heretic and a Gentile, I would contend that there is no injunction against reciting words of heresy under circumstances of coercion with a mental reservation, especially when the coercer realizes that the object of his coercion doesn't believe in what he is saying. (p. 249)

I have no quarrel with this restatement. The problem lies in what it omits. It fails to address three major problems that I highlighted in my study.[2] First and foremost, assenting to the primacy of the Mohammedan revelation is

[1] 'Iggeret ha-Shemad la-Rambam: Halakhah o Retorikah?', in I. Varhaftig, ed., *Sefer ha-Yovel Minhah le-'Ish: Kovets Ma'amarim Muggash be-Hokarah le-ha-Rav Avraham Yeshayahu Dolgin* (Jerusalem, 1991), 242–75; page references to this article are given in the text. My references to Maimonides' text follow the pattern outlined in my original essay, 'Maimonides' *Iggeret ha-Shemad*: Law and Rhetoric' (above, Ch. 12, n. 3).

[2] Above, pp. 291–300.

heresy, for it denies the eternal validity of the Torah. The primacy of the Mosaic revelation is the cornerstone of the Jewish religion, and no one ever emphasized this more than Maimonides. Seeing that he writes in the *Iggeret* that heresy (*minut*) is worse than idolatry with regard to the martyr imperative (*yehareg ve-'al ya'avor*), why is the heresy of Islam any different? Second, if heresy does fall under the rubric of 'idolatry', any word–deed distinction is precluded, as the Mishnah specifically states that idols can be worshipped by speech, no less than by deed. Third, as to inner disbelief conjoined with the coercer's awareness of the dissimulation as mitigating factors, these ingredients are present in all cases of religious coercion, and yet the halakhah demands martyrdom rather than compliance. My distinguished critic simply assumes that the recitation of *shahada* does not entail heresy and, if it does, inner disbelief together with the persecutor's awareness of disbelief neutralizes a heretical statement, even though it would never neutralize an idolatrous one. Nowhere in his essay does he provide any evidence for the validity of these far-reaching claims.

Rabbi Strikovsky further invokes the principle of 'self-benefit' (*hana'at 'atsmo*—*San.* 74b) (pp. 249, 258–60), namely, that, should someone threaten to kill me unless I drive a car for him on the Sabbath—not because he wishes me to desecrate the Sabbath but because he needs a getaway car for a robbery—I am allowed to drive the car. The coercion that elicits the martyrdom imperative must have a religious purpose; it must intend to force the coerced to violate his religion. Forcing someone to do something that *happens* to entail a religious transgression, though the coercer never intended it as such, does not constitute 'religious persecution' and martyrdom is uncalled for. He contends that Maimonides invokes this principle when he writes, 'They know very well that we do not mean what we say, and that what we say is only to escape the ruler's punishment and to satisfy him [*le-hafis da'ato*] with a simple confession.'[3]

I have several reservations. First, that of context: I do not believe that Maimonides intends to invoke the argument of *hana'at 'atsmo* when he speaks of 'satisfying' the ruler with empty words. The purpose of both passages that speak of *le-hafis da'ato* is to argue the meaninglessness of the recitation of the

[3] *Iggeret ha-Shemad*, *Rambam la-'Am* (Jerusalem, 1960), 61; Y. Shilat, *Iggerot ha-Rambam*, i (Jerusalem, 1987), 53; A. Halkin, *Crisis and Leadership: Epistles of Maimonides* (Philadelphia, 1985), 30. Variant readings: *Rambam la-'Am*, 61 (= A. Geiger, *Moses ben Maimon: Studien* [Breslau, 1850], fo. 5a): להפיס דעתו בדיבורים מן הדבור; Z. H. Edelmann, *Ḥemdah Genuzah* (Königsberg, 1856), 11: להפיס דעתו בדבור דתו; Shilat, *Iggerot ha-Rambam*, i. 53: די להפיס דעתו בעילוי דתו; Y. Kafih, *Iggerot ha-Rambam* (Jerusalem, 1972), 118: להפיס דעתו בדבור פשוט—this, however, is Kafih's own emendation.

shahada, as the persecutors themselves know that we do not believe what we say. Second, it is a misapplication of the criterion of *hana'at 'atsmo*. What pleases the ruler is that Jews should recite the *shahada*, the confession of Muslim faith; such a satisfaction does not fall under the rubric of *hana'at 'atsmo*. Most religious persecutors derive the same satisfaction as did the Almohad ruler. Taking pleasure from the results of religious coercion does not, however, nullify or even lessen the fact of 'religious coercion'. Only if the purpose (and, consequently, the satisfaction) is ulterior and extraneous, only if the coercion has a goal other than that of religious persecution, is the martyr imperative abated.

Lastly, *hana'at 'atsmo* annuls only the martyr imperative arising from religious persecution (*sha'at ha-gezerah*), not that which arises in instances of murder, idolatry, or adultery/incest. Because of their intrinsic severity, these acts cannot be performed under any circumstances, regardless of what motivates the coercer.[4] My colleague would have it that the passage in *Sanhedrin* 74b which permits giving lit braziers to idol worshippers who seek to warm themselves in their temple supplies evidence that *hana'at 'atsmo* allows even 'cultic acts of full-fledged idolatry'. He writes: 'From this we see that we expand the allowance of *hana'at 'atsmo* even to cultic acts of full-fledged idolatry; how much more so, then, can one expand it to include a statement which has lost its cultic meaning [i.e. the *shahada*]' (p. 260).

With all respect, I simply don't understand this statement. In the case in *Sanhedrin*, there is no cultic performance on the Jew's part, nor is the injunction that the Jew would ordinarily transgress by providing such fires that of idolatry—in any form. A Gentile is enjoined from idolatry by Jewish law. A Jew who provides him with the wherewithal to worship idols transgresses the injunction on placing a stumbling block before the blind (Lev. 19: 14, *lifnei 'iver lo titen mikhshol*). Unlike American and Israeli law, Jewish law does not consider the criminal facilitator or abettor to be a partner to the specific crime facilitated. A Jew who provides his co-religionist with a ham sandwich has transgressed no law of *kashrut*; a Jew who provides another Jew or a Gentile with the instruments of idol worship has transgressed no injunction on idolatry. He has simply facilitated a crime. This is a crime in and of itself, but it does not bear the legal taint of the crime facilitated. One cannot infer from the above passage in *Sanhedrin* that *hana'at 'atsmo* permits idolatry, in any of its permutations (*avizraya*). What one may infer at the most (should the brazier be used for idolatrous purposes) is that a decree requiring Jews to transgress the injunction on *lifnei 'iver* does not constitute religious persecution, if the

[4] *Iggeret ha-Shemad*, 51; Shilat (above, n. 3), 46; Halkin (above, n. 3), 24.

facilitation demanded has no religious purpose but is solely for the personal convenience of those who issued the decree (as saving themselves the bother of purchasing these braziers on their own).

My colleague would further have it that the Almohad persecution, since it was economically motivated (the goal was to drive successful Jewish businessmen from the realm), falls under the allowance of *hana'at 'atsmo*.[5] Passing over the issue whether this was in fact the case, I still fail to grasp his argument. The financial benefit does not arise from the recital of the *shahada* by the Jews but from their emigration. The purpose of the persecution may be emigration, but the purpose of the decree to recite the *shahada* is religious persecution. That this persecution is a means to a wider economic, diplomatic, or military end does not alter in any way its nature, and the martyr imperative remains in full force.

Rabbi Strikovsky then writes: 'Soloveitchik argues that Maimonides does not discuss the issue of mental reservation as the basis of the allowance' (p. 257). I ask the reader to turn to pp. 305–8 above, where I devote several pages to analyzing Maimonides' use of mental reservation. I contend that Maimonides' invocation of mental reservation was problematic, but nowhere do I deny that he invoked the concept. My colleague further argues that Maimonides' position in the *Iggeret* conforms to his position in *Moreh Nevukhim*, namely, that belief is entirely a mental state (pp. 258–9). Indeed it is. However, the issue at bar in the *Iggeret* is not the nature of belief but the nature of idolatry, of what constitutes an idolatrous act. Can the crime of idolatry be committed by word as well as by deed and is inner belief necessary for this criminal act? The *mishnah* stating that the utterance of 'Thou art my God' constitutes idolatry answers the first question unambiguously, and the subsequent talmudic ruling of 'intent to mock' (*mekhaven le-vizuyeh*), as understood by Maimonides—not to speak of his position in his early years that the ruling is *ha-'oved mi-'ahavah o mi-yir'ah ḥayyav* (one who worships an idol out of ulterior motives but does not accept it as a deity is nevertheless culpable of idolatry)—answers the second no less clearly.[6] The only line of defense is that heresy has different rules from idolatry. That may well be; the burden of proof, however, is on the claimant, and the absence of such proof is one of the major problems of the *Iggeret*.

Rabbi Strikovsky does not explain the astonishing absence of martyrdom from Maimonides' definition of *kiddush ha-shem* or the parallel omission of

[5] See p. 246 n. 8; p. 249 (*be-tseruf ha-reka' ha-kalkali*), p. 259. (It is somewhat strange to put the documentation of a central argument in a footnote to a passing remark unrelated to the argument that will be advanced on its basis.)

[6] *'Avodah Zarah* 60b, 64a. See above, pp. 295–6.

the failure to suffer martyrdom in his definition of *ḥillul ha-shem*.[7] He does address the baffling proof that Maimonides advanced from the efficacy of mental reservations in vows to 'murderers, robbers, and publicans'.[8] He contends that Maimonides did not deal with the problem of failing to live up to the demands of martyrdom but an entirely different one, namely, why the recitation of the *shahada* should not constitute *ḥillul ha-shem*, seeing that in Islamic law the *shahada* has the force of a vow. To this Maimonides replies that mental reservations are permissible in coerced vows.[9] Whether or not the *shahada* has the force of a vow in Islamic law I am not competent to say; however, I think my distinguished colleague is reading things into the text that are not there. The issue of mental reservation is discussed by Maimonides at pp. 294 and 307–8. In these passages the question at bar, put pointedly by Maimonides, is whether or not failure to live up to the martyr imperative renders a man culpable for his actions. The notion of the *shahada* as oath is an interesting one, and one that a comprehensive defense of its recitation should include. However, nowhere in the *Iggeret* is this issue raised, either by Maimonides or by his opponent, and I think it ahistorical to inject it into that work. What Maimonides should have argued or what a rounded treatment of the *shahada* must entail is a question for jurists and halakhists; the historian's concern is what Maimonides actually did argue, and this should be determined on the basis of his actual words.

[7] See above, pp. 309–10. [8] See above, pp. 307–8.
[9] pp. 252–5; documentation in nn. 29b, 30a.

IV

A RESPONSE TO HILLEL NOVETSKY

THE MOST TRENCHANT and sustained criticism of my essay on *Iggeret ha-Shemad* did not appear in print but in a private essay that a former student of mine, Rabbi Hillel Novetsky, sent me. Not only does he carefully scrutinize every one of my arguments but, equally, he offers a detailed alternative reading of the *Iggeret*. I find his central argument unpersuasive; however, the essay is well grounded and tightly argued, and some readers may well feel that his is the better reading of Maimonides' epistle. Rabbi Novetsky has graciously allowed me to place it on my website.[1] The reader can thus weigh his words against mine and arrive at his or her own conclusion.

As I have pointed out in previous chapters, the two most striking problems in *Iggeret ha-Shemad* are the logical fallacy of 'the undistributed middle' in Maimonides' argument based on a *mishnah* in *Nedarim* and the interpretation given to that *mishnah* contrary to the interpretation of all commentators, including Maimonides himself.[2] If Maimonides, indeed, took these two gross missteps, he did so intentionally. *Iggeret ha-Shemad* was, then, not written primarily as a halakhic work but as a rhetorical one, designed to counteract the despair that was sweeping through the Marrano community of Morocco. I will address Rabbi Novetsky's alternative interpretation of Maimonides' remarks on the *mishnah* in *Nedarim*, which, if it is correct, undermines my central argument, and then turn to four other basic critiques of his.

An Alternative Reading of Maimonides

I questioned the invocation of the above *mishnah* seeing that the coercion (*ones*) that relieves of culpability is the threat of death (or serious physical harm), whereas the Mishnah here also deals with the threat of monetary loss. In response to this, Rabbi Novetsky quotes the remarks of Rashbash (R. Shelomoh ben R. Shim'on Duran, Algiers, d. 1467), who claims that monetary coercion is also deemed coercion and who cites as evidence Mai-

[1] 'Halakhah, Polemikah ve-Retorikah be-'Iggeret ha-Shemad shel ha-Rambam', <www.haym-soloveitchik.org>. Page references to this article are given in the text.

[2] Above, pp. 307–8.

monides' comments in *Perush ha-Mishnayot* on *Ketubbot* 2: 3 (pp. 17–18). That *mishnah* states that witnesses who recant and claim that they were coerced by a financial threat are not believed, as that would be self-incrimination (*ein adam mesim 'atsmo rasha'*). The crime to which the witnesses have admitted, Maimonides writes, is that of saving one's own property at the expense of another's (*matsil 'atsmo be-mamon ḥavero*). The simplest explanation is that they are guilty of false testimony. Rashbash infers from this that Maimonides is of the opinion that since they testified under financial coercion, they are not guilty of false testimony.[3]

Coercion can be a factor in many different areas, for example in divorce (*get me'usseh*), sale (*talyuhu ve-zaben*), the fulfillment of vows (*ḥalah hu o beno*), and the exculpation of criminal acts. That financial pressure could be reckoned as coercion in the first three areas poses no problem. Not so in the fourth. It would mean that should someone say to me, 'Beat up the little old lady or I will take away the candy bar that you are eating', I would not be liable for any of the fivefold damages imposed upon the batterer if I proceeded to beat up the little old lady.[4] I find this intolerable, both morally and legally. (A $100,000 loss is equally intolerable.) As for Maimonides' remarks in *Ketubbot* (of which I was unaware): before I would attribute to him what to my mind is an appalling and shocking doctrine, I would sooner characterize his comment as *lav davka*, that is to say, Maimonides was of the opinion that the witnesses were guilty of both false testimony and saving oneself at the expense of another; he simply cited one rather than the other, for no particular reason. There are limits to strict construction, and exculpating every crime in the book (other than murder, idolatry, and incest/adultery) for the sake of a candy bar is one of them. If the reader does not share my visceral reaction, Novetsky's argument is compelling.

As to the logical fallacy of the undistributed middle that the argument from the *mishnah* in *Nedarim* entails,[5] Novetsky contends that Maimonides was not addressing the issue of whether coercion exculpates someone who has committed the sin of idolatry; were that the case, his argument would, indeed, be grossly fallacious. Maimonides was rebutting another charge altogether, though not one made by his opponent. Since the Mishnah in *Avot* (4: 4) states that Divine punishment is meted out for *ḥillul ha-shem*, whether committed intentionally (*mezid*) or in error (*shogeg*), he feared that someone might infer that one was punished equally in instances of coercion. Hence he sought out another instance of an injunction whose transgression constitutes *ḥillul ha-*

3 *She'elot u-Teshuvot Rashbash* (Jerusalem, 1998), #379.

4 *Nezek, tsa'ar, rippui, shevet, boshet* (damage, pain, medical expenses, loss of income due to disablement, shame).

5 Above, pp. 307–8.

shem, that against swearing falsely, and for which the individual is not held culpable if the false vow was made under coercion (pp. 17–18).

I have two objections. First, the context in which the Mishnah is cited is one in which Maimonides argues against the charge that the imperative of martyrdom (*yehareg ve-'al ya'avor*) precludes the plea of coercion. If he then moves on to argue against a mistaken inference from *Avot*, I find it strange that he does not spell this out, especially as the *Iggeret*'s target audience is, as I shall further emphasize, the ignorant (*'am ha-'arets*) as well as the scholarly. There should have been at least a half-sentence to the effect—'Should one argue that coercion does not exculpate in matters involving *ḥillul ha-shem* because of the passage in *Avot*?'—and then continue, 'this is disproven by the Mishnah in *Nedarim*'. Because of the differing translations, the text of *Iggeret ha-Shemad* is rich in variants, yet no version of that work reflects the purpose attributed by Novetsky to the citation.[6]

Second, Rabbi Novetsky realizes that invoking the passage in *Nedarim* to this end entails a novel interpretation of the Mishnah. All commentators have taken the allowance to be based on the presence of a mental reservation. Mental reservations are generally not allowed in matters of vows; however, when a coercer is present and the person is prevented from uttering what he actually thinks, mental reservations are then taken into consideration. The exculpation is based on the presence of mental reservations; coercion simply provides the circumstances when such reservations are admitted. According to this widely held view, coercion here plays a purely ancillary role, thus no inference can be drawn from this passage as to the exculpatory power of coercion in instances of *ḥillul ha-shem*.

Novetsky suggests that Maimonides entertained a novel reading of the *Nedarim* passage. The exculpating factor is coercion, including financial coercion. The Mishnah, however, also allows such vows to be taken *ab initio* (*le-khatḥilah*). This *ab initio* allowance is based on the utterer's mental reservation. The difference between these two explanations will express itself in an instance of coercion where no mental reservation was made. According to the standard explanation, the oath-taker has sworn falsely and is fully culpable. According to Novetsky's interpretation, he is not culpable since he was coerced, though he should not have taken the oath to begin with, as he made no mental reservation. Novetsky draws upon an observation of Radbaz in one of his responsa, where he interprets Maimonides' formulation in the *Mishneh Torah* (in 'Shevu'ot' 3: 3 and 'Nedarim' 4: 1), 'and the [utterer] should direct

[6] As to Novetsky's contention (p. 17) that, when Maimonides was discussing the *mishnah* in *Avot* several pages before, he wrote **וכל זה שיהיה מחלל שם שמים ברצונו, כמו שנבאר**, see below, pp. 361–2.

himself in his heart to something permissible [i.e. make a mental reservation]'. Radbaz claims that the verb 'should' (*ve-tsarikh*) implies a *le-khatḥilah*, a desirable but not an indispensable condition. Should the speaker not make this mental reservation, he is still not held culpable.

This is an original, well-thought-out argument; however, I believe that it places more weight on the word *ve-tsarikh* than it can bear. Radbaz suggests such a reading of Maimonides in a passing remark in a responsum and, significantly, he does not make this point in his commentary on the same passage in the *Mishneh Torah*. More importantly: while it is true that a CD-ROM check of the *Mishneh Torah* yields far more instances of *ve-tsarikh* being used to designate a legal preference (*le-khatḥilah*) rather than a *sine qua non* (*be-di'avad*), nevertheless, there are sufficient cases of its clear use by Maimonides as a *sine qua non* condition.[7] To my mind, its precise meaning always depends on its context, and there is little in the context of either of the two passages in *Mishneh Torah* to indicate that this is a *le-khatḥilah* only, and that Maimonides entertained here a novel interpretation of the Mishnah. The fact that Maimonides does not mention mental reservations in his brief remarks in *Perush ha-Mishnayot* in *Nedarim* is not, to my mind, convincing. Anyone who regularly uses that commentary knows how often Maimonides' explanatory remarks are incomplete, indeed, at times, even fragmentary. Again, the reader may well prefer here Novetsky's interpretation.

One should also be careful not to take an ivory-towered view of the *Iggeret*. That work may well be a valid halakhic essay; it is also, unquestionably, a work of rhetoric, written to save a host of 'sinners' from despair and conversion. Arguments that hold true in the talmudic academy are not persuasive in the marketplace, and, I might add, books readily available today were scarcely so in the medieval period. Rabbi Novetsky asks: seeing that Maimonides had an irrefutable proof from the *Sifra*, what need had he of another from a *mishnah*? Reply: how many ordinary Jews in Fez in the twelfth century had ever heard of the *Sifra*? How many ordinary Jews in eastern Europe over the past half-millennium have ever heard of the *Sifra*? If its moniker, *Torat Kohanim*, did ring some vague bell in their memory, it was because the abbreviation ת"כ appears at times in Rashi on *Ḥumash*, and their teacher (*rebbe*) in the *ḥeder* had told them what it stood for. Did they ever see an actual copy of the *Torat Kohanim*? I doubt it. (My impression is that the *Sifra* was not readily available until the latter half of the twentieth century, certainly not before the second half of the nineteenth century.[8]) Had they any notion of what its authority

[7] To give two examples from 'Tefillin': *mukaf gevil* in 1: 9 and *saḥ mevarekh shetayim* in 4: 6.

[8] As anecdotal evidence for this estimate, see Y. A. Karelitz, *Ḥazon Ish, Kelim* (Vilna, 1936), #1: 6:

was? How could they? Maimonides needed a source of unquestioned authority if he was to prove to the masses that coercion mitigates guilt in instances where martyrdom is demanded, and a passage from a tome called *Sifra* would scarcely suffice. He needed an authoritative text to dispel the fears and quiet the anxieties of the common folk, and there are few texts more authoritative in rabbinic Judaism than a *setam mishnah*.

If I am correct about the two central weaknesses, indeed, absurdities, in the argument from *Nedarim*, *Iggeret ha-Shemad* is clearly a rhetorical tract designed to assuage widespread guilt, and not a bona fide work of halakhah.

Novetsky's Other Critiques and Alternative Readings

Let me now turn to Rabbi Novetsky's other major criticisms and suggestions.

1. My colleague contends (pp. 6–8) that Maimonides' argument from the story of R. Eli'ezer—who proclaimed 'I take the Judge's word for it'—was not intended to answer the charge that recitation of the *shahada* was idolatrous; rather, it was a response to his opponent's claim that acting like a Gentile in public was equivalent to idolatry.[9]

Maimonides invokes *midrashim* to demonstrate that the most righteous of men in the Bible were punished for broadly characterizing Jews as being wicked, even when there were many among them who had worshipped idols and were, further, guilty of murder. How much more misguided, he continues, is one who says of the entire Moroccan community that they are 'sinners and wicked men, Gentiles and individuals who are not qualified to testify, and apostates who have denied the God of Israel' (פושעים ורשעים, גוים ופסולי עדות, וכופרים בה' א-לקי ישראל)?[10] Maimonides proceeds to invoke the case of R. Me'ir,

וצ"ע בפנים הת"כ ואינו ת"י [תחת ידי]. My father had no copy of the *Torat Kohanim* until a photo-offset of I. H. Weiss's 1862 edition of *Rabad's Commentary on the Sifra* appeared in 1947. (That reprint appeared because of the importance that Rabbi Rosemarin, the head of Om Publishing House, attached to the writings of Rabad, not because of the significance attributed by him to the *Sifra*.) Perhaps Malbim's commentary on the Torah gave the *Sifra*—on which he commented in *Sefer Va-Yikra*—some diffusion, but even granting a widespread familiarity among talmudic scholars with the works of Malbim (a questionable proposition in itself), this only pushes back cognizance of the *Sifra* to the latter half of the 19th century.

[9] Note that the opponent did not only say that the Marrano was legally a *rasha'* and disqualified from testimony, but also that he was a *goy*. This is a variant of the position to be developed by R. Mei'r of Rothenburg (d. 1293) that to state that one is a Gentile is equivalent to denying one's faith (see above, p. 271). Maimonides' opponent spoke of living outwardly in a way that proclaimed one's being a Gentile, and R. Me'ir speaks of stating that one is a Gentile; both, however, share a common outlook.

[10] *Iggeret ha-Shemad*, ed. M. D. Rabinovitz, in *Rambam la-'Am* edn. (Jerusalem, 1960), 38; ed. Y. Shilat in his *Iggerot ha-Rambam* (Jerusalem, 1987), i. 36.

who simulated eating non-kosher food to demonstrate that the charge of public comportment as a Gentile is equivalent to idolatry. He then invokes the case of R. Eli'ezer, who made an ambiguous statement of disbelief. There is no mention of public comportment in Maimonides' discussion here, only of the meaninglessness of oral statements when accompanied by inner disbelief—the crux of his claim that recitation of the *shahada* is halakhically meaningless. For this reason and one other that I will come to, I took this passage as addressing the central charge of *apostasy* (*kefirah*). I realized that this was a construction of Maimonides' words and, therefore, wrote, 'I take it that Maimonides now reasons'.

Novetsky argues that Maimonides' language—'In this persecution, we do not *show* [emphasis Novetsky's] that we worship idols but that we believe what they say' (**ובזה השמד אין אנו מראים בו שאנו עובדים עבודה זרה אלא שנאמין מה שהם אומרים בלבד**) (p. 8)—proves that the point is public comportment as a Gentile. Were my interpretation correct, the text should have read 'we do not worship idols' (**אין אנו עובדים עבודה זרה**). This is a good close reading.

However, according to Novetsky's interpretation, Maimonides never adduced any proof against the central charge of the accuser, namely, that by reciting the *shahada* one has professed Islam. That charge is the elephant in the room. Novetsky would have it that Maimonides disposed of the entire issue of the *shahada* at the very outset by simply stating that all one has done is to state that Mohammed is a prophet. The meaning of that sentence is determined by the intention of the speaker. Maimonides never elaborates on this position in the epistle, nor does he adduce any legal evidence for this crucial distinction. And this, to my mind, is deeply problematic.

The *shahada* is not simply a declarative sentence; it is *the* profession of Muslim faith—that's why the Almohads demanded its recitation by Jews and Christians—and the words 'is His prophet' mean that Mohammed is His *supreme* prophet, whose revelation supersedes those of Moses and Jesus. It was because of this tenet that Maimonides declared, in his *Perush ha-Mishnayot*, one of the thirteen central doctrines of Judaism to be that Moses is the supreme prophet (*av ha-nevi'im*).[11] *Shahada* means 'attestation' (very similar to 'confessio' in Latin, whence the English 'confession of faith'). One is attesting not to *a* prophecy but to the supremacy of *the* prophecy, which constitutes a profession of Islam. The *shahada* is thus either idolatry (if Islam is not monotheistic) or heresy (if it is). Suppose 'Hail Mary, full of grace, the Lord is with thee, blessed art thou among women and blessed is the fruit of thy womb,

[11] *Mishnah 'im Perush le-Rabbenu Mosheh b. Maimon, Nezikin*, ed. Y. Kafih (Jerusalem, 1965), 212–14, and see 'Teshuvah', 3: 8.

Jesus' were the formal confession, the 'credo' of Christianity. To claim that the statement of the *shahada* is purely informational and, in a time of persecution, should be taken literally (its confessional nature depends on the speaker's intent) is as persuasive in the Islamic world as would be the claim in a Christian context that the 'Hail Mary' refers, in a time of persecution, to my cleaning woman, Maria, and her son, Jesus (a common name among Latin Americans).[12]

Who would buy into this interpretation without some proof? Maimonides was confronted with a wave of despair that threatened to sweep his community into the outstretched arms of Islam. If by recitation of the *shahada* the Jews have embraced Islam and are already deemed apostates, why suffer the dangers and indignities of their covert Judaism? This unproven contention of Maimonides might have won acceptance if it had issued from the pen of a world-famous halakhic authority. However, the author of *Iggeret ha-Shemad* was not yet the 'chief of the Jews' (*ra'is al yahud*) of Egypt, not yet 'the great eagle' (*ha-nesher ha-gadol*) of the *Mishneh Torah*, not yet even the author of the Mishnah commentary. He was a total unknown. Who would pay him heed? As I have stated above, the accuser's charge of *'avodah zarah*, be it here idolatry or heresy, is the elephant in the room and it can't be banished without a 'proof', certainly not by a novice. The need to 'prove' his answer to the central charge of *shemad* was the second reason for my taking Maimonides' invocation of the story of R. Eli'ezer as addressing the profession of Islam. If one accepts Novetsky's interpretation, it radically diminishes Maimonides' skills as polemicist, consoler, and defender of the religious integrity of his community, and it was those skills that the hour called for and which Maimonides most needed to demonstrate.

2. Rabbi Novetsky then argues (pp. 19–21) that my interpretation of the opponent's charge that a Marrano who performs any *mitsvah* will receive no reward is mistaken, as is then inevitably my analysis of Maimonides' response. He contends that the opponent's remarks were confined to prayer and to prayer alone: the opponent claimed that the Marranos committed a double sin when, after praying at the mosque, they went home and prayed to the God of their fathers, and cited the *midrash* on the verse in Jeremiah 2: 13.

That the opponent concentrated on the issue of prayer, and that Maimonides feared, above all else, the loss of prayer and its healing power is clear,

[12] The analogy, admittedly, is not an absolutely strict one. In the *shahada* there is only one referent (Mohammed), the distinction being between the explicit and implicit meaning, whereas in 'Hail Mary' each of the two differing referents contains its own meaning. However, it still makes the point.

and I emphasized this in the essay, writing:

The charge that had caused the greatest consternation was more difficult to reply to. The anonymous writer had driven home, with great effectiveness, the accusation that the religious performances of the Marranos were absolutely worthless, and their prayer simply blasphemy. Prayer, with its confession and supplication, was the great purgative of the *anusim*. Maimonides recognized this no less than had his father, who had emphasized in his letter to the same oppressed communities how vital it was to maintain this intimate link with a living and cleansing God, for without it the burden of guilt and despair would be overwhelming.[13]

The question is whether the opponent included all other *mitsvot*, no less than prayer, in a sweeping dismissal of the Marranos' religious performances. I answered in the affirmative on the basis of the central statement of Maimonides:

We feared that this [i.e. the opponent's] responsum (which drives man away from God) would reach the masses, and they shall discover therein that there is no reward for their prayer, so they shall cease praying. And similarly other commandments, if they shall do them, they will not be rewarded for any one of them [so they will cease from performing them].[14]

Rabbi Novetsky claims that this is a misreading. The opponent never claimed that there was no reward for religious performances; rather, Maimonides feared that the masses would draw this inference. He points to the reading in Y. Shilat's edition of *Iggeret ha-Shemad* (based on MS JTS 2380), published some seven years after the appearance of my article:

לפיכך פחדנו שתגיע מאחר ימים בידי עם הארץ וימצא בה שאין לו שכר בתפילה ולא יתפלל עוד. וכמו כן יתר המצות-התבאר מדבריו [emphasis Novetsky] **שאין לו שכר במעשה אחת מהן.**

Therefore we feared that after some days[?] this letter would fall into the hands of the ignorant and he will find [written] therein that he has no reward in prayer and he will pray no more. Similarly [for] other commandments: it would be clear [i.e. inferred] from his [Maimonides' opponent's] words that he receives no reward for the performance of any of them.

Given this reading, Novetsky is correct; the issue, however, is far from settled. All the manuscripts (and consequently all the printed versions) are derived from one basic translation, from which, in the course of numerous transcriptions, minor variants emerged, making it difficult to determine which best

[13] Above, p. 318.

[14] *Iggeret ha-Shemad*, ed. Rabinovitz, 46; ed. Shilat, 43–4.

reflects the original.[15] In 1984 Y. Shilat published a wholly different translation, based on a manuscript of Me'ir Benayahu, which, as he noted, allows us to go behind the variants of the more widespread translation and catch a glimpse of the underlying Arabic text.[16] Though incomplete, this translation does contain our passage, and it reads:

> **לפיכך חששנו ונתיראנו שמא תגיע תשובה זו, המשיבה מאחרי ה', ליד עם הארץ, וימצא בה שכל מי שיתפלל אין לו שכר, וימנע מלהתפלל. וכן הדין לכל שאר מצוות בשווה [emphasis Soloveitchik], שאין לאדם מן האנוסים שום שכר בעשייתו אחת מהן.**

Therefore we were concerned and fearful lest this responsum, which casts man away from God, would reach an ignoramus and he will find [written] therein that one who prays receives no reward and will refrain from praying; *and the same is equally true for other commandments*, [namely,] that none of the Marranos will receive any reward for performing any of them. [emphasis mine][17]

Here Maimonides writes 'and the same is equally true for other commandments'. To all appearances, this describes what the ignorant man (*'am ha-'arets*) will find in the opponent's letter, not what he will infer from it.

In light of this, let us turn to the variants of the common translation, reflected in the different editions. Geiger, transcribing accurately MS Munich 315 (fo. 21a), published:

> **לפיכך פחדנו שתגיע התשובה ההיא המשיבה מאחרי ה' בידי עם הארץ וימצא בה שאין לו שכר בתפילה ולא יתפלל. וכמו יתר המצות אם יעשם, שלא יהיה לו שכר במעשה אחת מהם.**

Therefore we were concerned and fearful lest this responsum, which casts man away from God, would reach an ignoramus and he will find [written] therein that one who prays receives no reward and will cease praying, and the same is equally true for other commandments, [namely,] that none of the Marranos will receive any reward for performing any of them.[18]

This version shares with that of Shilat the phrase **המשיבה מאחרי ה'** (rather than the enigmatic **מאחר ימים**) and equally speaks of what the reader will find in the letter, not what he will infer from it.[19]

15 As I noted at the outset of my own essay (Ch. 12, n. 3 above).

16 'Targum Bilti-Yadua' shel Iggeret ha-Shemad la-Rambam', *Sinai*, 95 (1984), 158.

17 Ibid. 164. To forestall confusion on the part of the reader, I add that one must not confuse Shilat's *edition* of the *Iggeret ha-Shemad* (based on the JTS manuscript) with Shilat's article in *Sinai*, where he printed the different text of the Benayahu manuscript.

18 *Moses b. Maimon: Studien* (Breslau, 1850), Hebrew section, p. 3. Lichtenberg employed Geiger's text in his *Teshuvot ha-Rambam ve-'Iggerotav* (Leipzig, 1859), ii, fo. 12c.

19 Note that it reads **כמו יתר המצות** and not **כמו כן יתר המצות**.

D. Edelmann's edition, based on MS Oxford, Bodley 2218, reads, however:

לפיכך פחדנו שתגיע התשובה ההיא המשיבה מאחרי ה' ביד עם הארץ וימצא בה שאין לו שכר בתפילה ולא יתפלל. וכמו כן יתר המצות ההקש בם אחת [emphasis Novetsky] אין לו שכר במעשה אחת מהן.

Therefore we were afraid lest this responsum reach an ignoramus and he will find [written] therein that one who prays receives no reward and will cease praying, and similarly other commandments *their analogy/inference is one*, [namely, that] there is no reward in the performance of any of them. [emphasis Novetsky's][20]

When I was working on the topic, the italicized phrase in Edelmann's text seemed meaningless; I wrote it off as one of the innumerable infelicities that plague all of the medieval translations of the *Iggeret* and followed Geiger's text. In light of the new reading of the JTS manuscript (*ve-hitba'er mi-devarav*), Edelmann's italicized *ha-hekesh bam eḥad* seems to be a clumsy attempt to say 'and similarly other *mitsvot*, which are inferentially the same',[21] thus supporting Novetsky's interpretation.

All in all, it would seem that my interpretation here is open to serious question. Everything hinges on the text, and the textual witnesses give differing accounts. At the moment, the issue seems irresolvable.

3. I would like to return to a point that I have mentioned briefly before, namely, the danger of an ivory-tower perception of the *Iggeret*.[22] Rabbi Novetsky, to my thinking, forgets what Maimonides repeatedly stated: that in this epistle he was addressing the masses, even the ignorant. Maimonides avowedly wrote the *Iggeret* to save people from despair; he was not composing here a scholarly essay or penning a *devar torah*. The *Iggeret* is, as I said, 'rhetoric' in the classic sense of the word, in the much-respected sense of the term in the Middle Ages. (One must remember that our pejorative use of the term as ornamental or superfluous speech is a seventeenth-century development.) It is a presentation aimed explicitly at swaying a group of people to a certain course of action, and the criterion of such an exposition is always 'How does this argument sound?' 'Will it have the desired effect?'

Rabbi Novetsky argues that the Mishnah in *Nedarim* was cited to forfend a possible misinterpretation of the Mishnah in *Avot* which had been mentioned a few pages before and that Maimonides made this clear for he wrote there

[20] *Ḥemdah Genuzah* (Königsberg, 1857), 8–9.

[21] See J. Klatzkin, *Otsar ha-Munaḥim ve-'Antologyah Filosofit* (Berlin, 1926), i. 206–10.

[22] Above, p. 395.

kemo she-neva'er, which means 'see infra'. 'See infra' is fine if you are writing to scholars, but if you are seeking to sway the masses it is best to spell out clearly just what misunderstanding you are trying to dispel and not rely on a cross-reference several pages before. Again, Novetsky states (p. 4) that I claimed that Maimonides agreed with his critic that Islam was idolatry and then proceeds to criticize this claim. However, what I contended was that, irrespective of what Maimonides thought of Islam at the time of writing *Iggeret ha-Shemad*, he *had* to address the problem as if Islam were *'avodah zarah*. To have maintained that Islam was not idolatry would have been—in Morocco in the early 1160s—a cure worse than the disease. If Islam was monotheistic, why should Jews risk their lives to uphold Judaism? Maimonides could not reply (irrespective of what he thought) on any assumption other than that Islam was idolatry (and, thus, thoroughly abhorrent); however, the Jews had not subscribed to it by the recitation of the *shahada*.[23] The impact that his decisions would have on his target audience dictated the positions that he articulated, but not his personal views.

Again, Novetsky argues (p. 16) that Maimonides openly admitted to the seriousness of *ḥillul ha-shem* committed by those who yielded to Islam. I tried to point out at what stage of the argument this admission was made, and, in what context, to throw light on how this concession must have sounded to ordinary readers. I pointed out that the admission is made just as Maimonides reveals his irrefutable proof from the *Sifra* of the non-culpability of coerced acts—a claim he had made repeatedly before, but without adducing any evidence. It was this crucial proof that impacted most upon the reader in this passage, and not the fact that Maimonides had just quietly admitted to what he had implicitly denied before.[24] Thus, Maimonides registered the fact of *ḥillul ha-shem* in religious persecution, while lessening the impact of this admission, as one might expect of someone seeking to fix enough guilt to stir people to action (flight), but not so much guilt as to induce despair. I may well have been mistaken in my analysis; however, I addressed the issue of the suasive structure of the *Iggeret* and readers' response to it—something every good advocate has constantly in mind. Novetsky's analysis, to my reading at least, ignores this essential dimension of the *Iggeret*.

4. Rabbi Novetsky then faults my critique of the second half of the *Iggeret*, namely, Maimonides' presentation of the laws of martyrdom. Novetsky points out that the entire notion of suffering martyrdom in an instance of private

23 Above, p. 317. 24 Above, pp. 321–2.

coercion (*be-tsin'ah*, in the presence of fewer than ten Jews) is an innovation of Maimonides, and adds that one cannot fault him for employing the generally accepted categories of his time (pp. 10–12). As the readers of my Afterword will know, that is a line of argument with which I have, in principle, great sympathy.[25] However, I believe it to be beside the point here.

Had Maimonides never mentioned his personal opinion about *private* martyrdom in the *Iggeret*, well and good. However, he does mention this point, but not in sections one and two, where one might reasonably expect to find it, but in section three. More importantly, I had in mind *public* persecution (*be-farhesya*), the forced conversion of communities—that is, after all, what happened in Morocco under the Almohads. All hands are here agreed that it falls under *kiddush ha-shem*; indeed, in common parlance *kiddush ha-shem* is often synonymous with dying for one's faith under such circumstances. The gravamen of my charge is not simply that public apostasy and martyrdom are missing in the *first* unit (*ha-min ha-rishon*) of Maimonides' work, but also—and mainly—that they do not appear in the *second* unit (*ha-min ha-sheni*), which is dedicated to the definitions of *kiddush ha-shem* and *ḥillul hashem*. If a scholar's buying on credit can be registered in *Iggeret ha-Shemad* under *ḥillul ha-shem*, how can public apostasy not be mentioned? *Kiddush ha-shem* is defined there simply as acting altruistically; nothing more than that. There is not a whisper of martyrdom. Novetsky contends that since the classification of the *Iggeret* is functional and since it never addresses the issue of apostasy, there was no need to mention it. Let us grant him his premise that the *Iggeret* doesn't treat the issue of apostasy; does it treat buying on credit or gossip-inducing behavior? Yet when Maimonides dedicates a section to the definition of *ḥillul ha-shem*, he mentions credit and gossip, for those are sub-units of *ḥillul ha-shem*; yet there is no sub-unit for public apostasy. *Iggeret ha-Shemad* does not deal with altruistic behavior; nevertheless, when Maimonides defines *kiddush ha-shem* he mentions altruism, for that is a sub-unit of this *mitsvah*. Yet he makes no mention of public martyrdom. To my mind, this is strange and indicates that things aren't what they seem to be in the *Iggeret ha-Shemad*. I have

[25] Above, pp. 325–7. As to the narrow issue itself: if Novetsky's point is that I spoke too sweepingly of the identification of *kiddush ha-shem* and martyrdom, he is right and I stand corrected. If his point is that Maimonides was the first to contend that *kiddush ha-shem* encompasses the instance of a private (*be-tsin'ah*) sacrifice of life, I would simply point out that a similar view is found centuries before in the *She'iltot*, ed. S. K. Mirsky (Jerusalem, 1964), ii. 40, #44; ed. N. T. Y. Berlin (repr. Jerusalem, 1948), i. 255, #42. In the tradition in which Maimonides worked (and this is what is controlling in assessing Maimonides' position, not the Ashkenazic tradition of *Semag* and *Semak*), the issue was an open question: the author of the *Halakhot Gedolot* did not include private sacrifice; the author of the *She'iltot* did.

attempted to explain what its hidden agenda was. I may well be mistaken in my interpretation; but to say that all is well in the *Iggeret ha-Shemad* strikes me, with all due respect, as somewhat naïve.

Such is my opinion; the reader, however, is invited to form his or her own.

PART III

MISHNEH TORAH

CHAPTER FOURTEEN

Classification of *Mishneh Torah*: Problems Real and Imaginary

THE HISTORY of *Mishneh Torah* interpretation has been the history of its interrogation. From the days of the scholars of Lunel in the closing decade of the twelfth century down to our own time, every advance in the understanding of that work has been a product of questioning. Talmudic scholars, like legal scholars everywhere, are concerned with specific rulings, and if the meaning of a ruling is not affected in any way by its position in the text, they generally ignore the context. Historians, on the other hand, attempt to understand the system as a whole, the principles of its arrangement and organization. This agenda is fine if scrutiny and query remain their basic tools, but there is a tendency in Maimonidean scholarship to sing the praises of *Mishneh Torah*. There is nothing wrong with this so long as we remember that Maimonides is in no need of our praise. We are in need of understanding him, and paeans yield no insight.

Query we must, but what types of question are fruitful? I would like to point out two lines of enquiry that I believe to be unproductive, and indicate a third and more gainful one and give some examples of it. In the span of a short lecture, I can only draw attention to some of the problems that emerge in scrutinizing the classification in *Mishneh Torah*; their resolution requires a far broader framework: an analysis of the multiple intentions that Maimonides had in composing *Mishneh Torah* and the web of jurisprudential principles that underlie that work.

This essay is a slightly altered version of a lecture at the Eleventh Quadrennial Congress of the World Union of Jewish Studies in Jerusalem, August 1993. I have attempted to answer the questions posed about the organization of 'Hilkhot Shabbat' in '*Mishneh Torah*: Polemic and Art' (Ch. 15 below).

In my youth, on one of those long Saturday afternoons in the summer, I heard my father casually remarking that there were two problems in Maimonides' classification: the placement of the laws of mourning in *The Book of Judges* (*Shofetim*) and of those of circumcision in the *Book of Adoration* (*Ahavah*), and Maimonides himself was aware of the problematic nature of the first. I mulled over the remark and told my father the next day that I didn't think either of the two placements merited criticism. If someone decides to classify a vast corpus into a preconceived number of units, be they four, fourteen or forty, inevitably he will be left with some topics that don't fit into any of these predetermined units. The best example is the third volume of 'Yoreh De'ah' in the standard Vilna edition of the *Shulḥan 'Arukh*. All the other volumes of that work treat coherent units: 'Oraḥ Ḥayyim' discusses Jewish ritual life, 'Ḥoshen Mishpat' civil law, 'Even ha-'Ezer' marital law. The first two volumes of 'Yoreh De'ah' treat the Jewish home: the Jewish kitchen (the laws of *kashrut*) and the Jewish bedroom (*toharat ha-mishpaḥah*, the laws governing marital relations during and immediately after menstruation). R. Ya'akov Ba'al ha-Turim was left, however, with a host of laws that fitted none of the above units, such as honoring one's parents, the laws of firstborn animals, vows and oaths, the injunction against *sha'atnez* (wearing clothes made of wool and linen), charity, mourning, and the like. So he deposited them in a third volume of 'Yoreh De'ah', which is simply a collection, better yet a catch-all, of everything that did not fit in elsewhere.[1] If anything, the problems raised above demonstrate the greatness of Maimonides' classification. Even though *Mishneh Torah* is of far greater range than the *Shulḥan 'Arukh*, encompassing the totality of Jewish law, including laws of agriculture (*zera'im*), purity (*toharot*), and temple service (*kodashim*), only two of its sub-units appear to be out of place.

Such was my youthful formulation. Today, I would put it somewhat differently: in treating the classification of *Mishneh Torah*, one should bear in mind the principle laid down by Maimonides in *The Guide of the Perplexed* with regard to rationales of Divine imperatives (*ta'amei mitsvot*); namely, that he will not give a reason why seven lambs are offered for the *musaf* sacrifice, for had it been eight lambs, a similar question would be asked: why eight? Put differently, one cannot object to the placement of a set of laws, a halakhic field, in *Mishneh Torah* unless one can suggest for it a more appropriate locus. For this reason, I would not challenge Maimonides' placement of 'not muzzling an ox while he is treading the granary' in the 'Laws of Hired Labor' ('Sekhirut'). He had to put the ban against muzzling someplace, and as the law of hire treats the right of the laborer to eat lightly of the fruit he is gathering, placing the

[1] 'Yoreh De'ah', ##203–403.

eating 'rights' of an ox adjacent to those of a laborer is as good a location as any in *Mishneh Torah*.

There is another unproductive sort of question, to my thinking, in studying the arrangement of *Mishneh Torah*. Someone classifying the commandments (*mitsvot*) on the basis of their teleological function, such as 'improvement of society' or 'improvement of the soul', will do so differently from someone who classifies them by legal criteria, be they jurisprudential or functional. For example, there can be no doubt that the purpose of *ma'aser sheni* (the second tithe), which must be eaten by the owners of the produce in Jerusalem, 'before the Lord' as the Bible puts it (Deut. 14: 26), differs radically from the purpose of *ma'aser 'ani* (tithe for the poor), given to the needy. However, from the point of view of the laws of tithes, they have so many things in common that they must be treated side by side. Both are regulated by the rules of tithing (*hafrashat ma'aser*), both apply only to agricultural produce, both are obligatory only in the Land of Israel and not outside it, and both obligations rotate in and out by the rhythm of the sabbatical-year cycle. Not surprisingly, they are placed alongside one another by Maimonides in the *Book of Seeds* (*Zera'im*, treating agriculture), though they are worlds apart teleologically. To be sure, one can occasionally garner an insight by juxtaposing the teleological with the legal. However, one cannot hope to understand Maimonides' classification by primarily employing such an approach, for one is comparing things that are inherently not comparable.

Maimonides' classification is one of the pinnacles of the halakhic thought of the past millennium. However, it has its problems: problems of placement of units (i.e. 'Laws of X') within a book, problems within the units themselves, and, at times, even problems in the internal organization of sub-units. Let me instantiate each of these difficulties.

Problems in the Placement of Units within a Book

The *Book of Torts* (*Nezikin*) treats all the laws dealing with a breach of law or of the duty of care, such as theft, robbery, murder, and personal and property damages. Obviously, you will say; why, however, are the laws of lost property (*avedah*) found in the *Book of Torts*? Why has Maimonides created a unit of 'Laws of Robbery and Lost Property' ('Gezelah ve-'Avedah')? If the reply is made that someone who does not return lost property is viewed as a robber (*gazlan*), there is the counter that someone who does not pay his workers is equally a robber. Maimonides, however, did not place the laws of hire in the *Book of Torts*. The same holds true for bailment. Conversion of a bailment is robbery, but the laws of bailment are not found in the *Book of Torts*. Correctly so. The fact that breach of certain obligations by either employer or bailee constitutes robbery turns neither bailment nor hire into a sub-unit of *Torts*.

One may contend that both in robbery and lost property there is a common religious obligation of returning the lost or stolen object (*hashavah*), and this imperative yokes the two together. Why then should one not combine the laws of the Sabbath with those of festivals (*yom tov*), for both share a common denominator of abstention from work? One might argue that the definitions of work on the Sabbath and on *yom tov* differ from one another: on *yom tov* cooking is permitted, on the Sabbath it is forbidden, and thus the two cannot be combined. Such an argument must answer an obvious question: does this difference outweigh the differences that exist between the obligation of returning lost property and that of returning stolen objects? Truth to tell, there is little in common between these two obligations other than the word *hashavah*. In lost property there is no actual 'obligation to return'. The obligation is to publicize the find, so that the rightful owner can come to recover his property. After having placed the poster in the public square or the notice in the newspaper, the finder can settle down in his easy chair, never budging until the owner of the lost property rings him up. Not so the thief or robber. He must actively seek out the owners, and even if they be found in the 'lands of the Medes and the Persians', he must travel there and return the stolen object to them.

If the existence of a common religious imperative, in this case that of *hashavah*, suffices to justify placement in the same category in *Mishneh Torah*, then why not position the laws regulating the nazirite (*nazir*) alongside those regulating the leper (*metsora'*)? Both share a common injunction against shaving (*giluaḥ*). Why shouldn't one combine *halanat sakhar*, *halanat ha-met*, and *halanat kodashim* (*notar*), as they all have a common injunction of *lo talin*? The simple answer is that other than this one shared characteristic, no member of either group has anything in common with the others. The same holds true for robbery (*gezelah*) and lost property (*avedah*).

What alternative placement can be offered for the laws of lost property? Could it be located with equal plausibility outside the *Book of Torts*? I suggest the *Book of Acquisition* (*Kinyan*), alongside the laws of *hefker* (abandoned or ownerless property) and *nikhsei ha-ger*, as, indeed, it is found in the *Tur* and the *Shulḥan 'Arukh*.[2]

In a similar vein: Maimonides placed the laws of conversion (*gerut*) in 'Laws of Forbidden Sexual Relations' ('Issurei Bi'ah').[3] True, conversion (plus

[2] 'Ḥoshen Mishpat', ##259–75. [3] Chs. 13 and 14.

marriage) permits a sexual relationship between a Jew and a former Gentile. However, is the purpose and *raison d'être* of conversion to permit sexual intercourse?[4] Conversion would fit far more properly in any one of three places in the *Book of Knowledge* (*Madda'*): (1) at the end of 'Laws of the Fundamentals of Faith' ('Yesodei ha-Torah'), which treats recognizing and acknowledging the one sole God. If erasure of the Divine Name (*meḥikat ha-shem*) has its place in 'Yesodei ha-Torah',[5] surely conversion, the classic recognition and acknowledgment of God, has an equal claim. (2) After 'Laws of Idolatry' ("Avodah Zarah'). Conversion would serve as a perfect foil to the denial of God discussed here. Doubly so, as Maimonides opened the laws of *'avodah zarah* with his famous portrait of Abraham, who began as an idolater and after a forty-year quest arrived at the recognition of the true God.[6] Moreover, Abraham is viewed as the father of all converts. Rounding off the laws of idolatry with the opening theme would give that section a literary unity, something that Maimonides was eminently aware of. (3) Lastly, they could have been placed at the end of 'Laws of Repentance', concluding the *Book of Knowledge* with conversion, for reasons I shall soon point out.

Had the laws of conversion been placed in the *Book of Knowledge*, the problem of the location of the laws of circumcision would have been solved, for circumcision is an essential component of conversion and the two fit naturally side by side;[7] indeed, they are so found in the *Tur* and the *Shulḥan 'Arukh*.[8] The issue goes deeper. Maimonides was wont to end each book of *Mishneh Torah* with a peroration, and, when possible, to link one book to the next. This makes ending the *Book of Knowledge* with conversion and circumcision especially appealing as he could have melded various sections of that book into one memorable ending that linked up with the coming *Book of Adoration* (*Ahavah*). He could have joined conversion and circumcision with his famous remarks about Abraham's long quest for the true God in 'Laws of Idolatry' and fused them with his ending of 'Laws of Repentance' ('Teshuvah')[9] and the timeless words that he wrote to 'Ovadyah the Proselyte in approximately this fashion:

[4] Reply cannot be made that these laws are located in the *Book of Holiness* (*Kedushah*), for this term is not used by Maimonides in the same sense as 'the sanctity of the Temple'. The root meaning of *kadosh* is 'separated', 'set apart from', 'taboo'. It is used here in the sense of voluntary abstinence, pursuant to the language of the *Torat Kohanim* (Lev. 19: 2), 'Thou shalt be holy'—you should abstain from forbidden intercourse (*'arayot*). Maimonides saw 'holiness' as restraint in food and in sex, the two basic animal drives of man. For this reason, the *Book of Holiness* consists of, and only of, the laws of *kashrut* ('Ma'akhalot Asurot' and 'Sheḥitah') and those of forbidden sexual relations ('Issurei Bi'ah').

[5] 'Yesodei ha-Torah', ch. 6.

[6] "Avodah Zarah', 1: 3.

[7] *Keritut* 9a; 'Issurei Bi'ah', 13: 1.

[8] 'Yoreh De'ah', ##262–9.

[9] 'Teshuvah', 10: 6.

על פי הדעה וההכרה תהיה האהבה, אם מעט מעט ואם הרבה הרבה. ומי ששטט בדעתו כמו אותו איתן עד שהכיר את בוראו ונכספה נפשו לאהוב את ה׳, ורדף אחריו והלך בדרך הקודש עד שנכנס תחת כנפי השכינה, הרי הוא מבניו של אברהם אבינו, שבבריתו נכנס, שנאמר אב המון גויים נתתיך, ועליו אמר הכתוב, זרע אברהם אוהבי.

According to the understanding and recognition will be the love. If [the former is] little, [so will the latter be] little; if [the former is] great, [so will the latter be] great. And he whose mind began to reflect [about the world] as did that titan [Abraham] until he came to recognize his creator and his soul longed for the love of God, and he pursued Him and went in the path of holiness until he came under the wings of the *Shekhinah*, he is, indeed, a son of Abraham our father, for he [the searcher-convert] has entered into his [i.e. Abraham's] covenant, for it is written [Gen. 4]: 'thou shalt be the father of many nations', and about him the verse was said [Isa. 41: 8], '[he is] of the seed of Abraham who did love me'.[10]

The placement of conversion is problematic, and as we have found a more fitting place for circumcision, its placement becomes equally so.

Problems of the Sub-Units in a Book

It's a halakhic commonplace that there are four types of bailee (*shomerim*)—the gratis bailee (*shomer ḥinnam*), the hired bailee (*shomer sakhar*), the renter (*sokher*), and the borrower (*sho'el*). These bailees are adumbrated in the Bible, enumerated in the Mishnah, and discussed and analyzed in the Gemara. Yet, astonishingly enough, we find no section dedicated to the laws of bailment (*hilkhot shemirah*) in *Mishneh Torah*. Instead, Maimonides divided these four types in two and placed them in different units. The regulations of *shomer ḥinnam* and *sho'el* are in 'Laws of Borrowing and Bailment' ('She'ilah u-Fikadon'), while the *shomer sakhar* and the *sokher* are placed in 'Laws of Hire' ('Sekhirut'), together with the regulations on the hired laborer (*po'el*). Admittedly, one can find some commonality between the hiring of people and the hiring of animals, but does this commonality outweigh the similarity between a *shomer ḥinam* and a *shomer sakhar*?

Moreover, not only did Maimonides divide the four *shomerim* into two different units, he placed 'Laws of Hire' before 'Laws of Borrowing and Bailment'. The result is that all the classic definitions of bailment—*ein shemirah be-karka'ot*, *shomer she-masar le-shomer*, *teḥilato bi-feshi'ah ve-sofo be-'ones*—are to be found in 'Laws of Hire' rather than in 'Laws of Bailment', where one could reasonably expect them to be.

10 *Teshuvot ha-Rambam*, ed. J. Blau (Jerusalem, 1960), ii. 548–50, #253.

Indeed, from the drafts of *Mishneh Torah* found in the Genizah, we see that Maimonides initially thought to have a separate unit entitled 'Laws of Borrowing' and only later did he change his mind and include in it the laws regulating the *shomer ḥinnam*.[11] It is also clear that the first three chapters currently found in 'Laws of Hire' were not initially there; rather, this unit began with what is now its fourth chapter.[12] In other words, Maimonides' initial plan was for 'Laws of Hire' to contain only the renter (*sokher*) and the laws of laborers and nothing more. He apparently thought of having a unit entitled 'Bailments' that would include all the fundamental principles of bailment together with *shomer ḥinnam*, for the breach of negligence (*peshi'ah*) applies equally to all the other bailees.[13] For some reason he changed his mind (perhaps because the *shomer sakhar* and the *sokher* are governed by the same laws, perhaps because a division into three separate sections seemed excessive). So he divided it in the way it is now found in *Mishneh Torah*.

However, one can't help asking oneself: is this the optimum classification? Let us grant Maimonides the division into no more than two books; but why didn't he create a block entitled 'Laws of Bailment and Borrowing' (note, *not* 'Borrowing and Bailment') and place there the basic rules of bailment, and then pass on to the rules of *shomer ḥinnam* and *sho'el*? *After* this unit would come 'Laws of Hire', which would contain the laws of the bailment of a hired bailee and of the renter, followed by laws of the laborer. In this way, the basic principles of bailment would be set forth at the outset, and the reader would then be presented with the laws of bailment as they apply to those who receive no money, such as the *shomer ḥinnam* and the *sho'el*, and then the laws of the hired bailee and renter followed by labor law. All this, however, is *ex post facto*. The simple original question remains: why not simply have one unit called 'The Laws of Bailment', and another 'The Laws of Laborers'?

Problems of Internal Classification

Maimonides opens 'Hilkhot Shabbat' with that magnificent first chapter laying down the fundamental definitions of work (*melakhah*) on the Sabbath.

11 *Keta'im mi-Sefer Yad ha-Ḥazakah le-Rabbenu Mosheh ben Maimon*, ed. S. Atlas (London, 1940), 43; reprinted with the notes of M. Lutzky as an addendum to the fifth volume of the Schulsinger edition of *Mishneh Torah* (New York, 1947), 14; reprinted once more with notes by K. Kahana in the Pardes edition of the *Mishneh Torah* (Jerusalem, 1967).

12 *Mishneh Torah*, ed. Atlas, 26; ed. Lutzky, 4; ed. Kahana, 4. What is now chapter 11 is chapter 8 in the draft, and the first three chapters are the only ones that could logically be removed from *Hilkhot Sekhirut*.

13 The claim of *force majeure*, the subject of the third chapter of *Sekhirut*, applies to all bailees other than the borrower, whose laws were intended for another unit.

We find there the rules of *davar she-'eino mitkaven*, *pesik reisha*, *melakhah she-'einah tserikhah le-gufah*, *mit'asek*, and *mekalkel*. From the vast number of talmudic discussions of work on the Sabbath, Maimonides educed the underlying principles that constitute the *sine qua non* of any *melakhah*. It is no exaggeration to say that only Maimonides could have penned such a chapter. One would expect that he would then proceed to spell out the individual *melakhot* and treat each one in detail. No such thing, however, occurs. Instead, Maimonides treats the laws of saving a life on the Sabbath (*pikuaḥ nefesh*). One might argue that he must have wanted to emphasize that the sanctity of human life is such that its preservation outweighs even Sabbath observance. The next three chapters, however, preclude this argument and only increase the confusion. Maimonides still does not address the individual *melakhot* but begins the third chapter with the preparations on Friday (*'erev Shabbat*), and moves from there to treating the laws of *gerufah* and *ketumah* (very roughly, the hot plate, the covering of the fire on the stove). How can one treat the laws of *gerufah* and *ketumah* if one hasn't been informed that cooking and lighting a fire are forbidden on the Sabbath, not to speak of not being informed about the law of *muktseh* (objects which may not be moved on the Sabbath), which is the principle underlying *hatmanah* (placing food under covers to keep it warm)? In the fifth chapter, Maimonides moves on to the requirement of light on the Sabbath and the Sabbath candles. Interestingly, in chapters 3–6 he adopts the sequence of the Mishnah. However, are the laws of the Sabbath in *Mishneh Torah* organized by temporal sequence, by the daily round of religious observances? Maimonides vigorously rejected this system of organization throughout his life, from his introduction to *Commentary on the Mishnah* down to his famous letter to R. Pinḥas the Judge, where he emphasized that he 'was not proceeding by the order followed in the Talmud nor by that of the Mishnah'.[14] He was employing conceptual categories (*le-fi mah she-yeḥayyev ha-'iyyun*), not functional or chronological ones.[15] This principle is writ large on every page of *Mishneh Torah*. Maimonides then proceeds, in the sixth chapter, with the law of *amirah le-'akum shevut* (the rabbinic injunction against asking a Gentile to perform work), a law that embodies no philosophical principle (as does, perhaps, *pikuaḥ nefesh*), nor a chronological one as do chapters 3–6, and equally does not appear in the early *mishnayot* of tractate *Shabbat*.

[14] The letter to R. Pinḥas ha-Dayyan is found in *Teshuvot ha-Rambam*, ed. A. Lichtenberg (Leipzig, 1859), i. 26, #140; *Iggerot ha-Rambam*, ed. Y. Shilat (Jerusalem, 1988), ii. 444: איני מהלך לא על סדר התלמוד ולא על סדר המשנה.

[15] *Sefer ha-Mitsvot*, ed. S. Frankel (Jerusalem, 1995), introduction, fo. 10b. See I. Twersky's remarks in his *An Introduction to the Code of Maimonides (Mishneh Torah)* (New Haven, 1980), 238 ff.

Only in the seventh chapter does Maimonides finally get around to discussing the specific *melakhot*, six chapters later than one might have expected.

The internal structure of 'Laws of the Sabbath' has yet further problems. Maimonides wishes to distinguish between rabbinic and pentateuchal injunctions. This is quite understandable, and he formulates these distinctions with a thoroughness that is admirable. However, distinguishing between the two doesn't necessarily mean physically separating them, so that the pentateuchal aspects of the laws of *borer* (selection), for example, all go into one section of 'Hilkhot Shabbat' and the rabbinic aspects into another. Yet this is precisely what Maimonides has done in the case of thirty-eight of the thirty-nine archetypical *melakhot*.[16] He gathered all the pentateuchal aspects of thirty-eight *avot melakhot* in chapters 7–12 and then placed the rabbinic aspects in chapters 21–24, separated by no fewer than eight chapters. Thus, the laws of any *melakhah* are found in two different places. Should one be dealing with the *melakhah* of cooking and baking, parts of which are found in the early chapters of 'Hilkhot Shabbat' that treat *'erev Shabbat*, one has to look in three places—in chapters 5, 9, and 22! One cannot help asking: is this really the best way to organize the material? Wouldn't it have been far simpler and more convenient for all concerned to treat all the laws of a *melakhah* in a single unit, as did the *Tur* and the *Shulḥan 'Arukh*, all the while distinguishing between those of pentateuchal and rabbinic origin? Isn't the gathering of widely dispersed laws the very purpose of *Mishneh Torah*? That is what Maimonides proudly averred to the old judge.[17] Did the necessary distinction between rabbinic and pentateuchal laws require such radical separation?

One might invoke here the doctrine of the 'decline of generations' (*nitma'atu ha-dorot*). We moderns, people of little stature, are stumped at times by Maimonides' classification, but to the *rishonim*, the great medieval scholars, that classification was crystal clear. That may well be. However, no less a *rishon* than R. Shelomoh ibn Aderet, the towering Rashba, lost his way in 'Hilkhot Shabbat'. In his *'Avodat ha-Kodesh*, Rashba criticizes Maimonides for omitting a Sabbath law mentioned in the Talmud. In fact, Maimonides did discuss the law, but in a place where Rashba never dreamed of looking for it. It is worth dwelling a moment on this case, for it illustrates another problematic aspect in Maimonides' 'Hilkhot Shabbat', the problem of hyper-classification,

16 In the *melakhah* of *hotsa'ah* (carrying), Maimonides saw no way to systematically split the pentateuchal from the rabbinic aspects and combined the two in his treatment, chs. 13–19.

17 אלא כל ענין וענין אקבץ כל הדינין שנאמר בו בכל מקום שהן עד שלא יהיו הלכות אותו הענין מפוזרות ומפורדות בין המקומות. זו היתה סוף מגמתי בזה החיבור. *Teshuvot ha-Rambam*, ed. Leipzig, #140, p. 26; *Iggerot ha-Rambam*, ed. Shilat, ii. 444.

what the famous Maimonidean commentator R. Vidal, author of *Maggid Mishneh*, called 'exaggeration in adhering to order' (*haflagah bi-shemirat ha-seder*).

Classification clarifies and, at the same time, eases access to material; hyper-classification, on the other hand, is an adherence to classificatory categories so rigorous that few can anticipate the results—as exemplified by the case of Rashba.

There is a law stating that one may not set out on a sea trip three days before the Sabbath; however, for a meritorious purpose (*devar mitsvah*) one is permitted to embark even on a Friday. Maimonides divides this brief law into two separate sections: he mentions the allowance of setting out on Friday in chapter 24, but only lists the injunction itself at the very end of 'Hilkhot Shabbat', in chapter 30. His reason for this placement is Alfasi's explanation that the rabbinic ordinance against setting out on a sea journey three days before the Sabbath was instituted for fear that the seafarers might initially suffer from seasickness, which would interfere with the enjoyment of the Sabbath (*'oneg Shabbat*).[18] Rashba sought this injunction in the section dealing with *shevut* (rabbinic laws of the Sabbath), for it is, indeed, a rabbinic measure. He found there only the Friday allowance for a meritorious purpose.[19] Perplexed, he asked why Maimonides didn't register the injunction itself. It never occurred to him that Maimonides would split the formulation of so short a talmudic ruling and, furthermore, place the injunction in the last chapter of 'Hilkhot Shabbat', where he discusses the commandment of *'oneg Shabbat*—the requirements of Sabbath candles, Sabbath meals, special clothes, and the like. Admittedly, since Alfasi categorized setting out on a journey as an issue of *'oneg Shabbat*, it belongs, strictly speaking, in the thirtieth chapter. But who would imagine that Maimonides would register this law only two sections before the very end of 'Hilkhot Shabbat', between the obligation of three festive meals on the Sabbath and that of marital relations? It never occurred to Rashba that Maimonides would carry adherence to his conceptual classification to such extremes. Ineluctably, one must ask: does the loss not outweigh the gain here, and if so, is this not hyper-classification?

[18] Up to *Shabbat* 19a (Vilna edn., fo. 7a–b).

[19] Rashba's original remarks in his *'Avodat ha-Kodesh* have apparently been censored. They are cited in the *Maggid Mishneh*; nevertheless, they are not to be found in the printed text of the *'Avodat ha-Kodesh*, neither in the *editio princeps* (Venice, 1512) nor in the two critical editions available of that work, i.e. that of H. G. Zymbalist (Tel Aviv, 1978) and that of Y. A. Schulman (Benei Berak, 2003).

From this brief survey we see that the classifications in *Mishneh Torah* are cut from the same cloth as its formulations. Its restatements of the Oral Law have earned the admiration of all; at the same time, no one will gainsay the numerous problems that they have raised. So, too, with Maimonides' classification. There are strokes of brilliance (the idea of 'Hilkhot To'en ve-Nit'an'—the laws of litigation—is one of them) and, with them, baffling inconsistencies. In both instances, the solution begins with recognizing the problems. In this brief lecture I have simply tried to define what types of question in classification are, to my thinking, productive, and to exemplify some of the more prominent ones.

R. Vidal noted the problem of hyper-classification and, after citing the instance of the Rashba, remarked, 'and there are many others like this' (*ve-kha-yotse ba-zeh yesh harbeh*).

CHAPTER FIFTEEN

Mishneh Torah: Polemic and Art

SEVERAL YEARS AGO I raised questions about the organization of *Mishneh Torah* and argued that, as great a classifier as Maimonides was, there are nevertheless serious problems in the structure and distribution of topics in the *Yad ha-Ḥazakah*, as *Mishneh Torah* is alternatively called, that have hitherto gone unnoticed.[1] I further suggested that more would be achieved in the way of appreciation of his code by critical enquiry than by panegyric, especially as Maimonides was scarcely in need of our praise. I would like to practice here what I preached there: suggest a solution to one of the difficulties that I raised and then attempt to see whether its resolution yields any deeper insights into the nature of *Mishneh Torah*.

Let me restate one of the points I raised in that article. The structure of 'Hilkhot Shabbat' is deeply problematic. In the great first chapter Maimonides lays down the definition of a *melakhah*—the characteristics deemed necessary for any act to be classified as one of the thirty-nine *avot melakhot* (archetypal acts of labor forbidden on the Sabbath). This chapter, which, in its scope and synthetic power bears Maimonides' inimitable stamp, would naturally lead one to expect that he would promptly begin itemizing and detailing the thirty-nine *avot melakhot*. No such thing, however, occurs. He proceeds to dedicate the second chapter to violating the Sabbath so as to save a human life (*pikuaḥ nefesh*). One could yet argue, though I would not, that he has a philosophical purpose in mind—to emphasize at the outset the nigh-supreme value placed by Jewish law on human life, for its preservation prevails even over Sabbath observance, the injunction about which is only somewhat less stringent than that prohibiting idolatry.[2] However, he proceeds to a further detour by

I would like to thank Menahem Ben-Sasson, Robert Brody, and Yaacov Sussmann for reading and commenting on this essay, and Prudence Steiner for editing it.

[1] 'Hirhurim 'al Miyyuno shel ha-Rambam be-Mishneh Torah: Be'ayot Amitiyot u-Medummot', *Maimonidean Studies*, 4 (2000), Heb. section, 107–15. See Ch. 14 above.

[2] See *Mishneh Torah*, 'Shabbat', 30: 15. The only difference between the two is the imperative of martyrdom. Idolatry demands martyrdom; the Sabbath does not (*Sanhedrin*, 74a).

presenting in the next two chapters the laws of placing food on the fire before the Sabbath and having it cook on the Sabbath (*shehiyah*, *ḥazarah*, and *hatmanah*). How can one discuss the laws regulating the |328| covering of the stove if one hasn't spelled out beforehand the injunction against cooking or that of *muktseh* (objects which may not be moved on the Sabbath)? Following this, he details the laws of lighting candles on Friday towards sundown. Here he seems to be following the chronological sequence of the Mishnah, first treating the laws of Friday evening (*'erev Shabbat*) and then those of the Sabbath. However, the organizing principle of *Mishneh Torah* is conceptual, rejecting both the idea of proceeding by chronological order and that of following the sequence found in the canonical sources. Maimonides proudly articulated this point in his introduction to *Sefer ha-Mitsvot*,[3] and again in his famous letter to Pinḥas ha-Dayyan.[4] If all this were not enough, he then proceeds in the sixth chapter to set forth the laws regulating work done by a Gentile on the Sabbath at a Jew's behest (*goy shel Shabbat*)—a topic that has none of the philosophical implications that the saving of life does, and one which is not linked to the sequence found in the Mishnah. Only in the seventh chapter does Maimonides finally get around to the thirty-nine *avot melakhot* and begin to spell out their details—something one might have reasonably expected him to have done long before.

The second major problem is the structure of his presentation of the thirty-nine *melakhot*. It is dominated by the distinction between those aspects of the *melakhot* that are pentateuchal and those that are of rabbinic origin. The difference is, of course, a crucial one. However, Maimonides does not simply distinguish between the two categories but proceeds to gather the pentateuchal aspects of *all* the *melakhot* in one group of chapters (7–12) and then records *all* the rabbinic rulings in a second group (chapters 21–24), with no fewer than eight chapters separating the two sections! The result is that to learn the laws of *borer* (selection), for example, one must turn to two widely separated chapters. And, if one seeks the laws of cooking one must turn to as many as three separate chapters: to chapter 5, which treats cooking that begins on Friday and continues into the Sabbath; to chapter 9 for the pentateuchal facets of cooking and warming food on the Sabbath, and, finally, to chapter 22 for the rabbinic aspects of such activities. Would it not have been far simpler and better to place all the laws of a *melakhah* in one chapter, as do the *Tur* and *Shulḥan 'Arukh*, while distinguishing in that chapter between its pentateuchal

[3] 'כפי מה שיחייב העיון'.

[4] 'ואיני מהלך לא על סדר התלמוד ולא על סדר המשנה', *Teshuvot ha-Rambam* (Leipzig, 1859), i. 26, #140; *Iggerot ha-Rambam*, ed. Y. Shilat (Jerusalem, 1988), ii. 444.

and rabbinic aspects? Would it not have been more appropriate for one whose avowed purpose was gathering and consolidating (*melekhet ha-kinnus*) to collect all the widely dispersed rulings on a given topic in *one* place and present them not only in a conceptually coherent but also in a functional manner? **|329|**

So I argued then. I now suggest that the reason for this cumbersome and counter-intuitive arrangement is quite simple—the Karaite challenge.[5] The Karaite injunctions against having any fire on the Sabbath, even if it has been lit before the Sabbath, or of having any cooking take place on the Sabbath even if it was begun before the Sabbath are, of course, well known. Indeed, to Rabbanites these restrictions became the popular litmus test of Karaism.[6] Karaism equally viewed work done by a Gentile at a Jew's behest on the Sabbath as work by the Jew. As Hadassi writes:

> He who orders others and they do so under [his orders] . . . is as if he had done it himself, as it is written, 'and Moses completed the work' [Exod. 40: 33] . . . 'and he made a feast for all his servants' [Esther 2: 18], and the like; he is viewed as having done it himself even though it is others who [actually] do his wish.[7]

Moses didn't build the tabernacle himself; rather, he caused it to be built. Thus, in common parlance, a verb of action means equally causing something to be done. Similarly, 'Thou shalt do no work' includes not having work done for you.

[5] After much of the research on the Karaite law of the Sabbath was done, I came across the work of Baruch Ehrlich, 'Laws of Sabbath in Yehudah Hadassi's *Eshkol ha-Kofer*' (Ph.D. diss., Yeshiva University, 1974). The author edited the sections on the Sabbath found in the *Eshkol ha-Kofer* on the basis of four manuscripts, including that of the Austrian National Library in Vienna. He then provided a line-by-line commentary, comparing first Hadassi's position with that of other Karaite writers and then contrasting each statement of Hadassi with its halakhic counterparts. Rather than clutter this essay—which is essentially interpretative—with cumbersome and probably incomplete references to the Karaite literature, I will simply supply the source of my remarks in the *Eshkol ha-Kofer* providing both page references to the printed edition (Gozlov, 1836) and to the heavily annotated one of Ehrlich. When appropriate, I will also refer to Ehrlich's introductory remarks. Karaism was scarcely monolithic and, like Rabbanism, it had a host of different views on most issues. I have used Hadassi's work primarily as a convenient point of reference, as it is both comprehensive and more contemporary with *Mishneh Torah* than any other Karaite work of comparable scope. The reader seeking the full spectrum of Karaite opinion on any specific point will find Ehrlich's work a useful guide.

[6] See R. Yehudah of Barcelona, *Sefer ha-'Ittim* (Cracow, 1903), 24–5, and see Ehrlich (above, n. 5), 78–85; *Eshkol ha-Kofer* א"ב קמה/נ–ט, דף נד ע"ד–נה ע"א; א"ב קעו, דף עא ע"ד–עב ע"א; תשרק/ת–מ, דף עב ע"א–ע"ב ; Ehrlich, 141–60, 308–14 and notes ad loc.

[7] המצווה לאחרים ועושים תחתיו מצוויו-הוא כעושה בעצמו נחשב ככתוב ויכל משה את המלאכה . . . ויעש משתה לכל שריו ועבדיו ודומיהן, כעושה נחשב, אף על פי שאחרים היו עושים כדעתך. תשרק קמו/מ, דף נה ע"ב; Ehrlich (above, n. 5), 171.

In one area alone does Maimonides allude to the Karaites in the opening chapters, and specifically to their forbidding work to save life, writing: 'It is of heretics—who assert that this [i.e. *pikuaḥ nefesh*] is, nevertheless, a violation of the Sabbath and therefore prohibited—that the Scriptures say, "wherefore I gave them also statutes that were not good and ordinances whereby they should not live" [Ezek. 20: 25].' Surprisingly, we lack solid documentation that the Karaites ever did forbid work in the |330| instance of *pikuaḥ nefesh*, as Bernard Revel long ago noted.[8] Kirkisani and Hadassi both permitted *pikuaḥ nefesh*, though not in cases when the saving of life is in doubt (*safek pikuaḥ nefesh*). Bashyatzi alone reports that the early Karaites would not desecrate the Sabbath because of *pikuaḥ nefesh*.[9] However, as our evidence is spotty and Maimonides' words are clear, it seems probable that the practice of not violating the Sabbath for the sake of *pikuaḥ nefesh* was more widespread in his time than our scant surviving sources might indicate.

To rephrase my solution to the problematic early chapters of 'Hilkhot Shabbat': chapters 2–6 are no detour but have the same purpose as the opening chapter, namely, to define the characteristics of *melakhah* according to *Torah she-be-'al peh* not only in talmudic categories but also in contradistinction to those of the Karaites. The first chapter formulates the three talmudic requirements: it must be a constructive (not *mekalkel*), intentionally performed action (and not *davar she-'eino mitkaven*), and one done for its own sake and not for the sake of any by-product of the action (not *melakhah she-'einah tserikhah le-gufah*). Chapters 2–6 add three more general prerequisites contrary to Karaite law: the act must be carried out by a Jew himself (and not by a Gentile at a Jew's behest), it must be done on the Sabbath itself (and not begun on *'erev Shabbat* and continuing of its own momentum into the Sabbath), and, finally, it cannot be done for the purpose of saving a life (*pikuaḥ nefesh*). Only after laying down these six essential characteristics of all *melakhot* in the first six chapters of 'Hilkhot Shabbat' does Maimonides begin, in the seventh chapter, to detail the individual *melakhot*.

The solution to our second set of problems now appears obvious: I queried why Maimonides grouped all the pentateuchal aspects of a *melakhah* in one set

[8] ואלו המינים שאומרים שזה חילול שבת ואסור, עליהן הכתוב אומר וגם אני נתתי להם חוקים לא טובים ומשפטים לא יחיו בהם; *Mishneh Torah*, 'Shabbat', 2: 3; B. Revel, *The Karaite Halakhah and its Relation to Saduccean, Samaritan and Philonic Halakhah* (Philadelphia, 1913), 48 n. 74, repr. (with identical pagination) in *Karaite Studies*, ed. P. Birnbaum (New York, 1971).

[9] E. Bashyazi, *Aderet Eliyahu* (Odessa, 1870), fo. 53a. See also Ehrlich (above, n. 5), 232–8, 332–4, and D. Lasker, *Ha-Kara'ut ve-Ḥeker ha-Yahadut*, Meḥkerei ha-Katedra 'al Shem Yosef Vasil Maizer 1 (Tel Aviv, 2000), 8–21: R. Brody, *Pirkoi ben Baboi ve-Toledot ha-Pulmus ha-Penim Yehudi*, Meḥkerei ha-Katedra 'al Shem Yosef Vasil Maizer 3 (Tel Aviv, 2003), 23–5.

of chapters and the rabbinical aspects in another set. First, he did so in order to highlight the very existence and legal force of rabbinic enactments—both of which were denied by the Karaites—and then to sharpen their sensed difference from pentateuchal ones. To further emphasize the essential dissimilarity of these categories and the fact that each constitutes a separate legal universe, Maimonides did not even allow the two sections to be contiguous but conspicuously separated one from the other by interposing discussion, over eight chapters, of the laws of *hotsa'ah* and *'eruv*.[10] This massive interruption distances the two sections from each other and emphasizes both the separate existence of and unbridgeable gap between the laws of the Torah and the enactments of the Sages. |331|

A further word about the Karaite Sabbath may be in place. Breaking off from rabbinic Judaism yet seeking adherents from the Rabbanite community, the Karaites were confronted with a host of deeply entrenched Sabbath practices, some going back to the time of the prophets, for example **אם תשיב משבת רגלך ממצוא חפצך ודבר דבר** (the ban on discussing business matters on the Sabbath) or those in the book of Nehemiah.[11] They did not seek to jettison these millennia-old observances, so they evolved a notion of *'edah*, *kibbuts*, or *sevel ha-yerushah*—namely, that any universal practice among Jews (that was not contradicted by a biblical verse) was binding, if only some anchor for it could be found in the Tanakh. They further adopted many of the exegetical principles **מידות שהתורה נדרשת בהן** of both R. Yishma'el and R. Yosei ha-Gelili, and their literature, from 'Anan on, is replete with **קל וחומר, גזירה שווה, בנין אב ממקום אחד, היקש, סמוכין** and the like, though they often deploy these methods in a distinctive, non-rabbinic fashion.[12] The discussions of the Talmud were also a rich source of Karaite law—only they often contested individual rulings and, in principle, opposed the use of any rule of thumb of adjudication such as **הלכה כבית הלל** (the ruling is always according to Bet Hillel in any controversy with Bet Shammai). Every issue was to be decided on its own merits and not by any formal rule. In the words of Hadassi:

The latter [*amora'im*], Ashi and Ravina and their associates, said that the law is in accordance with the position of Bet Hillel [as stated] in the Talmud . . . To us it appears more [correct that this is not so] for from the day that the Holy Spirit and prophecy were taken from us, how can one declare that the law is in accordance with A rather than B without any proof from the Torah?[13]

[10] Chs. 13–20.

[11] Isa. 58: 13; Neh. 10: 32, 13: 18–22.

[12] Ehrlich (above, n. 5), 38–41.

[13] **ואחרונים אשי ורבינא וסיעתן אמרו הלכה כבית הלל בגמרין . . . זה לנו יותר כי מיום שנסתלקה רוח הקדש והנבואה מבינינו ואורים ותומים, איך יכשר לנו לאמר ולחרוץ שאין הלכה כפלוני אלא כפלוני בלא ראיות מן תורה. תשרק קנב/ד, דף נז ע"ד; א"ב קנג/ז, דף נז ע"ב**; Ehrlich (above, n. 5), 281, 285.

In instances of controversy between Bet Shammai and Bet Hillel, for example, the Karaites ruled as often as not according to Bet Shammai and inclined to other inversions of standard rules of adjudication, most notably that of majority rule.[14]

The upshot was that, except for such famous differences as the one concerning fire and warm food on the Sabbath and whether enjoyment or asceticism was to be cultivated on that day,[15] the Karaite Sabbath was similar in many ways to the rabbinic one. Most of the *shevutim* were taken over wholesale (only classified now as pentateuchal injunctions): *muktseh*,[16] for example, or the bans against horse riding,[17] |332| the making of music,[18] or climbing a tree,[19] to mention just a few. If one turns to their legal writings, one is confronted by not only a high degree of similarity but also a surprising measure of likeness in certain fundamental rubrics. Hadassi, for example, has thirty-nine *avot melakhot*;[20] he also distinguishes between *avot* and *toladot*,[21] and further rules, apparently, that it is permissible to tie an impermanent knot קשר שאינו של קיימא.[22] One who is steeped in rabbinic law and immerses himself in Karaite literature and reconstructs their Sabbath feels much like Alice stepping through the looking glass: the landscape is quite familiar (with a few objects upside down), only the people reason differently there.

However, most people don't learn the laws of the Sabbath by reasoning from written literature but rather from the daily practice imbued in them in childhood by home and by street—what I have called elsewhere mimetic transmission.[23] Two communities living side by side, sharing a common destiny and a way of life far closer to one another than to that of their Muslim neighbors, would discover that the walls between them were more permeable than they had thought. Given the daily intercourse that existed in many places between Rabbanites and Karaites, it would scarcely be surprising if the notions and practices of the Karaite Sabbath—not the radical ones of no cooking or the absence of all fire, but those of the numerous other *melakhot* held in common by the two communities—would, all unawares, begin to percolate into popular Rabbanite observance (and conversely, Rabbanite practices percolate into

[14] Ehrlich (above, n. 5), 42–53.
[15] See below, nn. 29–30.
[16] א"ב קמה/ט–כ, דף נה ע"ג; תשרק קמח/ק–צ, דף נו ע"א; Ehrlich, 130–4, 227–8.
[17] א"ב קמט/ב–ד, דף נו ע"א; Ehrlich, 241.
[18] א"ב קמט/פ, דף נו ע"ג; Ehrlich, 248.
[19] א"ב קמט/ה–ו, דף נו ע"ג; Ehrlich, 242.
[20] א"ב קמה/ל, דף נד ע"ד; תשרק קפ/א–ח, דף עג ע"ב; Ehrlich, 135, 339–41.
[21] א"ב קמה/ח–ת, דף נד ע"ד–נה ע"א; Ehrlich, 134–60.
[22] א"ב קמה/ח, דף נד ע"ד; Ehrlich, 128–9.
[23] 'Rupture and Reconstruction: The Transformation of Contemporary Orthodoxy', *Tradition*, 28 (1994), 64–130.

Karaite observance). Maimonides' need to delineate ever more sharply the distinctive contours of the Rabbanite Sabbath and to highlight the fundamental distinction between *de-'oraita* and *de-rabbanan*—the touchstone of Rabbanism—is, then, more easily understood.

A parting word of caution is in place. *Mishneh Torah* is in no way or manner an anti-Karaitic tract as some have claimed. I do not even believe that many other questions about the organization of *Mishneh Torah* are explainable by the sectarian challenge. I have simply argued for an anti-Karaite dimension in the structure of 'Hilkhot Shabbat'. Though my claim is narrow, its implications, I believe, are wide, and I would contend that this other dimension allows us to see afresh the nature of *Mishneh Torah*. It is to this larger issue that I would now like to turn. |333|

We may best obtain this new perspective on *Mishneh Torah* by taking a detour—moving to a different vantage point and returning only later to our initial point of departure. The Ba'alei ha-Tosafot generally ignored Maimonides just as they ignored the developments in Provence. Like most revolutionaries, they operated on the assumption—even if, as faithful sons of a traditional society, they would have adamantly denied it in theory—that neither the past, in the form of the Geonim, nor the present, in the shape of non-Tosafists, had much to teach them, nor could they help them solve the new problems which they had uncovered. The attitude of R. Mosheh of Coucy, the author of the *Semag*, was essentially the same. True, he realized that Maimonides had explicated and rephrased in transparent Hebrew many obscure dicta of both the Bavli and the Yerushalmi and that these formulations deserved to be reproduced. Indeed, he proceeded to do so—massively—in his *Sefer Mitsvot Gadol*. He also realized that Maimonides had coordinated vast quantities of information in such sections as 'Hilkhot Shabbat', and the author of the *Semag* drew freely on the structural arrangement of these laws in *Mishneh Torah*. Great as R. Mosheh's innovations were, he nonetheless used the numerous Maimonidean passages in a cut-and-paste manner. He was utilizing Maimonides' writing and organizational skills, not grappling with his thought, let alone attempting a modified reception of his code. Only one figure in Ashkenaz was free of any sense of cultural superiority: R. Me'ir of Rothenburg. He recognized greatness when he saw it and availed himself of it from whatever source he could. For example, he used extensively and unhesitatingly the commentary on *Mo'ed Katan* of the Provençal scholar Rabad of

Posquières,[24] and in this spirit instructed or inspired his student R. Me'ir ha-Kohen to write a massive Ashkenazic gloss to the *Mishneh Torah*, known as the *Haggahot Maimuniyot*. R. Me'ir of Rothenburg realized that Maimonides' work was not to be excerpted or epitomized but needed to be taken in all its fourteen-volume entirety—from *Sefer Madda'* to *Sefer Shofetim*.[25] It required updating—that is to say, it needed to be annotated and emended with tosafist notes—and then incorporated into the Ashkenazic canon. In other words, it was to be glossed and 'Ashkenized', much in the same fashion as R. Mosheh Isserles was later to do |334| with the next great Sephardic code, the *Shulḥan 'Arukh*—and his emendations would, indeed, serve to canonize the *Shulḥan 'Arukh* in eastern Europe.

At the time, and even in retrospect, there was every reason to believe that the effect of the *Haggahot Maimuniyot* on *Mishneh Torah* would be the same as that of Isserles' *Mappah* on the *Shulḥan 'Arukh*—reception through emendation and update. The authority behind the *Haggahot Maimuniyot* was R. Me'ir of Rothenburg, the last of the German Ba'alei ha-Tosafot, the greatest decisor (*posek*) of Ashkenaz and one whose personal conduct and rulings were scrupulously reported and generally viewed as normative. Yet this 'Ashkenization' was a failure. Never for a moment did the *Mishneh Torah* (or its relevant sections) become the basis of an Ashkenazic code, and the *Haggahot Maimuniyot* did not become the *Mappah* to the *Mishneh Torah*. It soon served simply as a source of information for Franco-Germanic works which were either lost—for example, the *Or Zarua'* and *Sefer Ravyah*—or hard to come by, as was the *Semag*. Moreover, no one ever tried to repeat this glossing of Maimonides' work—to update it again or Ashkenize it differently. Something in *Mishneh Torah* resisted glossing and transformation. What was it?

Let us turn to a page of any widely used edition of the *Shulḥan 'Arukh*—for example, the massive Lemberg edition of 'Oraḥ Ḥayyim' or the famed Vilna one of 'Yoreh De'ah'. The classic commentators on the *Shulḥan 'Arukh*, the Taz, Shakh, and Magen Avraham, do explain the words of the *Shulḥan 'Arukh*, clarify obscurities, disagree with some rulings, and add new ones. Subsequent commentators almost invariably discuss new cases—real or hypothetical. When confronted with a halakhic question, one seeks the section in the

[24] *Teshuvot, Pesakim u-Minhagim shel R. Me'ir (Maharam) mi-Rotenburg*, iii: *Hilkhot Semaḥot* (Jerusalem, 1963).

[25] See my remarks in the entry 'R. Meir ben Barukh of Rothenburg' in R. Y. Z. Werblowski and G. Wigoder, eds., *Oxford Dictionary of the Jewish Religion* (New York and Oxford, 1997), 451. (The editors, wishing to improve upon my scant bibliography, added S. Argaman, *The Captivity of the Maharam: A Narrative of the Events Surrounding the Arrest and Captivity of the Maharam of Rothenburg* [New York, 1990]—a children's storybook published by the Lakewood *ḥeder*.)

Shulḥan 'Arukh where the general topic is discussed and hopes that the case at bar is treated, if not in the code itself, then in the commentators. Put differently, after the text of the *Shulḥan 'Arukh* was clarified—and that was done within some seventy or eighty years of its publication—the subsequent commentarial literature is centrifugal. It does not move towards the text of the *Shulḥan 'Arukh*, focusing on understanding its formulations, elucidating in greater detail the nuances of its positions, but moves away from the text to address new, allied cases.

The reverse holds true of *Mishneh Torah*. Its commentarial literature is centripetal—for centuries after centuries, writers have focused on decoding the meaning of Maimonides' words. Indeed, while there exists a vast commentarial literature on it, there is no supercommentarial literature as there is on the *Shulḥan 'Arukh*. Sensibly so; if you are moving away from the text to treat new cases and variations of the doctrines mentioned in the *Shulḥan 'Arukh*, one of the most effective ways of doing so is to comment on the commentators—for your initial database is then larger.[26] One doesn't begin with the three cases found in the *Shulḥan 'Arukh* but with the six or seven discussed in the *Shakh* and |335| *Magen Avraham*, two of the more expansive commentaries on the *Shulḥan 'Arukh*. If, however, your focus is on the words of Maimonides, if your goal is plumbing his meaning, it would be silly to do so in the form of a commentary on someone else's writings, such as the authors of the *Kesef Mishneh* or *Maggid Mishneh*. Put differently, the *Shulḥan 'Arukh* has functioned for centuries as a springboard for discussions of other matters; it has served as a base for accreted, generational layers of new cases and rulings. Indeed, it is largely this flexibility, this openness to expansion, this ability to serve as a substructure for something larger than its original self that ensured that work's success. *Mishneh Torah*, on the other hand, has commanded the attention of scholars for 800 years and has sucked into its vortex nearly everyone who has sat down to write on it. Other than an initial thought of R. Yosef Karo to cast his *Bet Yosef* around *Mishneh Torah* rather than the *Tur*,[27] I know of no attempt

[26] The *Peri Megadim* is an outstanding example of this approach.

[27] *Bet Yosef*, 'Oraḥ Ḥayyim', introduction. R. Yosef Karo further writes that he decided to base his work on the *Tur* for technical reasons. Clearly, then, he did not subscribe to the view presented below, though he, too, was subsequently sucked into the Maimonidean vortex and produced the *Kesef Mishneh*. Benayahu further mentions a manuscript in his personal possession by an unknown author who lived in Safed, entitled *Yarketei ha-Mishkan*, which fuses the *Mishneh Torah* with the *Shulḥan 'Arukh* including the *haggahot* of the Rema. Every generalization has its exceptions—some significant, some trivial—and mine is no different. {The author of *Yarketei ha-Mishkan* has recently been identified as R. Mosheh Galanti; see 'Teshuvah Ḥadashah le-Rabbenu Betsal'el Ashkenazi bi-Shevaḥ Limmud ha-Talmud be-Filpul', *Mekabtsi'el*, 37 (2001), 510–11. Pinchas Roth drew my attention to this article.}

to use the *Mishneh Torah* as the base of a layered text or as a springboard for things beyond itself.[28]

Both *Mishneh Torah* and the *Shulḥan 'Arukh* are towering works, but *Mishneh Torah* is that rarest of things—a book of law, a work of discursive reasoning that is, at the same time, a work of art. And a work of art creates its own imaginative universe. You can decline to enter that universe as did Ashkenaz in the late medieval and early modern period; it rejected *Mishneh Torah* even as emended by the *Haggahot Maimuniyyot*. However, if you choose to enter that world, you must do so on its terms rather than your own. For a work of art is self-justificatory; it commands rather than seeks attention. It constitutes an end in itself and resists any attempt to turn it into a means, to have it serve a purpose other than its own. You can take the *Mona Lisa* or you can leave it, but you can't turn it into something other than what it is or use it as an instrument to attain some other artistic goal.

The *Shulḥan 'Arukh* is a great work, especially its functional classification—indeed, in ease of use it far exceeds Maimonides' code—but it is not a work of art. It is a pastiche, a great pastiche if you will, but a pastiche nonetheless. You can gloss it; you can tear the fabric of its prose with no sense of violation or even |336| of diminution. You can equally transform it, Ashkenize it, as, so successfully, did R. Mosheh Isserles. You can no more Ashkenize *Mishneh Torah* than you can Americanize *The Brothers Karamazov* or Russify *Huckleberry Finn*, for a work of art is the product of an innate development. It is an organic form that unfolds from within, according to laws derivable from its own essence.[29] Once this essence has been completely realized, once it has achieved full expression and attained its entelechy, it cannot be altered. R. Me'ir of Rothenburg recognized the greatness of *Mishneh Torah*; he did not perceive—how could he at so early a date?—that it was also a work of art whose very nature resists conversion. The *Haggahot Maimuniyot* was an attempt to emend the *Mishneh Torah*,

[28] The reply to the obvious objection of the instance of the *Mishneh la-Melekh* is that the work was never composed as a commentary on *Mishneh Torah*. The author's pupil, R. Ya'akov Coli, decided to arrange the writings of his deceased teacher according to the Maimonidean sequence, as he stated explicitly in his introduction to the work.

[29] I am not contending that this is the only definition of a work of art, but rather that the artistic dimension of *Mishneh Torah* is best grasped in terms of the categories provided by Romantic criticism. Their applicability is not universal. For example, the one other work in medieval halakhah that merits, to my thinking, the appellation 'work of art', is Rashi's *Commentary on the Talmud*. Here, however, the definitions of Schlegel and Coleridge would be useless, as they can assess an independent, self-standing oeuvre but not a work that is intercalated with another. On the artistic character of Rashi's commentary and its multiple agendas, see my brief remarks in 'Can Halakhic Texts Talk History?', *AJS Review*, 3 (1978), 170–1; repr. in the first volume of this series (*Collected Essays* [Oxford, 2013], i. 169–223, at 192–3).

to modify and adapt it for Ashkenazic use. Not surprisingly, it withstood this transformation. So strong was the intuited sense of the innate unity of *Mishneh Torah*, so universal the perception of its resistant integrity and immutability, that no one ever attempted again to emend it and assimilate it to another culture—Ashkenazic, Yemenite, North African, or what you will.[30]

The singularity of *Mishneh Torah* goes yet further. What you see in the *Shulḥan 'Arukh* is what you get, and after the various obscurities in its formulations are cleared up, there's nothing more to say. So you must begin to discuss other things, that is, new cases. What you see in a work of art is not what you get, or, not just what you get. *Moby-Dick* is a story about a whale; it is also more than that. The lucid and exquisitely calibrated formulations of *Mishneh Torah* also have a remarkable lexical subtlety; its spare, almost chaste words are somehow freighted with a richness of meaning. Under the surface clarity of its formulations there are further layers of creative ambiguity. These uncertainties of intent have fascinated readers for generations and scholars have labored tirelessly to resolve them. And the quest never ends.

Allow me to explain. To interpret is to highlight a passage. This passage, in turn, spotlights other passages which link naturally with it, in complement or contrast, to form an interpretative pattern. To be creatively ambiguous means that passages of the work can be linked up in varying, even mutually exclusive, ways, each making a comparable claim to fidelity; much, as it were, like a kaleidoscope, |337| each shift redistributes the alignment and creates a different configuration of parts that in themselves cannot be changed.

If this equivocality, this multivalence, is deep and complex enough, as it is in a few masterpieces, what are called 'supreme works of art', people then find themselves reflected in it. The work becomes, so to speak, all things to all men. Think of the history of Shakespearean interpretation. Maimonides' prose is so burnished that it is almost mirror-like, and many schools of halakhic thought, peering in, have found there their own likeness. One doesn't find one's own reflection in *Tosafot* or in the *Ḥiddushei ha-Ramban* or those of his school. The authors' thoughts are deep—very deep—but they say one thing; and peer as long and as intently as you will, the meaning of their words will be their meaning, not yours. *Their* formulations do not carry an abundance of meanings, a wealth of significations. Absent, beneath the plane of their overt content, are those added levels of provocative ambiguity, the capacity of forming diverse interpretative networks—a susceptibility that invites self-projection—and

[30] The initial thought of R. Yosef Karo (above, n. 27) was not to gloss or emend *Mishneh Torah*, as did the *Haggahot Maimuniyot*, but to use it as the base or point of departure of a much-expanded discussion. See also the appendix to this chapter below.

thus of meaning different things to different people. Over the long centuries, many diverse schools of halakhic thought have used and benefited immeasurably from the writings of Ba'alei ha-Tosafot and those of Ramban and his school, but they never found themselves embodied in them—as they so often have in the words of Maimonides.

In speaking of *Mishneh Torah* as a masterpiece, I have made analogies to works of the imagination in literature and art; perhaps an analogy from philosophy, a field—like law—of discursive thinking and articulation, may be in place. I would put the matter this way: there are some thinkers who wrote poorly, as did Kant and Hegel; there are some thinkers who wrote well—Descartes, Berkeley, and Hume come quickly to mind; and there are a few, a very few, who wrote too well—as did Plato and Nietzsche—so well that one sometimes doesn't know what they said. This is not a matter of opaqueness. Kant is only too often opaque but the range of possible meanings is restricted, and all interpretations will yield a solution that is distinctly Kantian; whereas diametrically opposed interpretations are offered of the thinkers who wrote too well. Despite their surface clarity, crucial passages allow a wide range of differing emphases and multiple, even conflicting, patterns of linkage. To this day we don't know whether Plato was a libertarian or a totalitarian or whether Nietzsche was a liberal or a proto-fascist. Put differently, Berkeley and Hume were pellucid stylists, Plato and Nietzsche were artists, and their writings have all the polysemy of literary masterpieces, the capacity to sustain in places the most contrary interpretations.

I suggest that Maimonides should be added to the small band of thinkers who wrote too well. Not simply the Maimonides of the *Guide of the Perplexed*, a book openly written as 'a riddle wrapped in an enigma', but also the Maimonides of the *Mishneh Torah*—a work of crystalline clarity and protean ambiguity. |338|

Indeed, Maimonides' artistic accomplishment exceeds that of Plato and Nietzsche, for it was attained in a far more constricting medium. To introduce ambiguity, Plato could at a further stage of the dialogue simply add an interlocutor's question, 'But, Socrates, didn't you previously say such and such?' Socrates could recapitulate his position using a word synonymous with the one in the prior discussion. No two words, however, are truly synonymous and the ground is laid for a creative ambiguity.[31] Maimonides, however, is writing

[31] The technique is easy; the accomplishment is anything but that—for the new meaning has then to form an interpretative pattern as philosophically suasive and powerful as the one invoked by the initial term. Not surprisingly, only two thinkers in twenty-five hundred years have performed this feat.

a code, and a code must be precise and maximally concise. Moreover, rarely is there an occasion for recapitulation, as the essence of a code is logical structure where each ruling has its necessary place and no other. Finally, a code isn't read; it is scrutinized piecemeal. One first studies the issue at bar, and then one reads very closely the short passage in the code that contains the relevant ruling. To have only one pass at formulation, and to successfully introduce ambiguity in compressed, closely examined statements of famed accuracy is the feat accomplished by Maimonides. His achievement is obvious; how he achieved it eludes me to this day.

And to come full circle and return to the organization of 'Hilkhot Shabbat': a work of art can have multiple agendas and function simultaneously on a number of different planes. *Mishneh Torah* is a code of law and that is its claim to immortality. It is also, in many places, a polemic—a polemic against Karaism, a polemic against the Geonim, a polemic against a host of competing views of halakhah, some sectarian, some misguided, but all ways of thinking that Maimonides found not only wrong but dangerous. You will ask, 'Why is this other dimension—polemic, of all things—a mark of greatness?' My answer is: not because of its content—the world, indeed, can do quite well without polemic—but because without reconstructing the world in which Maimonides lived and the practical problems he faced, one would never know that this other dimension existed. *Mishneh Torah* functions flawlessly on the level of codification: guiding practice, enunciating principles, and providing closure to innumerable talmudic ambiguities. Indeed, people have been scrutinizing and expounding his 'Hilkhot Shabbat' for some 835 years and excepting an occasional grumble (I assume)—why in the world does one have to turn to several places to find all the laws of cooking (*bishul*)?—no one has discerned any flaws that would so much as hint that this Olympian code was, at the same time, a work of contention, a tract with a contemporary agenda. Not that Maimonides' formulations are interwoven with polemic as in the works of mere mortals; rather, the very same words serve—simultaneously and with no mark of strain—both as timeless formulations |339| and as deliverances of contemporary import. One set of words speaks simultaneously in two voices, in two dissimilar keys.

It is in this fashion that Maimonides opened his 'Hilkhot Shabbat' and structured it, and in the same fashion he also closed it. From studying a legal or even a theological system one can rarely, if ever, get at the experiential core of a religion. One can be conversant with the entire literature of the Church Fathers and the dogmas of Christianity and little know how irrelevant God the Father has been to the lived Christianity of the past millennium and how central the Virgin Mary. One can master the entire *Shulḥan 'Arukh* in all its multi-volume complexity and never have an inkling of the centrality of *talmud torah* in Judaism. Similarly, but on a lesser scale, one can be conversant with the entire *hilkhot Shabbat* in the *Shulḥan 'Arukh*, and all that one would know of the Sabbath would be an endless series of 'No! No! No!' Almost everything that goes into the experience of the Sabbath, all that has made it so essential for Jewish survival, is not to be found there. Maimonides realized this, and, possessing a sense of architectonics (as the author of the *Tur* did not), he felt that the thirty chapters of uninterrupted injunctions should end on an uplift and not on yet more nay-saying. So he postponed the discussion of *kibbud ve-'oneg*—the two commandments that address the celebration and mood of the Sabbath and could well have been treated early on in 'Hilkhot Shabbat', seeing that it treats both kiddush and the preparations before the Sabbath—to the end, to the concluding two chapters of that unit. Then, expanding on the nature of these two *mitsvot*, he built up to a peroration, as was his wont, and wrote:

And he who observes the Sabbath in full accordance with the law and honors it and delights in it [**ומענגה**] to the utmost of his abilities, [to him does] the prophet describe explicitly his reward in this world, over and above the reward laid up to him in the world to come, in the following verse: 'Then shalt thou delight thyself [**תתענג**] in the Lord and I shall cause thee to ride up unto high places of the earth and I will feed thee with the heritage of Jacob thy father, for the mouth of the Lord has spoken' [Isa. 58: 14].[32]

People have always understood the conclusion of 'Hilkhot Shabbat' thus, and correctly so; this is, indeed, one of its purposes. The other is a final highlighting of the difference between the Sabbath of Maimonides and that of the Karaites, who saw the Sabbath as a day of ascetic retreat and allowed only the barest minimum of eating and sleeping—in Hadassi's words **לאכול ולשתות די מחייתו וקיום נפש ולנוח מעט במשכבך** ('to eat and drink just enough for one's sustenance and to rest a little in your bed')—and forbade, to use again Hadassi's formulations, any 'delight and indulgence' (**ענג ודישון**).[33] Hadassi forbade 'delight' (*'oneg*) and Maimonides concluded |**340**| with the obligation of 'delight', thus ending 'Hilkhot Shabbat' exactly as he had begun it—with a polemic

[32] **וכל השומר את שבת כהלכתה ומכבדה ומענגה כפי כוחו, כבר מפורש בקבלה שכרו בעולם הזה יותר על השכר הצפון לעולם הבא, שנאמר אז תתענג על ה' והרכבתיך על במותי ארץ והאכלתיך נחלת יעקב אביך כי פי ה' דבר** *Mishneh Torah*, 'Shabbat', 30: 15.

[33] **תשרק קמו/ר, דף נה ע"א; תשרק קמד/ל, דף נד ע"ב ('להשתשע ולהתעדן')** Ehrlich (above, n. 5), 106–7, 163.

encoded in his classic, halakhic formulations.[34] Once again, one set of words speaks simultaneously in two different keys, delivering two separate messages.

The final touch of the master of multiple meanings was to conclude his 'Hilkhot Shabbat' with words that, at that time, spoke not in two but in three different voices—halakhic, philosophical, and polemical—if one was attuned to hear them. The very last *halakhah* prior to the above-cited peroration, the *halakhah* that Maimonides felt most appropriate to conclude his vast presentation of the laws of the Sabbath—the largest single unit in the entire *Mishneh Torah*—is that of *'onah* (marital relations) as part of *'oneg Shabbat*. While the Talmud speaks approvingly of marital relations on the Sabbath,[35] nowhere does it state that they are a component of *'oneg Shabbat*. Maimonides draws here, as on innumerable other occasions, his own halakhic inference—which is scarcely surprising. What is surprising is the prominence bestowed upon *'onah* by the author of the *Guide*, by the advocate of the controversial position that sexual relations are an expression of man's animality.[36] The placement of the *halakhah* of *'onah* is a final, pointed affirmation not simply of difference but of radical difference. Maimonides literally ends 'Hilkhot Shabbat' by stating—to the philosophically enlightened—that not only is the Sabbath not a day of ascetic practices, a mini-Day of Atonement as the Karaites believed, but its very opposite—a day chosen by God, for reasons best known to Him, on which man should not only indulge his physical nature (food and drink), but even find release for his animal instincts. This concluding, pointed thrust draws on three levels of meaning, the philosophical and halakhic dimensions being here placed in service of the polemical.[37]

While penning the stately and imperishable prose of *Mishneh Torah*, Maimonides, at the same time and with those very same timeless words, was sharply etching the identity borders of rabbinic Judaism and heightening the awareness of his contemporary audience to just how large an extent the

[34] On the Karaite injunction against sexual relations on the Sabbath, see **א"ב קמז/ו, דף נח ע"ד**; **תשרק קנ/ע, דף נו ע"ד; תשרק קעט/כ, י, א, דף עג ע"א–ע"ב; א"ב קפ/ב, דף עג ע"ב**; Ehrlich, 187, 260–1, 334–8. This was not simply theory but part of the Karaite way of life. There is a *ketubbah* in the Genizah in which the Rabbanite groom contracts not to insist on sexual relations on Friday nights with his Karaite bride. See J. Mann, *The Jews in Egypt and in Palestine under the Fatimid Caliphs* (repr. New York, 1970), ii. 211–12.

[35] *Ketubbot* 62b; *Bava Kamma* 82a.

[36] *Guide of the Perplexed*, II. 36.

[37] Note again that juridically the formulation is in no way problematic. No eyebrows are raised here when *Mishneh Torah* is read on its own terms, simply as a code. The passage becomes problematic only if one is aware of Maimonides' views expressed in his philosophical work. Its covert purpose becomes clear only when dimensions other than legal are explored in *Mishneh Torah*, namely, those of philosophy and polemics.

Sabbath of *torah she-be'al-peh* differed from the competing alternatives of sectarians. |341|

APPENDIX

The objection has been made that while the broader point of the artistic nature and unity of *Mishneh Torah* is unquestionable, the example of the *Haggahot Maimuniyot* may not illustrate the point. The *Mishneh Torah* was soon replaced by the *Tur* as the definitive code. Just as updates and commentaries on the *Tur* swiftly ceased upon the acceptance of the *Shulḥan 'Arukh*, so, too, updates of the *Mishneh Torah* ceased upon the acceptance of the *Tur*. The underlying premises of the objection seem to be twofold. First, the *Mishneh Torah* as emended by R. Me'ir of Rothenburg failed to become the controlling code of Ashkenaz for reasons other than the one presented in my essay. Second, the *Tur* rapidly achieved widespread acceptance in Ashkenaz.

If Maharam's effort failed, it was scarcely for lack of authority. There was no mightier name in late medieval Ashkenaz than that of R. Me'ir of Rothenburg. When the *Piskei ha-Rosh* reached Germany there was no reason why some of the new material found therein should not have been glossed to the *Haggahot Maimuniyot*. No sooner had the *Piskei ha-Rosh* become known in Germany—and people noted the nigh-total absence in that work of the German Ba'alei ha-Tosafot, such as Ravyah and R. Yitsḥak Or Zarua'—than the *Haggahot Asheri* was penned. Germany had no hesitation in glossing the *Sha'arei Dura* and other authoritative works; why not the *Mishneh Torah* of Maharam? Answer may be made that three of the fourteen books of *Mishneh Torah* were inapplicable, as were some sections of the other books, for example 'Hilkhot Nezirut'. If this is so, why not simply employ the relevant units? 'Ahavah' and 'Zemanim' as glossed by the *Haggahot Maimuniyot* and the equivalent of the *Haggahot Asheri* would have served as an admirably functional code.

As to the swift acceptance of the *Tur*, this was hardly the case. It became authoritative in Poland in the sixteenth century; in Germany, even as late as the mid-sixteenth century, it did not. R. Shelomoh of Neustadt did not reckon with the *Tur*. His pupil, Maharil, would look in it in the synagogue if the cantor's singing prolonged the services, but this scarcely constitutes acceptance of its authority. In the fifteenth and sixteenth centuries the *Tur* was popular in Germany; the author of the *Leket Yosher* followed its sequence in his own work. It was also studied and annotated, but it was not authoritative. Some scholars ignored it and others did not hesitate to disagree with it. One doesn't know if the remarks of R. Yehudah Minz, a German rabbi who served in Italy in the latter half of the fifteenth century, reflect the attitude of the rabbis of Germany proper or only of those of Italy who were within the German cultural ambience. However, it does give some indication of |342| the contested standing of the *Tur* in that culture: ויש מהרבנים שאינם רוצים אפילו לקרות בטור א"ח [אורח חיים] ונותנין טעם שבעלי בתים לומדים אותו (there are some rabbis who do not want to even look into the *Tur*, explaining that it is a work that laymen study).[38]

This is not surprising in view of the fact that the *Tur*, unlike the *Shulḥan 'Arukh*, is a radically uneven work both in the range of sources used in its different units and in the degree of authorial intervention in the decision-making process. Were the title pages removed from its 'Oraḥ Ḥayyim' and 'Even ha-'Ezer' sections and the sources annotated, few readers would surmise that these are two volumes of one and the same work.[39] The *Semag* was a much more accepted authority in Germany and it was for this audience that the *'Ein Mishpat*, first printed in a mid-sixteenth-century edition of the Talmud, contained references to the *Semag*. On the latter work extensive running commentaries were written by R. Yitsḥak Stein in the late fifteenth century and R. Yehudah b. Natan Zak, better known as R. Zelkele Zak, of Schweinfort in the sixteenth. As the *Tur* had won acceptance in Poland, R. Shelomoh Luria (Rashal) gave classes on it to his students and cited it frequently in his writings. Nonetheless, when it came to the personal statement of authorship, he parted company from his Polish compatriots and pointedly wrote an extensive commentary on the *Semag*, while penning only brief notes on the *Tur*.[40] Indeed, as Elhanan Reiner has pointed out, even those brief notes are probably the jottings of Rashal's pupils, not of the master himself.[41] In the Ashkenazic world, full-fledged commentaries on the *Tur* were first produced in sixteenth-

[38] *Shut R. Yehudah (Mahari) Mints*, ed. A. Ziv (New York, 1995), 61, #15. See Y. A. Dinari, *Ḥakhmei Ashkenaz be-Shilhei Yemei ha-Beinayim: Darkheihem ve-Khitveihem ba-Halakhah* (Jerusalem, 1984), 165; Y. Y. Yovel, 'Rishonim ve-'Aḥaronim', *Zion*, 59 (1999), 378 n. 26.

[39] See Y. D. Galinsky, 'Arba'ah Turim ve-ha-Sifrut ha-Hilkhatit shel Sefarad ba-Me'ah ha-'Arba'-'Esreh: Aspektim Historiyim, Sifrutiyim ve-Hilkhatiyim' (Ph.D. diss., Bar Ilan University, 1999), 86–194.

[40] See *Sefer Mitsvot Gadol*, ed. A. Merzbach and Y. M. Peles (Jerusalem, 1993), for the running commentaries of the aforementioned German rabbis and Rashal's commentary in the supplement, pp. 401–632. Contrast the length of this commentary with the brevity of Rashal's notes on the *Tur* published in the recent *Hadrat Kodesh* edition of *Tur ve-Shulḥan 'Arukh*, 6 vols. (Jerusalem, 1991–2001). {For further instances of Rashal's following German rather than Polish tradition, see E. Wistreich, 'Ḥashivah Mishpatit be-Mishnatam shel Ḥakhmei Polin ha-Rishonim', in A. Enker and S. Deutsch, eds., *'Iyyunim be-Mishpat 'Ivri u-ve-Halakhah* (Ramat Gan, 1998), 183–204.}

[41] E. Reiner, 'Temurot bi-Yeshivot Polin ve-'Ashkenaz ba-Me'ot ha-Tet-Zayin–Yod-Zayin,

century Poland. In other words, Germany had some 250 years in which to attempt another update of the *Mishneh Torah*, or relevant sections thereof, but never did.

The common error about the reception of the *Tur* arises from a natural retrojection of the swift acceptance of the *Shulḥan 'Arukh* onto its predecessor. The flawless encyclopedic knowledge displayed in the *Bet Yosef* awed the author's contemporaries, and his authority was further enhanced by the appearance of his commentary on *Mishneh Torah*, the *Kesef Mishneh*. In these two works, R. Yosef Karo demonstrated a command of the entire talmudic corpus, the likes |343| of which had not been seen for centuries. This won for his code, the *Shulḥan 'Arukh*, swift acceptance, despite some pockets of opposition. It was only natural to assume that the *Tur*, too, enjoyed universal authority, especially as the most important commentators of the *Shulḥan 'Arukh*, R. Mosheh Isserles (Rema) and R. Shabbetai ha-Kohen (Shakh), wrote, and frequently refer to their works, on the *Tur*. R. David ha-Levi (Taz) also makes constant reference to his father-in-law's work (*Baḥ*) on that code. The two works, the *Tur* and the *Shulḥan 'Arukh*, seemed twinned, and it was only natural to assume that the acceptance of the former was similar to that of the latter. The truth of the matter is that the *Tur*, as I have remarked, is anything but comprehensive, and the history of its acceptance in Ashkenaz was hardly swift.[42]

(Despite the profound reverence in which Maimonides was held in Yemen, no one ever tried to update or employ the *Mishneh Torah* as the basis of a larger work. Taken by itself, Yemen is *sui generis* in so many ways that one might well hesitate before inferring anything broader from this. When, however, it conforms to what is observed in other communities of the Diaspora, its conduct is telling.)

ve-ha-Vikuaḥ 'al ha-Pilpul', in I. Bartal et al., eds., *Ke-Minhag Ashkenaz u-Polin: Sefer Yovel le-Ḥone Shemeruk—Kovets Meḥkarim be-Tarbut Yehudit* (Jerusalem, 1993), 21 n. 20.

42 In the Sephardic world the *Tur* became authoritative earlier, though the process was somewhat more complex than is commonly thought. See the dissertation of Yehudah Galinsky (above, n. 39), pp. 292–304, and his recent article 'Ve-Zakhah zeh he-Ḥakham Yoter mi-Kulam she-ha-kol Lamdu mi-Sefarav: 'Al Tefutsat "Arba'ah Turim" le-Rabbi Ya'akov ben ha-Rosh mi-Zeman Ketivato ve-'ad le-Sof ha-Me'ah ha-Ḥamesh-'Esreh', *Sidra*, 19 (2004), 25–45.

Bibliography of Manuscripts

Most manuscripts have been cited by the catalogue number of the Institute of Microfilmed Hebrew Manuscripts at the National Library of Israel, not by the shelf mark of the library of origin, the reason being that, given the Institute's vast collection of microfilms from all over the world, for decades most scholars worked there rather than moving around to different libraries in a host of countries. They naturally cited the manuscripts as they were registered in the Institute's catalogue, and these numbers have entered the scholarly literature.

Generally there are three numbers in the lists below: the catalogue number registered at the Institute in the left-hand column, taken from the catalogues of the respective libraries of origin; the library of origin's shelf mark in the middle column; and the reel number of the microfilm at the Institute in the right-hand column (where the catalogue number is not that of the Institute this is noted in the relevant left-hand column heading).

Where the library of origin did not have a catalogue, the Institute registered the manuscripts by the library's shelf mark, and the only references given below are that library's shelf mark and the Institute's reel number. Where the library of origin arranged its manuscripts by the order of its catalogue, the catalogue number together with the Institute's reel number are the only references.

The collection of Jews' College (Montefiore), London, has been sold and the manuscripts dispersed, many to private parties. Such manuscripts are nevertheless entered below as they are registered in the card catalogue of the Institute.

Berlin, Staatsbibliothek

Catalogue no.	Shelf mark	Reel no.
160	Or. Qu. 685	1798

Cambridge, University Library

Stefan C. Reif's catalogue of Cambridge University Library's manuscripts came out long after the microfilms of Cambridge had been accessed by the Institute. These manuscripts were therefore registered at the Institute by Cambridge's shelf mark. For the manuscripts below, Cambridge's catalogue number is in the left-hand column, the shelf mark in the middle, and the Institute's reel number on the right.

Catalogue no.	Shelf mark	Reel no.
SCR 359	Add. 667.1	16997

Florence, Biblioteca Nazionale Centrale

Catalogue no.	Shelf mark	Reel no.
—	Magl. II. 1.7	18623

Frankfurt am Main, Stadts- und Universitätsbibliothek (now Universitätsbibliothek Johann Christian Senckenberg)

Catalogue no.	Shelf mark	Reel no.
72	8vo 69	25909

Hamburg, Staats- und Universitätsbibliothek, Levy Collection

Catalogue no.	Shelf mark	Reel no.
70	—	1533

Jerusalem, National Library of Israel

Catalogue no.	Shelf mark	Reel no.
4to 689	B305	689 = 4
28vo 3182	B499	3182 = 28

London, British Library

Catalogue no.	Shelfmark	Reel no.
1056	Add. 11639	4948 G

London, Jews' College, Montefiore Collection

Catalogue no.	Shelfmark	Reel no.
65	—	4583
98	—	4613
134	—	7304

Mantua, Comunità Israelitica

Catalogue no.	Shelfmark	Reel no.
33	—	813

Milan, Biblioteca Ambrosiana

Catalogue no.	Shelfmark	Reel no.
14	C 116 Sup	12263

Moscow, Russian State Library, Günzburg Collection

Catalogue no.	Shelfmark	Reel no.
—	1	6682
—	73	6753

Munich, Bayerische Staatsbibliothek

Catalogue no.	Shelfmark	Reel no.
315	hebr. 315	1683

New York, Jewish Theological Seminary

Catalogue no.	Reel no.
Rabbinica 673	41418
Rabbinica 1077	43192
Rabbinica 1087 (= ENA 2717)	41627
ENA 2093-5/6 (Genizah fragments)	33306
2380	28633
8259	53135

Oxford, Bodleian Library

Catalogue no.	Shelf mark	Reel no.
268	Opp. 27	16736
416	Hunt. 200	18404
566	Opp. 276	19437
678	Opp. 42	20593
875	Opp. 340	21834
877	Mich. 41	21836
1103	Can. Or. 86	17709
1106	Opp. 642	17712
1317	Mich. 491	22131
2218	Poc. 280 B	20501

Paris, Bibliothèque Nationale

Catalogue no.	Shelf mark	Reel no.
326	Héb. 326	23495
392	Héb. 392	20243
393	Héb. 393	4428
1391	Héb. 1391	34252
1408	Héb. 1408	15770

Parma, Biblioteca Palatina

Giovanni B. De Rossi published a catalogue of his personal Hebraica collection in 1803. That collection was acquired by the Biblioteca Palatina. In 2001 a more precise and detailed catalogue was published by Benjamin Richler, long after the collection had been accessed by the Institute. Its card catalogue registers the De Rossi number.

De Rossi catalogue no.	Shelfmark	New catalogue no.	Reel no.
86	Parm. 2758	Richler 859	13607
189	Parm. 1940	Richler 804	13095
425	Parm. 2439	Richler 860	13443
813	Parm. 1941	Richler 876	13096
1133	Parm. 3280	Richler 1367	13957
1292	Parm. 3155	Richler 727	13896

Vatican, Biblioteca Apostolica

Catalogue no.	Shelfmark	Reel no.
Ebr. 136	136	8613
Ebr. 142	142	221
Ebr. 176	176	236
Ebr. 304	304	8634

Warsaw, Żydowski Instytut Historyczny

Catalogue no.	Shelfmark	Reel no.
204	—	10112

Source Acknowledgments

The following essays were originally published as detailed below.

CHAPTER 1: 'Berurim ba-Halakhah shel Ashkenaz ha-Kedumah 1: Agobard mi-Lyons, Megillat Aḥima'ats ve-ha-Halakhah ha-'Erets-Yisra'elit', in Yosef Hacker and Yaron Harel, eds., *Lo Yasur Shevet mi-Yehudah: Hanhagah, Rabbanut u-Kehillah be-Toledot Yisra'el: Meḥkarim Muggashim li-Professor Shimon Schwartzfuchs* (Jerusalem, 2011), 207–18.

CHAPTER 2: 'Berurim ba-Halakhah shel Ashkenaz ha-Kedumah 2: Di'alektikah, Skholastikah ve-Reshitan shel ha-Tosafot', *Sidra*, 24–5 (2011), 267–71.

CHAPTER 6: A partial translation of the ninth chapter of *Ha-Yayin bi-Yemei ha-Beinayim: Yein Nesekh—Perek be-Toledot ha-Halakhah be-'Ashkenaz* (Jerusalem, 2008).

CHAPTER 10: 'Bein Ḥevel 'Arav le-Ḥevel Edom', in Y. M. Gafni and A. Ravitzky, eds., *Kedushat ha-Ḥayyim ve-Ḥeruf ha-Nefesh: Kovets Ma'amarim le-Zikhro shel Amir Yekutiel* (Jerusalem, 1993), 149–52.

CHAPTER 11: 'Halakhah, Hermeneutics and Martyrdom in *Ashkenaz*', *Jewish Quarterly Review*, 94 (2004), 77–108, 278–97.

CHAPTER 12: 'Maimonides' *Iggeret ha-Shemad*: Law and Rhetoric', in L. Landman, ed., *Rabbi Joseph Lookstein Memorial Volume* (New York, 1980), 281–319.

CHAPTER 13/I: 'Beḥanim li-Fesikah Hilkhatit: Teshuvah le-Dr D. Hartman', *Meḥkerei Yerushalayim be-Maḥshevet Yisra'el*, 3 (1984), 683–6.

CHAPTER 13/II: 'A Response to Lorberbaum and Shapira, "Maimonides' Epistle on Martyrdom in the Light of Legal Philosophy"', *Dine Israel*, 28–9 (2011–12), 163–72.

CHAPTER 14: 'Hirhurim 'al Miyyuno shel ha-Rambam be-Mishneh Torah: Be'ayot Amitiyot u-Medummot', *Maimonidean Studies*, 4 (2000), 107–15.

CHAPTER 15: 'Mishneh Torah: Polemic and Art', in Jay M. Harris, ed., *Maimonides 800 Years After: Essays on Maimonides and his Influence* (Cambridge, Mass., 2007), 327–43.

Index of Names

A

Abu Aharon ben R. Shemu'el ha-Nassi 142, 157, 200
Abun family 188, 193
Agobard of Lyons:
De Insolentia Iudaeorum 5, 6 n. 3, 16, 18, 141 n. 37; on Jews selling non-kosher meat to Gentiles 5
feels harassed by Jews 13
Jewish practice as described by, disagrees with Palestinian halakhah 11–13, 16, 18–19, 22
Agus, I. A. 46 n. 39, 74 n. 5, 89 n. 66
R. 'Akiva, martyrdom of 235, 237, 245–7, 283
Al-Farabi 315 n. 58
Alfasi (R. Yitsḥak of Fez) 78 and n. 22, 79, 113, 376
continues geonic culture 203
manuscript tradition in *Sukkah* 123
occasional talmudic dialectics of 26
omits all topics in *kodashim* 33–4 n. 10
produces abridgements of the *sugya* 33, 159
R. Zeraḥyah ha-Levi's critiques of 31
al-Ghazali 315 n. 58
Almohads:
conduct of Jews under 322–3, 332, 336, 347
forced conversion under 223, 289 and n. 1, 294, 296–7, 330, 357
persecution of Jews 178, 305, 317, 323, 349, 363; economically motivated 350
radical monotheism of 288, 317, 326
R. 'Amram (Gaon) 77, 78 n. 23
Anselm of Canterbury 27–8
Aristotle, *Rhetoric* 312 n. 48, 315 n. 58, 336–7
R. Asher ben David ha-Levi 111
R. Asher ben Meshullam 286
R. Asher ben Yeḥi'el (Rosh) 38, 240 n. 21, 279 n. 139
on posing as a Gentile 271 and n. 104, 272 n. 105, 273
Averroës 315 n. 58
Avicenna 315 n. 58
R. Avraham Av Bet-Din 33–4 n. 10
R. Avraham ben David of Posquières, *see* Rabad
R. Avraham ben Efrayim, *Kitsur Sefer ha-Mitsvot* 256 n. 59, 270
R. Avraham ben Yitsḥak of Narbonne 12 n. 26, 31, 114 n. 24, 203

B

Ba'al ha-Ma'or, *see* R. Zeraḥyah ha-Levi of Lunel
Bartenura, *see* R. 'Ovadyah ben Avraham
Bashyatzi 381
Be'eri, Tovah 194
Benei ha-Makhiri, *see* Makirites
Ben-Sasson, Menahem 155 n. 11, 223, 226 n. 9, 314 n. 54
Berger, David 80 n. 34, 202, 206–15, 283
Bernold of Constance 260
Bonfid, R. David 299–300 n. 21, 306 n. 34, 343
Bonfil, Reuven 3, 5–6, 8–9, 13–21
Brody, Robert 13 n. 27, 179 n. 58, 196, 204

C

Charlemagne 128, 134, 137, 199
Charles the Bald 129
Chavel, Isaac 329–30
Coli, R. Ya'akov 387 n. 28
Constantine (emperor) 228

D

Danzig, Neil 152 n. 5, 204
R. David ha-Levi (Taz) 395
R. David ha-Levi of Mainz 65–6 n. 104, 111
R. David ben Zimra (Radbaz) 89–90, 293 n. 8, 354–5
Davidson, Herbert 330
Dönitz, Saskia 264 nn. 79–80, 284
Duran, R. Shelomoh ben R. Shim'on 352
Dworkin, Ronald 338–40

E

Edrei, A. 143–4
R. Efrayim of Regensburg 55
R. El'azar Roke'aḥ, *see* Kalonymos, R. El'azar ben Yehudah
R. El'azar of Worms, *see* Kalonymos, R. El'azar ben Yehudah
Eldad ha-Dani, *Hilkhot Sheḥitah* 15
R. Eli'ezer ha-Gadol 46, 77, 88 n. 62, 93–4, 97 and n. 86, 188–9 n. 78
  extant responsa of 46, 76 n. 13, 86
  on *sekhakh* 57 and n. 82
R. Eli'ezer of Metz 269, 306 n. 34
R. Eli'ezer ben Natan of Mainz (Ravan) 78 and n. 23, 79, 80, 82, 147
R. Eli'ezer ben Yo'el ha-Levi (Ravyah) 80, 147, 156 n. 12, 158 n. 19, 251, 254 n. 54, 393
  on child murder to avoid apostasy 256 n. 59, 287
  on following Palestinian rite 55, 84
  poem on *'akedah* 256 n. 59
Elitsur, Shulamit 194, 256 n. 59
R. Eliyahu of Vilna (Vilna Gaon) 60, 73, 86 and n. 57, 208–9
Emanuel, Simcha 93 n. 77
Emmanuel of Rome 250 n. 47
Epstein, J. N. 14, 32 n. 5, 163–4 n. 32, 165

F

Fleischer, Ezra 114, 143, 146 n. 4
Flusser, David 263, 264 n. 79
Friedman, Shamma 123–5, 174 n. 52, 204
Fulbert of Chartres 27

G

Galanti, R. Mosheh 386 n. 27
Gerbert of Aurillac 27
R. Gershom, *see* Rabbenu Gershom Me'or ha-Golah
R. Gershom, author of *Sefer ha-Shalman* 263
Goldin, Simha 259 n. 68, 282–3
Goldschmidt, Daniel 78 n. 23, 146 and n. 4
Gombiner, R. Avraham 56
Grabmann, Martin 28
Gregory of Tours, chronicle of 136
Groner, Zvi 61, 167
Gross, Abraham 243 n. 30, 283
Grossman, Avraham 50, 64, 120 n. 47, 188–9 n. 78, 223
  on *derashot* in halakhic decision-making 85–6, 90, 94 n. 78, 95 n. 80
  on employing aggadah in halakhic decision-making 85–6, 101, 103
  holds that Early Ashkenazic scholars disregarded the Bavli 71, 76 n. 14, 77, 82
  on Kalonymide relocation to Mainz 43, 193
  magnitude of scholarly achievement 3–4
  on martyrdom 262 and n. 74
  on Rabbenu Sasson 25, 106–7, 111–13, 116–19
  on scholastic influence on Tosafists 23–8
  on R. Yehudah ha-Kohen 46–7 n. 43, 47 n. 45, 48
Grossman, R. Yitzhak (*Bein Din le-Din*) 285, 287

H

Hadassi 380 and n. 5, 381–3, 391
R. Hai Gaon 55, 78, 169, 187, 188–9 n. 78
  command of Aramaic 160–1
  on halakhic matters 83 and n. 45, 84 n. 48, 326, 345 n. 13
  on matters of *minhag* 112, 113 n. 19, 114 nn. 24–5
  sister's alleged marriage to Rabbenu Gershom 201 n. 112
R. Ḥanan'el, *see* Rabbenu Ḥanan'el
R. Ḥanina ben Tradyon, martyrdom of 235–9, 241, 249
Hart, Herbert 338, 344
Hartman, David 331–2, 334–6, 338–9, 341
Hartz, Louis 192
Henry IV, grants privileges to Jews of Worms and Speyer 260

I

Ibn Tibbon, Shemu'el 315 n. 58
Ibn Tumrat 288
Ibrâhim ben Yaq'ub 127
Isserlein, R. Yisra'el 86, 271 n. 104
Isserles, R. Mosheh (Rema) 56, 385, 387, 395
Ivo of Chartres 28 n. 11

J
Josephus 194, 262, 267

K
Kalir, R. El'azar 114, 163
Kalonymide family 200, 215
guardians of esoteric tradition 157, 193, 266
migration from Lucca to Mainz 43, 142, 156 n. 13, 188–9 n. 78, 193 and n. 91, 198–9
Kalonymos, R. El'azar ben Yehudah (Roke'aḥ, also known as El'azar of Worms) 80, 104–5, 243 n. 30, 279
esoteric traditions of 86, 199–200
Perush ha-Tefillot 199
Sefer Roke'aḥ 65 n. 104, 105, 215, 275 n. 118
R. Kalonymos of Lucca 53 n. 66, 142
R. Kalonymos of Rome 24
R. Kalonymos ben Yehudah (*paytan*) 253
Karo, R. Yosef 87, 386 and n. 27, 388 n. 30, 395
Katz, Jacob 58, 115 n. 27, 281 n. 147
Kedar, B. Z. 259 n. 68, 260
Kirkisani 381
Kolon, R. Yosef, defense of *minhag* 56

L
R. Leon 43, 46, 207–10, 214
teacher of Rabbenu Gershom 45, 71, 153, 156–7, 169, 187, 209
R. Leontin, *see* R. Leon
Lorberbaum, Yair 338–41, 343–4
Lotter, Friedrich 42, 44–5 n. 36
Louis IX, anti-Jewish attitude 272–3
Louis the Pious, Carolingian emperor 44–5 n. 36, 45, 128–9
Agobard's letter to 5, 141
Luria, R. Shelomoh (Rashal) 156 n. 13, 193 n. 91, 394

M
McCormick, Michael 128–9, 135 n. 24, 136
Maharil, *see* R. Ya'akov ha-Levi Moellin
R. Maimon, father of Maimonides, Letter of Consolation 316, 318
Maimonides:
Commentary on the Mishnah, *see* Index of Subjects: *Perush ha-Mishnayot*
covert polemic against Karaites 380–2, 384, 391–2
defends forced converts in Morocco, *see* Index of Subjects: *Iggeret ha-Shemad*
defends persecuted Jews of Yemen 317
doctrine of non-culpability in instances of duress 306, 319
Epistle on Martyrdom, *see* Index of Subjects: *Iggeret ha-Shemad*
Epistle to 'Ovadyah the Convert 326, 371
familiar with philosophical rhetorical tradition 315 n. 58
forbids voluntary martyrdom 233, 276, 330 n. 88; opposed in Germany 234, 276
Guide of the Perplexed 312, 350, 368, 389, 392
Iggeret ha-Shemad, *see* Index of Subjects: *Iggeret ha-Shemad*
letter to R. Pinḥas the Judge 374
on martyrdom, *see* Index of Subjects: *Iggeret ha-Shemad*
Mishneh Torah, *see* Index of Subjects: *Mishneh Torah*
Perush ha-Mishnayot, *see* Index of Subjects: *Perush ha-Mishnayot*
possibly challenges the principle of direct inheritance 84 and n. 48
resolves, at times, talmudic contradictions 26
revolutionary redefinition of idolatry 291–5, 297, 327
sees heresy as a form of idolatry 293, 298, 325, 348
Sefer ha-Mitsvot 299, 306 n. 34, 310, 329–30, 379
Treatise on Logic 315 n. 58
R. Makhir of Mainz 29, 161 n. 24
Makirites (Benei ha-Makhiri) 118, 188–9 n. 78, 201 n. 113
compiled *Ma'aseh ha-Ge'onim* 29, 35, 65–6 n. 104
defend custom 36
Ma'aseh ha-Makhiri 147
mediocre scholars 35, 39, 62, 76
nephews and acolytes of R. Yitsḥak ben Yehudah 48–9, 54
write about varying customs of *haftarot* 114 and n. 25
Malkiel, David, rejection of his account of *kiddush ha-shem* 268 n. 92

R. Manoaḥ Hendel ben Shemaryahu 247 n. 37
R. Me'ir Abul'afia (Ramah) 82, 123, 140, 299–300 n. 21
R. Me'ir ha-Kohen 84–5, 385
R. Me'ir of Ramerupt 111 n. 17, 112
R. Me'ir of Rothenburg 84, 393
 forbids posing as a Gentile to escape danger 271, 273, 356 n. 9
 free of cultural superiority—uses work of Rabad and Maimonides 384–5
 on killing children to avoid baptism 251, 254, 387
 Teshuvot R. Me'ir mi-Rotenburg (*Maharam*) 46–7 n. 43, 247 n. 38
 towering reputation of 385
Me'iri, *see* R. Menaḥem ha-Me'iri
R. Menaḥem ha-Me'iri 33–4 n. 10, 37, 263
Mendels, D. 143–4
R. Meshullam ben Kalonymos of Lucca 86 n. 55, 94, 188–9 n. 78, 193 and n. 91, 201 n. 112
R. Meshullam of Lunel 116
R. Meshullam of Mainz 79
R. Meshullam ben Mosheh ben Iti'el 188 n. 78
Minz, R. Yehudah 394
Mohammed 294
 accepting the prophetic character of 317, 319, 324; is a denial of the supremacy of the Mosaic revelation 293, 303, 334, 347, 357; is not idolatry 291, 294
 massacres Jews 292, 313, 330
R. Mordekhai ben Hillel, florilegia of 37
R. Mosheh of Bari 188
R. Mosheh of Coucy 276, 281 n. 147, 384
R. Mosheh ha-Darshan of Narbonne 188
R. Mosheh Kalfo of Bari 188
R. Mosheh ben Kalonymos 156 n. 13
R. Mosheh ben Maimon, *see* Maimonides
R. Mosheh of Pavia 188
R. Mosheh ben Ya'akov ben Mosheh ben Abun of Narbonne 188
R. Mosheh of Zurich 254 n. 54, 255, 256 n. 59, 270

N
Naḥmanides (Ramban) 25, 189, 303 n. 27
 novellae of 38, 388–9
R. Naḥshon Gaon 32 n. 5
R. Natan ben Makhir 35, 54, 76, 188–9 n. 78
R. Natan of Rome 160–1, 188
 Sefer he-'Arukh 32 n. 5, 160–1, 169, 187–8
R. Natronai Gaon 140
Noam, Vered 123–4, 140
Novetsky, Hillel 352–4, 357–9, 361–3

O
R. 'Ovadyah ben Avraham (Bartenura) 287

P
R. Perets of Corbeil 270, 276 n. 126
Peter Damian 27
Philip IV 273
R. Pinḥas ha-Dayyan (also Pinḥas the Judge) 374, 379
Pirenne, Henri 142
Pirkoi ben Baboi 10, 21 n. 50

R
Rabad (R. Avraham ben David of Posquières) 82, 315 n. 57, 355–6 n. 8
 commentary on the Talmud 33–4 n. 10, 384–5; did not challenge traditional Provençal practice 31, 155; of a lesser caliber than Rashi's commentary 31, 159
Rabbenu Asher, *see* R. Asher ben Yeḥi'el (Rosh)
Rabbenu Gershom Me'or ha-Golah 27, 76 n. 13, 94, 127, 161 n. 24, 188–9 n. 78, 215
 alleged marriage to Hai Gaon's sister 201 n. 112
 allegedly copied *Sefer Yosippon* 263
 allegedly invented halakhic *derashot* 85–6, 91, 93
 attitude to *minhag* 44 and n. 36, 46
 bans emendation of the Talmud 125–6
 disciple of R. Leon 43, 45, 71, 153, 156–7, 187, 209
 dismissive attitude to the Geonim 153–4, 156, 187, 200, 204, 210, 213–14
 does not use the Yerushalmi 80, 147, 158 and n. 18
 explicates the entire Talmud 42
 founding father of Ashkenaz 42–3, 46, 71, 157

notion of *kehillah kedoshah* in the writings of 190
Perush Rabbenu Gershom, so-called, actually commentary of Mainz academy 31, 35, 50, 83, 149, 187–8; glossed with French words 215; new conception of talmudic interpretation in 207; in *sub verbo* style 62–3
pre-eminence of 45, 46 n. 39, 85, 108, 177
responsa of 74 and n. 9, 77, 85, 87–8, 92, 99, 151; allegedly written in dialectical style 23, 26; reflect independence 204, 213
rulings of 77, 79–80, 86–91, 107–8, 147
school of 50, 80, 160, 169, 187
textual emendation of 126
use of biblical and midrashic passages in halakhic decisions 86, 88–90, 92
Yerushalmi: not available to 158 n.18; not cited in rulings of 79–80, 147
Rabbenu Ḥanan'el of Kairouan 78 and n. 22
command of Aramaic 160
continuation of geonic culture 203
different textual traditions of Talmud in the writings of 123, 140
Talmud commentary of 32–3, 35, 126, 159 and n. 21; tractates treated in 33–4 n. 10, 169 n. 41; version of talmudic text cited in *Tosafot* 39
Rabbenu Leontin, *see* R. Leon
Rabbenu Nissim of Barcelona (Ran) 117
Rabbenu Nissim (Gaon) of Kairouan 32
Rabbenu Sasson (R. Shelomoh ben Shimshon) 26, 48, 108, 148
academy of 23
alleged reliance on *Halakhot Gedolot* 106, 118–20
alleged traditionalism of 48–9, 106, 112, 114–15, 117–18
alleged use of dialectical method 23–5
on inspection of slaughtered animals 111, 119
on *kashrut* of a fallen animal 118
a leading scholar of 11th-cent. Ashkenaz 48, 187
liturgical rulings of 112–13, 116–17, 120
on moneylending 107–8
murdered in Crusades 48
responsa of 76, 107
on transportation of wine 110
upholds the ban on vinegar 116
Rabbenu Tam (R. Ya'akov of Ramerupt) 56, 79 and n. 26, 82, 189
doctrine of *she'at ha-shemad* 248 n. 42, 283
on following Palestinian rite 55
forbids apostasy under torture 239–41, 249
on martyrdom 236, 238–9, 241, 244, 269, 283; contradictions in reasoning 253–4, 256 n. 59
revives talmudic dialectic 190, 238
rulings on *setam yeinam* 110, 115–16
selective use of biblical and aggadic passages in rulings 86, 103–4, 241–9
on suicide 239–41, 249, 250 n. 47, 256 n. 59, 274
Radbaz (R. David ben Zimra) 89–90, 293 n. 8, 354–5
Ramah, *see* R. Me'ir Abul'afia
Rambam, *see* Maimonides
Ramban, *see* Naḥmanides
Ran, *see* Rabbenu Nissim of Barcelona
Rashba (R. Shelomoh ibn Aderet) 38, 190, 315 n. 57, 375–6 and n. 19
Rashbam (R. Shemu'el ben Me'ir) 79, 82 and n. 41, 91 n. 73, 116, 276 n. 125
Rashbash, *see* Duran, R. Shelomoh ben R. Shim'on
Rashi 114 and n. 22, 188
command of Aramaic 160, 170, 212
commentary on Talmud 30–1, 62, 71, 119, 189–90, 210; artistic dimension of 387 n. 29; consults R. Yitsḥak ben Yehudah on difficult passages 50, 76, 110; intentionally does not explicate entire *sugya* 63 n. 99; leads to revision of Ashkenazic practices 30; occasionally resolves talmudic contradictions 26; pedagogical genius of 31, 33, 63; perfects the *sub verbo* method 32–3, 63 and n. 99; reintroduces *'Avodah Zarah* into talmudic curriculum 30, 147, 192; reputedly inspired by the Holy Spirit 151, 210
disciples of 30
does not believe in the binding force of custom 44

Rashi (*cont.*):
exegesis of 4, 212, 355
indifferent to geonic rulings 156 n. 12, 213
responsa of 35
school of, *see* disciples of
studied in Worms and Mainz 30, 32, 187
talmudic texts available to 114 n. 25, 123–5, 140
teachers of 45–6, 49, 111–12, 120
Ravan, *see* R. Eli'ezer ben Natan of Mainz
Ravyah, *see* R. Eli'ezer ben Yo'el ha-Levi
Reich, Eitan 283–4
Reiner, A. (Rami) 106, 118–20, 152 n. 5
Reiner, Elhanan 394
Rema, *see* Isserles, R. Mosheh
Ri (R. Yitsḥak ben Shemu'el of Dampierre, also known as Ri ha-Zaken) 238, 271 n. 100
on conflict between Talmud and *minhag* 55
justifies execution of informers 102, 286–7
on martyrdom 238–9, 248–9, 269
revives, together with Rabbenu Tam, talmudic dialectic 190
on suicide 240, 254, 274
Ri Kolon, *see* Kolon, R. Yosef
Ri ha-Zaken, *see* Ri
Ritva, *see* R. Yom Tov al-Sevilli
Riva, *see* R. Yitsḥak ben Asher of Speyer
Rosenthal, Eliezer Shimshon 123, 204
Rosh, *see* R. Asher ben Yeḥi'el

S

R. Sa'adyah Gaon 182, 184, 194
Schütte, S. 43 n. 32
Secunda, Shai 124 and n. 4
Segan ha-Levi, *see* R. Yitsḥak ha-Levi of Worms
Shapira, Hayyim 338–40, 344–5
R. Shelomoh ibn Aderet, *see* Rashba
R. Shelomoh of Neustadt 393
R. Shelomoh ben Shimshon, *see* Rabbenu Sasson
R. Shemu'el he-Ḥasid 84 n. 49
R. Sherira Gaon 88 n. 62, 153–4 n. 7, 210, 214
R. Shimshon of Sens 254, 278
on direct inheritance of grandchildren 82, 83 n. 47
on forced apostasy 238 n. 20, 244–5
on martyrdom 270, 279 and n. 137
permits suicide under persecution 249–50
R. Simḥah of Speyer 82, 83 n. 46
Stein, R. Yitsḥak 394
Strikovsky, Aryeh 347–8, 350
Sussmann, Yaacov 172, 181 n. 61, 204
on oral transmission of the Talmud 171
precludes involvement of Sura/Pumbedita in inscription of the Talmud 175, 196, 205
on study of *Kodashim* in Provence 33–4 n. 10
on the Yerushalmi: medieval diffusion of 149 n. 9, 158 n. 18; text of 39, 61 n. 94

T

Tachau, R. Mosheh, challenges Kalonymide esoteric traditions 200
Ta-Shma, I. M. 39, 48–9, 53 n. 66, 59, 61 n. 94
on aggadah as basis for halakhah 101–4
on the controlling role of *minhag* in Ashkenaz 3, 29, 36, 41–2, 44 and n. 36, 46, 71
on *Ma'aseh ha-Ge'onim* 30, 38, 40
on the origins of the Ashkenazic community 43–4
on *Perush Rabbenu Gershom* 31, 62, 64
Tertullian 228
Toch, Michael 42–4, 136–7
R. Tsadok Gaon 77, 78 n. 23
R. Tsidkiyahu ha-Rofé, author of *Shibbolei ha-Leket* 79–80

V

R. Vidal of Tolosa (*Maggid Mishneh*) 376 and n. 19
Vilna Gaon, *see* R. Eliyahu of Vilna

W

Weinreich, Max 72
William of Newburgh 267

Y

R. Ya'akov ben Asher, Ba'al ha-Turim 80, 368
R. Ya'akov ha-Levi Moellin (Maharil) 73, 86, 107, 393
R. Ya'akov of Ramerupt, *see* Rabbenu Tam
R. Ya'akov ben Yakar 46, 120, 187, 188–9 n. 78

R. Ya'ir ben Me'ir, unknown figure 80–1, 147
R. Yeḥezkel Landau 86
R. Yehudah of Barcelona 31, 203
R. Yehudah he-Ḥasid 104, 280
R. Yehudah ben Kalonymos 47 n. 45
R. Yehudah ha-Kohen, Ba'al Sefer ha-Dinim 23–4, 26, 65–6 n. 104, 187
based in Mainz 47
finesses disagreement with *Halakhot Gedolot* 48, 154 and n. 8, 213
proponent of children mourning for grandparents 81–4
relies on the Bavli in his rulings 42, 77, 85, 93–4
responsa of 46–7, 74–5, 93; on communal organization 95, 97; mostly found in 1607 Prague edition of *Teshuvot R. Me'ir mi-Rotenburg* 74 n. 9; reflect decisiveness and independence 46–8, 204; on Sabbath of Hanukkah falling on Rosh Hodesh 48
student of Rabbenu Gershom 71, 74
R. Yehudah ha-Levi 33–4 n. 10
R. Yehudah ben Natan, *see* Zak
R. Yehudah of Paris, *Tosafot* of 281, 299–300 n. 21
R. Yehudai Gaon 10 and n. 18, 33, 48, 78, 152 n. 5, 154–5
R. Yishma'el 18, 281, 382
R. Yitsḥak ben Asher of Speyer (Riva) 84 n. 49, 306 n. 34
R. Yitsḥak ben Avraham of Dampierre 276
R. Yitsḥak of Corbeil 279–80
R. Yitsḥak of Dampierre, *see* Ri (ha-Zaken)
R. Yitsḥak ben Dorbelo 184
R. Yitsḥak of Fez, *see* Alfasi
R. Yitsḥak ibn Gi'at 113, 117
R. Yitsḥak ha-Levi of Worms (Segan ha-Levi) 44, 65–6 n. 104, 76, 111
innovative 112–14, 116–17, 119
leading authority of late 11th-cent. Ashkenaz 48, 187
no deference to Babylonian authorities 155, 213
Rashi's teacher 45
ruling on *sekhakh* 57
R. Yitsḥak ben Menaḥem 76 n. 13
R. Yitsḥak Or Zarua' of Vienna 54 n. 71, 84, 89–90, 393
R. Yitsḥak ha-'Orliani (of Orléans) 188–9 n. 78
on presenting oneself as a Gentile 271, 273
R. Yitsḥak ben Yehudah:
attitude to *minhag* 49, 51, 53–4, 57 n. 82, 59–62
influence on Makirites 49
leading authority of late 11th-cent. Ashkenaz 48, 187
mourning on *yom tov* 65 n. 104
Rashi sends talmudic queries to 50, 76, 110–12
responsa of 54, 56, 64, 76; on Birkat Kohanim while in mourning 59; on circumcision on a fast day 51–3; on *pelugat ha-re'ah* 111–12, 119; on *sekhakh* 57–8; strongly based on the Bavli 77; on transportation of wine 110
role in the composition of *Perush Rabbenu Gershom* 50
R. Yitsḥak ben Yitsḥak 76
R. Yom Tov al-Sevilli (Ritva) 38, 83, 117, 250 n. 47
R. Yosef ibn Megas 26, 33–4 n. 10, 126, 209
R. Yosef Tov 'Elem of Limoges 99
responsa of 71, 75, 77
use of biblical verses and *midrashim* in halakhic ruling 86, 95–7

Z

Zak, R. Yehudah ben Natan (Zelkele) 394
R. Zeraḥyah ha-Levi of Lunel (Ba'al ha-Ma'or) 11, 31, 33–4 n. 10
Zfatman, Sara 165 n. 33, 201 n. 112
Zunz, Leopold, on *Sefer Yosippon* 264

Index of Places

A

Aachen 5, 22, 44–5 n. 36, 140–1, 157

Anjou, expulsion of Jews from 272

Arles 185, 214

Ashkenaz:

- ban on vinegar 116
- commentaries: on Talmud 32–3 and n. 10, 164, 172–3 n. 49, 187; on *Tur* 394
- community: alleged isolation of 123; beginnings of 42, 135 n. 22, 161, 193; considered its non-Jewish neighbors barbarians 258–9; involvement in trade 96, 127–9, 136–7, 140, 183, 185; *kehillah kedoshah* a central concept 151, 190–1, 194; knowledge of Aramaic in 126, 161, 163; level of knowledge of in early 11th cent. 75; martyrdom in 229, 250–1, 254, 256 n. 59, 264 n. 80, 267, 284; organization of 76 n. 13, 77, 94–5, 96–9, 101, 105 n. 13; reverence for tradition, greater than in other Diaspora communities 36; self-image 192, 225 n. 7
- culture, halakhic 37, 39, 125, 144, 284; alleged Palestinian origin of 29, 44, 122, 142, 149, 202–3; centrality of Bavli in 43, 70, 100, 102, 142; independence of 200; insularity of 151, 190; origins of 151, 156–7, 202–3, 208
- curriculum: *'Avodah Zarah* not included in 147, 192; includes tractates unstudied in Sura/Pumbedita 33–4, 42–3, 163–4, 169, 187, 189, 204
- has no foundation myth 198–201
- indifference to surrounding culture 177–8, 192
- liturgy 59–1, 113, 142–3, 193, 250
- manuscript traditions of Talmud 114 n. 25, 123–5, 140, 196
- martyrdom in, *see* Index of Subjects: martyrdom
- *minhag*, role of in 29, 42, 55–6
- no disparity between popular and elite conduct 58
- Palestinian origins of 29, 44, 122, 142–3; in halakhah, alleged 5, 13, 19–21, 141, 145–7, 202–3; in liturgy and ritual 113, 122–3, 142–3, 145–6, 162, 193
- priestly blessing no longer recited daily in 59–60
- responsa 36, 120
- rite, Palestinian influence on 122, 142, 145–6
- scholars, *see* Early Ashkenaz
- self-image 36, 190, 192, 201 n. 112
- survival of rabbinic literature in 33, 38
- Talmud-centric intellectual life 86
- *see also* Early Ashkenaz; France; Germany

B

Babylonia:

- academies 72, 82; attitude to Geonate 166, 176–8, 186, 206–7; editing of Talmud in multiple centers 165–7, 170, 172–6, 194–8, 205–6; Sura and Pumbedita, *see* Sura and Pumbedita; Third Yeshivah, *see* Index of Subjects: Third Yeshivah of Bavel
- agricultural society until Muslim conquest 168, 190
- Aramaic 125 n. 8, 126, 160–1, 163, 187, 208, 211–12
- clash of cultures after Abbasid takeover 176, 178, 180–5, 190, 201, 206
- contact with Ashkenaz 137, 140–1, 143, 185, 203
- custom, role of in 44
- founding fathers of Ashkenazic culture came from 182, 184–5, 187, 189, 193, 207, 210
- halakhah 10–12, 16, 18–19, 203; followed in Early Ashkenaz 209
- Jewish population 167, 176, 194
- migration to Ashkenaz from 158, 163, 185;

impact of 187, 189; reasons for 170, 175, 181, 184, 190–1, 206
orientation of scholars: in Early Ashkenaz 17, 22, 94, 141, 159, 203–4; in Italy 19, 21; in Kairouan 22
orthography, in Ashkenazic manuscripts 124
rite 112, 143, 146; followed in Early Ashkenaz 17, 194
Talmud, *see* Index of Subjects: Bavli
tradition 12, 14–15, 18, 87; on martyrdom, restrictive 266, 283–4
Baghdad 129, 134–5, 140, 176, 178 n. 57
Abbasid capital 179, 181 n. 61, 184
Jews living outside 167
yeshivot of Sura and Pumbedita move to 163
Bari 193
Bavel, *see* Babylonia
Black Sea 127, 185, 214
Breslau, anti-Jewish decrees of church council 273
Byzantium 185, 214

C
Cairo, *see* Index of Subjects: Cairo Genizah
Catalonia 25, 37, 38 n. 20
Champagne 114 n. 25, 115–16, 125 n. 8
Cologne 43–5, 79, 110–11
Constantinople 128–9, 137
Córdoba 288

D
Damascus 140, 179, 181 n. 61
Dampierre 238

E
Early Ashkenaz (*c.*950–1096), lands of:
alleged use of biblical passages and aggadah in 70–1, 82, 85–6, 90–1, 93–5, 97–8, 102–3
Babylonian orientation of 17, 22, 94, 141, 159, 203–4
contact with Bavel 137, 140–1, 143, 185, 203
founding fathers of 182, 184–5, 187, 189, 193, 207, 210
'fragment society' 192–3
historiography of 107, 136, 145, 148, 268
Jewish settlement in 42–3, 44–5 n. 36, 135 n. 22, 157, 193–4; allegedly from the Mediterranean 143–4; by the Kalonymides 43, 142, 156 n. 13, 193 and n. 91, 198–9; from the Third Yeshivah of Bavel 158, 163–4, 170, 175, 184–7
levels of knowledge among population of 75
Ma'aseh ha-Ge'onim, see Index of Subjects: *Ma'aseh ha-Ge'onim*
Mainz Commentary, see Index of Subjects: *Perush Rabbenu Gershom*
popular practice in 30–1, 35, 40, 42, 141 n. 37; allegedly overrides the Talmud 29; justified by Tosafists 36 and n. 13, 44 n. 36, 58–9; *see also* Index of Subjects: *minhag*
religious regimen altered by tosafist revolution 30, 190
respect for ancestors' wisdom in 36
rich culture from mid-10th cent. on 157–8
role of Bavli in 43, 70–2, 100, 122, 142, 145, 151
scholars of 46 n. 39, 48, 61, 71, 264; Aramaic-speakers 126, 161–3, 170, 187, 208, 211; attitude to Geonim 168, 177, 179, 181–2, 187, 200–1; control a large library 158; culture of anonymity among 155, 175, 188–9 n. 79, 201, 214; experienced and confident *posekim* 158, 168; explicate tractates of Bavli not studied in Sura and Pumbedita 33–4, 42–3, 163–4, 169, 187, 189, 204; French-speakers 215; on martyrdom, *see* Index of Subjects: martyrdom; no deference to the Geonim 168, 177, 179, 181–2, 187, 200–1; 'Puritan migration' of 158, 163, 170, 175, 181, 184–7, 190–1
talmudic commentaries in 32–3 and n. 10, 71, 187; all-encompassing 42–3, 61, 149, 158–9, 161, 164; included aggadic passages 159, 161, 210–11; lack Rashi's clarity 33; mostly lost 33; novel scope of 33, 207; *sub verbo* 32 and n. 7, 35 and n. 12, 51, 62–4, 157–9
wealth of 141, 183

Early Ashkenaz (*cont.*):
Yerushalmi marginal in 80, 149, 158–9, 163, 203
see also Ashkenaz; France; Germany
England 199
persecution of Jews in 272, 273 n. 112, 280–1
trade in kosher wine 110, 115

F
Fez 161, 203, 288, 316, 355
France:
academies of 23
anti-Jewish measures of Louis IX 272–3
communal organization in 96, 99
emergence of *Tosafot* in 12th cent. 23
persecution in 38, 272–3, 280–1
religious regimen altered by tosafist revolution 30
Roman law appears in 40–1
Fustat 140, 143, 166–7, 186, 211

G
Gascony, expulsion of Jews from 272
Germany:
alleged emergence of *Tosafot* in 11th cent. 23
Good Werner pogrom 272
imperial power protects against antisemitism 269, 272
Jewish badge 273
no empire-wide expulsion 38
no independent urban centers in 10th–11th cents. 128
pre-Crusade wave of popular piety 260
Rintfleisch massacres 273
wine shipped to England from 110
see also Ashkenaz; Early Ashkenaz

I
Ingelheim 128, 140
Italy 113, 137, 185, 188, 263, 394
contact with Rhineland 129, 282
piyyut in 123, 142, 162, 193, 266
southern, alleged shift from Palestinian to Babylonian orientation 19–21

J
Jerusalem 137, 140, 184, 284

K
Kairouan 54–5, 59, 167, 185
Babylonian orientation in 22 n. 52, 124, 160, 166, 200, 203
contact with Rhineland 129
Pirkoi ben Baboi 10
religious autonomy of 199
Koblenz, massacre of 1265 251

L
Languedoc 38 n. 28, 41
Le Mans 193
Limoges 96–7
Lorraine 125 n. 8
Lotharingia 44–5 n. 36, 111, 141 and n. 37, 143–4
Lotir, *see* Lotharingia
Lucca 188 n. 78, 193
Kalonymide move from 43, 142, 156 n. 13, 193, 199
Lyons 16
archbishop of 5, 13
Jews of, follow Babylonian halakhah 5, 22, 157
significant Jewish presence 44–5 n. 36

M
Magentsa, *see* Mainz
Maghreb 143
Almohad persecution 223, 229, 332
Babylonian influence 124, 140, 155 and n. 11, 166
curriculum in 159 n. 21
see also Kairouan
Maḥoza 165
Mainz:
academy 71, 80, 85, 161; curriculum of 191; disregard for Geonim 156; exegesis of Talmud in 31–2, 33–4 n. 10, 61, 63, 84 n. 49, 188 n. 78, 209; founded in mid-10th cent. 157–8, 185, 214; subgroups of 160
Commentary, *see* Index of Subjects: *Perush Rabbenu Gershom*
economic role of 127–9, 135 n. 22, 183
Ingelheim, imperial palace, close to 127–8
Jewish self-government 97
Kalonymide relocation to 43, 142, 193, 199

local customs in 40, 47–9, 66, 79
relocation of Third Yeshivah to 158, 170, 175, 183, 186, 214
viticulture around 109–10
R. Yehudah ha-Kohen based in 47–8
R. Yitsḥak ben Yehudah based in 49
Masada 262, 265–6
Mecca 292, 313, 316
Medina (Yathrib), massacre of Jews at 330
Morocco 324, 326, 346, 362
apostasy of Jews in 303, 314, 316, 363; despair over their situation 289, 312, 316, 320, 352; Maimonides' *Iggeret ha-Shemad* in response to 290, 304, 329, 346, 356
persecution of Jews in 288, 294

N
Narbonne 33–4 n. 10, 37, 44, 203
Nevers, expulsion of Jews from 272

O
Otranto 193, 266

P
Palestine 82–3, 114
academies 82
directives sent to Bavel (*shalḥu mi-tam*) 82
halakhah: allegedly followed by European Jews 5, 13, 19–21, 145–7, 203; attitude to martyrdom and suicide 262, 265–6, 282, 284; in conflict with Babylonian 9–11, 14–17, 20, 29; in disagreement with Agobard's description 16
influence on Ashkenaz: in attitude to martyrdom, alleged 229, 232, 262, 265–6, 282–4; in custom 22, 114; in halakhah, alleged 5, 13, 17, 146–8, 202–3; in liturgy 141–3, 146, 148, 162, 194; in ritual 122, 145–6
influence on Italian Jewry 19–22, 142, 162, 265
origin of Ashkenaz, alleged 29, 44, 122, 142–3, 149, 158, 229; insufficient evidence for 141, 146–7, 202–3
origin of *piyyut* 162, 193
rite, followed in minor matters by Ashkenazic Jews 55, 142, 146, 148, 194
Talmud, *see* Index of Subjects: Yerushalmi
traditions 12, 14, 18–19; definition 15
Paris, persecution of Jews in 272–3
Poitiers, expulsion of Jews from 272
Provence:
gap between popular and elite conduct in 58
literature of 41, 155, 254, 277–8; ignored by most Tosafists 384; manuscripts published by M. Y. H. Blau 38; *Sefer Asufot* published by B. Z. Benedict 37; *Shitah lo Noda' le-Mi 'al Kiddushin* 37; talmudic exegesis 33–4 n. 10, 37–8, 44, 159; *Temim De'im* 286; *Teshuvot Ḥakhmei Provintsya* 37
reverence of Geonim 155, 177
Spanish exiles import Judeo-Arabic culture to 178
traditional practice 31, 35–6, 60, 113
Pumbedita, academy of, *see* Sura and Pumbedita

R
Ramlah 140
Rheims 96, 115
Rhineland:
academies of 30, 116, 125, 187
centrality and affluence of 128, 140, 143, 183, 191
command of Aramaic among Jewish settlers in 125 n. 8, 161, 163, 212–13
extensive connections of 128–9, 140–1, 185
first Jewish settlement in 42–3, 157
French spoken by Jews of 215
martyrdom of Jews in 229, 265 n. 80, 282, 284
pre-Crusade scholarship of 28 n. 11, 32, 40, 70, 148, 204
range of talmudic texts available to scholars in 114 n. 25
scholars of, disregard Geonim 177
Third Yeshivah's move to 158, 170, 175, 183, 186, 214
wine trade in 110, 115–16, 191
Rhone 185
Rome 44, 160, 188–9 n. 78, 259

S
Sens 96
Spain 113, 124, 129, 180

foundation myth of community in 200
literature of 30, 140, 160 n. 22, 178; only greatest works survive 38; reverence for Geonim 155, 166, 177; talmudic manuscript tradition 123–4, 277
mass conversion of Jews in 223–4, 226, 289 n. 2
persecution: by the Almohads 178; expulsion of 1492 224; 'great persecution' of 1391 224; Jewish responses to 223–4, 226–7
role of custom in 36
Talmud scholarship in 159, 196, 199, 283, 308
trade connections of 129, 141
Speyer 40, 260
Sura and Pumbedita, academies of 137, 184, 187, 194, 207
almost no discussion of martyrdom in 228
authority of 72, 85, 154–6, 166, 175, 178–9
curriculum of 33, 163 and n. 31, 165 and n. 35, 168–9, 180, 209–10
invested in oral transmission 134, 171–2, 174–5, 196–7, 205
move to Baghdad 163
overshadow the rest of Bavel 166, 170, 175, 194
unstudied (*lashon meshunah*) tractates 33, 163–5, 169, 172–3, 187, 204, 207–9; *Keritut* (*Karetot*) 33, 163, 172–3 n. 49, 316; *Me'ilah* 33, 163–4, 191; *Nazir* 33, 62, 163 and n. 32, 168, 180, 191; *Nedarim* 33, 62, 163 and n. 32, 165, 168–9; *Tamid* 33, 163; *Temurah* 33, 163–4, 173, 191

T

Tiberias 140
Troyes 95–8, 110, 112, 125
blood libel and execution of Jews in 272
liturgical tradition in 114 n. 25, 117

V

Venice 127 and n. 12, 141
Vienna, anti-Jewish decrees of church council 273

W

Worms 119, 184
academy of 23–4, 32, 61, 71, 125
local custom in 40, 66, 113, 114 n. 22, 116
martyrdom of Jews in 262
privileges granted by Henry IV to the community of 260
wine trade in 109–10

Y

Yathrib (Medina), massacre of Jews at 330
Yemen 123–5, 140–1, 395
culture of 143, 388
persecution in 223, 317

Index of Subjects

A

Abbasid Caliphate 179, 181 n. 61, 184, 201

abutment, right of (*bar metsra*) 89–90

academies:

of Bavel, outside Sura/Pumbedita 198; attitude to the Geonate 166, 176–8, 186, 206–7; inscription of Talmud in 165–6, 170, 172–3, 176, 195–7, 205–6

of France 23, 30–1

of Mainz, *see* Index of Places: Mainz

of Palestine 82

of Rhineland 30, 116, 125, 187

Sura and Pumbedita, *see* Index of Places: Sura and Pumbedita

'Third Yeshivah', *see* Third Yeshivah of Bavel

Worms 23–4, 32, 61, 71, 125

acculturation vs. assimilation 192

aggadah:

invocation of, in halakhic reasoning 70–1, 88, 93–4; only when no guidance is found in Bavli 72–3, 101, 104, 202, 235, 243

talmudic, exegesis of, innovation of Early Ashkenazic scholars 159, 161, 206, 210–11

used by Maimonides in his defense of Marranos 301, 316, 318–19

used by Tosafists to justify suicide 101, 234–5, 241–3

see also *midrashim*

aggadic prescriptions, not valid if contradicted by halakhic ones 235

amora'im 14–15, 54, 182, 185

annulment by one court of the decrees of another 98–9

anonymity:

discarded by the Geonim 168, 176, 181, 206

practiced in talmudic exegesis by Early Ashkenazic scholars 155, 156 n. 12, 175, 188–9 n. 79, 201, 214

practiced in the unnamed academies of Bavel 176, 181, 197, 206

uniformly employed in amoraic responsa and savoraic writings 166–7, 201

anusim, *see* Marranos

apostasy, *see* conversion

apotropsut, *see* guardianship

Aramaic 73, 161, 188, 207

Ashkenazic *piyyutim* written in 162

command of, among scholars of Early Ashkenaz 126, 161–3, 170, 187, 208, 211

Eastern vs. Western 211

familiarity with, among Jews of late 11th-cent. Ashkenaz 160, 162–3, 212

lack of familiarity with, among Jews of early 11th-cent. Ashkenaz 72, 73 n. 4, 125 n. 8

possibly language of instruction in Ashkenazic *battei midrash* 212

Arba'ah Turim (*Tur*) 370–1, 375, 379, 386, 391

authority of 393–5

assimilation vs. acculturation 192

autonomy, local communal 96–7

avelut, *see* mourning

avizaraihu de-'avodah zarah 248 nn. 40, 42

'avodah zarah, *see* idolatry

'Avodah Zarah (tractate):

not studied in Rhineland academies 116, 147, 191–2

returned by Rashi to the curriculum 30, 192

textual variants of 124–5

avot melakhot 375, 378–9, 383

see also *melakhot*

B

Ba'alei ha-Tosafot, *see* Tosafists

bailment, laws of, in *Mishneh Torah* 369–70, 372–3

Banu Qurayza, Jewish tribe massacred by Mohammed 226 n. 9, 330

baptism, *see* conversion

bar metsra, *see* abutment, right of

Bava Batra 38, 96, 316

Bava Batra (*cont.*):
on coercing others to give charity 97–8
laws of inheritance in 92
Mainz commentary on 33
on mourning for grandparents 81, 84–5
Bava Metsi'a 37–8, 123, 125
Bavli:
authority of, in Early Ashkenaz 70–2, 122, 142, 145, 151
contradictions in 25–7, 171, 230
Early Ashkenazic exegesis of 31–3 and n. 8, 71, 207; all-encompassing 42–3, 61, 149, 158–9, 161, 164; anonymous 188–9; included aggadic passages 159, 161, 210–11; Mainz Commentary, see *Perush Rabbenu Gershom*; Rashi's 30–1, 50, 62–3, 187; *sub verbo* 32 and n. 7, 35 and n. 12, 51, 62–4, 157–9; *see also* lemmata
editing of 163 n. 31, 165 and n. 34, 170–6, 195, 204–6
inscription of 172, 196, 205; completed by mid-8th cent. 174, 195, 205; took place outside Sura/Pumbedita 172–3, 175, 205
North African exegesis of 32–3, 35, 126, 159 and n. 21, 196
oral transmission of 171–2, 196–7, 205
Palestinian traditions in 14–15
Provençal exegesis of 31, 33–4 n. 10, 37–8, 44, 159
Romm edition of 32 n. 6, 83 n. 47, 151; commentaries of Early Ashkenazic scholars in 33 n. 8, 163 n. 32, 164; containing *Perush Rabbenu Gershom* 31, 62–3, 149
study of: all-encompassing in Early Ashkenaz 33, 164, 186–7, 190, 192, 208–10; horizontal vs. vertical 26; selective, pragmatic 33, 180, 186; tractates not taught in Sura and Pumbedita 163–5, 169, 187, 204
text of, variant manuscripts 123, 149, 171, 196; emendation of, forbidden by R. Gershom 125–6
Benei ha-Makhiri, *see* Index of Names: Makirites
besamim, recitation of blessing over 77–81, 147
Bet ha-Beḥirah 37
Bet Yosef 386, 395
Bible:
commentary 4, 182, 254
passages of, in the Rosh Hashanah service 112, 116–17
verses of, allegedly used in halakhic reasoning by Ashkenazic scholars 70–1, 82, 85–6, 90–1, 93–5, 97–8, 102–3; justified when no guidance is found in Bavli 72–3, 88, 202; in a suasive function 92, 100
Birkat Kohanim, *see* priestly blessing
Book of Acquisition (*Mishneh Torah*) 370
Book of Adoration (*Mishneh Torah*) 368, 371
Book of Holiness (*Mishneh Torah*) 371 n. 4
Book of Knowledge (*Mishneh Torah*) 371
Book of Torts (*Mishneh Torah*) 369–70

C
Cairo Genizah 114, 226 n. 9, 373, 392 n. 34
anonymous Babylonian works in 167, 175, 197
does not inform us of unofficial centers of learning in Bavel 166
manuscript variants found in 123, 124 n. 4, 140, 152 n. 5
presents a partial picture 172, 174–5, 182, 204, 206, 210
source of information on liturgy 146
source of most of our knowledge of Geonim 166
Carolingian Empire 44–5 n. 36, 137, 143
Jews of, allegedly follow Palestinian halakhah 6, 17, 22, 141
Catalonian school of dialectics 25, 37
child murder:
allegedly justified in Palestinian sources 262, 265–7
appears in Crusade chronicles and in liturgy 264 n. 80
became a cultural norm in Ashkenaz 270, 284
justified by Tosafists 101, 229, 270
to prevent their apostasy 228–9, 234, 250–1, 254–60, 268–9
Christianity 27, 134, 192, 390
conversion to, *see* conversion
positive view of martyrdom in 225–6, 228, 275

profession of, under persecution 272 n. 105, 281
repulsive to Ashkenazic Jews 258–9, 268–9 n. 92
Christians 15, 134–5
non-kosher meat sold to 5–6, 16
persecuted by the Almohads 330, 357
raising Jewish children, fear of 101, 228, 231, 250, 254, 259, 260–1
trade with 136–7, 191
see also Gentiles
circumcision:
on a fast day 51–3
laws of, in *Mishneh Torah* 368, 371–2
to precede *shofar*-blowing 86
coercion 99, 247 n. 38, 348
to give to charity 97–8
kefiyyah/'issui 97–8
in the Mishnah in *Nedarim* 307–8, 352
monetary 352–3
religious 319, 329–30, 344, 349; absolute vs. relative 232–3, 239; mental reservations when subjected to 294, 297–9, 347–8, 351, 354; not culpable according to Maimonides 305–7, 310–11, 321–3, 346, 354, 356, 362; in public (*be-farhesya*) vs. in private (*be-tsin'ah*) 233, 265, 281, 309, 363; sins committed under 294–5, 303 n. 27
Commentary on the Mishnah (Maimonides), see *Perush ha-Mishnayot*
communal practice, in Ashkenaz 36 n. 13, 40, 55
conversion, forced 223, 272, 278, 363
of children 260, 269, 278; protection granted by Henry IV against 260
communal 223–7
forbidden in Christianity and Islam 223
Jewish responses to 225 n. 7, 259, 266; in Ashkenaz 226, 257–61, 267–9, 280, 324; in Islamic countries 224–6, 289 nn. 1–2, 324; in Spain 224, 226–7
in Yemen 317
conversion to Judaism, laws of, in *Mishneh Torah* 370–2
Crusade, First 261, 268
chronicles of 250, 259 n. 68; martyrdom highly valued in 264 n. 80; selective and hortatory 267, 282; speeches of martyrs in 262, 266
communal conduct during 229, 231, 254, 268–9, 282
preceded by wave of popular piety in rural Germany 260
religious atmosphere during 260, 269
religious persecution in 228
Rhineland academies destroyed in 187
Crusade, Third, chronicle of 267
custom, see *minhag*

D
damages, laws of, in *Mishneh Torah* 353, 369
De Insolentia Iudaeorum 5, 8, 16, 18
derashot 85–6, 91–3, 95 and n. 80, 243 n. 30
allegedly invented by Rabbenu Gershom 91
invoked by R. Yehudah Ba'al Sefer ha-Dinim 94 n. 78
dialectic:
Christian, influence of 23, 27–8
definition of 25–6
Rabbenu Sasson's alleged use of 24–5
scholastic vs. Socratic 25
Tosafists' method of study 23, 25
various meanings of 25
dibbur hamatḥil, see lemmata; *sub verbo* exegesis
Differences between the Men of the East and Those Who Dwell in Erets Yisra'el 20
direct inheritance of grandchildren 81–4, 94 n. 78, 95
distinction, a tosafist tool 25, 27, 39

E
Early Ashkenaz, *see* Index of Places: Early Ashkenaz
Eikhah Rabbati, editorial revision of 174
ein sheliḥut le-goy 108–9
elite conduct vs. popular conduct 58
Epistle on Martyrdom, see *Iggeret ha-Shemad*
Epistle to 'Ovadyah the Convert 326, 371
Esau, a symbol for Christianity 259
Eshkol ha-Kofer 380 n. 5
excommunication 75, 96–9
exegesis:
biblical 4, 160, 182, 212

exegesis (*cont.*):
of Talmud 33–4 n. 10, 164; in Early Ashkenaz 31–3, 149, 161 n. 25, 209, 211; included aggadic passages 159, 161, 210; Mainz Commentary, see *Perush Rabbenu Gershom*; Rashi's 30–1, 50, 62, 187; *sub verbo* 32, 35 and n. 12, 51, 62–4, 157–9
expulsion 38, 272
'extracurricular' tractates, *see under* Bavli: study of

F

fasting on the Sabbath 19, 21
festival, see *yom tov*
florilegia 61 and n. 94, 148, 158 n. 18, 278
of R. Mordekhai ben Hillel 37
from Rashi's academy 30
'fragment society' 192–3
free will vs. coercion 304, 322
French, spoken by Jews of Rhineland 215

G

gall bladder, see *terefot*
garsanim 134, 171, 197, 205
Gentiles:
accounts of Jewish rites 8
bread, forbidden 19–20
culture, Jewish response to 177, 182–3, 186, 192
Jew posing as 270–2, 274, 356–7
Jew serving as agent of 107–8
laws applying to 253, 349
selling non-kosher meat and wine to 5–6, 16
sending meat via 13
slaughter 8
trade with 44–5 n. 36, 136–7, 190–1
wine, ban on 109, 115–16, 141, 146, 151, 190–1
work done on the Sabbath by 374, 379–81
Geonate 140, 177–8, 180
a creation of the Abbasid Caliphate 179, 201
emergence of 166, 176, 179, 181 n. 61
not authoritative in Ashkenaz 177, 206, 214
see also Geonim
Geonim 77–8, 140, 166, 168, 206, 390
authority of 72, 85, 153, 203
halakhic monographs of 135, 152 n. 5
no monopoly of knowledge or of authority in Babylonia itself 165, 167–8, 175, 178, 210
responsa of 32, 152 n. 5, 167; cited anonymously in Early Ashkenaz 155, 156 n. 12; focus on contemporary needs 168, 186
scholars of Early Ashkenaz show no deference to 153–4, 168, 177, 179, 181–2, 186–7, 213
seemingly unaware of *Midrash Rabbah* 174
talmudic exegesis of 26, 32, 165
German Pietists (Ḥasidei Ashkenaz) 103–4, 243, 274–5, 279 n. 137
Good Werner pogrom 272
grandchildren:
direct inheritance of 81–4, 94 n. 78, 95
mourning for grandparents 47–8, 83, 84 and n. 49
guardianship (*apotropsut*) 90
Guide of the Perplexed 312, 315 n. 58, 350, 368, 389, 392

H

haftarah, changes made locally to 48, 54–6, 59
Haggahot Asheri 393
Haggahot Maimuniyot 85, 385, 387, 388 n. 30, 393
halakhah:
Babylonian vs. Palestinian 9–12, 19–21, 147, 149
ground rules of 220–1, 332–3
history of 3–4, 70–1, 73, 106, 146–8
insularity of Ashkenaz in 151, 190
level of knowledge of, in Ashkenaz 42
'measurable deflection' 231–2
vs. *minhag* 29, 42, 44, 49, 54, 59–61, 73
halakhic arguments, use of aggadah in 71–3, 82, 86–90, 94, 101–5
halakhic literature, surviving, of Ashkenaz 37–9
Halakhot Gedolot 48, 106, 164, 172–3 n. 49, 208
Ashkenazic lack of deference to 118–21, 154–5, 213
Palestinian influence on 12
variant texts of 12 n. 26, 152 n. 5
Halakhot Pesukot 152 and n. 5, 181 n. 61
Rabbenu Gershom's lack of deference to 153, 156, 210
hashavat avedah/gezelah (returning lost/stolen property) 99, 369–70

hasidim have no special aspiration to martyrdom 275–6
Ḥasidei Ashkenaz, *see* German Pietists
havdalah 77–80, 147
Hebrew, command of, in Ashkenaz 72–3, 75
hefker bet din hefker 94
heresy 298–9, 302, 318, 350, 357–8
  definition of 293 and n. 8, 327, 335–6
  equated with idolatry by Maimonides 325, 346–8
Hilkhot Sheḥitah of Eldad ha-Dani 13, 15
ḥillul ha-shem 310, 320–1
  avoidance of martyrdom regarded as 225, 351
  false oaths constitute 307, 353–4
  Maimonides' treatment of 307–9, 320–3, 334–5, 350–1, 353–4, 362–3
ḥillul Shabbat, charge of, against Marranos 304 n. 30
hiring (*sekhirut*), laws of, in *Mishneh Torah* 368, 372

I
idolatry 272 n. 105
  acting like a Gentile regarded as 356–7
  Christianity as 258
  coerced, requires martyrdom 266, 276–7, 281, 305, 346
  forbidden to Gentiles 349
  hana'at 'atsmo in 348–50
  the idol of Nebuchadnezzar, rabbinic discussions of 244–6, 248
  Islam as 290–1, 317, 322, 326, 362; recitation of *shahada* 293–4, 326–7, 347–8, 356–7
  laws of, in *Mishneh Torah* 371
  Maimonides' equation of heresy with 325, 327, 348
  Maimonides' redefinition of 291, 293, 295, 306, 327, 343–4; distinction between word and deed 295, 297–300, 311, 317, 323, 348, 350
  requirement of inner belief for 295–7, 326, 328–9, 342, 345
  talmudic definition of 295–6
Iggeret ha-Shemad 290, 293, 304 n. 30, 362
  editions of 289 n. 1, 290 n. 3
  flawed reasoning in 325, 330 n. 88, 340–1, 345–6, 350, 352
  on *ḥillul ha-shem* 307–9, 320–3, 334–5, 350–1, 353–4, 362–3
  on importance of prayer for the Marranos 301, 318 and n. 64, 358
  incompatible with Maimonides' early writings 325, 327–8, 342
  as a legal work 340–1, 346, 355–7
  martyrdom (*kiddush ha-shem*) in 295, 297, 305–7, 310, 322, 334–5; omitted from discussion of *ḥillul ha-shem* 309–10, 321, 350–1, 363
  a response to the Marranos' ostrich policy 320
  textual variants of 354, 359–61
  use of aggadah in 301, 316, 318–19
  on voluntary martyrdom 330 n. 88
  word–deed distinction in 295, 297–300, 311, 317, 323, 348, 350
  a work of rhetoric 288, 312, 315 n. 58, 325, 329, 332
informers, execution of 102–3, 286
Islam 225 n. 7
  acceptance of is heresy 295 n. 14, 316, 322, 357–8
  forbids forced conversion 223
  as idolatry 290–4, 326, 336
  imperative to die for Allah in battle 225
  involvement in slave trade 135–6
  Jews converting to 226–7, 289, 314, 316–17
  monotheistic according to Maimonides 292, 317, 347, 362
  shahada as vow 351
  taqiyya (lit. caution, i.e. dissimulation) in times of persecution 225
'issui 98
  see also *kefiyyah*

J
Jewish–Gentile relations 190–1
Jews:
  arrogance of, described by Agobard 5, 16, 44–5 n. 36
  required to wear badge 273
  resent Christian oppression 259
Judeo-Arabic culture 178, 182, 186, 190, 206
Judeo-Iranian culture 181–2, 206
judicial formalism vs. realism 219

K

kallah (scholarly gathering) 195–6
Karaites 185
daily interaction with Rabbanites 383
Maimonides' polemic against 380, 384, 392
Sabbath laws of 380–3, 392
war against 169
kefiyyah 97–8
see also *'issui*
kehillah kedoshah, a unique self-image of Ashkenaz 151, 190–1, 194
Kesef Mishneh 296 n. 16, 386 and n. 27, 395
ke-targumo 160, 212
kiddush, combined with *havdalah* 77–80, 147
kiddush ha-shem, *see* martyrdom
Kitsur Sefer ha-Mitsvot (*Semag*) 256 n. 59, 270
Kodashim:
contains most *lashon meshunah* tractates 173 n. 50
included in its entirety in Ashkenazic curriculum 33–4, 42, 159 and n. 21, 163, 189, 210
only parts of it studied in Sura and Pumbedita 33, 163, 169
kohen:
apostate, who has repented 76, 87–8
in mourning 59
see also priestly blessing
kosher meat 6, 13–14, 16
Kuntresim (*Notebooks*) 246–7

L

lashon meshunah tractates 163–5, 172–3, 187, 204, 207–9
Lateran Council, prescribes Jewish badge 273
'Laws of Borrowing and Bailment' (*Mishneh Torah*) 372–3
'Laws of Forbidden Sexual Relations' (*Mishneh Torah*) 370
'Laws of the Fundamentals of Faith' (*Mishneh Torah*) 371
'Laws of Hire' (*Mishneh Torah*) 368, 372–3
'Laws of Idolatry' (*Mishneh Torah*) 371
'Laws of Litigation' (*Mishneh Torah*) 377
'Laws of the Nazir' (*Mishneh Torah*) 393
'Laws of Repentance' (*Mishneh Torah*) 371
'Laws of Robbery and Lost Property' (*Mishneh Torah*) 369
'Laws of the Sabbath' (*Mishneh Torah*) 373, 384, 390–2
problematic structure 375–6, 378, 381
response to Karaite challenge 384
Leket Yosher 38, 393
lemmata, initial and embedded 63–4
see also *sub verbo*
lishna aḥarina in *Temurah* 173
liturgical poetry, see *piyyut*
liturgy, Ashkenazic 60–1, 73, 78, 142–3
has a life of its own 60, 194
slow to change 117, 194
variegated origins of 141–3, 146, 194
liver, punctured or missing, see *terefot*
lung, see *terefot*

M

ma'arufya 107–9, 137
Ma'aseh ha-Ge'onim 30, 37–8, 47, 49, 113, 187
anonymous geonic material in 155
authored by the Makirites 29, 35, 66
halakhic rulings in 40, 80, 93 n. 77
minhag constitutes small part in 35, 40
significance trivial in comparison with Talmud commentary 32, 35
Ma'aseh ha-Makhiri 147
Ma'aseh Roke'aḥ 105 and n. 13
Magen Avraham 56, 385–6
Maḥzor Vitry 30, 78–9 n. 23, 187
Mainz Commentary, see *Perush Rabbenu Gershom*
Marranos, in Morocco 289 and n. 2, 346, 356 n. 9
defended by Maimonides 291, 293–4, 298, 304–5, 318–19, 347
nature of the transgression of 291, 294, 303 n. 27, 304 and n. 30, 322
paralysed by guilt 313–14, 320, 352
prayer has important purgative function for 300–1, 358
religious observance of 302–3, 311, 318, 334, 342–3, 359
martyrdom:
aggadic sources on 229, 234–5, 237–46, 283–4

among Jews in Islamic lands 289–90, 293 n. 8
application to Noahides 266 n. 84
in Ashkenaz 264 n. 80; generates sudden writing of chronicles 267; not discussed in pre-Crusade sources 262, 269; real and alleged Palestinian influence on 262, 265–6, 283–4
attitude to, in Christianity and Judaism vs. Islam 224–6, 228
discussions of, halakhically often problematic 228–9, 235–61, 282
en masse 226 n. 9, 229, 261–2, 284
German Pietists on 274–6
imperative of 311; in the face of forbidden sexual relations 236; in the face of idolatry 248, 281, 327, 378 n. 2; overrides *pikuaḥ nefesh* 306; under private vs. public coercion 233, 265, 281, 309, 336, 363
laws of, set out in Talmud 235, 261, 265–6, 270, 276, 293
legal distinctions, important in 232
little discussed in talmudic literature 228
Maimonides' definition of 233, 295, 297, 305, 307; applied to the Almohad persecution 289 n. 1, 294, 296–7, 322; problematic 291–312, 330; in *Sefer ha-Mitsvot* 329
omitted from Maimonides' discussion of *ḥillul ha-shem* 309–10, 321, 350–1, 363
Rabbenu Tam on 236, 238–45, 248–9, 283
in *Sefer Yosippon* 262, 265–6, 284
Spanish Jews cannot fulfill the demand of 226–7
voluntary 269–70, 270 n. 96, 276–7; Ashkenazic views on, change in late 13th cent. 276, 280; based on aggadah 234, 252; forbidden by Maimonides and others 233–4, 250 n. 47, 276, 330; justified by Tosafists 36, 103, 232, 250–2, 255–7, 279–80; strange reasoning 231, 247; in the Talmud 265, 277–8, 283–4
'measurable deflection' 219–21, 230–1, 254, 273–4
meat, *see* kosher meat; pork
Megillat Aḥima'ats 3, 5, 19, 200
mekom ha-sheḥitah 7 n. 11
melakhot 373–5, 378–9, 381, 383
see also *avot melakhot*
mepakh shevu'ah, *see* oaths: inversion of
merchants, Jewish 96, 136–7, 140, 183, 185
on Europe's trade routes 127, 129
participate in trade with East 127
purveyors to courts 137
Radhanites 128
messianism, in late 11th-cent. Germany 268
Ashkenaz/Sefarad dichotomy 315 n. 38
midrashim 14, 157–8, 188, 265, 318
customs rooted in 73
editorial revisions of, in Bavel 174
halakhists rely on 88, 93–7, 100, 105 n. 13, 333; to justify voluntary martyrdom 244, 249–50, 253, 262, 284
never used in certain cases 103–4
often invoked in Early Askhenaz 75, 86, 101
Palestinian traditions embedded in 15
quoted by Maimonides in *Iggeret ha-Shemad* 302, 316, 356
milah, *see* circumcision
mimetic religion 41, 43, 135, 383
minhag:
adherence to, in Ashkenaz: allegedly of Palestinian origin 29, 142–3, 150, 167; of Rabbenu Sasson, alleged 116–18
allegedly central in *Ma'aseh ha-Ge'onim* 29–30, 36, 40
Ashkenaz ha-Kadmon 3, 46–7, 62, 148, 202–3
avoteinu Torah 49–52
controlling in civil law 47 n. 44, 62
different meanings of 40
invoked by R. Yitsḥak ben Yehudah 49–50, 52, 57–9, 61, 64
mevattel halakhah 29, 44
often has aggadic justification 73, 101, 105 n. 13
written law superior to 42, 44, 60
Mishneh Torah 308–9, 328–9
artistic dimension of 387–90, 393
classification of laws in 367–9, 377, 390; problems of 372–3, 375–6, 378–9

Mishneh Torah (*cont.*):
commentaries on 254, 376, 385–6, 387 n. 28, 388 n. 30, 395
multiple levels of meaning in 367, 375
never became the basis of another larger work 385–7, 393, 395
no supercommentaries on 386
as polemic 384, 390–2
Semag partly based on 276, 384
see also under titles of individual books and laws
Mo'ed Katan 81, 84–5, 92, 96
Early Ashkenazic commentaries on 33, 62
Rabad's commentary on 384
moneylending 36, 44–5 n. 36, 95, 107–8
Moreh Nevukhim, see *Guide of the Perplexed*
mosrim, *see* informers
mourning:
of grandchildren for grandparents 47–8, 81, 83–4
of *kohanim* 59
laws of, in *Mishneh Torah* 368
on Purim 90, 103
on second day of festivals 65–6, 93 n. 77
murder 252–3, 285–6
of children, *see* child murder
distinction between committing and enabling 233 n. 8
Muslim Empire, Jewish communities in 135, 168, 179–80, 184
muwahhidun vs. *mujassima* 326

N
Nedarim:
editing of 165
not taught in Babylonia 163–4 n. 32, 169
taught in Ashkenaz 33, 62, 163
Noahide Laws 253, 266 n. 84, 285
Notebooks (*Kuntresim*) 246–7

O
oaths:
false 306–8, 341, 354
inversion of (*mepakh shevu'ah*) 89, 103, 152–3, 213–14
shahada as 351
On Jewish Insolence, see *De Insolentia Iudaeorum*
Or Zarua' 25, 80, 107, 119, 271, 385
oral transmission, of Bavli 171–2, 196–7, 205
organs, damaged, see *terefot*
orthopraxis, by atheists 303 n. 27

P
paganism, cultic not credal according to Maimonides 344
Palestinian Talmud, *see* Yerushalmi
patria potestas 255, 259 n. 60
persecution, religious (*she'at ha-shemad*) 223, 228, 248 n. 42, 272–3, 297
conduct in times of 231, 233, 254, 290, 301; murder of children 254–6, 265; as prescribed by Maimonides 305, 308, 311, 320, 323; suicide 249, 253, 262, 265
definition of purpose of 350
dissimulation forbidden in times of 226
expulsion of Jews from European countries 38, 272
in Islamic countries 178, 223, 316–17, 322–3, 330; in Maghreb 223, 288, 289 n. 1, 294, 363; in Yemen 223, 317
no formative impact in early Judaism 228
Perush ha-Mishnayot (Maimonides) 296, 312, 341, 374
on coercion 308 and n. 38, 346, 353
early editions of 296 n. 16, 326, 328, 345
on idolatry 325–6, 328
on mental reservations 341, 355
Perush Rabbenu Gershom 'al ha-Talmud 158, 172–3 n. 49, 187, 215
on all of the Talmud 42–3, 149, 207
Avraham Epstein on 50
collective work of school of Rabbenu Gershom 31, 50, 188, 215 n. 23
groundbreaking 35, 207
multi-layered, as shown by Ta-Shma 35
neglected today 35
no individual names mentioned in 187–8 and n. 78
printed in Romm edition of the Talmud 31, 149
realia in 212–13
a *sub verbo*-type commentary 62–3, 207
Perush ha-Tefillot 199

Perushei Magentsa 63 n. 99, 160, 204
piety, Christian, pre-Crusade wave of 260
pikuaḥ nefesh 305–7, 374, 378, 381
piyyut:
in Aramaic 162–3
Ashkenazic, patterned on Italian models 142, 266
important genre in Early Ashkenaz 143, 148, 157, 193–4
originated in Palestine and arrived via Italy 123, 142, 162, 193
Rashi's exegesis of 4
route of migration of 193–4
scholarship on 4, 142–3
polemics 4, 141
in Maimonides' *Iggeret ha-Shemad* 311, 315, 322, 327, 330 n. 88, 340
in *Mishneh Torah* 390–2
pork, revulsion for 224, 240 n. 21
prayer, *see* liturgy
priestly blessing 59–60, 87, 88 n. 62, 103

R
Radhanites 128, 135
rebellious son (*ben sorer u-moreh*) 256–7, 259, 285–7
reportatio 84 n. 49, 238, 244–5
responsa 111 n. 17, 147–8, 167, 180, 198
anonymous until the time of the Geonim 155, 156 n. 12, 167, 176, 188
of R. Yehudah Ba'al Sefer ha-Dinim 46–8, 70, 73, 76 n. 13, 93 and n. 77
of R. Yitsḥak ha-Levi 76 n. 14
of R. Yitsḥak ben Yehudah 64–5, 76, 111
re'uta (negative symptom) 8, 11
rhetoric 89, 92, 95 n. 80, 211
in *Iggeret ha-Shemad* 312 and n. 48, 327, 329, 332, 334, 347; rooted in Aristotle's *Rhetoric* 315 n. 58, 336, 361
Rintfleisch massacres 273
robbery, laws relating to, in *Mishneh Torah* 369–70
Rosh Hashanah, *musaf* on 112, 116–17

S
Sabbath:
activities forbidden on 104, 373–4, 378
desecration of 240 n. 21, 256, 278, 304, 348
fasting on 19, 21
Karaite injunctions on 380–4
most Jews have no knowledge of formal rules of 41–2
vs. *yom tov* 370
savora'im 54, 163 n. 31, 165, 187–8, 201
anonymous editors of the Talmud 175–6
culture of, in contrast to geonic culture 181–2, 185–6
scholastic dialectic 25–8
scholasticism 23, 27
Schwabenspiegel 273
seder Kodashim, see *Kodashim*
Seder Tanna'im ve-Amora'im 152 n. 5
Sefer he-'Arukh 32 n. 5, 160–1, 169, 187–8
Sefer Asufot 37
Sefer ha-'Eshkol 12 n. 26, 31, 155, 203
Sefer Halakhot Gedolot, see *Halakhot Gedolot*
Sefer Halakhot Pesukot, see *Halakhot Pesukot*
Sefer Ḥasidim 84 n. 49, 271, 274, 279, 280 n. 141
Sefer ve-Hizhir 13
Sefer ha-'Ittim 31, 155, 203
Sefer ha-'Ittur 12, 77, 113
Sefer ha-Kabbalah 199
Sefer ha-Manhig 113
Sefer ha-Minhagim of R. Ya'akov ha-Levi Moellin 73
Sefer ha-Mitsvot 299, 306 n. 34, 310, 329–30, 379
Sefer Mitsvot Gadol (*Semag*) 269, 276, 281 n. 147, 363 n. 25, 384–5, 394
Sefer Mitsvot Katan (*Semak*) 255, 269, 270 nn. 96–7, 279, 280 nn. 140–1, 363 n. 25
Sefer ha-'Oreh 155
Sefer ha-Pardes 46–7 n. 43, 54, 64–6, 93 n. 77, 154 n. 8, 155
Sefer Ravyah 107, 148, 385
Sefer ha-Roke'aḥ 65 n. 104, 105, 215
Sefer ha-Shalman 263
Sefer ha-Terumot 37
Sefer Yere'im 269
Sefer Yosippon 262–4, 267, 284
describes the suicides at Masada 262, 266
influence of, in Early Ashkenaz 262, 264–6
never invoked in halakhic discussions 264–5

sekhirut (hiring), laws of, in *Mishneh Torah* 368, 372
Semag, see *Sefer Mitsvot Gadol*
Semak, see *Sefer Mitsvot Katan*
setam mishnah 18, 287, 345, 356
setam yeinam, *see* Gentiles: wine, ban on
setama'im 175–6, 187–8, 201
sevara 39, 152 n. 5, 213–14, 240
Sha'arei Dura 393
shahada, recital of:
as apostasy 294, 348, 357–8, 362
demanded by the Almohads 289 and n. 1, 330, 349–50
does not require martyrdom 327, 329
mental reservations during 299 n. 21, 308 and n. 38, 347, 350–1, 354–5
Shakh (*Siftei Kohen*) 386
shalḥu mi-tam 82, 84 n. 48
she'at ha-shemad, *see* persecution
'She-heḥiyanu' 52–3, 120
sheḥitah 5–8, 13, 15, 111
She'iltot 12, 87, 181 n. 61, 363 n. 25
Shemini 'Atseret, debate over Torah reading on 112–14
shevut 374, 376, 383
Shibbolei ha-Leket (*ha-Shalem*) 25, 64, 68, 79, 111, 113, 147
Shibbolei ha-Leket II 68
Shitah Mekubbetset 26 n. 6, 173 n. 50, 246–7
Shitah lo Noda' le-Mi 'al Kiddushin 37
Shi'ur Komah 134
shiv'ah:
for grandparents 47–8, 81, 83–4
on second day of festivals 65–6, 93 n. 77
shofar-blowing, preceded by circumcision 86
Shulḥan 'Arukh 270, 272, 368, 385, 387–8, 391
commentaries on 9, 56, 73, 385–6
swift acceptance of 393–5
Siddur Rabbenu Shelomoh mi-Germaiza 46 n. 43, 64
Siddur shel Rashi 30–1, 78–9 n. 23, 187
Siddur Rav 'Amram Gaon 78 and n. 23, 112
Siddur R. Sa'adyah, contains *piyyut* 194
Sifra (*Torat Kohanim*) 319, 355–6, 371 n. 4
on idolatry committed under coercion 296 n. 17, 306 and n. 34, 321, 346, 362
Sifrut de-Vei Rashi 25, 30, 107, 187
Issur ve-Heter shel Rashi 30–1
Maḥzor Vitry 30, 78–9 n. 23, 187
Siddur shel Rashi 30–1, 78–9 n. 23, 187
slaughter of animals 5–8, 13, 15, 111
slave trade 135–6, 138, 140
sod 157, 193, 199
sub verbo exegesis 62–4, 159
first practiced by scholars of Early Ashkenaz 32 and n. 7, 35 and n. 12, 51, 62–3
perfected by Rashi 63
see also lemmata
suicide 104, 235 n. 13, 236, 243, 253, 274
in the face of apostasy 249, 268 n. 92, 269–70, 283–4; justified by Tosafists 101, 102–3 n. 8, 229, 231–3, 239–41, 256 n. 59; permissibility of, derived from aggadah 234, 241–2, 249–55
forbidden by Noahide Law according to a *midrash* 253
Masada 262, 265–6
sukkah, laws of 57–8

T

ta'amei mitsvot 368
Talmud, *see* Bavli; Yerushalmi
taqiyya 225
Targum Onkelos 160
taxation, communal 75, 95, 97, 99
Temim De'im 286 n. 151
terefot 5, 8–9, 11–13, 17–18
gall bladder 6, 12–13, 17–19
Hilkhot Terefot 12, 15–16
inspection of organs 8–9
liver 8–9, 11, 15–16
lung 6–11, 16–17
missing organs 11–13, 16–19
Teshuvot u-Fesakim me'et Ḥakhmei Ashkenaz ve-Tsarfat 85 n. 54, 88
Teshuvot Ḥakhmei Provintsya 37
Teshuvot Ḥakhmei Tsarfat ve-Lotir 25, 64–5, 74, 76, 120
Teshuvot R. Me'ir mi-Rotenburg 37, 73, 299–300 n. 21
Third Yeshivah of Bavel 165 n. 33
attitude to Geonate 168, 177, 179, 181–2, 187, 200–1

curriculum of 163–5, 169, 187, 189–91, 204, 206–7
ideology of 188, 190–1, 201
involved in editing the Talmud 196
no official standing 169
no records exist of 165–7, 198, 200
origin of first scholars of Ashkenaz 164–5, 169
relocation to Ashkenaz 158, 170, 175, 183, 186–7, 214; reason for 170, 175, 190
Toledot Tanna'im ve-'Amora'im 214
Torat Kohanim, see *Sifra*
torat ha-sod 157, 193, 199
torture 234, 239, 244–7, 249, 274
obligation to endure 245, 269–70
suicide in the face of 231, 235 n. 13, 239, 241, 250, 269–70
Tosafists 33–4 n. 10, 53, 240 n. 21, 269, 281
defend communal practice 36 and n. 13, 58 n. 83
do not invoke aggadah in halakhic arguments if talmudic source is available 71, 83 n. 47, 101, 103–4, 234–5
ignore Maimonides 234, 276, 384
justify murder and suicide in the face of conversion 229, 240–2, 248, 282
on martyrdom, strange reasoning 230–2, 234, 238, 250, 253–4
method of study 23–7, 39
reportatio common among 84 n. 49, 238, 244–5
revolution of, alters religious regimen in Ashkenaz 30, 190
Tosafot 249, 270, 276 and n. 126, 279, 281
dialectical method in 230
emendations rare in 39
of R. Elḥanan 238–9
traditional society 35, 61, 335, 384
mimetic culture in 41–2
slow to change prevailing custom 56, 117
Treatise on Logic 315 n. 58
Tur, see *Arba'ah Turim*

U
usury 3, 41, 109

V
vinegar, treated as wine 112, 115–16
Vox Talmudica 172, 174, 196, 205

W
wedding, priority over funeral 86
wine 52–3, 77
touched by Gentiles (*yein nesekh*) 115–16, 141, 146, 151, 190–1
transportation of 107, 109–10
turned into vinegar 115–16
Wissenschaft des Judentums 122, 142

Y
Yad ha-Ḥazakah, see *Mishneh Torah*
Yarketei ha-Mishkan 386 n. 27
yehareg ve-'al ya'avor, *see* martyrdom
yein nesekh, see Gentiles: wine, ban on
Yerushalmi (Palestinian Talmud) 79, 143, 147, 270–3
abridged quotations from, in rabbinic literature 278
alleged prominence of custom in 29, 49, 61
in conflict with Bavli 9–10, 20–1, 81, 147
lacks an interpretative tradition 207
marginal in Ashkenaz 80, 149, 158–9, 163, 203
on martyrdom 265–6, 277–8
not available in Early Ashkenaz 61 and n. 94, 149, 158 and n. 18, 203
Palestinian traditions in 15
R. Eliyahu of Vilna's writings on 208
yesh lomar 25
yeshivot, *see* academies
Yiddish 72, 212
Yiḥusei Tanna'im ve-'Amora'im 47 n. 45
yom tov 59, 370
commencing on Saturday night 77–8, 80
sheni shel galuyot 82, 119, 167; mourning on 47, 65–6 n. 104, 93 n. 77
Yosippon, see *Sefer Yosippon*